Beginning XSLT 2.0

From Novice to Professional

JENI TENNISON

Apress®

Beginning XSLT 2.0: From Novice to Professional

ISBN (pbk): 1-59059-324-3

Printed and bound in the United States of America 9 8 7 6 5 4 3 2 1

Lead Editor: Chris Mills
Technical Reviewer: Norman Walsh
Editorial Board: Steve Anglin, Dan Appleman, Ewan Buckingham, Gary Cornell, Tony Davis, Jason Gilmore, Jonathan Hassell, Chris Mills, Dominic Shakeshaft, Jim Sumser
Assistant Publisher: Grace Wong
Project Manager: Kylie Johnston
Copy Manager: Nicole LeClerc
Copy Editor: Ami Knox
Assistant Production Director: Kari Brooks-Copony
Production Editor: Kelly Winquist
Compositor and Artist: Kinetic Publishing Services, LLC
Proofreader: Elizabeth Berry
Indexer: Kevin Broccoli
Cover Designer: Kurt Krames
Manufacturing Manager: Tom Debolski

Distributed to the book trade in the United States by Springer-Verlag New York, Inc., 233 Spring Street, 6th Floor, New York, NY 10013, and outside the United States by Springer-Verlag GmbH & Co. KG, Tiergartenstr. 17, 69112 Heidelberg, Germany.

In the United States: phone 1-800-SPRINGER, fax 201-348-4505, e-mail orders@springer-ny.com, or visit http://www.springer-ny.com. Outside the United States: fax +49 6221 345229, e-mail orders@springer.de, or visit http://www.springer.de.

For information on translations, please contact Apress directly at 2560 Ninth Street, Suite 219, Berkeley, CA 94710. Phone 510-549-5930, fax 510-549-5939, e-mail info@apress.com, or visit http://www.apress.com.

The source code for this book is available to readers at http://www.apress.com in the Downloads section.

Contents at a Glance

Contents

About the Author

JENI TENNISON is an independent consultant and author specializing in XSLT and XML schema development. She trained as a knowledge engineer, gaining a PhD in collaborative ontology development, and since becoming a consultant has worked in a wide variety of areas, including publishing, water monitoring, and financial services. She is author of *XPath and XSLT On The Edge* (Hungry Minds, 2001) and *Beginning XSLT* (Wrox, 2002) and one of the founders of the EXSLT initiative to standardize extensions to XSLT and XPath. She is an invited expert on the XSL Working Group at the W3C. She lives with her family, cats, and computers in Nottingham, England.

About the Technical Reviewer

NORMAN WALSH is an XML standards architect at Sun Microsystems, Inc. He is an active participant in a number of standards efforts worldwide, including the XML Core and XSL Working Groups of the World Wide Web Consortium, where he is also an elected member of the Technical Architecture Group, and the RELAX NG, Entity Resolution, and DocBook Technical Committees at OASIS. In addition to chairing the DocBook Technical Committee, he is the principal author of *DocBook: The Definitive Guide* (O'Reilly & Associates, 1999) and a lead designer of the widely used DocBook XSL Stylesheets.

Acknowledgments

This book has had a long and drawn-out gestation as it matched the slow progress of XSLT 2.0. My thanks to all those at Apress who helped in the process, particularly Kylie Johnston, Martin Streicher, and Ami Knox. My thanks to Norm Walsh for somehow finding the time to do a technical review; much as I'd like to blame them on him, the remaining errors are mine, of course. And many thanks to Michael Kay for letting me have a copy of Schema-Aware Saxon to use. Finally, thanks to those in the XML and XSLT community for their questions, opinions, and encouragement: I learned all I know from you.

Introduction

Welcome to *Beginning XSLT 2.0*, a comprehensive introduction to the Extensible Stylesheet Language: Transformations 2.0. This book introduces you to transforming XML with XSLT 2.0, helping you to create tailored presentations for all the information you have accessible as XML.

I wrote this book, like *Beginning XSLT*, based on my own experience as an XSLT user, but also based on my familiarity, from training people in XSLT, with the practical and conceptual hurdles that newcomers often face. My aim is to provide a step-by-step, how-to manual for the kind of the real-world transformation problems that you will come across.

Who This Book Is For

This book is primarily for newcomers to XML and XSLT. It's particularly aimed towards web developers who have some knowledge of HTML, CSS, and a smattering of JavaScript; but none of these are essential, and the techniques you learn in this book can just as easily be applied to transforming between XML-based markup languages as to web pages.

Seasoned users of XSLT 1.0 will learn about the new datatypes, expressions, and functions of XPath 2.0 and the new facilities in XSLT that make tasks such as text processing, grouping, and creating multiple documents much easier. Although much will look familiar, there are also some fundamental changes in the XPath data model and the XSLT processing model that may take you by surprise.

How This Book Is Structured

This book starts gently, introducing XML and XSLT bit by bit and gradually demonstrating the techniques that you need to generate HTML (and other formats) from XML.

The first eight chapters are ideally read in sequence, since they build on each other and together introduce you to the fundamental concepts involved in transforming XML with XSLT. Chapters 9 to 15 provide guides to particular facilities in XSLT that you may or may not find useful depending on your particular project. You can dip into these chapters as you see fit, although the examples do continue to build on each other.

Because each of these chapters introduces new material, they contain a lot of exercises that you can follow to try out the new techniques that you've read about. In addition, each chapter has a set of review questions at the end to help reinforce the information that you've taken in.

The final two chapters, 16 and 17, pull together the techniques that you've learned in isolation earlier in the book, so that you get a feel for how a stylesheet is developed from scratch. These chapters round off with a set of ideas for future development of the stylesheet that give you an opportunity to try out your XSLT skills.

- Chapter 1, "Introducing XML":

  This chapter introduces you to XHTML and XML and discusses the design of markup languages, and how you can validate documents against schemas and apply CSS stylesheets to XML. If you already know about XML, then you may want to skip this chapter, although you may find it useful to go through the review questions to refresh your memory. You'll also be introduced to the TV guide example that's used throughout the book, and here translate an original HTML page to an XHTML equivalent and into an XML format.

- Chapter 2, "Creating HTML from XML":

  This chapter introduces simplified XSLT stylesheets and describes how to create HTML pages using them. In this chapter, you'll create a stylesheet that transforms the TV guide XML that you generated in the previous chapter into a basic HTML page for a daily listing.

- Chapter 3, "Templates":

  This chapter introduces templates as a way of breaking up larger XSLT stylesheets into separate components, each handling the generation of a different portion of the HTML page. Here you'll create your first full XSLT stylesheet for the TV guide, learn how to process document-oriented XML, and make your stylesheet more maintainable. XSLT 1.0 users will learn about the new instruction `<xsl:next-match>` and using templates with multiple modes.

- Chapter 4, "Conditions":

  This chapter discusses ways of creating conditional portions of a document, depending on the information that's available to the stylesheet. In this chapter, you'll tackle the creation of some more complex HTML whose structure depends on the information that's available about a program—for example, adding an image to the page if a program has been flagged. XSLT 1.0 users will learn about new value comparisons, node comparisons, and the `if` XPath statement.

- Chapter 5, "Manipulating Atomic Values":

  This chapter introduces the datatypes that are available in XSLT, including strings, numbers, and dates and times. It describes the various functions and operators that you can use to manipulate them (including processing strings using regular expressions), perform calculations, and extract components such as the year of a date. Almost all the content of this chapter will be new to XSLT 1.0 users.

- Chapter 6, "Variables and Parameters":

  This chapter examines how to store pieces of information in variables so that you can reuse them, and how to pass parameters between templates and into XSLT stylesheets in order to change the output that's created. Learning about variables and parameters will allow you to simplify your stylesheet, and to create a stylesheet that can be used to generate guides for different series when passed the name of a series. XSLT 1.0 users will learn how to declare the types of their variables and about the new concepts of temporary trees and sequence constructors.

- Chapter 7, "Paths and Sequences":

  This chapter looks at how to extract information from XML documents and create sequences of values. While this chapter has a lot of theoretical content, it will equip you with the skills to move around XML information with ease. XSLT 1.0 users will learn about the new properties of nodes and the functions to access them, and how to create and process sequences of atomic values (such as numbers).

- Chapter 8, "Result Trees":

  This chapter explores the various methods of creating parts of an HTML document. In this chapter, you'll learn how to create conditional attributes, how to add comments within the HTML page, and several techniques that give you more control over the precise look of the HTML that you generate. XSLT 1.0 users will be particularly pleased to learn how to create multiple output documents from a single transformation.

- Chapter 9, "Sorting and Grouping":

  This chapter introduces methods for sorting and grouping together the components that you generate in the HTML page. For example, you'll see how to list programs alphabetically or by the time that they're shown, and how to group episodes according to the series they belong to. XSLT 1.0 users will be introduced to the new `<xsl:perform-sort>` and `<xsl:for-each-group>` instructions.

- Chapter 10, "IDs, Keys, and Numbering":

  This chapter shows you how to follow links between separate pieces of information and how to generate identifiers, such as numbers, that can be used within the HTML page you generate. While trying these techniques out on the TV guide, you'll see how to manage when data about series is kept separate from the data about individual programs, and you'll learn how to assign each program a unique number so that you can link between them.

- Chapter 11, "Named Templates, Stylesheet Functions, and Recursion":

  This chapter introduces you to how to create named templates or functions that you can call to carry out a series of XSLT instructions. You'll learn how to use recursion (when a template or function calls itself) within XSLT. Here you'll develop a number of utility templates or functions that allow you to perform sophisticated calculations. XSLT 1.0 users will find the ability to create user-defined functions with XSLT code particularly helpful.

- Chapter 12, "Building XSLT Applications":

  This chapter discusses how to manage XSLT stylesheets that are divided between several files, and how to generate HTML based on information from multiple separate XML or text documents. Here you'll learn how to create stylesheets that hold utility code that you can use in all the stylesheets for the TV Guide web site. You'll also learn what to do when the TV guide information is divided between several physical files. XSLT 1.0 users will learn about the new `unparsed-text()` function, amongst others.

- Chapter 13, "Schemas":

  This chapter describes how to use schemas to make your stylesheets simpler by using type annotations on nodes. You'll also learn how to invoke validation of the output that your stylesheet generates, which can help ensure that the result of the transformation is as it should be. All this chapter will be new to XSLT 1.0 users.

- Chapter 14, "Backwards Compatibility and Extensions":

  This chapter discusses how to write stylesheets that can be run with both XSLT 1.0 and XSLT 2.0 processors and how to deal with partial implementations of XSLT 2.0. It also discusses the use of extension attributes, functions, and instructions that are available in different processors and some of the ways in which you can debug your code.

- Chapter 15, "Dynamic XSLT":

  This chapter discusses how to use XSLT in two environments that have built-in support for running transformations: client side in browsers such as Internet Explorer or Firefox (with the Sarissa library), and server side in Cocoon (a Java servlet). You'll learn how to create dynamic XSLT applications that provide different presentations depending on a user's input. For example, you'll learn how to create forms that let users request summaries of particular TV series, so that the series guides can be created dynamically on demand.

- Chapter 16, "Creating SVG":

  This chapter introduces you to SVG, Scalable Vector Graphics, which is a markup language that represents graphics. You'll learn the basics of SVG, and experiment with it to create a pretty, printable image displaying the programs showing during a particular evening.

- Chapter 17, "Interpreting RSS with XSLT":

  This chapter examines RSS, or RDF Site Summaries, as a way of receiving syndicated information from other sites. We'll examine how to use TV listings and news received from other online sources in our own TV guide.

Conventions

You will encounter various styles of text and layout as you browse through this book. These have been used deliberately in order to make important information stand out. These styles are as follows:

Exercises

Exercises provide you with practical examples that you can step through using the source code that's available online via the Apress website.

SIDEBARS

Sidebars provide additional information that's offset from the main text. You can read them as you first go through the chapter or come back to them later.

Note Notes appear like this, as do tips, cautions, and summaries of sections.

When first introduced, new topics and names will appear as **important new topic**.

Within normal text, if you see something like `code`, then it's a piece of code that you might find in an XML document or stylesheet. Functions will be shown as `function()`; HTML, XML, and XSLT elements will be shown as `<element>`; and variables as `$variable`.

```
Lines of code appear like this
with important lines in bold
```

The result of a transformation is shown similarly

```
with lines of code like this
```

Prerequisites

As XML is text-based, all you really need to create an XML or XSLT file is a simple text editor, such as Notepad, which comes with Windows. However, I recommend getting hold of a good XML editor, such as <oXygen/> from SyncRO Soft (`http://www.oxygenxml.com/`), which also provides XSLT debugging facilities.

In order to run the XSLT transformations in this book, you will need at least one XSLT 2.0 processor. At the moment, that means getting hold of Saxon-B (currently version 8.4), available from `http://saxon.sourceforge.net/`. To run the examples in Chapter 13, you will need a Schema-Aware XSLT 2.0 processor, which at the moment means Saxon-SA (currently version 8.4), available from `http://www.saxonica.com/`.

You'll also want to look at the HTML that's generated from your transformations in a browser, but I suspect you have a favorite one of those already. The HTML's been tested in Internet Explorer.

Downloading the Code

As you work through the examples in this book, you might decide that you prefer to type all the code in by hand. Many readers do prefer this, because it's a good way of getting familiar with the coding techniques that are used.

If you are one of those readers who like to type in the code, you can use our files to check the results you should be getting. They should be your first stop if you think you have typed in an error. If you don't like typing, then downloading the source code from the Apress web site is a must! Either way, it will help you with updates and debugging.

All the source code for this book is available at this web site: `http://www.apress.com/book/download.html`.

Contacting the Author

Comments on this book (especially positive ones!) are welcome: just email me at `jeni@jenitennison.com`. If you've found a mistake, you should submit it as an erratum via the Apress website at `http://www.apress.com/`.

If you're having problems with your own XSLT, I recommend joining the XSL-List (details at `http://www.mulberrytech.com/xsl/xsl-list`). The mailing list is packed full of extremely helpful and knowledgeable XSLT users, a great resource for learners, and you're likely to get an answer much more promptly from them than from me. The XSLT FAQ at `http://www.dpawson.co.uk/xsl/` and my own web site at `http://www.jenitennison.com/` may also prove useful resources.

CHAPTER 1

Introducing XML

Welcome to *Beginning XSLT 2.0*. This book will lead you through the basics of markup and transformations, on the way equipping you with the skills you need to create XML-based web sites and other XML applications.

In this first chapter we're going to look at how to separate the **dynamic information** in a web page—the content that we'll want to change over time—from the **static information** that stays the same over a longer period. We're going to store this dynamic information as a separate XML file so that it can be repurposed—used in other places in addition to this web page, such as in other web pages, or presented in a different form such as PDF for print or text for an email message.

To illustrate this process, we'll look at some web pages from the example that we'll be using throughout this book—a web-based TV guide. By the end of the chapter we'll have an XML document on which we can use a variety of **XSLT** stylesheets in the rest of the book.

The material that you learn in this chapter is essential for the rest of the book because everything else we look at, including XSLT, is based on XML. In this chapter you'll learn

- What XML is and where it comes from
- How to make HTML XML-compliant
- How to create some XML to hold the information that you have
- What things to bear in mind when you're designing a markup language
- How to write a description of your markup language
- How to use CSS to present an XML document

Markup Languages

When you think of the Web, you think of HTML, the Hypertext Markup Language. Like a natural language, there are two parts to a markup language: its **vocabulary** and its **grammar**.

The vocabulary tells you the names of the components that you can use in a document. Those things are

- **Elements** like `<P>` and `<A>`
- **Attributes** like `class` and `href`
- **Entities** like ` ` and `é`

The grammar tells you the rules that tie the parts of the vocabulary together. These are rules like the following:

- An <A> element has an href attribute
- A <UL> element can contain one or more <LI> elements
- The <HEAD> element must contain a <TITLE> element

Now, you could imagine a different markup language that uses a different vocabulary and grammar. Instead of a <P> element, it might use the name <para>; rather than having <H1> to <H6> for headings, it might use <section> elements with <title> elements inside them, and so on.

Extending HTML

Why would you need this other language? Well, have a look at the HTML that we're using for our TV guide in Listing 1-1.

Listing 1-1. TVGuide.html

```
<HTML>
<HEAD>
  <TITLE>TV Guide</TITLE>
  <LINK rel="stylesheet" href="TVGuide.css">
  <SCRIPT type="text/javascript">
    function toggle(element) {
      if (element.style.display == 'none') {
        element.style.display = 'block';
      } else {
        element.style.display = 'none';
      }
    }
  </SCRIPT>
</HEAD>
<BODY>
  <H1>TV Guide</H1>
  <H2><SPAN class="day">Thursday</SPAN> 5 July</H2>
  <TABLE width="100%">
    <TR>
      <TH width="16%">Channel
      <TH colspan="6" width="12%">7:00
      <TH colspan="6" width="12%">7:30
      ...
    <TR>
      <TH class="channel">BBC1
      <TD colspan="6" class="quiz">
        <SPAN class="title">A Question Of Sport</SPAN><BR>
      <TD colspan="6" class="soap">
        <IMG src="flag.gif" alt="[Flagged]" width="20" height="20">
        <SPAN class="title">EastEnders</SPAN><BR>
```

```
        Mark's health scare forces him to reconsider his future with Lisa,
        while Jamie is torn between Sonia and Zoe.
        <SPAN onclick="toggle(EastEndersCast);">[Cast]</SPAN>
        <DIV id="EastEndersCast" style="display: none;">
          <UL class="castlist">
            <LI>
              <SPAN class="character">Zoe Slater</SPAN>
              <SPAN class="actor">Michelle Ryan</SPAN>
            <LI>
              <SPAN class="character">Jamie Mitchell</SPAN>
              <SPAN class="actor">Jack Ryder</SPAN>
            <LI>
              <SPAN class="character">Sonia Jackson</SPAN>
              <SPAN class="actor">Natalie Cassidy</SPAN>
          </UL>
        </DIV>
      ...
  </TABLE>
</BODY>
</HTML>
```

HTML has elements that allow us to say that a particular word or phrase is a link or should be emphasized, but it doesn't let us state that this part of the TV description is the title of the program, that bit its running length, this other section lists its cast, and so on. Identifying those parts is important for two reasons:

It affects the way that information looks on the page. The presentation of a piece of content is often tied to its meaning. If we had elements to indicate the meaning of these words and phrases, we would be able to display them in different ways with CSS.

It helps other people, and more importantly applications, look at the page and draw some conclusions about the information that it contains. If we used `<B>` to indicate the program's title and the name of a character, then all an application could tell was that those phrases should be in bold. If we had more descriptive element names, like `<title>` and `<character>`, then the application could distinguish between the two and could actually make use of that information.

Changing CSS Classes to Elements

We're currently using the `class` attributes on HTML elements and using `<SPAN>` and `<DIV>` elements in our HTML page to indicate the meaning of the parts of the page. This is fine as far as it goes, but it doesn't give us the flexibility and control that an element and attributes would. For example, currently the `TVGuide.html` HTML page contains the following structure for cast lists:

```
<UL class="castlist">
  <LI>
    <SPAN class="character">Zoe Slater</SPAN>
    <SPAN class="actor">Michelle Ryan</SPAN>
```

```
  <LI>
    <SPAN class="character">Jamie Mitchell</SPAN>
    <SPAN class="actor">Jack Ryder</SPAN>
  <LI>
    <SPAN class="character">Sonia Jackson</SPAN>
    <SPAN class="actor">Natalie Cassidy</SPAN>
</UL>
```

In this structure the cast list contains a number of character-actor pairs, but there's nothing in the grammar of HTML that determines this—it's just a rule that we know about. We assume that this rule holds true in the CSS that we use to present the cast list. Instead, we could design a markup language that uses elements to mark up the cast list as shown in Listing 1-2.

Listing 1-2. `castlist1.xml`

```
<castlist>
  <member>
    <character>Zoe Slater</character>
    <actor>Michelle Ryan</actor>
  </member>
  <member>
    <character>Jamie Mitchell</character>
    <actor>Jack Ryder</actor>
  </member>
  <member>
    <character>Sonia Jackson</character>
    <actor>Natalie Cassidy</actor>
  </member>
</castlist>
```

Using elements means that it's easy to write the grammar for the cast list:

- `<castlist>` elements contain one or more `<member>` elements.
- `<member>` elements contain a `<character>` element followed by an `<actor>` element.
- <character> and <actor> elements contain text.

It also means that we can add attributes to these elements if we want to, perhaps indicating the gender of the different characters as we do in Listing 1-3.

Listing 1-3. `castlist2.xml`

```
<castlist>
  <member>
    <character gender="female">Zoe Slater</character>
    <actor>Michelle Ryan</actor>
  </member>
```

```
  <member>
    <character gender="male">Jamie Mitchell</character>
    <actor>Jack Ryder</actor>
  </member>
  <member>
    <character gender="female">Sonia Jackson</character>
    <actor>Natalie Cassidy</actor>
  </member>
</castlist>
```

Including structured information would be a lot harder to do using just the `class` attribute in HTML. Even if we did include it in the `class` attribute, it would be hard to use because you have to be able to list all the possible classes in order to use them. While that's easy for an attribute like gender—its value can be either "male" or "female"—if we were to include the character's age, or the date the actor joined the series, then it would become impossible.

Summary Using your own elements and attributes to mark up your information gives you more flexibility in how to represent it and makes it more accessible and meaningful to other people and programs.

Meta-Markup Languages

You'll notice in the example we used previously that the new markup language for the cast list still uses the same general syntax as HTML—tags are indicated with angle brackets, attributes with names, and values are separated by an equals sign. A document written in this new markup language would look much the same as the same document written in HTML, except that the names of the elements and attributes might change and perhaps things would be moved around a little.

But how do you decide that this is the syntax you will use? Why not use parentheses to indicate elements and slashes to escape special characters? Well, you could, and some markup languages do, but HTML, along with a number of other markup languages, is based on the ISO standard **SGML**, the **Standard Generalized Markup Language**. SGML is what's known as a **meta-markup language**—it doesn't define a vocabulary or a grammar itself, but it does define the general syntax that the members of a family of markup languages share.

The benefit of sharing a meta-markup language is that you can create basic applications that can handle *any* markup language in that family. An SGML **parser** can read and interpret SGML because it recognizes, for example, where an element starts and ends, what attributes there are, what their values are, and so on. SGML editors can support authors who are writing in SGML-based markup languages by adding end tags where necessary. Standard tools can format and present SGML no matter which SGML-based markup language is used in a particular document. Indeed, SGML-based markup languages have been used in many large projects; HTML is just the most popular of these languages.

However, SGML has some drawbacks as a meta-markup language that mean it doesn't quite fit the bill as a meta-markup language for the Web. The most important of these drawbacks is that it is *too* flexible, *too* configurable, which means that the applications such as web browsers that read it and manipulate it have to be fairly heavy weight. You can see some of this in HTML—certain elements in HTML, like `<LI>`, don't need to have literal close tags whereas others, like `<EM>`, do. Other markup languages in the SGML family use close tags without names in, and so on. The variation that SGML allows means that any application that covers all the possibilities is going to be huge.

XML: The Extensible Markup Language

What the Web needed was a cut-down version of SGML, a meta-markup language that gave just enough flexibility, but retained its simplicity. This is the role of **XML**, the Extensible Markup Language.

XML is a meta-markup language, like SGML, but it's specifically designed to be easy to use over the Web, to be human-readable and straightforward for applications to read and understand. The XML Recommendation was released by the W3C in February 1998, followed by a "Second Edition" in October 2000 and a "Third Edition" in February 2004, which just incorporate minor errata from the previous editions. You can download a copy of the XML 1.0 Recommendation from `http://www.w3.org/TR/REC-xml`.

XML VERSION 1.1

XML 1.1 (see `http://www.w3.org/TR/xml11`) makes three minor, and pretty obscure, changes to XML 1.0:

- Some characters added to Unicode after Unicode 2.0 are now allowed in element, attribute, and entity names in XML 1.1 but aren't in XML 1.0. The characters that have been added to Unicode are mainly additional Chinese, Japanese, or Korean ideographs, historical scripts, and mathematical and currency symbols.
- XML 1.0 only considers certain combinations of newlines (#xA) and carriage returns (#xD) as line ends. In XML 1.1, next line (NEL—`#x85`), which is used to indicate line endings on IBM and IBM-compatible mainframes, and the Unicode line separator character (`#x2028`) are also considered to be line ends. All line ends are normalized to newline (#xA) characters during parsing.
- You can't include most of the control characters between `#x1` and `#x1F` in XML 1.0; in XML 1.1, you can include them, but only as character references (such as  for a form feed character), not as literal characters. Also, while the control characters between `#x7F` and `#x9F` are allowed to be used literally in XML 1.0, in XML 1.1 they have to be represented as character references.

In addition to these changes, parsers of XML 1.1 documents will recognize namespace use as defined in Namespaces in XML 1.1 (see `http://www.w3.org/TR/xml-names11/`) rather than Namespaces in XML 1.0. Namespaces are ways of labeling elements and attributes with a URI that indicates which markup language they belong to. The main change between namespaces in XML 1.1 and XML 1.0 is that namespaces can be undeclared in 1.1 whereas they can't in 1.0, which just makes it slightly easier to embed XML documents inside each other. We'll have a look at what that means in Chapter 7, where we look at namespaces in more detail.

If you can use XML 1.0 then you should, since XML 1.1 is pretty new and there are fewer implementations that support it. You only need to use XML 1.1 if

- You want to use post-Unicode 2.0 characters in the names of your element, attributes, or entities.
- You're using XML on IBM or IBM-compatible mainframes.
- You want to include control characters in your XML document.
- You need to have self-contained fragments in your XML document that don't inherit namespace nodes from their ancestors.

None of these are true for the XML that we're using, so we'll be using XML 1.0 throughout this book, except where illustrating the effect of namespace undeclarations.

There are now lots of tools that can help you to author XML and to write applications that use XML. One important group of these tools is XML parsers. XML parsers know the syntax rules that XML documents follow and use that knowledge to break down XML documents into their component parts, like elements and attributes. This process is known as **parsing** a document.

Most XML parsers make the information held in the document available through a standard set of methods and properties. Most parsers support **SAX**, the Simple API for XML. SAX parsers generate events every time they come across a component in an XML document, such as a start tag or a comment. Many parsers also support **DOM**, the Document Object Model, which is an API defined by the W3C. DOM parsers hold the structure of the XML document in memory as a tree.

Note You can find out more about the SAX and DOM APIs, and lots more, in *XML in a Nutshell, Third Edition*, by Elliotte Rusty Harold and W. Scott Means (O'Reilly, 2004, ISBN 0596007647).

Summary XML is a meta-markup language that defines the general syntax of markup languages for use on the Web and elsewhere.

There are a large and growing number of markup languages that are based on XML, that are part of the family that follow the syntactic rules that are defined by XML. There are markup languages in all areas—documentation, e-commerce, metadata, geographical, medical, scientific, graphical, and so on—often several. Because all these languages are based on XML, you can move between them very easily—all you have to learn is the new set of elements, attributes, and entities. So what are the syntactic rules that these markup languages all have in common?

XML Rules

We've already seen that HTML is a markup language that uses SGML, and how XML is a cut-down version of SGML. As you might expect, then, the syntax that XML defines involves a lot that's familiar from HTML: it has elements and attributes, start tags and end tags, and a number of entities for escaping the characters that are used as part of the markup.

In this section, we'll go through the rules that govern XML documents in general. These rules are known as **well-formedness constraints**, and XML documents that follow them are known as **well-formed documents**. Unlike with HTML, where browsers are notoriously lazy about checking the HTML that you give them, XML has to be well-formed to be recognized and usable by XML applications. When people talk about an XML document or XML message, then they are talking about well-formed XML.

Well-formedness constraints are distinct from the rules that come from the vocabulary and grammar of a particular markup language (like HTML). An XML document that adheres to the rules of a particular markup language is known as a **valid document**; we'll see how to declare the rules that a valid document must follow later in this chapter.

Testing Whether an XML Document Is Well-Formed

Before we launch into a look at what the well-formedness rules are, we'll first look at how to check whether an XML document is well-formed or not. Knowing how to check well-formedness will enable you to try out different examples as we go through the individual rules.

Most XML editors will let you test whether a document you create is well-formed and show you the error if it isn't. If you're not using an XML editor, you can test whether a document is a well-formed XML document by opening it in Internet Explorer or Firefox: by default a well-formed XML document will display as a collapsible tree.

Try looking at the `castlist2.xml` XML document that we created earlier in this chapter in Listing 1-3 using Internet Explorer. You should see a tree representation of the XML file, as in Figure 1-1.

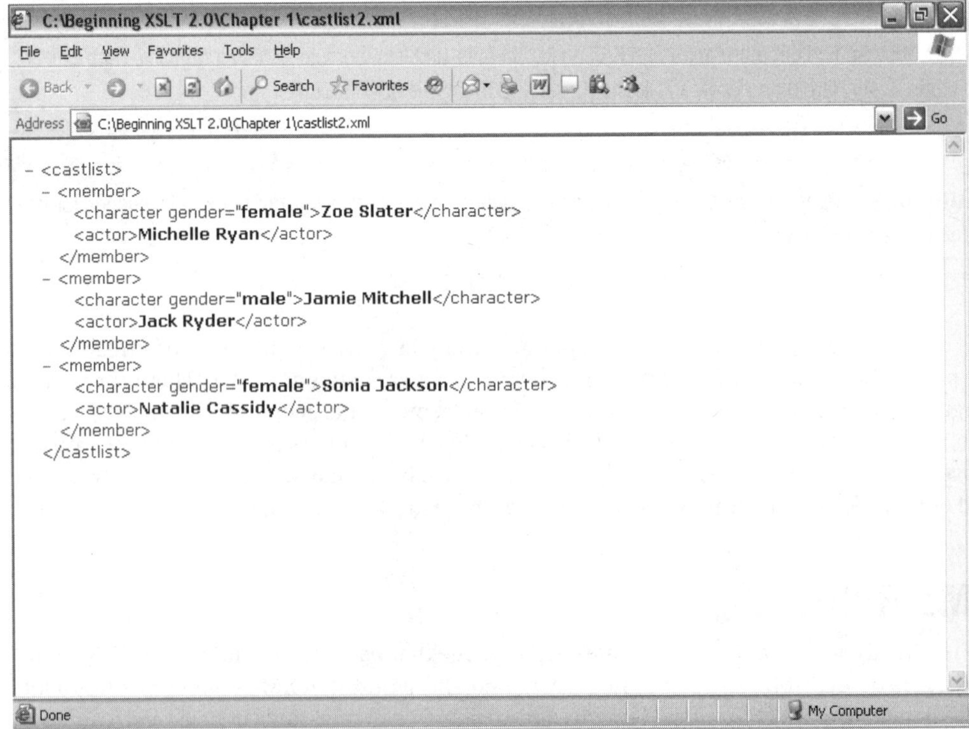

Figure 1-1. *Viewing* `castlist2.xml` *in Internet Explorer*

You can click any of the minus signs next to the start tags of the elements to collapse those elements. For example, Figure 1-2 shows all the `<member>` elements collapsed except for the first.

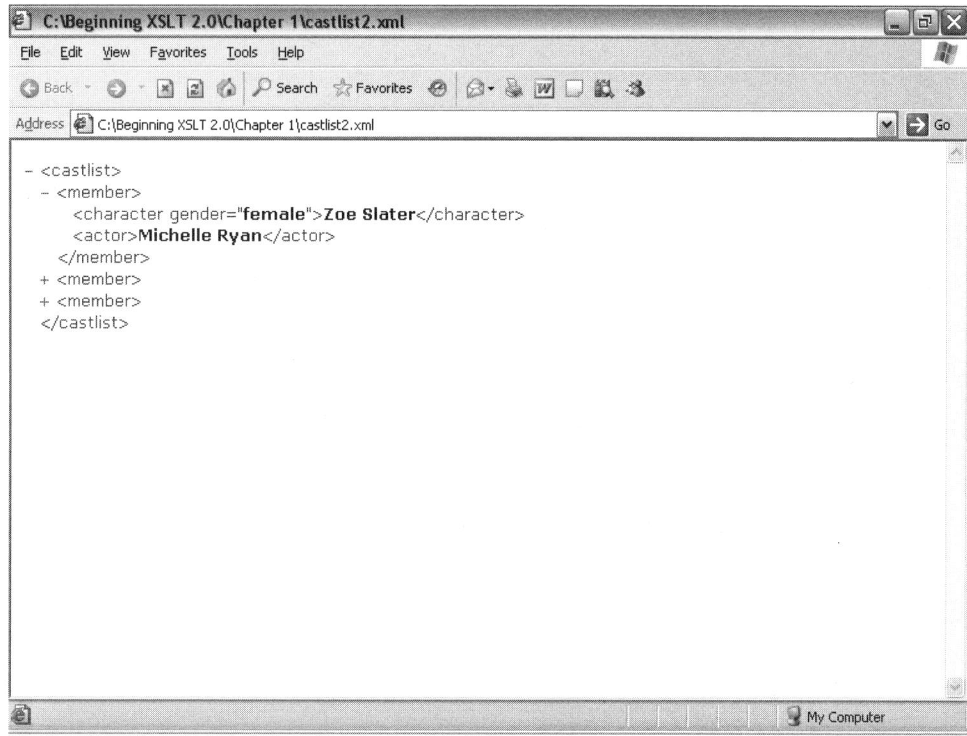

Figure 1-2. *Collapsing elements when viewing XML in Internet Explorer*

Now try adding the extension `.xml` to `TVguide.html` to create `TVGuide.html.xml`. Adding this extension will make Internet Explorer treat the HTML file as an XML file. But the HTML file doesn't adhere to XML rules, so you get an error reported, as shown in Figure 1-3.

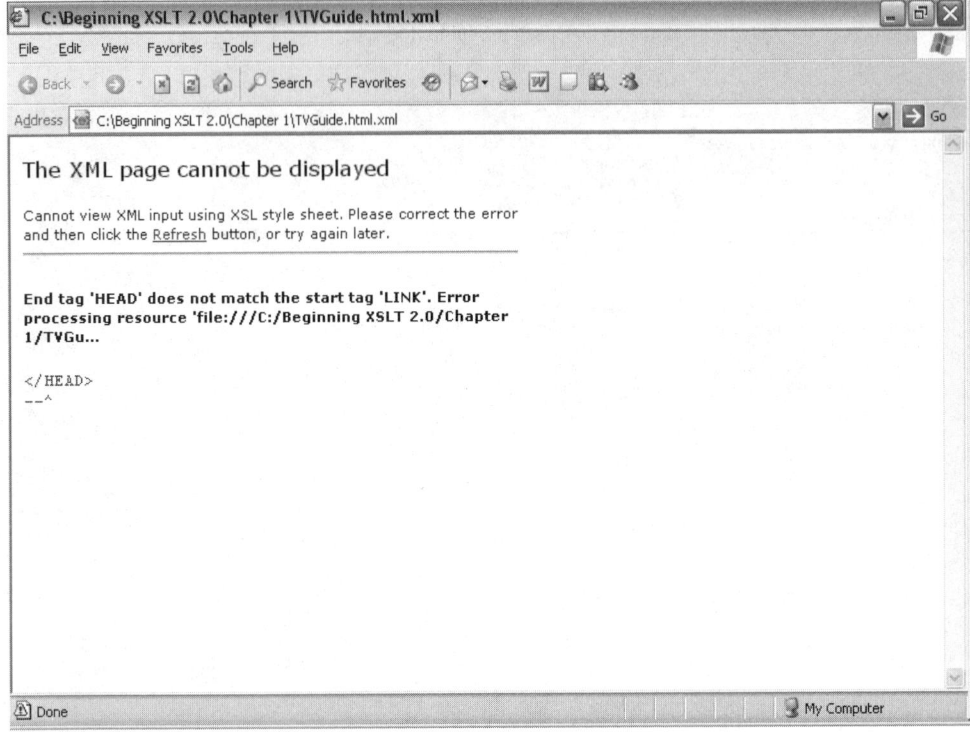

Figure 1-3. *Viewing a non-well-formed XML document in Internet Explorer*

By simply opening your document in Internet Explorer or Firefox, you can use any error messages that it shows you to identify the problems in your XML documents.

XHTML

As you've seen, HTML doesn't follow the XML rules. However, you can turn HTML into **XHTML**. In the XHTML 1.0 Recommendation at `http://www.w3.org/TR/xhtml1`, XHTML is called "The Extensible HyperText Markup Language", but really its subtitle, "A Reformulation of HTML 4 in XML 1.0," is more accurate. As we've seen, HTML is a markup language in the SGML family; XHTML is the same markup language (the same vocabulary and grammar) as HTML, but this time in the XML family.

In the rest of this section, we'll take the HTML document that we put together in the last section and turn it into XHTML bit by bit. By the end of this section, you'll be able to open up the XHTML document with an `.xml` extension in Internet Explorer or Firefox, and it will display as a tree.

Naming Conventions

Names are used in several places in XML, the most important of which are element names, attribute names, and entity names. In general, the names that you use in XML only have to follow a few rules:

- Names can contain letters, digits, hyphens (-), periods (.), colons (:), or underscores (_), but they must start with a letter, colon, or underscore.
- Names cannot start with xml in any case combination (that is, they can't start with XML or Xml either) as these names are reserved for XML standards from the W3C.
- Names should only use a colon if they use **namespaces**, which are ways of indicating the markup language that a particular element or attribute comes from. We will see more about namespaces in the next chapter.

Table 1-1 compares a few valid and invalid names.

Table 1-1. *Valid and Invalid XML Names*

Invalid XML Names	Valid XML Names
2nd	second
XmlDoc	Doc
tv:castlist:member	tv.castlist.member

There aren't any fixed conventions for names in XML, so if you're designing your own markup language you can use whatever naming convention you like. However, XML is case-sensitive, so if you use a particular case convention for the name of an element in a start tag, you must use the same convention in the end tag. Many markup languages use camel case, where new words are indicated by a capital letter, either starting with an uppercase letter (for example, CastList) or lowercase letter (castList). Several markup languages use lowercase with hyphens (cast-list) or capital case with periods (Cast.List).

Note As we'll see later on, XSLT uses a naming convention of all lowercase with hyphens separating words, for example, <value-of>.

The first big difference between HTML and XHTML is that whereas you can use any case you like for the names of elements and attributes in HTML, in XHTML they are standardized to all be lowercase. If you revisit the HTML that we looked at earlier in the chapter, and change all the element and attribute names to use lowercase, creating TVGuide2.html, you can see the (small) difference that this makes. For example, the cast list now looks like this:

```
<ul class="castlist">
  <li>
    <span class="character">Zoe Slater</span>
    <span class="actor">Michelle Ryan</span>
  <li>
    <span class="character">Jamie Mitchell</span>
    <span class="actor">Jack Ryder</span>
  <li>
    <span class="character">Sonia Jackson</span>
    <span class="actor">Natalie Cassidy</span>
</ul>
```

■ **Summary** XHTML uses all-lowercase element and attribute names.

Elements in XML

This section looks at the main component in an XML document—the elements—and the rules that they must follow.

End Tags

In XML, all elements must have both start and end tags, each holding the name of the element, with the name in the closing tag prefixed with the / character.

Therefore, unlike in HTML, every element in XHTML has to have an end tag. The HTML that we looked at before didn't have end tags for the `<LI>` elements; the equivalent XHTML must look like the following:

```
<ul class="castlist">
  <li>
    <span class="character">Zoe Slater</span>
    <span class="actor">Michelle Ryan</span>
  </li>
  <li>
    <span class="character">Jamie Mitchell</span>
    <span class="actor">Jack Ryder</span>
  </li>
  <li>
    <span class="character">Sonia Jackson</span>
    <span class="actor">Natalie Cassidy</span>
  </li>
</ul>
```

Empty Elements

Some elements, such as `<IMG>` and `<BR>` in HTML, don't have end tags because they don't contain anything. In XML, these **empty elements** can use a special syntax: a forward-slash before the closing angle bracket of the start tag rather than having an end tag.

Here are a couple of examples from XHTML:

```
<img src="star.gif" />
<br />
```

■ **Tip** I put a space before the forward-slash out of habit—it's not necessary in XML, but including one in XHTML means that older browsers that only understand HTML don't balk at empty XHTML elements, particularly those that don't have attributes such as `<br>` and `<hr>`.

This syntax means exactly the same thing to an XML application as having a start tag immediately followed by an end tag:

```
<img src="star.gif"></img>
<br></br>
```

Nested Elements

Elements in XHTML have to nest properly inside each other—you can't have the end tag in the content of an element unless its start tag is also within that element. In fact, this is the case in HTML as well (it's a rule from SGML), but some web browsers don't pick up on errors where elements overlap each other. For example:

```
Some <B>bold and <I>italic</B> text</I>.
```

should be

```
Some <B>bold and <I>italic</I></B><I> text</I>.
```

The Document Element

Finally, XML only allows there to be a single element at the top level of the document, known as the **document element**. This element contains everything in the XML document. In XHTML, the document element is the `<html>` element, for example. Compare this well-formed XML document:

```
<Chars>
  <Char>Zoe Slater</Char>
  <Char>Jamie Mitchell</Char>
  <Char>Sonia Jackson</Char>
  ...
</Chars>
```

with the following non-well-formed document:

```
<Char>Zoe Slater</Char>
<Char>Jamie Mitchell</Char>
<Char>Sonia Jackson</Char>
...
```

Summary Elements nest inside each other to form a tree, with the document element at the top of the tree. Elements must have a start and end tag, although empty elements can use a special syntax.

Attributes in XML

XML attributes are name-value pairs located within an element's start tag, with the value given in quotes following an equals sign after the name of the attribute. You can use either single or double quotes for any particular attribute value, but they must match: if you start the attribute value with a single quote, then you must use a single quote to end it.

Like element names, attribute names must be valid XML names. However, unlike elements, there are some attributes that are built in to XML:

- `xml:lang`—Indicates the language of the element, its attributes, and its contents
- `xml:space`—Controls whether whitespace is retained (`preserve`) or dealt with by the application (`default`)
- `xml:base`—Provides the base URI for the element, its attributes, and its contents
- `xml:id`—Assigns a unique ID to the element, which can then be used for linking to that element

---

Note Only `xml:lang` and `xml:space` are actually defined as part of XML; `xml:base` is defined in the XML Base Recommendation at `http://www.w3.org/TR/xmlbase/` and `xml:id` in the xml:id specification at `http://www.w3.org/TR/xml-id/`.

In addition to these attributes, there is a class of special attributes known as namespace declarations, as we'll see later, all of which begin with the string `xmlns`.

As well as forcing attributes to use quotes around values, XML differs from SGML in that it cannot have attributes that are indicated solely by their name, without a value—the presence of a attribute implies a true value and its absence a false one. These are termed **Boolean attributes** in HTML, and occur in several places, most especially in forms. Take an example drop-down menu in HTML:

```
<SELECT name="channels" multiple>
  <OPTION selected>BBC1
  <OPTION selected>BBC2
  <OPTION>ITV
  <OPTION selected>Channel 4
  <OPTION>Channel 5
</SELECT>
```

The `<SELECT>` element can take a `multiple` Boolean attribute and the `<OPTION>` element can take a `selected` Boolean attribute. These Boolean attributes aren't allowed in XML because every attribute must have a value. Instead, each of these attributes takes a value equal to the name of the attribute. Thus the equivalent in XHTML (remembering to use lowercase and to add end tags) would be

```
<select name="channels" multiple="multiple">
  <option selected="selected">BBC1</option>
  <option selected="selected">BBC2</option>
  <option>ITV</option>
  <option selected="selected">Channel 4</option>
  <option>Channel 5</option>
</select>
```

Summary All attributes must use either single or double quotes. Boolean attributes have values that are equal to their name.

Entities, Characters, and Encodings

There are several characters that are significant in XML—a less-than sign signals the start of a tag, for example. But what if you want to include one of these characters in the data that the XML document holds, such as a less-than sign in some code held by an XML element? In these cases, you have to **escape** the character so that an XML parser knows that it's not part of the markup you're using in this particular instance. As in HTML, the significant characters in XML markup are escaped with **entities**. This means that the ampersand, which indicates the start of an entity, also has to be escaped. These special characters should be familiar from HTML:

- `<`—Less-than sign (<)
- `>`—Greater-than sign (>)
- `"`—Double quotes (")
- `'`—Single quotes or apostrophe (')
- `&`—Ampersand (&)

Note You have to use `<` to escape the less-than sign and `&` to escape ampersands wherever they occur in attribute values or element content. You only have to use `"` in an attribute value that's delimited by double quotes and `'` in an attribute value that's delimited by single quotes (these are the only places where they are significant). The only time you have to use `>` to escape a greater-than sign is after double close square brackets (`]]`). But if in doubt, use the entity!

The big difference between HTML and XHTML in this regard lies in the fact that these are the only entities that are recognized in XML applications. In HTML, you're used to having a whole range of other entities at your disposal, giving symbols, accented characters, and things like non-breaking spaces. These aren't available as entities in XML, but they are available in different guises.

XML uses **Unicode** to represent characters. Unicode is a standard that assigns numerical values to characters in almost every language under the sun, as well as symbols and mathematical notations. Using Unicode means that XML supports internationalization fairly easily. Almost all Unicode characters can be included in your XML document if you use a **character reference**. A character reference looks a bit like an entity—it starts with an ampersand (&) and ends with a semicolon (;)—but it has a hash (#) right after the ampersand. The hash is followed by the number of a character in Unicode, either as a decimal or in hexadecimal if the number starts with an `x`. For example, a lowercase `e` with an acute accent could be represented as any of the following:

```
&#233;
&#xE9;
&#xe9;
```

■ **Tip** One good place to find numbers for the characters that you're used to from HTML is Section 24 ("Character entity references in HTML 4") in the HTML 4 Recommendation at `http://www.w3.org/TR/html401`. To find the numerical values for all characters, go to the Unicode site at `http://www.unicode.org/`.

Using Character References

One of the characters in *EastEnders* is called Zoe, and so far we've glossed over the fact that it should be spelled with an ë as the last character. It's easy to use an ë in HTML, because HTML defines the entity `ë`. We'll use a simple HTML document (`eastenders.html`) to look at this in detail, containing just the information about *EastEnders*. In the `eastenders.html` HTML document, we can use this entity as follows:

```
<ul class="castlist">
  <li>
    <span class="character">Zo&euml; Slater</span>
    <span class="actor">Michelle Ryan</span>
  </li>
  ...
</ul>
```

The HTML browser shows the `ë` entity as an ë character when you view `eastenders.html` and click the `[Cast]` link, as shown in Figure 1-4.

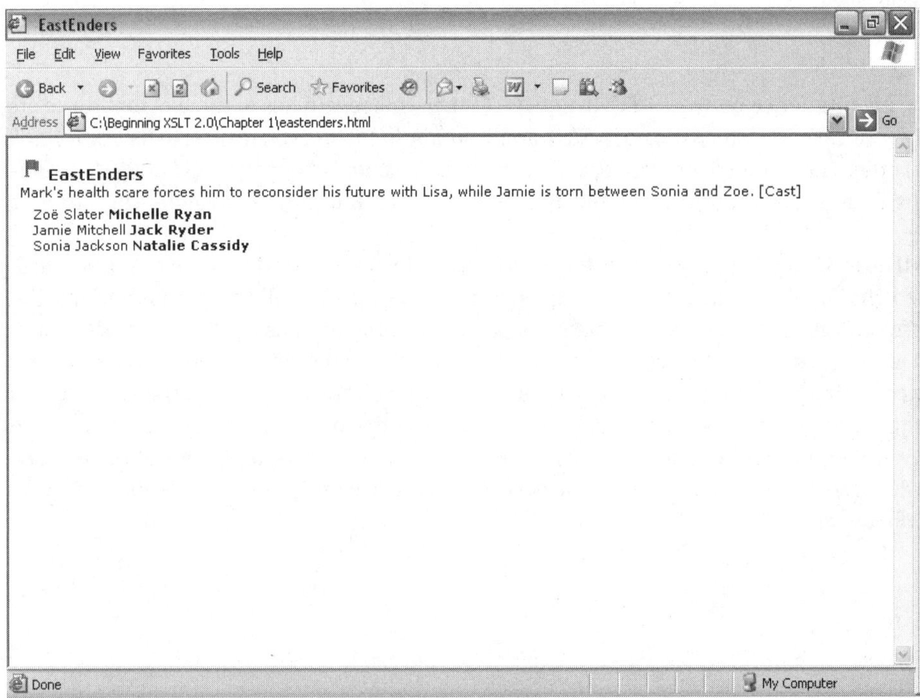

Figure 1-4. *Viewing the* `ë` *entity in an HTML document*

However, try using the `ë` entity in the `castlist3.xml` XML document, as in Listing 1-4.

Listing 1-4. `castlist3.xml`

```
<castlist>
  <member>
    <character gender="female">Zo&euml; Slater</character>
    <actor>Michelle Ryan</actor>
  </member>
  ...
</castlist>
```

When you open up this document in Internet Explorer, you get an error message, as shown in Figure 1-5.

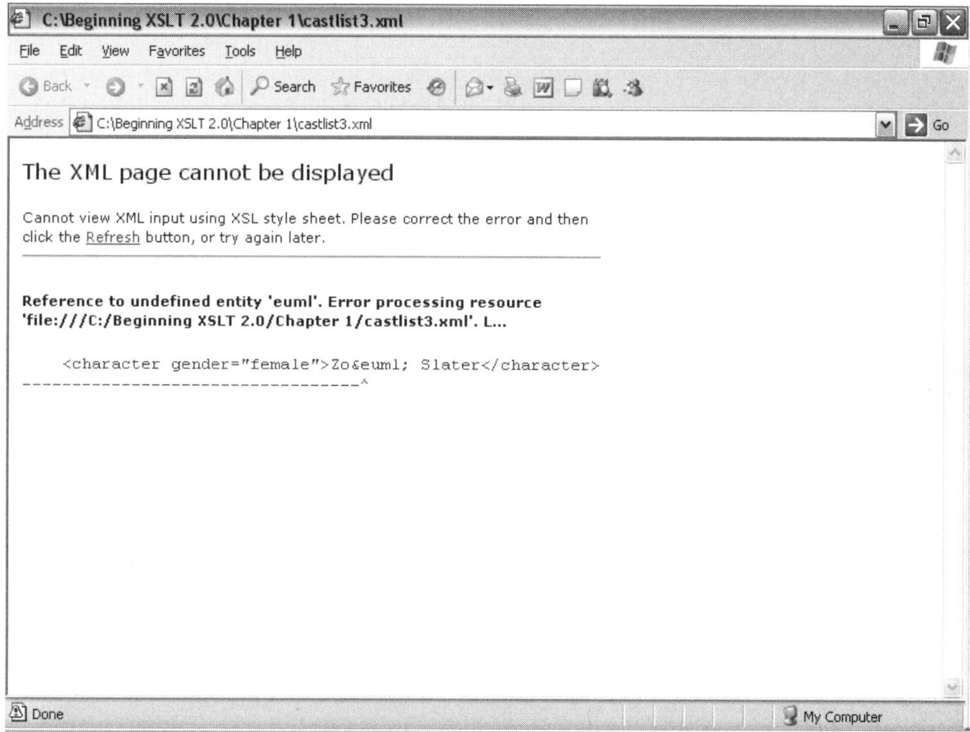

Figure 1-5. *Viewing the undeclared* `ë` *entity in an XML document*

The XML parser in Internet Explorer doesn't recognize the `ë` because it's not a character reference and it's not one of the five entities that are built into XML. Instead, you have to use a character reference for the ë character. If you look at the definitions in HTML, you'll see that the ë character is assigned the number 235, which equates to `EB` in hexadecimal. Therefore, you can use either of the following character references to get an ë in your XML:

```
&#235;
&#xEB;
```

If you replace the `ë` reference with either of these entities, to create `castlist4.xml`, and then load `castlist4.xml` into Internet Explorer, you'll see the result shown in Figure 1-6.

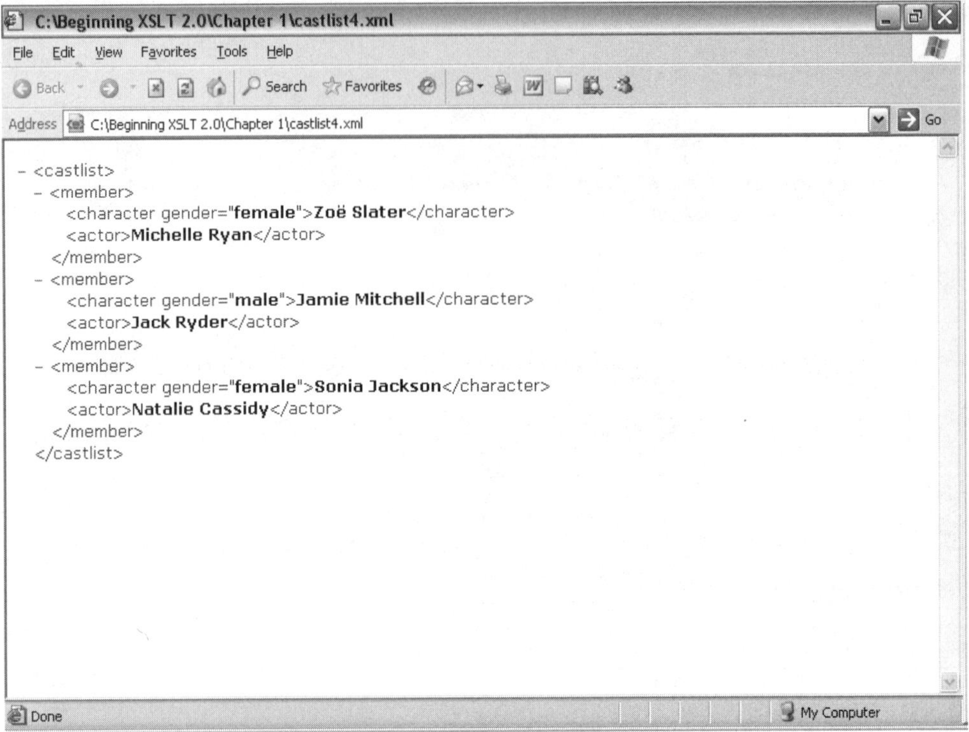

Figure 1-6. *Viewing a character reference in an XML document*

The XML parser in Internet Explorer recognizes the character reference and decodes it. Internet Explorer displays the ë character despite the fact that you used a character reference for it. You can use character references for any of the data in the file—text in element content or attribute values. Try using ` ` in place of spaces, for example.

The XML Declaration

You can also just include any character in your document as it is, natively, but if you do so then you need to make sure that the application that uses your XML can understand the **encoding** that you use when you save your document. An encoding is a way of representing characters with bytes. Some encodings, like **UTF-8** and **UTF-16**, map very closely onto the Unicode character numbers whereas others, like **ISO-8859-1** and **Shift-JIS**, are specifically designed for representing characters in particular languages. Applications that are designed for a particular locale usually expect the encoding that's used in that locale—programs in the US will usually assume ISO-8859-1, while those in Japan will assume Shift-JIS.

All XML applications must understand UTF-8 and UTF-16, so if you have an editor that saves files in one of these encodings then you don't have to do anything special. In fact, ASCII uses the same encoding as UTF-8, so you're also OK if you only use ASCII characters. However, if you have an editor that uses a different encoding—such as Notepad in Windows 98, which uses ISO-8859-1—then you need to indicate what encoding you've used for the document.

You can indicate the encoding of your XML document using an **XML declaration**. If you use an XML declaration, it must be the very first thing in your document, on the first line, without even a space in front of it. The basic XML declaration looks like:

```
<?xml version="1.0"?>
```

Having this at the start of a file indicates that the file is XML and that it conforms to version 1.0 of XML.

If you don't include an XML declaration in your XML document, then an XML application will assume that it's an XML 1.0 document encoded using UTF-8 or UTF-16. If you want to indicate the encoding that you're using, you can do this in the XML declaration. For example, to indicate that your XML document has been saved using ISO-8859-1, you should use

```
<?xml version="1.0" encoding="ISO-8859-1"?>
```

You can see here that the XML declaration contains a couple of things that look like attributes. These are known as **pseudo-attributes** because they look like attributes but, unlike real attributes, they don't live in the start tag of an element.

Summary There are only five entities built into XML, and you must always use `<` to escape less-than signs and `&` to escape ampersands. You can use character references to include non-ASCII characters, or include them directly as long as you use an XML declaration to specify the encoding that you save your document in.

Changing the Encoding of an XML Document

In the previous section, you worked out various ways of including an ë character in the castlist4.xml XML document. Now try including the ë character as an ë character instead, to give castlist5.xml, as in Listing 1-5.

Listing 1-5. castlist5.xml

```
<castlist>
  <member>
    <character gender="female">Zoë Slater</character>
    <actor>Michelle Ryan</actor>
  </member>
  ...
</castlist>
```

Open up the document in Internet Explorer. If you're using an editor that saves in something other than UTF-8 or UTF-16, then you will get an error like the one shown in the screenshot in Figure 1-7.

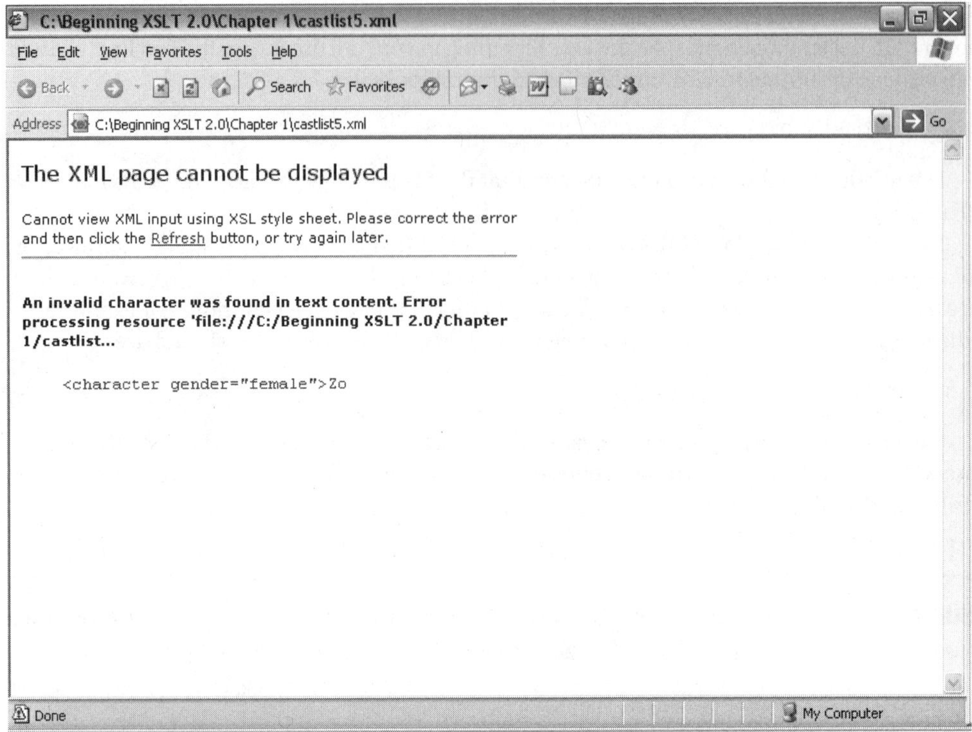

Figure 1-7. *Viewing a document in an encoding other than UTF-8 or UTF-16*

Probably your editor saves documents using ISO-8859-1, but we haven't included an XML declaration yet, so the XML parser thinks that the document is encoded using UTF-8. When the XML parser comes across the bytes that make up the character ë in ISO-8859-1, it tries to interpret them as bytes in UTF-8, and therefore can't figure out what the character is and shows the error message.

Now add the XML declaration to state that you're using ISO-8859-1 to save the file, to create `castlist6.xml` as in Listing 1-6.

Listing 1-6. `castlist6.xml`

```
<?xml version="1.0" encoding="ISO-8859-1"?>
<castlist>
  <member>
    <character gender="female">Zoë Slater</character>
    <actor>Michelle Ryan</actor>
  </member>
  ...
</castlist>
```

When you open this file up in Internet Explorer, you should see the collapsible tree as before, this time with the XML declaration that you used shown at the top, as in Figure 1-8.

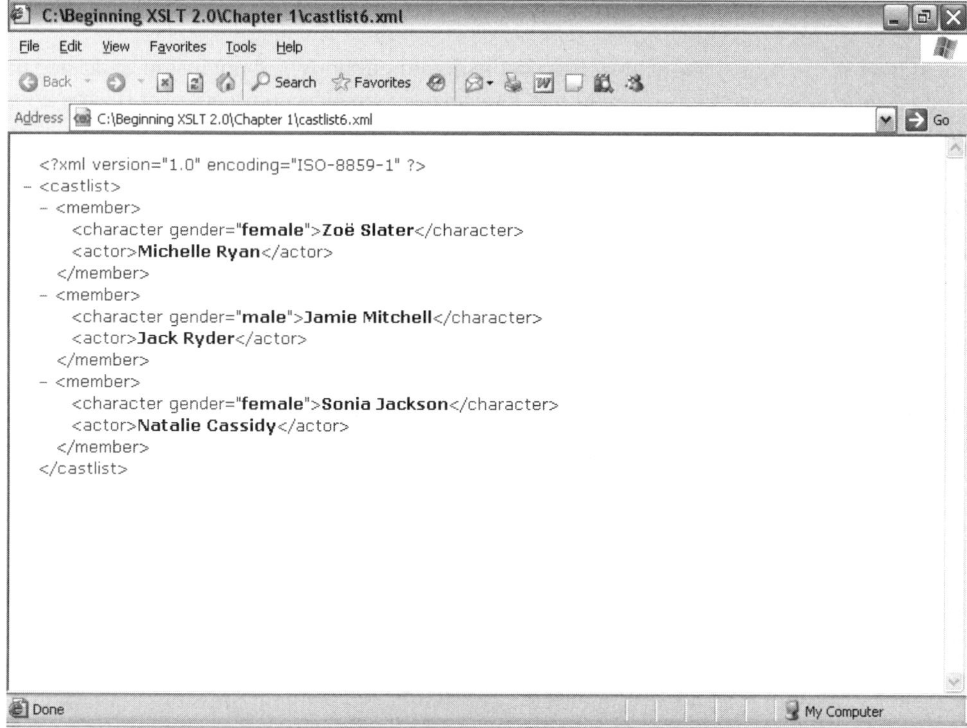

Figure 1-8. *Viewing a document with the correct encoding in the XML declaration*

If Internet Explorer still gives you an error, your editor is using some other encoding when it saves the file. You need to read your editor's documentation to find out what encoding it's using, and then state that encoding within the `encoding` pseudo-attribute in the XML declaration.

Other Components of XML

There are three other components of XML documents that we haven't yet touched on:

- Comments
- Processing instructions
- CDATA sections

Comments

Comments in XML (and therefore in XHTML) work in exactly the same way as those in HTML. They start with the characters `<!--` and end with the characters `-->`. You can have anything you like between the start and end of a comment; you don't have to escape any characters within them. The only thing you need to watch out for is that you cannot have two hyphens next to each other in the middle of a comment, because that would make the parser think that it was the end of the comment. Here is an example:

```
<!-- Document written February 18th 2002 -->
```

Comments can go just about anywhere in the document body, but not inside a start tag or an end tag, nor within an empty element tag. You can even spread a comment over several lines if you wish.

Processing Instructions

A component in XML that you probably won't have seen in HTML is the **processing instruction**. As their name suggests, processing instructions (or **PIs**) are instructions destined for the application that processes the XML document. Processing instructions start with `<?`, are immediately followed by a name and then some content, and end with `?>`.

Processing instructions aren't used very often, but there's one use for processing instructions that is particularly relevant for this book, and that's to link an XML document with a stylesheet that can be used to present it. For example, if we were writing the TV guide in XML (which we will do in detail later in this chapter), then we could link it to the CSS stylesheet (`TVGuide.css`) for formatting it using the `xml-stylesheet` processing instruction:

```
<?xml-stylesheet type="text/css" href="TVGuide.css"?>
```

You can see here that the `xml-stylesheet` processing instruction contains a couple of pseudo-attributes. The syntax of the content of processing instructions in general isn't something that's fixed in XML, but the application that understands the processing instruction will know what to do with it. The only limit on the content of a PI is that it must not contain the characters `?>`, as that indicates the end of the processing instruction.

Summary Processing instructions can control the processing of an XML document.

CDATA Sections

There are a couple of elements in HTML where the normal parsing of HTML is suspended, namely in `<SCRIPT>` and `<STYLE>` elements. Things work differently in these elements because they contain content that isn't HTML, but that may use characters such as less-than signs, which are usually used as part of markup, in other ways. Take a simple piece of JavaScript in HTML, for example:

```
<SCRIPT type="text/javascript">
  function validHour(hour) {
    if (hour >= 0 && hour < 24) {
      return true;
    }
    else {
      return false;
    }
  }
</SCRIPT>
```

Here, the less-than sign and the ampersand character have all been included in the HTML literally rather than being escaped. As we've already seen when looking at entities, this isn't legal XML—you have to escape less-than signs and ampersands throughout the document. In XHTML, you could therefore use the following:

```
<script content="text/javascript">
  function validHour(hour) {
    if (hour >= 0 &amp;&amp; hour &lt; 24) {
      return true;
    }
    else {
      return false;
    }
  }
</script>
```

However, it's difficult to read code that's been escaped like this and it's tedious to write. If you have an element that contains lots of characters that you need to escape, you can use a **CDATA section.** CDATA stands for "character data," and a CDATA section indicates that a piece of text only contains characters, so the meaning of the characters is no longer significant. CDATA sections begin with the special series of characters `<![CDATA[` and end with the sequence `]]>`.

In this example, we can create a CDATA section to wrap around the JavaScript code:

```
<script content="text/javascript">
  <![CDATA[
  function validHour(hour) {
    if (hour >= 0 && hour < 24) {
      return true;
    }
    else {
      return false;
    }
  }
  ]]>
</script>
```

One problem with doing this is that browsers that don't recognize XHTML will not know how to interpret the CDATA section, and will report it as a JavaScript syntax error. To avoid this, you can use JavaScript comments to comment out the CDATA section:

```
<script content="text/javascript">
  // <![CDATA[
  function validHour(hour) {
    if (hour >= 0 && hour < 24) {
      return true;
    }
    else {
      return false;
    }
```

```
  }
  // ]]>
</script>
```

Even better, you can use an external JavaScript file to hold the script and then refer to it:

```
<script content="text/javascript" src="TVGuide.js" />
```

■Caution Internet Explorer doesn't recognize `<script>` elements that don't have content, so to make the preceding work with Internet Explorer, you should use start and end tags, with a comment or a space between them.

As you might expect, the only sequence of characters that *isn't* allowed in a CDATA section is the sequence used to close it, `]]>`.

■Summary CDATA sections are a way of saving you from having to escape characters using entities.

Moving to XHTML

Most web browsers can understand XHTML, so converting your HTML documents into XHTML is a good way to start the journey to using XML. The easiest way to convert an HTML document into XHTML is to use HTML Tidy from Dave Raggett at W3C. You can get HTML Tidy from `http://tidy.sourceforge.net/`.

Let's review the changes that you have to make to your HTML to turn it into XHTML:

- Change the names of elements and attributes to lowercase.
- Add end tags if they are missing.
- Use empty element syntax for empty elements.
- Make sure that the elements don't overlap each other.
- Add matching quotes to all attribute values.
- Turn Boolean attributes into normal attributes by giving them their name as a value.
- Change any entity references in your document into character references.
- Add an XML declaration that specifies the encoding that you're using to save the file.
- Wrap the content of `<script>` and `<style>` elements in CDATA sections.

Converting HTML to XHTML

If we follow these steps with the HTML document that we looked at earlier in the chapter, then we get the document shown in Listing 1-7, TVGuide.xhtml.

Listing 1-7. TVGuide.xhtml

```
<?xml version="1.0" encoding="ISO-8859-1"?>
<html>
<head>
  <title>TV Guide</title>
  <link rel="stylesheet" href="TVGuide.css" />
  <script type="text/javascript">
    // <![CDATA[
    function toggle(element) {
      if (element.style.display == 'none') {
        element.style.display = 'block';
      }
      else {
        element.style.display = 'none';
      }
    }
    // ]]>
  </script>
</head>
<body>
  <h1>TV Guide</h1>
  <h2><span class="day">Thursday</span> 5 July</h2>
  <table>
    <tr>
      <th>Channel</th>
      <th colspan="6">7:00</th>
      <th colspan="6">7:30</th>
      ...
    </tr>
    <tr>
      <th class="channel">BBC1</th>
      ...
      <td colspan="6" class="soap">
        <img src="flag.gif" alt="[Flagged]" width="20" height="20" />
        <span class="title">EastEnders</span><br />
        Mark's health scare forces him to reconsider his future with Lisa,
        while Jamie is torn between Sonia and Zoe.
        <span onclick="toggle(EastEndersCast);">[Cast]</span>
        <div id="EastEndersCast" style="display: none;">
          <ul class="castlist">
            <li>
              <span class="character">Zo&#235; Slater</span>
```

```
              <span class="actor">Michelle Ryan</span>
            </li>
            ...
          </ul>
        </div>
      </td>
      ...
    </tr>
    ...
  </table>
</body>
</html>
```

When you view `TVGuide.xhtml` in Internet Explorer, as shown in Figure 1-9, it has exactly the same appearance as the original HTML file, `TVGuide.html`.

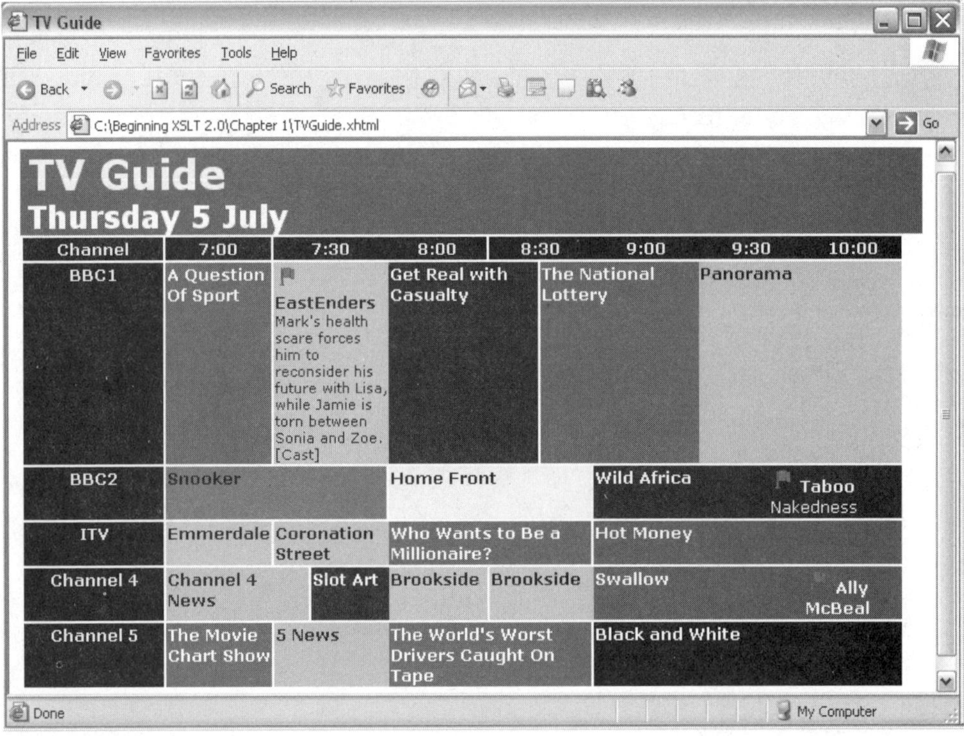

Figure 1-9. *Viewing XHTML in Internet Explorer*

Creating Markup Languages

Despite the fact that it uses XML, XHTML, like HTML, is still oriented around the presentation of documents. Looking at the kind of elements that XHTML uses illustrates this: <p> for paragraphs,

`<em>` for emphasis, `<ul>` for unordered lists, and so on. XHTML elements are designed to mark up documents, not for data, and they're certainly not tailored for the data that we're using.

To get the full benefit of XML, we need to design our own markup languages or reuse an existing one if we can find one that fulfills our requirements. We can design a markup language to hold the information in our TV guide; one that specifically indicates what a cast list is, what a program title is, and so on.

In this section, I'll briefly go through some of the issues involved in designing your own markup language and look at how to articulate the rules that you come up with so that an application can check whether an XML document adheres to those rules. Both these topics are big areas, so we won't have space to go into a lot of detail on them, but I'll show you enough to get by and point you in the direction of more information if you're interested.

Designing Markup Languages

Designing a markup language involves two steps:

1. Analyzing how the information fits together and how it will be used in your system
2. Deciding how to represent this in XML

To analyze the information that you need to represent, you can use much the same methodologies as you might when designing a database or an object-oriented program. The kinds of questions that you need to ask are as follows:

- What are the main things (concepts) that are used in the system?
- How do these different concepts fit together?
- What do you need to know about the concepts?
- Which parts of the application use what information?
- Is the information transient or does it hang around and get reused?

Often it's a good idea to sketch out the properties of and relationships between the concepts that you want to cover in your XML in a diagram. For example, Figure 1-10 shows each of the concepts used in a TV guide as a rectangle. A concept's associated properties are shown inside its rectangle; for example, a series has a title and a description.

The lines between the rectangles show the relationships between the concepts. An asterisk at the end of a line indicates a one-to-many relationship. For instance, the asterisk above the program rectangle (and next to the line from the channel rectangle) indicates that each channel can contain one or many programs. A triangle at the end of a line indicates a subtype relationship. For example, characters, actors, writers, directors, and producers are all people, so they all have names.

Note I've used basic UML (Unified Modeling Language, see `http://www.uml.org`) conventions in this diagram, but there are many methods of representing conceptual models, and you should use the one that you're most comfortable with.

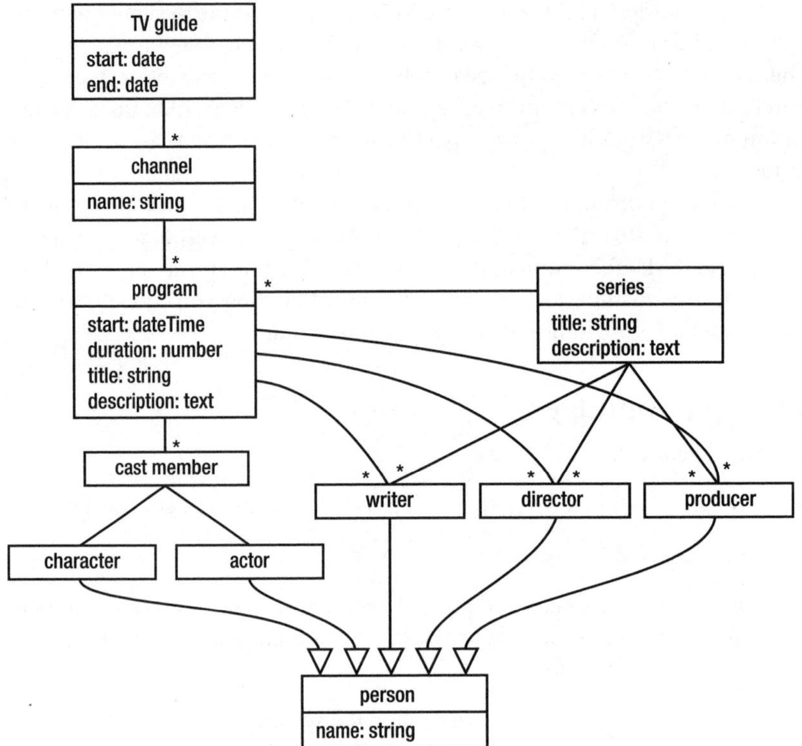

Figure 1-10. *Diagram of an information model for a TV guide*

Summary An information model is the starting point for designing a markup language.

Once you have this type of model, you need to map it onto an XML structure. In the rest of this section, we'll look at how you do this mapping and the different choices you might make while doing it, but before we start, it's worth getting our priorities in order.

Deciding Our Criteria

Whenever you design something, you need to know the requirements of the design. Knowing what your requirements are helps you to make decisions because it enables you to tell the difference between a good design (one that meets the requirements) and a bad design (one that doesn't).

There are usually four types of requirements in systems involving XML:

- **Human readability**—How easy it is for someone to understand the XML document.

  This is especially important if people have to author the XML documents by hand, but is also relevant for people programming applications that deal with the XML document.

- **Processing efficiency**—How easy it is for an application to process the XML document.

  The ease with which relevant information can be accessed within your XML document affects how simple it is to program applications that use it, and the speed with which they work. Different types of applications make different demands on markup languages, so it's not the case that one design will suit every type of processing.

- **Size**—How big the XML document is.

  XML is a verbose syntax—one of the initial requirements for XML was that it not be too concerned about verbosity—and it compresses well, so size is rarely crucial. However, it can be important in storage, processing, and transmission.

- **Extensibility**—How easy it is to reuse or make changes to the markup language later on.

  Extensibility involves giving room in a markup language for people to add their own extras and designing parts of the structure so that they can be used easily elsewhere. Both increase the lifespan and utility of the markup language. Of course, you don't have to worry about this if you never make explicit any rules about how your elements and attributes should fit together (such as in a schema or DTD).

These types of requirements have to be balanced against each other for any particular project, and even for particular XML documents within an application. You might not care very much about size when storing some information, for example, but it starts to be an issue when that same information needs to be transmitted over the Internet.

In our example, human readability and extensibility are the most important aspects because we're going to be using this as an example throughout the book, and I want you to be able to understand the examples we use, as well as to be able to extend the markup language to illustrate particular points. Processing efficiency is also important—we're going to be processing this with XSLT, and we want that XSLT to be fairly simple. Size, on the other hand, isn't really important.

Summary How an XML document is going to be used has a big effect on how it is best structured.

Deciding on a Naming Convention

The second decision to make before progressing on to the really hard work is to decide what naming convention to use. You'll remember from earlier in the chapter that there is no prescribed naming convention for XML markup languages, so it's up to you what you use. You may even wish to adopt different naming conventions for the different types of names (element, attribute, and entity names, and enumerated values) that you use in your document.

XML is case-sensitive, but which case convention you use is really a matter of preference. It can be helpful to use a case convention that makes your markup stand out from the languages that you're using to process it. In this book we'll be using XSLT, which uses all-lowercase words, separated by hyphens, to process our XML, and we'll also be using XHTML, which uses lowercase names, so using something that stands out from both of those would be useful.

A second thing to consider when deciding on names is how much abbreviation to use. Using abbreviations can make a big difference to the size of the document that you create and the amount of typing you have to do to create it! For example, consider the difference between HTML names `tr` and `td` and the names `table-row` and `table-cell`. The longer names are less ambiguous, but long element names can make the markup dominate the content of a document, as well as make a document larger.

Along the same lines as the issue of abbreviation is the question of how much context to add to element and attribute names. Some markup languages add a lot of context, for example, using names like `Cast.Member.Character` and `Cast.Member.Actor`. Other markup languages use the context in which an element appears to indicate what an element means. For example, a `<Character>` element gets its context from its parent `<Member>` element, which gets its context from its parent `<CastList>` element. Using context from the tree rather than in the element name is easier when processing with languages (such as XSLT) where the tree of the XML document is readily available.

For the purposes of the examples in this book, then, I will use camel case names, starting with an uppercase letter for elements and a lowercase letter for attributes. I will not use abbreviations, but neither will I add context information to element names. So the cast list will look like this:

```
<CastList>
  <CastMember>
    <Character>Zoe Slater</Character>
    <Actor>Michelle Ryan</Actor>
  </CastMember>
  <CastMember>
    <Character>Jamie Mitchell</Character>
    <Actor>Jack Ryder</Actor>
  </CastMember>
  <CastMember>
    <Character>Sonia Jackson</Character>
    <Actor>Natalie Cassidy</Actor>
  </CastMember>
</CastList>
```

Summary The naming convention that you use doesn't matter, as long as it's consistent so that it's easy to guess what the name of an element or attribute will be.

Mapping to Elements and Attributes

Now that we know what our priorities are and how we're going to name everything, we can start thinking about the components that we're going to use in our markup language. We need to decide what elements and attributes we're going to have and what kind of values they can take.

You have to use elements to hold structured or complex information in an XML document, so each of the concepts in the TV guide model can map onto an element in our XML structure. However, you can represent properties as either elements or attributes. Whether you use an element or attribute for a particular property is largely a matter of preference, although here are a couple of guidelines:

- Use an element if you might want to add more structure later on. For example, I might later want to add markup within descriptions or break down people's names into forenames and surnames.
- Use an attribute if the property holds information about information (**meta-information**). For example, the start and end dates for the TV guide are information about the information held in the TV guide, not a feature of the TV guide itself.
- If in doubt, use an element.

Using these mapping rules and the naming conventions that we've decided, we can come up with preliminary structures for those concepts and properties in the information model for our TV guide in Figure 1-10. These elements aren't arranged in a document yet—we're just looking at what the concepts and their properties might look like as elements and attributes individually:

```
<TVGuide start="date" end="date">...</TVGuide>
<Channel>
  <Name>string</Name>
  ...
</Channel>
<Program>
  <Start>dateTime</Start>
  <Duration>duration</Duration>
  <Title>string</Title>
  <Description>text</Description>
  ...
</Program>
<Series>
  <Title>string</Title>
  <Description>text</Description>
  ...
</Series>
<Character><Name>string</Name></Character>
<Actor><Name>string</Name></Actor>
<Writer><Name>string</Name></Writer>
<Director><Name>string</Name></Director>
<Producer><Name>string</Name></Producer>
```

While you're looking at the simple values that you need to hold in your XML document, it's worth thinking about how to represent them and what rules will govern whether a value is acceptable for that element or attribute. The closer the representation that you use is to the one used by the source or destination of the data, the easier it will be to process. Another factor that might influence the representations that you use is the availability of a standard representation, which we'll come to soon.

Summary You can hold simple data in either attributes or elements, but you have to use elements to hold structured information.

Representing Relationships

In the last section, we created some basic XML for the important information in our TV guide. What we didn't do, though, was fit that information together to show how the parts related to each other. We need to represent things like the following:

- A TV guide has listings for a number of channels.
- A channel shows a number of programs.
- A program has a number of cast members.
- A program may be part of a series.
- A cast member is a pairing of a character and an actor.

There are two ways of representing this kind of information in XML: by **nesting** and by **reference**.

Using nesting involves placing the element representing one piece of information within the element it's associated with. For example, we could show that a TV guide is made up of a number of channels by nesting the `<Channel>` elements within the `<TVGuide>` element, and show that a channel shows a number of programs by nesting the `<Program>` elements within the corresponding `<Channel>` elements:

```
<TVGuide start="date" end="date">
  <Channel>
    <Name>string</Name>
    <Program>...</Program>
    <Program>...</Program>
    ...
  </Channel>
  <Channel>
    <Name>string</Name>
    <Program>...</Program>
    <Program>...</Program>
    ...
  </Channel>
  ...
</TVGuide>
```

When you use nesting to indicate a one-to-many relationship, it's sometimes worth using a **wrapper element** to hold the nested elements. Using a wrapper element makes it easy to see where the list begins and ends, especially if you have several other elements nested in the same parent element. For example, we could use a wrapper element called `<CastList>` to hold all the `<CastMember>` elements in a `<Program>`:

```
<Program>
  <Start>dateTime</Start>
  <Duration>duration</Duration>
  <Title>string</Title>
  <Description>text</Description>
  <CastList>
```

```
    <CastMember>
      <Character><Name>string</Name></Character>
      <Actor><Name>string</Name></Actor>
    </CastMember>
    <CastMember>
      <Character><Name>string</Name></Character>
      <Actor><Name>string</Name></Actor>
    </CastMember>
    ...
  </CastList>
  ...
</Program>
```

Using references involves referencing a set of information using a unique identifier. For historical reasons, these identifiers and references often use attributes rather than elements, but you can use either, especially if you are using XSLT to process your XML. A good example where references would be appropriate here is in representing the link between a program and a series. We don't really want to nest the <Series> element inside the <Program> element because that would mean repeating the information about the series multiple times in the TV guide, whenever a program in that series was shown. On the other hand, we don't want to nest the <Program> element within the <Series> element because that would break the association between the channel and the program.

Instead, we could use the title of the series as a unique identifier for that series, and use that title within the information about the program. In the following code, a program uses the title of the series (*EastEnders*) to reference information about the series. The first <Series> element defines the series at the top level of the document:

```
<Series>
  <Title>EastEnders</Title>
  <Description>Soap set in the East End of London.</Description>
</Series>
```

The second <Series> element, used inside the <Program> element, gives a pointer to the series description (notice that the <Title> element here is empty as it represents the title of the episode, and the *EastEnders* series does not use episode titles):

```
<Program>
  <Start>2001-07-05T19:30:00</Start>
  <Duration>PT30M</Duration>
  <Series>EastEnders</Series>
  <Title></Title>
  <Description>
    Mark's health scare forces him to reconsider his future with Lisa, while
    Jamie is torn between Sonia and Zoe.
  </Description>
  ...
</Program>
```

Using references allows you to reuse the same information without repeating it. The referenced material may be in the same document as the references to it (you could nest the <Series> elements within the <TVGuide> element), or it could be in a separate document (you could create a series.xml document that contains the <Series> elements). However, using too many references may make it hard to work out how all the information ties together.

Summary You can use nesting or references to show the links between different sets of information in your document. References prevent duplication of information, but generally lead to documents that are harder to process.

TV Guide XML Document

It's always helpful to create a sample XML document when you design a new markup language, both to show people what you mean it to look like and to test that the decisions you've made hold up against data in the real world. So Listing 1-8 shows a sample document for our TV guide—TVGuide.xml.

Listing 1-8. TVGuide.xml

```
<?xml version="1.0" encoding="ISO-8859-1"?>
<TVGuide start="2001-07-05" end="2001-07-12">
  <Channel>
    <Name>BBC1</Name>
    ...
    <Program>
      <Start>2001-07-05T19:30:00</Start>
      <Duration>PT30M</Duration>
      <Series>EastEnders</Series>
      <Title></Title>
      <Description>
        Mark's health scare forces him to reconsider his future with Lisa,
        while Jamie is torn between Sonia and Zoe.
      </Description>
      <CastList>
        <CastMember>
          <Character><Name>Zoe Slater</Name></Character>
          <Actor><Name>Michelle Ryan</Name></Actor>
        </CastMember>
        <CastMember>
          <Character><Name>Jamie Mitchell</Name></Character>
          <Actor><Name>Jack Ryder</Name></Actor>
        </CastMember>
        <CastMember>
          <Character><Name>Sonia Jackson</Name></Character>
          <Actor><Name>Natalie Cassidy</Name></Actor>
        </CastMember>
        ...
      </CastList>
```

```
      <Writers>
        <Writer><Name>Nick Saltrese</Name></Writer>
        <Writer><Name>Julie Wassmer</Name></Writer>
      </Writers>
      <Director><Name>Stewart Edwards</Name></Director>
      <Producer><Name>Emma Turner</Name></Producer>
    </Program>
    ...
  </Channel>
  ...
</TVGuide>
```

We also have a supplementary document—series.xml—that holds information about TV series, as shown in Listing 1-9.

Listing 1-9. series.xml

```
<SeriesList>
  ...
  <Series>
    <Title>EastEnders</Title>
    <Description>Soap set in the East End of London.</Description>
  </Series>
  ...
</SeriesList>
```

This XML structure is the structure that we'll use throughout this book as the basis of our XSLT transformations. We've got a sample document, and we've discussed the rules that the document follows, but to share that description with other people, and to enable computers to check our documents, we need to write down those rules in a formal way. In the next section, we look at how to validate markup languages by describing them with DTDs and schemas.

Validating Markup Languages

Earlier in this chapter, we looked at the differences between well-formed XML documents, which follow the rules governing the syntax of XML, and valid XML documents, which follow the specific rules for a particular markup language. To enable an application to check whether a document you write is valid, you have to tell it the rules governing the vocabulary and grammar of the markup language that you're using. Validating helps you check the XML that you generate and the XML that you receive, to make sure that it has the structure that you're expecting.

The other important reason to validate an XML document when using XSLT is that the process of validation may **annotate** the XML document, adding information about the **types** of the elements and attributes that it contains. These annotations can help you, as an XSLT author, when writing and maintaining stylesheets. We'll be looking at using type annotations in Chapter 13.

There are two general ways of defining a markup language: using a **document type definition,** or **DTD**, and using a **schema**.

Document Type Definitions

DTDs are the basic means of defining XML structures. They use a subset of the syntax for describing markup languages that SGML uses, rather than XML, and they are fairly restricted in the rules that they allow you to put together about a markup language. However, DTDs are well-supported: most XML editors enable you to validate an XML document against a DTD and most applications that use XML will use a DTD if one is available.

Associating Documents with DTDs

You can associate a DTD with an XML document using a **DOCTYPE declaration** at the top of your XML document, just underneath the XML declaration. A DOCTYPE declaration can link to an external DTD or define an internal DTD, called an **internal subset**, or do both. For example, you could link your XHTML document to an external XHTML DTD with the following:

```
<?xml version="1.0" encoding="ISO-8859-1"?>
<!DOCTYPE html PUBLIC "-//W3C//DTD XHTML 1.0 Strict//EN"
                      "DTD/xhtml1-strict.dtd">
<html>
...
</html>
```

The string after the PUBLIC keyword is known as a **public identifier** and it gives a unique identity for the markup language. Some applications might be able to recognize the public identifier and use that to access their own set of internal rules to apply to the document. After the public identifier comes the **system identifier**, which is a URI for the DTD for the XML document.

An internal DOCTYPE declaration for our TV guide XML might look like the following:

```
<?xml version="1.0" encoding="ISO-8859-1"?>
<!DOCTYPE TVGuide [
<!ELEMENT TVGuide (Channel+)>
<!ATTLIST TVGuide
   start CDATA #REQUIRED
   end   CDATA #REQUIRED>
<!ELEMENT Channel (Name, Program+)>
...
]>
<TVGuide start="2001-07-05" end="2001-07-12">
...
</TVGuide>
```

This code snippet shows that the <TVGuide> element can contain one or more <Channel> elements and has two attributes: start and end. The <Channel> element contains a <Name> element followed by one or more <Program> elements.

Writing DTDs

There isn't enough space here to go into how to write DTDs in detail, but there's one aspect of DTDs that will be useful for you to know about: defining **entities**.

Note You can find details of DTD syntax in *XML in a Nutshell, Third Edition*, by Elliotte Rusty Harold and W. Scott Means (O'Reilly, 204, ISBN 0596007647).

If you remember back a couple of sections, we talked about how XML only uses five entities to escape the special characters in XML, and doesn't support all those useful entities that you have in HTML. Well, you can use a DTD to define whatever entities you want. These can be character entities, for example for a nonbreaking space or an é character, or longer ones if you want, holding standard or repeated text or XML, such as disclaimers.

You can define an entity with an entity definition, which gives the name of that entity and the value it holds. For example, you could define a ` ` entity for a nonbreaking space (which is ` ` as a character reference) with

```
<!ENTITY nbsp ' '>
```

Naturally, the XHTML DTD includes all the entities that you can use in HTML. If you want to use them in your XML document, you can define **parameter entities** (which are entities that can be used within a DTD) for the files and include them in an internal DTD. To use these entities in the TV guide document, for example, we could use the following:

```
<!DOCTYPE TVGuide [
<!ENTITY % HTMLlat1 SYSTEM "xhtml-lat1.ent">
%HTMLlat1;
<!ENTITY % HTMLsymbol SYSTEM "xhtml-symbol.ent">
%HTMLsymbol;
<!ENTITY % HTMLspecial SYSTEM "xhtml-special.ent">
%HTMLspecial;
]>
```

Note These `.ent` files are available along with the XHTML DTDs from `http://www.w3.org/TR/xhtml1`.

Summary You can use DTDs to define entities and make it easier to include non-ASCII characters in your document.

Defining Entities

Earlier in this chapter, we looked at a couple of ways of including an ë character in the cast list XML document and found that the usual HTML entity `ë` wouldn't work. Let's look now at how to define an entity for that character, so that we can use the `ë` entity in our XML document.

We'll start off with an internal DTD, in `castlist7.xml`. You need to create a `DOCTYPE` declaration in the XML document, and put the entity definition inside this `DOCTYPE` declaration, as shown in Listing 1-10.

Listing 1-10. `castlist7.xml`

```
<?xml version="1.0" encoding="ISO-8859-1"?>
<!DOCTYPE castlist [
<!ENTITY euml '&#235;'>
]>
<castlist>
  <member>
    <character gender="female">Zo&euml; Slater</character>
    <actor>Michelle Ryan</actor>
  </member>
  ...
</castlist>
```

Have a look at this XML document using Internet Explorer, and you should see the ë character without any problems. The DOCTYPE declaration is indicated at the top of the page, but Internet Explorer doesn't show you its contents, as in Figure 1-11.

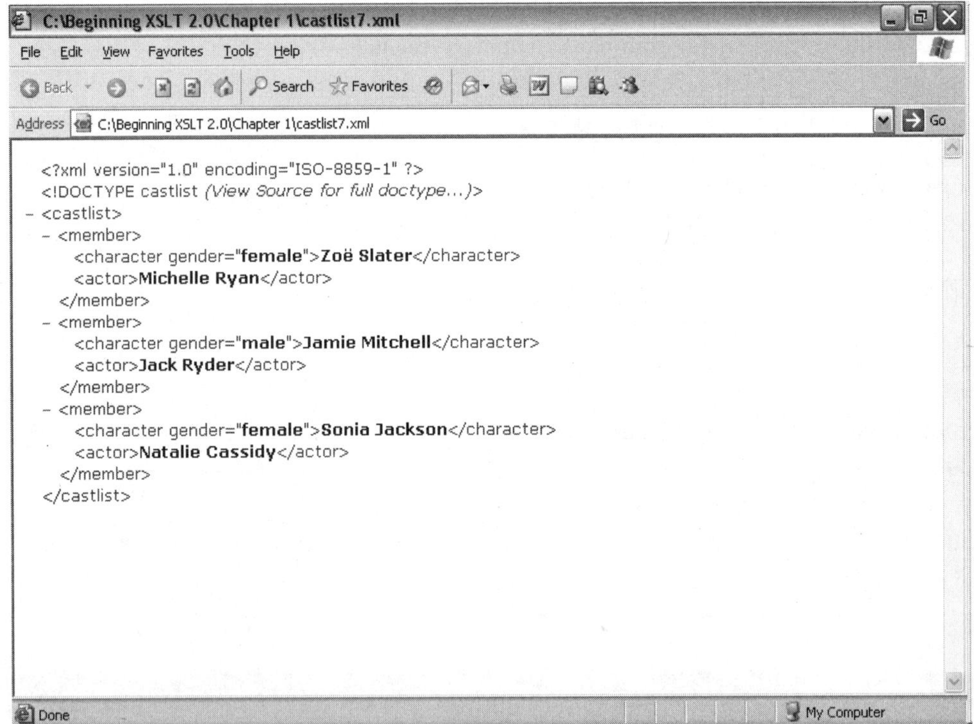

Figure 1-11. *Viewing the declared* `ë` *entity reference*

Now try moving the content of the DOCTYPE declaration into its own file, `castlist.dtd`. The DTD document is very small, only containing one line, shown in Listing 1-11.

Listing 1-11. castlist.dtd

```
<!ENTITY euml '&#235;'>
```

In the castlist8.xml XML document, you need to point to this external DTD from the DOCTYPE declaration. Change the DOCTYPE declaration from castlist7.xml so that it reads like the code in Listing 1-12.

Listing 1-12. castlist8.xml

```
<?xml version="1.0" encoding="ISO-8859-1"?>
<!DOCTYPE castlist SYSTEM 'castlist.dtd'>
<castlist>
  <member>
    <character gender="female">Zo&euml; Slater</character>
    <actor>Michelle Ryan</actor>
  </member>
  ...
</castlist>
```

Moving the entity definition to an external DTD makes absolutely no difference to how Internet Explorer displays the XML document—it looks the same as in Figure 1-10.

Finally, try using the entity definitions available from XHTML. Download the three entities files from http://www.w3.org/TR/xhtml1 and reference them from castlist2.dtd DTD, as in Listing 1-13.

Listing 1-13. castlist2.dtd

```
<!ENTITY % HTMLlat1 SYSTEM "xhtml-lat1.ent">
%HTMLlat1;
<!ENTITY % HTMLsymbol SYSTEM "xhtml-symbol.ent">
%HTMLsymbol;
<!ENTITY % HTMLspecial SYSTEM "xhtml-special.ent">
%HTMLspecial;
```

Now you can use whatever entities you like from HTML within castlist9.xml, which refers to this DTD.

Schemas

Schemas are XML documents that define a particular markup language. There are several different schema markup languages around; at the time of writing three schema languages are heading the field:

- **XML Schema** from W3C—The official W3C schema language
- **RELAX NG**—A schema language from OASIS, now an ISO standard
- **Schematron**—A very flexible rule-based schema language, currently undergoing ISO standardization

Each of these schema languages is able to articulate different kinds of rules that might apply to your markup language. Indeed, often it's worth using several of these schema languages in combination, depending on how rigorous you need the validation to be.

The schema language that is most significant for XSLT authors is XML Schema. As we'll see in Chapter 5, the datatypes available in XPath are based on those defined in XML Schema. It's also likely that most **Schema-Aware XSLT processors** will use XML Schema schemas (as well as DTDs) to annotate elements and attributes with their types. We'll be looking at how XSLT processors use type information in Chapter 13.

When designing XML documents, the format of the values that you use can make a big difference to how easy it is to validate the document, and to how easy it is to process the document using XSLT. If you can, it will make life a lot easier if you follow the formats of the datatypes used in XPath. This is particularly the case for the date/time and duration types, but also for Boolean values and for languages. The formats that you should use are

- `xs:dateTime` format—`CCYY-MM-DDThh:mm:ss`, for example, `2001-07-05T19:30:00`
- `xs:date` format—`CCYY-MM-DD`, for example, `2001-07-05`
- `xs:time` format—`hh:mm:ss`, for example, `19:30:00`
- `xdt:yearMonthDuration` format—`PyYmM`, for example, `P1Y` for a duration of one year
- `xdt:dayTimeDuration` format—`PdDThHmMsS`, for example, `PT30M` for a duration of 30 minutes
- `xs:boolean` format—`true` or `1` for true, and `false` or `0` for false
- `xs:language` format—As defined by RFC 1766, for example, `en-US` for US English

---

■ **Note** If you want to learn more about XML Schema in general, then you should have a look at *XML Schema*, by Eric van der Vlist (O'Reilly, 2002, ISBN 0596002521).

■ **Summary** XML Schema is used for typing in XSLT, so you should use the formats that it defines if you can.

Presenting XML

The reason that HTML is so ubiquitous is because there are lots of applications that understand HTML. HTML editors and most importantly web browsers know how to parse HTML, and they know how to present HTML—they know that an `<H1>` element should be large and bold, that a `<TABLE>` element and its content defines a table, that an `<EM>` element should be rendered in italics, and so on. These presentational rules might be overridden by CSS, but usually the default behavior of the web browser gives a baseline, with CSS tweaking the details.

On the other hand, a web browser has absolutely no idea about what to do with an XML document. It can't know how a `<CastList>` element should be displayed because it doesn't know anything about our TV guide XML. However, we can still use CSS to tell the browser how to display the XML.

Presenting XML with CSS

The CSS that you use for XML documents is similar to that for HTML documents, except that the names that you use in the CSS rules are those of the XML elements rather than the HTML elements.

One thing that's particularly important in CSS for XML documents is the `display` property. The `display` property governs the general layout of the content of the element within the page, for example, whether it should create a new block, be rendered inline, be a list item, and so on. The `display` property is also useful for *hiding* certain parts of the document if you don't want them to be displayed, which you can do by setting it to the value `none`.

As an example, Listing 1-14 shows a CSS file—`TVGuide.xml.css`—for displaying the TV guide XML.

Listing 1-14. `TVGuide.xml.css`

```
TVGuide {
  font-family: Verdana, sans-serif;
  font-size: small;
}
Duration, Writer, Director, Producer {
  display: none;
}
Start {
  margin-top: 1em;
  display: block;
}
Channel Name, Series, Title {
  display: block;
  margin-bottom: 0em;
  padding: 0.3em;
}
Channel Name {
  margin-top: 1em;
  background: #C00;
  color: white;
  font-weight: bold;
  font-size: 1.44em;
}
Series {
  background: black;
  color: yellow;
  font-weight: bold;
  font-size: 1.2em;
}
Title {
  background: black;
  color: white;
}
```

```
CastList {
  display: block;
  padding: 0.5em 1em;
}
CastMember {
  display: list-item;
  list-style-type: none;
}
Character Name, Actor Name {
  display: inline;
  background: transparent;
  color: black;
  margin-bottom: 0em;
  padding: 0em;
  font-weight: normal;
  font-size: 1em;
}
Actor Name {
  font-weight: bold;
}
```

Summary You can use CSS to style XML in the same way as you use it with HTML.

Associating Stylesheets with XML

In HTML, you can either nest CSS within a `<STYLE>` element or use a `<LINK>` element to point to a separate CSS file. An XML document can't use either of these methods because a web browser doesn't know what these elements mean for a random markup language. So how does the web browser know to use this CSS with the XML document without having a `<LINK>` element to point to it? Well, you might remember the `xml-stylesheet` processing instruction from earlier in this chapter:

```
<?xml-stylesheet type="text/css" href="TVGuide.css"?>
```

If you add this processing instruction to the top of your XML document, right underneath the XML declaration and before any DOCTYPE declaration, then an XML-aware and CSS-capable web browser (like Internet Explorer) will use the CSS stylesheet you point at to display the XML document. The top of `TVGuide2.xml` looks like Listing 1-15.

Listing 1-15. `TVGuide2.xml`

```
<?xml version="1.0"?>
<?xml-stylesheet type="text/css" href="TVGuide.css"?>
<TVGuide start="2001-07-05" end="2001-07-12">
  ...
</TVGuide>
```

Summary The `xml-stylesheet` processing instruction links a document to a stylesheet that can be used to present it.

Viewing XML with CSS

Save the CSS shown in the last section as `TVGuide.xml.css` and add an `xml-stylesheet` processing instruction to the `TVGuide.xml` file that we've developed, pointing to the `TVGuide.xml.css` file, to create `TVGuide2.xml`. Now open the `TVGuide2.xml` file in Internet Explorer. Instead of the collapsible tree that you saw before, you'll see something that looks like an HTML page as shown in Figure 1-12.

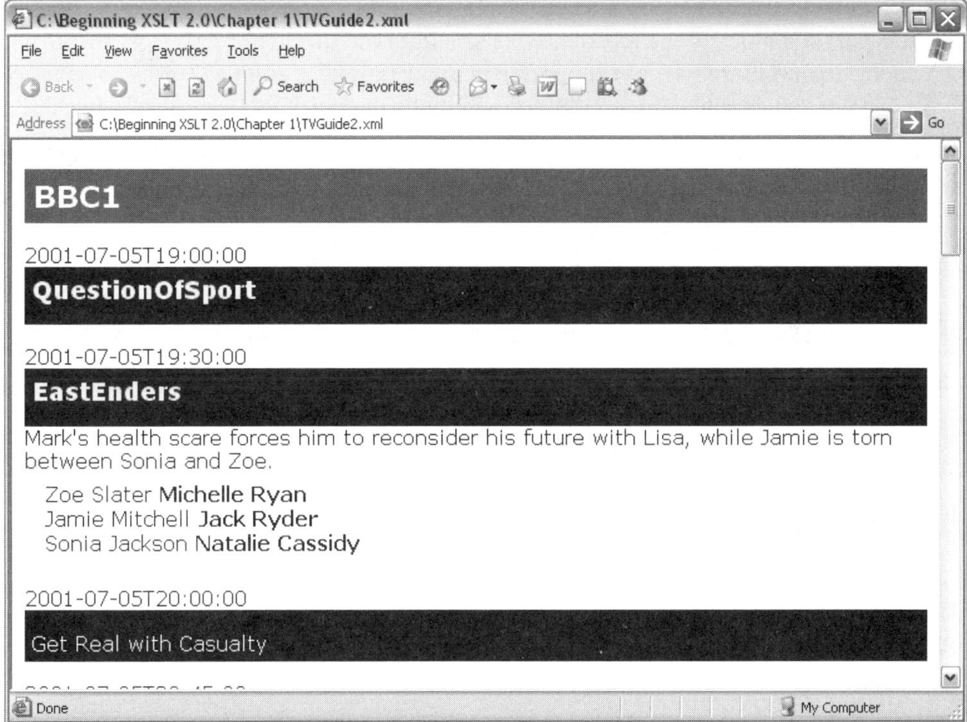

Figure 1-12. *Viewing an XML document using CSS styles*

You can play around with the CSS to hide and show different parts of the XML document.

Limitations of CSS

We've managed to get a reasonably nice view of our XML document using CSS, but it isn't perfect—in fact it looks nothing like the pretty display that we had with our HTML document. CSS has several limitations that stop us from getting the display the way we want with the XML that we have:

- The XML elements are displayed in the order that they're given in the XML document. We can't make the start time of a program display after the series title, for example.
- CSS can't display attributes. We can't use CSS to display the start and end dates of the TV guide as they're held in attributes.
- Element content is shown exactly as it is. Our XML specifies the start date/time of a program using a standard date/time format that isn't particularly easy to read, but we can't use CSS to reformat it.
- You can't add much in the way of text. CSS2 allows you to add text or images before or after elements, but this is not supported in many browsers, and CSS2 gives no support for adding static content like headings, descriptions, or disclaimers when displaying XML.
- Content held in other documents is hard to access. We've put the information about the series that programs can be part of in a separate document, but we can't now access that information and display it in the page.
- An element can only be of one type. If you want to use CSS to display tables, you have to have elements that follow the same kind of structure as tables in HTML. We couldn't display the TV guide as a table with each column being a different channel, for example.
- CSS doesn't support dynamic content. We can't create links from our page, much less use scripting to show and hide parts of the page.

All in all, CSS is fairly limited when it comes to displaying XML documents, especially ones that are **data oriented** like ours is, where the structure of the XML doesn't necessarily mirror the way that we want to see it.

■ **Summary** You can't use CSS to restructure your XML or your data, which is a big limitation.

Summary

This chapter has given a speedy introduction to XML. XML is a meta-markup language: it defines a syntax that a family of markup languages should follow. Documents that follow these rules are known as well-formed XML documents. An HTML document can be turned into an XHTML document by making it follow XML rules.

But the real power of XML comes from being able to make up your own markup language. You can design a markup language that is specifically designed to hold the information that you need it to hold for your application. Once you've designed it, you can describe the language using a DTD or a schema. Having a DTD or schema enables applications to check whether a document adheres to the rules of your markup language—to validate XML documents.

We've created an XML document that holds the dynamic information in our HTML page, the core set of information that makes up our TV guide. We can render this XML document using CSS, but it doesn't look anything like the HTML document that we had in the first place.

So haven't we painted ourselves into a corner? We did have a lovely HTML page that displayed the information we had in the way that we wanted to see it, gave us links and images, and had dynamic content. Now we have an XML document that we can't view in the way we want to view it. What's the point of that? Well, the content that our XML document holds can now be used by applications without them having to wade through lots of irrelevant HTML. This means our TV guide can be **repurposed**—used by lots of different applications in lots of different ways.

However, we still want to be able to use that information in the way that we were originally using it—to display it on a web page. To do that, we need a mechanism for transforming our XML into something that web browsers can understand more easily, back to the HTML that we had originally. And to do that, we need XSLT, which leads us nicely to the next chapter.

Review Questions

1. Why is it beneficial to use your own elements and attributes rather than using HTML?
2. What are the relationships between XML, SGML, HTML, and XHTML?
3. What naming convention does XHTML use?
4. What are the differences between start tags, end tags, and empty element tags?
5. What is the term for the element in an XML document that contains all the other elements in the document?
6. What two ways could you use to give an attribute a value that contains an apostrophe?
7. How do you translate Boolean attributes from HTML to XHTML?
8. What two characters must always be escaped using entities within an XML document? Which other three characters can be represented by entities in an XML document?
9. What four ways could you use to include a nonbreaking space character in an XML document?
10. In which two XHTML elements are `CDATA` sections most useful, and why?
11. What considerations do you need to take into account when you're designing an XML-based markup language?
12. What kinds of information can attributes hold?
13. What two ways can you use to indicate an association between different sets of information in an XML document?
14. How do you associate a DTD with an XML document?

15. What is the difference between a well-formed XML document and a valid XML document?
16. Name some schema markup languages.
17. How can you associate a stylesheet with an XML document?
18. What are the limitations of using CSS to style XML?

CHAPTER 2

Creating HTML from XML

In the last chapter, we developed two main XML documents. The first was an XHTML document—the same HTML document that we started with, but represented in XHTML. The XHTML document gets displayed just like an HTML document would, but you can also edit it and display it like XML, in a tree. The XHTML document doesn't really take full advantage of XML, though. We're still stuck using a markup language that doesn't really tie in with the content of our document. So the second XML document we developed used a markup language we specifically invented to hold information for our TV guide.

The XML document written in the specialized markup language is a lot cleaner—it doesn't say anything at all about the way in which a particular piece of information should be presented. On the other hand, that's its big weakness—even people who are used to reading XML will find it a lot harder to work out what TV program is showing when and on what channel. Somehow we need to add information to the XML document to say how it should be shown in a web browser.

In this chapter, we'll start looking at XSLT as a way of telling a browser how to display an XML document. This whole book is about XSLT, so we're not going to cover everything, just enough to get an XML document displayed as an HTML page. In this chapter, you'll learn

- What the goals of XSLT are and how it fits with other XML standards
- How to use XSLT processors to transform XML into HTML
- How to write simplified stylesheets
- What the XSLT namespace is
- How to access information from an XML document
- How to iterate over elements in an XML document
- How to get a value into an attribute

XSL: The Extensible Stylesheet Language

XML goes a long way towards making information accessible—it's a text-based format that you can use to hold data on different platforms and in different kinds of applications. But just because some information is held in XML doesn't mean that it's immediately useful. You still need to write a program to manipulate the data. One of the most common things that you'll want to do with XML is to present that information—as HTML pages on the Web, as PDF documents for printing, as text for emailing, and so on.

The W3C started developing a standard language for presenting information held in XML in 1998, around the time XML was being finalized. This language was named the Extensible Stylesheet Language (**XSL**). The goal of XSL was to develop a stylesheet language that could overcome the limitations of CSS that we saw at the end of the last chapter—a stylesheet language that could restructure information and add things like headings to a page. To manage this, XSL borrowed heavily from the Document Style Semantics and Specification Language (**DSSSL**), which is a standard stylesheet language that's used in SGML applications. Another early design decision was that XSL should use **XML syntax** to represent the rules about how XML should be presented—XSL should be an XML-based markup language.

Not long into the development of XSL, it became clear that there were really three parts to the stylesheet language:

- A markup language for describing presentational details, like the margin around a block or the color of a table cell
- A markup language for defining how to map from some XML into the presentational markup language
- An expression language for pointing to information in an XML document and performing calculations

The Extensible Stylesheet Language therefore split into two markup languages and a third text-based language. The first markup language is purely presentational and describes how **formatting objects** should be laid out on a page. This language is known as XSL Formatting Objects, or **XSL-FO**. The second markup language defines how to **transform** from any XML-based markup language into another markup language (or into plain text). This language is known as XSL Transformations, or **XSLT**. The third, text based, language is used within XSLT to point to pieces of information in an XML document, and this is the XML Path Language, or **XPath**.

■ **Note** XSL-FO is a fairly large markup language in its own right, so we're not going to have space to cover it in detail in this book, but you don't need to know about XSL-FO in order to use XSLT to transform into other useful markup languages, such as XHTML. XSL-FO is usually used as an intermediary format on the way to something like PDF or PostScript, for printing.

■ **Summary** XSL is made up of two markup languages: XSL-FO for describing how information should be displayed and XSLT for describing how to transform from one markup language to another format. XSLT uses a third language, XPath, to select parts of XML to process and to perform calculations.

The first versions of XSLT and XPath became W3C Recommendations in November 1999. XSLT 1.0 and XPath 1.0 have been around for over five years now and have experienced fairly heavy use in that time, with a number of conformant processors and many editors and other support tools.

Note The XSLT 1.0 Recommendation is available at `http://www.w3.org/TR/xslt` and the XPath 1.0 Recommendation is available at `http://www.w3.org/TR/xpath`.

The XSLT 1.0 Recommendation was followed in December 2000 by a Working Draft for XSLT 1.1, which involved supposedly minor changes to XSLT 1.0 such as support for multiple result documents and user-defined functions. Unfortunately, some of these minor changes proved to be more work, or more contentious, than the Working Group developing XSLT anticipated; XSLT 1.1 never reached completion, and work on it officially ended in August 2001.

Caution There are some XSLT processors around that support features from XSLT 1.1. Obviously if you use these features, you won't be able to use a processor that doesn't support them, so your stylesheet won't be portable.

In February 2001, the W3C produced a set of requirements for XSLT 2.0 and XPath 2.0, and work has been ongoing on these versions since then. Most of the changes in XPath 2.0 have been to bring it into line with XML Schema and with XQuery, such as the introduction of strong data typing; most of the changes in XSLT 2.0 have been to make it easier to do those things that were hard in XSLT 1.0, such as grouping and string processing.

The XPath 2.0 spec is split over several documents, most of which are shared with XQuery 1.0:

- **"Data Model"** defines the data model that XPath uses for atomic values and for XML documents; available at `http://www.w3.org/TR/xpath-datamodel`.
- **"XPath 2.0 Language"** defines the syntax and semantics of the XPath expression language; available at `http://www.w3.org/TR/xpath20`.
- **"Function and Operators"** defines the behavior of the functions and operators that are built in to XPath 2.0; available at `http://www.w3.org/TR/xpath-functions`.
- **"Formal Semantics"** provides a formal definition of the XPath language, including the static type inferencing that's allowed; available at `http://www.w3.org/TR/xquery-semantics`.

Note There's rarely any need to look at the "Formal Semantics" document. XSLT 2.0 doesn't use the static type inferencing that it defines, and the other behavior that it details is described in a more accessible way in the "XPath 2.0 Language" document.

The XSLT 2.0 spec is also split over a couple of documents:

- **"XSLT 2.0"** defines the syntax and semantics of XSLT; available at `http://www.w3.org/TR/xslt20`.
- **Serialization** defines how the node trees that result from a transformation or query can be serialized into a physical document; available at `http://www.w3.org/TR/xslt-xquery-serialization`.

Unsurprisingly, there aren't currently as many tools for XSLT 2.0 as there are for XSLT 1.0, but this should change when XSLT 2.0 becomes a Recommendation and becomes more widely adopted.

Summary There are three versions of XSLT. XSLT 1.0 is stable but lacks functionality; XSLT 1.1 only got to the stage of Working Draft and shouldn't be used; XSLT 2.0 has a lot of useful features but has not been around for very long so still lacks support.

An XML document that is written in XSLT is commonly known as an **XSLT stylesheet**, and it's usually given the extension `.xsl`. Each XSLT stylesheet describes how a set of XML documents—the **source** documents—should be converted into other documents—the **result** documents—whether they are XSL-FO, XHTML, comma-delimited text, or in any other text-based format such as HTML. Usually, an XSLT stylesheet will take source documents written in one particular markup language, such as the TV guide XML that we're using, and produce a result in another markup language that can be used by a specialist application, such as XHTML for presentation in a browser.

To perform a transformation, XSLT needs to be able to point to information in the source document, so that it can process it and include it in the result, and this is where XPath comes in. The most important role of XPath is to collect information from an XML document by navigating through the document. A secondary role of XPath is as a general expression language, to allow you to perform calculations, such as averaging the ratings given to TV programs.

Summary XML documents written in XSLT are known as stylesheets. Stylesheets can transform source XML documents into result documents in a range of formats.

Using XSLT Processors

To use XSLT, you need an **XSLT processor**. XSLT processors are applications that understand what to do with XSLT stylesheets. You tell an XSLT processor to use a particular stylesheet with a particular XML document, and it runs the stylesheet to give you a result, as shown in Figure 2-1.

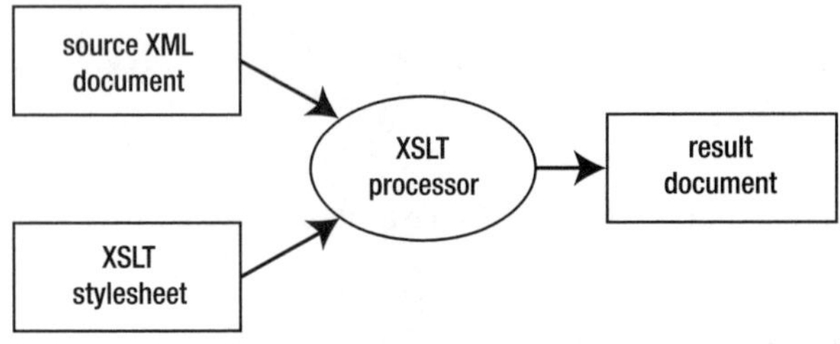

Figure 2-1. *Using an XSLT processor*

XSLT 2.0 processors fall into two categories: **Basic XSLT processors** support all the basic functionality that's needed for carrying out a transformation; **Schema-Aware XSLT processors** additionally understand how to validate a document against a schema, and they can use the information that arises from this validation to help process the document. We'll be mainly focusing on Basic XSLT processing in this book, although Chapter 13 will look at features that are only available in Schema-Aware XSLT processors.

There are lots of different XSLT 1.0 processors available for different platforms, many of which are free and open source. The three major XSLT 1.0 processors are

- **MSXML** from Microsoft—Download from `http://msdn.microsoft.com/`.
- **Saxon** version 6.5.3 from Michael Kay—Download from `http://saxon.sourceforge.net/`.
- **Xalan** from the Apache project—Download from `http://xml.apache.org/`.

■ Note There are lots and lots of other stand-alone XSLT processors that you can use. Go to `http://www.xmlsoftware.com/xslt/` for a complete list. There are also XSLT processors embedded in frameworks and applications, for example, the `System.Xml.Xsl` class in Microsoft's .NET Framework.

These three processors have all been around for some time and have gone through a lot of testing, so they're pretty much guaranteed to be conformant to the XSLT 1.0 Recommendation. However, they do often differ in little ways, and in particular in the types of error message that they give when there's something wrong with your stylesheet, so sometimes it's useful to try a stylesheet with several processors to help isolate what's wrong with it.

XSLT 2.0 processors are a lot thinner on the ground. The ones that are available at time of writing are

- **Saxon** version 8.4 from Saxonica—Download from `http://www.saxonica.com/`.
- **Altova XSLT Engine** from Altova—Download from `http://www.xmlspy.com/resources_xsltengine.html`.
- **Saxon.NET** from X2x2X, which is a port of Saxon 8.0B to .NET—Download from `http://www.x2x2x.org/x2x2x/home/`.
- **Gestalt** by Colin Paul Adams, which is a port of Saxon to Eiffel—Information from `http://sourceforge.net/projects/gestalt`.
- **oraxsl** in Oracle's XML Developer's Kit version 10i and above—Download from `http://otn.oracle.com/tech/xml/xdk/content.html`.

Most of these processors are Basic XSLT processors, so they don't support the features of XSLT 2.0 that require schema awareness. Saxon, however, comes in two flavors: Saxon Basic, which is free and open-source, and Saxon Schema-Aware, which is a commercial product. A version of Xalan that supports XSLT 2.0 is also under development.

Caution None of these XSLT 2.0 processors fully implement the most recent version of XSLT 2.0, so do check the documentation to see what's missing. Also, unlike XSLT 1.0 processors, XSLT 2.0 processors haven't been under heavy enough use for long enough to be bug-free, so it's especially important to test your stylesheet with multiple processors to make sure that you're not exploiting a bug in your particular processor.

Summary XSLT stylesheets are interpreted by XSLT processors, which generate a result from source XML.

In the rest of this section, I'll describe how to use Saxon, which is the most well-developed and conformant of the XSLT 2.0 processors, and MSXML, which, despite only being an XSLT 1.0 processor, is worth a mention because it's built into Internet Explorer. As is traditional, we'll use a very simple Hello World example. The XML document for this example is `HelloWorld.xml`, as shown in Listing 2-1.

Listing 2-1. `HelloWorld.xml`

```
<?xml version="1.0" encoding="ISO-8859-1"?>
<greeting>Hello World!</greeting>
```

The `HelloWorld.xsl` stylesheet, shown in Listing 2-2, is also very straightforward. It looks a lot like a well-formed HTML document but has some special XSLT-related elements and attributes in it.

Listing 2-2. `HelloWorld.xsl`

```
<?xml version="1.0" encoding="ISO-8859-1"?>
<html xmlns:xsl="http://www.w3.org/1999/XSL/Transform"
      xsl:version="2.0">
  <head>
    <title>Hello World Example</title>
  </head>
  <body>
    <p>
      <xsl:value-of select="/greeting" />
    </p>
  </body>
</html>
```

Note The more astute amongst you will have noticed that this XML document contains a special attribute, beginning with `xmlns`. This attribute declares a namespace and associates the namespace with the prefix `xsl`. As we'll see later on, prefixes are used on element and attribute names to say what markup language they come from.

Using Saxon

Saxon is an XSLT 2.0 processor written in Java by Michael Kay, the Basic version of which is open source. Make sure that you get the most recent version (8.4 at time of writing) to get the best coverage.

As well as using Saxon on the command line to test a transformation, you can use Saxon in any Java application. As we'll see in Chapter 15, one of the places where it's most useful is within the **Cocoon** servlet. Cocoon is a servlet that sits on a web server and manages the transformations of XML documents into HTML, which it then sends back to the client. These transformations are known as **server-side transformations** because they occur on the server.

Transforming with Saxon

First, make sure that you've got `saxon8.jar` in your `CLASSPATH`, so that Java knows where to find it.

Then open a command prompt in the directory in which you've saved `HelloWorld.xml` and use the following command line:

```
java net.sf.saxon.Transform -o HelloWorld.saxon.html HelloWorld.xml
  HelloWorld.xsl
```

This command line tells Saxon to transform `HelloWorld.xml` using `HelloWorld.xsl` and directs the output of the transformation to `HelloWorld.saxon.html`. If you open this HTML file up, you'll see the following:

```
<html>
   <head>
      <meta http-equiv="Content-Type" content="text/html; charset=UTF-8">

      <title>Hello World Example</title>
   </head>
   <body>
      <p>Hello World!</p>
   </body>
</html>
```

If you open up `HelloWorld.saxon.html` using a web browser, you should see the simple HTML page shown in Figure 2-2.

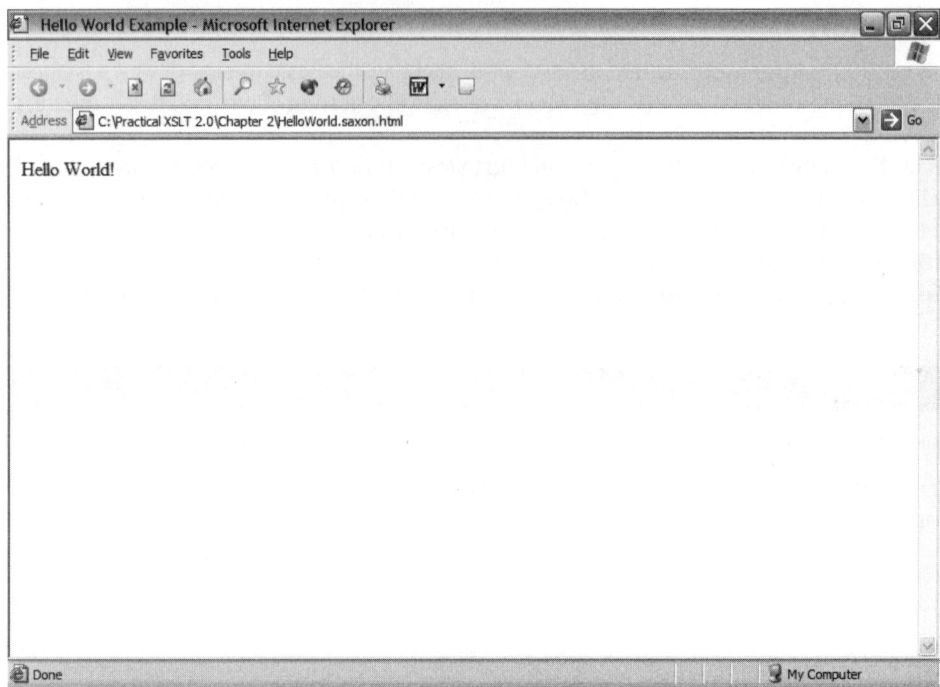

Figure 2-2. *Viewing* `HelloWorld.saxon.html` *in Internet Explorer*

In the last chapter, you saw how you could associate a stylesheet with an XML document by adding an `xml-stylesheet` processing instruction at the top of the XML document. In that example, we used a CSS stylesheet, but you can do the same with an XSLT stylesheet. Here, we want to associate the `HelloWorld.xml` document with the `HelloWorld.xsl` stylesheet. Edit `HelloWorld.xml` to add an `xml-stylesheet` processing instruction and create `HelloWorld2.xml` as in Listing 2-3.

Listing 2-3. `HelloWorld2.xml`

```
<?xml version="1.0" encoding="ISO-8859-1"?>
<?xml-stylesheet type="text/xsl" href="HelloWorld.xsl"?>
<greeting>Hello World!</greeting>
```

If you want Saxon to use the `xml-stylesheet` processing instruction to work out which XSLT stylesheet to use to transform a document, you need to add the `-a` flag to the command line and remove the reference to the stylesheet, as follows:

```
java net.sf.saxon.Transform -a -o HelloWorld.saxon.html HelloWorld2.xml
```

This should give you exactly the same output as before: if you view `HelloWorld.saxon.html` in Internet Explorer, you should see the same as before, as shown in Figure 2-2.

Using MSXML

MSXML is Microsoft's XML parser, schema validator, and XSLT processor rolled into one package. MSXML comes with Internet Explorer, so if you have Internet Explorer installed on your machine, you will have a version of MSXML as well.

MSXML is mainly used with **client-side transformations**. In a client-side transformation, the source XML and the stylesheet for transforming it are both shipped to a client (like Internet Explorer) and then the client carries out the transformations and displays the result. Of course, you can use this facility to automatically transform and view XML documents on your machine—they don't have to come from a distant server.

Note You can also run MSXML from a script in Internet Explorer or server-side from ASP pages. You'll learn more about this in Chapter 15, when we look at writing dynamic applications using XSLT.

You have to be careful with MSXML because there are several different versions. MSXML only supports XSLT in version 3 and above. The version that comes with Internet Explorer 5 and 5.5 is MSXML2, which doesn't support XSLT. MSXML3 comes with Internet Explorer 6, but you can install it in replace mode to make it work in Internet Explorer 5 and above. There's no version of MSXML that supports XSLT 2.0 at the moment.

Caution MSXML2 does support a transformation language, but it's based on an early version of XSL and isn't XSLT. You can tell that a stylesheet is using this transformation language by the fact that it uses the namespace `http://www.w3.org/TR/WD-xsl` rather than `http://www.w3.org/1999/XSL/Transform`.

To work with XSLT in Internet Explorer, you need to either download and install Internet Explorer version 6 or download and install MSXML3. To make it work automatically, you have to install MSXML3 in replace mode by running a utility called `xmlinst` to replace the existing MSXML2 with MSXML3. You cannot use MSXML4 to get automatic transformations with Internet Explorer; you must use MSXML3.

Tip A very useful FAQ on MSXML is available at `http://www.netcrucible.com/xslt/msxml-faq.htm`. You might also find Chris Bayes's site at `http://www.bayes.co.uk/xml` useful for identifying what version of MSXML you have installed.

There are two other tools available from Microsoft at `http://msdn.microsoft.com/XML/XMLDownloads/default.aspx` that you will find helpful if you're using MSXML to transform your documents:

- **Internet Explorer Tools for Validating XML and Viewing XSLT Output**—Gives a context-menu option for viewing the result of XSLT transformations in Internet Explorer
- **MSXSL Command Line Transformation Utility**—Allows you to carry out transformations using MSXML from the command line

---

Note The MSXSL command-line utility uses MSXML4 by default. You can also use MSXML4 if you run the transformation from a client-side or server-side script.

Transforming with MSXML

The easiest way to transform XML with MSXML is to use Internet Explorer to activate the transformation. When you include an `xml-stylesheet` processing instruction in the XML document and then open that XML document, Internet Explorer reads the `xml-stylesheet` processing instruction and automatically retrieves the stylesheet you've pointed to. Internet Explorer uses MSXML to process the stylesheet and shows you the result in an HTML page.

If you try opening, in Internet Explorer, `HelloWorld2.xml` (shown in Listing 2-3), which includes an `xml-stylesheet` processing instruction that points to `HelloWorld.xsl`, you should see something like the screenshot shown in Figure 2-3.

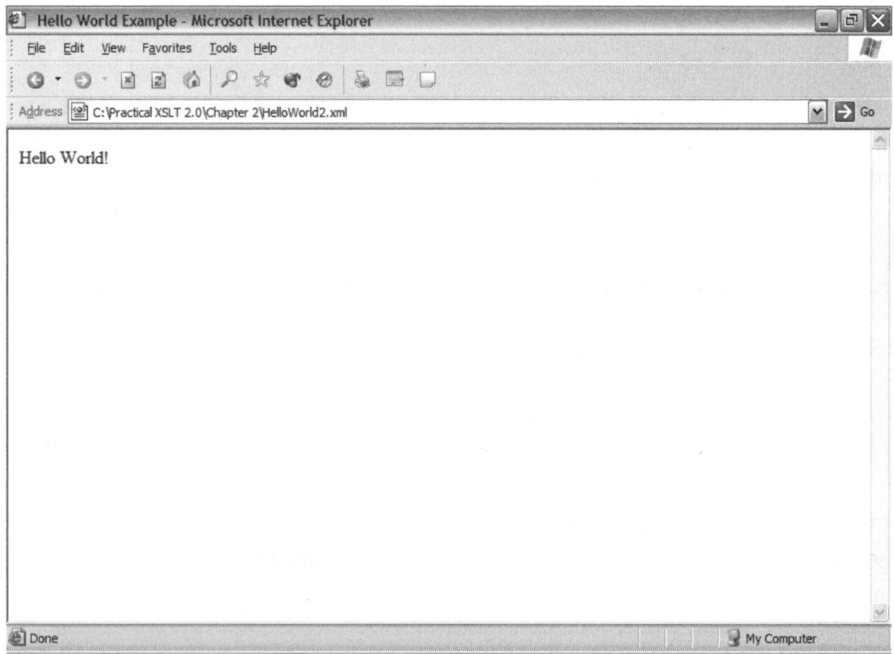

Figure 2-3. *Client-side transformation in Internet Explorer*

You can see that the XSLT stylesheet's been used properly because the title bar of the window shows the title that we used in the XSLT stylesheet. You can check the XML source by viewing the source of the document (either through the View Source option in the context menu or through the Source option in the View menu). The XML document will probably open up in Notepad, as shown in Figure 2-4.

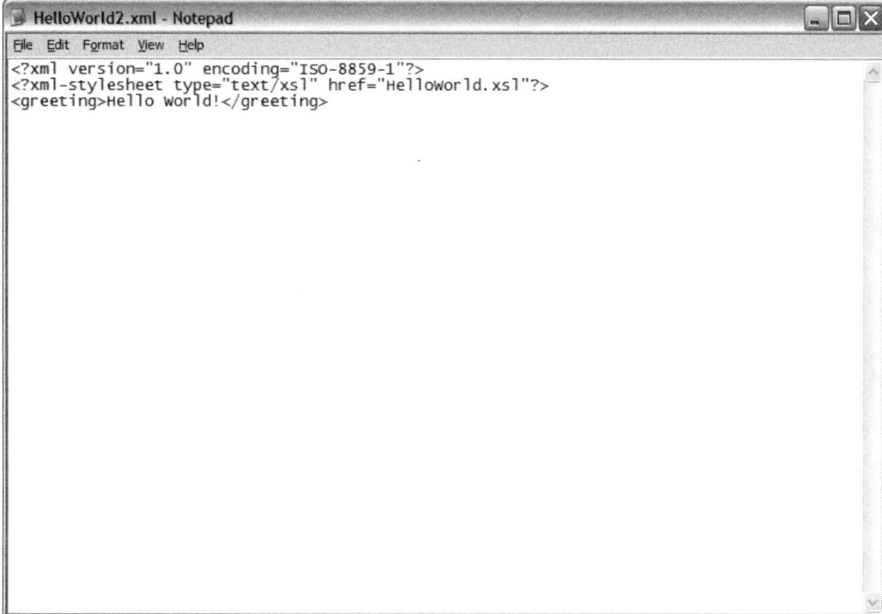

Figure 2-4. *Viewing XML source in Notepad*

If you've installed the Internet Explorer XML tools, then you can also view the source code of the result of the transformation. Open the context menu and select the View XSL Output option. Another window will open up to show you the result of the transformation, as shown in Figure 2-5.

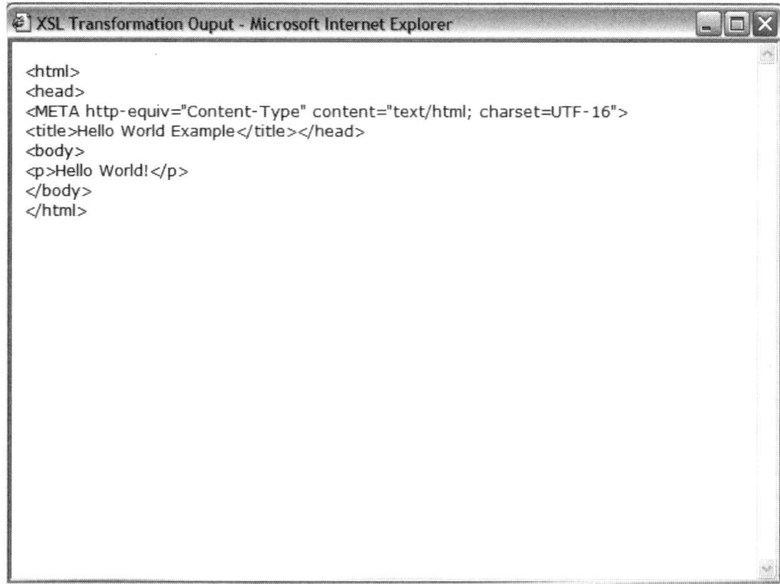

Figure 2-5. *Viewing the output of a transformation*

■ **Caution** Notice that the result of the transformation is encoded in UTF-16 rather than ISO-8859-1. We'll get on to how you control the encoding of the result of a transformation in Chapter 8, but the encoding of the result really doesn't matter when you're doing a client-side transformation because in fact the result is never saved as a physical file, only manipulated by the browser in memory.

If you've installed the MSXML command line transformation utility, then you can also run transformations from the command line. It will make things easier if you have the MSXSL executable in your path, so either edit your `PATH` environment variable or copy/move `msxsl.exe` into the `System32` directory on your machine.

Now open a command prompt in the directory in which you've saved `HelloWorld2.xml` and type the following command line:

```
msxsl HelloWorld2.xml HelloWorld.xsl -o HelloWorld.msxml.html
```

■ **Tip** This command line will use MSXML4 to transform `HelloWorld2.xml`. If you want to use MSXML3 instead, include the option `-u 3.0` at the end. This should make no difference to the result.

MSXSL ignores the `xml-stylesheet` processing instruction, and instead uses whatever stylesheet you specify on the command line. In the preceding command line, we direct the output to `HelloWorld.msxml.html`. If you now open up `HelloWorld.msxml.html` in a text editor, you'll see the same result for the transformation:

```
<html>
<head>
<META http-equiv="Content-Type" content="text/html; charset=UTF-16">
<title>Hello World Example</title></head>
<body>
<p>Hello World!</p>
</body>
</html>
```

■ **Tip** If your text editor doesn't understand the UTF-16 encoding, then you may find that `HelloWorld.msxsl.html` looks strange, with spaces or Å characters every other character. This is because UTF-16 stores each character as 2 bytes, but editors that don't understand UTF-16 interpret the first of each of these bytes as a separate character. It's a good idea to find an editor that understands UTF-16—I use EditPlus from `http://www.editplus.com/`.

■ **Note** There are three differences between the result from MSXML and that from Saxon. First, Saxon indents the output, MSXML doesn't. Second, MSXML uses a `<META>` element, whereas Saxon uses a `<meta>` element (though this doesn't matter since HTML is not case-sensitive). Finally, MSXML uses UTF-16 as its default output encoding, whereas Saxon uses UTF-8 (this is reflected in the `content` attribute of the `<meta>` element).

Simplified Stylesheets

Hopefully you'll have been able to get at least one of the processors to transform the HelloWorld2.xml document into HTML. Now let's have a closer look at the HelloWorld.xsl stylesheet so we can see what it's doing. Listing 2-4 shows the stylesheet again.

Listing 2-4. HelloWorld.xsl

```
<?xml version="1.0" encoding="ISO-8859-1"?>
<html xmlns:xsl="http://www.w3.org/1999/XSL/Transform"
      xsl:version="2.0">
  <head>
    <title>Hello World Example</title>
  </head>
  <body>
    <p>
      <xsl:value-of select="/greeting" />
    </p>
  </body>
</html>
```

The first thing you'll notice is that the document element of the XML document is an <html> element rather than one with a name that indicates that the XML document is a stylesheet. This is because this stylesheet is a **simplified stylesheet**. Simplified stylesheets are intended for basic transformations, and are a good first step on the road to more complicated stylesheets. We'll start seeing more complicated (and more representative) stylesheets in the next chapter.

The second thing that you should notice from the XSLT stylesheet is that it's a well-formed XML document. It has elements, attributes, and an XML declaration. XSLT stylesheets have to be well-formed XML documents.

Checking the Well-Formedness of Stylesheets

Even with practice, it's often difficult to write well-formed XML in a normal text editor (although XML editors can help a lot). One of the main types of errors you'll find as you write XSLT stylesheets just occurs because you've made a mistake with the XML. To see what happens when you try to transform XML with a non-well-formed stylesheet, try changing HelloWorld.xsl so that it's not well-formed: take away the close tag for the <p> element, for example, as in HelloWorld2.xsl, shown in Listing 2-5.

Listing 2-5. HelloWorld2.xsl

```
<?xml version="1.0" encoding="ISO-8859-1"?>
<html xmlns:xsl="http://www.w3.org/1999/XSL/Transform"
      xsl:version="2.0">
  <head>
    <title>Hello World Example</title>
  </head>
  <body>
    <p>
```

```
      <xsl:value-of select="/greeting" />
  </body>
</html>
```

Now try transforming `HelloWorld2.xml` with this non-well-formed stylesheet. The XSLT processor will report an error with the stylesheet. For example, using Saxon you should get an error reported, as shown in Figure 2-6.

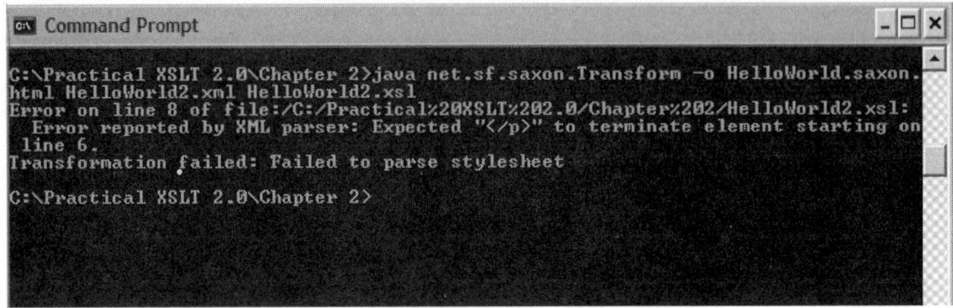

Figure 2-6. *Error with Saxon from non-well-formed stylesheet*

Alternatively, amend `HelloWorld2.xml` to reference the new non-well-formed stylesheet and save it as a new file called `HelloWorld2a.xml`, shown in Listing 2-6.

Listing 2-6. `HelloWorld2a.xml`

```
<?xml version="1.0" encoding="ISO-8859-1"?>
<?xml-stylesheet type="text/xsl" href="HelloWorld2.xsl"?>
<greeting>Hello World!</greeting>
```

If you try to open this file in Internet Explorer, you'll get the error shown in Figure 2-7.

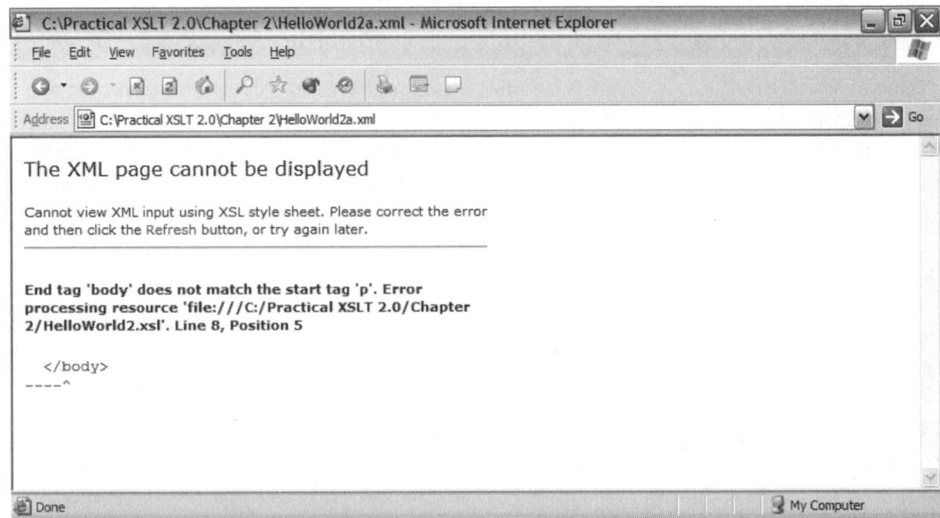

Figure 2-7. *Error in Internet Explorer from non-well-formed stylesheet*

You can also open up an XSLT stylesheet directly within Internet Explorer to see whether it is well-formed, in the same way as you can any XML document. Try opening the original (well-formed) `HelloWorld.xsl` stylesheet in Internet Explorer. You should see the usual XML display as shown in Figure 2-8.

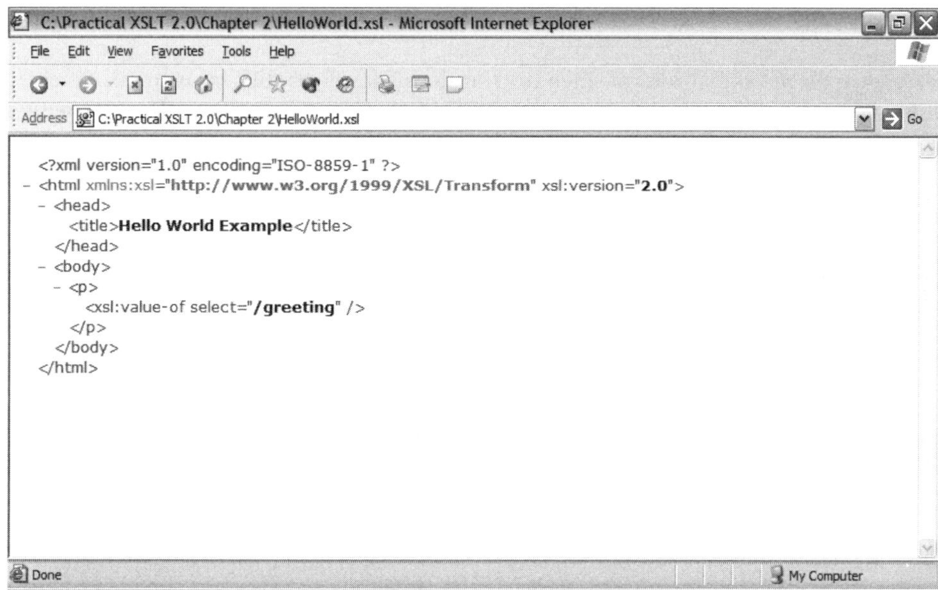

Figure 2-8. *Viewing a well-formed stylesheet in Internet Explorer*

■ **Summary** XSLT stylesheets must be well-formed XML documents; you can check the well-formedness of stylesheets in exactly the same ways as you can check normal XML documents, for example, by opening them in Internet Explorer.

Literal Result Elements

Most of the elements in the stylesheet are well-formed HTML elements. These elements are given literally in the stylesheet just as if you were creating a normal HTML document. The start and end tags of these elements are highlighted here:

```
<?xml version="1.0" encoding="ISO-8859-1"?>
<html xmlns:xsl="http://www.w3.org/1999/XSL/Transform"
      xsl:version="2.0">
  <head>
    <title>Hello World Example</title>
  </head>
```

```
  <body>
    <p>
      <xsl:value-of select="/greeting" />
    </p>
  </body>
</html>
```

Now look at the result that you got when you transformed HelloWorld2.xml with HelloWorld.xsl. You'll see that the elements that you gave in the stylesheet are output literally in the result:

```
<html>
   <head>
      <meta http-equiv="Content-Type" content="text/html; charset=utf-8">
      <title>Hello World Example</title>
   </head>
   <body>
      <p>Hello World!</p>
   </body>
</html>
```

■ **Note** The one element in the result that wasn't in the stylesheet is the <meta> element. XSLT processors add this element automatically whenever you create an HTML document.

When you include an element literally in a stylesheet so that it's output in the result, these elements are known as **literal result elements**. You'll also have noticed that the text that you included in the stylesheet (namely the "Hello World Example" text in the <title> element) was also included literally in the result, and you'll see later that attributes are as well.

■ **Summary** Any non-XSLT elements and attributes, and any text in a stylesheet, are given literally in the result. Elements that are generated like this are known as literal result elements.

The <xsl:value-of> Instruction

The one element in HelloWorld.xsl that isn't output literally to the result is the <xsl:value-of> element. The <xsl:value-of> element is a special element that the XSLT processor recognizes as an **instruction**. The <xsl:value-of> element usually takes an attribute called select. When the XSLT processor encounters an <xsl:value-of> instruction in the stylesheet, it inserts the value specified by the <xsl:value-of> element's select attribute.

In the Hello World example, the <xsl:value-of> instruction tells the XSLT processor to insert the value of the <greeting> element from the source document (HelloWorld2.xml) in the result. The `select` attribute holds an XPath—`/greeting`. The XPath acts a bit like a file path. It tells the processor to go to the very top of the document and then down to the `<greeting>` element.

We'll look at a few more XPaths a bit later on in this chapter.

Summary The `<xsl:value-of>` instruction gives the result of evaluating the XPath held in its `select` attribute as some text in the result document.

The XSLT Namespace

We can see from the result of the transformation that the XSLT processor recognizes the `<xsl:value-of>` element as an XSLT instruction. How does it know that `<xsl:value-of>` is an XSLT instruction rather than a literal result element like the other elements in the stylesheet?

Stylesheets are a particular example of a problem in XML: what do you do when you have a document that contains a mixture of elements and attributes from different markup languages? It would be possible, even likely, that elements and attributes from different markup languages would have the same names, and so you need a way of distinguishing between them. XML distinguishes between elements and attributes from different markup languages with **namespaces**.

Most markup languages have their own namespace, which is identified with a unique identifier—a **namespace URI**. Namespace URIs are often (though not always) URLs. For example, the namespace URI for XSLT is

```
http://www.w3.org/1999/XSL/Transform
```

You've seen this URL in the Hello World example. Let's look at the `HelloWorld.xsl` stylesheet again:

```
<?xml version="1.0" encoding="ISO-8859-1"?>
<html xmlns:xsl="http://www.w3.org/1999/XSL/Transform"
      xsl:version="2.0">
  <head>
    <title>Hello World Example</title>
  </head>
  <body>
    <p>
      <xsl:value-of select="/greeting" />
    </p>
  </body>
</html>
```

The XSLT namespace is the value of the `xmlns:xsl` attribute on the `<html>` element. Attributes that start with `xmlns` have a special significance in XML; they're known as **namespace declarations**. A namespace declaration associates a short string, known as the **namespace prefix**, with a namespace URI. The prefix is the part of the attribute name after the colon. In this case, the XSLT namespace URI is being associated with the prefix `xsl`.

You can also have namespace declarations that don't specify a prefix. For example, we could add a namespace declaration without a prefix to the stylesheet, one that points to the XHTML namespace. Listing 2-7 shows the file HelloWorld3.xsl.

Listing 2-7. HelloWorld3.xsl

```
<?xml version="1.0" encoding="ISO-8859-1"?>
<html xmlns:xsl="http://www.w3.org/1999/XSL/Transform"
      xmlns="http://www.w3.org/1999/xhtml"
      xsl:version="2.0">
  <head>
    <title>Hello World Example</title>
  </head>
  <body>
    <p>
      <xsl:value-of select="/greeting" />
    </p>
  </body>
</html>
```

A namespace declaration that doesn't specify a prefix indicates the **default namespace**. So now the default namespace of our stylesheet is the XHTML namespace.

When an XML parser goes through a document, it looks at each element and attribute and tries to work out what namespace the element or attribute belongs to. It treats the name of each element and attribute as a **qualified name** or **QName** for short—a name that is qualified by the namespace to which the element or attribute belongs. If a qualified name contains a colon (:), then the part before the colon indicates a namespace prefix. The part after the colon is known as the **local part** or **local name** of the element. So in the case of <xsl:value-of>, the prefix is xsl and the local part is value-of.

Once it's worked out what prefix is being used in a particular qualified name, the XML parser tries to work out which namespace URI the prefix has been associated with by looking at the namespace declarations. In this case, the prefix xsl has been associated with the XSLT namespace, so the XML parser knows that the <xsl:value-of> element is part of the XSLT namespace.

■ **Note** By convention, the XSLT namespace is usually associated with the prefix xsl. In this book, I use <xsl:value-of> to indicate the value-of element in the XSLT namespace even though you can use a different prefix for it if you want to.

Qualified names that don't have colons are treated a little differently. If an element's name doesn't contain a colon, then the element belongs to the default namespace. On the other hand, if an attribute's name doesn't contain a colon, then the attribute doesn't belong to any namespace.

When the XML parser passes on information about the XML document, it tells the application about the namespace to which the element or attribute belongs. So the XSLT processor sees some XML where every element and attribute has a namespace.

Let's look back at the HelloWorld3.xsl stylesheet again, with the default namespace declaration that we included. Most of the elements don't have a prefix, so they are in the default namespace, which is the XHTML namespace. The <xsl:value-of> element does have a prefix, xsl, which is associated with the XSLT namespace, so <xsl:value-of> is part of XSLT. The xsl:version attribute has a prefix as well, so it is also part of XSLT. On the other hand, the select attribute on <xsl:value-of> has no prefix, and attributes without a prefix don't use the default namespace, so that attribute is in no namespace. Let's have a look at the XML document as a tree, shown in Figure 2-9, to make this clearer.

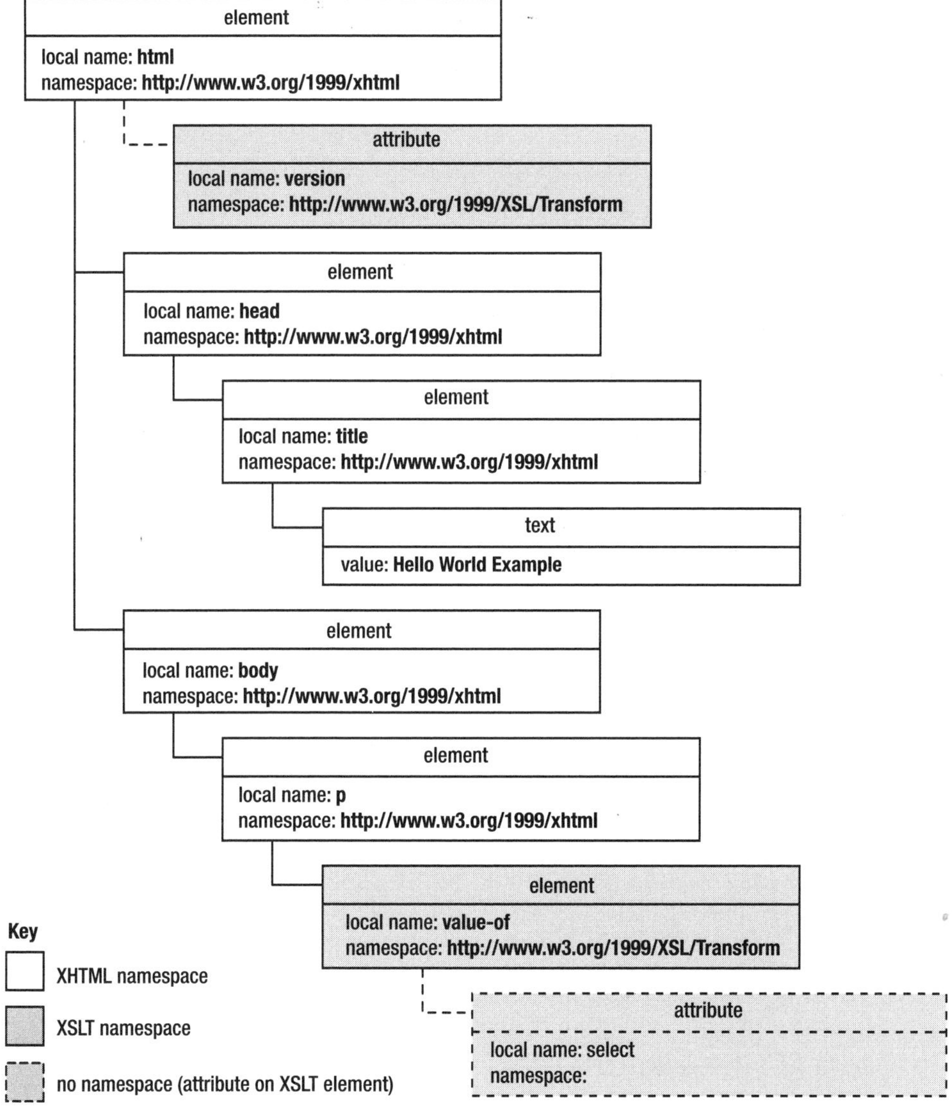

Figure 2-9. *XML document viewed as a tree*

■ **Summary** Namespaces allow you to distinguish between elements and attributes that come from different markup languages. A namespace declaration associates a prefix with a namespace URI in a particular document. Elements and attributes that use that prefix belong to that namespace. Elements that don't have a prefix belong to the default namespace, if one is declared with an `xmlns` attribute.

Controlling Namespaces

The prefix that you use in a particular XML document for a namespace doesn't matter, as long as the namespace URI is the same. Try editing the `HelloWorld.xsl` XSLT stylesheet so that you use a different namespace prefix, `test:`, instead, to give `HelloWorld4.xsl`, as shown in Listing 2-8.

Listing 2-8. `HelloWorld4.xsl`

```
<?xml version="1.0" encoding="ISO-8859-1"?>
<html xmlns:test="http://www.w3.org/1999/XSL/Transform"
      test:version="2.0">
  <head>
    <title>Hello World Example</title>
  </head>
  <body>
    <p>
      <test:value-of select="/greeting" />
    </p>
  </body>
</html>
```

Now change the `href` attribute in `HelloWorld2.xml` to `HelloWorld4.xsl` to use this stylesheet and save the new file as `HelloWorld2b.xml`; use `HelloWorld4.xsl` to transform `HelloWorld2b.html` and look at the result. You'll see that the changed prefix makes no difference to the result of the transformation. The XSLT application uses the namespace URI of the element or attribute to work out whether it's an XSLT instruction (if it has a namespace URI of `http://www.w3.org/1999/XSL/Transform`) or a literal result element (otherwise); it doesn't care about the prefix that you use.

The XML parser will give an error if you try to use a prefix but you haven't specified a namespace declaration for that prefix. Try removing the namespace declaration for the XSLT namespace to give `HelloWorld5.xsl` as shown in Listing 2-9.

Listing 2-9. `HelloWorld5.xsl`

```
<?xml version="1.0" encoding="ISO-8859-1"?>
<html xsl:version="2.0">
  <head>
    <title>Hello World Example</title>
  </head>
```

```
  <body>
    <p>
      <xsl:value-of select="/greeting" />
    </p>
  </body>
</html>
```

Now amend `HelloWorld2.xml` to reference `HelloWorld5.xsl` and call the new file `HelloWorld2c.xml`. If you try to open `HelloWorld2c.xml` in Internet Explorer, then you'll see the error shown in Figure 2-10.

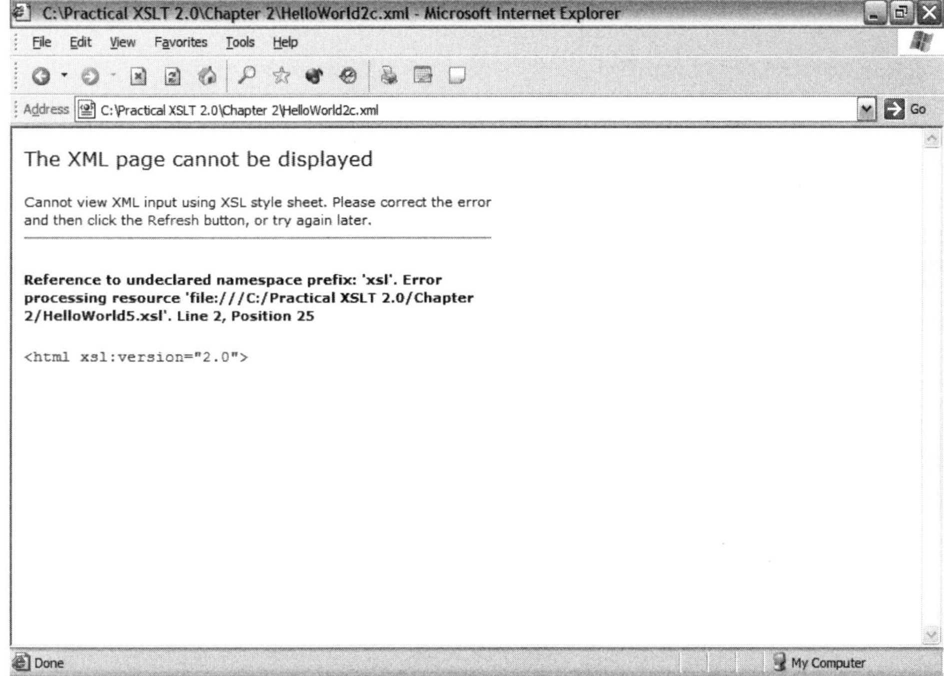

Figure 2-10. *Error from undeclared namespace prefix in Internet Explorer*

The XML parser can't work out what namespace the `xsl` prefix is supposed to indicate.

■ **Note** The XSLT stylesheet is still a well-formed XML document. Namespaces work at a level above basic XML syntax.

The other kind of change that you can try out is using a different namespace URI for the namespace declaration. Try the stylesheet shown in Listing 2-10, `HelloWorld6.xsl`.

Listing 2-10. HelloWorld6.xsl

```
<?xml version="1.0" encoding="ISO-8859-1"?>
<html xmlns:xsl="http://www.example.com/bogus/namespace"
      xsl:version="2.0">
  <head>
    <title>Hello World Example</title>
  </head>
  <body>
    <p>
      <xsl:value-of select="/greeting" />
    </p>
  </body>
</html>
```

This is one of those times when the processor that you use makes a difference. MSXML3 treats the <xsl:value-of> element as a literal result element—they just include it in the result in the same way that they include the other elements in the stylesheet, to give the following:

```
<html xmlns:xsl="http://www.example.com/bogus/namespace" xsl:version="2.0">
  <head><title>Hello World Example</title></head>
  <body>
    <p>
      <xsl:value-of select="/greeting" />
    </p>
  </body>
</html>
```

On the other hand, Saxon and MSXML4 raise errors because they don't find a version attribute in the XSLT namespace on the document element, so don't believe that HelloWorld6.xsl is a stylesheet. The Saxon error message is shown in Figure 2-11.

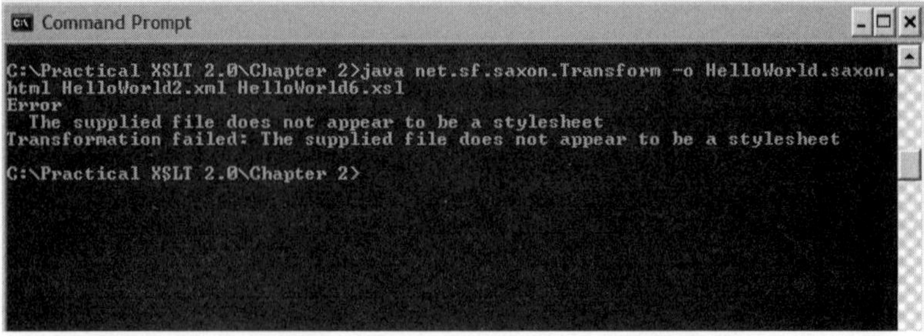

Figure 2-11. *Error from Saxon due to incorrect namespace in stylesheet*

Simplified stylesheets like the one that we're using here must have an `xsl:version` attribute on the document element, but some XSLT processors accept any XML document as a stylesheet, in which case they copy the XML document as the result of the transformation. The `xsl:version` attribute indicates the version of XSLT that is used in the stylesheet, which in our case is `2.0`.

Note As you've seen, XSLT 1.0 processors such as MSXML don't just reject XSLT 2.0 stylesheets—they try to interpret them as if they were XSLT 1.0 stylesheets. We'll be looking at how to make 2.0 stylesheets backwards compatible so that they are guaranteed to work with 1.0 processors in Chapter 14.

Generating HTML Pages

We've looked through a nice, simple example of how to create an HTML page using a simplified stylesheet. Now it's time to try to use what you've learned about XSLT with our TV guide.

From the last chapter, we've got two main XML files associated with our TV guide:

- `TVGuide.xhtml`—An XHTML version of the original HTML TV guide
- `TVGuide.xml`—An XML file that just holds the information about the programs in the TV guide

We want to generate some HTML that looks something like `TVGuide.html`, but use the information from `TVGuide.xml` to fill in the details. You've seen from the Hello World example that a simplified XSLT stylesheet for generating HTML looks a lot like a well-formed HTML file. We can use `TVGuide.html` as a template for the stylesheet to transform `TVGuide.xml` into HTML.

As a first step, we should use a simple version of `TVGuide.html` so that it's a bit easier to manage—filling in the table cells properly would involve some complicated calculations that we should leave for a later chapter. So instead, we'll just list the programs that are on for each channel. We'll start with some XHTML that looks like that in Listing 2-11.

Listing 2-11. `TVGuide.html`

```
<?xml version="1.0" encoding="ISO-8859-1"?>
<html>
<head>
  <title>TV Guide</title>
  <link rel="stylesheet" href="TVGuide.css" />
  <script type="text/javascript">
    function toggle(element) {
      if (element.style.display == 'none') {
        element.style.display = 'block';
      }
      else {
        element.style.display = 'none';
      }
    }
  </script>
</head>
```

```
<body>
  <h1>TV Guide</h1>
  <h2 class="channel">BBC1</h2>
  ...
  <div>
    <p>
      <span class="date">2001-07-05T19:30:00</span><br />
      <span class="title">EastEnders</span><br />
      Mark's health scare forces him to reconsider his future with Lisa,
      while Jamie is torn between Sonia and Zoe.
      <span onclick="toggle(EastEndersCast);">[Cast]</span>
    </p>
    <div id="EastEndersCast" style="display: none;">
      <ul class="castlist">
        <li>
          <span class="character">Zoe Slater</span>
          <span class="actor">Michelle Ryan</span>
        </li>
        <li>
          <span class="character">Jamie Mitchell</span>
          <span class="actor">Jack Ryder</span>
        </li>
        <li>
          <span class="character">Sonia Jackson</span>
          <span class="actor">Natalie Cassidy</span>
        </li>
        ...
      </ul>
    </div>
  </div>
  ...
</body>
</html>
```

In Internet Explorer, TVGuide.html looks as shown in Figure 2-12.

■ **Note** Note that TVGuide.html still links to a CSS stylesheet to make the page look pretty.

We can use TVGuide.html as the basis of our stylesheet, which we'll call TVGuide.xsl. As you'll remember from the end of the last section, the one necessity in a simplified stylesheet is that the document element (<html> in this case) has an xsl:version attribute on it. The xsl:version attribute is in the XSLT namespace, so the first change from TVGuide.html to TVGuide.xsl is to add these attributes to the <html> element:

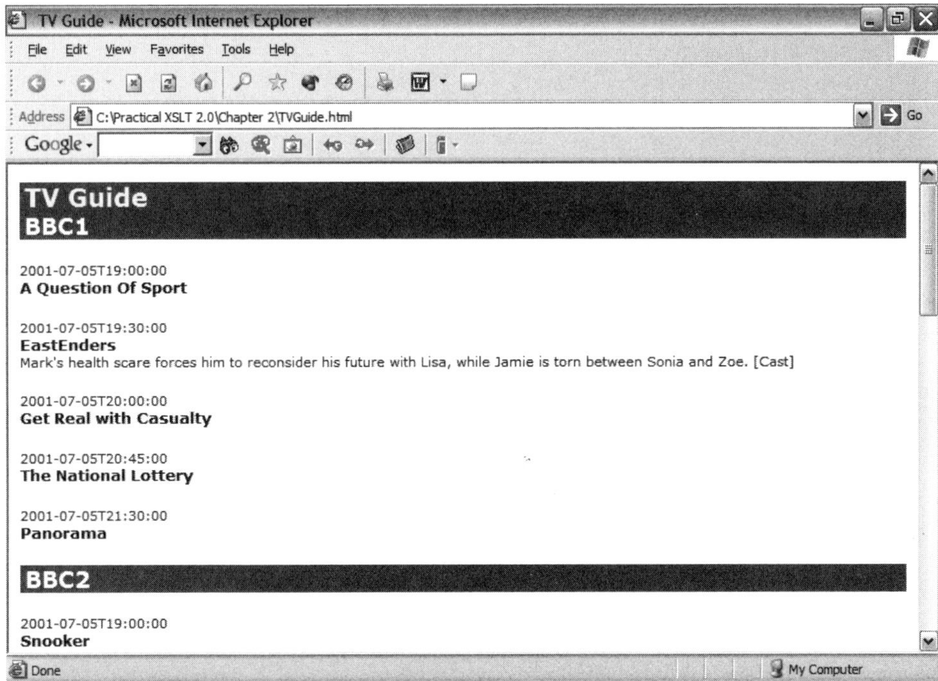

Figure 2-12. *Viewing* TVGuide.html *in Internet Explorer*

```
<?xml version="1.0" encoding="ISO-8859-1"?>
<html xmlns:xsl="http://www.w3.org/1999/XSL/Transform"
      xsl:version="2.0">
  ...
</html>
```

If you transform TVGuide.xml with this stylesheet, you should get a result that looks pretty much identical to TVGuide.html. But not so fast—all of the information about all of the programs is written in the stylesheet, whereas we want the stylesheet to get that information from TVGuide.xml. So let's look at how to do that in more detail.

Iterating Over Elements

If you examine the content of TVGuide.html closely, you should be able to relate the content that we have in the HTML that we want to generate to the content that's held in TVGuide.xml. The first thing we can see is that some of the content of TVGuide.html should never change even if the content of TVGuide.xml changes—things like the title, the link to the CSS stylesheet, and the script are just static. The static parts are the parts highlighted in the following:

```
<html>
<head>
  <title>TV Guide</title>
  <link rel="stylesheet" href="TVGuide.css" />
```

```
  <script type="text/javascript">
    function toggle(element) {
      if (element.style.display == 'none') {
        element.style.display = 'block';
      }
      else {
        element.style.display = 'none';
      }
    }
  </script>
</head>
<body>
  <h1>TV Guide</h1>
  <h2 class="channel">BBC1</h2>
  <div>
    ...
  </div>
  ...
</body>
</html>
```

The rest of the content is influenced by the content of `TVGuide.xml`. Let's look at `TVGuide.xml` again, as shown in Listing 2-12.

Listing 2-12. `TVGuide.xml`

```
<?xml version="1.0" encoding="ISO-8859-1"?>
<TVGuide start="2001-07-05" end="2001-07-05">
  <Channel>
    <Name>BBC1</Name>
    ...
    <Program>
      <Start>2001-07-05T19:30:00</Start>
      <Duration>PT30M</Duration>
      <Series>EastEnders</Series>
      <Title></Title>
      <Description>
        Mark's health scare forces him to reconsider his future with Lisa,
        while Jamie is torn between Sonia and Zoe.
      </Description>
      <CastList>
        <CastMember>
          <Character><Name>Zoe Slater</Name></Character>
          <Actor><Name>Michelle Ryan</Name></Actor>
        </CastMember>
        <CastMember>
          <Character><Name>Jamie Mitchell</Name></Character>
          <Actor><Name>Jack Ryder</Name></Actor>
        </CastMember>
```

```
      <CastMember>
        <Character><Name>Sonia Jackson</Name></Character>
        <Actor><Name>Natalie Cassidy</Name></Actor>
      </CastMember>
      ...
    </CastList>
    <Writers>
      <Writer><Name>Nick Saltrese</Name></Writer>
      <Writer><Name>Julie Wassmer</Name></Writer>
    </Writers>
    <Director><Name>Stewart Edwards</Name></Director>
    <Producer><Name>Emma Turner</Name></Producer>
  </Program>
  ...
</Channel>
...
</TVGuide>
```

In TVGuide.xml, the <TVGuide> element contains a number of <Channel> elements. In the output, for every <Channel> element in TVGuide.xml, we want to have an <h2> element naming the channel, and then some information about each of the programs available on that channel.

The <xsl:for-each> Element

You can go through each of the <Channel> elements one by one using an XSLT instruction—<xsl:for-each>. The <xsl:for-each> element has a select attribute, which you use to point to the things that you want to iterate over. So, you can iterate over each of the <Channel> elements that are children of the <TVGuide> element with the following XSLT instruction:

```
<xsl:for-each select="/TVGuide/Channel">
  ...
</xsl:for-each>
```

The XSLT processor goes through the **items** in the **sequence** that you select with the select attribute one by one. In this case, the sequence contains the <Channel> elements in the order that they appear in the XML document. Anything that you put in the content of the <xsl:for-each> instruction gets processed once for each of the items in that sequence.

Summary The <xsl:for-each> element iterates over the items in the sequence specified by the XPath in its select attribute.

Absolute and Relative Paths

We saw in the "Hello World" example how to get the value of an element with <xsl:value-of>. In that example, we used an **absolute path** to point to the value of the <greeting> document element. Absolute paths start from the top of the document and work down from there, just like an absolute file path or absolute URL.

But here we want to give the name of each channel, which is contained in the <Name> element under each <Channel> element. To let you point to the name of this particular channel, you can use **relative paths** in the select attribute of <xsl:value-of>. Relative paths don't start with a /, and are similar to relative file paths or relative URLs. In the TV guide stylesheet, we can give the name of each channel, inside an <h2> element, with the following:

```
<xsl:for-each select="/TVGuide/Channel">
  <h2 class="channel"><xsl:value-of select="Name" /></h2>
</xsl:for-each>
```

Relative paths are always evaluated relative to the **context node**. The context node is the element (or attribute, comment, or other kind of node) that you're currently processing. So when the XSLT processor selects the first <Channel> element to process in the preceding <xsl:for-each> instruction, the context node becomes that first <Channel> element. When the XSLT processor evaluates the select attribute of the <xsl:value-of> instruction, it looks for the <Name> element under the first <Channel> element. When the processor moves on to the second <Channel> element, the context node becomes the second <Channel> element, so the <xsl:value-of> gives the name of the second channel.

Summary Absolute paths start with a / and reference nodes starting from the top of the XML document. Relative paths are evaluated starting from the context node, which is whatever node is currently being processed.

Giving a Title for Every Channel

It's time to try out iterating over all the <Channel> elements in TVGuide.xml and giving each of their names in the HTML. The stylesheet needs to contain an <xsl:for-each> element that selects all the <Channel> elements. For each of those, it needs to create an <h2> element, and inside it give the name of the channel, which is held in the <Name> element under the <Channel> element. The stylesheet contains all the static information that it did before, but the main body of the stylesheet outputs the channel names. TVGuide2.xsl looks as shown in Listing 2-13.

Listing 2-13. TVGuide2.xsl

```
<html xmlns:xsl="http://www.w3.org/1999/XSL/Transform"
      xsl:version="2.0">
<head>
  <title>TV Guide</title>
  <link rel="stylesheet" href="TVGuide.css" />
  <script type="text/javascript">
    function toggle(element) {
      if (element.style.display == 'none') {
        element.style.display = 'block';
      }
      else {
        element.style.display = 'none';
      }
    }
  </script>
</head>
```

```
<body>
  <h1>TV Guide</h1>
  <xsl:for-each select="/TVGuide/Channel">
    <h2 class="channel"><xsl:value-of select="Name" /></h2>
  </xsl:for-each>
</body>
</html>
```

Run an XSLT processor to transform TVGuide.xml with TVGuide2.xsl as the stylesheet to produce TVGuide2.html. For instance, using Saxon, use the following at the command prompt:

```
java net.sf.saxon.Transform -o TVGuide2.html TVGuide.xml TVGuide2.xsl
```

The source code of the result of the transformation is as follows:

```
<html>
  <head>
    <link rel="stylesheet" href="TVGuide.css">
    <script type="text/javascript">
      function toggle(element) {
        if (element.style.display == 'none') {
          element.style.display = 'block';
        }
        else {
          element.style.display = 'none';
        }
      }
    </script>
  </head>
  <body>
    <h1>TV Guide</h1>
    <h2 class="channel">BBC1</h2>
    <h2 class="channel">BBC2</h2>
    <h2 class="channel">ITV</h2>
    <h2 class="channel">Channel 4</h2>
    <h2 class="channel">Channel 5</h2>
  </body>
</html>
```

The static parts of the page are added, and for each channel that you've listed in TVGuide.xml, you get an <h2> element in the result. When you look at this in Internet Explorer, you see the page shown in Figure 2-13.

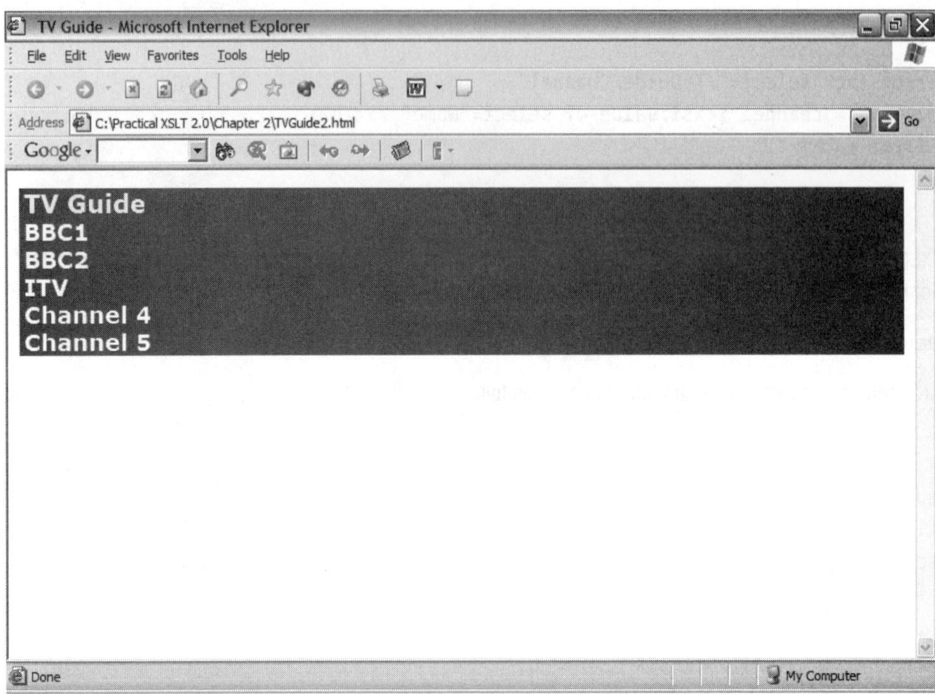

Figure 2-13. *Viewing* TVGuide2.html *in Internet Explorer*

As before, the alternative method is to reference the stylesheet from within the XML document itself. Insert an xml-stylesheet processing instruction into TVGuide.xml to create TVGuide2.xml as shown in Listing 2-14.

Listing 2-14. TVGuide2.xml

```
<?xml version="1.0" encoding="ISO-8859-1"?>
<?xml-stylesheet type="text/xsl" href="TVGuide2.xsl"?>
<TVGuide start="2001-07-05" end="2001-07-05">
  ...
</TVGuide>
```

The output you see in Internet Explorer should be the same as with TVGuide2.html, shown in Figure 2-12.

You can nest <xsl:for-each> elements as much as you want. So let's try adding some more information to the output. We'll aim to generate something like the following for each program in TVGuide.xml:

```
<div>
  <p>
    <span class="date">2001-07-05T19:30:00</span><br />
    <span class="title">EastEnders</span><br />
    Mark's health scare forces him to reconsider his future with Lisa,
    while Jamie is torn between Sonia and Zoe.
  </p>
```

```
  <ul class="castlist">
    <li>
      <span class="character">Zoe Slater</span>
      <span class="actor">Michelle Ryan</span>
    </li>
    <li>
      <span class="character">Jamie Mitchell</span>
      <span class="actor">Jack Ryder</span>
    </li>
    <li>
      <span class="character">Sonia Jackson</span>
      <span class="actor">Natalie Cassidy</span>
    </li>
    ...
  </ul>
</div>
```

Inside the loop that's iterating over the <Channel> elements, after giving the name of the channel, we need to loop over each of the <Program> elements. As we did when we were giving the name of the channel, we want a relative path to select only the <Program> elements that are within this particular <Channel> element:

```
<xsl:for-each select="/TVGuide/Channel">
  <h2 class="channel"><xsl:value-of select="Name" /></h2>
  <xsl:for-each select="Program">
    ...
  </xsl:for-each>
</xsl:for-each>
```

For each of the <Program> elements, we create a <div> element. Inside the <div> element we need a <p> element to hold the start date and time, the series name, and the description of the program. Because we're within an <xsl:for-each> instruction that's selected <Program> elements, the current node is a <Program> element, and the paths that we use should be relative to the <Program> element:

```
<xsl:for-each select="/TVGuide/Channel">
  <h2 class="channel"><xsl:value-of select="Name" /></h2>
  <xsl:for-each select="Program">
    <div>
      <p>
        <span class="date"><xsl:value-of select="Start" /></span><br />
        <span class="title"><xsl:value-of select="Series" /></span><br />
        <xsl:value-of select="Description" />
      </p>
      ...
    </div>
  </xsl:for-each>
</xsl:for-each>
```

After the <p> element, we need a <ul> element. To get the contents of the <ul> element, we need to iterate over the <CastMember> elements in the cast list for the program and for each of those give an <li> element containing the value of the <Character> and <Actor> elements from the source, so TVGuide3.xsl contains

```
<xsl:for-each select="/TVGuide/Channel">
  <h2 class="channel"><xsl:value-of select="Name" /></h2>
  <xsl:for-each select="Program">
    <div>
      <p>
        <span class="date"><xsl:value-of select="Start" /></span><br />
        <span class="title"><xsl:value-of select="Series" /></span><br />
        <xsl:value-of select="Description" />
      </p>
      <ul class="castlist">
        <xsl:for-each select="CastList/CastMember">
          <li>
            <span class="character">
              <xsl:value-of select="Character" />
            </span>
            <span class="actor">
              <xsl:value-of select="Actor" />
            </span>
          </li>
        </xsl:for-each>
      </ul>
    </div>
  </xsl:for-each>
</xsl:for-each>
```

Now create TVGuide3.html by running TVGuide3.xsl against TVGuide.xml, or alternatively, you can generate the same result by amending the href attribute in TVGuide2.xml to reference TVGuide3.xsl, thus creating TVGuide3.xml. You'll see roughly the result that we were aiming for, as shown in Figure 2-14, though there are still a few bits that could be neater.

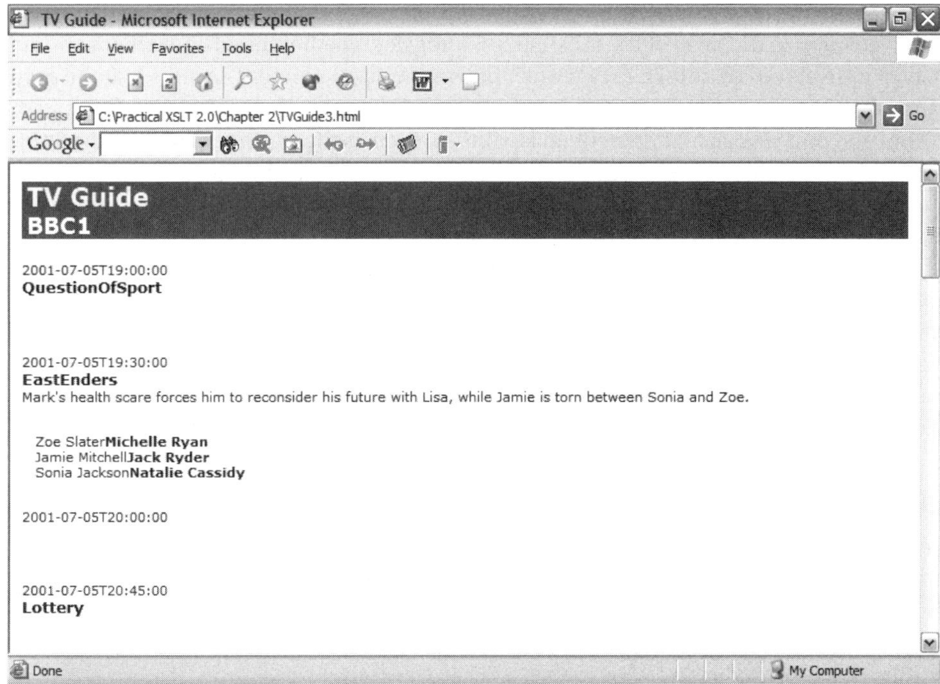

Figure 2-14. *Viewing* TVGuide3.html *in Internet Explorer*

Generating Attribute Values

In the original well-formed HTML that we were aiming for, we had a bit of dynamic HTML so that the end user could show or hide the cast list for a program. For the *EastEnders* program, the dynamic HTML looked like this:

```
<div>
  <p>
    <span class="date">2001-07-05T19:30:00</span><br />
    <span class="title">EastEnders</span><br />
    Mark's health scare forces him to reconsider his future with Lisa,
    while Jamie is torn between Sonia and Zoe.
    <span onclick="toggle(EastEndersCast);">[Cast]</span>
  </p>
  <div id="EastEndersCast" style="display: none;">
    <ul class="castlist">
      ...
    </ul>
  </div>
</div>
```

The onclick attribute in the <span> element calls the toggle() function that we defined in a <script> element in the head of the HTML page. It toggles whether the <div> element around the cast list is displayed or not. The style attribute on the <div> element ensures that the cast list starts off hidden.

We've seen that we can add predefined attributes, such as the style attribute on the <div> element, to the HTML that we generate with our stylesheet just by including them on the literal result elements in the stylesheet. But the dynamic HTML uses attributes that have values that are dependent on the identity of the program. For this program, the <div> has an id attribute equal to EastEndersCast, and the onclick attribute of the <span> references that id. For another program, the id would be different, so that clicking on [Cast] for different programs would display different cast lists.

Here, we want to make the id attribute of the <div> around the cast list be dependent on the <Series> to which the program belongs. For <Series>EastEnders</Series>, we want it to be EastEndersCast. For <Series>Friends</Series>, we'd want it to be FriendsCast.

Attribute Value Templates

You can dynamically generate the value of an attribute using an **attribute value template**. If you put curly brackets ({}) in an attribute value, then whatever you have inside the curly brackets is evaluated as if it were in the select attribute of an <xsl:value-of>, and the result is inserted into the attribute value. For example, if we have

```
<div id="{Series}Cast" style="display: none;">
  ...
</div>
```

then the {Series} part of the id attribute value is interpreted by the XSLT processor and it puts the value of the <Series> element in its place.

Tip You can insert as many values as you like within an attribute's value with separate pairs of curly brackets. If you want to insert a curly bracket literally into an attribute's value, then double it up—alt="{{flag}}" will be output as alt="{flag}".

Not all attributes in a stylesheet are interpreted as attribute value templates, so you can't just use curly brackets in attribute values wherever you like. Most attributes on XSLT elements aren't attribute value templates; you couldn't dynamically evaluate the value of the select attributes of <xsl:for-each> or <xsl:value-of>, for example.

Summary You can use pairs of curly brackets ({}) in attribute values on literal result elements to generate attribute values based on information in the source XML.

Using Attribute Value Templates

Now that you know how to give attributes values based on values from the source XML, let's try adding the dynamic HTML for showing and hiding the cast list. The well-formed HTML we want to generate is shown here:

```
<div>
  <p>
    <span class="date">2001-07-05T19:30:00</span><br />
    <span class="title">EastEnders</span><br />
    Mark's health scare forces him to reconsider his future with Lisa,
    while Jamie is torn between Sonia and Zoe.
    <span onclick="toggle(EastEndersCast);">[Cast]</span>
  </p>
  <div id="EastEndersCast" style="display: none;">
    <ul class="castlist">
      ...
    </ul>
  </div>
</div>
```

So in the paragraph describing each program, you need to add a `<span>` element whose `onclick` attribute's value is based on the value of the `<Series>` element under the program. Similarly, you need to generate a `<div>` element with an `id` attribute based on the program's series. You can do both with an attribute value template in `TVGuide4.xsl`, as follows:

```
<xsl:for-each select="Program">
  <div>
    <p>
      <span class="date"><xsl:value-of select="Start" /></span><br />
      <span class="title"><xsl:value-of select="Series" /></span><br />
      <xsl:value-of select="Description" />
      <span onclick="toggle({Series}Cast);">[Cast]</span>
    </p>
    <div id="{Series}Cast" style="display: none;">
      <ul class="castlist">
        ...
      </ul>
    </div>
  </div>
</xsl:for-each>
```

Create `TVGuide4.html` and `TVGuide4.xml` using the same methods as before, and look at the result in a web browser. You should see something like the page shown in Figure 2-15.

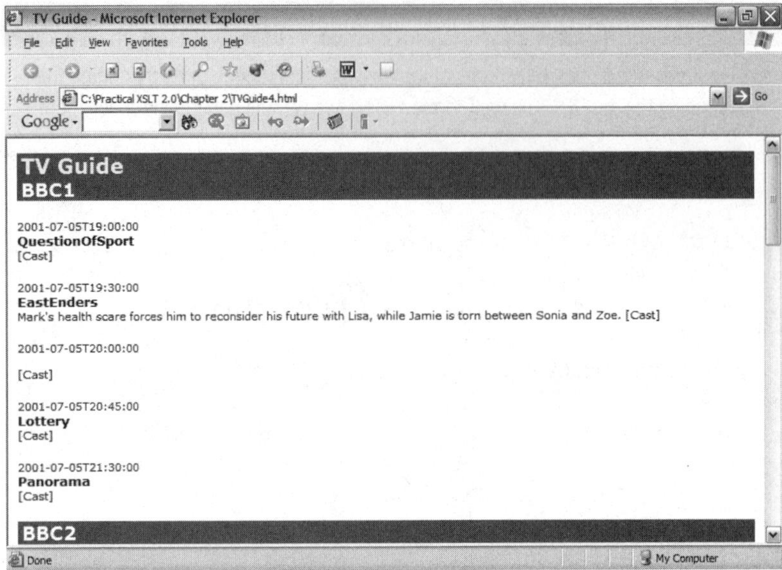

Figure 2-15. *Viewing* `TVGuide4.html` *in Internet Explorer*

You'll see the information that you've pulled out from `TVGuide.xml`. Try clicking the `[Cast]` link for `EastEnders` and you should see the cast list displayed, as in Figure 2-16.

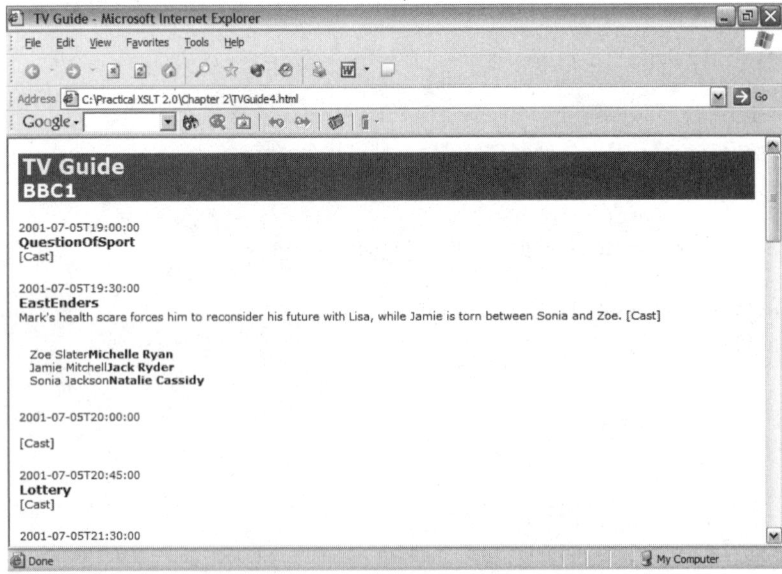

Figure 2-16. *Viewing cast in* `TVGuide4.html` *in Internet Explorer*

The script that you originally had in the well-formed HTML works just as well when it's generated from a stylesheet.

Summary

This chapter has introduced you to the basic features of XSLT, and it's proved enough to generate quite a nice looking web page. Sure, there are a few things that could be smartened up—it would be good to have the programs given in a table again, and really it would be nice to use a different date format than the one we have at the moment—but all in all, it's not bad for a first shot.

You've learned a bit about the background of XSLT, how it originated as part of a language for styling XML documents, and how it's evolved into something that you can use to generate any text-based format. You've seen how to use XSLT processors embedded in web browsers or run from the command line to run stylesheets; you can use them embedded within other programs as well, but running them like this helps you to test stylesheets.

You've been introduced to the concept of namespaces. Namespaces are really useful in XSLT because they enable XSLT processors to discriminate between literal result elements (which are just added to the output) and XSLT instructions. We're going to return to namespaces in Chapter 7.

You've seen two XSLT instructions in action:

- `<xsl:value-of>` to get the value of an expression
- `<xsl:for-each>` to iterate over a sequence

You've also generated attributes with values taken from the XML source using attribute value templates.

But the type of stylesheet that you've seen here is the most basic kind, known as a simplified stylesheet. You can turn any XML document into a simplified stylesheet by adding an `xsl:version` attribute and a namespace declaration for the XSLT namespace to the document element, so they're often a good starting point when you're creating some XSLT. However, they're not very flexible, so in the next chapter, we'll move on to more complex stylesheets and see a different way of approaching transformations with XSLT.

Review Questions

1. What are the relationships between XSLT, XPath, XSL-FO, XSL, XML, DSSSL, and SGML?
2. What are XML documents written in XSLT called, and what extension do they usually use?
3. What class of documents can act as the input to an XSLT processor?
4. What kinds of documents can you generate with XSLT?
5. Name two XSLT processors.
6. Do XSLT processors live on the client or the server in client-server architecture?
7. How can you associate an XML document with a particular XSLT stylesheet?
8. What is the term for elements that are specified in the stylesheet and output literally in the result?
9. What XSLT instruction can you use to give the value of an element?

10. What is the significance of the URL `http://www.w3.org/1999/XSL/Transform`?

11. Why would you use a namespace declaration?

12. What does an `xmlns` "attribute" do?

13. What namespace prefix is commonly used with XSLT?

14. What attribute must be given on the document element of a simplified stylesheet? What else must be specified on the document element for the attribute to be recognized?

15. What XSLT instruction can you use to iterate over a sequence?

16. How does an XSLT processor resolve paths that don't begin with /?

17. How can you insert a value from your source XML into an attribute value?

CHAPTER 3

Templates

In the last chapter, you saw how to take a well-formed HTML document and turn it into a stylesheet by adding the XSLT elements `<xsl:value-of>` and `<xsl:for-each>` to pick out information from an input XML document and produce an HTML result. The stylesheets that we looked at were **simplified stylesheets**. Simplified stylesheets are good as a starting point when you're creating a stylesheet, and they can be all you need in some cases. However, to utilize the more sophisticated functionality of XSLT, you need to use full stylesheets.

In this chapter, we'll take the simplified stylesheet that we developed during the last chapter and turn it into a full stylesheet. I'll also introduce you to **templates** as a way of breaking up your code and look in a bit more detail at how XSLT processors construct a result from some input XML. You'll learn

- What full stylesheets look like
- How the XSLT processor navigates the input document to create a result
- How to break up your code into separate templates
- How templates help with document-oriented and unpredictable XML
- How to create tables of contents or indexes in your pages using template modes

XSLT Stylesheet Structure

The simplified stylesheets that we used in the last chapter are a specialized form of stylesheet that make a good starting point when we're creating an XSLT stylesheet. Simplified stylesheets aren't all that common in larger applications because they're fairly restricted in what they can do, especially with document-oriented XML.

Technically, simplified stylesheets are defined in XSLT in terms of how they map to full stylesheets. In the last chapter, we developed the simplified stylesheet shown in Listing 3-1 (`HelloWorld.xsl`) to take the Hello World XML document (`HelloWorld.xml`) and convert it to HTML.

Listing 3-1. `HelloWorld.xsl`

```
<?xml version="1.0" encoding="ISO-8859-1"?>
<html xmlns:xsl="http://www.w3.org/1999/XSL/Transform"
      xsl:version="2.0">
```

```
  <head><title>Hello World Example</title></head>
  <body>
    <p>
      <xsl:value-of select="/greeting" />
    </p>
  </body>
</html>
```

The equivalent full stylesheet for the simplified stylesheet looks very similar. The content of the simplified stylesheet is wrapped in two elements—<xsl:template> and <xsl:stylesheet>—to create HelloWorld2.xsl, shown in Listing 3-2. The <xsl:stylesheet> element takes the version attribute and the XSLT namespace declaration instead of them being on the <html> element.

Listing 3-2. HelloWorld2.xsl

```
<?xml version="1.0" encoding="ISO-8859-1"?>
<xsl:stylesheet version="2.0"
                xmlns:xsl="http://www.w3.org/1999/XSL/Transform">

<xsl:template match="/">
  <html>
    <head><title>Hello World Example</title></head>
    <body>
      <p>
        <xsl:value-of select="/greeting" />
      </p>
    </body>
  </html>
</xsl:template>

</xsl:stylesheet>
```

In the next couple of sections, we'll look at what these new XSLT elements do.

Stylesheet Document Elements

The document element of a full stylesheet is <xsl:stylesheet> (a <stylesheet> element in the namespace http://www.w3.org/1999/XSL/Transform—as usual I'm using the prefix xsl here, but you can use whatever prefix you like as long as it's associated with the XSLT namespace with a namespace declaration). Like the document element in simplified stylesheets, the <xsl:stylesheet> element needs to declare the XSLT namespace and give the version of XSLT that's used in the stylesheet with a version attribute. This time, though, the version attribute doesn't need to be qualified with the xsl prefix because it already lives on an element in the XSLT namespace, so the processor knows it's part of XSLT.

■ **Note** You can also use <xsl:transform> as the document element in a full stylesheet, rather than <xsl:stylesheet>. There is no difference in functionality between the two document elements—they each use exactly the same attributes and do exactly the same thing. Some people prefer to use <xsl:transform> when doing transformations that aren't producing presentation-oriented formats such as XSL-FO or XHTML. Personally, I use <xsl:stylesheet> all the time.

Defining Templates

Inside the <xsl:stylesheet> document element, XSLT stylesheets are made up of a number of templates, each of which matches a particular part of the input XML document and processes it in whatever way you define. The templates are rules that define how a particular part of the input XML document maps on to the result that you want. Thus a full stylesheet has a structure that's quite similar to the structure of CSS stylesheets—a set of rules that match different elements and describe how they should be presented.

■ **Note** There are some fundamental differences between CSS stylesheets and XSLT stylesheets, though. First, while CSS always processes all the elements in a document, you can use XSLT to pick and choose which elements to display. Second, while multiple rules can be applied to style a particular element in CSS, only one template can be applied at a time in XSLT. Third, XSLT templates can match a lot of things that CSS templates can't, such as attributes and comments.

Templates are defined using the <xsl:template> element. The match attribute on <xsl:template> indicates which parts of the input document should be processed with the particular template and the content of the <xsl:template> element dictates what is done with that particular part of the input document. You can use literal result elements, <xsl:value-of>, and <xsl:for-each> inside a template in exactly the same way as you do within a simplified stylesheet to generate some output.

■ **Summary** A full XSLT stylesheet has an <xsl:stylesheet> document element, which contains a number of <xsl:template> elements, each of which defines the processing that should be carried out on a particular part of the input XML.

Converting a Simplified Stylesheet to a Full Stylesheet

In this exercise, you'll convert the simplified stylesheet TVGuide.xsl that we created in the last chapter into a full stylesheet and test that the full stylesheet gives exactly the same result for TVGuide.xml as the simplified stylesheet did.

The simplified stylesheet TVGuide.xsl is shown in Listing 3-3.

Listing 3-3. TVGuide.xsl

```
<?xml version="1.0" encoding="ISO-8859-1"?>
<html xmlns:xsl="http://www.w3.org/1999/XSL/Transform"
      xsl:version="2.0">
<head>
  <title>TV Guide</title>
  <link rel="stylesheet" href="TVGuide.css" />
  <script type="text/javascript">
    function toggle(element) {
      if (element.style.display == 'none') {
        element.style.display = 'block';
      } else {
        element.style.display = 'none';
      }
    }
  </script>
</head>

<body>
  <h1>TV Guide</h1>
  <xsl:for-each select="/TVGuide/Channel">
    <h2 class="channel"><xsl:value-of select="Name" /></h2>
    <xsl:for-each select="Program">
      <div>
        <p>
          <span class="date"><xsl:value-of select="Start" /></span><br />
          <span class="title"><xsl:value-of select="Series" /></span><br />
          <xsl:value-of select="Description" />
          <span onclick="toggle({Series}Cast);">[Cast]</span>
        </p>
        <div id="{Series}Cast" style="display: none;">
          <ul class="castlist">
            <xsl:for-each select="CastList/CastMember">
              <li>
                <span class="character">
                  <xsl:value-of select="Character" />
                </span>
                <span class="actor">
                  <xsl:value-of select="Actor" />
                </span>
```

```
            </li>
          </xsl:for-each>
        </ul>
      </div>
    </div>
  </xsl:for-each>
</xsl:for-each>
</body>
</html>
```

If you use TVGuide.xsl to transform TVGuide.xml into TVGuide.html, and then view TVGuide.html in Internet Explorer, you should see the page shown in Figure 3-1.

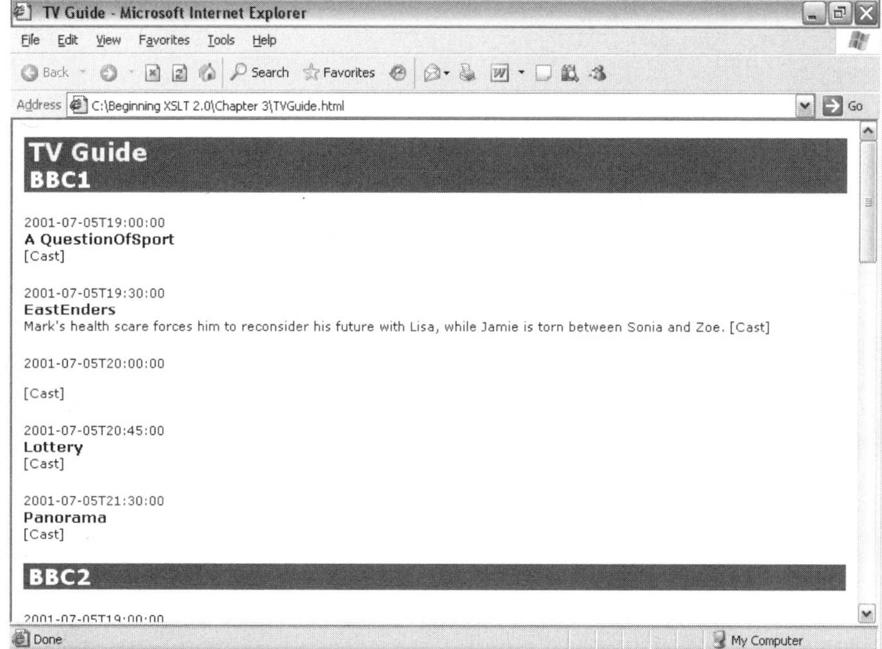

Figure 3-1. *Viewing* TVGuide.html *in Internet Explorer*

To create a full stylesheet from this simplified stylesheet, you need to do the following:

- Add an <xsl:template> element whose match attribute has the value / around the <html> element.
- Add an <xsl:stylesheet> element around the new <xsl:template> element.
- Move the XSLT namespace declaration from the <html> element to the <xsl:stylesheet> element.
- Remove the xsl:version attribute from the <html> element and add an equivalent version attribute on the <xsl:stylesheet> element.

The result of these four steps is TVGuide2.xsl, with the outline shown in Listing 3-4.

Listing 3-4. TVGuide2.xsl

```
<?xml version="1.0" encoding="ISO-8859-1"?>
<xsl:stylesheet version="2.0"
                xmlns:xsl="http://www.w3.org/1999/XSL/Transform">

<xsl:template match="/">
  <html>
    <head>
      ...
    </head>
    <body>
      ...
    </body>
  </html>
</xsl:template>

</xsl:stylesheet>
```

Now run the transformation of TVGuide.xml, this time with the full stylesheet TVGuide2.xsl. You should get exactly the same result as shown in Figure 3-1.

The Node Tree

Before we start looking at templates in detail, we first need to look at an XML document in the way that an XSLT processor does. When an XSLT processor reads in a document, it generates a representation of the XML as a **node tree**. As you might expect from its name, the node tree is a bunch of **nodes** arranged in a tree. Nodes are a general term for the components of an XML document, such as

- Element nodes
- Attribute nodes
- Text nodes
- Comment nodes
- Processing-instruction nodes

The nodes are arranged in a tree such that the tree forms a new branch for every node contained in an element. The relationships between the nodes in the tree are described in terms of familial relationships, so the nodes that an element contains are called its **children** and an element node is its children's **parent**. Similarly, all the children of an element node are **siblings**, and you can also talk about the **descendants** of an element node or a node's **ancestors**.

At the very top of the node tree is the **root node** (for some reason node trees grow down rather than up). In most cases, the root node is a **document node**, which is equivalent to the XML document itself. In a tree created from a well-formed XML document, a document node's children are the document element and any comments or processing instructions that live outside the document element.

Note Node trees aren't necessarily created from well-formed XML documents. Technically, the root node can be any kind of node, and a document node can have text node children or have any number of element node children. But when we're dealing with well-formed XML documents, the root node is always a document node, and the document node has just one element child: the document element.

Attribute nodes are a bit special because attributes are not contained in elements in the same way as other elements or text, but they are still associated with particular elements. The element that an attribute is associated with is still known as its parent, but attributes are not their parent element's children, just its attributes.

Note Comments and processing instructions are nodes and part of the node tree, so you need to take them into account if you count nodes or iterate over them. As we'll see in Chapter 7, text nodes that consist purely of whitespace might also be part of the node tree, but you have some control over which are and which aren't.

The view of XML as a node tree is a very natural view because of the way that XML is structured, with elements nesting inside each other. In XML, the relationship between an element and its contents is a one-to-many relationship—each element can have many children but only have one parent—which fits the pattern of a tree structure. Processing XML as a tree of nodes is also useful because it means you can focus down on a particular branch of the tree (the content of a particular element) very easily. Other models of XML documents, such as the Document Object Model (DOM) and the XML Infoset, also view XML documents as tree structures, although the models are just slightly different from the node tree that XSLT uses.

Note You can find out more about the DOM at `http://www.w3.org/DOM/Activity.html` and more about the XML Infoset at `http://www.w3.org/TR/xml-infoset/`.

Summary XSLT processors treat documents as a node tree in which the contents of an element are represented as its children. Every node in a node tree descends from the root document node.

Having a picture of the node tree can be very useful because it lets you view the XML document in the same way as the XSLT processor does. Here's a simplified version of the XML that we're using to hold the information in our TV guide:

```
<?xml version="1.0" encoding="ISO-8859-1"?>
<?xml-stylesheet type="text/xsl" href="TVGuide.xsl"?>
<TVGuide start="2001-07-05" end="2001-07-05">
  <Channel>
```

```
    <Name>BBC1</Name>
    ...
    <Program>
      <Start>2001-07-05T19:30:00</Start>
      <Duration>PT30M</Duration>
      <Series>EastEnders</Series>
      ...
    </Program>
    ...
  </Channel>
  ...
</TVGuide>
```

Every node tree created from a well-formed XML document like this one has a document node as its root node, so that's the starting point for our diagram. The document node of the tree represents the document itself. The XML document has two nodes at the top level, the `xml-stylesheet` processing instruction and the document element—the `<TVGuide>` element. The document element is the top-most element in the node tree, but other things (like comments and processing instructions) can occur at the same level. We can also draw the children of the document node in, as in Figure 3-2.

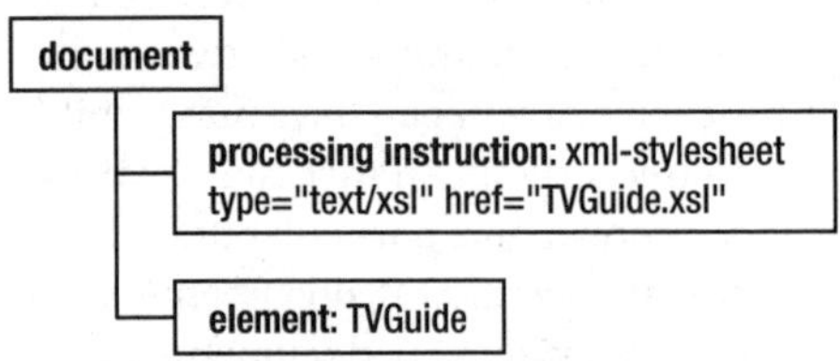

Figure 3-2. *Node tree: children of the document node*

■ Note An XSLT processor doesn't see the XML declaration (the first line of an XML file). The information held in the XML declaration relates to how the XML document has been stored, which the XSLT processor doesn't care about. Also, note that the pseudo-attributes in the `xml-stylesheet` processing instruction aren't nodes (unlike proper attributes), they're just part of the value of the processing instruction.

Now, the `<TVGuide>` element has a couple of attributes: `start` and `end`. These attributes shouldn't be added to the tree in the same way as the children of the `<TVGuide>` would be, so we'll place them off to one side and use a different kind of line for them, as in Figure 3-3.

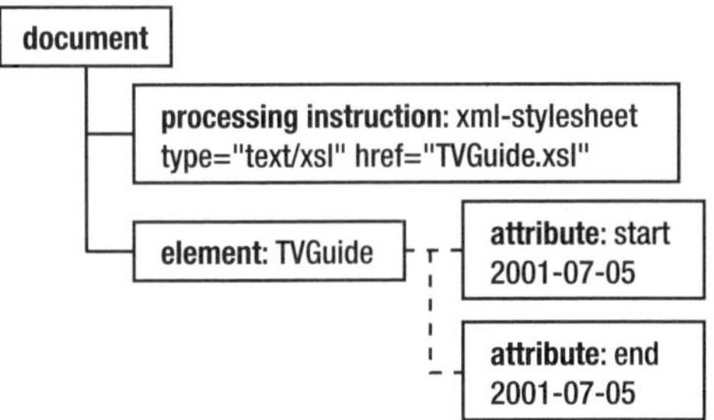

Figure 3-3. *Node tree: attributes on the* `<TVGuide>` *element*

Now let's look at the content of the `<TVGuide>` element. The `<TVGuide>` element contains a `<Channel>` element, which in turn contains a `<Name>` element and a `<Program>` element. The `<Name>` element contains some text. Pieces of text are represented as separate nodes in the node tree, so the `<Name>` element node contains a text node, as shown in Figure 3-4.

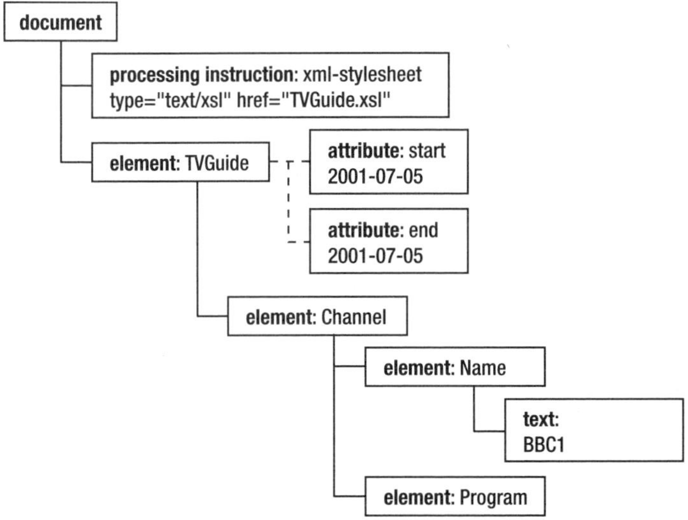

Figure 3-4. *Node tree: children of the* `<Channel>` *element*

The child elements of the `<Program>` element are treated in the same way—they each have a single text node as a child, as shown in Figure 3-5.

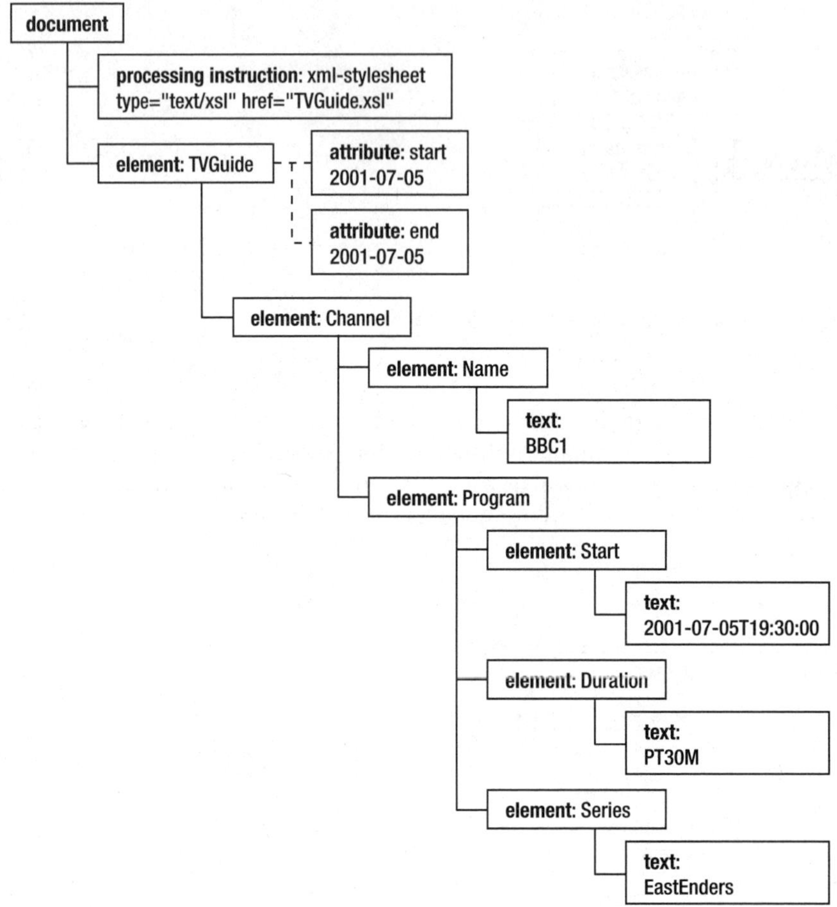

Figure 3-5. *Node tree: children of the* `<Program>` *element*

The rest of the tree follows a similar pattern: element nodes having either other elements or text nodes as children. It's often very useful to keep a picture of the node tree of the input document that you're working with close at hand, to help you work out what nodes you're selecting and processing.

Tip Many XSLT editors help with you gain a picture of the node tree by providing a simple tree view on an input document. Alternatively, you can use a stand-alone tool such as Mike Brown's Pretty XML Tree Viewer (`http://skew.org/xml/stylesheets/treeview/html/`).

XSLT Processing Model

Templates in stylesheets each match particular nodes in the node tree. The `match` attribute on a template tells the XSLT processor what kind of nodes they match. In a full stylesheet, you tell the XSLT processor what nodes you want to be processed (using an `<xsl:apply-templates>`

instruction, as you'll see later) and the XSLT processor goes through the nodes you've selected one by one trying to find a matching template for each in turn. When it looks for a template, it searches the whole stylesheet, so it doesn't matter where the template is within that stylesheet.

When the XSLT processor finds a matching template, it uses the content of that template to process the matching node and generate some output. The content of the template might include instructions that tell the processor to apply templates to a particular set of nodes, in which case it goes through those nodes finding and processing matching templates, and so on.

In this section, we'll look at the implications of this processing model and the kinds of changes that we can make to our stylesheet to take advantage of templates.

Summary XSLT processing involves telling the processor to apply templates to some nodes in the input document. The XSLT processor locates a template that matches the node, and processes its content to generate a result. The location of the template within the stylesheet doesn't matter.

The Initial Template

This process of applying templates to nodes in the node tree has to start somewhere. In the majority of cases, the input to the stylesheet is an XML document, and the processor starts at the root of the node tree, on the document node for that XML document. After building the node tree, the XSLT processor takes the document node and tries to find a template that matches it. If the XSLT processor finds one, it processes the content of that template to generate the output.

Tip If you're running a stylesheet from code, then you can make the stylesheet start from a node other than the document node if you want. This is useful if you want to only process a section of a larger document, for example. In these cases, you need templates that match the nodes that you use as the input to the transformation—a template that matches the document node will only be used if you tell the processor to process the document node.

A template that matches the document node of a node tree has a `match` attribute with a value of `/`, one that looks like this:

```
<xsl:template match="/">
  ...
</xsl:template>
```

If you're familiar with programming, you can think of this template as analogous to the main entry point in a program or the `main()` method on a class. Whatever happens, when you process a document with the stylesheet, the XSLT processor will process the contents of this template, so it gives you top-level control over what the stylesheet does.

If you look back at `TVGuide2.xsl`, the full stylesheet that you created based on the simplified stylesheet from the last chapter, you'll see that it contains only one template, which matches the document node. The stylesheet works because the XSLT processor always activates that template.

Summary A template that matches the document node of the input acts as high-level control over the result of the stylesheet.

Matching Elements with Templates

At the moment, we use <xsl:for-each> to tell the XSLT processor to go through the <Channel> elements one by one. That's one place where we could use templates instead. In this section, we'll look at how we can replace this <xsl:for-each> with a separate template and an <xsl:apply-templates> instruction.

First, we need a template that tells the XSLT processor what to do when it's told to process a <Channel> element. You can match an element with a template by giving the name of the element in the `match` attribute of the <xsl:template> element. So the following template will match <Channel> elements and process them to generate the same result as is currently generated inside <xsl:for-each>:

```
<xsl:template match="Channel">
  <h2 class="channel"><xsl:value-of select="Name" /></h2>
  <xsl:for-each select="Program">
    <div>
      <p>
        <span class="date"><xsl:value-of select="Start" /></span><br />
        <span class="title"><xsl:value-of select="Series" /></span><br />
        <xsl:value-of select="Description" />
        <span onclick="toggle({Series}Cast);">[Cast]</span>
      </p>
      <div id="{Series}Cast" style="display: none;">
        <ul class="castlist">
          <xsl:for-each select="CastList/CastMember">
            <li>
              <span class="character">
                <xsl:value-of select="Character" />
              </span>
              <span class="actor">
                <xsl:value-of select="Actor" />
              </span>
            </li>
          </xsl:for-each>
        </ul>
      </div>
    </div>
  </xsl:for-each>
</xsl:template>
```

Summary If a template's `match` attribute gives the name of an element, the XSLT processor will use that template for elements with that name.

You can put this template wherever you like at the top level of the stylesheet (at the same level as the other <xsl:template> elements). The XSLT processor will find it and use it whenever it needs to process a <Channel> element. In TVGuide3.xsl, I've put this template after the template that matches the document node, so the top level of the stylesheet looks like this:

```
<?xml version="1.0" encoding="ISO-8859-1"?>
<xsl:stylesheet version="2.0"
                xmlns:xsl="http://www.w3.org/1999/XSL/Transform">

<xsl:template match="/">
  ...
</xsl:template>

<xsl:template match="Channel">
  ...
</xsl:template>

</xsl:stylesheet>
```

■ **Tip** I usually order the templates in my stylesheets starting from the template matching the document node and working down the levels of the node tree. But you are free to arrange your templates however you like.

However, the XSLT processor will never use this template unless you tell the processor to process (apply templates to) a <Channel> element. You instruct the XSLT processor to apply templates to some nodes using the <xsl:apply-templates> instruction. Like <xsl:for-each>, the result of the <xsl:apply-templates> instruction gets inserted into the result of the transformation at the point where you use the instruction, so while the location of <xsl:template> doesn't matter, the positioning of <xsl:apply-templates> is very important.

The <xsl:apply-templates> instruction has a select attribute, which tells the XSLT processor which nodes to apply templates to. The select attribute on <xsl:apply-templates> works in the same way as the select attribute on <xsl:for-each>—you give a path that points to the nodes to which you want to apply templates.

We want the result to appear at the same place as the result of the original <xsl:for-each>, and we already know the path to those nodes because we're already using it on the <xsl:for-each>. So you can apply templates instead by replacing the <xsl:for-each> with an <xsl:apply-templates> element that has exactly the same select attribute. Doing this in TVGuide4.xsl gives a template matching the document node as follows:

```
<xsl:template match="/">
  <html>
    <head>
      <title>TV Guide</title>
      ...
    </head>
    <body>
```

```
      <h1>TV Guide</h1>
      <xsl:apply-templates select="/TVGuide/Channel" />
    </body>
  </html>
</xsl:template>
```

Using templates instead of <xsl:for-each> breaks up the stylesheet into manageable chunks in a similar way to functions and methods in standard programming languages. One advantage of this is that you don't have XSLT with lots and lots of indentation, which can really help with readability! A bigger advantage is that you can use the same template for similar nodes in different places or on the same node multiple times, as we'll see later in the chapter. On the down side, the stylesheet no longer looks as similar to the HTML document that we're producing as it used to, and to work out how to change the result of the stylesheet, you may have to navigate between multiple templates.

Summary You can replace an <xsl:for-each> element with a template holding its contents and an <xsl:apply-templates> element selecting the nodes you want to process.

Replacing <xsl:for-each> with Templates

We've still used <xsl:for-each> in a couple of other places within TVGuide4.xsl, so let's convert those instances in the same way as we've done with the one that iterated over <Channel> elements.

The next <xsl:for-each> is where we iterate over the <Program> elements, which is within the template that matches <Channel> elements. We can convert it by first replacing the <xsl:for-each> with an <xsl:apply-templates> element that has the same value for its select attribute:

```
<xsl:template match="Channel">
  <h2 class="channel"><xsl:value-of select="Name" /></h2>
  <xsl:apply-templates select="Program" />
</xsl:template>
```

and then creating a template that matches <Program> elements. The new template has the same contents as the old <xsl:for-each> did:

```
<xsl:template match="Program">
  <div>
    <p>
      <span class="date"><xsl:value-of select="Start" /></span><br />
      <span class="title"><xsl:value-of select="Series" /></span><br />
      <xsl:value-of select="Description" />
      <span onclick="toggle({Series}Cast);">[Cast]</span>
    </p>
    <div id="{Series}Cast" style="display: none;">
      <ul class="castlist">
        <xsl:for-each select="CastList/CastMember">
          <li>
            <span class="character">
```

```
          <xsl:value-of select="Character" />
        </span>
        <span class="actor">
          <xsl:value-of select="Actor" />
        </span>
      </li>
    </xsl:for-each>
  </ul>
</div>
  </div>
</xsl:template>
```

This template also contains an <xsl:for-each>, one that iterates over the <CastMember> element children of <CastList> elements. Again, we can replace this <xsl:for-each> with an <xsl:apply-templates>:

```
<xsl:template match="Program">
  <div>
    <p>
      <span class="date"><xsl:value-of select="Start" /></span><br />
      <span class="title"><xsl:value-of select="Series" /></span><br />
      <xsl:value-of select="Description" />
      <span onclick="toggle({Series}Cast);">[Cast]</span>
    </p>
    <div id="{Series}Cast" style="display: none;">
      <ul class="castlist">
        <xsl:apply-templates select="CastList/CastMember" />
      </ul>
    </div>
  </div>
</xsl:template>
```

and create a separate template that deals with giving output for <CastMember> elements:

```
<xsl:template match="CastMember">
  <li>
    <span class="character"><xsl:value-of select="Character" /></span>
    <span class="actor"><xsl:value-of select="Actor" /></span>
  </li>
</xsl:template>
```

We now have four templates in TVGuide5.xsl, matching

- The document node
- <Channel> elements
- <Program> elements
- <CastMember> elements

If you run TVGuide5.xsl with TVGuide.xml, you should get exactly the same result as the original, simplified stylesheet. Splitting up the processing into separate templates hasn't changed the result of the transformation.

The Built-in Templates

We've seen that when you apply templates to a node, the XSLT processor tries to find the template that matches that node. But what happens when there isn't a template that matches a node? For example, if we applied templates to the <Name> child of the <Channel> element, as follows, but didn't have a template to match the <Name> element:

```
<xsl:template match="Channel">
  <h2 class="channel"><xsl:apply-templates select="Name" /></h2>
  <xsl:apply-templates select="Program" />
</xsl:template>
```

When the XSLT processor can't find a template to match the node that it's been told to process, it uses a **built-in template**. If you find that the result of your stylesheet includes text you didn't expect, chances are that it's due to the built-in templates. Just because there isn't a template for a particular node doesn't mean that the node's not processed.

For elements, the built-in template is as follows:

```
<xsl:template match="*">
  <xsl:apply-templates />
</xsl:template>
```

This template uses two bits of syntax that we haven't seen before:

- The `match` attribute of the template takes the value *. Templates with a match pattern of * match all elements.
- The `<xsl:apply-templates>` element doesn't have a `select` attribute. If you use `<xsl:apply-templates>` without a `select` attribute, the XSLT processor collects all the children of the current node (which is the node that the template matches) and applies templates to them.

To see the effect of this, take another look at the part of the node tree containing the <Name> element, shown in Figure 3-6.

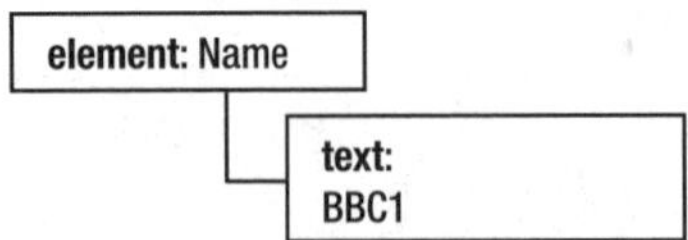

Figure 3-6. *The* <Name> *element and its text node child*

The <Name> element has only one child node, a text node with the value `BBC1`. When you tell the XSLT processor to apply templates to the <Name> element, it will use the built-in template for elements, and hence apply templates to that text node.

Now, again, we don't have a template that matches text nodes in our stylesheet, so the processor uses a built-in template. The built-in template for text nodes is

```
<xsl:template match="text()">
  <xsl:value-of select="." />
</xsl:template>
```

Again, this template uses a couple of new bits of syntax:

- The `match` attribute of the `<xsl:template>` element takes the value `text()`. Templates with a match pattern of `text()` match text nodes.
- The `select` attribute of the `<xsl:value-of>` element takes the value `.` (dot). The XPath expression `.` selects the context item, so `<xsl:value-of select="."/>` gives the value of the context item, in this case the text node.

With these built-in templates, if you apply templates to an element, but don't have a template for that element (or any elements it contains), then you'll get the value of the text held within the element. So applying templates to the `<Name>` element means that you get the value `BBC1` in the result.

Summary If a processor can't find a template that matches a node, it uses the built-in template for that node type. In effect, these give the value of the elements to which you apply templates.

Using the Built-in Templates

There are quite a few places in our stylesheet where we want to just get the value of an element. Rather than using `<xsl:value-of>` to get these values, we could apply templates to the elements and let the built-in templates do their work to give us the element values.

We've already done this with the template for `<Channel>` elements, to get the name of the channel:

```
<xsl:template match="Channel">
  <h2 class="channel"><xsl:apply-templates select="Name" /></h2>
  <xsl:apply-templates select="Program" />
</xsl:template>
```

We can also replace the `<xsl:value-of>` instructions in the template for `<Program>` elements to get the values of the `<Start>`, `<Series>`, and `<Description>` elements:

```
<xsl:template match="Program">
  <div>
    <p>
      <span class="date"><xsl:apply-templates select="Start" /></span>
      <br />
      <span class="title"><xsl:apply-templates select="Series" /></span>
      <br />
      <xsl:apply-templates select="Description" />
      <span onclick="toggle({Series}Cast);">[Cast]</span>
    </p>
    <div id="{Series}Cast" style="display: none;">
      <ul class="castlist">
        <xsl:apply-templates select="CastList/CastMember" />
      </ul>
```

```
    </div>
  </div>
</xsl:template>
```

and in the template for <CastMember> elements, to get the values of the <Character> and <Actor> elements:

```
<xsl:template match="CastMember">
  <li>
    <span class="character">
      <xsl:apply-templates select="Character" />
    </span>
    <span class="actor">
      <xsl:apply-templates select="Actor" />
    </span>
  </li>
</xsl:template>
```

■ **Note** Both the <Character> and <Actor> elements actually contain <Name> elements giving the name of the character or actor. With the built-in templates, you get the value of the text held in these <Name> elements.

The stylesheet TVGuide6.xsl still contains the same number of templates, but applies templates to all the elements that it processes rather than simply getting their values. If you run TVGuide6.xsl with TVGuide.xml to produce TVGuide6.html, you should get exactly the same result as you did before. Changing the <xsl:value-of> elements to <xsl:apply-templates> elements hasn't altered the result of the stylesheet.

Extending Stylesheets

As you've seen in the previous section, the effect of the built-in templates is that if you apply templates to a single element, you get all the text that's contained in that element, at any level. This is the same as what you get when you use <xsl:value-of> and select the element. In other words, if you don't have a template that matches <Name> elements or any of their descendants, then the following instructions give you exactly the same result:

```
<xsl:apply-templates select="Name" />
<xsl:value-of select="Name" />
```

There are pluses and minuses to using <xsl:apply-templates> rather than <xsl:value-of>. The biggest downside is that it's less efficient to use <xsl:apply-templates> because it forces the XSLT processor to search through the stylesheet for templates that match the node rather than directly giving the value of the node. For this reason, I would generally only apply templates to elements that I know could contain other elements, and not to text nodes, attributes, or elements that I know only have text content.

On the plus side, using <xsl:apply-templates> makes it a lot easier to change the format of the value that you get from an element, just by adding a template for that element. For example, if I wanted to change the way I give the name of the series so that it's given as a link to a page on that series instead, I can add a template that matches the `<Series>` element and generates an `<a>` element in the result giving a link to the page.

```
<xsl:template match="Series">
  <a href="{.}.html">
    <xsl:value-of select="." />
  </a>
</xsl:template>
```

Note This uses an attribute value template (which we met in the last chapter) to give the URL for the page, using the value of the context node (the `<Series>` element) plus the string `.html`. For example, the element `<Series>EastEnders</Series>` will result in a link to `EastEnders.html`.

This flexibility is also very useful when the XML format that you're converting from isn't finalized. If we added `<Description>` elements to the `<Character>` and `<Actor>` elements, as in `TVGuide2.xml` in the code download, then we could update the stylesheet to cope with the change by adding templates for these elements so that they only generate the value of the `<Name>` rather than including the description. We do this in `TVGuide7.xsl`, which contains

```
<xsl:template match="Actor">
  <xsl:apply-templates select="Name" />
</xsl:template>

<xsl:template match="Character">
  <xsl:apply-templates select="Name" />
</xsl:template>
```

Note If you didn't add these templates, then applying templates to the `<Actor>` or `<Character>` elements would result in text containing both the name and description of the actor or character, concatenated.

Summary Using templates allows you to extend your stylesheet more easily than you can if you use `<xsl:for-each>` and `<xsl:value-of>`.

Templates As Mapping Rules

We've been a little formulaic in our conversion from the simplified stylesheet to the full stylesheet that we have now—we take every `<xsl:for-each>` and `<xsl:value-of>` and turn it into an `<xsl:apply-templates>`. The introduction of templates has really just been a way of modularizing the code.

But there's another way of thinking about templates that can make your stylesheets more elegant and more extensible, and that's to consider them as mapping rules. Each template describes how to map a particular node in the input XML onto a result that you're after. In this section, we'll first look at using templates with mixed content, and at how using templates as mapping rules is particularly useful when processing document-oriented XML. Then, we'll go on to look at how we could apply the same kind of technique to our stylesheet and the impact of doing so.

Processing Document-Oriented XML

Let's first look at the problem of generating output from document-oriented XML. Document-oriented XML arises when you take a paragraph of text and mark up particular words and phrases within that paragraph, giving mixed content—elements and text intermingled. This is in contrast to data-oriented XML, which is concerned with storing data and usually results in element-only and text-only content.

Take another look at the XML structure that we're using to store information about TV programs:

```
<Program>
  <Start>2001-07-05T19:30:00</Start>
  <Duration>PT30M</Duration>
  <Series>EastEnders</Series>
  <Title></Title>
  <Description>
    Mark's health scare forces him to reconsider his future with Lisa,
    while Jamie is torn between Sonia and Zoe.
  </Description>
  ...
</Program>
```

While most of the XML structure is oriented around providing data, the description of the TV program is more document-oriented. You could imagine wanting to add a bit of document-oriented markup to the <Description> element, perhaps a link to the *EastEnders* biography for Jamie and highlights around the names of the characters:

```
<Description>
  <Character>Mark</Character>'s health scare forces him to reconsider his
  future with <Character>Lisa</Character>, while
  <Link
    href="http://www.bbc.co.uk/eastenders/characters/jamie_m_biog.shtml">
    <Character>Jamie</Character>
  </Link> is torn between <Character>Sonia</Character> and
  <Character>Zoe</Character>.
</Description>
```

The <Description> element now holds mixed content. Looking at the node tree representation of that piece of XML, as shown in Figure 3-7, makes this clearer.

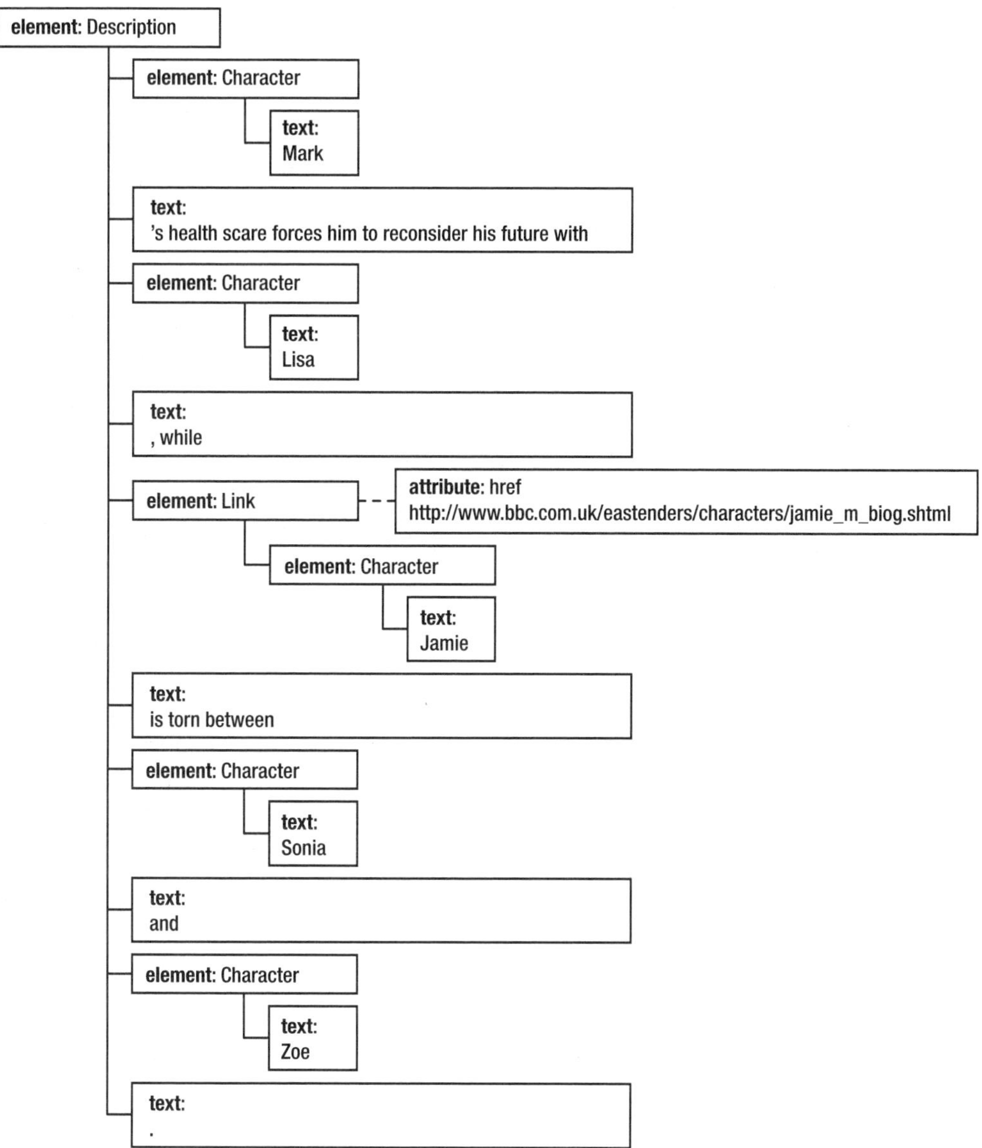

Figure 3-7. *Mixed content in a node tree*

We want the elements that we use in the description to be transformed into HTML elements instead. In the HTML version of the page, we want to use `<span>` elements around the character names, and transform the `<Link>` elements into `<a>` elements, to give the following:

```
<p>
  <span class="date">2001-07-05T19:30:00</span><br />
  <span class="title">EastEnders</span><br />
  <span class="character">Mark</span>'s health scare forces him to
  reconsider his future with <span class="character">Lisa</span>, while
  <a href="http://www.bbc.co.uk/eastenders/characters/jamie_m_biog.shtml">
  <span class="character">Jamie</span></a> is torn between
  <span class="character">Sonia</span> and
  <span class="character">Zoe</span>.
  <span onclick="toggle(EastEndersCast);">[Cast]</span>
</p>
```

If you imagine processing the content of the <Description> element with <xsl:for-each>, you'll see that you run into problems. We haven't looked at how to yet, but it's possible to iterate over all the nodes that are children of the <Description> element, and test what kind of node they are to decide what to do with them. But even if you did that, you still need to take account of nested elements (like the <Character> element inside the <Link> element), so you'd get very long and very deep conditional processing to cover all levels of nesting.

However, with templates it's a lot easier. You can create a template for each kind of element that you know can occur in the content of the <Description> element, which describes how to map between that element and the result that you want. In this example, there are two elements, <Character> and <Link>, so you need a template for each. Within the <span> and <a> elements that these templates create, you apply templates to the content of the <Character> or <Link> element to account for possible nested elements:

```
<xsl:template match="Character">
  <span class="character"><xsl:apply-templates /></span>
</xsl:template>

<xsl:template match="Link">
  <a href="{@href}"><xsl:apply-templates /></a>
</xsl:template>
```

Whenever you add a new type of element that you might include in the description, you can add a new template that describes how to map that onto HTML.

Summary Templates are particularly suited to processing document-oriented XML. Each template acts as a mapping rule from input to result.

Creating Presentation Rules

We can add support for lots of different elements that we want to be able to use within the <Description> element. Highlighting character names and providing links to other web sites is useful, but you might also want to add elements for emphasis, foreign words, names of directors, series, channels, films, and so on—different elements for the different types of words and phrases that can appear in descriptions of TV programs and series.

We'll add just a few of these elements in TVGuide2.xml, to create TVGuide3.xml, shown in Listing 3-5.

Listing 3-5. TVGuide3.xml

```
<?xml version="1.0" encoding="ISO-8859-1"?>
<TVGuide start="2001-07-05" end="2001-07-05">
<Channel>
  <Name>BBC1</Name>
  ...
  <Program rating="5" flag="favorite">
    <Start>2001-07-05T19:30:00</Start>
    <Duration>PT30M</Duration>
    <Series>EastEnders</Series>
    <Title></Title>
    <Description>
      <Character>Mark</Character>'s health scare forces him to reconsider
      his future with <Character>Lisa</Character>, while
      <Link
      href="http://www.bbc.co.uk/eastenders/characters/jamie_m_biog.shtml">
        <Character>Jamie</Character>
      </Link> is torn between <Character>Sonia</Character> and
      <Character>Zoe</Character>.
    </Description>
    <CastList>
      <CastMember>
        <Character>
          <Name>Zoe Slater</Name>
          <Description>
            The youngest Slater girl, <Character>Zoe</Character> really
            makes the most of the fact she's the baby of the family.
          </Description>
        </Character>
        <Actor>
          <Name>Michelle Ryan</Name>
          <Description>
            For more details, see
            <Link href="http://www.ajmanagement.co.uk/michelle-ryan.htm">
              <Actor>Michelle Ryan</Actor>'s Agency
            </Link>.
          </Description>
        </Actor>
      </CastMember>
      <CastMember>
        <Character>
          <Name>Jamie Mitchell</Name>
          <Description>
            Jamie's a bit of a heartthrob (who could resist that
            little-boy-lost look?) but until <Character>Janine
```

```
          Butcher</Character> came along he'd steered clear of girls.
        </Description>
      </Character>
      <Actor>
        <Name>Jack Ryder</Name>
        <Description>
          Won Best Newcomer for <Character>Jamie Mitchell</Character>
          in the 1999 TV awards.
        </Description>
      </Actor>
    </CastMember>
    <CastMember>
      ...
    </CastMember>
  </CastList>
  ...
 </Program>
 ...
</Channel>
...
</TVGuide>
```

Try using TVGuide6.xsl with TVGuide3.xml, which uses <xsl:apply-templates> to apply templates to the <Description> element. There aren't any templates for <Character> or <Link> elements, so the built-in templates are used instead. The result of the transformation of the <Description> element looks just the same as before, because the built-in templates automatically show any text within an element.

We want a new version of the stylesheet (TVGuide8.xsl), which generates HTML where the words and phrases in the description that we've picked out with <Character> and <Link> elements are displayed and behave slightly differently from the rest of the text. Links should *be* links, for example, and character names should be slightly larger than the surrounding text.

To make the marked-up text display and act differently, we need to introduce templates for these new elements: one for the <Link> element, to create a hypertext link with an HTML <a> element:

```
<xsl:template match="Link">
  <a href="{@href}"><xsl:apply-templates /></a>
</xsl:template>
```

and one for the <Character> element, to create a <span> element with a class of character around the character names:

```
<xsl:template match="Character">
  <span class="character"><xsl:apply-templates /></span>
</xsl:template>
```

To make the character names slightly bigger, we'll add a rule to TVGuide.css, to create TVGuide2.css, which contains

```
.character {
  font-size: larger;
}
```

Putting the final touches on TVGuide8.xsl, we need the HTML that it creates to point to TVGuide2.css rather than TVGuide.css, so the <link> element generated in the template matching the document node needs to be altered slightly:

```
<xsl:template match="/">
  <html>
    <head>
      <title>TV Guide</title>
      <link rel="stylesheet" href="TVGuide2.css" />
      ...
    </head>
    ...
  </html>
</xsl:template>
```

Having made this final change, transform TVGuide3.xml with TVGuide8.xsl. When viewed in a browser, the result of the transformation—TVGuide8.html—should look something like the screenshot shown in Figure 3-8.

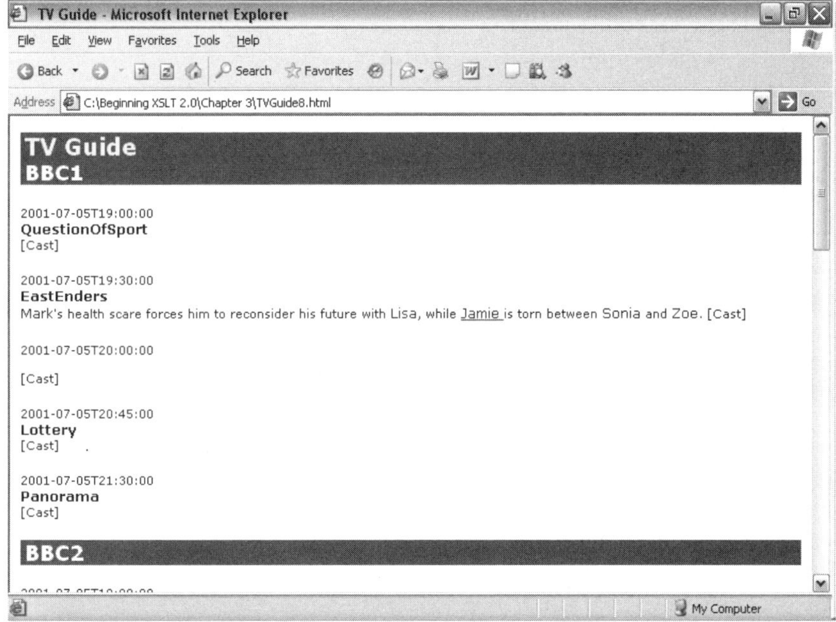

Figure 3-8. *Viewing* TVGuide8.html *in Internet Explorer*

The character names are slightly larger than the rest of the text, and clicking the word "Jamie" takes you to the *EastEnders* site with Jamie Mitchell's biography. Feel free to add your own elements to that description, and add your own templates matching them to present the document-oriented XML.

Context-Dependent Processing

We've now introduced a number of elements into our XML structure that we're actually using elsewhere in different ways. For example, we use the <Character> element to indicate the name of a character in a description, and to hold information about a character within the <CastMember> element. The template makes no distinction between these two uses of the <Character> element, and does the same thing for each, making a <span> element with a character class:

```
<xsl:template match="Character">
  <span class="character">
    <xsl:apply-templates />
  </span>
</xsl:template>
```

At the moment, we're also creating a <span> element when we create the cast list, in the template matching the <CastMember> element:

```
<xsl:template match="CastMember">
  <li>
    <span class="character">
      <xsl:apply-templates select="Character" />
    </span>
    <span class="actor">
      <xsl:apply-templates select="Actor" />
    </span>
  </li>
</xsl:template>
```

This means we end up with two <span> elements around the names of the characters in the cast list. We can get rid of the superfluous <span> element either by reverting back to using <xsl:value-of> to get the name of the character, or by removing the <span> element in the template that matches <CastMember> elements (and the same applies for the <Actor> elements as well, since we might name actors in a description):

```
<xsl:template match="CastMember">
  <li>
    <xsl:apply-templates select="Character" />
    <xsl:apply-templates select="Actor" />
  </li>
</xsl:template>
```

So now we have the same template being used to process <Character> elements in different contexts. However, one of the extensions that we made earlier in this chapter was to have the <Character> and <Actor> elements within <CastMember> actually give both a name and a description of the character. When we take this into account, we have a problem because we don't want the <span> element to contain both the name and the description of the character. We need a different template for the <Character> and <Actor> elements when they are children of <CastMember> elements (ones that just apply templates to the <Name> element child of the <Character> or <Actor> element). The new templates for the <Character> elements that occur in <CastMember> elements need to look like the following:

```
<xsl:template match="Character">
  <span class="character">
    <xsl:apply-templates select="Name" />
  </span>
</xsl:template>
```

But we can't use this template with the <Character> elements that occur in <Description> elements because they don't contain <Name> elements. If we use this template with those elements, the <span> elements won't have any content.

So we need some way of having different templates for the different contexts in which these elements are allowed. We can do this by changing the value of the match attribute of <xsl:template>, and this is where we need to use patterns, which is why they are introduced next.

Patterns

So far we've seen four kinds of values for the match attribute of <xsl:template>:

- / matches the document node.
- * matches any element.
- text() matches text nodes.
- The name of an element matches that element.

These values are all examples of **patterns**. An XSLT processor uses the pattern specified in the match attribute of <xsl:template> to work out whether it can use a template to process a node to which you've told it to apply templates. In our case, we need one pattern to match <Character> elements that are children of <CastMember> elements, and another pattern to match <Character> elements that appear at any level within <Description> elements. In both cases, we're checking the context in which the <Character> element appears. The two patterns we need are

- CastMember/Character to match <Character> elements that occur within <CastMember> elements
- Description//Character to match <Character> elements that occur nested to any level within <Description> elements

These types of patterns are technically known as **path patterns**. As you can see, path patterns look a lot like the paths that we use to select nodes to process in select attributes, and it can be easy to get confused between the two. You use paths to *select* nodes: they point from the current node to a set of other nodes in the tree, stepping down from element to child. You use path patterns to *match* nodes: they test whether a particular node has particular ancestors, looking up the node tree to work out the context of the node.

A path pattern is made up of a number of **pattern steps**, separated by either / or //. If the separator is a /, then the pattern tests a parent-child relationship. For example, the pattern Description/Character matches <Character> elements whose immediate parent is a <Description> element. If the separator is //, on the other hand, then the pattern tests an ancestor-descendant relationship. For example, the pattern Description//Character matches <Character> elements that have a <Description> element as an ancestor at any level.

■ **Summary** Path patterns enable you to match elements according to the context in which they occur.

Identifying Elements in Different Contexts

In our XML document, TVGuide3.xml, there are some elements that have different meanings in different contexts. If you remember back that far, it was one of our design decisions when we first put together our XML structure that we would make use of the context an element was in, rather than use different names for elements in different contexts, to work out what an element meant and what we should do with it.

So now we have to deal with that decision by creating different templates with different match patterns for the different contexts in which an element can occur. The contexts within which different elements can occur are shown in the following table:

Element	Contexts
<Name>	Child of <Channel> Child of <Character> Child of <Actor>
<Description>	Child of <Program> Child of <Character> Child of <Actor>
<Character>	Child of <CastMember> Descendant of <Description>
<Actor>	Child of <CastMember> Descendant of <Description>
<Series>	Child of <Program> Descendant of <Description>
<Program>	Child of <Channel> Descendant of <Description>
<Channel>	Child of <TVGuide> Descendant of <Description>

A stylesheet that deals with documents that follow our markup language really needs to have templates that deal with elements occurring in each of these possible contexts, using patterns that include ancestry information.

Creating Templates for Context-Dependent Elements

At this stage, we'll create a new version of the stylesheet, TVGuide9.xsl, which contains separate templates for each of these elements in each of these contexts. You should be able to put together different templates for the elements in their different contexts as mapping rules. For example, the <Name> element can occur in three contexts—<Channel>, <Character>, and <Actor>—so there should be three corresponding templates:

```
<xsl:template match="Channel/Name">...</xsl:template>
<xsl:template match="Character/Name">...</xsl:template>
<xsl:template match="Actor/Name">...</xsl:template>
```

As you add these templates, you should consider whether some of the HTML that you're currently generating in higher-level templates can be generated in lower-level templates instead. For example, my feeling is that the <Name> element in the <Channel> element maps onto the <h2> heading element in the result, so the template should look like this:

```
<xsl:template match="Channel/Name">
  <h2 class="channel"><xsl:value-of select="." /></h2>
</xsl:template>
```

But if you create the <h2> element in the preceding template, you don't need to create it in the template for the <Channel> element. So you need to change that template too, removing the <h2> element that you were creating within it:

```
<xsl:template match="TVGuide/Channel">
  <xsl:apply-templates select="Name" />
  <xsl:apply-templates select="Program" />
</xsl:template>
```

■ **Note** This template only applies to <Channel> elements that are children of the <TVGuide> element, not those that are descendants of <Description> elements.

If you go through this process religiously, you should end up with about 19 different templates, as in TVGuide9.xsl. Using TVGuide9.xsl with TVGuide3.xml results in TVGuide9.html, in which both the <Character> elements within the cast list and those within the <Description> are treated properly, so the result looks like that shown in Figure 3-9 when you view it in Internet Explorer.

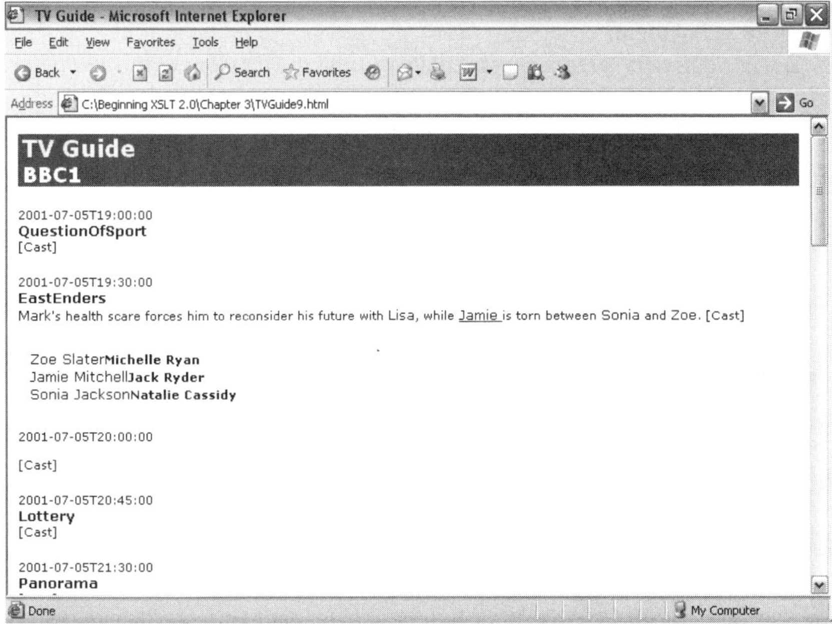

Figure 3-9. *Viewing* TVGuide9.html *in Internet Explorer*

This process of adding templates on an element-by-element basis, taking account of the different contexts in which an element can occur, has left us with a lot of templates, but it has made the stylesheet more robust. We've handled the problem that we had with <Character> elements being treated differently in different contexts, and we've included templates to handle the possibility of things that aren't actually present in TVGuide3.xml, but which could happen in more complete documents that follow the markup language, such as <Channel> elements in <Description> elements.

Unnecessary Templates

Adding templates to deal with every kind of element, in every context, within a stylesheet can leave you with a stylesheet that contains lots of templates that actually don't do very much. This makes the stylesheet harder for you to maintain (because it's longer), and it makes more work for the processor when it needs to identify which template to apply in a particular situation. You need to find a judicious balance between the two.

First, you don't need to create a template for every element in every context. Remember that if the XSLT processor can't find a template that matches a node, then it will use a built-in template. If an element (and all its content) gets processed by the built-in templates, then you'll just get the value of the node. So, if you have templates that look like either of the following:

```
<xsl:template match="...">
  <xsl:value-of select="." />
</xsl:template>

<xsl:template match="...">
  <xsl:apply-templates />
</xsl:template>
```

then you may as well get rid of them.

Second, you can get rid of templates that essentially process the children of the element that they match in the order that they appear. For example, the revised template for the <Channel> elements that are children of <TVGuide> elements is like that:

```
<xsl:template match="TVGuide/Channel">
  <xsl:apply-templates select="Name" />
  <xsl:apply-templates select="Program" />
</xsl:template>
```

When a <Channel> element appears as a child of a <TVGuide> element, then it can only contain a <Name> element followed by any number of <Program> elements. So telling the processor to apply templates first to the <Name> element and then to the <Program> elements has the same effect as telling the processor to apply templates to all the <Channel> element's children in the order they occur, which would be the template:

```
<xsl:template match="TVGuide/Channel">
  <xsl:apply-templates />
</xsl:template>
```

This template has the same effect as the built-in template for elements, so you can delete it without affecting the result of the stylesheet.

Finally, you can get rid of templates that match elements that are never selected for processing. Remember that a template is never actually used if the processor never gets told to apply templates to a node that matches that template. A template that is never matched will never be used, and can therefore be safely removed.

Removing Unnecessary Templates

TVGuide9.xsl does contain a few templates that aren't really necessary, and to make it easier to understand we could prune it to create TVGuide10.xsl.

There are three templates that do the same thing as the built-in templates, and just contain an <xsl:apply-templates> or an <xsl:value-of> instruction that gives the value of the current node. They are the one matching <Name> element children of <Character> elements, the one matching <Name> element children of <Actor> elements, and the one matching <Description> element children of <Program> elements—you can safely delete them:

```
<xsl:template match="Character/Name">
  <xsl:value-of select="." />
</xsl:template>

<xsl:template match="Actor/Name">
  <xsl:value-of select="." />
</xsl:template>

<xsl:template match="Program/Description">
  <xsl:apply-templates />
</xsl:template>
```

We identified the template matching <Channel> element children of the <TVGuide> element as falling into the second category. It had two <xsl:apply-templates> in it, but these selected nodes in the same order as they occurred in the input document, essentially the same as applying templates to all the children, which again is just what the built-in templates do. So you can safely delete the following template:

```
<xsl:template match="TVGuide/Channel">
  <xsl:apply-templates select="Name" />
  <xsl:apply-templates select="Program" />
</xsl:template>
```

Finally, in TVGuide9.xsl there are two templates that can never be applied—the one matching <Description> elements within <Character> elements, and the one matching <Description> elements within <Actor> elements. These templates will never get activated because the templates that match <Character> and <Actor> elements (within <CastMember> elements) never apply templates to their child <Description> elements. So these two templates can also be deleted:

```
<xsl:template match="Character/Description" />
<xsl:template match="Actor/Description" />
```

Once you've done all that, you should have something like the stylesheet shown in Listing 3-6, TVGuide10.xsl. The ordering of the templates within the stylesheet doesn't matter.

Listing 3-6. TVGuide10.xsl

```
<?xml version="1.0" encoding="ISO-8859-1"?>
<xsl:stylesheet version="2.0"
                xmlns:xsl="http://www.w3.org/1999/XSL/Transform">

<xsl:template match="/">
  <html>
    ...
  </html>
</xsl:template>

<xsl:template match="Channel/Name">
  <h2 class="channel"><xsl:value-of select="." /></h2>
</xsl:template>

<xsl:template match="Channel/Program">
  <div>
    ...
  </div>
</xsl:template>

<xsl:template match="Program/Series">
 <span class="title"><xsl:value-of select="." /></span>
</xsl:template>

<xsl:template match="CastMember">
  <li>
    <xsl:apply-templates select="Character" />
    <xsl:apply-templates select="Actor" />
  </li>
</xsl:template>

<xsl:template match="CastMember/Character">
  <span class="character">
    <xsl:apply-templates select="Name" />
  </span>
</xsl:template>

<xsl:template match="CastMember/Actor">
  <span class="actor">
    <xsl:apply-templates select="Name" />
  </span>
</xsl:template>

<xsl:template match="Description//Character">
  <span class="character">
```

```
    <xsl:apply-templates />
  </span>
</xsl:template>

<xsl:template match="Description//Actor">
  <span class="actor">
    <xsl:apply-templates />
  </span>
</xsl:template>

<xsl:template match="Link">
  <a href="{@href}">
    <xsl:apply-templates />
  </a>
</xsl:template>

<xsl:template match="Description//Program">
  <span class="program"><xsl:apply-templates /></span>
</xsl:template>

<xsl:template match="Description//Series">
  <span class="series"><xsl:apply-templates /></span>
</xsl:template>

<xsl:template match="Description//Channel">
  <span class="channel"><xsl:apply-templates /></span>
</xsl:template>

</xsl:stylesheet>
```

Using `TVGuide10.xsl` with `TVGuide3.xml` should give the same result as `TVGuide9.xsl` did.

Resolving Conflicts Between Templates

Whenever you have rules in a language, such as rules in CSS or templates in XSLT, you need some way to resolve conflicts when two of the rules apply to the same situation. What would happen, for example, if you had one template that matched all `<Character>` elements and another template that matched only those `<Character>` elements that had `<CastMember>` as their parent:

```
<xsl:template match="Character">
  <span class="character"><xsl:apply-templates /></span>
</xsl:template>

<xsl:template match="CastMember/Character">
  <span class="character"><xsl:apply-templates select="Name" /></span>
</xsl:template>
```

A <Character> element in a <Description> element only matches one of the templates, because it doesn't have a <CastMember> element as its parent, so obviously the XSLT processor uses that template with it. But what about a <Character> element in a <CastMember> element? It matches both of the template's patterns, so what should the XSLT processor do?

Template Priority

Well, the XSLT processor will only ever process one template when you apply templates to a node, so it has to choose between the two templates that it's presented with in some way. It does this by looking at the template's **priority**. A template with a high priority is chosen over a template with a lower priority.

You can specifically assign a template a priority using the priority attribute on the <xsl:template> element. The priority attribute can be set to any number, including decimal and negative numbers. For example, you can give the two templates different specific priorities, as follows:

```
<xsl:template match="Character" priority="-1">
  <span class="character"><xsl:apply-templates /></span>
</xsl:template>

<xsl:template match="CastMember/Character" priority="2">
  <span class="character"><xsl:apply-templates select="Name" /></span>
</xsl:template>
```

Default Priorities

However, it would be very difficult to assign and keep track of priorities if the priority attribute was your only option. If you don't specify a priority attribute on a template, the XSLT processor assigns it a priority based on how specific its match pattern is. XSLT processors recognize three levels of priority in the kind of patterns that we've looked at so far:

- Patterns that match a class of nodes, such as *, which matches all elements, are assigned an implicit priority of -0.5.
- Patterns that match nodes according to their name, such as Character, which matches <Character> elements, are assigned an implicit priority of 0.
- Patterns that match nodes according to their context, such as CastMember/Character, which matches <Character> elements whose parent is a <CastMember> element, are assigned an implicit priority of 0.5.

■ **Caution** When assigning priorities based on patterns, it doesn't matter how specific the context information is: if you specify any context for a node, then the template has a priority of 0.5. For example, Description/Link/Character has exactly the same priority as Description//Character.

Technically, it's an error if you have two templates that match the same node and the match patterns for the two templates have the same specificity. However, most processors recover from the error, which means they use the last template that you've defined in the stylesheet. You should try to avoid having templates that have the same priority and can feasibly match the same node; use the `priority` attribute to assign them specific, different priorities.

Summary If two templates match the same node, the processor uses the one with the highest priority. Priority can be assigned explicitly with the `priority` attribute or determined implicitly from the template's match pattern. As a last resort, the processor will select the last matching template in the stylesheet.

Using Priorities

Currently, the templates that our stylesheet contains don't have any conflicts with each other because each of them only matches elements in a fairly specific context. To try out priorities, let's try making some of the templates conflict by removing some of that context information from one of them. For example, in `TVGuide11.xsl`, let's change the template that matches `<Program>` elements within `<Description>` elements to match any `<Program>` element:

```
<xsl:template match="Program">
  <span class="program"><xsl:apply-templates /></span>
</xsl:template>
```

Now a `<Program>` element will always be matched by this template, and if it's a child of a `<Channel>` element, then it will also match the following template:

```
<xsl:template match="Channel/Program">
  <div>
    <p>
      <span class="date"><xsl:apply-templates select="Start" /></span>
      <br />
      <xsl:apply-templates select="Series" />
      <br />
      <xsl:apply-templates select="Description" />
      <span onclick="toggle({Series}Cast);">[Cast]</span>
    </p>
    <div id="{Series}Cast" style="display: none;">
      <ul class="castlist">
        <xsl:apply-templates select="CastList/CastMember" />
      </ul>
    </div>
  </div>
</xsl:template>
```

However, if you run `TVGuide11.xsl` with `TVGuide3.xml`, it won't make any difference to the result because the latter template, matching `<Program>` element children of `<Channel>` elements, has a higher priority. When the `<Program>` element that the XSLT processor is trying to process is a child of a `<Channel>` element, it will use the latter template, with the match pattern of `Channel/Program`; when it's not (such as when it's a child of a `<Description>` element), the processor will use the former template, with the match pattern of `Program`.

But we can change that in two ways. First, we can assign different priorities to the two templates using the `priority` attribute. Assign the general template a priority of 1, to create `TVGuide12.xsl`:

```
<xsl:template match="Program" priority="1">
  <span class="program"><xsl:apply-templates /></span>
</xsl:template>
```

This explicit priority is higher than the implicit priority of the second template. If you run `TVGuide12.xsl` with `TVGuide3.xml` to give `TVGuide12.html` you get the mess shown in Figure 3-10.

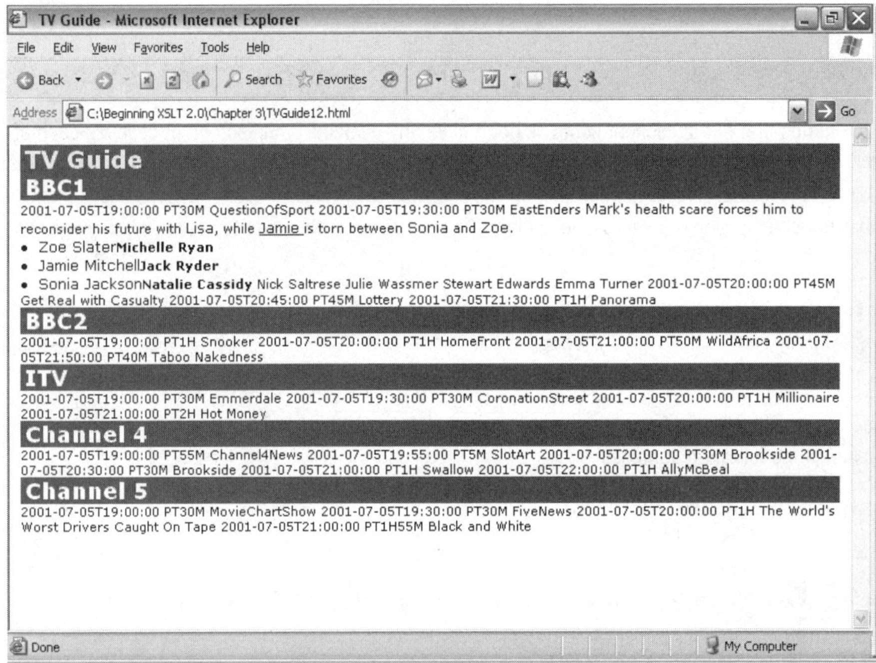

Figure 3-10. *Viewing* `TVGuide12.html` *in Internet Explorer*

Some of the formatting is still present because the elements inside the `<Program>` element still get processed by this template. However, the parts of the result that were generated by the second template, such as the `<div>` and `<p>` elements, are no longer present. You can get the same effect by removing the priority on the template matching all `<Program>` elements and giving the template matching `<Program>` elements within `<Channel>` elements a priority lower than -0.5.

A second way of manipulating the priority of the templates is to remove the context from the path for the second template (and remove the `priority` attributes that you just added), so the template that's supposed to be used to process `<Program>` elements within `<Channel>` elements looks like the following:

```
<xsl:template match="Program">
  <div>
    <p>
      <span class="date"><xsl:apply-templates select="Start" /></span>
```

```
      <br />
      <xsl:apply-templates select="Series" />
      <br />
      <xsl:apply-templates select="Description" />
      <span onclick="toggle({Series}Cast);">[Cast]</span>
    </p>
    <div id="{Series}Cast" style="display: none;">
      <ul class="castlist">
        <xsl:apply-templates select="CastList/CastMember" />
      </ul>
    </div>
  </div>
</xsl:template>
```

Now the templates both apply to the same `<Program>` elements and have the same priority, which is an error. Move the template that's supposed to be for `<Program>` elements within `<Description>` elements below the preceding code in the stylesheet (if it's not there already), to give `TVGuide13.xsl`. Most likely your processor will use the lower template in the stylesheet to process the `<Program>` elements, and you'll get the same mess as when you changed the priority explicitly. Processors are within their rights to terminate the stylesheet and give you an error, though, and some processors might warn you that there are two templates that match the same node with the same priority. Saxon, for example, gives reams of recoverable error messages as shown in Figure 3-11, though it produces the result perfectly well.

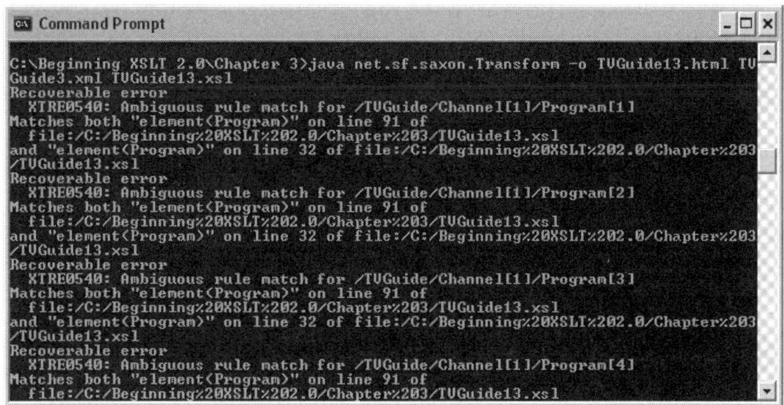

Figure 3-11. *Recoverable error messages from multiple template matches in Saxon*

It's often simpler to make templates whose match patterns don't include any information about the ancestry of the element, and it's easier for the processor too, because it doesn't have to check. For our TV guide stylesheet, we could adopt one of two styles to deal with elements that need to be treated differently in different places—add ancestry information for those templates that deal with elements in the descriptions, or add ancestry information to the other templates, those that deal with the bulk of the result. I think it makes more sense to keep ancestry information on the templates that deal with descriptions, because that way it's easy to tell which templates are those that deal with descriptions and which aren't. `TVGuide14.xsl` shows the result of doing that.

Choosing the Next Best Template

As we've seen, a particular node can match more than one template. When this happens, the templates are prioritized, based on their explicit or implicit priority or, if all else fails, their position in the stylesheet.

Sometimes the behavior of different matching templates at different priorities can be very similar. For example, look at the templates that match <Character> elements in TVGuide14.xsl:

```
<xsl:template match="Character">
  <span class="character">
    <xsl:apply-templates match="Name" />
  </span>
</xsl:template>

<xsl:template match="Description//Character">
  <span class="character">
    <xsl:apply-templates />
  </span>
</xsl:template>
```

Both these templates create a <span> element with a class attribute with the value character. If we changed the CSS class that we use to indicate character names, we'd have to change both templates.

What we'd really like to do here is say that whenever any <Character> element is processed, you get a <span> element with a class attribute with the value character, and that the content of that <span> element is determined by finding another template for the <Character> element, in which the ancestry of the <Character> element (whether it is within a <Description> element or a <CastMember> element) determines what happens.

We can arrange this with the <xsl:next-match> instruction. The <xsl:next-match> instruction tells the XSLT processor to take the current node (the one that's matched by this template) and to use whatever template was next in the list to process it. Looking at it another way, it tells the processor to process this node just as it would if this template didn't exist, and to insert the result.

Processing with the Next Matching Template

Let's try to use the <xsl:next-match> element to cut down on the repetition between the two templates in TVGuide14.xsl that match <Character> elements:

```
<xsl:template match="Character">
  <span class="character">
    <xsl:apply-templates match="Name" />
  </span>
</xsl:template>

<xsl:template match="Description//Character">
  <span class="character">
    <xsl:apply-templates />
  </span>
</xsl:template>
```

First, we want to say that whatever else happens, processing a <Character> element should result in a <span> element with a class attribute whose value is character. This needs to be our highest priority template, but the pattern for matching all <Character> elements—Character—doesn't have a very high default priority, so we need to use an explicit priority for it. The content of the <span> element will be determined by the next best template, using a <xsl:next-match> instruction:

```
<xsl:template match="Character" priority="2">
  <span class="character">
    <xsl:next-match />
  </span>
</xsl:template>
```

If we only had this template, then the next best template for the <Character> element would be the built-in template, which would process the <Character> element by applying templates to its content. This is exactly what we want to happen when the <Character> element appears within a <Description> element. However, if the <Character> element appears as a child of a <CastMember> element, we only want to process the child <Name> element.

So we need another template, at a lower priority to the preceding one, that matches <Character> elements that are children of <CastMember> elements and applies templates to their child <Name> elements:

```
<xsl:template match="CastMember/Character">
  <xsl:apply-templates select="Name" />
</xsl:template>
```

■ **Note** This template has an implicit priority of 0.5.

You can do the same kind of thing with the templates that match <Actor> elements. These templates are used in TVGuide15.xsl. Transforming TVGuide3.xml using TVGuide15.xsl gives you exactly the same result as you get with TVGuide14.xsl.

Processing with Push and Pull

Using templates as mapping rules really makes explicit the correspondence between a bit of the input XML and the result that you desire from it. As we've seen in the recent stylesheets such as TVGuide15.xsl, we can adopt this approach in data-oriented XML as well as document-oriented XML—you can have different templates matching different elements, even if those elements follow the traditionally "data-oriented" pattern of just having element or text children. The approach that we were working with at the start of this chapter was quite different. There, we had very few templates (we started with just one!), and where we did use them it was really to make the stylesheet more manageable and to get reuse.

These two approaches to transformations with XSLT are termed **push** and **pull**.

Processing with Push

In the push approach, templates specify fairly low-level rules and the input XML document gets pushed through the stylesheet to be transformed on the way. Stylesheets that use the push approach tend to have a lot of templates, each containing a snippet of XML with an `<xsl:apply-templates>` instruction that moves the processing down to all an element's children. The final structure of the result is highly determined by the structure of the input.

Listing 3-7 shows a stylesheet, `TVGuide16.xsl`, which demonstrates a push approach. You can see how multiple templates are used to build up the result, but without knowing the structure of the input XML document it's hard to tell exactly what result you'll get (I've highlighted the main changes from `TVGuide15.xsl`, though it was actually quite push-like already).

Listing 3-7. `TVGuide16.xsl`

```
<?xml version="1.0" encoding="ISO-8859-1"?>
<xsl:stylesheet version="2.0"
                xmlns:xsl="http://www.w3.org/1999/XSL/Transform">

<xsl:template match="/">
  <html>
    <head>
      ...
    </head>
    <body>
      <h1>TV Guide</h1>
      <xsl:apply-templates />
    </body>
  </html>
</xsl:template>

<xsl:template match="Channel/Name">
  <h2 class="channel"><xsl:apply-templates /></h2>
</xsl:template>

<xsl:template match="Program">
  <div>
    <p>
      <xsl:apply-templates select="Start" /><br />
      <xsl:apply-templates select="Series" /><br />
      <xsl:apply-templates select="Description" />
      <span onclick="toggle({Series}Cast);">[Cast]</span>
    </p>
    <div id="{Series}Cast" style="display: none;">
      <ul class="castlist">
        <xsl:apply-templates select="CastList" />
      </ul>
    </div>
  </div>
</xsl:template>
```

```
<xsl:template match="Start">
  <span class="date"><xsl:apply-templates /></span>
</xsl:template>

<xsl:template match="Series">
 <span class="title"><xsl:apply-templates /></span>
</xsl:template>

<xsl:template match="CastMember">
  <li><xsl:apply-templates /></li>
</xsl:template>

<xsl:template match="Character">
  <span class="character"><xsl:apply-templates /></span>
</xsl:template>

<xsl:template match="Actor">
  <span class="actor"><xsl:apply-templates /></span>
</xsl:template>

<xsl:template match="Character/Description" />
<xsl:template match="Actor/Description" />

<xsl:template match="Description//Character">
  <span class="character"><xsl:apply-templates /></span>
</xsl:template>

<xsl:template match="Description//Actor">
  <span class="actor"><xsl:apply-templates /></span>
</xsl:template>

<xsl:template match="Description//Link">
  <a href="{@href}"><xsl:apply-templates /></a>
</xsl:template>

<xsl:template match="Description//Program">
  <span class="program"><xsl:apply-templates /></span>
</xsl:template>

<xsl:template match="Description//Series">
  <span class="series"><xsl:apply-templates /></span>
</xsl:template>

<xsl:template match="Description//Channel">
  <span class="channel"><xsl:apply-templates /></span>
</xsl:template>

</xsl:stylesheet>
```

Note In this stylesheet I've used empty templates to do nothing with the <Description> elements within <Character> and <Actor> elements within the cast list. I apply templates to both the <Name> and <Description> children of these elements, but then ignore the <Description> element. This contrasts with a pull approach, which would only apply templates to the <Name> element in the first place.

Processing with Pull

In the pull approach, the stylesheet pulls in information from the input XML document to populate a template structure. Stylesheets that use the pull approach tend to have only a few templates and to use <xsl:for-each> and <xsl:value-of> to generate the result. The final structure of the result is mainly determined by the structure of the stylesheet and how the templates fit together.

Listing 3-8 shows a stylesheet that demonstrates a pull approach (actually, it's TVGuide2.xsl—the first stylesheet we used in this chapter, more or less). As you can see, there's only one template, and its content follows the structure of the result that it generates very closely.

Listing 3-8. TVGuide2.xsl

```
<?xml version="1.0" encoding="ISO-8859-1"?>
<xsl:stylesheet version="2.0"
                xmlns:xsl="http://www.w3.org/1999/XSL/Transform">

<xsl:template match="/">
  <html>
    <head>
      ...
    </head>
    <body>
      <h1>TV Guide</h1>
      <xsl:for-each select="/TVGuide/Channel">
        <h2 class="channel"><xsl:value-of select="Name" /></h2>
        <xsl:for-each select="Program">
          <div>
            <p>
              <span class="date"><xsl:value-of select="Start" /></span>
              <br />
              <span class="title"><xsl:value-of select="Series" /></span>
              <br />
              <xsl:value-of select="Description" />
              <span onclick="toggle({Series}Cast);">[Cast]</span>
            </p>
            <div id="{Series}Cast" style="display: none;">
              <ul class="castlist">
                <xsl:for-each select="CastList/CastMember">
                  <li>
                    <span class="character">
```

```
                <xsl:value-of select="Character/Name" />
              </span>
              <span class="actor">
                <xsl:value-of select="Actor/Name" />
              </span>
            </li>
          </xsl:for-each>
        </ul>
      </div>
    </div>
  </xsl:for-each>
</xsl:for-each>
    </body>
  </html>
</xsl:template>

</xsl:stylesheet>
```

If you look carefully, you'll notice that I haven't even tried to style the content of the <Description> element in this stylesheet—it's very hard to process document-oriented XML with a pull style.

When to Use Push and Pull

Push and pull approaches both have their own advantages and disadvantages, and the best stylesheets use both approaches in tandem to process different parts of a particular XML document. You might use pull for the data-oriented parts of the XML and push for the document-oriented parts, for example. Here are some general guidelines about where to use push and where to use pull:

- Use multiple templates, each matching different types of nodes (a push approach) to process document-oriented XML.
- Select the nodes that you specifically want to process (a pull approach) to change the order in which the input is processed or to only process certain portions of the input. This is very common in data-oriented XML where the order in which information is contained in the input is not the same as the order in which it is required in the result.
- Apply templates to nodes directly (a push approach), rather than getting their value, to allow for extensibility in areas where the structure of the input XML, or the result that you want to generate from it, might change in the future.
- Access the values of nodes directly (a pull approach) when the structure of the input XML is fixed and you know exactly what result you want from it.

Taking these guidelines into account, TVGuide17.xsl gives a stylesheet that balances the push and pull approaches. It mainly uses a push style, but selects nodes directly for processing in certain places, notably to get only the <Name> child of <Character> and <Actor> elements and ignore the <Description>.

■ **Summary** Using templates to match nodes is a push approach, which is good for document-oriented XML and for extensibility. Selecting nodes to process is a pull approach, which is good for changing the structure of a document.

Using Templates with Modes

We've seen how to use separate templates to process different nodes in different ways. However, one thing that we might lose when we use templates like this is the ability to process the *same* node in different ways in different situations. For example, say we want to create a table of contents for the HTML page that we're generating, giving a list of the channels that the TV guide offers, as shown in Figure 3-12.

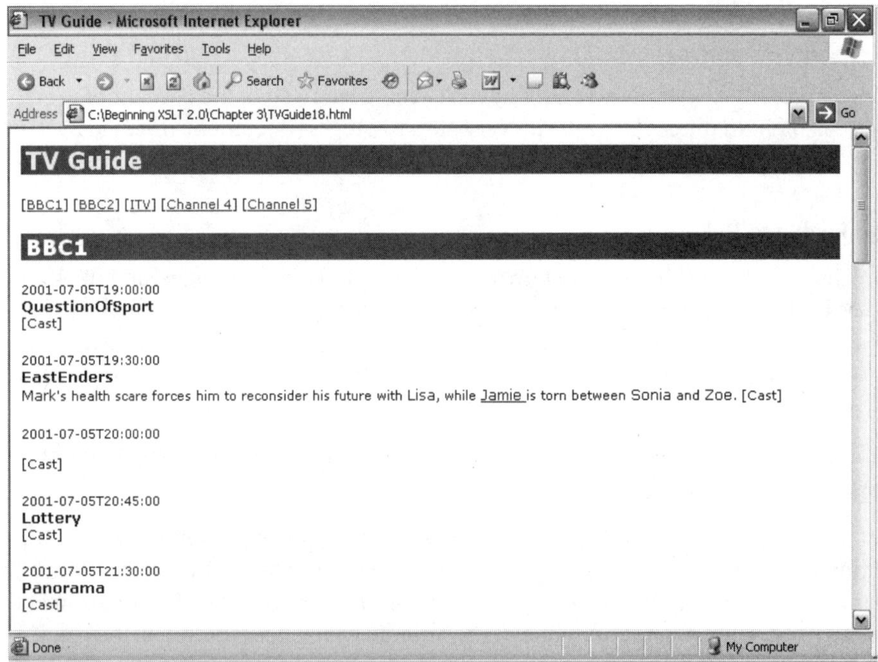

Figure 3-12. *A channel list in the TV guide*

The HTML underlying the preceding page is as follows:

```
...
<h1>TV Guide</h1>
<p>
  [<a href="#BBC1">BBC1</a>]
  [<a href="#BBC2">BBC2</a>]
  [<a href="#ITV">ITV</a>]
  [<a href="#Channel 4">Channel 4</a>]
  [<a href="#Channel 5">Channel 5</a>]
</p>
<h2 class="channel"><a name="BBC1" id="BBC1">BBC1</a></h2>
...
```

We can get this table of contents by processing the `<Channel>` elements, but we're already processing the `<Channel>` elements to get the lists of the programs available on each channel. We want to process the same `<Channel>` elements twice: once for their entry in the channel list and once to get their details.

This is fairly easy with `<xsl:for-each>` because the content of the particular `<xsl:for-each>` determines the result that you get. So we could do the following:

```
<h1>TV Guide</h1>
<p>
  <xsl:for-each select="TVGuide/Channel">
    [<a href="#{Name}"><xsl:value-of select="Name" /></a>]
  </xsl:for-each>
</p>
<xsl:apply-templates />
```

to get the entries in the channel list, and then either use another `<xsl:for-each>` or apply templates (as previously) to the `<Channel>` elements to get their content later on.

However, you can also achieve this by using template **modes**. Modes allow you to process the same node with different templates in different situations. You can define the modes for a template with the `mode` attribute on `<xsl:template>`. The `mode` attribute either holds the special value `#all`, or a whitespace-separated list of modes, which can include the special value `#default`.

You can apply templates in a particular mode using the `mode` attribute on `<xsl:apply-templates>`, which either holds the name of a mode or the special value `#current`, which means that whatever mode was used for this template gets used again. When you apply templates in a particular mode, then the XSLT processor will only look at those templates with that mode or that cover all modes.

■ Note When you use `<xsl:next-match>` within a template that's invoked in a particular mode, you'll pick up the next best template with that mode.

With modes, then, you can apply templates to the same node in different modes to get different results. So in this case, we can use a template in ChannelList mode to generate the result for each channel in the channel list, as follows:

```
<xsl:template match="Channel" mode="ChannelList">
  [<a href="#{Name}"><xsl:value-of select="Name" /></a>]
</xsl:template>
```

This template will only match <Channel> elements if you apply templates in ChannelList mode. So we need to have an <xsl:apply-templates> element in the template for the document node that applies templates in ChannelList mode:

```
<h1>TV Guide</h1>
<p>
  <xsl:apply-templates select="TVGuide/Channel" mode="ChannelList" />
</p>
<xsl:apply-templates />
```

■ **Note** When you apply templates without setting the mode, then the processor uses templates that either don't have a mode attribute or that include the values #default or #all in their mode attribute.

■ **Summary** You can use templates with modes to get different processing for the same node in different situations.

Built-in Templates Revisited

As you'll recall, when an XSLT processor can't find a template that matches a particular node, then it will use a built-in template instead. In fact, the built-in templates get used for all modes and carry through whatever mode is being used when they're invoked. The built-in template for elements simply applies templates to their content in the current mode:

```
<xsl:template match="*" mode="#all">
  <xsl:apply-templates mode="#current" />
</xsl:template>
```

The built-in template that matches text nodes matches in any mode and gives the value of the text node:

```
<xsl:template match="text()" mode="#all">
  <xsl:value-of select="." />
</xsl:template>
```

These built-in templates mean that you can get rid of superfluous templates and apply templates without explicitly specifying the nodes to which you're applying them in exactly the same way as you can with the default mode.

When applying templates in ChannelList mode, then, we don't have to specify the nodes to which we're applying templates and can just use the following:

```
<h1>TV Guide</h1>
<p>
  <xsl:apply-templates mode="ChannelList" />
</p>
<xsl:apply-templates />
```

The current node in the template (which matches the document node) is the document node, so the `<xsl:apply-templates>` in `ChannelList` mode with no `select` attribute will apply templates to the document element—the `<TVGuide>` element—in `ChannelList` mode. There isn't a template for the `<TVGuide>` element in `ChannelList` mode, so the processor will apply the built-in template. This template selects the children of the `<TVGuide>` element, the `<Channel>` elements, and applies templates to them in `ChannelList` mode.

■ **Summary** The built-in templates cover every mode. The built-in template for elements applies templates to the element's children in the same mode as was used to invoke the built-in template.

Creating a Channel List

There are three things that we need to do to `TVGuide17.xsl` to create a linked list of channels in our page:

1. Add anchors to the headings for the channels in the main body of the page.
2. Create a template in `ChannelList` mode to give the link to each channel.
3. Apply templates in ChannelList mode at the point at which the channel list should be given on the page.

We'll make these three changes to create a new version of our stylesheet, `TVGuide18.xsl`.

You can add the anchors to the headings by changing the template for the `<Name>` element child of the `<Channel>` element to include an `<a>` element whose `name` and `id` attributes give the name of the channel:

```
<xsl:template match="Channel/Name">
  <h2 class="channel">
    <a name="{.}" id="{.}"><xsl:value-of select="." /></a>
  </h2>
</xsl:template>
```

■ **Tip** The XHTML Recommendation advises that you use both the `name` and `id` attributes when creating anchors for backward and forward compatibility. We're not yet generating proper XHTML, but it's a good guideline to follow, as that's our final goal.

You can create the template for `<Channel>` elements in `ChannelList` mode to reference these links, as follows:

```
<xsl:template match="Channel" mode="ChannelList">
  [<a href="#{Name}"><xsl:value-of select="Name" /></a>]
</xsl:template>
```

Finally, you can apply templates in ChannelList mode in the template matching the document node to insert the channel list just under the title. The main content of the page comes after this channel list and is generated by applying templates in the default mode:

```
<xsl:template match="/">
  <html>
    <head>
      ...
    </head>
    <body>
      <h1>TV Guide</h1>
      <p>
        <xsl:apply-templates mode="ChannelList" />
      </p>
      <xsl:apply-templates />
    </body>
  </html>
</xsl:template>
```

You could repeat the same list again at the bottom of the page very easily, by repeating the same instruction after the <xsl:apply-templates> that generates the main body of the page:

```
<xsl:template match="/">
  <html>
    <head>
      ...
    </head>
    <body>
      <h1>TV Guide</h1>
      <p>
        <xsl:apply-templates mode="ChannelList" />
      </p>
      <xsl:apply-templates />
      <p>
        <xsl:apply-templates mode="ChannelList" />
      </p>
    </body>
  </html>
</xsl:template>
```

This demonstrates one of the advantages of using templates over using <xsl:for-each>—you can reuse the same code by applying the same template. Transforming TVGuide3.xml with TVGuide18.xsl gives the display that we were aiming for, with a list of channel names at the top and the bottom of the page. Clicking the channel name takes you to the program listing for that channel.

Summary

We've covered a lot of ground in this chapter. We've looked at full stylesheets for the first time—XML documents whose primary markup language is XSLT. You've learned how to convert from the starting point of a simplified stylesheet into a full stylesheet, by adding an `<xsl:stylesheet>` document element and an `<xsl:template>` element to give a template for the document node.

You've seen how an XSLT processor sees an XML document, as a node tree, and learned how to make an XSLT processor give you the output you want by telling it to apply templates to a bunch of nodes and providing the templates that it should use with them. You've discovered how to create templates that match various types of nodes:

- The document node
- Text nodes
- All element nodes
- Element nodes with particular names
- Element nodes with particular parents or ancestors

XSLT processors can only use one template to process a node when you apply templates to it. We've talked about how the processor deals with finding more than one template that matches a node by looking at the templates' priorities, and how it handles not finding one at all by using the built-in templates. You've seen how to get the processor to use the result of using the next-best matching template, and you've also learned how to use modes to get the XSLT processor to use different templates in different situations.

Templates are the main constituent of a stylesheet, and the templates that you produce and the way you fit them together has a big effect on the stylesheet. You've now experienced the two main approaches used in stylesheets—push and pull—and we discussed the advantages and disadvantages of using each of them.

The XSLT that you've learned in this chapter hasn't much changed what you can generate from a stylesheet, just the way in which you get it. In the next chapter, we'll start looking at how to get a stylesheet to do more complicated processing dependent on the values of elements and attributes.

Review Questions

1. Turn the following simplified stylesheet into a full stylesheet:

```
<?xml version="1.0" encoding="ISO-8859-1"?>
<html xmlns:xsl="http://www.w3.org/1999/XSL/Transform"
      xsl:version="2.0">
  <head><title>Films</title></head>
  <body>
    <ul>
      <xsl:for-each select="/Films/Film">
        <li><xsl:value-of select="Name" /></li>
      </xsl:for-each>
```

```
    </ul>
  </body>
</html>
```

2. What is the term for the node at the top of the node tree? What relationship does it have to the document element?

3. Draw a node tree for the following XML document:

```
<?xml version="1.0" encoding="ISO-8859-1"?>
<?xml-stylesheet type="text/xsl" href="Films.xsl"?>
<Films>
  <Film rating="12">
    <Name>Crouching Tiger Hidden Dragon</Name>
    <Notes>
      Directed by <Director>Ang Lee</Director>.
    </Notes>
  </Film>
</Films>
```

4. Which template is the first template to be processed when you use a stylesheet with an entire document?

5. What kind of nodes does the following template process, and what does it do with them?

```
<xsl:template match="Description//Film">
  <a href="http://www.imdb.com/Find?for={.}">
    <xsl:value-of select="." />
  </a>
</xsl:template>
```

6. What will be the result of applying the following stylesheet to a document:

```
<?xml version="1.0" encoding="ISO-8859-1"?>
<xsl:stylesheet version="2.0"
                xmlns:xsl="http://www.w3.org/1999/XSL/Transform">
<xsl:template match="/">
  <xsl:apply-templates />
</xsl:template>
</xsl:stylesheet>
```

7. Which of the following templates will be applied to a `<Film>` element that's a child of a `<Link>` element that's a child of a `<Description>` element:

```
<xsl:template match="Description/Link/Film">...</xsl:template>
<xsl:template match="Film" priority="1">...</xsl:template>
<xsl:template match="Description//Film" priority="-1">...</xsl:template>
<xsl:template match="Description/Link/Film" mode="#all">...</xsl:template>
<xsl:template match="*">...</xsl:template>
<xsl:template match="Film" mode="#default Description">...</xsl:template>
<xsl:template match="*" mode="Description">...</xsl:template>
```

8. If the template from the previous question contains a `<xsl:next-match>` instruction, what will it do?

9. Which of the templates given in Question 7 will be applied to the `<Film>` element if it's selected with this instruction:

```
<xsl:apply-templates mode="Description" />
```

CHAPTER 4

Conditions

The last couple of chapters have given us a good foundation in XSLT. You've learned how to generate elements and attributes, and how to use the values of elements in XML as the values of the new nodes you create. You've learned how to iterate over elements in two ways—using `<xsl:for-each>` and using templates—and you've seen how to use patterns and modes to generate different content in different circumstances.

So far, we've been treating the information that's held in the source XML document as precisely the information we want in the result. In the TV guide example, we've been listing all the programs in all the channels, and if a piece of information is there, then we use it (more or less). Normally processing a document is more complex than that—perhaps you want to filter out some information, or only add something to the result if a particular case is true. For these cases, you need **conditional processing**, so you can choose to do something on the basis of an expression that can return either `true` or `false`.

In this chapter, you'll learn a number of ways of carrying out conditional processing in XSLT. Over the course of the chapter, you'll gain an understanding of

- How to generate content only under certain positive and negative conditions
- How to supply default values when information is missing
- How to test whether an element or attribute is present or not
- How to test whether two nodes are the same
- How to test the values of elements and attributes
- How to filter a set of elements

Conditional Processing

Conditional processing is all about doing different things in different circumstances, such as only showing a cast list if there is a `<CastList>` element that holds information to present, or only adding a flag image to the description of a program if the `<Program>` element has a `flag` attribute.

In fact, we've already seen a certain amount of conditional processing, so before we move on to the new methods that this chapter introduces, we'll remind ourselves of the kinds of conditional processing we can do already. There are three types of conditional processing that we've encountered from previous chapters:

- Creating different results if an element is present or missing
- Creating different results for elements with different ancestry
- Creating different HTML for the same element in different locations in the result

Processing Optional Elements

The first and most obvious type of conditional content is when we only want to generate a piece of HTML in the result when there is an element in the source. Take the example of the cast list. Here's the XML that we use in TVGuide.xml to represent the cast list for a program:

```
<Program>
  ...
  <CastList>
    <CastMember>
      <Character><Name>Zoe Slater</Name>...</Character>
      <Actor><Name>Michelle Ryan</Name>...</Actor>
    </CastMember>
    <CastMember>
      <Character><Name>Jamie Mitchell</Name>...</Character>
      <Actor><Name>Jack Ryder</Name>...</Actor>
    </CastMember>
    <CastMember>
      <Character><Name>Sonia Jackson</Name>...</Character>
      <Actor><Name>Natalie Cassidy</Name>...</Actor>
    </CastMember>
  </CastList>
  ...
</Program>
```

When we generate the HTML for this cast list, we generate one <li> element for each <CastMember> element in the list. If there are only three cast members, we only generate three items. We make sure we don't generate more (or fewer) list items than we need by telling the processor to collect the <CastMember> elements together in a sequence and process them, either by iterating over them with <xsl:for-each> or by applying templates to them with <xsl:apply-templates>.

Some TV programs, such as documentaries, don't have a cast; when we represent the information about these programs in XML, we don't include a <CastList> element in the <Program> element for the program. Take a look at the XSLT that we're currently using to deal with the <CastList> element. In the template for the <Program> element, we apply templates to the <CastList> element:

```
<xsl:template match="Program">
  <div>
    <p>
      <xsl:apply-templates select="Start" /><br />
      <xsl:apply-templates select="Series" /><br />
      <xsl:apply-templates select="Description" />
      <span onclick="toggle({Series}Cast);">[Cast]</span>
```

```
    </p>
    <div id="{Series}Cast" style="display: none;">
      <xsl:apply-templates select="CastList" />
    </div>
  </div>
</xsl:template>
```

and later on we have a template that matches the <CastList> element. This generates the <ul> element that wraps around the list and populates the <ul> element with the result of transforming the <CastMember> elements that the <CastList> element contains:

```
<xsl:template match="CastList">
  <ul class="castlist"><xsl:apply-templates /></ul>
</xsl:template>
```

If the <CastList> element is missing from the XML, the processor won't find a <CastList> element node to which to apply templates. Without finding a node to process, the XSLT processor won't process any template, so you won't get the <ul> element or any <li> elements added to the result.

Summary If you tell an XSLT processor to apply templates to a type of node, but the node doesn't exist in the source, then the processor will not generate any output at that point.

Using the Ancestry of Source XML

We've used context information from the source XML to generate different results when an element occurs with different parents or ancestors in the last chapter. For example, we had a template that matched <Character> elements wherever they appear:

```
<xsl:template match="Character" priority="2">
  <span class="character"><xsl:next-match /></span>
</xsl:template>
```

The <xsl:next-match> instruction then locates the next best template to use. For the <Character> elements occurring as a child of a <CastMember> element, it's this one:

```
<xsl:template match="CastMember/Character">
  <xsl:apply-templates select="Name" />
</xsl:template>
```

whereas the built-in template is used for <Character> elements appearing elsewhere, such as within a <Description> element:

```
<xsl:template match="*">
  <xsl:apply-templates />
</xsl:template>
```

Another example is the template that matches <Name> element children of <Channel> elements. This template isn't used, for example, for <Name> elements that are children of the <Character> or <Actor> elements.

```
<xsl:template match="Channel/Name">
  <h2 class="channel">
    <a name="{.}" id="{.}"><xsl:apply-templates /></a>
  </h2>
</xsl:template>
```

Summary You can create different templates for elements with different ancestry by using different patterns in the templates' `match` attributes.

Using the Location of Result XML

We've also seen how to use modes to generate different HTML based on the location at which the HTML is used in the page. So we have one template for `<Channel>` elements that gives just the name of the channel, for the top of the page:

```
<xsl:template match="Channel" mode="ChannelList">
  [<a href="#{Name}"><xsl:value-of select="Name" /></a>]
</xsl:template>
```

and we use the built-in templates for `<Channel>` elements when we generate the body of the page:

```
<xsl:template match="*">
  <xsl:apply-templates />
</xsl:template>
```

The `<xsl:apply-templates>` instruction tells the processor what mode should be used; the location of the `<xsl:apply-templates>` indicates where on the page it should go. In `TVGuide.xsl`, for example, we have the following:

```
<xsl:template match="/">
  <html>
    <head>
      ...
    </head>
    <body>
      <h1>TV Guide</h1>
      <p>
        <xsl:apply-templates select="Channel" mode="ChannelList" />
      </p>
      <xsl:apply-templates select="Channel" />
      <p>
        <xsl:apply-templates select="Channel" mode="ChannelList" />
      </p>
    </body>
  </html>
</xsl:template>
```

So you get one set of content for the <Channel> elements to create the main listing (when templates are applied without a mode) and a channel list before and after this main listing, generated by applying templates to the same elements, but this time in ChannelList mode.

Summary You can create different output for different locations in the result using moded templates.

Generating Content for an Optional Cast List

We can use the fact that an XSLT processor will not generate a result for elements that don't exist to our advantage. If you take another look at the way we're generating a result for the program in TVGuide.xsl, you'll see that we still get some information that we don't want if the <CastList> element is missing, namely a <div> element around the cast list and a <span> element that acts to show or hide the cast:

```
<xsl:template match="Channel/Program">
  <div>
    <p>
      <xsl:apply-templates select="Series" /><br />
      <xsl:apply-templates select="Description" />
      <span onclick="toggle({Series}Cast);">[Cast]</span>
    </p>
    <div id="{Series}Cast" style="display: none;">
      <xsl:apply-templates select="CastList" />
    </div>
  </div>
</xsl:template>
```

The <div> doesn't matter too much, because it doesn't actually get displayed unless it has some content, but the <span> containing the text [Cast] shows up for programs even when we really don't want it to. Look at the *Question of Sport* and *Lottery* programs in Figure 4-1—they don't have a cast, but still have a [Cast] "button."

Let's try to get rid of that extra <div> and toggling <span> in the next version of our stylesheet, TVGuide2.xsl.

We can make sure that the <div> element isn't generated if the <CastList> element isn't present by moving the <div> element inside the template for the <CastList> element. That way, if there isn't a <CastList> element to have templates applied to, we won't get the <div> in the result. The new template for <CastList> elements looks as follows:

```
<xsl:template match="CastList">
  <div id="{../Series}Cast" style="display: none;">
    <ul class="castlist"><xsl:apply-templates /></ul>
  </div>
</xsl:template>
```

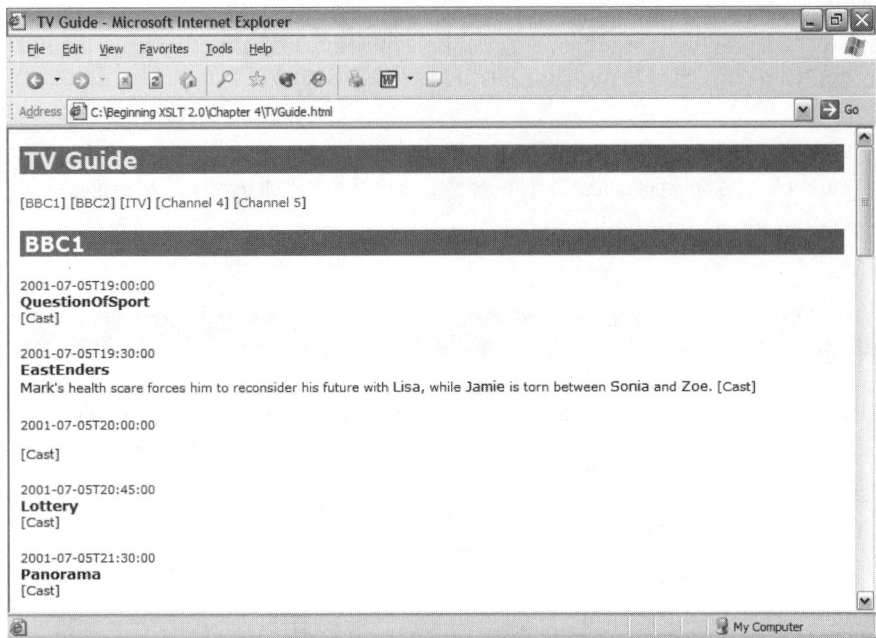

Figure 4-1. *Viewing* `TVGuide.html` *in Internet Explorer*

Note The attribute value template we use in the `id` attribute has to change a little because the current node in this template is the `<CastList>` element, which is a sibling of the `<Series>` element rather than its parent. The new attribute value template uses a path that goes up a level (to the `<Program>` element), before going down again to the `<Series>` element.

The other piece of content that we don't want to generate if there isn't a `<CastList>` element is the `<span>` element that acts as the toggle for displaying or hiding the cast list. We can't move that inside the template for the `<CastList>` element because it needs to be generated inside the paragraph that holds the title and description of the program.

However, we can still use the same principle of trying to apply templates to a node if we use a moded template. As you'll remember from the last chapter, a moded template allows you to generate different content for the same node in different situations. So in this case we can apply templates to the `<CastList>` element in a different mode (`DisplayToggle`, for example) to generate the `<span>` element. The `DisplayToggle` mode template for the `<CastList>` element looks as follows:

```
<xsl:template match="CastList" mode="DisplayToggle">
  <span onclick="toggle({../Series}Cast);">[Cast]</span>
</xsl:template>
```

The template for the `<Program>` element now just needs to apply templates to the `<CastList>` element at the relevant places, first in `DisplayToggle` mode, then in normal mode:

```
<xsl:template match="Program">
  <div>
    <p>
      <xsl:apply-templates select="Start" /><br />
      <xsl:apply-templates select="Series" /><br />
      <xsl:apply-templates select="Description" />
      <xsl:apply-templates select="CastList" mode="DisplayToggle" />
    </p>
    <xsl:apply-templates select="CastList" />
  </div>
</xsl:template>
```

Now transform `TVGuide.xml` using `TVGuide2.xsl`. `TVGuide.xml` includes the following XML for the *Question of Sport* program:

```
<Program>
  <Start>2001-07-05T19:00:00</Start>
  <Duration>PT30M</Duration>
  <Series>QuestionOfSport</Series>
  <Title></Title>
</Program>
```

This `<Program>` element doesn't contain a `<CastList>` element, so it gets transformed to the following HTML:

```
<div>
  <p>
    <span class="date">2001-07-05T19:00:00</span><br>
    <span class="title">QuestionOfSport</span><br>
  </p>
</div>
```

On the other hand, the XML for the *EastEnders* program contains the extra HTML because it does have a `<CastList>` element, so it gets transformed into the following HTML:

```
<div>
  <p>
    <span class="date">2001-07-05T19:30:00</span><br>
    <span class="title">EastEnders</span><br>
     ...
    <span onclick="toggle(EastEndersCast);">[Cast]</span>
  </p>
  <div id="EastEndersCast" style="display: none;">
    <ul class="castlist">
     ...
    </ul>
  </div>
</div>
```

You can also see the effect if you look at the page in a web browser, as in Figure 4-2.

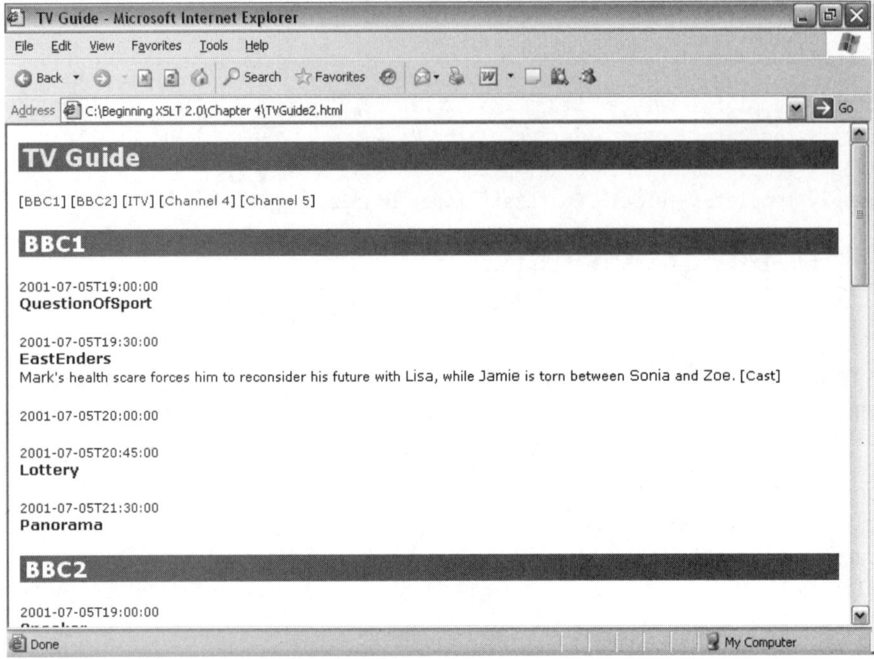

Figure 4-2. *Viewing* `TVGuide2.html` *in Internet Explorer*

The *Question of Sport* program (and many other programs) no longer has a toggle "button" for its cast, since the source XML doesn't contain a `<CastList>` element.

Conditional Elements in XSLT

We've seen three situations where we can use what we know already to generate results conditionally:

- Generate content only when an element is present.
- Generate content only if an element has a particular ancestry.
- Generate content for a particular location in the result.

But these three situations are special cases because they can be handled through template processing as we've seen. We can't use these techniques in all cases—what if we want to generate particular content if an element is absent, has a particular child or attribute, or has a particular value? In these cases we need to use a conditional construct. In XSLT there are two conditional constructs, which we'll be looking at in this section: an `if` statement and a `choose` statement.

`if` Statements

The most basic conditional construct in XSLT is `<xsl:if>`. The `<xsl:if>` element takes a single attribute, `test`, which holds an XPath expression. If the XPath expression evaluates to `true`, then the content of `<xsl:if>` is processed; otherwise nothing happens. The basic form of the `<xsl:if>` element is as follows:

```
<xsl:if test="...">
  ...
</xsl:if>
```

There are all sorts of conditions that you can put in a test attribute, as you'll see in the next section. One of the simplest is testing for the presence of an element or attribute, which you do with a path that points to the element or attribute for which you want to test. If the XSLT processor finds any nodes when it evaluates that path, then the condition evaluates to true, and the XSLT processor processes the content of the <xsl:if> element; if it doesn't find any nodes, the condition evaluates to false, and the content of the <xsl:if> element is ignored. For example, take this if statement:

```
<xsl:if test="Program">
  There are programs showing on this channel.
</xsl:if>
```

The content of the <xsl:if> will be processed (and thus the text "There are programs showing on this channel" added to the result) if the current node (a <Channel> element) has any <Program> element children.

Note Conditions that consist of a path actually work because the sequence of nodes that's returned by the path is implicitly converted to its effective Boolean value because it's in a test attribute. You can also convert a sequence to its effective Boolean value explicitly, with the boolean() function, as you'll see later in this chapter.

Summary The <xsl:if> instruction only generates output if the condition held in its test attribute evaluates as true.

Adding Conditional Content

In the previous section, you saw how to use templates and modes to generate the elements associated with a cast list only in cases where there was a <CastList> element child of the <Program> element that was being processed. Here, we'll look at how to use <xsl:if> to achieve the same effect.

The original template, in TVGuide.xsl, was as follows; the highlighted <span> and <div> elements should only be generated if the <Program> element has a <CastList> element child:

```
<xsl:template match="Program">
  <div>
    <p>
      <xsl:apply-templates select="Start" /><br />
      <xsl:apply-templates select="Series" /><br />
      <xsl:apply-templates select="Description" />
      <span onclick="toggle({Series}Cast);">[Cast]</span>
    </p>
```

```
    <div id="{Series}Cast" style="display: none;">
      <xsl:apply-templates select="CastList" />
    </div>
  </div>
</xsl:template>
```

We can add content under a particular condition using an `<xsl:if>` element. To test whether the current node has a particular element child, we can just use the name of the element in the `test` attribute. So, to test whether the `<Program>` element (which is the current node in a template matching `<Program>` elements) has a `<CastList>` child element, and add something to the result if it does, we can use

```
<xsl:if test="CastList">
  ...
</xsl:if>
```

In this example, we need two `<xsl:if>` elements—one to wrap around the `<span>` element and the other to wrap around the `<div>` element. The amended template for the `<Program>` element, in `TVGuide3.xsl`, is as follows:

```
<xsl:template match="Program">
  <div>
    <p>
      <xsl:apply-templates select="Start" /><br />
      <xsl:apply-templates select="Series" /><br />
      <xsl:apply-templates select="Description" />
      <xsl:if test="CastList">
        <span onclick="toggle({Series}Cast);">[Cast]</span>
      </xsl:if>
    </p>
    <xsl:if test="CastList">
      <div id="{Series}Cast" style="display: none;">
        <xsl:apply-templates select="CastList" />
      </div>
    </xsl:if>
  </div>
</xsl:template>
```

■ **Note** Unlike `<xsl:for-each>`, an `<xsl:if>` does not change the current node—the paths within the `<xsl:if>` are still evaluated relative to the node that the template matches, rather than the node whose presence you are testing for (for example).

If you run `TVGuide3.xsl` with the `TVGuide.xml` document to create `TVGuide3.html`, you'll see that the [Cast] "buttons" do not appear when there's no cast to show, in just the same way as they weren't generated when we used modes in `TVGuide2.xsl`. `TVGuide3.html` is shown in Figure 4-3.

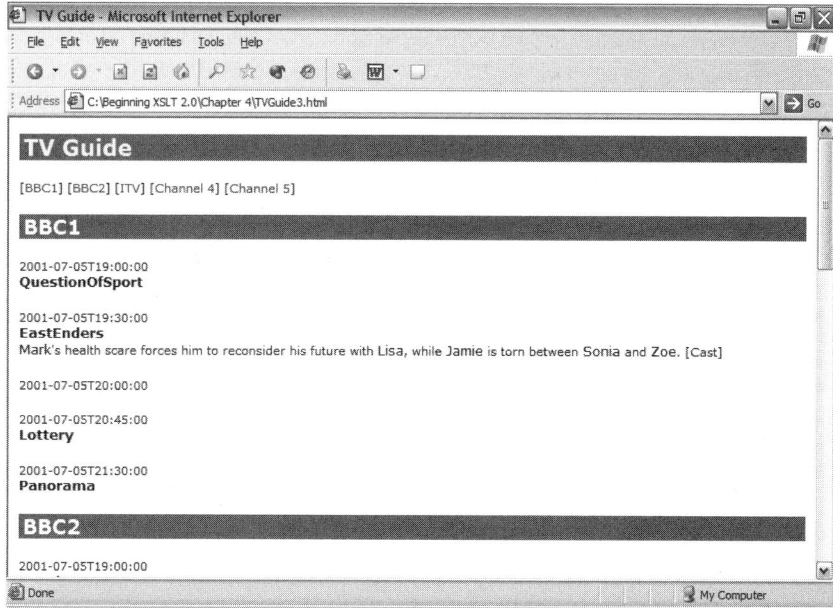

Figure 4-3. *Viewing* `TVGuide3.html` *in Internet Explorer*

---

choose Statements

XSLT doesn't have an `else` statement, but instead uses `<xsl:choose>`. The `<xsl:choose>` element contains a number of `<xsl:when>` elements, which can be followed by an `<xsl:otherwise>` element. Each of the `<xsl:when>` elements tests for a particular condition with a `test` attribute that works in exactly the same way as the `test` attribute on `<xsl:if>`. The basic form of the `<xsl:choose>` element is as follows:

```
<xsl:choose>
  <xsl:when test="...">...</xsl:when>
  <xsl:when test="...">...</xsl:when>
  ...
  <xsl:otherwise>...</xsl:otherwise>
</xsl:choose>
```

The XSLT processor works through the `<xsl:when>` elements one at a time. When it comes across an `<xsl:when>` element whose `test` attribute evaluates to `true`, then it processes the content of that `<xsl:when>` element and ignores the rest of the `<xsl:choose>`. If the XSLT processor doesn't find an `<xsl:when>` whose condition is `true`, then it processes the content of the `<xsl:otherwise>` if there is one and does nothing if there isn't.

Summary The <xsl:choose> instruction gives a choice between different outputs based on different conditions. The content and conditions are defined in separate <xsl:when> elements and their test attribute. If no condition is true, the XSLT processor processes the content of <xsl:otherwise>.

Merging Templates That Share Content

You've already seen how to use the match patterns of templates to generate different results for elements with different ancestors or parents. Here, we'll look at how to use <xsl:choose> to do the same thing.

In TVGuide3.xsl, we currently have two templates to deal with <Character> elements in different contexts:

```
<xsl:template match="Character" priority="2">
  <span class="character"><xsl:next-match /></span>
</xsl:template>

<xsl:template match="CastMember/Character">
  <xsl:apply-templates select="Name" />
</xsl:template>
```

As you can see, wherever the <Character> element appears, we generate a <span> element with a class attribute that's given the value character. To get the content of the <span> element, when the <Character> element appears within a <CastMember> element, we only apply templates to its child <Name> element, whereas when it appears elsewhere, we apply templates to all its children (via the built-in template). Instead of this setup, we could use a single template with an <xsl:choose> within the <span> element to decide whether to give the value of the <Character> element or apply templates to its child <Name> element.

We haven't yet looked at how to select parents or ancestors of an element (we'll come to that in Chapter 7). However, we know that the only <Character> elements that have a <Name> element child are those in the cast list, so instead of testing whether the parent of the <Character> element is a <CastMember> element, we can test whether it has a <Name> element as a child. The template looks like this:

```
<xsl:template match="Character">
  <span class="character">
    <xsl:choose>
      <xsl:when test="Name">
        <xsl:apply-templates select="Name" />
      </xsl:when>
      <xsl:otherwise>
        <xsl:apply-templates />
      </xsl:otherwise>
    </xsl:choose>
  </span>
</xsl:template>
```

This template replaces the two templates in TVGuide3.xsl, and the same kind of thing can be done for the templates that deal with the <Actor> element, to give TVGuide4.xsl. When you transform TVGuide.xml with TVGuide4.xsl, the result (TVGuide4.html) is shown in Figure 4-4.

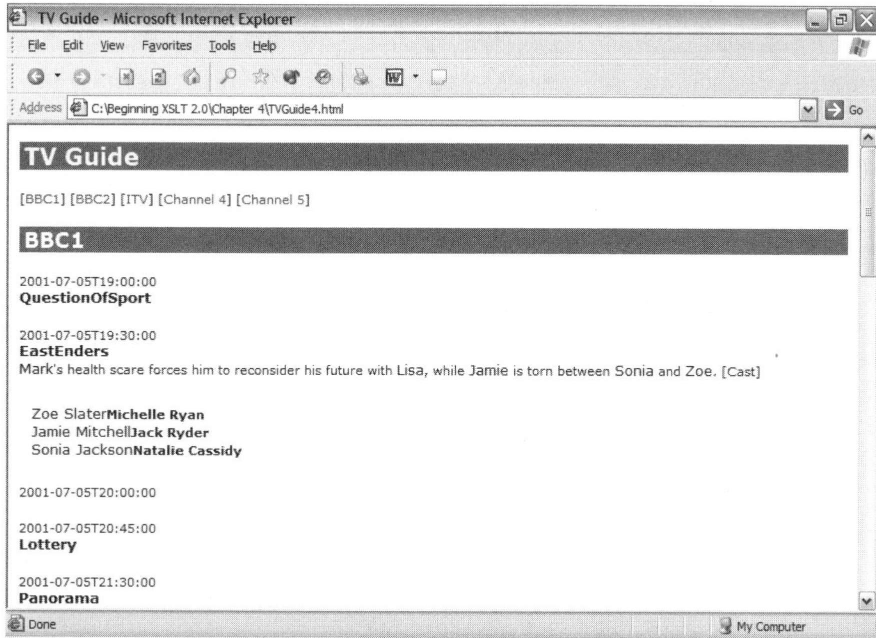

Figure 4-4. *Viewing* `TVGuide4.html` *in Internet Explorer*

As you can see, the descriptions of the characters are not included in the cast list, and character names in the description of the program are highlighted as usual (by being slightly larger).

Conditional Expressions in XPath

The conditional elements in XSLT are essential when the output that you want to generate contains XML structures like elements and attributes. Sometimes, however, you need to use conditions to create different strings or numbers within an XPath. XPath 2.0 provides `if` expressions, which look like the following:

```
if (...) then ... else ...
```

You can string `if` expressions together to test for multiple possibilities:

```
if (...) then ...
else if (...) then ...
else if (...) then ...
else ...
```

The `if` expression is really useful when you're creating an attribute whose content needs to change based on some condition, because you can use it within an attribute value template. It's also useful if you want to select different nodes in different conditions.

Summary The `if` expression provides a short way to give different values based on some condition within an XPath.

Selecting Different Sets of Nodes

In the last example, we looked at how to apply templates to different nodes based on a condition using an <xsl:choose> instruction. In TVGuide4.xsl, the template that matches <Character> elements looks like this:

```
<xsl:template match="Character">
  <span class="character">
    <xsl:choose>
      <xsl:when test="Name">
        <xsl:apply-templates select="Name" />
      </xsl:when>
      <xsl:otherwise>
        <xsl:apply-templates />
      </xsl:otherwise>
    </xsl:choose>
  </span>
</xsl:template>
```

Whether the <Character> element has a <Name> element child or not, we want to apply templates to something: when the <Name> element is present, that's what we want to apply templates to; when it isn't, we want to apply templates to all the children of the <Character> element.

We can therefore restructure this template so that we always apply templates, but select different things to which to apply templates in the two conditions, using an if expression as follows:

```
<xsl:template match="Character">
  <span class="character">
    <xsl:apply-templates select="if (Name) then Name else node()" />
  </span>
</xsl:template>
```

■ **Note** The expression node() selects all the children of the context node—text and elements. We'll see more about this and other node tests in Chapter 7.

If you make this change to this template and a similar change to the template that matches <Actor> elements, as in TVGuide5.xsl, and transform TVGuide.xml, you'll see exactly the same result as in Figure 4-4.

Testing Elements and Attributes

The various conditional constructs we've looked at are only as powerful as the conditions that you test with them. You've seen how to test whether an element has a particular child element by using the name of the child element in the test attribute or in the condition of an if expression. In this section, we'll look at the other kinds of tests that you can use there.

Testing for Attributes

You can test for the presence of an attribute in a very similar way to testing for the presence of an element. You use a location path to select the attribute; if the XSLT processor finds an attribute when it evaluates the path, then the condition is true; otherwise it's false.

You select an attribute on the current element by giving the name of the attribute preceded by an @ sign. For example, if the current node is the <TVGuide> element, you could test whether it has a start attribute with the following <xsl:if> instruction:

```
<xsl:if test="@start">
  ...
</xsl:if>
```

You can select attributes from further down the node tree, on descendant elements of the current node, by stepping down the node tree in exactly the same way as you do when selecting elements, except that once you get to an attribute there's no further to go. The @ sign in front of the name indicates that you want to select an attribute rather than an element. For example, to get the value of the start attribute of the <TVGuide> element from wherever you are within the stylesheet, you could do

```
<xsl:value-of select="/TVGuide/@start" />
```

You can use the attributes you select in just the same way as you can an element—you can get the values of attributes with <xsl:value-of>, iterate over them with <xsl:for-each>, and apply templates to them with <xsl:apply-templates>.

Summary You can select an attribute in a location path by giving an @ sign before its name.

Changing the Result Based on Attribute Presence

Consider the extract from a node tree shown in Figure 4-5.

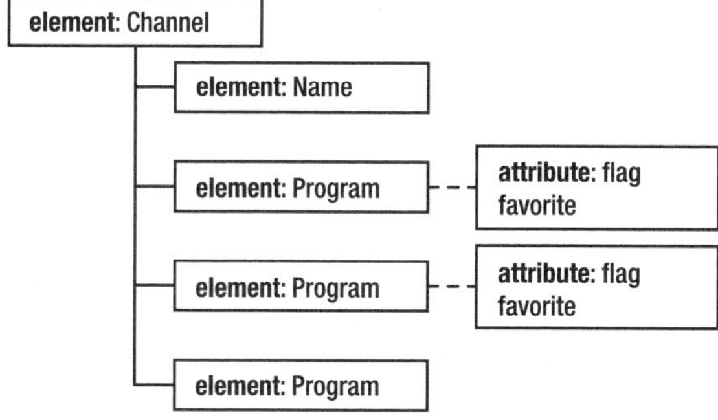

Figure 4-5. <Program> *elements with* flag *attributes*

Two of the `<Program>` elements have `flag` attributes. Say that in the next version of our stylesheet, `TVGuide6.xsl`, we don't want to show a channel if it doesn't have any flagged programs. We don't have a specific template for `<Channel>` elements (in default mode) at the moment—we just use the built-in templates to process each `<Channel>` element and all its content. One method of approaching this problem would be to introduce a template for a `<Channel>` element, in which you test the content of the `<Channel>` element to see whether its content should be processed at all, as follows:

```
<xsl:template match="Channel">
  <xsl:if test="...">
    <xsl:apply-templates />
  </xsl:if>
</xsl:template>
```

In this template for the `<Channel>` element, you could test whether *any* of the `<Program>` elements have `flag` attributes by stepping from the current `<Channel>` element down to the `<Program>` elements, and then across to their `flag` attributes. The location path `Program/@flag` selects the `flag` attributes that are the children of `<Program>` elements that are the children of the current (`<Channel>`) element. As with tests that test for the presence of an element, if the node set contains some `flag` attributes, then the test evaluates as true; if the processor doesn't manage to find any `flag` attributes, then it evaluates as false. The effect is that we only apply templates to the content of the `<Channel>` element if we find any `flag` attributes:

```
<xsl:template match="Channel">
  <xsl:if test="Program/@flag">
    <xsl:apply-templates />
  </xsl:if>
</xsl:template>
```

To prevent frustration, it would probably also be a good idea not to display links in the channel listing at the top and bottom of the page to those channels that are not actually shown within the page. The template for `<Channel>` elements in `ChannelList` mode also needs a similar `<xsl:if>` added, as follows:

```
<xsl:template match="Channel" mode="ChannelList">
  <xsl:if test="Program/@flag">
    [<a href="#{Name}"><xsl:value-of select="Name" /></a>]
  </xsl:if>
</xsl:template>
```

We're still showing all the programs for these channels, but we want the flagged programs to be marked by an image. In the template for the `<Program>` element, we want to add a flag image before the title of the program if the `<Program>` element has a `flag` attribute. Again, we use an `<xsl:if>` instruction to add the conditional content, as follows:

```
<xsl:template match="Channel/Program">
  <div>
    <p>
      <xsl:if test="@flag">
        <img src="flag.gif" alt="[Flagged]" width="20" height="20" />
      </xsl:if>
      <xsl:apply-templates select="Series" /><br />
      <xsl:apply-templates select="Description" />
      <xsl:apply-templates select="CastList" mode="DisplayToggle" />
```

```
    </p>
    <xsl:apply-templates select="CastList" />
  </div>
</xsl:template>
```

Transforming `TVGuide.xml` with `TVGuide6.xsl` to create `TVGuide6.html` only shows the channels that have flagged programs, both in the channel list at the top of the page and in the main content of the page. It also adds an image to those programs that are flagged, such as *EastEnders*, as shown in Figure 4-6.

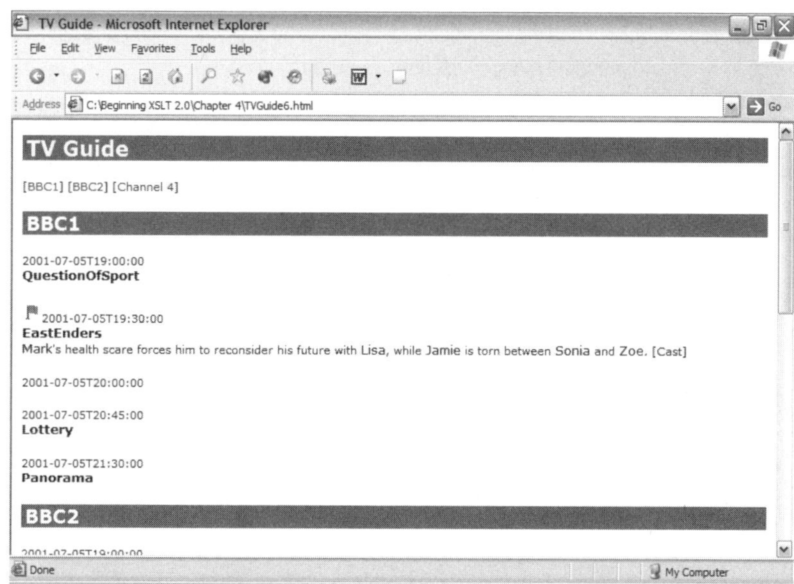

Figure 4-6. *Viewing* `TVGuide6.html` *in Internet Explorer*

So, in `TVGuide6.xsl` we're both omitting content conditionally and adding content conditionally, based on the presence or absence of attributes.

Comparing Values

XPath has a number of **operators** that allow you to compare the value of an element or attribute to a string or a number. Operators are symbols that sit between two expressions and perform some operation on the results of those expressions. For example, you can test whether the `flag` attribute on the current `<Program>` element is equal to the string `'favorite'` with the following expression, which uses an = (equals) operator:

```
@flag = 'favorite'
```

This is the first time that we've seen a literal string being used in an expression. Note the single quotes around the string `'favorite'`. Putting single or double quotes around a string makes the XPath processor recognize it as a string, as opposed to a path. If you missed out the quotes (and it's an easy mistake to make!) and did `@flag = favorite`, then you'd be testing whether the `flag` attribute has the same value as the `<favorite>` child element of the context node, which isn't what you want at all.

■ **Tip** Whether you use single or double quotes is up to you, but XPaths in XSLT are always held within attribute values, so if you use double quotes around an attribute value, and double quotes around a literal string in an XPath, then you have to escape the double quotes in the XPath with `"`. Similarly, if you use single quotes around an attribute value, and single quotes around a literal string in an XPath, then you have to escape the single quotes in the XPath with `'`. I usually use double quotes around attribute values and single quotes around literal strings in XPaths to prevent having to escape too much.

Like most things in XML, comparisons between strings are case-sensitive. The preceding expression will only return `true` if the `flag` attribute has exactly the value `favorite`. The comparison will not return `true` for any of the following `<Program>` elements:

```
<Program flag="interesting">...</Program>
<Program>...</Program>
<Program flag="Favorite">...</Program>
<Program flag="FAVORITE">...</Program>
<Program flag=" favorite ">...</Program>
```

■ **Note** We'll look at how to do case-insensitive comparisons when we look at the `matches()` function later in this chapter.

Comparison Operators

There are two sets of comparison operators in XPath 2.0. One set performs **value comparisons** and the other set performs **general comparisons**.

Value comparisons perform simple comparisons between two values. The values must be of the same type (for example, both strings or both numbers) and untyped nodes (all nodes in Basic processing) are always treated in the same way as strings. The set of value comparison operators are shown in Table 4-1.

Table 4-1. *Value Comparison Operators*

Name	Operator	Example	Explanation
Equals	`eq`	`@flag eq 'favorite'`	Returns true if the value of the `flag` attribute is equal to the string `'favorite'`
Not equals	`ne`	`@flag ne 'favorite'`	Returns true if the value of the `flag` attribute is not equal to the string `'favorite'`
Less than	`lt`	`@flag lt 'favorite'`	Returns true if the value of the `flag` attribute comes before `'favorite'` in alphabetical order

Name	Operator	Example	Explanation
Less than or equal to	`le`	`@flag le 'favorite'`	Returns true if the value of the `flag` attribute is equal to, or comes before `'favorite'` in alphabetical order
Greater than	`gt`	`@flag gt 'favorite'`	Returns true if the value of the `flag` attribute comes after `'favorite'` in alphabetical order
Greater than or equal to	`ge`	`@flag ge 'favorite'`	Returns true if the value of the `flag` attribute is equal to or comes after `'favorite'` in alphabetical order

General comparisons can perform comparisons between sequences of values (rather than just single values) and convert untyped node values to the type of the value that you're testing against. The set of operators for performing general comparisons is shown in Table 4-2.

Table 4-2. *General Comparison Operators*

Name	Operator	Example	Explanation
Equals	`=`	`@flag = 'favorite'`	Returns true if the `flag` attribute is equal to the string `'favorite'`
Not equals	`!=`	`@flag != 'favorite'`	Returns true if the `flag` attribute is not equal to the string `'favorite'`
Less than	`<`	`@rating < 2`	Returns true if the `rating` attribute is less than 2
Less than or equal to	`<=`	`@rating <= 4`	Returns true if the `rating` attribute is less than or equal to 4
Greater than	`>`	`@rating > 8`	Returns true if the `rating` attribute is more than 8
Greater than or equal to	`>=`	`@rating >= 6`	Returns true if the `rating` attribute is more than or equal to 6

■ **Caution** If you compare the values of two nodes, those values will always be compared alphabetically rather than numerically. For example, if you had a `<Program>` element with a `viewerRating` attribute with the value `'8'` and `criticRating` with the value `'10'`, then the comparison `@viewerRating > @criticRating` would be true because `'8'` comes before `'10'` alphabetically. This is a change from the behavior in XPath 1.0.

Value comparisons and general comparisons look as though they do exactly the same thing, but in fact value comparisons are stricter about the types of the arguments. Assuming that you're using a Basic XSLT processor, the test `@rating lt 4` will raise an error because the rating attribute will be treated as a string, and it's an error to use a value comparison to compare a string with a number. On the other hand, the test @rating < 4 will convert the value of the rating attribute to a number automatically before testing.

The other big difference between value comparisons and general comparisons is that general comparisons can be used to compare sequences, whereas value comparisons can only be used to compare single values. We'll see how comparing sequences can be useful in the next section.

Caution If one of the operands to a value comparison is an empty sequence, then it returns an empty sequence, whereas a general comparison will return false. For example, @flag eq 'favorite' returns an empty sequence if there's no flag attribute on the context node, whereas @flag = 'favorite' returns false. When you're using the expression in a test, this won't make any difference, since an empty sequence is treated as false in that case anyway, but if you were simply outputting the result of the test using <xsl:value-of>, you'd get nothing in the result rather than the string 'false'.

Unless you really want the extra strict checking that you get with value comparisons, you'll probably find general comparisons easier to use. On the other hand, using value comparisons might make your stylesheets easier for processors to optimize.

Summary There are six operators for performing comparisons between values: eq, ne, lt, le, gt, and ge. There are also six operators for performing general comparisons: =, !=, <, <=, > and >=.

ESCAPING OPERATORS IN XSLT

You always have to escape the less-than (<) operator as < and the less-than-or-equal-to (<=) operator as <= when you use them in XSLT because XSLT is XML and less-than signs must always be escaped in XML. For example, if you want to do the test @rating < 2 in an XSLT stylesheet, then you actually need to write

```
<xsl:if test="@rating &lt; 2">
  ...
</xsl:if>
```

If you want to, you can escape the greater-than (>) operator as > and the greater-than-or-equal-to (>=) operator as >=. However, people often use the fact that the greater-than sign doesn't have to be escaped to prevent any escaping at all. For example, you can turn around the test @rating < 2 to give 2 > @rating, which you could happily write in XSLT without any escaping as

```
<xsl:if test="2 > @rating">
  ...
</xsl:if>
```

XPath defines these operators and is designed to be used in languages other than XSLT, including text-based languages where you don't need to do this escaping. Fortunately, the less-than and less-than-or-equal-to operators are the only operators that need to be escaped in XSLT.

Comparing Sequences and Values

Comparisons between a sequence (such as the sequence of nodes you select with a path) and values work in a special way when using general comparisons. For example, say that the current node is the <Channel> element and we want to test the flag attributes on its <Program> child elements. Look at the following expression:

```
Program/@flag = 'favorite'
```

The path Program/@flag evaluates to a sequence containing a number of flag attributes, namely all the flag attributes that were found on <Program> element children of the current <Channel> element. When you compare this sequence to the string 'favorite', the XSLT processor goes through each of the flag attributes in turn. If it finds *any* flag attribute that has the value favorite, then the comparison returns true. So the preceding condition is true if *any* programs have been flagged as favorite programs.

Now consider the following condition:

```
Program/@flag != 'favorite'
```

As previously, the Program/@flag path gives a sequence of flag attributes. The XSLT processor goes through each of the flag attributes in turn, this time checking whether they are *not* equal to the string 'favorite'. If it finds *any* flag attribute that does not have the value favorite, then the comparison returns true. So the preceding condition is true if *any* programs have not been flagged as favorite programs.

This is different from testing whether there are *no* programs that have been flagged as favorite programs. Testing whether there are no flag attributes that have the value favorite is the opposite of testing whether there are *any* flag attributes that have the value favorite. You can reverse a condition with the not() function, as follows:

```
not(Program/@flag = 'favorite')
```

Note The not() function takes a single argument, which is interpreted as a Boolean value. Note that all function names in XPath are case-sensitive—in fact they are usually lowercase, with hyphens separating words where necessary.

The same technicality applies to the other general comparisons. If you compare a sequence to a value, then the comparison returns true if there are any items in the sequence for which the comparison is true. This distinction doesn't matter if you're only picking a single node, but it does if you're selecting more than one. This can be confusing, because it looks like the test works differently in different circumstances. For example, if you have the following test:

```
Series != 'EastEnders'
```

then the test returns true if the <Series> element child of the current <Program> element is not equal to the value 'EastEnders' (if the current program isn't an *EastEnders* episode). There can only be one <Series> element child of the <Program> element, so it's a one-to-one comparison, and it works as you expect. On the other hand, with this test:

```
Program/Series != 'EastEnders'
```

you get a `true` result if *any* of the `<Series>` element children of the `<Program>` element children of the current `<Channel>` element are *not* equal to the value `'EastEnders'` (in other words, if any of the programs showing on the channel are not *EastEnders* episodes). Unless a channel shows *EastEnders* episodes exclusively, round the clock, the test will return `false`. More than likely, what you're after is actually this:

```
not(Program/Series = 'EastEnders')
```

which returns `true` if *none* of the programs showing on the channel are *EastEnders* episodes.

Note We'll look in more detail at using general comparisons with sequences in Chapter 7. In that chapter, you'll also see how to use the `some` and `every` expressions, which you can use to perform more complex versions of the kinds of tests between sequences and values described previously.

Summary A general comparison between a sequence and a value is true if the comparison is true for any item in the sequence.

Generating Different Results for Different Attribute Values

In `TVGuide6.xsl`, we use the same kind of flag no matter what the value of the `flag` attribute. But say we have different kinds of flags for favorite programs and interesting programs, and we want those flags to be indicated with different images (`favorite.gif` and `interest.gif`).

Rather than using an `<xsl:if>` as we do in `TVGuide6.xsl`, in `TVGuide7.xsl`, the template for the `<Program>` element can use an `<xsl:choose>` that tests whether the `flag` attribute is equal to the string `'favorite'` or `'interesting'` and gives an appropriate image, as follows:

```
<xsl:template match="Program">
  <div>
    <p>
      <xsl:apply-templates select="Start" /><br />
      <xsl:choose>
        <xsl:when test="@flag = 'favorite'">
          <img src="favorite.gif" alt="[Favorite]" width="20" height="20" />
        </xsl:when>
        <xsl:when test="@flag = 'interesting'">
          <img src="interest.gif" alt="[Interest]" width="20" height="20" />
        </xsl:when>
      </xsl:choose>
      <xsl:apply-templates select="Series" /><br />
      <xsl:apply-templates select="Description" />
      <xsl:if test="CastList">
        <span onclick="toggle({Series}Cast);">[Cast]</span>
      </xsl:if>
```

```
    </p>
    <xsl:if test="CastList">
      <div id="{Series}Cast" style="display: none;">
        <xsl:apply-templates select="CastList" />
      </div>
    </xsl:if>
  </div>
</xsl:template>
```

The condition `@flag = 'favorite'` will only be `true` if there is a `flag` attribute with the value `favorite`. We use another `<xsl:when>`, rather than an `<xsl:otherwise>`, to make sure we only add an image under those conditions, not if the `flag` attribute is missing. The result of transforming `TVGuide.xml` with `TVGuide7.xsl` is `TVGuide7.html`, which is shown in Figure 4-7.

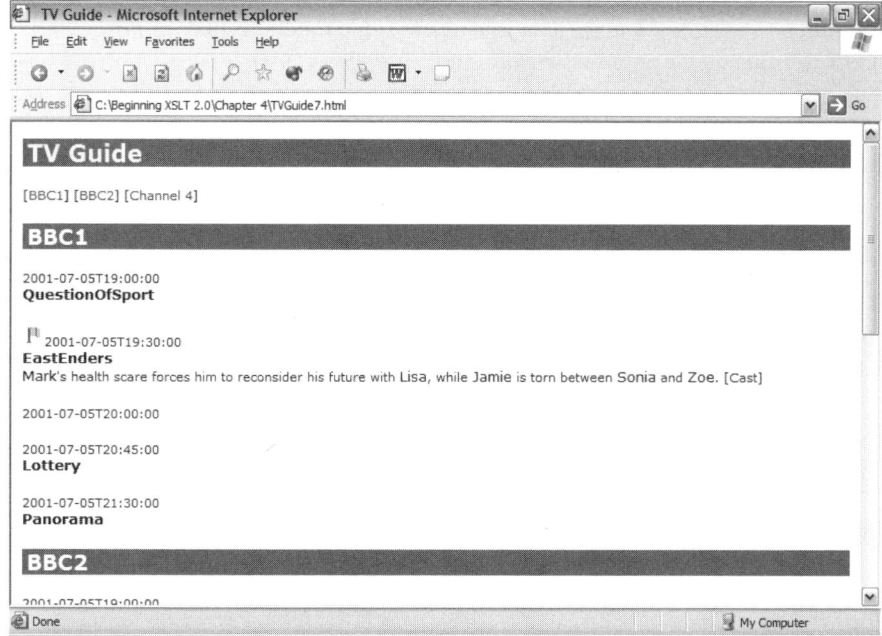

Figure 4-7. *Viewing* `TVGuide7.html` *in Internet Explorer*

As you can see, *EastEnders* is flagged with a green flag now, indicating that it's a favorite program (rather than a particularly interesting one). If you scroll down, you'll see blue flags next to some of the other programs, those that have a `flag` attribute with a value of `'interesting'`.

Assuming that `'favorite'` and `'interesting'` are the only legal values for the `flag` attribute, another way to approach this problem would be to test whether the `flag` attribute exists, and if it does, create the `<img>` element, and use `if` expressions within attribute value templates to determine the values of the `src` and `alt` attributes. If the `flag` attribute is `'favorite'`, the `src` attribute needs to contain `'favorite.gif'`, otherwise it needs to contain `'interest.gif'`; the `alt` attribute needs to contain `'[Favorite]'` if the `flag` attribute is `'favorite'` and `'[Interest]'` otherwise:

```
<xsl:if test="@flag">
  <img src="{if (@flag = 'favorite') then 'favorite' else 'interest'}.gif"
       alt="[{if (@flag = 'favorite') then 'Favorite' else 'Interest'}]"
       width="20" height="20" />
</xsl:if>
```

Make this change to `TVGuide7.xsl` in order to create `TVGuide8.xsl` and transform `TVGuide.xml` with `TVGuide8.xsl` to get `TVGuide8.html`. `TVGuide8.html` should look exactly the same as `TVGuide7.html`, as shown in Figure 4-7.

Testing with Functions

As well as operators, XPath defines a number of **functions** that are particularly useful in tests. Functions are often passed **arguments**, which are listed in brackets after the function name, separated by commas. In this section, we'll have a look at some functions that are particularly useful when testing values; we'll come across a lot more functions as we progress with the rest of the book.

Effective Boolean Values

When we first started looking at conditions, we saw how if you use a path in a `test` attribute, it evaluates to `true` if the path manages to select any nodes. In more technical terms, the path evaluates to a **sequence** and this sequence is converted to its **effective Boolean value**—`true` if the sequence contains items and `false` if it doesn't.

In XPath 2.0, sequences can contain any number of items, which are of two kinds: nodes or **atomic values**. Atomic values are things like

- Booleans
- Numbers
- Strings
- Dates or times
- Durations

Note We'll be looking in detail at the different kinds of atomic values in the next chapter.

Every expression evaluates to a sequence; for example, a path evaluates to a sequence of nodes. Some expressions evaluate to a sequence that contains only a single value, which is treated in exactly the same way as the single value on its own; for example, a comparison (with one of the operators that we saw earlier) evaluates to a Boolean value.

When you test a sequence or a value in a `test` attribute or in the condition of an `if` expression, an XSLT processor looks at its **effective Boolean value**. The effective Boolean value of a value (i.e., a sequence that contains a single value) is calculated as described in Table 4-3.

Table 4-3. *Effective Boolean Values*

Value	Effective Boolean Value
Node	`true`
String	`true` if the string contains any characters, `false` otherwise
Number	`false` if number is `0` or `NaN`, `true` otherwise
Boolean	`true` if `true`, `false` if `false`
Other value	Raises an error

The effective Boolean value of a sequence is `false` if the sequence is empty. If the sequence contains more than one item, then its effective Boolean value is `true` if the first item is a node. Trying to get the effective Boolean value of a sequence whose first item is of another type raises an error.

You can get the effective Boolean value of a value explicitly using the `boolean()` function, but it's very rare that you'll need to do so. For example, doing this:

```
<xsl:if test="boolean(Name)">...</xsl:if>
```

is exactly the same as doing this:

```
<xsl:if test="Name">...</xsl:if>
```

Caution The `boolean()` function behaves very differently from the `xs:boolean()` function. The former gives you the effective Boolean value of its argument, whereas the latter converts its argument to a Boolean value using the normal casting rules. For example, `boolean('false')` evaluates to `true` (because the string argument contains characters), whereas `xs:boolean('false')` evaluates to `false` (because the string argument is a valid lexical representation of the `xs:boolean` value `false`).

Summary When you use an expression in a `test` attribute or the condition of an `if` expression, the effective Boolean value of the result of evaluating the expression is used to determine whether the test succeeds or fails.

Converting Values

As we've seen, the `boolean()` function converts its argument to a Boolean value, by getting the effective Boolean value of the argument. There are a whole set of functions that convert their argument to a particular atomic type, which we'll look at in detail in the next chapter, but two are especially useful:

- `number()`—Converts to a number
- `string()`—Converts to a string

The `number()` function converts its argument to a number as described in Table 4-4.

Table 4-4. *Result of* `number()` *Function*

Value	Result of `number()` Function
Sequence	`NaN` if the sequence is empty; raises an error if it contains more than one item.
Node	The number if the node can be converted to a number, `NaN` otherwise; `'INF'` and `'-INF'` are recognized.
String	The number if the string can be converted to a number, `NaN` otherwise; `'INF'` and `'-INF'` are recognized.
Number	The number itself.
Boolean	`1` if `true`, `0` if `false`.
Other atomic value	`NaN`.

■ **Caution** There are some changes here from the behavior of the `number()` function in XPath 1.0. You now get an error if you attempt to convert a sequence that contains more than one node, and the function recognizes the special values `'INF'` and `'-INF'`.

The `string()` function converts its argument to a string as described in Table 4-5.

Table 4-5. *Result of* `string()` *Function*

Value	Result of `string()` Function
Sequence	An empty string if the sequence is empty; raises an error if it contains more than one item
Node	The string value of the node
String	The string itself
Number	The lexical representation of the number
Boolean	`'true'` if `true`, `'false'` if `false`
Other atomic value	The lexical representation of the atomic value

■ **Caution** There are some changes here from the behavior of the `string()` function in XPath 1.0. You now get an error if you attempt to convert a sequence that contains more than one node, and when converting a number to a string you get `'INF'` rather than `'Infinity'` and `'-INF'` rather than `'-Infinity'`, and the string representation of the number might include an exponent. The `string()` function also behaves subtly differently from the `xs:string()` function; in particular, it gives you the string value of a node rather than the string value of the typed value of the node (the distinction is only important if you're using Schema-Aware processing) and returns an empty string from an empty sequence (whereas `xs:string()` will return an empty sequence).

■ **Summary** The `number()` function converts a value to a number, and the `string()` function converts a value to a string.

Testing If an Element Has a Value

We've seen how to test if an element is present, but what if the element is present but doesn't have a value? For example, the *EastEnders* program is represented by the following XML in TVGuide.xml:

```
<Program>
  <Start>2001-07-05T19:30:00</Start>
  <Duration>PT30M</Duration>
  <Series>EastEnders</Series>
  <Title></Title>
  <Description>
    ...
  </Description>
  ...
</Program>
```

The <Title> element is empty because *EastEnders* episodes don't have individual titles. Other programs have individual titles for episodes in a series, and still others aren't part of a series. We've chosen to represent this in our XML by always having a <Series> element and a <Title> element. If the program isn't part of a series, then the <Series> element is empty; if the program hasn't got an individual title, then the <Title> element is empty.

When it comes to the HTML, we have the following possibilities:

```
<span class="title">Series</span>
<span class="title">Series - <span class="subtitle">Title</span></span>
<span class="title">Title</span>
```

■ **Note** We're currently only recognizing the first possibility, which is why several of the programs in the program listing haven't got titles at the moment.

Which of these possibilities we use depends on the string values of the <Series> and <Title> elements. If they don't have a string value, then they are empty. You can get the string value of an element using the string() function. If the resulting string has any characters in it, then it will evaluate as true in a test attribute; if the element is empty, the string is empty, and the condition will evaluate to false. Therefore we can use the following XSLT in the template for the <Program> element to insert the correct XML:

```
<xsl:template match="Program">
  ...
  <xsl:apply-templates select="Start" /><br />
  <span class="title">
    <xsl:choose>
      <xsl:when test="string(Series)">
        <xsl:value-of select="Series" />
        <xsl:if test="string(Title)">
          - <span class="subtitle"><xsl:value-of select="Title" /></span>
        </xsl:if>
      </xsl:when>
```

```
      <xsl:otherwise>
        <xsl:value-of select="Title" />
      </xsl:otherwise>
    </xsl:choose>
  </span>
  <br />
  ...
</xsl:template>
```

This version is used in TVGuide9.xsl. When you transform TVGuide.xml with TVGuide9.xsl and look at the result (TVGuide9.html) you should see that every program has a title, and that some of them have subtitles as well. For example, BBC2 is showing four programs, the last of which has a pretty racy subtitle (which may contribute to the fact that it's flagged as interesting!), as shown in Figure 4-8.

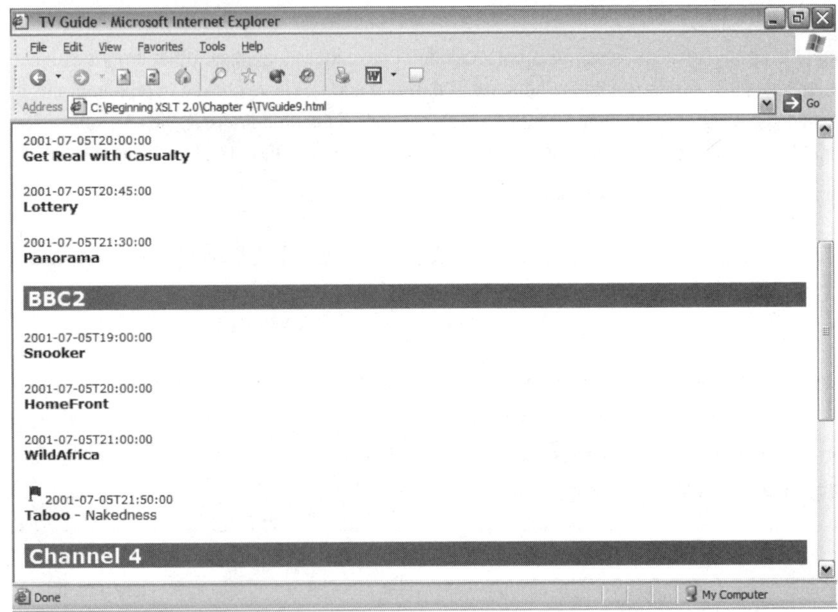

Figure 4-8. *Viewing* TVGuide9.html *in Internet Explorer*

Alternatively, you could use similar conditions within the templates for the <Series> and <Title> elements. See if you can achieve the same output as shown previously using separate templates for <Series> and <Title> elements instead.

Testing the Contents of Strings

There are several functions that come in handy when testing the content of element and attribute values:

- `compare()`
- `starts-with()`
- `ends-with()`
- `contains()`
- `matches()`

COLLATIONS

Strings are usually compared, in XSLT 2.0, by comparing the Unicode codepoints of the characters that they contain. For example, `'a'` comes before `'b'` because the Unicode codepoint for `'a'` (`#x61`) is less than the Unicode codepoint for `'b'` (`#x62`), and `'C'` comes before `'c'` because the Unicode codepoint for `'C'` (`#x43`) is less than the Unicode codepoint for `'c'` (`#x63`).

However, there are other ways to compare strings. For example, you might want to compare strings such that capital letters are sorted after their lowercase equivalents. Or you might want to do a case-insensitive comparison, such that `'C'` and `'c'` are treated as the same character. For some languages, you might even want to have particular combinations of characters be treated specially; the XPath 2.0 Functions and Operators spec uses the example of `'uve'` and `'uwe'` being the same in some European languages.

To carry out string comparisons and sorting based on something other than Unicode codepoints, you need to use **collations**. Collations are definitions of how strings should be compared, and are identified via a URI. For example, the URI for the collation based on Unicode codepoints is

```
http://www.w3.org/2005/04/xpath-functions/collation/codepoint
```

■ **Caution** This URI is the one used in the latest version of the Functions and Operators document as I write this. Check the latest version of the Functions and Operators document at `http://www.w3.org/TR/xpath-functions/#collations` to get the correct URI when you're reading this.

Whenever you use a function that needs to compare strings, such as the `compare()` function or the `contains()` function, you can specify a collation to use for the comparison as the last argument. For example, to see whether the string value of the `<Description>` element contains the string `'sport'`, based on the Unicode codepoint collation, you can use

```
contains(Description, 'sport',
         'http://www.w3.org/2005/04/xpath-functions/collation/codepoint')
```

If you don't specify a collation explicitly, then the XSLT processor will use a default collation. Different processors support different sets of collations, and may have different default collations (though it's likely that most will use the Unicode codepoint collation as their default), so you should look at the documentation of the processor that you're using to determine which collations are available and which will be used as the default. It's likely that in the future, IANA will provide a registry for collations, and that XSLT processors will pick the collations that they support from that register.

As we'll see in Chapter 9, you can also use collations when sorting or grouping items based on a string value. It's also worth noting that whenever you compare strings using the value or general comparison operators, they are compared using the default collation.

The `compare()` function takes two or three strings as arguments and compares the first string with the second string based on the **collation** specified by the third string. See the "Collations" sidebar for information about what collations are and how they work. If the first string is less than the second string (according to the collation), the `compare()` function returns `-1`; if the first string is more than the second string, the `compare()` function returns `1`; and if the two strings are equal, it returns `0`. For example, to see, on a `<CastMember>` element, whether the character's first name comes in the first half of the alphabet, you can use this test:

```
compare(Character/Name, 'N') = -1
```

■ **Tip** The `compare()` function is only really useful if you want to compare strings using a collation other than the default one. Otherwise, you may as well just use a comparison operator. For example, rather than the above expression you could just use: `Character/Name lt 'N'`.

The `starts-with()` and `ends-with()` functions take two or three strings as arguments. The first string is the string to test—usually the value of an attribute or element—and the second string gives the starting or ending string for which you want to test. The third argument is a collation. The function returns `true` if the first string starts with (or ends with) the second string according to the collation. For example, with the current node being a `<CastMember>` element, the following tests whether the character's first name is Mark:

```
starts-with(Character/Name, 'Mark ')
```

■ **Note** The space at the end of the string `'Mark '` ensures that we don't select people whose first name is `'Marko'` or `'Markie'` for example.

Similarly, with the current node being a `<CastMember>` element, the following tests whether the character's last name is Slater:

```
ends-with(Character/Name, ' Slater')
```

The `contains()` function also takes two or three strings as arguments, but this time returns `true` if the first string contains the second string at any point (based on the collation supplied by the third string). For example, with the current node being a `<Program>` element, the following tests whether the description of the program contains the string `'sport'`:

```
contains(Description, 'sport')
```

The `matches()` function is one of a set of functions in XPath 2.0 that support **regular expressions**. It takes two or three arguments, which are all strings, and returns `true` if the first string matches the regular expression held in the second string. The third argument is a list of flags that change details about how the match works. For example, if the current node is a `<Program>` element, you can test whether the description of the program contains the *word* "sport", possibly starting with a capital S using

```
matches(Description, '(^|\W)[Ss]port(\W|$)')
```

■ **Note** We'll be looking in detail at regular-expression processing in XSLT 2.0 in the next chapter.

The `matches()` function is the easiest way to do case-insensitive comparisons. If you specify the character `i` in the third argument, then the comparison will be case-insensitive. So the case-insensitive version of the preceding `contains()` example is simply

```
matches(Description, 'sport', 'i')
```

You can use ^ at the start of the regular expression to test whether the string starts with another string. For example, to see whether the character's first name is Mark in any case combination, you can use

```
matches(Character/Name, '^mark', 'i')
```

Similarly, you can use $ at the end of the regular expression to test whether the string ends with another string. For example, to see whether the character's last name is Slater in any case combination, you can use

```
matches(Character/Name, 'slater$', 'i')
```

■ **Note** There are two other ways to do case-insensitive comparisons. First, you can specify a case-insensitive collation as the last argument in the function call. Second, you can convert both the strings to upper- or lowercase using the `upper-case()` or `lower-case()` functions, which we'll meet in the next chapter, and then compare them.

These functions don't work in the same way as the comparison operators. If you use a path to give the first argument, then the sequence that it returns must either be empty or contain a single item; otherwise you'll get an error.

■ **Caution** This is a change from XPath 1.0, in which the first node from the node-set would have been used.

■ **Note** We'll see how to get around this limitation a little later on in this chapter, by using predicates.

Summary The `compare()` function tests whether one string comes before another alphabetically. The `starts-with()` and `ends-with()` functions test whether a string starts with or ends with another string. The `contains()` function tests whether a string contains another string, and the `matches()` function tests whether a string matches a regular expression.

Identifying Elements That Start with a String

A new feature that we'll introduce to our TV guide in `TVGuide10.xsl` is that we use a special icon alongside every *Star Trek* episode of whichever series (*Star Trek*, *Star Trek: The Next Generation*, *Star Trek: Deep Space Nine*, *Star Trek: Voyager*, and *Star Trek: Enterprise*). To identify these programs, we can test whether the series starts with the string `'StarTrek'`; if it does, we add the relevant image after the image added if the program is flagged:

```
<xsl:template match="Program">
  ...
  <xsl:if test="starts-with(Series, 'StarTrek')">
    <img src="StarTrek.gif" alt="[Star Trek]" width="20" height="20" />
  </xsl:if>
  ...
</xsl:template>
```

Add this instruction to the template for the `<Program>` element so that it shows a logo prior to the title for all the *Star Trek* programs. Actually, `TVGuide.xml` doesn't contain any *Star Trek* programs, so we'll add a new channel (Sky One) that includes some to create `TVGuide2.xml`, which lets us test out the logo. The new channel includes the following XML:

```
<Channel>
  <Name>Sky One</Name>
  ...
  <Program rating="8">
    <Start>2001-07-05T20:00:00</Start>
    <Duration>PT1H</Duration>
    <Series>StarTrekVoyager</Series>
    <Title>Renaissance Man</Title>
  </Program>
  ...
  <Program flag="favorite">
    <Start>2001-07-05T22:00:00</Start>
    <Duration>PT1H</Duration>
    <Series>StarTrekNextGeneration</Series>
    <Title>The Inner Light</Title>
  </Program>
</Channel>
```

When you transform `TVGuide2.xml`, which includes *Star Trek* programs, with `TVGuide10.xsl`, which highlights *Star Trek* programs, to get `TVGuide10.html`, you get logos next to the two *Star Trek* episodes, as shown in Figure 4-9.

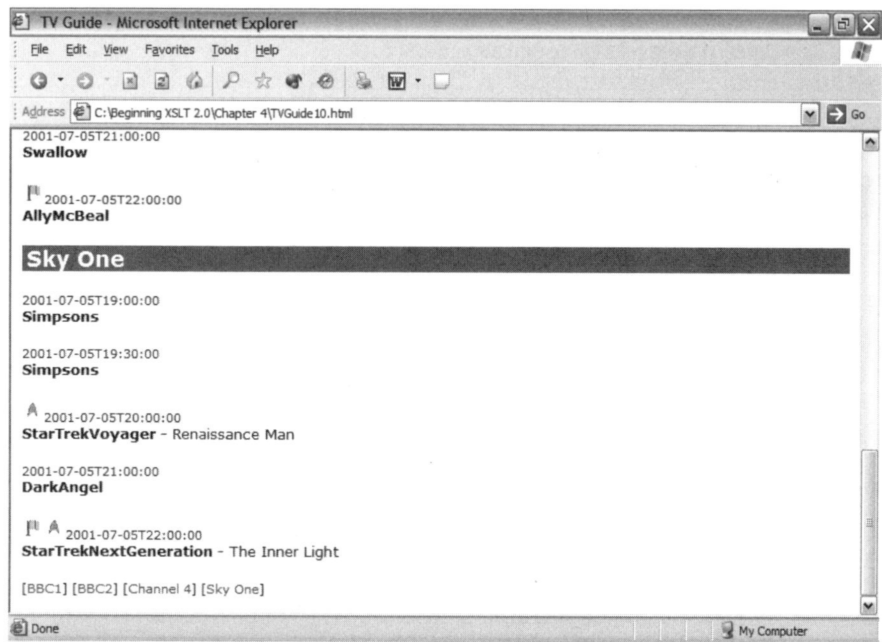

Figure 4-9. *Viewing* `TVGuide10.html` *in Internet Explorer*

The *Star Trek* logo only appears when the `<Series>` element starts with the string `'StarTrek'`.

Combining Tests

Often constructing the tests that you want requires you to combine tests together. You can combine tests with the operators `and` and `or` in XPath, and use brackets (`()`) to collect multiple tests together.

> **Note** The main reason that XPath uses `and` and `or` rather than `&&` and `||` (which are commonly used in other programming languages) is that if it used `&&`, then the ampersands would have to be escaped when XPath was used with XSLT, so you'd end up with `&&` all over the place, which is pretty ugly! Like the rest of XPath, `and` and `or` are case-sensitive, so `AND` won't work, for example.

For example, you could test whether a program both belongs to a series (a nonempty `<Series>` element) and has a title (a nonempty `<Title>` element) with this condition:

```
string(Series) and string(Title)
```

You can test whether a program either is flagged as a favorite (has a `flag` attribute with the value `favorite`) or has a high rating (has a `rating` attribute with a value greater than `6`) with this condition:

```
@flag = 'favorite' or @rating > 6
```

Summary You can combine tests with the operators and and or.

Using Logical Operators to Highlight Interesting Programs

There are lots of factors that might make a program interesting to a user of the TV guide:

- Being flagged as interesting or a favorite
- Having a high rating
- Containing one of several keywords in its title or description

We can create a new version of the stylesheet, TVGuide11.xsl, which shows all the programs and highlights those interesting programs. If a program isn't interesting, then it is contained in an attribute-less <div> element, as in

```
<div>
  <p>
    <span class="date">2001-07-05T21:30:00</span><br>
    <span class="title">Panorama</span><br>
  </p>
</div>
```

However, if it is interesting, then the <div> element should take a class attribute with the value interesting, as well as have any other icons attached to it as desired. For example, if "News" is a keyword, then the *Channel 4 News* should be highlighted with

```
<div class="interesting">
  <p>
    <span class="date">2001-07-05T19:00:00</span><br>
    <span class="title">Channel4News</span><br>
  </p>
</div>
```

The TVGuide.css CSS stylesheet needs to be updated to pick up on these interesting programs. We'll create a new version, TVGuide2.css, which highlights them by giving them a yellow background, with the following rule:

```
div.interesting {
     background: yellow;
}
```

and remember to change the <link> element generated by TVGuide11.xsl so that it points to TVGuide2.css.

The template for the <Program> element in TVGuide11.xsl needs to test for the various conditions that make a program interesting, and use the relevant <div> element around the HTML for the program:

```
<xsl:template match="Program">
  <xsl:choose>
    <xsl:when test="@flag = 'favorite' or @flag = 'interesting' or
                    @rating > 6 or contains(Series, 'News') or
                    contains(Title, 'News') or
                    contains(Description, 'news')">
      <div class="interesting">...</div>
    </xsl:when>
    <xsl:otherwise>
      <div>...</div>
    </xsl:otherwise>
  </xsl:choose>
</xsl:template>
```

Adding conditional parent elements is difficult because it requires you to repeat the same content within the XSLT. In the preceding example, the content of both <div> elements is the same. For now, we can get around this problem by using a template in Details mode that matches all <Program> elements and generates the content for them:

```
<xsl:template match="Program" mode="Details">
  <p>
    ...
  </p>
  <xsl:if test="CastList">
    ...
  </xsl:if>
</xsl:template>
```

In the main template for the <Program> elements, we can apply templates to the current node (the <Program> element) in Details mode to get the content of the two <div> elements.

```
<xsl:template match="Program">
  <xsl:choose>
    <xsl:when test="@flag = 'favorite' or @flag = 'interesting' or
                    @rating > 6 or contains(Series, 'News') or
                    contains(Title, 'News') or
                    contains(Description, 'news')">
      <div class="interesting">
        <xsl:apply-templates select="." mode="Details" />
      </div>
    </xsl:when>
    <xsl:otherwise>
      <div>
        <xsl:apply-templates select="." mode="Details" />
      </div>
    </xsl:otherwise>
  </xsl:choose>
</xsl:template>
```

■ Note We'll see a couple of other ways of handling the same problem in the next few chapters—with variables in Chapter 6 and using instructions that generate attributes independently of elements in Chapter 8. In Chapter 12 and later in Chapter 15, you'll also see how to enable a user to customize these kinds of queries according to their preferences.

The result of applying `TVGuide11.xsl` to `TVGuide2.xml` is `TVGuide11.html`, which includes several highlighted programs, including *EastEnders*, as shown in Figure 4-10.

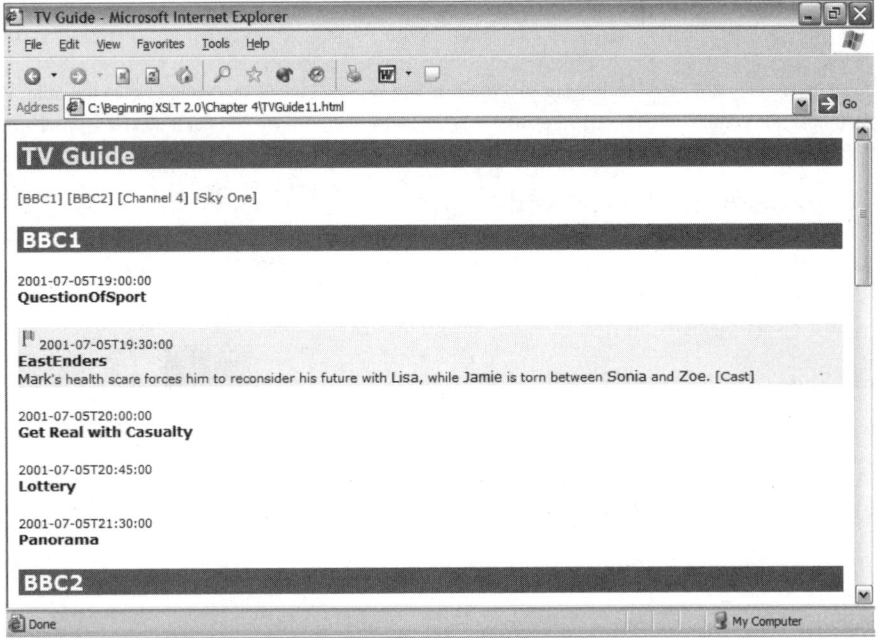

Figure 4-10. *Viewing* `TVGuide11.html` *in Internet Explorer*

Other programs are highlighted if they're interesting, have a high rating, or if their series, title, or description contains the word "News".

Filtering XML

Thus far, this chapter has focused on using conditions to generate different content in different circumstances. You can also use these tests to only select particular elements and attributes based on their values (for example), so that you can apply templates to them, iterate over them, or get their values. You do this by placing the test in square brackets (`[]`) after the location path. The square brackets and the test inside them are known as a **predicate**.

For example, with the current node being a `<Channel>` element, you can select all `<Program>` elements that have a `flag` attribute with a value of `favorite` using the following path:

```
Program[@flag = 'favorite']
```

The component [@flag = 'favorite'] is a predicate that filters the <Program> elements returned by the rest of the path to include only those <Program> elements for which the condition is true. Without the predicate, the path Program would return *all* the <Program> element children of the context node. With the predicate, the path only returns those <Program> elements that have a flag attribute whose value is favorite. You can apply templates to only this filtered set of <Program> elements with the following <xsl:apply-templates> instruction:

```
<xsl:apply-templates select="Program[@flag = 'favorite']" />
```

Note As we'll see in Chapter 7, you can also use predicates in patterns, for example, to make a template match only a particular type of element based on the element's value.

Summary You can filter a sequence with a predicate, which is a test in square brackets. Items for which the predicate is not true are filtered out of the sequence.

Selecting Elements Based on Their Content

In the previous sections, we've highlighted *Star Trek* episodes within the main program listing using icons. A more useful resource for *Star Trek* fans, though, would be a separate list including all the *Star Trek* episodes that are shown on the various channels. We'll aim to do this in the new stylesheet, StarTrek.xsl, which is based on TVGuide11.xsl.

The first change is to make sure that the listing for a channel only displays *Star Trek* episodes. We can do that by altering the template for the <Channel> elements, so that it explicitly applies templates to its <Name> element child, and then only applies templates to the <Program> elements whose <Series> element starts with the string 'StarTrek', as follows:

```
<xsl:template match="Channel">
  <xsl:apply-templates select="Name" />
  <xsl:apply-templates select="Program[starts-with(Series, 'StarTrek')]" />
</xsl:template>
```

The second problem is a bit trickier. In this new stylesheet, we only want to list a channel if any of the programs that it shows are *Star Trek* episodes. As we saw earlier, with the current node being a <Channel> element, the test

```
starts-with(Program/Series, 'StarTrek')
```

will give an error because the first argument returns a sequence containing more than one item (there are lots of <Program> elements within a particular <Channel>).

However, we've seen that we can make a sequence made up of <Program> elements that represent *Star Trek* episodes, and we know that an empty sequence evaluates as false when you use it as a test. Therefore, if we construct a sequence containing the *Star Trek* episodes for a channel, we can find out whether there are any *Star Trek* episodes on that channel. We can do this inside the template for the <Channel> elements, as follows:

```
<xsl:template match="Channel">
  <xsl:if test="Program[starts-with(Series, 'StarTrek')]">
    <xsl:apply-templates select="Name" />
    <xsl:apply-templates
        select="Program[starts-with(Series, 'StarTrek')]" />
  </xsl:if>
</xsl:template>
```

We should make a similar change to the template in ChannelList mode, so the channel list at the top and bottom of the page only displays those channels showing *Star Trek* episodes as well:

```
<xsl:template match="Channel" mode="ChannelList">
  <xsl:if test="Program[starts-with(Series, 'StarTrek')]">
    [<a href="#{Name}"><xsl:value-of select="Name" /></a>]
  </xsl:if>
</xsl:template>
```

The result of applying StarTrek.xsl to TVGuide2.xml, StarTrek.html, is shown Figure 4-11.

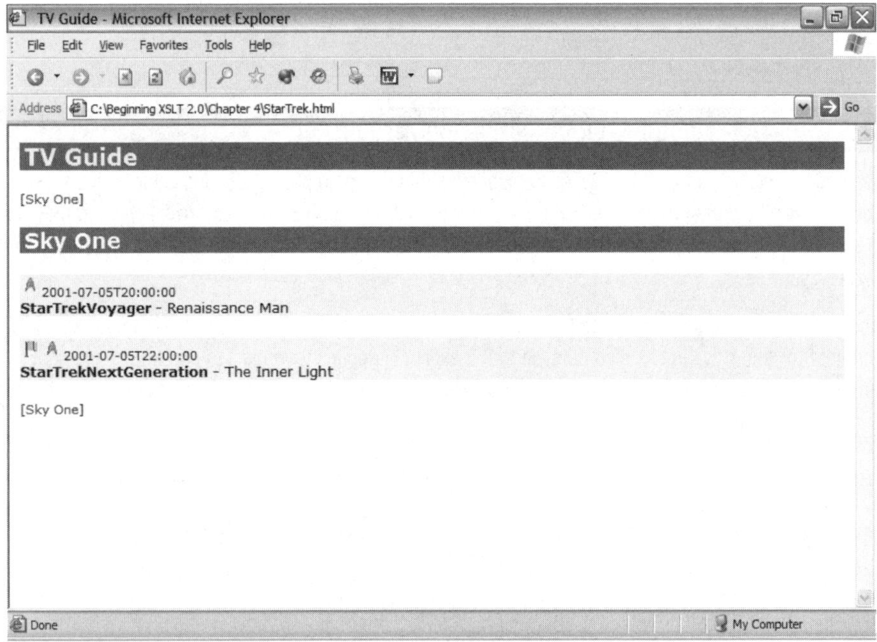

Figure 4-11. *Viewing* StarTrek.html *in Internet Explorer*

The only channel that's showing any *Star Trek* episodes is Sky One, so that's the only channel that gets shown in either the channel listing at the top and bottom of the page or the main body of the page.

■ **Note** Both *Star Trek* episodes are highlighted—the *Voyager* episode because it has a high rating, the *Next Generation* episode because it's flagged as a favorite program.

There's no prohibition on nesting predicates. Just as with the `<Program>` elements, rather than apply templates to all channels but only give a result for those that show *Star Trek* episodes, we could just apply templates to those channels that show *Star Trek* episodes. You can select the `<Channel>` elements that have a `<Program>` element child whose `<Series>` element child starts with the string `'StarTrek'` with this location path:

```
Channel[Program[starts-with(Series, 'StarTrek')]]
```

So, in another version of the stylesheet, `StarTrek2.xsl`, within the template that matches the root node, you can make sure that you only display information for channels that show *Star Trek* episodes, and give a message if there are no such channels, with the following:

```
<xsl:template match="/">
  ...
  <xsl:choose>
    <xsl:when test="TVGuide/Channel[Program[starts-with(Series, 'StarTrek')]]">
      <xsl:apply-templates
          select="TVGuide/Channel[Program[starts-with(Series, 'StarTrek')]]" />
    </xsl:when>
    <xsl:otherwise>
      <p>No Star Trek showing this week!</p>
    </xsl:otherwise>
  </xsl:choose>
  ...
</xsl:template>
```

When we use `StarTrek2.xsl` on `TVGuide2.xml` to create `StarTrek2.html`, we get exactly the same display as we did before, shown in Figure 4-11—Sky One is showing some *Star Trek* episodes, so it gets shown. On the other hand, if you try using `StarTrek2.xsl` with `TVGuide.xml`, which doesn't include Sky One, to create `StarTrek2a.html`, you should get the result shown in Figure 4-12.

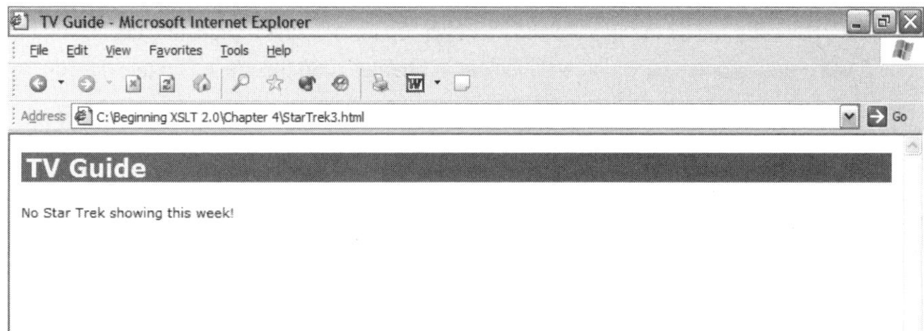

Figure 4-12. *Viewing* `StarTrek2a.html` *in Internet Explorer*

The stylesheet has detected that none of the channels are showing *Star Trek* episodes, and it's given a different message.

Testing Positions

A predicate can hold any expression, and it's usually evaluated as a Boolean, just as if the expression were used in a test attribute. However, if the expression evaluates to a number, then it's taken as the position of the item in the sequence that you've selected with the beginning bit of the path. Have a look at the following XPath with the current node being a <Channel> element:

```
Program[1]
```

This expression selects just the first <Program> element in the list for the channel. You can use the last() function to get the last element in a list. For example, the following selects the last <CastMember> element in the <CastList>, assuming the current node is the <Program> element:

```
CastList/CastMember[last()]
```

Using a number in a predicate is actually shorthand for testing the number returned by the position() function. The two paths given previously are shorthand for the following:

```
Program[position() = 1]
CastList/CastMember[position() = last()]
```

The position() function returns the index of the item you're looking at in the sequence that you're selecting. You can test whether the position of an item is in a particular range using less-than and greater-than operators. For example, with the <TVGuide> element as the current node, the following XPath applies templates to the third, fourth, and fifth <Channel> elements:

```
<xsl:apply-templates select="Channel[position() >= 3 and
                                     position() &lt;= 5]" />
```

■ Note You can also perform this test by taking advantage of the way that general comparisons work when one operand is a sequence: by creating a sequence that contains the integers 3, 4, and 5 and testing that sequence against the value returned by the position() function. You can create a sequence containing the integers 3, 4, and 5 using the to operator, which we'll look at in Chapter 7. So the preceding could be done with the expression Channel[position() = (3 to 5)].

You can also test the position of a node outside a predicate, in the test attribute of <xsl:if> or <xsl:when>. If you do so, you test the position of the current node (the node that the template matches) in the sequence of nodes that have had templates applied to them. We'll look at the implications of this in Chapter 10 when we look at numbering.

Summary A numerical predicate indicates the position of the selected node; you can use the `last()` function to get the index of the last node in a list. You can also use the `position()` function to test the position of a node explicitly.

Testing the Position of Nodes

When we list the channels that are available in our TV guide, they are given in a line that looks like the following:

```
[BBC1] [BBC2] [ITV] [Channel 4] [Channel 5] [Sky One]
```

This formatting is easy because every channel is treated in exactly the same way. Instead, say we wanted to create the links separated by pipe symbols:

```
BBC1 | BBC2 | ITV | Channel 4 | Channel 5 | Sky One
```

With this formatting, every channel name has a pipe after it except the last channel, which doesn't have a pipe symbol. In `TVGuide12.xsl`, we'll go back to listing all the channels, and add a pipe sign only if the channel isn't the last channel in the list. If you recall, we made this list of channels with a template matching `<Channel>` elements in `ChannelList` mode, which was applied to all `<Channel>` elements at once. In `TVGuide11.xsl`, this template looks like the following:

```
<xsl:template match="Channel" mode="ChannelList">
  <xsl:if test="Program/@flag">
    [<a href="#{Name}"><xsl:value-of select="Name" /></a>]
  </xsl:if>
</xsl:template>
```

We need to first change this template to remove the `<xsl:if>` so that we show all the channels:

```
<xsl:template match="Channel" mode="ChannelList">
  [<a href="#{Name}"><xsl:value-of select="Name" /></a>]
</xsl:template>
```

We can then alter this template to add an `<xsl:if>` that adds a pipe symbol conditional on the position of the `<Channel>` element, as follows:

```
<xsl:template match="Channel" mode="ChannelList">
  <a href="#{Name}"><xsl:value-of select="Name" /></a>
  <xsl:if test="position() != last()"> | </xsl:if>
</xsl:template>
```

Don't forget to also change (or simply remove) the template matching the `<Channel>` elements in the default mode, since we want to list all the channels.

If you transform `TVGuide2.xml` with `TVGuide12.xsl`, to give `TVGuide12.html`, you should get the page shown in Figure 4-13.

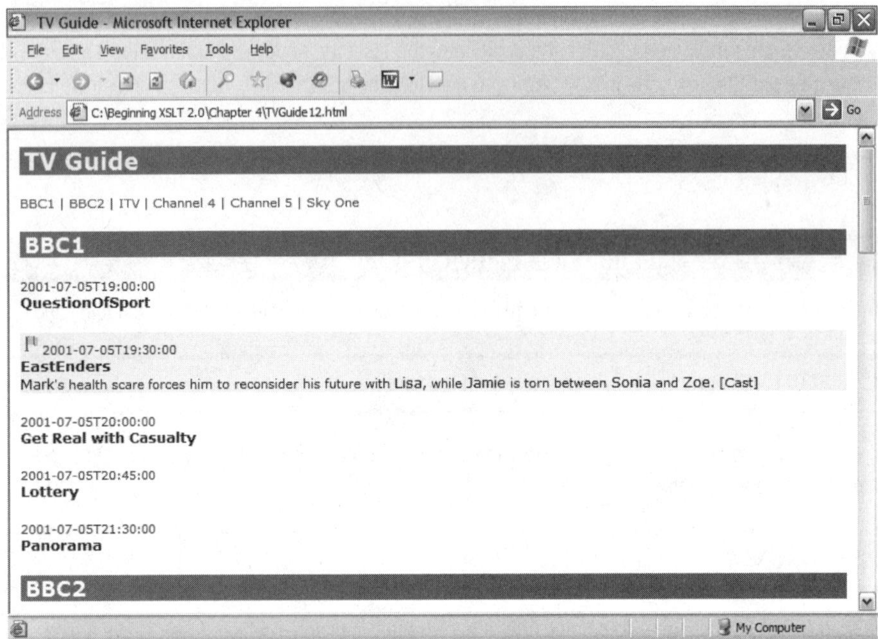

Figure 4-13. *Viewing* TVGuide12.html *in Internet Explorer*

The channel names are separated by pipe symbols. The only channel that doesn't have a pipe symbol after its name is Sky One, because that's the last channel in the list.

■ **Tip** This technique is often very handy when you're creating comma-separated or space-separated lists of values, but if the values are just strings (rather than XML), then you can use the `separator` attribute on `<xsl:value-of>` to do the same thing much more easily. We'll see this in action in Chapter 7.

Summary

This chapter has covered how to generate output conditionally, based on the presence of information in some source XML. You've learned how to generate different HTML dependent on

- The presence or absence of elements and attributes
- The ancestry of an element or attribute
- The values of elements and attributes

You've seen two new XSLT instructions: `<xsl:if>` to generate optional content and `<xsl:choose>` to generate different content in different situations. You've also seen a new conditional expression—the `if` expression—which you can use within an XPath to create different values in different circumstances.

Both <xsl:if> and the <xsl:when> elements inside <xsl:choose> use a test attribute to hold an XPath expression that's interpreted as a Boolean value, and the condition in an if expression is treated in the same way. In this chapter, we introduced the different value types that XPath expressions could evaluate as—sequences, Booleans, numbers, strings, and so on—and saw how the effective Boolean value of each is calculated when an expression is used in a condition. You've also seen how to use the boolean(), number(), and string() functions to convert between the different value types.

Many tests involve comparing values, and you've learned about the six value comparison operators that enable you to do comparisons between values—eq, ne, lt, le, gt, and ge—and the six general comparison operators that enable you to do comparisons between sequences— =, !=, <, <=, >, and >=. You've discovered how to combine tests together with and and or, and negate them with the not() function. As well as testing the value of an element or attribute exactly, you've also seen how to test the content of a string using compare(), starts-with(), ends-with(), contains(), and matches().

The expressions that we've tried out in this chapter have been more complex than the ones we've looked at before. In particular, we've seen how to use predicates to filter sequences. We'll be looking in more detail at paths and sequences in Chapter 7, but in the next chapter we're going to investigate the various atomic values that you might need to manipulate and the functions and operators that you can use to perform calculations with them.

Review Questions

1. What output do you get when you try to apply templates to a node that doesn't exist?
2. How can you use templates to generate different output for a <Film> element that's a descendant of a <Description> element and for a <Film> element that's a child of a <Channel> element?
3. What does the following code do?

```
<div>
  <xsl:apply-templates select="Film" />
  <xsl:if test="not(Film)">No films showing on this channel.</xsl:if>
</div>
```

4. Rewrite the preceding code using an <xsl:choose> element. What are the advantages and disadvantages of the two forms?
5. What does the following code do?

```
<xsl:choose>
  <xsl:when test="@flag = 'favorite'">
    <img src="favorite.gif" alt="[Favorite]" width="20" height="20" />
  </xsl:when>
  <xsl:when test="@flag = 'interesting'">
    <img src="interest.gif" alt="[Interest]" width="20" height="20" />
  </xsl:when>
  <xsl:when test="@flag">
```

```
    <img src="flag.gif" alt="[Flagged]" width="20" height="20" />
  </xsl:when>
</xsl:choose>
```

6. Rewrite the preceding code as a sequence of <xsl:if> elements. What are the advantages and disadvantages of the two forms?

7. Rewrite the preceding code as a combination of an <xsl:if> and `if` expressions within attribute value templates. What are the advantages and disadvantages of this version?

8. Write an expression that tests whether any <Film> element children of the current node have a `year` attribute whose value is greater than `1950`.

9. Write an expression that selects all the <Film> element children of the current node whose <Title> element child starts with the string `'Romeo'`.

10. Write an expression that tests whether the current node's value is a nonzero number.

11. Write an expression that tests whether the current node's value is a number (including zero).

CHAPTER 5

Manipulating Atomic Values

The last chapter focused on how to create conditional content using XSLT, and along the way introduced **XPath expressions**. XPath expressions are simple bits of code that a processor evaluates to get a value. XPath expressions are used by XSLT a lot, but they're used in other places too, such as XPointer, XQuery, and in the DOM API.

In the last chapter you learned about the kinds of values that XPath expressions can evaluate to: **atomic values** such as strings, numbers, Booleans, dates, and times; **nodes** such as elements and attributes; and **sequences** of items, which can be atomic values or nodes. So far we've focused on the basic kinds of atomic values: strings, numbers, and Booleans. In this chapter, we're going to look at the other kinds of atomic values that are available to you.

Expressions can combine values in various ways. In the last chapter, you saw how to use **operators** to compare values and **functions** to test values. There are lots of other operators and functions available to you, allowing you to manipulate the various kinds of atomic values supported by XPath. We'll be looking at many of these functions and operators in this chapter. Don't feel that you have to memorize every feature of each of them, but skimming through this chapter should give you enough familiarity to know that a function exists to do what you need to do, even if you have to look up the details in Appendix A later.

In this chapter, you'll learn

- What kinds of atomic values are available
- How to process strings, including how to process them with regular expressions
- How to use numbers, including how to format them
- How to manipulate dates, times, and durations
- How to process URIs

Atomic Values

Atomic values are the basic kind of value that you encounter in XPath. Every atomic value has a **type**, which determines what you can do with that value. The type of an atomic value is identified by its name, which is qualified (just like the names of elements) through a namespace. For example, the atomic value `'StarTrek'` has a type called `string` in the namespace `http://www.w3.org/2001/XMLSchema`.

XPath has a large number of types of atomic value built-in, most of which were originally defined by XML Schema and therefore live in the XML Schema namespace. XPath itself defines a few extra types that you can use; these live in the following namespace:

```
http://www.w3.org/2005/04/xpath-datatypes
```

■**Caution** The namespace used for the datatypes defined by XPath changes each time a new version of the specification comes out. Make sure that the namespace you use in your stylesheets is the same as that supported by the processor that you're using.

■**Note** In the rest of this book, I'll use the prefix `xs` to indicate the namespace `http://www.w3.org/2001/XMLSchema` and the prefix `xdt` to indicate the namespace `http://www.w3.org/2005/04/xpath-datatypes`. For example, a qualified name with a local name of `string` and a namespace URI of `http://www.w3.org/2001/XMLSchema` will be expressed as `xs:string`.

Basic XSLT processors, which we're using at the moment, support most XML Schema and XPath datatypes. As we'll see in Chapter 13, with Schema-Aware processing you can also define your own types within a schema and then import them into your stylesheet. Individual XSLT processors are also free to define their own types, so check your processor's documentation to see if it supplies any special types that you can use.

■**Summary** Atomic values have types, which determine how they're treated. The types that are available in a stylesheet include the built-in types (which are defined in XML Schema or in XPath), types imported from schemas, and types defined by the processor you're using.

The Atomic Type Hierarchy

The types of atomic values are arranged in a type hierarchy, which is shown in Figure 5-1. The type immediately above a particular type in the hierarchy is known as the type's base type or supertype. For example, the type `xs:integer` is the base type of `xs:nonNegativeInteger`. Conversely, the types immediately below a particular type in the hierarchy are known as the type's derived types or subtypes, so `xs:nonNegativeInteger` is a subtype of `xs:integer`. A subtype is a specialized version of its supertype. For example, while `xs:integer` values can be negative or positive, values of type `xs:nonNegativeInteger` have to be `0` or more (nonnegative).

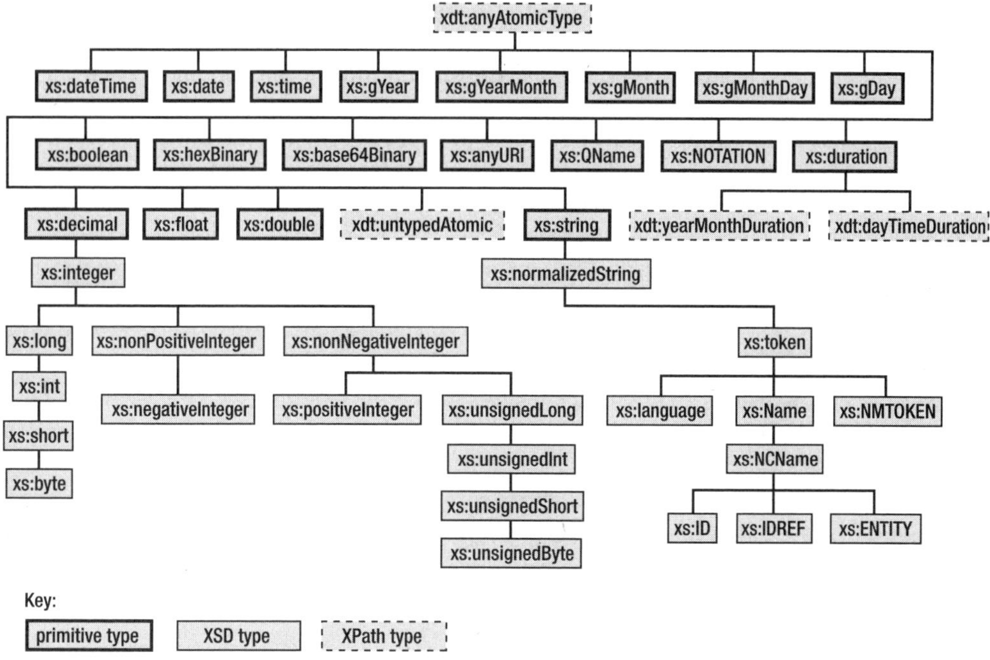

Figure 5-1. *The hierarchy of built-in types*

At the very top of the hierarchy is a type called `xdt:anyAtomicType`, which is the most general atomic type that you can get. Below it are a number of primitive types; it's at the level of primitive types that the real distinctions between the types start. The primitive types can be categorized as follows:

- `xdt:untypedAtomic`
- `xs:string`
- Numeric types: `xs:double`, `xs:float`, and `xs:decimal`
- Date/time types: `xs:dateTime`, `xs:date`, `xs:time`, `xs:gYear`, `xs:gYearMonth`, `xs:gMonth`, `xs:gMonthDay`, and `xs:gDay`
- `xs:duration`
- Binary types: `xs:base64Binary` and `xs:hexBinary`
- `xs:boolean`
- `xs:QName`
- `xs:anyURI`
- `xs:NOTATION`

We'll look at most of these types in detail in the rest of this chapter, but there are two that are worth mentioning specially here.

First, the `xdt:untypedAtomic` type is unlike the other primitive types, in that it's really used to indicate a value whose type isn't known. This type actually crops up all over the place, especially in Basic XSLT processing, because it's the type that's assigned to the values of nodes. As we'll see later on in this section, unlike atomic values of other types, atomic values of the type `xdt:untypedAtomic` are automatically cast to the type that they need to be based on how they're used. For example, if you pass a value of type `xdt:untypedAtomic` to a function that expects an `xs:date` value, then the `xdt:untypedAtomic` value will be cast to an `xs:date` value, and that value used in the function.

Second, the `xs:NOTATION` type is only any use if you have a schema that declares notations. Notations are a legacy DTD mechanism for defining the type of elements, and it's very rare to see a schema that actually uses them. So I'm going to ignore `xs:NOTATION` for the remainder of this book.

■ **Summary** Types are arranged in a hierarchy, with each subtype inheriting from its supertype. The very top of the atomic type hierarchy is `xdt:anyAtomicType`, whose subtypes are the primitive types.

Creating Atomic Values

You've already seen how to create some kinds of atomic values using simple expressions. To create a string, you just use the value of the string that you want, with quotes around it; for example, to create the `xs:string` value `'StarTrek'` you use either of the following:

```
'StarTrek'
"StarTrek"
```

QUOTES AND STRING LITERALS

Including quotes in string literals has traditionally been a problem in XSLT. Say that you wanted to test whether a string contains an apostrophe. To test that, you need to create a string that contains a single apostrophe character. If you delimit the string literal with apostrophes, as in

```
contains(Name, ''')
```

then the processor will interpret the apostrophe character in the string as ending the string literal, and will complain that the XPath expression isn't legal. You can use double quotes around the apostrophe instead:

```
contains(Name, "'")
```

But then, what if you need to create a string that contains both an apostrophe and a double quote? If you delimited the string literal with apostrophes, the apostrophe in the string would be interpreted as the end of the string literal; if you delimited it with double quotes, the double quote in the string would be interpreted as the end of the string literal.

To get around this problem, XPath 2.0 allows you to escape apostrophes or double quotes within a string by doubling them. For example, the following call to the `contains()` function would be legal:

```
contains(Name, '''')
```

Another level of complication arises because these expressions are embedded in XML attribute values, which themselves use either apostrophes or double quotes as delimiters. It's not well-formed XML to include a double quote inside an attribute value that's delimited by double quotes. For example, the following isn't well-formed XML:

```
<xsl:if test="contains(Name, "'")">...</xsl:if>
```

If an attribute value is delimited by double quotes, then you have to escape any double quotes within the attribute value using the XML escape `"`. Likewise, if an attribute value is delimited by apostrophes, then you have to escape any apostrophes within the attribute value using the XML escape `'`. So the following are all legal ways of testing whether the `<Name>` element child of the current node contains an apostrophe, both at the XML level and the XPath level:

```
<xsl:if test="contains(Name, &quot;'&quot;)">...</xsl:if>
<xsl:if test='contains(Name, "&apos;")'>...</xsl:if>
<xsl:if test="contains(Name, '''')">...</xsl:if>
<xsl:if test='contains(Name, &apos;&apos;&apos;&apos;)'>...</xsl:if>
```

To create a number, you just include the number literally; for example, to create the number `6`, you can just use

```
6
```

In fact, this literal creates a value of type `xs:integer`. To create values of other numeric types, you need to use slightly different syntax. To create a value of type `xs:decimal`, you need to include a decimal point:

```
6.0
```

To create a value of type `xs:double`, you need to include an exponent; any of the following will create the `xs:double` value `6E0`:

```
6E0
6.0E+0
6e0
0006e0
```

Note When creating a number with a numeric literal, you can include whatever leading or trailing zeros you want; the value will be the same.

To create values of any other type, it's usually easiest to use a constructor function. Constructor functions are special functions that are designed for constructing atomic values. Each is named after the type of value that it constructs, and takes a single argument, usually a string, which specifies the value. For example, to create the `xs:time` `18:00:00`, you would use

```
xs:time('18:00:00')
```

■ **Caution** You will get an error if the argument you pass to a constructor function isn't a legal value for the type that you're trying to create. For example, the call `xs:time('6pm')` will raise an error.

In most cases, the string that you pass in as the argument to the constructor function can come from anywhere: it can be a string literal; the value of a node; or a substring of another string, calculated using the `substring()` function, for example. So the following is perfectly fine:

```
xs:time(concat(substring(dc:date, 17, 5), '00'))
```

However, for arcane implementation-related reasons, the `xs:QName` constructor function (and the `xs:NOTATION` constructor function, which you will never use) can only be called with an argument that is a string literal. Thus, the following works:

```
xs:QName('xs:string')
```

but the following gives an error because the argument is not a string literal:

```
xs:QName(concat('xs', ':', 'string'))
```

■ **Note** The string literal passed as the argument of `xs:QName()` will be interpreted based on the namespace declarations that are present in your stylesheet. If the string doesn't have a prefix, then the default namespace for element and type names, which is set using the `xpath-default-namespace` attribute, will be used. If there's no `xpath-default-namespace` attribute, then the unprefixed string will be interpreted as being a local name only (in no namespace). The default namespace declared in the stylesheet is never used.

Using constructor functions is actually a specialized form of casting, which we'll look at in the next section.

■ **Summary** Strings and numbers can be created using literals. Values of other types are usually created using constructor functions, each of which has the same name as the type that they're used to create.

Casting Between Types

In XPath 2.0, if a function or operator expects an atomic value of a particular type, and you instead pass an atomic value of a different type, you will get a type error. Smart processors, which analyze the stylesheet before trying to use it, might be able to pick up type errors before you even run your stylesheet; otherwise, you'll be informed of the type error when you try to run your transformation. There's no way to recover from a type error, so if your code contains a type error, then your stylesheet won't work.

■ Note Values that have a type that is a subtype of the expected type for an argument won't give a type error, because by definition a value of a particular type is also of that type's supertype. For example, if a function expects an `xs:decimal` and you pass it an `xs:integer`, then that's fine.

For example, say that you wanted to check whether a number includes a decimal point (which is one way of testing whether the number is a whole number). If you tried passing the number to the `contains()` function as follows, you would get an error:

```
contains(number(@rating), '.')
```

■ Note In this case, the number is being created using the `number()` function, which you met in the last chapter. The `number()` function actually creates an `xs:double` value.

■ Tip There are a number of better ways of testing whether a value is a whole number, including testing whether the number is equal to the floored version of the number (`number(@rating) = floor(@rating)`) and testing whether the number is equal to the result of casting the number to an `xs:integer` (`number(@rating) = xs:integer(number(@rating))`).

This is an error because the `contains()` function expects an `xs:string` as its first argument, but you've supplied an `xs:double`. To provide the correct type of value to the `contains()` function, you must cast the `xs:double` to an `xs:string`. There are two ways of casting a value from one type to another: using a constructor function, as you saw just now, and using a `cast` expression.

Constructor functions are usually the easiest method to use to cast a value to a new type. For example, you could cast the `xs:double` to an `xs:string` using the `xs:string()` constructor function as follows:

```
contains(xs:string(number(@rating)), '.')
```

■ Caution The `xs:string()` constructor function works in almost exactly the same way as the `string()` function. The only difference arises when the argument is a node that has been assigned a type (by validation against a schema), in which case the `xs:string()` function gives you the string value of the node's typed value, whereas the `string()` function gives you the original string value of the node itself. We'll revisit this distinction when we look at using schemas with XSLT 2.0 in Chapter 13.

The alternative method of casting is a `cast` expression. A `cast` expression looks like

```
value cast as type
```

The *value* is the value that you want to cast and the *type* is the type that you want to cast it to. For example:

```
contains(number(@rating) cast as xs:string, '.')
```

The `cast` expression gives you a little more control than constructor functions when it comes to dealing with empty sequences. Passing a constructor function an argument that is an empty sequence will always give an empty sequence as a result. With a `cast` expression, you can indicate that an empty sequence is acceptable by appending a question mark (?) after the name of the type; if you don't include the question mark, then a type error will be raised if you try to cast an empty sequence to the desired type. For example, consider the following `cast` expression:

```
@rating cast as xs:decimal?
```

If the `rating` attribute exists, this expression returns the value of the `rating` attribute cast to an `xs:decimal`. If the `rating` attribute doesn't exist, then the path `"@rating"` returns an empty sequence, and the expression as a whole likewise returns the empty sequence. On the other hand, the following expression will raise a type error if there is no `rating` attribute:

```
@rating cast as xs:decimal
```

The requirement that arguments must be of the required type could lead to your code being littered with constructor functions and `cast` expressions, but thankfully, for usability, there are three exceptions to the general rule that an argument must be of the type expected by the function:

- If the value is of type `xdt:untypedAtomic` (such as the value of a node under Basic XSLT processing), then it will be automatically cast to the type expected by the function.
- If the value is of type `xs:decimal`, then it can be used when a value of type `xs:float` or `xs:double` is expected; similarly, a value of type `xs:float` can be used when the expected type is `xs:double`. This is known as **numeric type promotion**.
- If the value is of type `xs:anyURI`, then it can be used when a value of type `xs:string` is expected. This is known as **URI type promotion**.

Summary You can cast a value to a different type using either a constructor function or a `cast` expression.

Testing Castability

There are two things that determine whether a value can be cast to a particular type: the type of the value and the value itself.

A value of a particular type can only be cast to certain other types. If you try to cast between two types where casting isn't allowed, you will get a type error. The casts that *are* allowed between the primitive types are as follows:

- xs:string and xdt:untypedAtomic values can be cast to any other type (though the cast won't always succeed), and any type can be cast to xs:string or xdt:untypedAtomic.
- Values of numeric types (xs:decimal, xs:float, and xs:double) can be cast to other numeric types, though casts from xs:double and xs:float to xs:decimal won't always succeed.
- Values of numeric types can be cast to xs:boolean and vice versa.
- xs:dateTime values can be cast to any of the date/time types.
- xs:date values can be cast to xs:dateTime, xs:gYear, xs:gYearMonth, xs:gMonth, xs:gMonthDay, and xs:gDay types.
- xs:base64Binary can be cast to xs:hexBinary and vice versa.

In addition, casts from supertype to subtype are always allowed (though aren't always guaranteed to succeed), and in general you can cast from a value to any type as long as you can cast from the primitive type from which the value's type is derived across to the primitive type from which the target type is derived. For example, you can cast from xs:token to xdt:yearMonthDuration because you can cast from xs:string (from which xs:token is derived) to xs:duration (from which xdt:yearMonthDuration is derived).

■ **Note** Casts from subtype to supertype succeed by definition, since a value can only be legal for a subtype if it is also legal for the supertype. You never *have* to cast from subtype to a supertype, but you can do if you want.

CASTING DOWN THE TYPE HIERARCHY

In general, when you cast down the type hierarchy, changing the type of an atomic value to one of its subtypes, the value must comply with all the extra requirements that the subtype defines. For example, if you cast an xs:integer value to xs:nonNegativeInteger, then the value must not be negative; if it is, the cast will raise a dynamic error.

There are two exceptions to this general rule, however:

- Values of type xs:decimal can be cast to xs:integer, even if they're not integers; the cast is done by removing any fractional part from the decimal (in other words, by rounding down if the value is positive and up if the value is negative).
- Values of type xs:duration can be cast to xdt:yearMonthDuration by removing any day, hour, minute, or second components from the duration; similarly, xs:duration values can be cast to xdt:dayTimeDuration by removing any year or month components from the duration.

As mentioned previously, just because a cast is legal doesn't mean that it will always work. For example, the following cast (from an xs:string to an xs:integer) is legal:

```
xs:integer('12.5')
```

but it won't work because the value '12.5' isn't a legal representation of an integer. If you try to carry out a cast and it turns out that the value isn't legal, then you will get a **dynamic error**. Dynamic errors are errors that the processor can usually only detect when it actually evaluates an expression.

So there are two kinds of errors that you might get when you attempt a cast: type errors and dynamic errors. You can't catch either kind of error to make sure the transformation as a whole succeeds, but you can test whether a cast is going to work before you actually do the cast using a `castable` expression. The general form of the `castable` expression is similar to that of the `cast` expression:

```
value castable as type
```

For example, if you weren't sure whether the `rating` attribute was formatted as an integer, you could check whether the cast was going to work before you tried it:

```
@rating castable as xs:integer
```

If the `rating` attribute weren't castable as an `xs:integer`, this test would return false. You could use an `if` expression to choose what to do in this case, for example, to return an empty sequence if the `rating` attribute isn't an integer:

```
if (@rating castable as xs:integer) then xs:integer(@rating) else ()
```

■ **Summary** You can check whether a cast is going to succeed using a `castable` expression. If you attempt a cast that isn't allowed at all, you will get a type error; if casting the particular value isn't successful, you will get a dynamic error.

Manipulating Strings

Now that we've seen the fundamentals of atomic values, let's move on to look at how to actually use them.

First up is the most common kind of atomic value in XML: strings. There are lots of functions for manipulating strings within XPath, for example, allowing you to break up strings, to combine them together, and to reformat them. Several of these functions have been added between XPath 1.0 and XPath 2.0, including functions that support matching and replacing based on regular expressions. XSLT 2.0 also introduces an `<xsl:analyze-string>` element for regular expression processing.

Splitting and Recombining Strings

The `substring-before()` and `substring-after()` functions are handy for splitting up character-delimited strings. They both take two or three arguments, the first being the original string, the second being the character or string at which it should be broken, and the optional third argument being a collation URI.

■ **Note** You learned about collations, which are used to compare strings, in the last chapter.

The substring-before() function returns the substring of the first argument before the first occurrence of the second argument, while the substring-after() function returns the substring of the first argument after the first occurrence of the second argument. If the character doesn't appear in the string, then both functions return an empty string. For example, you could use these functions to get someone's forename and surname given just their name:

```
substring-before('Jeni Tennison', ' ')
substring-after('Jeni Tennison', ' ')
```

The substring() function is useful when you have strings that follow a fixed-width format. It normally takes three arguments: the original string, the index of the first character in the string that you want (starting from 1), and the number of characters you want to get in the substring. You can omit the third argument to get all the remaining characters in a string. For example, both the following calls return the string 'xyz':

```
substring('abcdefghijklmnopqrstuvwxyz', 24, 3)
substring('abcdefghijklmnopqrstuvwxyz', 24)
```

Note There's no limit in XPath to the number of characters that a string can contain, though it will be limited in particular implementations, or by the memory capacity of the computer on which you're running the transformation. There are limits on the numbers that XPath can handle, since most XPath numbers are double-precision 64-bit floating point numbers. I've never seen either limit be a real problem.

When you're trying to get the last part of a string, it's often useful to know the string's length. You can do this with the string-length() function. For example, you can get the last letter in a string with the following:

```
substring($string, string-length($string))
```

Once you've broken up a string, you often want to recombine the component parts in a different way. You can do this with the concat() function, which takes two or more string arguments and combines them into a single string. For example, once you've pulled out the forename and surname from a string, you might want to combine them back together in a sortable format, with the surname first and a comma separator:

```
concat($surname, ', ', $forename)
```

If you have a sequence of strings, such as the values of all the <Name> elements of the <Channel> elements in the TV guide, you can concatenate them together with the string-join() function. The string-join() function takes a sequence of strings as the first argument, and a separator string as the second argument; each string in the sequence is concatenated with the next, with the separator in between. For example, to create a comma-separated list of the channels in our TV guide, we can use

```
string-join(Channel/Name, ', ')
```

Summary You can split up a string with the substring(), substring-before(), and substring-after() functions and put a string together with the concat() and string-join() functions. The string-length() function tells you the length of a string.

Parsing Dates and Times

The TV guide markup language holds the start date and time of a program in a `<Start>` element, which uses the format `YYYY-MM-DDThh:mm:ss`. This format is a good standard format to use, but it isn't very readable. Instead, it would be good to just use a US date format and just give the hours and minutes when the show starts. The start date of `2001-07-05T19:30:00` should be shown as something like

```
7/5/2001 19:30
```

We'll try to generate this format in the next version of our stylesheet, `TVGuide2.xsl`, which is based on `TVGuide.xsl`.

■ **Note** In this example, we'll do this formatting using string manipulation. Later you'll see how much easier it is to format dates directly using the `format-date()` function.

The date and time format held in the `<Start>` element is a fixed-width format: the first four characters always give the year and the last eight characters give the time. Therefore we can split the string up with the `substring()` function. For example, we can get the month using

```
substring(., 6, 2)
```

We can then construct the new string by concatenating the various components together in a different order (and inserting two /s and a space), using the `concat()` function as follows:

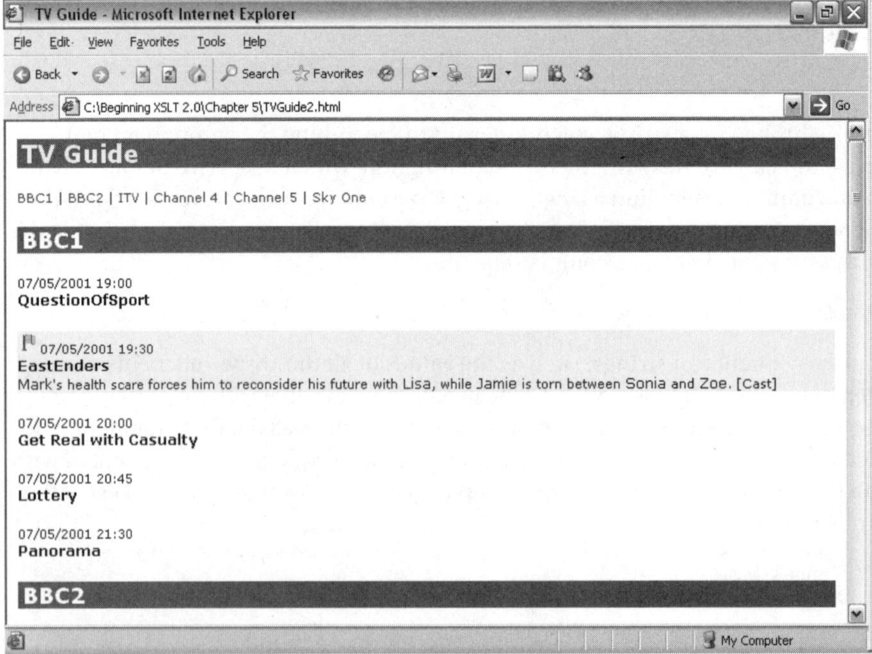

Figure 5-2. *Viewing* `TVGuide2.html` *in Internet Explorer*

```
<xsl:template match="Start">
  <span class="date">
    <xsl:value-of select="concat(substring(., 6, 2), '/',
                                 substring(., 9, 2), '/',
                                 substring(., 1, 4), ' ',
                                 substring(., 12, 5))" />
  </span>
</xsl:template>
```

This gives a much more readable format to the dates, as you can see in Figure 5-2.

However, the substrings are, unsurprisingly, strings—the month and day components are the strings `'07'` and `'05'` respectively—so we get leading zeros to the resulting format. The neatest way of getting rid of those zeros in the next version, `TVGuide3.xsl`, is to convert the variables into numbers first, using the `number()` function. Since the `concat()` function expects strings as its arguments, these numbers then need to be turned back into strings using the `string()` function, as follows:

```
<xsl:value-of select="concat(string(number(substring(., 6, 2))), '/',
                             string(number(substring(., 9, 2))), '/',
                             substring(., 1, 4), ' ',
                             substring(., 12, 5))" />
```

With this change made in `TVGuide3.xsl`, the leading zeros on the month and the day disappear, as shown in Figure 5-3.

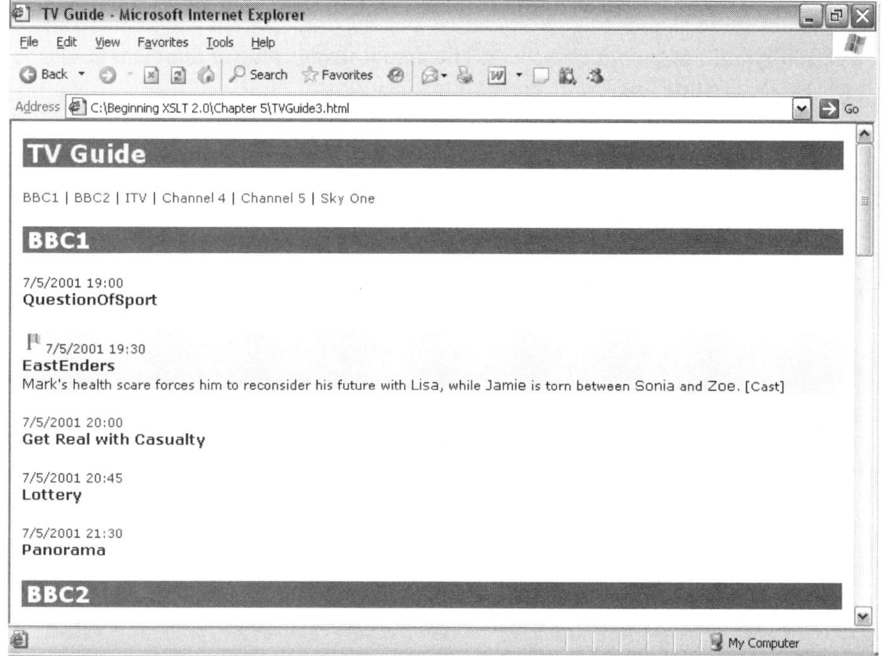

Figure 5-3. *Viewing* `TVGuide3.html` *in Internet Explorer*

Reformatting Strings

There are five other string-manipulation functions that are mainly useful when formatting strings: `normalize-space()`, `normalize-unicode()`, `translate()`, `upper-case()`, and `lower-case()`.

Normalizing Whitespace

The `normalize-space()` function strips leading and trailing whitespace from a string and substitutes all the whitespace within the string with single spaces. It can take a single argument (it defaults to the string value of the context node if you don't give an argument), and is particularly useful when the XML that you're processing has had whitespace added within it to help with readability. For example, `TVGuide2.xml` includes elements with a lot of whitespace within them:

```
<Program rating="5" flag="favorite">
  <Start>
    2001-07-05T19:30:00
  </Start>
  <Duration>
    PT30M
  </Duration>
  <Series>
    EastEnders
  </Series>
  ...
</Program>
```

When the values of these elements are accessed as strings, they contain line breaks and tabs where really they should only contain spaces. The actual string value of the `<Start>` element is as follows (`
` is a line break and ` ` is a space):

```
&#xA;&#x20;&#x20;&#x20;&#x20;&#x20;&#x20;2001-07-05T19:30:00&#xA;➥
&#x20;&#x20;&#x20;&#x20;
```

This means that when you try to extract the year, month, day, and time from the `<Start>` element, you get a different set of characters from the ones that you're expecting. Trying to transform `TVGuide2.xml` with `TVGuide3.xsl`, for example, gives you `TVGuide3a.html`, which is shown in Figure 5-4.

You can get rid of the spurious whitespace in the string by passing the value of the `<Start>` element as the argument to `normalize-space()` as follows in the template for the `<Start>` element:

```
normalize-space(.)
```

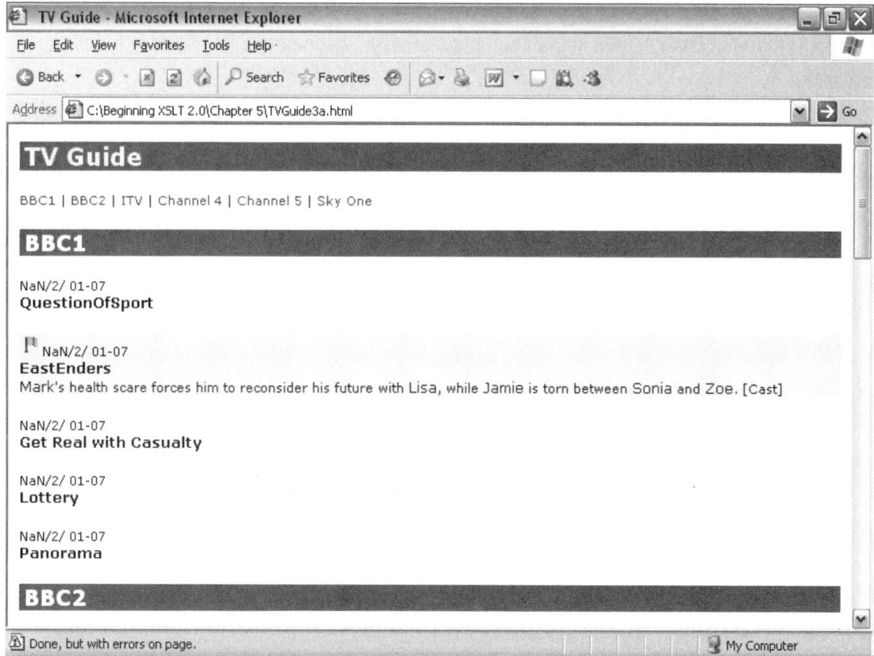

Figure 5-4. *Viewing* TVGuide3a.html *in Internet Explorer*

Note If you don't explicitly pass a node as the argument to the `normalize-space()` function, it assumes that you want the normalized value of the current node. Thus `normalize-space(.)` is equivalent to simply `normalize-space()`.

The result is the following string; all the trailing and leading whitespace is removed. If the string had line breaks or tabs in the middle, these would be substituted with a single space:

```
2001-07-05T19:30:00
```

You can see the effect of this by looking at TVGuide4.xsl, which includes

```
<xsl:template match="Start">
  <span class="date">
    <xsl:value-of
      select="concat(string(number(substring(normalize-space(.), 6, 2))), '/',
                     string(number(substring(normalize-space(.), 9, 2))), '/',
                     substring(normalize-space(.), 1, 4), ' ',
                     substring(normalize-space(.), 12, 5))" />
  </span>
</xsl:template>
```

Note As we'll see in the next chapter, this kind of complicated expression gets a lot easier to manage when you use variables.

When TVGuide2.xml is transformed using TVGuide4.xsl to give TVGuide4.html, you get the dates formatted correctly once more.

Summary You can normalize a string to get rid of superfluous whitespace using the normalize-space() function.

Normalizing Unicode

The normalize-unicode() is somewhat similar to normalize-space(), in that it takes a string and returns a normalized version of that same string. However, rather than whitespace normalization, normalize-unicode() performs Unicode normalization.

Unicode has a certain amount of redundancy in the characters that it defines; some characters are cursive versions of others, or simply have different widths, and sometimes one Unicode character is equivalent to two or three other Unicode characters in combination (for example, the character Å is equivalent to a capital A combined with a "combining ring above," ˚).

Unicode defines four ways of normalizing strings, so that you can guarantee which variants or combinations of characters the string contains, which is useful if you want to search that string. These are known as Unicode Normalization Forms, and they're described in detail in Unicode Standard Annex #15, available at http://www.unicode.org/reports/tr15/.

The normalize-unicode() function takes one or two arguments, the first of which is the string to be normalized and the second of which is the normalization form that you want to use. The possible normalization forms are 'NFC', 'NFD', 'NFKC', 'NFKD', and 'FULLY-NORMALIZED' (this second argument has leading and trailing whitespace removed and is converted to uppercase, so supplying the value ' nfc ' is OK). Full normalization is similar to NFC normalization except that it guarantees that the string can't start or end with a combining character. The NFC normalization form is the default if you don't specify a second argument; if the second argument is an empty string, then the first argument doesn't get changed at all.

Caution There are open issues about what full normalization actually means, and the current Working Draft at time of writing uses the string 'FULLY_NORMALIZED' in one place and 'FULLY-NORMALIZED' in another. You should check the definition of the normalize-unicode() function at http://www.w3.org/TR/xpath-functions/#func-normalize-unicode to see the current status. Also note that Saxon 8.4 doesn't support the normalize-unicode() function.

Caution There's no requirement for implementations to support any normalization form other than 'NFC', and there's no way to tell from within the stylesheet which normalization forms the processor supports. If you tell the processor to use a normalization form that it doesn't support, you will get an error, so you should be careful about using normalization forms other than 'NFC' if you want your stylesheet to be portable.

The `normalize-unicode()` function is useful if you want to search a document for a particular character, but that character is one of the ones that's equivalent to other characters in Unicode and so might have been entered, by the author of the XML document, in a number of different ways. For example, the Ohm sign (`#x2126`) is equivalent to capital omega (Ω, `#x03A9`), and a physicist might have used either character when writing about resistance. If you want to see if the current paragraph contains an Ohm sign, you need to make sure that the paragraph's string value is Unicode normalized, so that every Ohm sign becomes a capital omega, and then search for the capital omega:

```
contains(normalize-unicode(.), '&#x03A9;')
```

Note The Character Model for the World Wide Web 1.0: Normalization Working Draft, available at `http://www.w3.org/TR/charmod-norm/`, states that text *should* be normalized early, such that any text you have to deal with within XSLT should already be Unicode normalized. However, if you're dealing with XML that's been generated from a database or authored by specialist mathematical or Japanese editors, then this might not be the case.

Summary The `normalize-unicode()` function normalizes a string according to one of the Unicode normalization forms.

Translating Strings

The `translate()` function allows you to delete all occurrences of specific characters in a string or replace them with other single characters. The first argument to the `translate()` function is the string that you want to alter; the second is a string containing the characters to search for in the original string; and the third is a string containing the replacement characters in the equivalent order.

To use the `translate()` function to remove all occurrences of a particular character from a string, use an empty string as the third argument. For example, you could remove all line breaks from the string value of the `<Description>` element with

```
translate(Description, '&#xA;', '')
```

Note When this code is included in an XSLT stylesheet, the character reference `
` counts as a single line break character rather than the separate characters `&`, `#`, `x`, `A`, and `;` because the character reference is substituted with a line break character when the XML that contains it is initially parsed. Also note that when the source XML document is initially parsed, the XML parser automatically converts all combinations of line breaks and carriage returns to single line breaks, so this method works no matter what platform your XML document is saved on.

To use the `translate()` function to replace all the instances of a particular character into another, the third argument needs to contain the new character in the equivalent position to the old character in the original string. For example, if you have numbers in a normal US format, such as '1,234.56' and you want them in a European format like '1 234,56', then you need to replace the commas in the first string with spaces and the periods in the first string with commas, as follows:

```
translate('1,234.56', ',.', ' ,')
```

■ **Note** To map whole words onto other words, you need to use the regular expression facilities, which we'll look at in a moment.

In XPath 1.0, one of the most common uses of the translate() function was in turning a word into uppercase or lowercase, for example:

```
translate('sport', 'abcdefghijklmnopqrstuvwxyz',
                   'ABCDEFGHIJKLMNOPQRSTUVWXYZ')
```

Fortunately, XPath 2.0 provides two new functions that allow you to translate a string into uppercase or lowercase really easily: upper-case() and lower-case(). Both functions take a single string and simply translate it into uppercase or lowercase, respectively. For example, to translate the string 'sport' into 'SPORT', you can now do

```
upper-case('sport')
```

■ **Caution** The result of mapping a string to uppercase or lowercase might be a string of a different length than the original. For example, the uppercase version of the single character 'ß' is the two characters 'SS'. Also, note that while you can create a title-case version of a word by capitalizing its first letter, this isn't necessarily the same as the title-case version of the word according to Unicode. See Section 3.13 Default Case Operations in the Unicode specification at http://www.unicode.org/versions/Unicode4.0.0/ch03.pdf.

■ **Summary** The translate() function replaces single characters with other single characters or with nothing at all. The upper-case() and lower-case() functions change the case of strings to upper- or lowercase, respectively.

Case-Insensitive Searches

In the last chapter, we created pages that highlighted programs that had particular words in their descriptions or titles. In TVGuide4.xsl, we search for the word "News" in the <Series>, <Title>, and <Description> children of the <Program> element and mark the program as interesting if they occur with the following template:

```
<xsl:template match="Program">
  <xsl:choose>
    <xsl:when test="@flag = 'favorite' or @flag = 'interesting' or
                    @rating > 6 or contains(Series, 'News') or
                    contains(Title, 'News') or
                    contains(Description, 'news')">
      <div class="interesting">
        <xsl:apply-templates select="." mode="Details" />
      </div>
    </xsl:when>
    <xsl:otherwise>
      <div>
        <xsl:apply-templates select="." mode="Details" />
      </div>
    </xsl:otherwise>
  </xsl:choose>
</xsl:template>
```

The `contains()` function, like all other functions in XPath, is case-sensitive. A program will only be marked as interesting if the word "News" occurs with a capital "N" within the program's `<Series>` or `<Title>`, or if the word "news" occurs completely in lowercase in the program's `<Description>`. However, the person reading the page would probably also be interested in the program if it contained "News" or "NEWS" in its description. To highlight those programs as well, we have to do a case-insensitive search.

You can do a case-insensitive search for a word within a string by making sure both strings use the same case throughout. If we changed the series, title, and description of the program to contain only lowercase characters, then occurrences of "News" and "NEWS" would both become "news" and therefore match the term for which we're looking.

In `TVGuide5.xsl`, in the condition that looks for the keyword, we need to translate the values of the `<Description>`, `<Series>`, and `<Title>` elements into lowercase using the `lower-case()` function:

```
<xsl:template match="Program">
  <xsl:choose>
    <xsl:when
      test="@flag = 'favorite' or @flag = 'interesting' or @rating > 6 or
            contains(lower-case(Series), 'news') or
            contains(lower-case(Title), 'news') or
            contains(lower-case(Description), 'news')">
      <div class="interesting">
        <xsl:apply-templates select="." mode="Details" />
      </div>
    </xsl:when>
    <xsl:otherwise>
      <div>
        <xsl:apply-templates select="." mode="Details" />
      </div>
    </xsl:otherwise>
  </xsl:choose>
</xsl:template>
```

When you transform TVGuide.xml with TVGuide5.xsl to create TVGuide5.html, programs with the string "News" in their <Series> are still highlighted, despite the fact that all the contains() functions were searching for the lowercase "news", as shown in Figure 5-5.

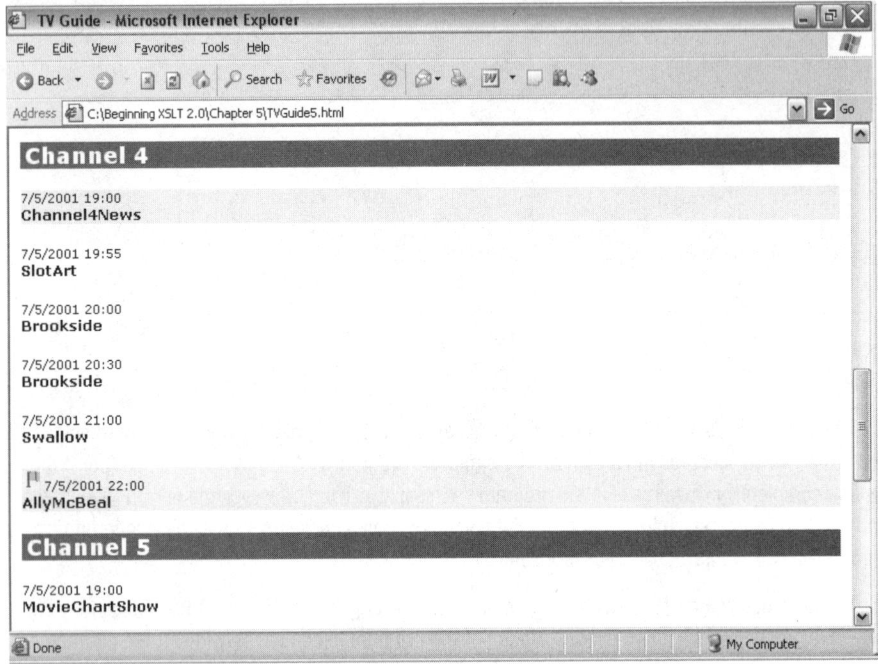

Figure 5-5. *Viewing* TVGuide5.html *in Internet Explorer*

■ **Tip** An alternative way to do a case-insensitive search is to use the matches() function with a third argument that includes the letter i. For example, you could use matches(Series, 'news', 'i') to test whether the series contains the word "news" in any case combination.

Regular Expression Processing

XPath and XSLT 2.0 both introduce new ways of processing strings using regular expressions. Regular expressions are patterns that match strings or substrings, and they're common in programming languages, particularly those that need to support string processing; if you've ever used Perl, Java, JavaScript, or virtually any other programming language, you've probably encountered them already.

We've already come across one function that uses regular expressions: the matches() function, which tests whether a string contains a match for a regular expression. In this section, we'll first look at the regular-expression syntax that XPath and XSLT use. We'll then go on to look at the other functions in XPath that use regular expressions, and finally see the <xsl:analyze-string> instruction from XSLT and how it works.

Regular Expression Syntax

The regular-expression syntax used in XPath and XSLT is similar to that used in other programming languages. It's actually based on the regular-expression syntax defined in XML Schema, which is itself based on the regular-expression syntax used in Perl.

The simplest kind of regular expression is just a literal substring that you want to look for. For example, the regular expression

```
sport
```

would match the substring 'sport' (including if it appeared in 'transport' or 'sporting').

> **SINGLE CHARACTER ESCAPES**
>
> Several characters have a particular meaning within regular expressions. For example, the character . matches any character, not just a period. If you want to include these characters as literal characters in a regular expression, you need to escape them. You can escape characters by prefixing a backslash (\).
>
> For example, the following matches the substring 'sport' followed by any other character:
>
> ```
> sport.
> ```
>
> whereas the following matches the substring 'sport' followed by a period:
>
> ```
> sport\.
> ```
>
> The full set of characters that you need to escape in this way is listed in Appendix A.

Choices

You can indicate a choice between two regular expressions using a vertical bar (|). For example, to match either the substring 'sport' or the substring 'Sport', you can use

```
sport|Sport
```

Character Class Expressions

A regular expression can include a character class expression, which describes a set of characters that might appear in a particular location in the substring. A character class expression is enclosed in square brackets: the content of the square brackets describes the characters that are allowed. The simplest kind of character class expression is just a list of the allowed characters. For example, to match the substrings 'sport' and 'Sport', you could use

```
[sS]port
```

and you could match a date in the format MM/DD/YY with

```
[0123456789][0123456789]/[0123456789][0123456789]/[0123456789][0123456789]
```

When a character class expression contains a sequence of characters that occur next to each other in Unicode, you can use a hyphen to indicate the range of characters. The same regular expression as just shown can be represented as

```
[0-9][0-9]/[0-9][0-9]/[0-9][0-9]
```

You can also have negative character groups, which match any character *except* those listed, by putting a caret (^) before the list of unacceptable characters. For example, you could match the substring 'sport' as long as neither the character before it nor the character after it was a letter with the following:

```
[^a-zA-Z]sport[^a-zA-Z]
```

The final thing you can do with character class expressions is subtract one set of allowed or disallowed characters from another using a hyphen followed by another character class expression. For example:

```
[a-z-[aeiou]]
```

matches any character from "a" to "z" aside from the vowels.

Character Class Escapes

Some character class expressions are so commonly used or so tedious to write that there are shorthands for them, known as character class escapes. The most commonly used shorthands are those shown in Table 5-1.

Table 5-1. *Multicharacter Escapes*

Escape	Description
`.`	Any character
`\s`	Any whitespace character (space, tab, newline, carriage return)
`\S`	Any nonwhitespace character
`\i`	Any character that is legal as the first letter of an XML name
`\I`	Any character that is not legal as the first letter of an XML name
`\c`	Any character that is legal within an XML name
`\C`	Any character that is not legal within an XML name
`\d`	Any digit (from any alphabet supported by Unicode)
`\D`	Any character that isn't a digit
`\w`	Any word character
`\W`	Any nonword character

Note As you can see, the uppercase escapes such as \D are the inverse of the lowercase escapes such as \d.

For example, to match the substring 'sport' as long as neither the character before it nor the character after it is a word character, you could use

```
\Wsport\W
```

There are also character class escapes that describe sets of Unicode characters based on which **Unicode block** or **Unicode category** they belong to. Unicode blocks are very roughly equivalent to alphabets and are matched by a regular expression in the form `\p{Is`*`Block`*`}`. For example, to match any Tibetan character, you can use

```
\p{IsTibetan}
```

Unicode categories indicate the way in which the character is used—for example, whether it's a letter or a number or a punctuation character—using a one or two-letter code. For example, to match any uppercase letter, you can use

```
\p{Lu}
```

Using `\P` rather than `\p` indicates the inverse set of characters. For example, to match any letter that *isn't* Tibetan, you can use

```
\P{IsTibetan}
```

■ **Note** Complete lists of the Unicode blocks and categories that you can refer to are available in Appendix A, and in the XML Schema Datatypes Recommendation at `http://www.w3.org/TR/xmlschema-2/`.

Occurrence Indicators

Sometimes you want to match any number of a particular character. You can indicate that a character (or set of characters, or even string) is repeated using occurrence indicators. The main set of occurrence indicators that are used in regular expressions are the same as those used in DTDs. For example, to match the substring `'sport'`, possibly with a trailing `'s'`, you can use

```
sports?
```

The set of occurrence indicators that you can use in regular expressions in XPath and XSLT are listed in Table 5-2.

Table 5-2. *Occurrence Indicators*

Occurrence Indicator	Description
`?`	Optional
`+`	One or more
`*`	Zero or more
`{N}`	Exactly `N` occurrences
`{N,}`	At least `N` occurrences
`{N,M}`	Between `N` and `M` occurrences

For example, to match a date in US format, we could use

```
[0-9]{2}/[0-9]{2}/[0-9]{2}
```

Normally, an expression will try to match as many characters as possible (known as a **greedy** match). For example, the regular expression

```
\w+
```

will match as many word characters in a row as it can. However, each of the preceding occurrence indicators can be followed by a ?; this indicates that as *few* characters as possible will be matched, as long as the regular expression as a whole continues to match (known as a **reluctant** match). For example, if we have the string `'07/05/01'`, then the regular expression

```
.+/
```

will match the substring `'07/05/'` because this is the longest substring that's comprised of any number of characters followed by a forward slash. On the other hand, the regular expression

```
.+?/
```

will match the substring `'07/'` because this is the shortest substring that's comprised of any number of characters followed by a forward slash.

■ **Note** The difference between greedy and reluctant qualifiers only becomes important if you're processing matched substrings, not if you're just checking if a string matches a regular expression.

Subexpressions and Backreferences

Indicating **subexpressions** within a regular expression is useful in two ways. First, it allows you to say that a particular *string* is repeated a certain number of times. Second, it allows you to refer to those subexpressions later on within the regular expression itself (known as a **back reference**), and when doing replacements or pulling information out of a string.

You can indicate a subexpression using brackets. For example, the following regular expression contains three subexpressions, indicating the month, day, and year in a US format date:

```
([0-9]{2})/([0-9]{2})/([0-9]{2})
```

An occurrence indicator that appears after the close bracket of a subexpression applies to the subexpression as a whole. For example, the following regular expression matches integers, without leading zeros, formatted with grouping separators, such as `'1,234,567'`:

```
[1-9][0-9]{0,2}(,[0-9]{3})*
```

Subexpressions are numbered, starting from 1, based on the position of their open bracket within the regular expression. Back references allow you to refer to the string matched by a subexpression using the syntax `\N` where `N` is the number of the subexpression. For example, the following regular expression matches strings that contain repeated words separated by only a space, such as `"This is so so interesting!"`:

```
\W(\w+) \1\W
```

Beginning and End of Strings

There are just two more special characters to mention: ^ and $. These characters match the start and the end of a string, respectively. For example, the regular expression

```
\Wsport\W
```

matches the substring 'sport' but only if it doesn't appear right at the start or right at the end of a string. If you want to also match the substring 'sport' if it appears right at the start or end of the string, you need to say that either the character before can be a nonword character, or be the start of the string, and similarly for the character at the end:

```
(^|\W)sport(\W|$)
```

Regular Expression Flags

There are four flags, used both by the XPath regular expression functions and by XSLT's regular expression processing, that govern the way a regular expression works.

The i flag indicates that the match is carried out in **case-insensitive mode**. Normally, regular expressions only match a string if the string contains exactly the characters specified in the regular expression. In case-insensitive mode, however, the case of the characters in the string doesn't matter.

For example, the regular expression 'news' will normally only match exactly the substring 'news'. In case-insensitive mode, it will match 'news', 'News', 'NEWS', or the string 'news' in any other case combination.

The s flag indicates that the match is carried out in **dot-all mode**. Normally, a . in a regular expression will match any character aside from a new-line character (#xA). In dot-all mode, . matches any character at all. Dot-all mode is useful if you need to ignore the line breaks within a string.

The m flag indicates that the match is carried out in **multiline mode**. Normally, regular expressions match against the string as a whole: a ^ matches the start of the string and a $ matches the end of the string. In multiline mode, the matches take place against separate lines within the string (each line aside from the last ending in a newline [#xA] character): a ^ matches the start of a line and a $ matches the end of a line.

For example, say you had an XML nursery rhyme such as the following:

```
<poem>
  Three wise men of Gotham
  Went to sea in a bowl;
  If the bowl had been stronger,
  My song would have been longer.
</poem>
```

Normally, the regular expression '^.*$' won't match the value of the <poem> element because the ^ and $ match the very start and end of the string, but the . only matches characters that aren't newlines, and in this case the string contains newline characters. In dot-all mode, the regular expression will match the string as a whole. In multiline mode, the same regular expression will match each line individually.

Finally, the x flag indicates that whitespace characters within the regular expression should be ignored. This is useful when you get really long regular expressions because it allows you to break up and indent the regular expression over several lines without the extra whitespace being interpreted as part of the regular expression. If you use the x flag, then you have to use \s within the regular expression when you do want to match whitespace characters.

■ **Summary** The regular expression syntax used in XPath and XSLT is similar to that used in Perl and other programming languages. XPath and XSLT use flags to indicate whether regular expressions should be applied in case-insensitive mode, in dot-all mode, in multiline mode, and/or with whitespace within the regular expression ignored.

Regular Expression Functions

There are three functions in XPath that use regular expressions: `matches()`, which tests whether a string matches a regular expression; `replace()`, which replaces matching substrings; and `tokenize()`, which splits a string at each matching substring.

In all of these functions, the final argument is optional, and contains a string that contains any flags that govern the regular expression. Also, in all cases it's an error if the regular expression matches an empty string: so the empty regular expression `''` is an error, as is anything that matches an empty string, such as `'\d?'`.

Matching Strings

As we saw in the last chapter, the `matches()` function tests whether the regular expression given in the second argument matches the string given in the first argument, based on the flags specified by the third argument. At a basic level, this works much like the `contains()` function. For example:

```
matches(Description, 'news')
```

will return true if the string value of the `<Description>` element includes the substring `'news'`. But of course you can do much more sophisticated matches using the `matches()` function, such as a case-insensitive match:

```
matches(Description, 'news', 'i')
```

or a match that tests for a number of keywords:

```
matches(Description, 'news|sport|weather', 'i')
```

Replacing Strings

The `replace()` function returns the first argument but with any substring matched by the regular expression given as the second argument replaced by the third argument. The optional fourth argument contains the flags that govern how the regular expression is interpreted.

At its simplest, you can use this to replace one substring with another; for example, to replace the substring `'.html'` at the end of a string with the substring `'.xml'`, you could use

```
replace(., '\.html$', '.xml')
```

When the regular expression held in the second argument is matched against the first argument string, the substrings that match against the subexpressions in the regular expression are stored. When the matching substrings are replaced, you can refer to the substrings that match the subexpressions using the syntax '$N' where N is the number of the subexpression that you want to use.

For example, in the regular expression '([0-9]{2})/([0-9]{2})/([0-9]{2})', which matches a US-formatted date, the first subexpression matches the month, the second matches the day, and the third matches the year. To reformat the date '07/05/01' into the standard CCYY-MM-DD format, you can use

```
replace(., '([0-9]{2})/([0-9]{2})/([0-9]{2})', '20$3-$1-$2')
```

Note If you want to include a $ in the replacement string, you must escape it as \$. If you want to include a \ in the replacement string, you must escape it as \\.

You can also use the replace() function to extract a substring from a string. If the regular expression given as the second argument matches the entire string, then replacing it effectively replaces the entire string with whatever you specify as the replacement. For example, to extract the surname from a string like 'Jeni Tennison', you can use

```
replace(Name, '^(\S+) (\S+)$', '$2')
```

Here, the entire string is replaced by the substring that matches the second subexpression in the string: the characters after the space.

Tokenizing Strings

The tokenize() function returns the sequence of strings created by splitting the first argument string at any occurrence of a string that matches the regular expression given by the second argument. The optional third argument contains the regular expression flags. You can then iterate over this sequence using <xsl:for-each>, for example.

A common use for the tokenize() function is to get the items in a whitespace-separated list:

```
tokenize(., '\s+')
```

Caution When you do this, if the string starts with whitespace, the first item in the sequence will be an empty string. Similarly, if the string ends with whitespace, the last item in the sequence will be an empty string. So you'll probably want to use the normalize-space() function on the first argument most of the time.

Summary The matches() function tests whether a string matches a regular expression. The replace() function replaces the matched substring with a replacement string, which can contain information from the matched substring. The tokenize() function splits up a string into tokens, based on a regular expression that matches delimiters within the string.

Analyzing Strings in XSLT

The regular-expression functionality of XPath can do quite a lot, but it's difficult to use it in combination with XSLT to construct elements. For example, while you can replace all the newline characters in a string with a space using the `replace()` function, you can't replace them with `<br>` elements. Analyzing a string in order to give it structure is generally known as **up-translation**, and XSLT 2.0 provides the `<xsl:analyze-string>` element for precisely this purpose.

The `<xsl:analyze-string>` element has three attributes:

- `select`—Selects the string to be analyzed
- `regex`—Contains the regular expression to match against
- `flags`—Contains any flags to be used during the matching (optional)

It contains two elements: `<xsl:matching-substring>` and `<xsl:non-matching-substring>`. Both of these elements are optional, but if you don't have either of them, then the `<xsl:analyze-string>` element won't produce anything, so there's no point in having neither.

The XSLT processor goes through the string selected by the `select` expression and divides it up into a sequence of substrings, each of which either matches the regular expression specified by the regex or doesn't. It then goes through this sequence of strings one at a time. Any string that matches the regular expression is processed by the content of the `<xsl:matching-substring>` element, while any substring that doesn't match the regular expression is processed by the content of the `<xsl:non-matching-substring>` element.

A simple use for the `<xsl:analyze-string>` element, as mentioned earlier, is to replace any newline character with a `<br>` element. For example, to turn the poem

```
<poem>
  Three wise men of Gotham
  Went to sea in a bowl;
  If the bowl had been stronger,
  My song would have been longer.
</poem>
```

into the following HTML paragraph:

```
<p><br />Three wise men of Gotham<br />Went to sea in a bowl;<br />If the bowl
had been stronger,<br />My song would have been longer.<br /></p>
```

you need to match the newline characters in the content of the `<poem>` element and replace them with `<br>` elements; any nonmatching substrings (the lines of the poem) need to be copied through, whitespace normalized to get rid of leading whitespace, as follows:

```
<xsl:analyze-string select="poem" regex="\n">
  <xsl:matching-substring>
    <br />
  </xsl:matching-substring>
  <xsl:non-matching-substring>
    <xsl:value-of select="normalize-space(.)" />
  </xsl:non-matching-substring>
</xsl:analyze-string>
```

Alternatively, you might want to up-translate the content of the <poem> element into a number of <line> elements. Again, you can match newline characters, but this time you just want to ignore them; the substrings between the newline characters are the lines of the poem, and as long as they have some content, you want to output them within a <line> element, as follows:

```
<xsl:analyze-string select="poem" regex="\n">
  <xsl:non-matching-substring>
    <xsl:if test="normalize-space(.)">
      <line><xsl:value-of select="normalize-space(.)" /></line>
    </xsl:if>
  </xsl:non-matching-substring>
</xsl:analyze-string>
```

This produces (with whitespace added here for readability) the following:

```
<poem>
  <line>Three wise men of Gotham</line>
  <line>Went to sea in a bowl;</line>
  <line>If the bowl had been stronger,</line>
  <line>My song would have been longer.</line>
</poem>
```

As with the replace() function, when a substring matches against the regular expression specified in the regex attribute, the XSLT processor keeps track of the substrings within it that match the subexpressions in the regular expression. The substrings that match the subexpressions are then available using the regex-group() function, which takes an xs:integer as an argument and returns the substring matching that subexpression.

You can use this facility to reformat strings. Say that we want to format the duration of a program as, for example, "1 hour, 30 minutes," or "15 minutes." We can do so as follows:

```
<xsl:analyze-string select="Duration" regex="PT((\d+)H)?((\d+)M)">
  <xsl:matching-substring>
    <xsl:if test="regex-group(1)">
      <xsl:value-of
        select="concat(regex-group(2), ' ',
                       if (regex-group(2) > 1) then 'hours' else 'hour',
                       if (regex-group(3)) then ', ' else '')" />
    </xsl:if>
    <xsl:if test="regex-group(3)">
      <xsl:value-of
        select="concat(regex-group(4), ' ',
                       if (regex-group(4) > 1) then 'minutes' else 'minute')" />
    </xsl:if>
  </xsl:matching-substring>
</xsl:analyze-string>
```

One thing that you have to be careful of when using the <xsl:analyze-string> element is that the regex attribute is interpreted as an attribute value template: anything within curly brackets is interpreted as an XPath expression, whose string value is inserted into the regular expression. This means that the regular expression that you use to analyze the string can be determined dynamically, based on information you get from the input document or elsewhere, but it also means that if you use occurrence indicators such as {2} or {1,4} in your regular expression, you must escape the curly brackets by doubling them up; otherwise they'll be interpreted wrongly.

For example, say you want to analyze a string using the following regular expression, which matches a phone number in the UK (the first subexpression matches an area code; the second the local number):

```
(\d{3,5}) (\d{6,7})
```

To analyze a phone number with this regular expression, the <xsl:analyze-string> element needs to look like the following, in which the curly brackets used in the regular expression are doubled in the regex attribute:

```
<xsl:analyze-string select="@phone" regex="(\d{{3,5}}) (\d{{6,7}})">
  ...
</xsl:analyze-string>
```

■ **Summary** The <xsl:analyze-string> element splits up a string into matching and nonmatching substrings. Matching substrings are processed by the <xsl:matching-substring> element and nonmatching substrings with the <xsl:non-matching-substring> element. Within the <xsl:matching-substring> element, the regex-group() function provides access to the substrings that match subexpressions within the matched substring.

Reformatting Dates Using Regular Expressions

In TVGuide5.xsl, we reformat the date/time strings that indicate when a program starts using string manipulation, as follows:

```
<xsl:template match="Start">
  <span class="date">
    <xsl:value-of
      select="concat(string(number(substring(normalize-space(.), 6, 2))), '/',
                     string(number(substring(normalize-space(.), 9, 2))), '/',
                     substring(normalize-space(.), 1, 4), ' ',
                     substring(normalize-space(.), 12, 5))" />
  </span>
</xsl:template>
```

This is a bit laborious, and it means counting characters in a string to work out how to access the day, month, year, and time components of the date/time, which is easy to get wrong.

An alternative approach, which we'll try in TVGuide6.xsl, would be to pick apart the date/time using a regular expression, and extract the significant parts of the date/time using the regex-group() function.

First, we need to put together a regular expression that will match the date/time strings that we're using. We can use the shorthand \d to indicate digits in the date/time string, and use occurrence indicators such as {2} to indicate that there are exactly two digits. Because we want to capture the year, month, day, and time, we need to put these parts of the regular expression in brackets. The regular expression we'll use is

```
(\d{4})-(\d{2})-(\d{2})T(\d{2}:\d{2}):00
```

The first set of brackets indicates the year, the second the month, the third the day, and the fourth the time.

In the template matching the <Start> element, we need to analyze the value of that <Start> element using this regular expression. Remember that the curly brackets need to be doubled; otherwise their content will be interpreted as XPath expressions, and you'll effectively be analyzing the string against the regular expression "(\d4)-(\d2)-(\d2)T(\d2:\d2):00". The <xsl:analyze-string> element needs to look like this:

```
<xsl:analyze-string select="."
                    regex="(\d{{4}})-(\d{{2}})-(\d{{2}})T(\d{{2}}:\d{{2}}):00">
  ...
</xsl:analyze-string>
```

We don't care about anything that doesn't match the regular expression, so we don't need an <xsl:non-matching-substring> element inside the <xsl:analyze-string> element. However, we do want to do something if we find a matching substring, so we need an <xsl:matching-substring> child element:

```
<xsl:analyze-string select="."
                    regex="(\d{{4}})-(\d{{2}})-(\d{{2}})T(\d{{2}}:\d{{2}}):00">
  <xsl:matching-substring>
    ...
  </xsl:matching-substring>
</xsl:analyze-string>
```

Within the <xsl:matching-substring> element, we want to generate the reformatted date/time. We can do this with an <xsl:value-of> instruction very similar to the one that we're currently using. The only difference is that rather than getting hold of the components of the date/time string using the substring() function, we can now use the regex-group() function: regex-group(1) will give us the year, regex-group(2) the month, and so on. The final <xsl:analyze-string> instruction looks like this:

```
<xsl:analyze-string select="."
                    regex="(\d{{4}})-(\d{{2}})-(\d{{2}})T(\d{{2}}:\d{{2}}):00">
  <xsl:matching-substring>
    <xsl:value-of
      select="concat(string(number(regex-group(2))), '/',
                     string(number(regex-group(3))), '/',
                     regex-group(1), ' ',
                     regex-group(4))" />
  </xsl:matching-substring>
</xsl:analyze-string>
```

If you transform TVGuide.xml using TVGuide6.xsl to create TVGuide6.html, you'll get exactly the same formatted date/time as you got before, as shown in Figure 5-5.

Manipulating Numbers

As you already know, there are three main kinds of numbers in XPath 2.0: doubles, decimals, and integers. You can convert a value into a number using a constructor function, or a `cast` expression, or use the `number()` function. We've also seen how you can create numeric values of these different types using literals.

XPath has a number of operators that you can use to perform basic mathematics, most of which work on any type of numeric values. The result of applying these operators is the same as the most general of the operands; for example, if you try to add an `xs:integer` to an `xs:double`, you will get an `xs:double`. If an operand to one of these operators is untyped (is the value of an unvalidated node), its value will usually get converted to an `xs:double`.

■ **Caution** Since most untyped operands are usually cast to `xs:double`, and when one of the operands is an `xs:double`, the result is an `xs:double`; operations that involve untyped nodes will usually return an `xs:double`, even if the other operand is an `xs:integer`. This means that while the expression `"@value to 10"` will work, because the `value` attribute will be cast to an `xs:integer` as expected, the expression `"(@value + 1) to 10"` will give a type error, because the operands to `to` must be `xs:integer` values.

The set of arithmetic operators is shown in Table 5-3.

Table 5-3. *Arithmetic Operators*

Name	Operator	Example	Explanation
Plus	+	`2 + 2`	Adds two numbers together
Minus	-	`3 - 2`	Subtracts one number from another
Multiply by	*	`2 * 2`	Multiplies two numbers together
Divide by	`div`	`3 div 2`	Divides a number by another using floating point division
Integer divide by	`idiv`	`3 idiv 2`	Divides an integer by another integer, discarding any remainder
Mod	`mod`	`3 mod 2`	Gives the remainder after integer division
Unary plus	+	`+2`	Returns the number
Unary minus	-	`-2`	Negates a number

Other than that, functions for numerical manipulation are fairly thin on the ground. XPath offers three functions for rounding numbers in various ways:

- `floor()`—Rounds the argument number down to the nearest integer.
- `ceiling()`—Rounds the argument number up to the nearest integer.
- `round()`—Rounds the argument number to the nearest integer, or rounds up if it is half way between two integers.
- `round-half-to-even()`—Rounds the first argument to the number of decimal places indicated by the second argument; a negative second argument rounds to a whole number of tens, hundreds, and so on; if rounding could go either way, rounds towards an even digit.

The round-half-to-even() function deserves a few examples:

```
round-half-to-even(12.345) = 12
round-half-to-even(12.345, 1) = 12.3
round-half-to-even(12.345, 2) = 12.34
round-half-to-even(12.355, 2) = 12.36
round-half-to-even(12.345, -1) = 10
```

Summary XPath supports the numeric operators +, -, *, div, idiv, mod, and unary + and -. You can round numbers with the functions floor(), ceiling(), round(), and round-half-to-even().

Formatting Numbers

While XSLT isn't spectacularly easy to use for doing sophisticated math, it has a lot more support for formatting numbers, provided by the format-number() function. The format-number() function usually takes two arguments: the first argument is the number that you want to format, and the second is a pattern that determines the format for the number. For example:

```
format-number(12345.6789, '#,##0.00')
```

will give the string '12,345.68'. Similarly, you can use format-number() to add leading zeros. For example:

```
format-number(5, '00')
```

will give the string '05'.

Format Patterns

The symbols shown in Table 5-4 are significant in the pattern string that's passed as the second argument to format-number().

Table 5-4. *Significant Characters in Format Patterns*

Name	Character	Description
Digit	#	Placeholder for optional digits in the formatted number—indicates the maximum number of fraction digits to be shown
Zero digit	0	Placeholder for required digits in the formatted number—indicates the minimum number of integer and fraction digits to be shown
Decimal separator	.	Separates the integer and fraction digit characters
Grouping separator	,	Indicates the number of digits in a group
Pattern separator	;	Separates the pattern for positive numbers from that for negative numbers
Minus sign	-	Shows the location of the minus sign in the negative pattern
Percent	%	Indicates that the number should be multiplied by 100 and shows the location of the percent sign
Per-mille	‰	Indicates that the number should be multiplied by 1000 and shows the location of the per-mille sign

---

■ **Note** You might have to use the character reference for the per-mille sign, if your editor or character encoding doesn't support it. The character reference you need is `‰`.

If the number that you pass as the first argument to `format-number()` is negative, the XSLT processor will use the negative pattern if you supply one, or prefix a minus sign to the positive pattern if you don't. If the number is not a number, then the `format-number()` function will return the string `'NaN'`. If the number is infinity, then `format-number()` will return the string `'Infinity'`.

■ **Summary** The `format-number()` function formats the number passed as its first argument according to the format pattern passed as its second argument.

Localized Numbers

As you can see from looking at the characters that are listed as being significant in the format pattern, the `format-number()` function uses a US numbering scheme by default, with the decimal point indicated by `.` and groups of digits separated by `,`. In other regions, people use different numerical formats. The French, for example, use a comma as the decimal point and a space to separate groups of numbers. However, the XSLT processor does not take the locale into account when it formats numbers. If you tried to format numbers in the French style, with

```
format-number(12345.6789, '# ##0,00')
```

then you would not get the string `'12 345,67'` even if you ran the stylesheet on a machine set up with a French locale.

■ **Caution** What you *do* get depends on the processor that you use. MSXML raises an error, saying "The '0' format symbol may not follow the '#' format symbol in this section of a format pattern." Saxon 6.5.3 and Xalan create the string `'1,23,45'`. These differences probably arise because the way that `format-number()` works is not particularly well specified in the XSLT 1.0 Recommendation. The XSLT 2.0 Recommendation is a lot more specific about how processors should behave, and Saxon 8.4 raises an error, saying that passive characters must not appear before active characters within the format string.

To format a number with a different locale, you need to tell the XSLT processor to use a different set of significant characters when interpreting the formatting pattern that you pass as the second argument to `format-number()`. You can do this with a decimal format. Decimal formats specify the characters that are significant in a formatting pattern and the special strings that are used when the number is `NaN` or `INF`.

You declare a decimal format with the `<xsl:decimal-format>` element, which lives at the top level of the stylesheet. You can name the decimal format using the `name` attribute. If you name a decimal format, then you can tell the XSLT processor to use that decimal format when formatting a specific number by passing that name as a third argument to the `format-number()` function. For example, if you set up a decimal format named `French`, then you could format a number in the French style with

```
format-number(12345.6789, '# ##0,00', 'French')
```

If you don't specify a name for a decimal format in the `<xsl:decimal-format>` element, then that decimal format is the **default decimal format**. This is useful when you format a lot of numbers in exactly the same way, whereas named decimal formats are handy if you want to format different numbers in different ways.

The special characters and strings that you use in particular decimal formats are set using attributes on the `<xsl:decimal-format>` element. The full details of the characters and strings that you can set are given in Appendix B at the back of this book, but, for example, you could set up a French decimal format with the following:

```
<xsl:decimal-format name="French"
                    decimal-separator=","
                    grouping-separator=" "
                    infinity="Infinit&#233;" />
```

Summary If you want to format numbers in non-US styles, you have to declare your own decimal formats that specify the characters used for the decimal point, for grouping separators, and so on.

Manipulating Dates, Times, and Durations

Dates, times, and durations are new and welcome additions to XPath 2.0, giving us the ability to insert the date and time of the transformation into our documents, and allowing us to perform date/time arithmetic and timezone-aware sorting.

There are five main date, time, and duration types in XPath 2.0:

- `xs:dateTime`—A date and time in the format `CCYY-MM-DDThh:mm:ss`
- `xs:date`—A date in the format `CCYY-MM-DD`
- `xs:time`—A time in the format `hh:mm:ss`
- `xdt:yearMonthDuration`—A duration of years and months in the format `P`*`N`*`Y`*`N`*`M`
- `xdt:dayTimeDuration`—A duration of days, hours, minutes, and seconds in the format `P`*`N`*`DT`*`N`*`H`*`N`*`M`*`N`*`S`

Note There are a bunch of other date/time types that are specifically related to the Gregorian calendar: `xs:gYear`, `xs:gYearMonth`, `xs:gMonth`, `xs:gMonthDay`, and `xs:gDay`. There's no real support for these types, aside from testing whether two values are equal and casting them to an `xs:date` or `xs:dateTime`. Similarly, the XML Schema duration datatype, `xs:duration`, doesn't have any real support in XPath 2.0: if you have values of that type, you should cast them to an `xdt:yearMonthDuration` and an `xdt:dayTimeDuration` and combine the results as necessary.

Date/time values may have a timezone associated with them, indicated by either a `Z` (which indicates UTC) or an offset from UTC in the format `±hh:mm`. We'll look at how timezones work in detail later in this section.

You can create values of any of these types using constructor functions as usual, or take values of these types from the XML that you're processing (for example, our TV guide contains `xs:date` values, `xs:dateTime` values, and `xdt:dayTimeDuration` values). You can also work out when the transformation is running using the following functions:

- `current-dateTime()`—Returns the `xs:dateTime` when the transformation started
- `current-date()`—Returns the `xs:date` when the transformation started
- `current-time()`—Returns the `xs:time` when the transformation started

■ **Caution** All these functions return the same date/time throughout a transformation. You can use them to add a date/time stamp to your output document, but you can't use them to time how long a particular part of your transformation takes.

■ **Summary** You can get the current date/time when the transformation starts using the `current-date()`, `current-time()`, and `current-dateTime()` functions.

The comparison operators that we looked at in the last chapter will work with date/time and duration values. For example, to test whether the TV guide covers the current day, you can test the values of the `start` and `end` attributes of the current `<TVGuide>` element against the result of calling the `current-date()` function:

```
current-date() >= @start and @end >= current-date()
```

Similarly, you could test whether the current `<Program>` element's `<Duration>` was less than 30 minutes using

```
xdt:dayTimeDuration('PT30M') > Duration
```

■ **Note** When you compare the value of a node with a date/time value, the node's value automatically gets cast to the same type as the date/time value. But if you want to compare the values of two nodes that hold date/time values, you must cast them to the appropriate type first. For example `xs:date(@end) >= xs:date(@start)` to compare the values of the `start` and `end` attributes as dates.

Many of the arithmetic operators that we looked at in the last section can also be used with date/times and durations. You can add or subtract two durations (of the same type) to get another duration, or add or subtract a duration from a date/time. For example, to get tomorrow's date, you can add the `xdt:dayTimeDuration` `P1D` to today's date:

```
current-date() + xdt:dayTimeDuration('P1D')
```

You can also subtract two date/times from each other in order to get an `xdt:dayTimeDuration`. For example:

```
xs:time('17:00:00Z') - xs:time('09:00:00Z')
```

returns the `xdt:dayTimeDuration` `PT8H`.

■ **Note** Although you can add `xdt:yearMonthDuration`s to `xs:date`s and `xs:dateTime`s, you can't subtract two `xs:date`s or two `xs:dateTime`s to get an `xdt:yearMonthDuration`.

You can multiply or divide a duration by an `xs:decimal` to get another duration of the same type. For example, to find the date halfway between the `start` and `end` attributes of the current `<TVGuide>` element, you can use

```
xs:date(@start) + ((xs:date(@end) - xs:date(@start)) div 2)
```

■ **Note** The values of the `start` and `end` attributes must be explicitly cast to dates in the preceding, since otherwise they will be interpreted as numbers and you will get the result `NaN`.

Finally, you can divide a duration by another duration (of the same type), for example to tell how many weeks there are in an `xdt:dayTimeDuration` or how many years in an `xdt:yearMonthDuration`. To tell how many 5-minute intervals there are in the duration of a program, we can use

```
xdt:dayTimeDuration(Duration) div xdt:dayTimeDuration('PT5M')
```

■ **Note** The value of the `<Duration>` attribute must be explicitly cast to an `xdt:dayTimeDuration` in the preceding or you will get an error. When you refer to an untyped node in an arithmetic expression, the XSLT processor will assume that it contains a numeric value, and since there's no way to divide a number by a duration, the processor will give you an error.

■ **Summary** Date/time and duration types can be compared using the normal comparison operators, and you can carry out most date/time arithmetic using the normal arithmetic operators.

Calculating End Times

To gain some experience with date/time arithmetic, we'll try to use XSLT to calculate the end times of the programs, based on their start time and duration, in TVGuide7.xsl.

The duration of a program is held in the <Duration> child of the <Program> element, in the format of an xdt:dayTimeDuration. We want to use the duration to work out the end time for the program based on the current <Start> element child of the <Program> element. We can do this with the following expression:

```
xs:dateTime(.) + xdt:dayTimeDuration(../Duration)
```

The constructor functions in the preceding expression are in different namespaces from usual: the xs:dateTime() constructor function is in the XML Schema namespace of http://www.w3.org/2001/XMLSchema, while the xdt:dayTimeDuration() constructor function is in the namespace http://www.w3.org/2005/04/xpath-datatypes. We need to declare these two namespaces in our stylesheet in order to use these functions; otherwise the processor will object that it doesn't understand which functions we're referring to. So the <xsl:stylesheet> element needs to look like this:

```
<xsl:stylesheet version="2.0"
                xmlns:xsl="http://www.w3.org/1999/XSL/Transform"
                xmlns:xs="http://www.w3.org/2001/XMLSchema"
                xmlns:xdt="http://www.w3.org/2005/04/xpath-datatypes">
  ...
</xsl:stylesheet>
```

If we convert the end time to a string, we can get just the hours and minutes using the substring() function:

```
substring(string(xs:dateTime(.) + xdt:dayTimeDuration(../Duration)), 12, 5)
```

We can add this information to the details that we give about the timing of the program as follows:

```
<xsl:template match="Start">
  <span class="date">
    <xsl:analyze-string select="."
      regex="(\d{{4}})-(\d{{2}})-(\d{{2}})T(\d{{2}}:\d{{2}}):00">
      <xsl:matching-substring>
        <xsl:value-of
          select="concat(string(number(regex-group(2))), '/',
                         string(number(regex-group(3))), '/',
                         regex-group(1), ' ',
                         regex-group(4))" />
      </xsl:matching-substring>
    </xsl:analyze-string>
    <xsl:value-of
      select="concat(' - ',
                     substring(string(xs:dateTime(.) +
                                      xdt:dayTimeDuration(../Duration)),
                               12, 5))" />
  </span>
</xsl:template>
```

The result of transforming TVGuide.xml with TVGuide7.xsl is TVGuide7.html, which is shown in Figure 5-6.

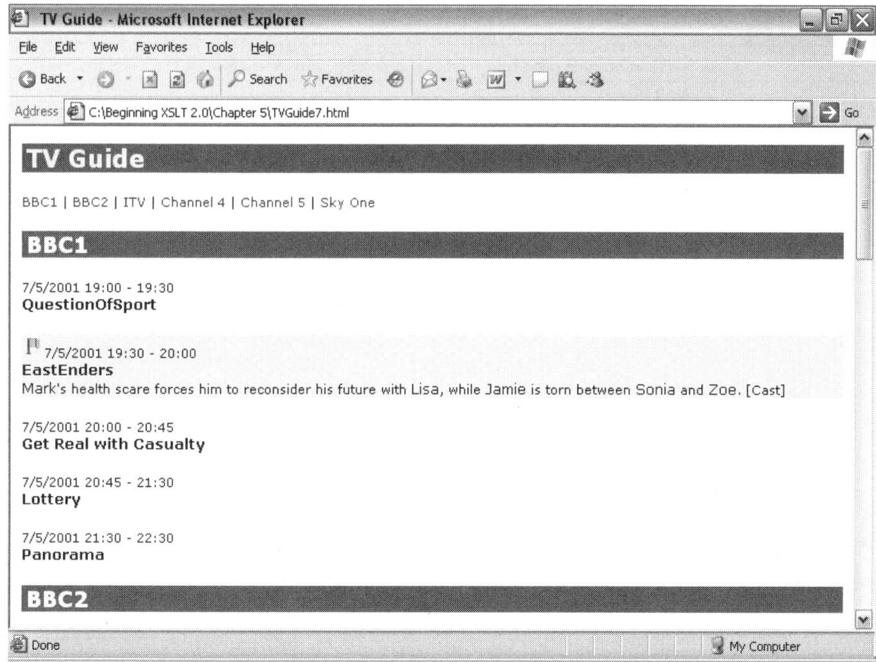

Figure 5-6. *Viewing* `TVGuide7.html` *in Internet Explorer*

■ **Note** For most programs—all those aside from the last showing on a particular channel—you could work out the program's end time by looking at the next program's start time, and that might be slightly quicker (and easier to understand) than going through the calculations. We'll see how to use the start time of the next program as the end time of this program in the next chapter.

Extracting Components

Date/time and duration values are actually made up of separate components: an `xs:date`, for example, has a year, month, and day, while an `xdt:dayTimeDuration` has a number of days, hours, minutes, and seconds. There are a number of functions that extract components from date/time and duration types, each of them named in the form

`component``-from-`*`datatype`*`()`

For example, to get the year component from an `xs:date`, you would use the function `year-from-date()`. To make life simpler, extracting components from `xdt:yearMonthDuration` and `xdt:dayTimeDuration` datatypes uses the syntax *`component`*`-from-duration()`, for example, `seconds-from-duration()`.

The components, and the datatypes that you can extract them from, are summarized in Table 5-5. A cross indicates that the component doesn't apply to that datatype, while a tick indicates that it does.

Table 5-5. *Date/Time and Duration Components*

Component	Type	xs:dateTime	xs:date	xs:time	xdt:yearMonthDuration	xdt:dayTimeDuration
years	xs:integer	✗	✗	✗	✔	✗
months	xs:integer	✗	✗	✗	✔	✗
days	xs:integer	✗	✗	✗	✗	✔
hours	xs:integer	✔	✗	✔	✗	✔
minutes	xs:integer	✔	✗	✔	✗	✔
seconds	xs:decimal	✔	✗	✔	✗	✔
year	xs:integer	✔	✔	✗	✗	✗
month	xs:integer	✔	✔	✗	✗	✗
day	xs:integer	✔	✔	✗	✗	✗
timezone	xdt:dayTimeDuration	✔	✔	✔	✗	✗

When you extract a component from one of the duration types, you get the value of that component from a **canonical lexical representation** of the duration. The canonical lexical representation of an `xdt:yearMonthDuration` represents the same amount of time, but limits the number of months in the representation to a maximum of 11. For example, the canonical representation of the `xdt:yearMonthDuration` `P30M` is `P2Y6M`, so if you did

```
months-from-duration(xdt:yearMonthDuration('P30M'))
```

you would get the integer `6`.

Similarly, the canonical representation of an `xdt:dayTimeDuration` limits the number of seconds and minutes to less than 60 and the number of hours to less than 24. If you did

```
hours-from-duration(xdt:dayTimeDuration('PT14H125M'))
```

you would get the integer `16`.

■ **Note** When you cast a duration type to a string, you also get its canonical lexical representation. For example `xs:string(xdt:yearMonthDuration('P30M'))` returns `'P2Y6M'`.

■ **Summary** You can extract components from date/time and duration values using functions whose names are in the form *`component-from-datatype`*`()`.

Adjusting Timezones

One of the trickier aspects of dealing with dates and times is how to handle timezones.

Firstly, some date/time values have timezones and some do not; those that do not are said to indicate **local time**. For example, in a bus timetable, you might want to say that the bus leaves at 09:30:00. It doesn't matter if the timezone changes (because daylight saving time comes into effect or stops being in effect), the time the bus leaves stays the same.

Other date/time values have timezones because they indicate precise moments in time. If you've ever had to schedule a teleconference involving people living in multiple timezones, you'll know that it's very important to state the timezone along with the time of the meeting or you'll never get people turning up on time. For example, you might schedule the meeting for 2005-03-17T18:00:00Z, which means that for people in the Eastern Standard Time timezone (-05:00), it will be held at 1 p.m.

So is the xs:dateTime 2005-03-17T18:00:00Z the same as the xs:dateTime 2005-03-17T13:00:00-05:00? Well, yes and no. When you're comparing two times, you want to take into account their timezones. In XPath 2.0, when you compare xs:dateTime values, you actually compare their normalized values, so

```
xs:dateTime('2005-03-17T18:00:00Z') = xs:dateTime('2005-03-17T13:00:00-05:00')
```

returns true. On the other hand, when you're serializing a date/time as a string, you want to be able to recover the original timezone that was used in that date/time. In XPath 2.0, when you cast a date/time to a string, you get back the original timezone that you used, so

```
xs:string(xs:dateTime('2005-03-17T13:00:00-05:00'))
```

returns the string '2005-03-17T13:00:00-05:00' rather than '2005-03-17T18:00:00Z'.

What about date/time values that use local time—those that don't specify a timezone? Well, for the purposes of comparison, these date/time values are assumed to belong to the **implicit timezone**. The implicit timezone is supplied by the XSLT processor that you use; usually it will be the same as the timezone used by the machine that the transformation is run on, but different XSLT processors might allow you to supply an implicit timezone through an API or command-line option.

So, if I'm running a transformation during the winter, here in the UK, the implicit timezone will be UTC, and

```
xs:dateTime('2005-03-17T18:00:00') = xs:dateTime('2005-03-17T18:00:00Z')
```

will be true because the local date/time 2005-03-17T18:00:00 is assumed to be in the UTC timezone. On the other hand, if I run the same transformation in the summer, the implicit timezone will be British Summer Time (+01:00), and the same comparison will be false.

Comparison operators actually compare the **starting instants** of date/time values other than xs:dateTime. The starting instant of a date/time value is constructed by filling in any missing components from the date/time value using the equivalent components from a reference xs:dateTime value, such as 1976-12-31T00:00:00. For example, the starting instant for the xs:time 13:00:00-05:00 is the xs:dateTime 1976-12-31T13:00:00-05:00 and the starting instant of 2001-07-05 is the xs:dateTime 2001-07-05T00:00:00.

This can have some peculiar side-effects. When a meeting is scheduled for 18:00:00Z, my Japanese colleagues have to get up in the middle of the night: 03:00:00+09:00. The xs:dateTime 2005-03-17T18:00:00Z and the xs:dateTime 2005-03-18T03:00:00+09:00 are equal, but if I do

```
xs:time('18:00:00Z') = xs:time('03:00:00+09:00')
```

the result is false. The starting instant for the xs:time 18:00:00Z is 1976-12-31T18:00:00Z, but the starting instant for the xs:time 03:00:00+09:00 is 1976-12-31T03:00:00+09:00, which is equivalent to 1976-12-30T18:00:00Z 6 p.m. on the previous day.

If you need to compare two xs:dates or xs:times in different timezones, you'll sometimes want to adjust the xs:dates or xs:times to use the same timezone before doing the comparison. You can add and remove timezones, and adjust date/time values to different timezones, using the three related functions:

- adjust-dateTime-to-timezone()—Adjusts xs:dateTime values
- adjust-date-to-timezone()—Adjusts xs:date values
- adjust-time-to-timezone()—Adjusts xs:time values

Each of these functions takes one or two arguments. The first is the date/time value to be adjusted and the second, optional, argument is a new timezone to use, represented as an xdt:dayTimeDuration. If you don't give a second argument, then it defaults to the implicit timezone. The result is a date/time value that uses the timezone specified by the second argument, or, if the second argument is an empty sequence, a date/time value in local time.

■ Note The xdt:dayTimeDuration supplying the timezone must be between -PT14H and PT14H.

Adjusting the existing timezone on a date/time value doesn't change the instant that the date/time represents, it just changes the timezone that's used when the date/time is serialized as a string or used when calculating its starting instant for the purpose of comparison. For example, if we adjust the xs:dateTime 2005-03-17T18:00:00Z to Eastern Standard Time (-05:00):

```
xs:string(adjust-dateTime-to-timezone(xs:dateTime('2005-03-17T18:00:00Z'),
                                      xdt:dayTimeDuration('-PT5H')))
```

we get the string '2005-03-17T13:00:00-05:00'. If we adjust the xs:time 03:00:00+09:00 to UTC:

```
adjust-time-to-timezone(xs:time('03:00:00+09:00'),
                        xdt:dayTimeDuration('PT0H'))
```

we get the xs:time 18:00:00Z.

On the other hand, adding or removing a timezone from a date/time value can change the instant that the date/time represents. For example, if I run the transformation in British Summer Time, then the local time 18:00:00 is equal to 18:00:00+01:00, which is the same as 19:00:00Z. If I adjust the xs:dateTime 2005-03-17T18:00:00 to Eastern Standard Time:

```
adjust-dateTime-to-timezone(xs:dateTime('2005-03-17T18:00:00'),
                            xdt:dayTimeDuration('-PT5H'))
```

then the result is 2005-03-17T18:00:00-05:00, which is the same as 2005-03-17T23:00:00Z.

■ Summary Date/times are normalized for the purposes of comparison, with local date/times being assumed to be in the implicit timezone, but the original timezone is retained for the purposes of formatting. You can change the timezone for a date/time using the adjust-dateTime-to-timezone(), adjust-date-to-timezone(), and adjust-time-to-timezone() functions.

Formatting Dates and Times

Even more so than with numbers, the default string representation of a date/time value isn't particularly pretty or readable. So, as with numbers, XSLT 2.0 supplies formatting functions that allow you to format date/time values. These functions are

- `format-dateTime()`—For formatting `xs:dateTime` values
- `format-date()`—For formatting `xs:date` values
- `format-time()`—For formatting `xs:time` values

Like the `format-number()` function, each of these functions usually takes two arguments: the first being the date/time value to be formatted and the second being a format pattern. For example:

```
format-date(xs:date('2001-07-05'), '[M]/[D]/[Y]')
```

returns the string `'7/5/2001'`.

Format Patterns

Unsurprisingly, the format patterns that are used by the `format-dateTime()`, `format-date()`, and `format-time()` functions are a lot more complicated than those used by the `format-number()` function.

Within the pattern string, anything inside square brackets ([]) acts as a placeholder for some information from the date/time value, and anything outside the square brackets, including whitespace, is treated as literal text to be inserted into the string.

Note If you want to insert a literal square bracket in the date/time format you're using, you need to double it within the format pattern.

The contents of the square brackets indicate exactly what should be inserted. The first letter specifies which component from the date/time value is required. This can be followed by one or two presentation modifiers, which determine how the component is presented. Finally, you can specify a minimum and maximum width for the component, which enables you to give abbreviated month or day names, or pad numbers with leading zeros.

Component Specifiers

Table 5-6 lists the letters that you use to indicate the component, and specifies the default presentation modifier used for the component.

Table 5-6. *Component Specifiers*

Specifier	Component	Default Presentation
Y	Year	1
M	Month of year	1
D	Day of month	1
d	Day of year	1
F	Day of week	n
W	Week of year	1
w	Week of month	1
H	Hour of day (24 hours)	1
h	Hour of half-day (12 hours)	1
P	Half-day (a.m./p.m.)	n
m	Minute of hour	01
s	Second of minute	01
f	Fractional seconds	1
Z	Timezone	1
z	Timezone as hours offset using GMT, for example 'GMT+1'	1
C	Calendar	n
E	Era	n

For example, to format the `<Start>` child of the current `<Program>` element as "5/7/2001 7p.m.," you could use

```
format-dateTime(Start, '[M]/[D]/[Y] [h][P]')
```

Presentation Modifiers

Table 5-7 lists the first set of presentation modifiers that can be applied to a component.

Table 5-7. *Primary Presentation Modifiers*

Modifier	Meaning
1	Decimal number
I	Uppercase Roman numeral
i	Lowercase Roman numeral
W	Uppercase number in words
w	Lowercase number in words
Ww	Title-case number in words
N	Uppercase name
n	Lowercase name
Nn	Title-case name

In addition to these nine presentation modifiers, you can use any Unicode character that has a decimal digit value of 1 to indicate decimal numbering starting from that Unicode character. For example, to format the date using Thai numbers, use the presentation modifier `๑`.

■Note Processors may also recognize other characters as being the start of a numbering scheme, but you should check the documentation of the processor that you're using to see which other numbering schemes it supports, if any.

Dates are often formatted using ordinal numbers; for example, "5th July 2001." If you use a decimal numbering scheme, you can specify that you want ordinal numbers using a secondary presentation modifier `o`. For example, to get "5th July 2001," you would use

```
format-date(xs:date('2001-07-05'), '[D1o] [MNn] [Y]')
```

In some languages, the same starting letter is used for two different numbering schemes. Normally, the `a` and `A` modifiers use the standard alphabetic numbering scheme, but you can add a secondary modifier, `t`, to indicate that you want to use the traditional numbering scheme that starts with that character. For example, the component `'[Dаt]'` specifies the day of month presented using Old Slavic numbering.

Width Modifiers

Whether or not you specify any presentation modifiers, you can specify how many characters should be used to represent the component using a width modifier, which comes after a comma. The simplest form of width modifier is simply a specification of the minimum width for the component. If the specified format for the component isn't long enough to satisfy this minimum width, it gets padded with either leading zeros (if it's a number) or with leading spaces. For example:

```
format-dateTime(Start, '[M,2]/[D,2]/[Y] [h,2]:[m,2][P]')
```

specifies that the month, day, hours, and minutes components must all be specified with at least two digits, which means you'd end up with a format like "07/05/2001 07:00p.m."

You can also specify a maximum number of characters, following the hyphen. For example:

```
format-date(@start, '[D] [MNn,3-4] [Y,2-2]')
```

specifies that the month name should be between three and four characters long, and the year should be exactly two characters long, so you might get a format like "5 July 01" or "15 Aug 01."

Both the minimum and maximum widths can be specified as *, which means that the processor should use whatever minimum or maximum is appropriate.

If you're formatting a component as a number, you can alternatively use leading zeros to indicate the minimum and maximum width of the number. The following examples are equivalent to the preceding ones:

```
format-dateTime(Start, '[M01]/[D01]/[Y] [h01]:[m01][P]')
format-date(@start, '[D] [MNn,3-4] [Y01]')
```

Summary You can format a date/time with the `format-dateTime()`, `format-date()`, or `format-time()` functions. The format pattern describes the components in the formatted string, and how they should be presented.

Reformatting Dates with format-dateTime()

We've gone through several methods of formatting date/times in this chapter. We started by extracting the components from a date/time string using the `substring()` function, then moved on to using the `<xsl:analyze-string>` instruction to pull out the components based on a regular expression. Now, finally, we can move on to the easiest method: using the `format-dateTime()` function.

The current code in `TVGuide7.xsl` for formatting the date/time given as the start time of a program is as follows:

```
<xsl:template match="Start">
  <span class="date">
    <xsl:analyze-string select="."
      regex="(\d{{4}})-(\d{{2}})-(\d{{2}})T(\d{{2}}:\d{{2}}):00">
      <xsl:matching-substring>
        <xsl:value-of
          select="concat(string(number(regex-group(2))), '/',
                         string(number(regex-group(3))), '/',
                         regex-group(1), ' ',
                         regex-group(4))" />
      </xsl:matching-substring>
    </xsl:analyze-string>
    <xsl:value-of
      select="concat(' - ',
                     substring(string(xs:dateTime(.) +
                                      xdt:dayTimeDuration(../Duration)),
                               12, 5))" />
  </span>
</xsl:template>
```

The `<xsl:analyze-string>` instruction in the preceding is the code that's reformatting the date/time string, by extracting the components using a regular expression. In `TVGuide8.xsl`, we want to use the `format-dateTime()` function; the new format for the start date/time is represented as a format pattern like this:

```
[M]/[D]/[Y] [H01]:[m]
```

and for the end time a format pattern like this:

```
[H01]:[m]
```

So to format the start time, we just need to call the `format-dateTime()` function, with the first argument being the `xs:dateTime` generated from the value of the `<Start>` element, and the second argument being the first of the preceding format strings. To format the end time, we calculate it as normal and then format it with `format-dateTime()` and the second format string:

```
<xsl:template match="Start">
  <span class="date">
    <xsl:value-of
      select="concat(format-dateTime(xs:dateTime(.),
                                      '[M]/[D]/[Y] [H01]:[m]'), ' - ',
                     format-dateTime(xs:dateTime(.) +
                                      xdt:dayTimeDuration(../Duration),
                                      '[H01]:[m]'))" />
  </span>
</xsl:template>
```

The result of transforming TVGuide.xml with TVGuide8.xsl is TVGuide8.html, which looks the same as TVGuide7.html, shown in Figure 5-6.

Localizing Date and Time Formats

There are many more considerations when localizing date and time formats than arise when localizing numbers. The format of a date/time can vary both in terms of the language that's used and in terms of the calendar in which the date/time is represented. We've seen a bit about how to use different digits for the numbering of components in the formatting date/time, but not how to change the language that's used for the names of months and days, or the calendar that's used for the formatting.

As well as the date/time to be formatted and the pattern that defines how it should be formatted, the format-dateTime(), format-date(), and format-time() functions can take three additional arguments: the language, calendar and country to be used. You must specify all three of these arguments if you want to specify any of them, but you can use the empty sequence as an argument to indicate that an implementation-defined default should be used for that particular argument.

The language argument gives the language code for the language that's used for the names of months and days of the week and for ordinal numbering, and is used by the processor to decide how to number hours (from 0 to 23 or from 1 to 24, for example), and how to count days within a week or weeks within a year. Language codes are usually two-letter languages, such as en for English and fr for French, but you can also specify subcategories, such as en-GB for British English or fr-CA for Canadian French. For example, if you format a date as follows:

```
format-date(xs:date('2001-07-05'), '[Fn] [D1o] [Mn], [Y]', 'fr', (), ())
```

then you should get "jeudi 5 juillet, 2001" (in France, ordinals are only applied on the 1st of the month).

The calendar argument specifies the calendar that should be used when formatting the date/time. There are a vast number of calendars in use currently and in the past. Examples are Common Era (CE), the Japanese calendar (JE), and Anno Mundi (the Jewish calendar, AM).

The country argument specifies the country in which the date occurred. This can be important for certain calendars and certain dates where different countries start or started the New Year on different dates.

Support for languages, calendars, and countries is completely dependent on the implementation, so you should check your processor's documentation to see what it supports.

■ **Summary** Five-argument versions of the `format-dateTime()`, `format-date()`, and `format-time()` functions can be used to specify a language, calendar, and/or a country that should be used when formatting the date/time.

Manipulating Qualified Names

Qualified names (values typed as `xs:QName`) are pairs of namespace URIs and local names. The idea of a qualified name was developed at the same time as namespaces, which you learned about in Chapter 2; the names of elements and attributes are qualified names: each element and attribute is associated with a namespace, and has its own, local, name.

■ **Note** As we'll see in Chapter 7, you can get the name of an element or attribute as a qualified name using the `node-name()` function.

Qualified names are also used in the values of elements and attributes, sometimes to refer to elements and attributes (for example, in a schema or in an XPath), and sometimes just as a way to ensure that different people use different unique names for things.

The interpretation of a string, such as `'xsl:template'`, as a qualified name depends on the namespace declarations that are in scope at the point at which the string is used. For example, if a document contained

```
<element name="xsl:template"
         xmlns:xsl="http://www.w3.org/1999/XSL/Transform">
  ...
</element>
```

then the value of the `name` attribute should be interpreted as a qualified name with the namespace URI `"http://www.w3.org/1999/XSL/Transform"` and the local name `"template"`. On the other hand, if a document contained

```
<element name="xsl:template"
         xmlns:xsl="http://www.example.com/">
  ...
</element>
```

then the value of the `name` attribute should be interpreted as a qualified name with the namespace URI `"http://www.example.com/"` and the local name `"template"`.

The `resolve-QName()` function allows you to resolve a string to a qualified name, based on the namespace declarations that are in scope for a particular element. The first argument is the string and the second argument is the element whose namespace declarations should be used. For example, to resolve the value of the `name` attribute when the `<element>` element is the current node, you'd use

```
resolve-QName(@name, .)
```

■ **Note** The `resolve-QName()` function uses the default namespace declaration that's in scope on the element when interpreting strings that don't have a prefix.

To create a qualified name directly, in order to compare it to another qualified name, for example, you can use the `QName()` function. The first argument is a namespace URI and the second argument is a local name. For example, to test whether the resolved value of the `name` attribute of the current `<element>` element is a qualified name whose namespace URI is `http://www.w3.org/1999/XSL/Transform` and whose local name is `template`, you could use

```
resolve-QName(@name, .) =
  expanded-QName('http://www.w3.org/1999/XSL/Transform', 'template')
```

You can alternatively use the `xs:QName()` constructor function, so long as the prefix that you use in the argument is declared within the stylesheet. For example, the following will only work if the prefix `xsl` is declared within the stylesheet:

```
resolve-QName(@name, .) = xs:QName('xsl:template')
```

If you have a qualified name, you can extract the prefix, namespace URI, and local name components from it using the following functions:

- `prefix-from-QName()`—Returns the prefix (as an `xs:NCName`)
- `namespace-from-QName()`—Returns the namespace URI (as an `xs:anyURI`)
- `local-name-from-QName()`—Returns the local name (as an `xs:NCName`)

For example, to see whether the resolved value of the `name` attribute was a qualified name in the `http://www.w3.org/1999/XSL/Transform` namespace, you could use

```
namespace-from-QName(resolve-QName(@name, .)) =
  'http://www.w3.org/1999/XSL/Transform'
```

■ **Summary** You can resolve a string as a qualified name using the `resolve-QName()` function, or create a qualified name from scratch using the `QName()` function. To get the components of a qualified name, use the `prefix-from-QName()`, `namespace-from-QName()`, and `local-name-from-QName()` functions.

Manipulating URIs

The final datatype that we'll look at in this chapter are URIs. As we saw earlier, XML Schema defined the primitive type `xs:anyURI` for URI values, but XPath 2.0 allows this type to be promoted to `xs:string` automatically when an argument of type `xs:string` is expected. In addition, those functions that you might expect would take `xs:anyURI` arguments actually take strings. This makes it easy to create URIs: you can use a string literal rather than having to use a constructor function. All in all, XPath 2.0 treats URIs as if they were a kind of string.

There are only a couple of functions that support the manipulation of URIs, but they're quite useful. The `resolve-uri()` function takes a relative URI as its first argument and resolves it against a base URI. The base URI can be specified directly in the second argument; otherwise it defaults to the base URI of the stylesheet itself.

Note We'll be looking more closely at how base URIs are determined in Chapter 12, where you'll also see how to get the base URI of an element using the `base-uri()` function.

For example, if you have an element such as

```
<link href="index.xml" />
```

then you can resolve this URI against the URI `http://www.example.com/` using

```
resolve-uri(@href, 'http://www.example.com/')
```

The result is the URI `http://www.example.com/index.xml`.

Note URI resolution is purely string manipulation; the URIs themselves aren't retrieved, so you don't have to be connected to the Internet for this to work.

The `escape-uri()` function escapes a string using the URI escapes (which basically means that non-ASCII characters are turned into escapes in the form `%HH`). It takes two arguments, the first being the string to be escaped, and the second which determines whether characters that are reserved within URIs, such as / and #, should be escaped.

When the second argument is `true`, the `escape-uri()` function is useful for converting strings into values that can be used within a URI, usually as part of a query. For example, if you wanted to construct a link to Google to search for a character's name, you'd have to escape the character's name, since otherwise it would contain a space or other characters that aren't allowed in a URI. With the current element being a `<Character>` element, you could use

```
concat('http://www.google.com/search?q=', escape-uri(Name, true()))
```

If the `<Name>` of the `<Character>` is "Zoë Slater," for example, you'd get this URI:

```
http://www.google.com/search?q=Zo%C3%AB%20Slater
```

When the second argument is `false`, the `escape-uri()` function is mainly useful for escaping whole URIs, since any characters that are significant within the URI won't be escaped. Using `escape-uri()` on whole URIs is useful when you want to compare URIs in a more sophisticated way than the normal character-by-character comparison, since `escape-uri()` will normalize them to using escapes for the same set of characters.

Summary You can resolve a relative URI against a base URI using the `resolve-uri()` function. You can escape either the whole or part of a URI using the `escape-uri()` function.

Summary

This chapter has looked in detail at the datatypes that are available in XPath 2.0, and, for some of them at least, the functions and operators that are available for manipulating them.

We looked first at the atomic type hierarchy and discussed how to create values of different types using constructor functions. We also saw how to cast a value to a different type, using a constructor function or a `cast` expression, and how to test whether such casting would give us an error using the `castable` expression.

We then looked at string manipulation: breaking apart strings with the `substring-before()`, `substring-after()`, and `substring()` functions, and putting them back together with the `concat()` and `string-join()` functions. We saw how to normalize the whitespace in strings with `normalize-space()` and the Unicode characters used in a string with `normalize-unicode()`. We also saw how to do simple string translation using the `translate()`, `upper-case()`, and `lower-case()` functions.

We spent a bit of time looking at regular expression processing in XPath and XSLT: the XPath functions `matches()`, `replace()`, and `tokenize()` and the XSLT element `<xsl:analyze-string>`. Regular expression processing makes a lot of things that used to be done with complicated templates in XSLT 1.0 much, much easier.

This chapter then turned to numeric manipulation, looking at the arithmetic operators for doing simple math, and at formatting decimal numbers into strings for presentation using `format-number()`.

The same arithmetic operators can be used with date/time and duration values, and you can format dates and times using similar functions to that used to format numbers, although the formatting, as you saw, is a lot more complicated. If you need to dive into the depths of date/times and durations, we saw in this chapter how to extract their components and adjust the timezones that they use.

Finally, the last couple of sections have looked at manipulating qualified names and URIs. These datatypes probably aren't used as extensively as strings, numbers, or dates and times, but XPath 2.0 still offers some useful mechanisms for creating them, extracting information from them, and normalizing them.

The datatypes, and the means of manipulating them, that you've learned about in this chapter form the basic building blocks for the complex processing that XSLT 2.0 supports. In the next chapter, we'll see how to use variables and parameters to create more complex expressions and thus do more complex processing.

Review Questions

1. What types of atomic values can you create using literals?
2. Write an XPath that creates an `xdt:dayTimeDuration` of two weeks.
3. Can you cast `xs:gYear('2003')` to an `xs:integer`? If not, what kind of error will you get if you try?

4. Can you cast `xs:string('12.5')` to an `xs:integer`? If not, what kind of error will you get if you try?

5. Can you cast `xs:decimal('12.5')` to an `xs:integer`? If not, what kind of error will you get if you try?

6. What does the following XPath do?

```
if (@start castable as xs:date) then xs:date(@start) else current-date()
```

7. Create an XPath that will take a date in the US date format `M/D/YYYY` and convert it to the standard date format `YYYY-MM-DD`. The date `9/4/2001` should get converted to `2001-09-04`.

8. Use the `<xsl:analyze-string>` element instead of an XPath to convert from the US date format into the standard date format.

9. Write at least two tests that will return true if the value of the `<Description>` element contains `'tiger'` or `'tigers'`, whatever the case.

10. Given the following decimal formats, create some XSLT that will output a number formatted in English, French, and German style:

```
<xsl:decimal-format name="French"
                    decimal-separator="," grouping-separator=" " />
<xsl:decimal-format name="German"
                    decimal-separator="," grouping-separator="." />
```

11. Create some XSLT that tells you how many days there are between the dates held by the `start` and `end` attributes of the current `<TVGuide>` element.

12. Under what circumstances would `xs:time('10:00:00') = xs:time('17:00:00+01:00')` be true?

13. Create an XPath that will take a time such as `19:00:00-05:00` and convert it to the format "7:00 EST." If the time represents a whole number of hours, it should be formatted as "7 o'clock EST."

14. What does the following code do?

```
<xsl:choose>
  <xsl:when test="namespace-from-QName(resolve-QName(@name, .)) =
                  'http://www.w3.org/1999/XSL/Transform'">
    <xsl:value-of
      select="concat('xsl:', local-name-from-QName(resolve-QName(@name, .))
  </xsl:when>
  <xsl:otherwise>
    <xsl:value-of select="@name" />
  </xsl:otherwise>
</xsl:choose>
```

CHAPTER 6

Variables and Parameters

The last chapter gave a rundown of the various **atomic types** that you might use in your stylesheet, and the **functions** and **operators** that you might use to manipulate them. In previous chapters, we've also looked at how you can use paths to create **sequences** of **nodes** in order to iterate over them, process them with templates, and so on.

As you've seen, as you get into using more complex XPath expressions, they can get a bit unwieldy. It soon becomes apparent that you need some way of storing the result of intermediate expressions, both to make the code easier to read and to enable you to reuse the same calculated value again and again. As with other programming languages, XSLT allows you to store these values within **variables**, which are the subject of this chapter. In this chapter, you'll learn

- How to define variables using XSLT
- How to use variables within XPaths
- How to generate snippets of XML to reuse or process later on
- How to declare and use parameters within templates and within the stylesheet as a whole

Defining Variables

Variables allow you to use a particular name to stand for a value within an expression. You define a variable in XSLT using an `<xsl:variable>` element. Each `<xsl:variable>` element usually has two attributes:

- `name`—Specifies the name of the variable
- `select`—Holds an expression that specifies the value of the variable

Variable names must follow the same rules as the names of attributes or elements, so they can't start with numbers, for example. The expression that you use in the `select` attribute can evaluate to any type of value. At the simplest level, you can just give a literal string or number, for example:

```
<xsl:variable name="daysInWeek" select="7" />
<xsl:variable name="myName" select="'Jeni Tennison'" />
```

■ **Caution** If you set a variable to a string, remember to put either single or double quotes around the string; otherwise the XSLT processor will try to interpret the content of the string as an expression, which may result in an error or (if it's just one word) may be interpreted as a location path and evaluate to an empty sequence. For example, `select="Program"` assigns a sequence of `<Program>` elements to the variable, whereas `select="'Program'"` assigns the string `'Program'` to the variable. You don't have to worry with numbers—element names can't start with a number, so XPath processors can tell that when you use a literal number, you mean that number rather than an element.

In fact, you can use any expression you like to give the value of a variable. For example, you could set a variable to a sequence containing all the `<Program>` element children of the current node using a location path, with

```
<xsl:variable name="programs" select="Program" />
```

Or you could set a variable to a Boolean value, `true` if the current program is interesting (has a `flag` attribute or a `rating` attribute with a value over 6), with

```
<xsl:variable name="isInteresting" select="@flag or (@rating > 6)" />
```

■ **Note** Remember that you can use brackets around subexpressions if you want to make the priority of different operators explicit. In the preceding expression, the result of the comparison `@rating > 6` is compared with the true or false result of the expression `@flag` (which tests whether a `flag` attribute is present).

■ **Summary** You can define a variable with the `<xsl:variable>` element; its `name` attribute specifies the name of the variable. The `select` attribute holds an expression that's evaluated to provide the value of the variable.

Declaring a Variable's Type

It's good practice to declare the type of a variable: the kind of value that the variable holds. Processors can use information about the type of a variable to help optimize their processing and to tell you about any errors that you might have made when using the variable. For example, if you declare the type of a variable as a string, but then you apply templates to the value of that variable, the processor can give you an error because it knows you can't apply templates to a string.

You can declare the type of a variable using the as attribute on the `<xsl:variable>` element. The `as` attribute holds a **sequence type**. A sequence type describes a sequence in terms of the kind of and number of items that it holds.

The simplest kind of sequence type is one that matches a single atomic value. These sequence types simply name the type of the atomic value that they match. For example, a sequence type that matches a string looks like this:

```
xs:string
```

so if you declare a variable that holds a string, you should add an as attribute to the variable declaration as follows:

```
<xsl:variable name="myName" select="'Jeni Tennison'" as="xs:string" />
```

Other sequence types match single nodes using **node tests**. You've already seen one node test: text() matches any text node. There are similar node tests for most kinds of nodes that you might encounter; the ones that we've looked at so far are

- document-node()—Matches a document node
- element()—Matches an element node
- attribute()—Matches an attribute node
- text()—Matches a text node

For example, if you wanted to create a variable that holds the <Series> child element of the current <Program> element, you could use

```
<xsl:variable name="series" select="Series" as="element()" />
```

■ **Note** We'll be looking at nodes and node tests in a lot more detail in the next chapter.

Any of the preceding sequence types can be followed by an **occurrence indicator**. The occurrence indicators that you can use in sequence types are just the same as those that you can use in DTDs, namely

- ?—Indicates that the item is optional
- *—Indicates that there's zero or more of the items
- +—Indicates that there's one or more of the items

For example, a variable that held all the <Program> element children of a <Channel> element can hold one or more elements. An appropriate declaration would therefore look like this:

```
<xsl:variable name="programs" select="Program" as="element()+" />
```

If you do declare the type of a variable, you need to make sure that the value of the variable is of that type or can be cast to that type implicitly; otherwise you will get an error. As we saw in the last chapter, there are restrictions on which types can be cast to which other types implicitly.

For example, the following declaration is fine because the integer that's provided as the value of the variable can be cast to an xs:double:

```
<xsl:variable name="daysInWeek" select="7" as="xs:double" />
```

On the other hand, the following declaration will give you an error because the string that's provided can't be cast to an xs:date implicitly:

```
<xsl:variable name="dueDate" select="'2003-12-08'" as="xs:date" />
```

■ **Note** Just because a value can't be cast implicitly doesn't mean that it can't be cast at all. As we saw in the last chapter, you can explicitly cast the string `'2003-12-08'` to a date using the `xs:date()` constructor function or using a `cast` expression.

As you'll remember, in Basic XSLT processing, the values of nodes can be cast implicitly to any type. In an earlier example, we created a variable called `series` to hold the `<Series>` element itself:

```
<xsl:variable name="series" select="Series" as="element()" />
```

If you were interested in reusing the *value* of the `<Series>` element, as a string, then you should declare the variable as holding an `xs:string` instead:

```
<xsl:variable name="series" select="Series" as="xs:string" />
```

As another example: if you've selected a sequence of more than one node, you can cast all of them to strings by declaring the type of the variable as being `xs:string+`. For example, to get a sequence of strings containing the names of the channels in the TV guide, you could use

```
<xsl:variable name="channels" select="/TVGuide/Channel/Name" as="xs:string+" />
```

■ **Summary** The `as` attribute of `<xsl:variable>` holds a sequence type that declares the type of the value held by the variable. The value that you provide for the variable must be implicitly castable to that type.

Referring to Variables

Knowing how to set variables isn't much use if you don't know how to use them. Once you've declared a variable with a particular value, you can refer to that variable's value within another XPath expression using the variable's name prefixed with a dollar sign ($). Like most things in XML, variable names are case-sensitive.

■ **Note** I'm going to use the same syntax when I talk about variables in the explanatory text in this book. So when I say "`$minRating` has the value `6`," I mean that the variable named `minRating` has the value `6`.

As a simple example, you could use a variable to hold a number that indicates the minimum rating that a program can have for it to count as an interesting program:

```
<xsl:variable name="minRating" select="6" as="xs:integer" />
```

You can generate some output that gives that number using `<xsl:value-of>`, giving a variable reference in its `select` attribute:

```
Minimum rating: <xsl:value-of select="$minRating" />
```

The result would then be

```
Minimum rating: 6
```

You could also use the $minRating variable within a larger expression, when testing whether a program is interesting or not in order to decide whether or not to generate some HTML for the program:

```
<xsl:if test="@rating > $minRating">
  ...
</xsl:if>
```

Summary You can refer to a variable within an expression by prefixing its name with a dollar sign. Names are case-sensitive as usual. When the expression is evaluated, the processor uses the value of the variable in place of the reference.

Reusing Node Sequences

Variables can make your XSLT more efficient if you use them to hold values that you use more than once in your code, especially if those values are time-consuming for the XSLT processor to evaluate, such as complicated paths. In Chapter 4, we looked at filtering TVGuide.xml to generate a page that only listed *Star Trek* programs and the channels that show them with StarTrek.xsl.

The template for <Channel> elements in StarTrek.xsl is as follows:

```
<xsl:template match="Channel">
  <xsl:if test="Program[starts-with(Series, 'StarTrek')]">
    <xsl:apply-templates select="Name" />
    <xsl:apply-templates select="Program[starts-with(Series, 'StarTrek')]" />
  </xsl:if>
</xsl:template>
```

As you can see, the expression Program[starts-with(Series, 'Star Trek')] is used twice in the preceding template, once to test whether there are any *Star Trek* programs showing on the channel and once (if there are such) to apply templates to those programs. Evaluating this expression could be fairly time-consuming because the XSLT processor has to go through all the <Program> element children of the <Channel> element to locate the relevant ones. Therefore, you don't want to evaluate this path twice if you can help it. Instead, you could use a variable to hold the resulting sequence of nodes and then refer to it in the two different locations. We'll do this in the next version of this stylesheet, in StarTrek2.xsl.

First, you need to set up a $StarTrekPrograms variable to hold all the *Star Trek* programs that are showing on a particular channel. The select attribute needs to hold a location path that points to all the <Program> element children of the current <Channel> element whose <Series> child starts with the string 'Star Trek', and the as attribute should indicate that the variable holds a sequence of zero or more elements, as follows:

```
<xsl:template match="Channel">
  <xsl:variable name="StarTrekPrograms"
                select="Program[starts-with(Series, 'StarTrek')]"
                as="element()*" />
  ...
</xsl:template>
```

■ **Note** As you'll see in the next section, you'll only be able to use this variable within this template.

Then you need to substitute the path where it's used in the `test` attribute of `<xsl:if>` and in the `select` attribute of the `<xsl:apply-templates>` instruction with a reference to the `$StarTrekPrograms` variable:

```
<xsl:template match="Channel">
  <xsl:variable name="StarTrekPrograms"
                select="Program[starts-with(Series, 'StarTrek')]" />
  <xsl:if test="$StarTrekPrograms">
    <xsl:apply-templates select="Name" />
    <xsl:apply-templates select="$StarTrekPrograms" />
  </xsl:if>
</xsl:template>
```

The result of running `StarTrek2.xsl` with `TVGuide.xml` is `StarTrek2.html`, which looks just the same as the one you get when using `StarTrek.xsl`, as shown in Figure 6-1.

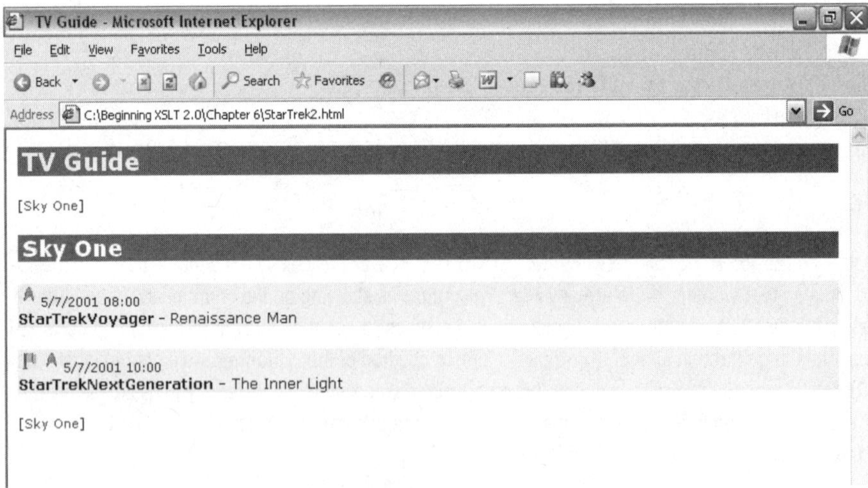

Figure 6-1. *Viewing* `StarTrek2.html` *using Internet Explorer*

You probably won't notice the difference, but it's likely to run slightly faster. Moreover, making this change has the benefit that you only have to write the complex XPath expression once, which makes it easier to maintain—if you make a mistake in it, or if you want to change it later on, you only have to adjust it in one location rather than two.

You can make the same kind of change to the template for the <TVGuide> element where you tell the user when there are no *Star Trek* programs showing. The next version of the stylesheet, StarTrek3.xsl, contains the following template for the <TVGuide> element:

```
<xsl:template match="TVGuide">
  <xsl:variable name="StarTrekChannels"
                select="Channel[Program[starts-with(Series, 'StarTrek')]]"
                as="element()*" />
  <p>
    <xsl:apply-templates select="$StarTrekChannels" mode="ChannelList" />
  </p>
  <xsl:choose>
    <xsl:when test="$StarTrekChannels">
      <xsl:apply-templates select="$StarTrekChannels" />
    </xsl:when>
    <xsl:otherwise>
      <p>No Star Trek showing this week!</p>
    </xsl:otherwise>
  </xsl:choose>
  <p>
    <xsl:apply-templates select="$StarTrekChannels" mode="ChannelList" />
  </p>
</xsl:template>
```

and, since the only channels that have templates applied to them in ChannelList mode are now those that are showing *Star Trek* programs, the test that was in the template matching the <Channel> elements in ChannelList mode can now be removed, to give the following:

```
<xsl:template match="Channel" mode="ChannelList">
  [<a href="#{Name}"><xsl:value-of select="Name" /></a>]
</xsl:template>
```

Again, StarTrek3.html, generated by transforming TVGuide.xml using StarTrek3.xsl, looks exactly the same as StarTrek.html, but is likely to be fractionally faster, and quite a bit easier to maintain.

Variable Scope

Where you declare a variable determines where you can refer to it. The area of the stylesheet in which a variable can be referred to is known as the variable's **scope**. The fact that variables have different scopes allows you to use the same names for variables in different templates, for example. You can define variables at two levels in XSLT: at the top level of the stylesheet, to give global variables, or within a template, to give local variables.

Global Variables

Variables that you declare at the top level of a stylesheet (as direct children of the <xsl:stylesheet> element) are known as **global variables**. Typically, global variables hold either constants or values that are used across a number of different templates (so that the processor doesn't have to evaluate them each time) or constants or values that you might change during the course of developing the stylesheet (to make the stylesheet easier to maintain). The `select` attribute of global variables is interpreted with the document node of the input XML document as the current node, so any paths that you use should be relative to that document node.

■ **Tip** I normally use absolute location paths (starting with a /) when I set global variables that hold nodes.

The order in which you declare global variables doesn't matter. For example, in the following code, the `$channelsShowingSeries` variable holds those channels that show programs in the series whose name is held in the `$series` variable. The `$channelsShowingSeries` variable can be declared *before* the `$series` variable, despite the fact that `$channelsShowingSeries` refers to `$series` (although it would be clearer if it were declared afterwards).

```
<xsl:variable name="channelsShowingSeries" as="element()*"
  select="/TVGuide/Channel[Program[starts-with(Series, $series)]]" />
<xsl:variable name="series" select="'Star Trek'" as="xs:string" />
```

However, you cannot have two global variables with the same name in the same stylesheet (or in included stylesheets, as we'll see in Chapter 12), and you cannot have circular references, where the value of one variable relies on the value of another variable, which relies on the first variable. For example, if you had variables to hold information about the size of a table, it would be an error to have them all depend on each other, as follows:

```
<xsl:variable name="rows"    select="$cells idiv $columns" as="xs:integer" />
<xsl:variable name="columns" select="$cells idiv $rows"    as="xs:integer" />
<xsl:variable name="cells"   select="$rows * $columns"     as="xs:integer" />
```

■ **Summary** Global variables are declared at the top level of the stylesheet and are visible throughout the stylesheet.

Local Variables

Variables that you declare within a template are known as **local variables**. Local variables are only accessible within the template in which they're declared, so you can't declare a variable in one template and then access it from another (you need to use parameters, which we'll come to later in this chapter, if you find yourself needing to do that).

What's more, a local variable is only accessible to the `<xsl:variable>` element's following siblings and their descendants, not to everything within the template. For example, in `TVGuide.xsl` we are currently using the following template to generate HTML for the details of the TV programs:

```
<xsl:template match="Program" mode="Details">
  <p>
    ...
```

```
    <xsl:apply-templates select="CastList" mode="DisplayToggle" />
  </p>
  <xsl:apply-templates select="CastList" />
</xsl:template>
```

The <CastList> element is referred to twice within the template: once to generate the cast list itself, and once to generate a clickable piece of text to toggle the display of the cast list. We could hold the <CastList> element child of the <Program> element within a variable, as follows:

```
<xsl:variable name="castList" select="CastList" />
```

We would then be able to refer to it in the two <xsl:apply-templates> instructions rather than using the path directly. However, we need to position the variable declaration so that both <xsl:apply-templates> instructions follow the variable declaration, either as siblings or as children of their siblings. If we put it just before the first <xsl:apply-templates>, as in TVGuide2.xsl, which contains the following:

```
<xsl:template match="Program" mode="Details">
  <p>
    ...
    <xsl:variable name="castList" select="CastList" as="element()?" />
    <xsl:apply-templates select="$castList" mode="DisplayToggle" />
  </p>
  <xsl:apply-templates select="$castList" />
</xsl:template>
```

we would run into problems because the second <xsl:apply-templates> is at a higher level in the tree than the variable declaration. If you try to run the stylesheet with this template, the XSLT processor should complain that there is no $castList variable in scope. For example, when running Saxon, you will see the error message shown in Figure 6-2.

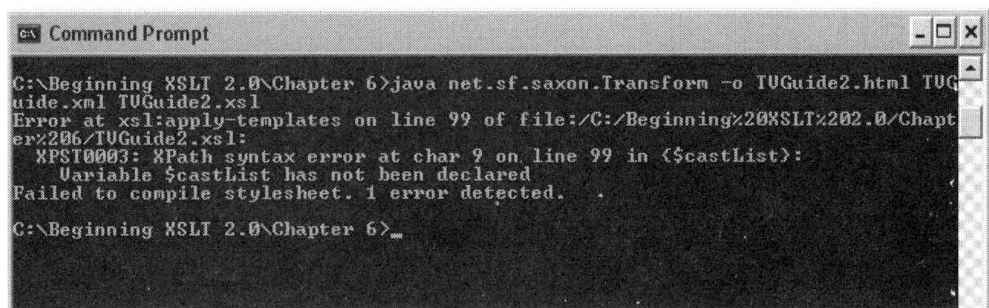

Figure 6-2. *Error message when transforming* TVGuide.xml *with* TVGuide2.xsl

The only legal location for the variable declaration to make it visible to both <xsl:apply-templates> instructions is before the <p> element, as in TVGuide3.xsl, as follows:

```
<xsl:template match="Program" mode="Details">
  <xsl:variable name="castList" select="CastList" as="element()?" />
  <p>
    ...
```

```
    <xsl:apply-templates select="$castList" mode="DisplayToggle" />
  </p>
  <xsl:apply-templates select="$castList" />
</xsl:template>
```

Unlike with global variables, you can declare a variable even if a local variable with the same name is in scope, so the template matching the `<Program>` element could hold other variable declarations for the `$castList` variable, despite the fact that it's declared right at the start of the template. You can also declare a local variable that has the same name as an existing global variable. This is known as **shadowing**. Within the scope of the new declaration, its value is used instead of the value of the shadowed variable.

■ **Caution** Unlike in procedural programming languages, there's no requirement for a shadowing variable to have the same type as the variable that it's shadowing.

Shadowing of variables is usually a bad idea, since it can make it hard to tell which value a particular variable reference is referring to, especially when you shadow a variable within a `<xsl:for-each>` loop, as you'll see later. If you can, try to come up with unique and descriptive names for variables so that your code is easier for others to follow.

■ **Summary** Local variables are declared within templates and are only visible to their following siblings and their descendants. A local variable can shadow a global variable or another local variable.

Declaring Global and Local Variables

To try out the distinction between global and local variables, let's try declaring some variables in `StarTrek4.xsl`. First, we'll create a global variable to hold the name of the series (`'StarTrek'`). This variable declaration goes at the top level of the stylesheet, as a direct child of the `<xsl:stylesheet>` element, as follows:

```
<xsl:stylesheet version="2.0"
                xmlns:xsl="http://www.w3.org/1999/XSL/Transform"
                xmlns:xs="http://www.w3.org/2001/XMLSchema"
                xmlns:xdt="http://www.w3.org/2005/04/xpath-datatypes">
<xsl:variable name="series" select="'StarTrek'" as="xs:string" />
...
</xsl:stylesheet>
```

We can use this `$series` variable wherever we want. There are two locations where we need to know the series that we want to look at. The first one is within the template for the `<TVGuide>` element, to identify those channels that show programs from the series. Here, we're putting these channels into a `$StarTrekChannels` variable, which is defined locally within the `<TVGuide>` template:

```
<xsl:template match="TVGuide">
  <xsl:variable name="StarTrekChannels"
                select="Channel[Program[starts-with(Series, $series)]]" />
  ...
</xsl:template>
```

The second is within the template matching the <Channel> elements. We know that this template will only be called if the channel shows programs in the relevant series, so we can get rid of the <xsl:if> that we had before (which means there's no point in declaring the $StarTrekPrograms variable), but we still want to identify those programs so that we only apply templates to the relevant <Program> elements, as follows:

```
<xsl:template match="Channel">
  <xsl:apply-templates select="Name" />
  <xsl:apply-templates select="Program[starts-with(Series, $series)]" />
</xsl:template>
```

The two templates use the value from the global $series variable. Transform TVGuide.xml with StarTrek4.xsl, in which the $series variable is set to 'StarTrek', and you'll get StarTrek4.html, which shows the *Star Trek* programs as shown in Figure 6-3.

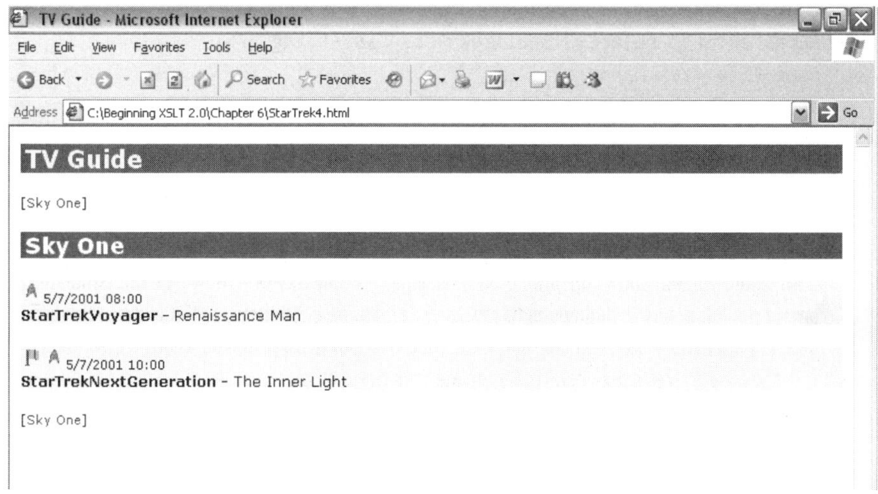

Figure 6-3. *Viewing* StarTrek4.html *in Internet Explorer*

On the other hand, if you make a copy of StarTrek4.xsl, called EastEnders.xsl, and in that stylesheet set the $series variable so it takes the value 'EastEnders', you'll get EastEnders.html, which shows only *EastEnders* episodes, as shown in Figure 6-4.

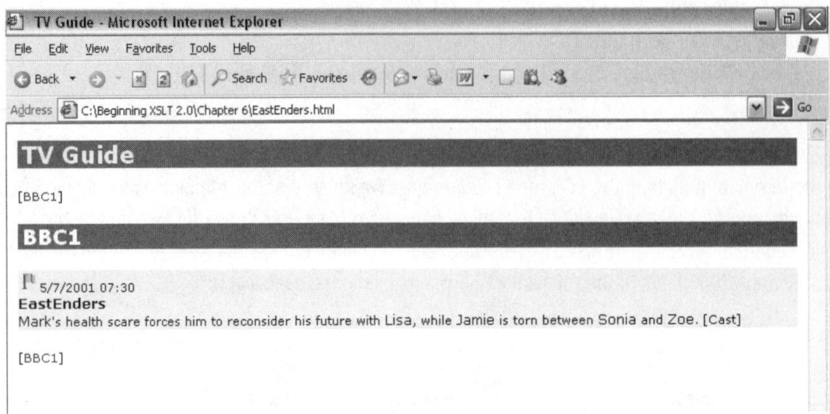

Figure 6-4. *Viewing* EastEnders.html *in Internet Explorer*

Now we'll shadow the $series variable within the template for the <TVGuide> element, in StarTrek5.xsl. We'll set the global variable to 'EastEnders' but have a local variable of the same name set to 'StarTrek', as follows:

```
<xsl:variable name="series" select="'EastEnders'" as="xs:string" />
<xsl:template match="TVGuide">
  <xsl:variable name="series" select="'StarTrek'" as="xs:string" />
  <xsl:variable name="StarTrekChannels"
                select="Channel[Program[starts-with(Series, $series)]]"
                as="element()*" />
  ...
</xsl:template>
```

Within the template for the <TVGuide> element, the $series variable is set to the string 'StarTrek', so we get templates applied to all the channels that show *Star Trek* programs, which is only Sky One. However, the templates for the <Channel> element don't have local definitions of the $series variable, so they use the global definition. The main part of the page is provided by the template in default mode, which is only applied to one <Channel> element (Sky One, since it shows *Star Trek* episodes). That template tries to list all the episodes of *EastEnders* on the channel. Unfortunately, there aren't any *EastEnders* episodes showing on Sky One, so we end up with no programs being listed for Sky One. The result is shown in Figure 6-5.

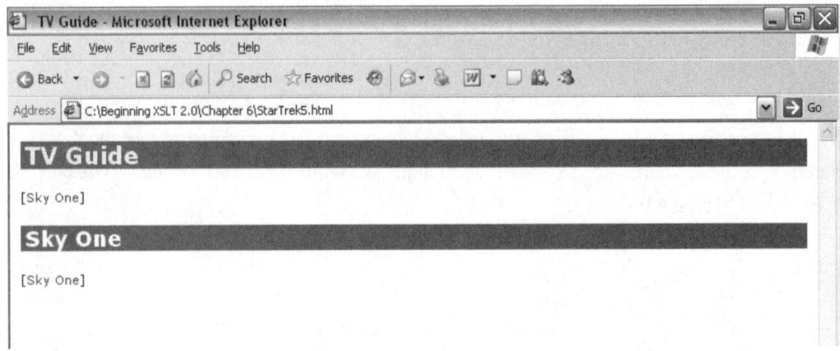

Figure 6-5. *Viewing* StarTrek5.html *in Internet Explorer*

Loops and Counters

XSLT variables have one quite peculiar feature: they can't vary. Once you've set the value of a local variable, it remains the same throughout its scope (even though it can be shadowed by other variables of the same name). This can appear strange, particularly if you're used to programming with procedural languages, such as JavaScript, but it does not limit what you can do with XSLT: there are other methods for achieving the same goals.

A common use of variables in procedural programming languages is in loops that use counters to index into arrays. For example, when programming with a document object model (DOM) in JavaScript, we could iterate over the <Channel> children of a <TVGuide> element with the following code:

```
var TVGuide = document.documentElement;
var Channels = TVGuide.getElementsByTagName('Channel');
for (var i = 0; i < Channels.length; i++) {
  var Channel = Channels.item(i);
  ...
}
```

In XSLT, the <xsl:for-each> element is specifically oriented towards iterating over the items in a sequence, so the equivalent code in XSLT would look something like the following:

```
<xsl:variable name="TVGuide" select="/TVGuide" as="element()" />
<xsl:variable name="Channels" select="$TVGuide/Channel" as="element()+" />
<xsl:for-each select="$Channels">
  <xsl:variable name="Channel" select="." as="element()" />
  ...
</xsl:for-each>
```

Variables that act as counters in procedural programming languages can be useful in numbering the items that they count, and in counting or summing them. For example, in JavaScript we could iterate over the programs shown on a channel, counting them and keeping track of the total rating for the channel as follows:

```
var Programs = Channel.getElementsByTagName('Program');
var count = 0;
var rating = 0;
for (; count < Programs.length; count++) {
  var Program = Programs.item(count);
  rating = rating + parseInt(Program.getAttribute('rating'));
  document.write(count);
  ...
}
document.write('Average Rating: ' + rating / count);
```

If you try to use the same kind of approach in XSLT, you'll run into problems. The literal equivalent of the preceding JavaScript code might look like the following:

```
<xsl:variable name="Programs" select="$Channel/Program" as="element()+" />
<xsl:variable name="count" select="0" as="xs:integer" />
<xsl:variable name="rating" select="0" as="xs:integer" />
<xsl:for-each select="$Programs">
```

```
  <xsl:variable name="Program" select="." as="element()" />
  <xsl:variable name="count" select="$count + 1" as="xs:integer" />
  <xsl:variable name="rating" as="xs:integer"
                select="$rating + $Program/@rating" />
  <xsl:value-of select="$count" />
  ...
</xsl:for-each>
Average Rating: <xsl:value-of select="$rating div $count" />
```

This code won't give you what you might expect. When you refer to the `$count` variable in the last line, the variable declaration that's in scope is the one on the second line, which sets the `$count` variable to `0`. Similarly, the reference in the last line to the `$rating` variable refers to the declaration in the third line, which sets the `$rating` variable to `0`. Nothing that goes on within the `<xsl:for-each>` can change the values of these variables; the variable declarations within the loop are new variables that are, as far as the XSLT processor is concerned, completely separate from those declared outside the loop.

So how do you number items or calculate averages using XSLT? Well, you've already seen how to find the number of an item in XSLT using the `position()` function in Chapter 4 (we'll see some more methods in Chapter 10). XPath also has specific functions for calculating values from a sequence:

- `count()`—Counts the number of items in the sequence
- `sum()`—Sums the values of the items in the sequence
- `avg()`—Gets the average value of the items in the sequence
- `min()`—Gets the minimum value of the items in the sequence
- `max()`—Gets the maximum value of the items in the sequence

Caution The `sum()`, `avg()`, `min()`, and `max()` functions use the type of the items in the sequence passed as the argument to work out what kind of sum, average, and so on you want. If you pass a sequence of strings to the `min()` function, for example, you'll get the string that appears first alphabetically; if you pass a sequence of dates, on the other hand, you'll get the earliest date. When you pass a sequence of nodes, they're implicitly cast to numbers.

All these functions can take a single argument—a sequence containing the items to count, sum, average, and so on as appropriate. Here's the equivalent to the preceding JavaScript in XSLT:

```
<xsl:variable name="Programs" select="$Channel/Program" as="element()+" />
<xsl:for-each select="$Programs">
  <xsl:variable name="Program" select="." as="element()" />
  <xsl:value-of select="position()" />
  ...
</xsl:for-each>
Average Rating: <xsl:value-of select="avg($Programs/@rating) " />
```

Note You can use a sequence held in a variable as if that sequence was created directly from the original location path: `$Programs/@rating` gives you the `rating` attributes of the nodes held in the `$Programs` variable, in this case exactly the same as `($Channel/Program)/@rating`.

The `min()` and `max()` functions can also take an optional second argument that specifies the collation that's used for comparing strings if the sequence given in the first argument contains strings. You learned about collations in Chapter 4.

This is a good place to quickly mention a subtlety of the `sum()` function. Imagine you were summing the durations of the programs of a channel, using the following:

```
<xsl:variable name="durations" as="xdt:dayTimeDuration*"
              select="Program/Duration" />
<xsl:variable name="total-duration" as="xdt:dayTimeDuration"
              select="sum($durations)" />
```

Usually this code would work fine. However, if you had a channel that didn't have any programs, then the `$durations` variable would hold an empty sequence. Despite the fact that you've declared the type of the `$durations` variable, the XSLT processor can't tell the difference between the empty sequence of durations and an empty sequence of another type. If you pass a single argument to the `sum()` function, and that argument is an empty sequence, the result is the `xs:integer` `0`. Since `0` is not an `xdt:dayTimeDuration`, it's not a legal value for the `$total-duration` variable, and the processor gives you an error.

To get around this problem, the `sum()` function takes an optional second argument, the value that's returned if the sequence passed as the first argument is empty. To prevent the error occurring with the preceding code, you should give the `xdt:dayTimeDuration` `PT0S` as the second argument:

```
<xsl:variable name="durations" as="xdt:dayTimeDuration*"
              select="Program/Duration" />
<xsl:variable name="total-duration" as="xdt:dayTimeDuration"
              select="sum($durations, xdt:dayTimeDuration('PT0S'))" />
```

Summary Once a variable's value is set, it cannot be changed. But you can number nodes using the `position()` function, count nodes with the `count()` function, sum their values with the `sum()` function, average them with the `avg()` function, and get their minimum or maximum with the `min()` or `max()` functions.

XSLT is a functional language. If you've done a lot of procedural programming, you might find the transition to using XSLT a bit confusing because you need to change the way that you think about problems. But you can usually get the result that you're after fairly easily despite the fact that XSLT variables cannot be updated. In more complex cases, you may have to use recursive templates, which is something that we'll look at in Chapter 11.

Counting the Number of *Star Trek* Episodes

Let's try out counting nodes by providing a count of the number of *Star Trek* episodes found within `TVGuide.xml`, using a new version of our stylesheet, `StarTrek6.xsl` (based on `StarTrek4.xsl`). When we do find channels showing *Star Trek* episodes, we'll state how many *Star Trek* episodes are being shown. For example:

```
There is 1 Star Trek episode showing this week.
There are 2 Star Trek episodes showing this week.
```

In the template for the `<TVGuide>` element, we can find all the *Star Trek* episodes, no matter what channel they're being shown on, with the following location path:

```
Channel/Program[starts-with(Series, $series)]
```

To count how many episodes there are, we can pass this node set of `<Program>` elements as the argument to the `count()` variable as follows:

```
count(Channel/Program[starts-with(Series, $series)]
```

Now we need to change the wording slightly depending on whether there's only one *Star Trek* episode or more than one *Star Trek* episode, which means using that count at least twice, so we'll store the count in a variable, `$NumberOfStarTrekEpisodes`:

```
<xsl:variable name="NumberOfStarTrekEpisodes" as="xs:integer"
              select="count(Channel/Program[starts-with(Series, $series)])" />
```

We'll also create another variable, `$Plural`, which will be a Boolean—`true` if the number of *Star Trek* episodes is more than one, `false` otherwise:

```
<xsl:variable name="Plural" as="xs:boolean"
              select="$NumberOfStarTrekEpisodes > 1" />
```

Now we can create the sentence that we want using a combination of literal text, conditional statements, and `<xsl:value-of>` instructions. We can use the `$Plural` variable to judge whether we need "are" or "is", and whether we need an "s" at the end of "episodes":

```
<p>
  There
  <xsl:choose>
    <xsl:when test="$Plural">are </xsl:when>
    <xsl:otherwise>is </xsl:otherwise>
  </xsl:choose>
  <xsl:value-of select="$NumberOfStarTrekEpisodes" />
  Star Trek episode<xsl:if test="$Plural">s</xsl:if>
  showing this week.
</p>
```

Putting this all together in the template for the `<TVGuide>` element in `StarTrek6.xsl`, we get the following:

```
<xsl:template match="TVGuide">
  <xsl:variable name="StarTrekChannels"
    select="Channel[Program[starts-with(Series, $series)]]" />
```

```
  <p>
    <xsl:apply-templates select="$StarTrekChannels" mode="ChannelList" />
  </p>
  <xsl:choose>
    <xsl:when test="$StarTrekChannels">
      <xsl:variable name="NumberOfStarTrekEpisodes" as="xs:integer"
        select="count(Channel/Program[starts-with(Series, $series)])" />
      <xsl:variable name="Plural" as="xs:boolean"
        select="$NumberOfStarTrekEpisodes > 1" />
      <p>
        There
        <xsl:choose>
          <xsl:when test="$Plural">are </xsl:when>
          <xsl:otherwise>is </xsl:otherwise>
        </xsl:choose>
        <xsl:value-of select="$NumberOfStarTrekEpisodes" />
        Star Trek episode<xsl:if test="$Plural">s</xsl:if>
        showing this week.
      </p>
      <xsl:apply-templates select="$StarTrekChannels" />
    </xsl:when>
    <xsl:otherwise>
      <p>No Star Trek showing this week!</p>
    </xsl:otherwise>
  </xsl:choose>
  <p>
    <xsl:apply-templates select="$StarTrekChannels" mode="ChannelList" />
  </p>
</xsl:template>
```

The result of transforming TVGuide.xml with StarTrek6.xsl is StarTrek6.html, which is shown in Figure 6-6.

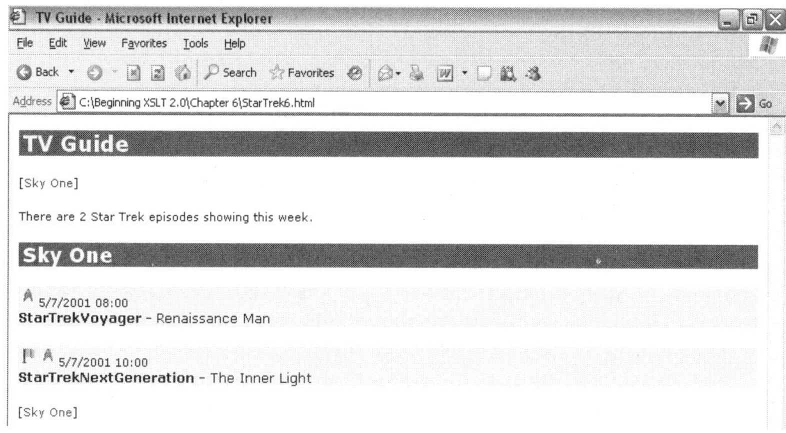

Figure 6-6. *Viewing* StarTrek6.html *in Internet Explorer*

Sequence Constructors

So far we've looked at how to use `<xsl:variable>` to define variables using the `select` attribute. There is another way to set the value of a variable: using its content. If you don't have a `select` attribute, the content of the `<xsl:variable>` element is used as a **sequence constructor**. The XSLT instructions that the `<xsl:variable>` element contains are used to create a sequence of nodes or atomic values (or a mixture of both), which are then assigned to the variable.

Each instruction in a sequence constructor contributes zero or more items to the sequence that gets created by the sequence constructor. Most instructions don't actually create items for the sequence themselves, but rather determine which other instructions are used to create the items. For example, consider the following:

```
<xsl:variable name="flagImage" as="element()?">
  <xsl:choose>
    <xsl:when test="@flag = 'favorite'">
      <img src="favorite.gif" alt="[Favorite]" width="20" height="20" />
    </xsl:when>
    <xsl:when test="@flag = 'interesting'">
      <img src="interest.gif" alt="[Interest]" width="20" height="20" />
    </xsl:when>
  </xsl:choose>
</xsl:variable>
```

The `<xsl:choose>` instruction (and the `<xsl:when>` elements that it contains) determines which set of instructions is used to construct the sequence: either the instructions held by the first `<xsl:when>` or the instructions held by the second `<xsl:when>`. Several other instructions play a similar role:

- `<xsl:if>`—Determines whether or not the instructions that it contains are used, based on the value of its `test` attribute, to construct a result sequence.
- `<xsl:for-each>`—Holds instructions that are repeated for each item in the sequence it selects with its `select` attribute, to construct a result sequence.
- `<xsl:apply-templates>`—Applies templates to the items in the sequence it selects with its `select` attribute. The templates that are applied contain instructions that are used to construct a result sequence.

Other instructions actually identify items that should be added to the result sequence. In the next few sections, we'll look at what you can do as a result.

Constructing Sequences Containing Atomic Values

The simplest kind of item that you can have in a sequence is an atomic value. There are two other ways of adding atomic values to a sequence: `<xsl:copy-of>` and `<xsl:sequence>`. Both instructions have a `select` attribute that selects the value to add to the sequence. The following variable declarations are all equivalent: they all set the `$dueDate` variable to the `xs:date` `2003-12-08`:

```
<xsl:variable name="dueDate" as="xs:date" select="xs:date('2003-12-08')" />
<xsl:variable name="dueDate" as="xs:date">
  <xsl:copy-of select="xs:date('2003-12-08')" />
```

```
</xsl:variable>
<xsl:variable name="dueDate" as="xs:date">
  <xsl:sequence select="xs:date('2003-12-08')" />
</xsl:variable>
```

Note There's not really any point in using `<xsl:copy-of>` or `<xsl:sequence>` to set variables in the way shown previously: using the `select` attribute of the `<xsl:variable>` element, or implicitly casting a text node to the required type, is a lot shorter and more readable.

One way in which `<xsl:copy-of>` and `<xsl:sequence>` come in handy is when using `<xsl:for-each>` to create a sequence of atomic values, one for each node in a sequence.

For example, say that we wanted to indicate, for the TV guide as a whole, the time span over which we have program information on all the channels. We can work out the start of this time span by looking at the start times of the first `<Program>` elements within each `<Channel>` element, and taking the maximum (the latest of these start times) using the `max()` function. We can get the start times for the first `<Program>` element in each `<Channel>` element with

```
Channel/Program[1]/Start
```

Each of the start times needs to be cast to an `xs:dateTime`; otherwise the `max()` function will interpret them as numbers and give an error, but we can do this easily enough using the implicit casting that we get when we declare a variable's type. Here, if we create a variable to hold the start times, we can declare it as being of type `xs:dateTime+`, and the `<Start>` elements' values will be automatically cast to that type:

```
<xsl:variable name="startTimes" as="xs:dateTime+"
              select="Channel/Program[1]/Start" />
```

The latest start time (the earliest time for which we have program information on all channels) can then be calculated using the `max()` function:

```
<xsl:variable name="latestStartTime" as="xs:dateTime"
              select="max($startTimes)" />
```

To create a similar sequence of end times, on the other hand, we're going to need to do some calculations. The sequence of end times needs to contain, for each channel, the end time of the last program on the channel. Given a `<Channel>` element, we can work out the end time of the last program using date/time arithmetic, as we saw in the last chapter:

```
xs:dateTime(Program[last()]/Start) +
xdt:dayTimeDuration(Program[last()]/Duration)
```

To create a sequence of these values, we need to iterate over the `<Channel>` elements using `<xsl:for-each>`, and for each of them create an atomic value, calculated as in the preceding code; we can use either `<xsl:copy-of>` or `<xsl:sequence>` to create the atomic value to add to the sequence:

```
<xsl:variable name="endTimes" as="xs:dateTime+">
  <xsl:for-each select="Channel">
```

```
    <xsl:sequence select="xs:dateTime(Program[last()]/Start) +
                          xdt:dayTimeDuration(Program[last()]/Duration)" />
  </xsl:for-each>
</xsl:variable>
```

Note We'll see a couple of other ways to create this sequence in the next chapter, when we look at paths and the `for` expression.

The earliest end time (the latest time for which we have program information on all channels) can then be calculated using the `min()` function:

```
<xsl:variable name="earliestEndTime" as="xs:dateTime"
              select="min($endTimes)" />
```

Summary You can add an atomic value to a sequence using either the `<xsl:copy-of>` element or the `<xsl:sequence>` element.

Constructing Sequences Containing Existing Nodes

You can also use the `<xsl:copy-of>` and `<xsl:sequence>` to add nodes to a sequence, and this is where their behavior diverges. If you select a sequence of nodes (using a path, for example) with its `select` attribute, the `<xsl:copy-of>` instruction creates *new* nodes in the sequence: copies of the nodes that you select. On the other hand, the `<xsl:sequence>` element adds the *original* nodes themselves to the sequence.

For example, in `TVGuide3.xsl`, we're currently setting the `$castList` variable as follows:

```
<xsl:variable name="castList" as="element()?" select="CastList" />
```

Another way to set it would be to use the content of the `<xsl:variable>` element, as in `TVGuide4.xsl`, in which the variable is set as follows:

```
<xsl:variable name="castList" as="element()?">
  <xsl:copy-of select="CastList" />
</xsl:variable>
```

If we use `<xsl:copy-of>`, as in the preceding code, the `$castList` variable actually holds a copy of the `<CastList>` element. It's a **deep copy**, which means that it includes copies of the `<CastList>` element's attributes and descendants as well as the `<CastList>` element itself, but it's a new node and doesn't have a parent. We apply templates to this element using

```
<xsl:apply-templates select="$castList" />
```

The template that is invoked is as follows:

```
<xsl:template match="CastList">
  <div id="{../Series}Cast" style="display: none;">
    <ul class="castlist"><xsl:apply-templates /></ul>
  </div>
</xsl:template>
```

See how the value of the id attribute is being set using the value of the <Series> element that's a child of the <CastList> element's parent? The <CastList> that we're processing here doesn't have a parent, so there's no way of working out what series the cast list relates to. The HTML that's generated (in TVGuide4.html) looks like this:

```
<div id="Cast" style="display: none;">
  <ul class="castlist">...</ul>
</div>
```

On the other hand, if you use <xsl:sequence> to add the <CastList> element to the sequence, as in TVGuide5.xsl:

```
<xsl:variable name="castList" as="element()?">
  <xsl:sequence select="CastList" />
</xsl:variable>
```

then the $castList variable holds the original <CastList> element, from which it's possible to navigate to the <Series> element. The resulting HTML, in TVGuide5.html, looks like this:

```
<div id="EastEndersCast" style="display: none;">
  <ul class="castlist">...</ul>
</div>
```

Usually, it's the behavior of <xsl:sequence> that you want: having the original nodes in the sequence means that you can move around the original node tree to get hold of information. In addition, creating new nodes is one of the more time-consuming of the operations that you can perform in XSLT, so avoiding creating new nodes is a good idea if you can help it.

Summary If you select nodes using <xsl:sequence>, then the nodes are added to the result sequence. If you select nodes using <xsl:copy-of>, they get copied and the new copies are added to the result sequence.

Constructing Sequences Containing New Nodes

If we include <xsl:copy-of>, we've now seen four ways to add new nodes to a sequence:

- Using a literal result element adds an element to the sequence.
- Using literal text adds a text node to the sequence.
- Using <xsl:value-of> adds a text node to the sequence.
- Using <xsl:copy-of> adds copies of whatever nodes you select to the sequence.

For example, the following variable declaration assigns a single <img> element as the value of the $flagImage variable:

```
<xsl:variable name="flagImage" as="element()">
  <img src="flag.gif" alt="[Flagged]" width="20" height="20" />
</xsl:variable>
```

and the following variable declaration assigns three text nodes as the value of the $formattedDate variable: one for the first <xsl:value-of> element, one for the literal text node (" - "), and one for the second <xsl:value-of> element:

```
<xsl:variable name="formattedDate" as="text()+">
    <xsl:value-of select="format-dateTime(xs:dateTime(.),
                                          '[M]/[D]/[Y] [H01]:[m]')" />
    -
    <xsl:value-of select="format-dateTime(xs:dateTime(.) +
                                          xdt:dayTimeDuration(../Duration),
                                          '[H01]:[m]')" />
</xsl:variable>
```

Sometimes you might want to create a variable that holds both text and elements. In this case, you need the as attribute of <xsl:variable> to reflect the fact that it holds nodes of any kind, which you can do using the node() node test. For example:

```
<xsl:variable name="copyright" as="node()+">
  Copyright <a href="mailto:jeni@jenitennison.com">Jeni Tennison</a>, 2005
</xsl:variable>
```

Summary Some instructions, such as <xsl:value-of> and literal result elements, create new nodes that are added to the sequence being generated.

CREATING ATOMIC VALUES VIA TEXT NODES

You can use a sequence constructor that creates nodes to assign a sequence of atomic values to a variable. As usual, the as attribute indicates the type of the variable, and the sequence generated by the sequence constructor will be cast to the type indicated by the as attribute (if it's possible to do so implicitly). For example, you can set the $dueDate variable to the xs:date 2003-12-08 using

```
<xsl:variable name="dueDate" as="xs:date">2003-12-08</xsl:variable>
```

When setting the $dueDate variable, the sequence constructor generates a sequence containing a single text node with the value '2003-12-08', and this gets automatically cast to an xs:date. The result is exactly the same as if you set the variable using

```
<xsl:variable name="dueDate" as="xs:date" select="xs:date('2003-12-08')" />
```

Beware, however, of using <xsl:value-of> when <xsl:sequence> (or <xsl:copy-of>) would give you the value more directly. For example, we saw how to use <xsl:sequence> to create a sequence of end times for the programs listed for the channels in the TV guide, using

```
<xsl:variable name="endTimes" as="xs:dateTime+">
  <xsl:for-each select="Channel">
    <xsl:sequence select="xs:dateTime(Program[last()]/Start) +
                          xdt:dayTimeDuration(Program[last()]/Duration)" />
  </xsl:for-each>
</xsl:variable>
```

Using <xsl:value-of> instead of <xsl:sequence> here would give exactly the same effect:

```
<xsl:variable name="endTimes" as="xs:dateTime+">
  <xsl:for-each select="Channel">
    <xsl:value-of select="xs:dateTime(Program[last()]/Start) +
                          xdt:dayTimeDuration(Program[last()]/Duration)" />
  </xsl:for-each>
</xsl:variable>
```

However, behind the scenes the processor would have to do a lot more work. The <xsl:value-of> instruction converts the sequence that it selects to a text node, and then the text nodes that are generated each get converted to xs:dateTime values. In contrast, using <xsl:sequence> just adds the xs:dateTime value directly to the sequence, which is obviously less work for the processor.

One way in which using a sequence constructor to hold new nodes is useful is that you can make a variable that holds a fragment of the result node tree, and then output the same nodes in multiple locations within the output, using <xsl:copy-of> or <xsl:sequence>.

For example, we can set up a global variable to hold the <img> element that we want in the output if a program is a *Star Trek* episode:

```
<xsl:variable name="StarTrekLogo" as="element()">
  <img src="StarTrek.gif" alt="[Star Trek]" width="20" height="20" />
</xsl:variable>
```

This variable is global, so we can refer to it from anywhere within the stylesheet. The template for the <Program> element in TVGuide6.xsl includes the following:

```
<p>
  ...
  <xsl:if test="starts-with(Series, 'StarTrek')">
    <xsl:sequence select="$StarTrekLogo" />
  </xsl:if>
  ...
</p>
```

The same <img> element is reused multiple times. You could use <xsl:copy-of> instead of <xsl:sequence> here; either way, the <img> element gets copied into the content of the <p> elements as required.

Summary You can reuse XML fragments by copying them into the result tree using either the <xsl:copy-of> or <xsl:sequence> instruction.

Repeating Channel Lists

When we create our TV listing with TVGuide6.xsl, we have a list of the channels shown at the top and bottom of the page, to help the person reading the page to navigate to the channel they want to look at. We generate these channel lists by applying templates in ChannelList mode in the template for the <TVGuide> element, as follows:

```
<xsl:template match="TVGuide">
  <p>
    <xsl:apply-templates select="Channel" mode="ChannelList" />
  </p>
  <xsl:apply-templates select="Channel" />
  <p>
    <xsl:apply-templates select="Channel" mode="ChannelList" />
  </p>
</xsl:template>
```

Each time the XSLT processor encounters these <xsl:apply-templates> instructions, it navigates the source node tree and constructs a list of channels using the following template:

```
<xsl:template match="Channel" mode="ChannelList">
  <a href="#{Name}"><xsl:value-of select="Name" /></a>
  <xsl:if test="position() != last()"> | </xsl:if>
</xsl:template>
```

Exactly the same HTML is generated each time templates are applied in ChannelList mode—we are performing exactly the same transformation twice over. Instead, we can store the results of doing the transformation in a variable and then copy this result into the HTML page wherever we want.

We'll make this change in TVGuide7.xsl, and make it a global variable because that will enable us to add the same channel list at other locations within our page if we want to later on (such as prior to the program listing for each channel). We want the variable to hold the result of applying templates in ChannelList mode, so we use the content of the <xsl:variable> element to set the variable value:

```
<xsl:variable name="ChannelList" as="element()+">
  <p><xsl:apply-templates select="/TVGuide/Channel" mode="ChannelList" /></p>
</xsl:variable>
```

To copy the value of that variable into the result HTML, you need either the <xsl:copy-of> instruction or the <xsl:sequence> instruction. This replaces the original <p> elements in the template that matches the <TVGuide> element, as follows:

```
<xsl:template match="TVGuide">
  <xsl:sequence select="$ChannelList" />
  <xsl:apply-templates select="Channel" />
  <xsl:sequence select="$ChannelList" />
</xsl:template>
```

Try transforming `TVGuide.xml` with `TVGuide7.xsl` to give `TVGuide7.html`. You should get the result shown in Figure 6-7.

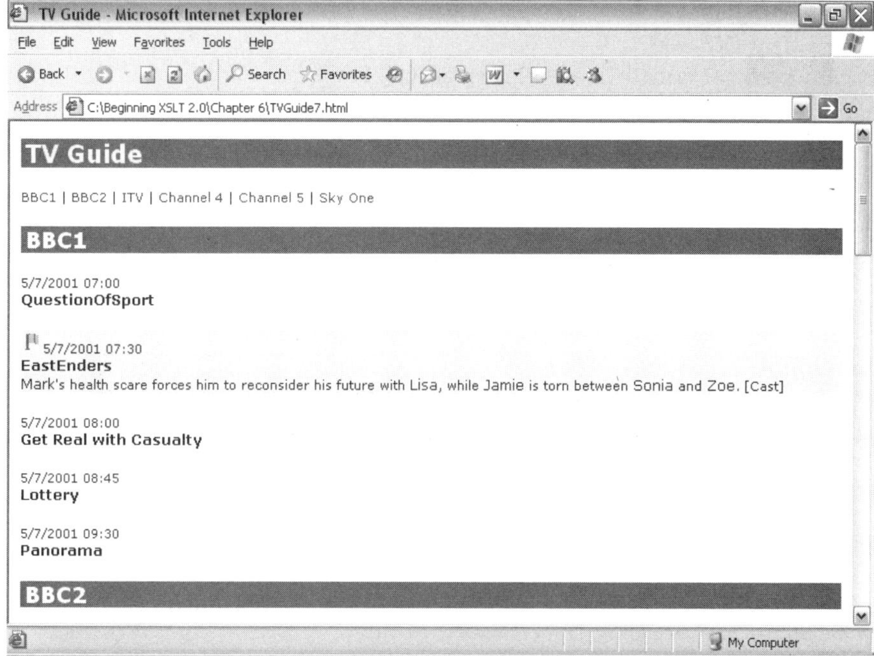

Figure 6-7. *Viewing* `TVGuide7.html` *in Internet Explorer*

Using a variable has made absolutely no difference to the result you get, and the speed increase is likely to be fractional, but using a variable has made your stylesheet easier to maintain and change later on.

Temporary Trees

In the last section, we introduced the notion of setting a variable using a sequence constructor in its content. All the examples that we looked at in the last section coupled the use of the content of the `<xsl:variable>` element with an `as` attribute. In fact, the presence of an `as` attribute has a big effect on the value that a variable gets assigned to it when you use the content of the variable to set its value. If you don't use an as attribute, and you set a variable using its content, you actually get a **temporary tree**.

Temporary trees are small node trees, with their very own document node. The main reason for having them in XSLT 2.0 is for backwards compatibility with XSLT 1.0, in which setting a variable using its content generated what was known as a **result tree fragment**. When you use the content of `<xsl:variable>` and you don't have an `as` attribute, the sequence created by the result is added to a new document node and the variable's value is that document node rather than the sequence itself.

If the sequence constructor used within the `<xsl:variable>` element generates a sequence of atomic values, you can get dramatically different results if you create a temporary tree instead. For example, if we left off the `as` attribute when creating the sequence of end times for the `<Channel>` elements, as follows:

```
<xsl:variable name="endTimes">
  <xsl:for-each select="Channel">
    <xsl:sequence select="xs:dateTime(Program[last()]/Start) +
                          xdt:dayTimeDuration(Program[last()]/Duration)" />
  </xsl:for-each>
</xsl:variable>
```

then rather than the `$endTimes` variable holding a sequence of `xs:dateTime` values, it would hold a single document node with a single text node as a child. Obviously this would completely change the result of the function call `max($endTimes)`.

■ **Note** As we'll see in Chapter 8, that text node would hold a concatenation of the string values of the end times, with spaces in between.

If the sequence constructor used within the `<xsl:variable>` element generates new nodes, then there are three subtle but significant differences between creating the sequence of new nodes and creating a temporary tree in which the children of the root document node are the new nodes:

- In a temporary tree, the new nodes will be siblings, which means that you can navigate from one to another; in a sequence, they are unrelated, which means you can't.
- In a temporary tree, any consecutive text nodes will be concatenated into a single text node child of the root document node; in a sequence, they will remain separate.
- The new nodes in the temporary tree have a parent—the root document node—whereas new nodes in a sequence are parentless.

In general, if the purpose of a variable is to hold a snippet of the result tree, I use a temporary tree, but if the purpose of a variable is to hold nodes for processing or lookup purposes, I have it hold a sequence of those nodes.

For example, the following variable holds a snippet of XML that will eventually be used in the result node tree, so I've omitted the `as` attribute:

```
<xsl:variable name="copyright">
  Copyright <a href="mailto:jeni@jenitennison.com">Jeni Tennison</a>, 2005
</xsl:variable>
```

On the other hand, the following variable holds elements that you might use for looking up the appropriate graphic and alternative text for a particular flag, so I've included an as attribute:

```
<xsl:variable name="flags" as="element()+">
  <flag name="interesting" src="interest.gif" alt="[Interest]" />
  <flag name="favorite" src="favorite.gif" alt="[Favorite]" />
  ...
</xsl:variable>
```

■ **Summary** If you don't have an as attribute on an <xsl:variable> element, and you set the variable using its content, then you generate a temporary tree.

Using Parameters

As we've seen, variables can hold information within a specific stylesheet or within a specific template. **Parameters** are like variables, but their values can be set from outside their scope, allowing values to be passed in to the stylesheet or to be passed in to a template.

Earlier in this chapter, we looked at how to create a global variable that could hold the string 'StarTrek' that we then used to create a page dedicated to *Star Trek* shows. The relevant piece of XSLT is the following from StarTrek6.xsl:

```
<xsl:variable name="series" select="'StarTrek'" />
<xsl:template match="TVGuide">
  <xsl:variable name="StarTrekChannels" as="element()*"
    select="Channel[Program[starts-with(Series, $series)]]" />
  <p><xsl:apply-templates select="$StarTrekChannels" mode="ChannelList" /></p>
  <xsl:choose>
    <xsl:when test="$StarTrekChannels">
      <xsl:variable name="NumberOfStarTrekEpisodes" as="xs:integer"
        select="count(Channel/Program[starts-with(Series, $series)])" />
      <xsl:variable name="Plural" as="xs:boolean"
        select="$NumberOfStarTrekEpisodes > 1" />
      <p>
        There
        <xsl:choose>
          <xsl:when test="$Plural">are </xsl:when>
          <xsl:otherwise>is </xsl:otherwise>
        </xsl:choose>
        <xsl:value-of select="$NumberOfStarTrekEpisodes" />
        Star Trek episode<xsl:if test="$Plural">s</xsl:if>
        showing this week.
      </p>
      <xsl:apply-templates select="$StarTrekChannels" />
```

```
    </xsl:when>
    <xsl:otherwise>
      <p>No Star Trek showing this week!</p>
    </xsl:otherwise>
  </xsl:choose>
  <p><xsl:apply-templates select="$StarTrekChannels" mode="ChannelList" /></p>
</xsl:template>

<xsl:template match="Channel">
  <xsl:apply-templates select="Name" />
  <xsl:apply-templates select="Program[starts-with(Series, $series)]" />
</xsl:template>
```

Despite the naming of the `$StarTrekChannels` and `$NumberOfStarTrekEpisodes` variables, and the messages that get displayed to say how many episodes are showing, if we changed the value of the `$series` variable, we could use this same XSLT to create a page dedicated to any series we wanted. Currently, changing the value of the `$series` variable would mean editing the stylesheet itself each time we want to create a different page (for example, we did this to create `EastEnders.xsl` earlier). However, XSLT provides parameters to allow you to change the values of variables on the fly, without editing the stylesheet. In this section, we'll look at how parameters work and how to use them.

Declaring and Referring to Parameters

Parameters are very similar to variables. When you declare a parameter, you do so with an `<xsl:param>` element rather than an `<xsl:variable>` element, but the syntax of the two elements is basically the same. As with variables, every parameter must have a name, defined through the `<xsl:param>` element's `name` attribute, and this is prefixed with a dollar sign ($) when it's referred to within an XPath.

You can give parameters values in the same ways as you can variables, either through the `<xsl:param>` element's `select` attribute or through its content. The main difference between variables and parameters, though, is that the value that you specify for a parameter when you declare it can be overridden from elsewhere—it acts as a default for the parameter.

Sometimes it's not sensible for a parameter to have a default, because the parameter *must* be given a value. The `<xsl:param>` element has an extra attribute—`required`—which indicates whether a value must be supplied for the parameter or not. If the value is `'yes'`, then the parameter cannot have a default value (it must not have a `select` attribute, nor any content), and a value for it must be supplied by the calling code. If the value is `'no'`, then the default value gets used if no other value is supplied.

Like variables, parameters can occur at two levels within a stylesheet—as top-level elements similar to global variables (children of the `<xsl:stylesheet>` element), or within a template similar to local variables. Parameters that are declared at the top level of a stylesheet are known as **stylesheet parameters**, while those that are declared within templates are known as **template parameters**.

■ **Note** Parameters are also used to declare the arguments for functions, which we'll see in Chapter 11. Function parameters work in a very similar way to template parameters.

The scoping rules for parameters are the same as those for variables, and their names are in the same symbol space, so if you have a variable in the same scope as a parameter with the same name, the variable will shadow the parameter.

■ **Summary** Parameters are like variables that you can set to different values on the fly.

Stylesheet Parameters

Stylesheet parameters are declared at the top level of the stylesheet. Once you've declared a stylesheet parameter you can use different values for that parameter each time you run a transformation with the stylesheet. For example, you can turn the `$series` global variable into a stylesheet parameter by changing the name of the element from `<xsl:variable>` to `<xsl:param>`:

```
<xsl:param name="series" select="'StarTrek'" as="xs:string" />
```

How you pass a value for the parameter into the stylesheet depends on the XSLT processor that you're using and how you're using it. That makes it difficult to state exactly how you do it in general.

If you're using a client-side transformation or if you're running your own script on the server side, then you have to use the methods available in the interface to the transformation to set the parameters. Some server-side frameworks, such as Cocoon, AxKit, and XSQL, allow you to pass parameters to a stylesheet using the URL that you use to access the XML document that's transformed with the stylesheet.

■ **Note** You can find out more about Cocoon at `http://xml.apache.org/cocoon/`, more about AxKit at `http://axkit.org/`, and more about XSQL at `http://technet.oracle.com/tech/xml/xdk_java/`.

For example, you would be able to use the URL

```
http://www.example.com/TVGuide.xml?series=EastEnders
```

to generate an HTML page that showed only the *EastEnders* programs. We'll be looking at how to pass parameters into stylesheets from code and using Cocoon in detail in Chapter 15.

■ **Caution** It is not an error to pass in a parameter to a stylesheet that doesn't declare that parameter, so watch out for spelling mistakes, especially wrong capitalization.

You can also pass parameters into stylesheets when you run them from the command line. With MSXML, the syntax is

```
msxsl TVGuide.xml Series.xsl -o EastEnders.html series=EastEnders
```

It's similar with Saxon:

```
java net.sf.saxon.Transform -o EastEnders.html TVGuide.xml Series.xsl
series=EastEnders
```

With Xalan, it's slightly different:

```
java org.apache.xalan.xslt.Process -IN TVGuide.xml -XSL Series.xsl
-OUT EastEnders.html -PARAM series EastEnders
```

■ **Note** When you pass in parameters using the command line, they are values of type `xs:string`. You should therefore declare any stylesheet parameters that you want to set using a command line as being of type `xs:string`.

■ **Summary** Stylesheet parameters are declared at the top level of the stylesheet. You can use different values for these parameters each time you run the stylesheet.

Creating Series-Specific TV Guides

The easiest way to test stylesheet parameters is to use a command line to run the transformation. First, we'll create a new stylesheet, called `Series.xsl`, in which the `$series` global variable is a stylesheet parameter instead; you could correct the messages generated by the template that matches the `<TVGuide>` element at the same time, so that it isn't specific to *Star Trek*:

```
<xsl:param name="series" select="'Star Trek'" as="xs:string" />
<xsl:template match="TVGuide">
  <xsl:variable name="channels" as="element()*"
                select="Channel[Program[starts-with(Series, $series)]]" />
  <xsl:choose>
    <xsl:when test="$channels">
      <xsl:apply-templates select="$channels" />
    </xsl:when>
    <xsl:otherwise>
      <p>No <xsl:value-of select="$series" /> showing this week!</p>
    </xsl:otherwise>
  </xsl:choose>
</xsl:template>
```

Run the stylesheet as it is, using the normal command line for the processor that you're using. The relevant command line for Saxon is

```
java net.sf.saxon.Transform -o StarTrekSeries.html TVGuide.xml Series.xsl
```

The `StarTrekSeries.html` page will list any *Star Trek* programs in the TV guide XML; the default value for the `$series` parameter is `'StarTrek'`, and in the absence of a different value being passed in at the command line, the stylesheet will use this default. Figure 6-8 shows you what `StarTrekSeries.html` looks like when you view it in Internet Explorer.

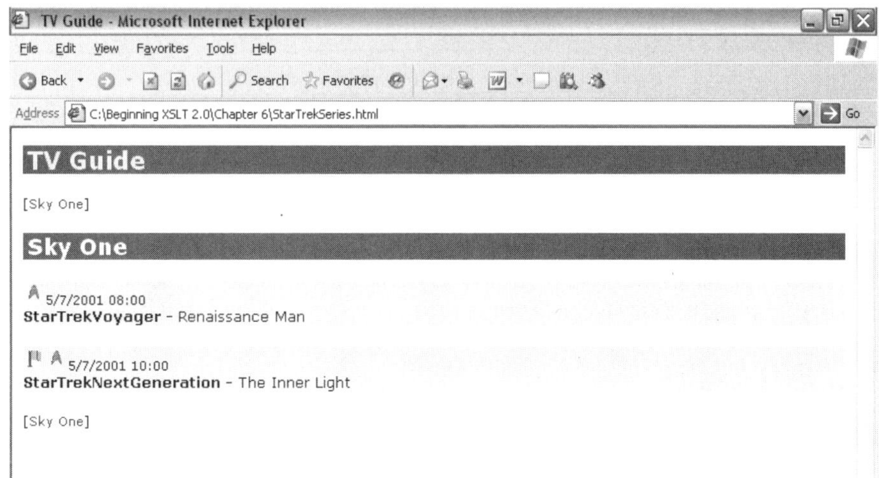

Figure 6-8. *Viewing* `StarTrekSeries.html` *in Internet Explorer*

Now try using the same stylesheet to generate an episode listing for *EastEnders*. To pass the string `'EastEnders'` as the value of the `$series` parameter to Saxon, you should use the following command line:

```
java net.sf.saxon.Transform -o EastEndersSeries.html TVGuide.xml Series.xsl
series=EastEnders
```

Figure 6-9 shows the `EastEndersSeries.html` HTML page in Internet Explorer.

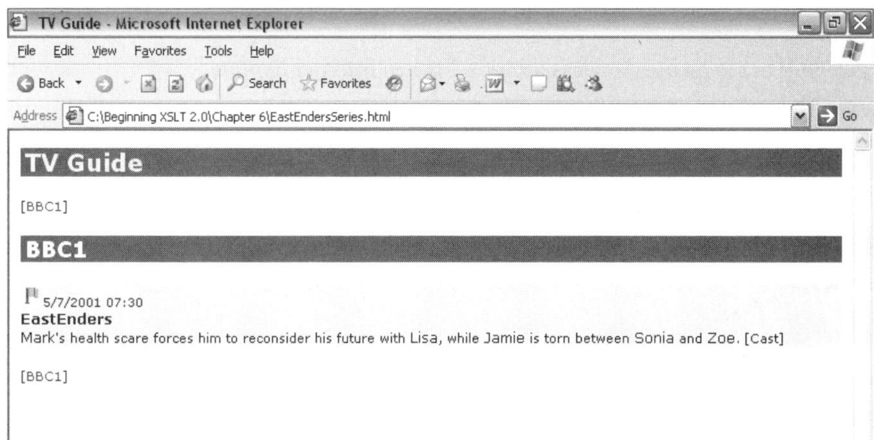

Figure 6-9. *Viewing* `EastEndersSeries.html` *in Internet Explorer*

You can do the same for any other series that you like by passing in different values for the `$series` stylesheet parameter. Being able to use the same stylesheet to generate lots of different pages drastically cuts down on the number of stylesheets you need to maintain, and makes it a lot easier to create dynamic applications, as we'll see in Chapter 15.

Before we move on, let's have a look at what happens if you misspell the name of the `$series` parameter, for example, accidentally capitalizing and calling it `$Series` instead:

```
java net.sf.saxon.Transform -o EastEndersSeriesMisspelled.html TVGuide.xml
Series.xsl Series=EastEnders
```

The resulting `EastEndersSeriesMisspelled.html` page looks exactly the same as that we got when we didn't provide a value for the `$series` parameter: it shows us the *Star Trek* episodes in the TV guide.

To avoid this kind of mistake, you could make the `$series` parameter a required parameter, so that you get an error if you don't provide a value for it. In `Series2.xsl`, the `$series` parameter is required: it has a `required` attribute with the value `'yes'` and it doesn't provide a default value:

```
<xsl:param name="series" as="xs:string" required="yes" />
```

What happens if we misspell the name of the `$series` parameter when transforming with `Series2.xsl`?

```
java net.sf.saxon.Transform -o EastEndersSeriesMisspelled2.html TVGuide.xml
Series2.xsl Series=EastEnders
```

Figure 6-10 shows the error that you get from Saxon as a result of misspelling the name of the required parameter.

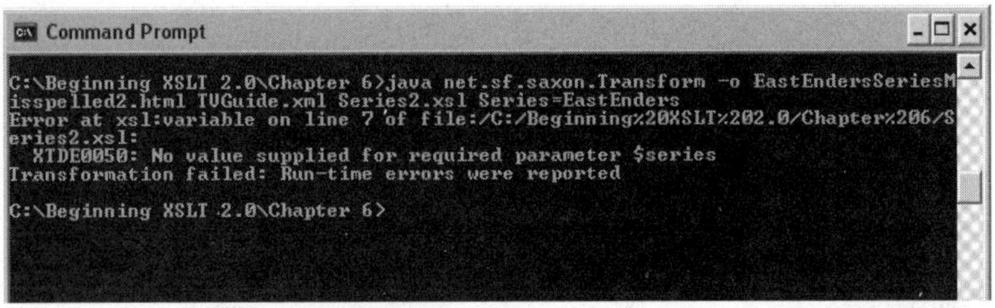

```
Command Prompt
C:\Beginning XSLT 2.0\Chapter 6>java net.sf.saxon.Transform -o EastEndersSeriesM
isspelled2.html TVGuide.xml Series2.xsl Series=EastEnders
Error at xsl:variable on line 7 of file:/C:/Beginning%20XSLT%202.0/Chapter%206/S
eries2.xsl:
  XTDE0050: No value supplied for required parameter $series
Transformation failed: Run-time errors were reported

C:\Beginning XSLT 2.0\Chapter 6>
```

Figure 6-10. *Viewing* `EastEndersSeriesMisspelled2.html` *in Internet Explorer*

You would get the same error if you didn't supply a value for the `$series` parameter at all. Supplying the value of the `$series` parameter correctly, as in the command line

```
java net.sf.saxon.Transform -o EastEndersSeries2.html TVGuide.xml Series2.xsl
series=EastEnders
```

works fine.

Template Parameters

You can also pass parameters to templates, which is particularly useful when you start using recursive templates, which we'll come to in Chapter 11. One place in which they would be useful in our stylesheet is when we create the HTML for the TV programs, specifically for the cast list. If you recall, in TVGuide7.xsl, we're currently applying templates to the <CastList> elements twice: once to create the cast list itself and once, in DisplayToggle mode, to create a link that shows or hides the cast list. The relevant templates are as follows:

```
<xsl:template match="Program" mode="Details">
  <p>
    ...
    <xsl:apply-templates select="Description" />
    <xsl:apply-templates select="$castList" mode="DisplayToggle" />
  </p>
  <xsl:apply-templates select="$castList" />
</xsl:template>

<xsl:template match="CastList" mode="DisplayToggle">
  <span onclick="toggle({../Series}Cast);">[Cast]</span>
</xsl:template>

<xsl:template match="CastList">
  <div id="{../Series}Cast" style="display: none;">
    <ul class="castlist"><xsl:apply-templates /></ul>
  </div>
</xsl:template>
```

Both of the templates need to use the same ID for the <div> that contains the cast list. As it stands, we're creating this ID twice in the same way in separate templates. If the code for creating the <div> and the reference to it were within the same template, we could create the ID once, use a variable to hold it, and refer to that variable in the two different locations. We can create the variable easily enough, but we need to pass the value of that variable to the two different templates to allow them to use it.

To use template parameters, you must both declare the parameter within the template that uses it and pass in values for that parameter when you apply templates to the nodes that are processed with that template. When you declare template parameters, the <xsl:param> elements must be the first elements in the content of the <xsl:template> element.

To pass parameters to a template, you use <xsl:with-param> elements within the <xsl:apply-templates> or <xsl:next-match> instruction that results in the template being processed. The <xsl:with-param> element is a lot like the <xsl:variable> and <xsl:param> elements, in that you use the name attribute to give the name of the parameter and either the select attribute or the content of the <xsl:with-param> element to specify the value for the parameter.

Note As we'll see in later chapters, you can also pass parameters using <xsl:with-param> when you call templates by name using <xsl:call-template> or when you invoke templates from an imported stylesheet using <xsl:apply-imports>.

The name that you use when you pass the parameter value into the template has to be the same as the name of the parameter that you've declared in the template. Usually, as with stylesheet parameters, the XSLT processor won't complain if you try to pass a parameter into a template that doesn't declare that parameter, or if you don't pass a value for a parameter that's not required. The XSLT processor will complain, however, if you don't pass a value for a required parameter (one that has a `required` attribute with the value `yes`).

Summary Template parameters have to be declared as the first thing in a template. You can use them to change what a template generates based on information from the template that causes it to be processed.

Passing Parameters to Templates

Let's look at how to use parameters so that we only create the ID for the `<div>` element once in `TVGuide8.xsl`. There are two templates that use the ID; both need to declare that they require a parameter (which we'll call `$divID`), which is a string, and then use that parameter in the HTML that they create:

```
<xsl:template match="CastList" mode="DisplayToggle">
  <xsl:param name="divID" as="xs:string" required="yes" />
  <span onclick="toggle({$divID});">[Cast]</span>
</xsl:template>

<xsl:template match="CastList">
  <xsl:param name="divID" as="xs:string" required="yes" />
  <div id="{$divID}" style="display: none;">
    <ul class="castlist"><xsl:apply-templates /></ul>
  </div>
</xsl:template>
```

In the template that applies templates to the `<CastList>` elements that these templates match, we need to construct the ID for the `<div>` element we're creating and then pass that ID into the two templates using `<xsl:with-param>` within the two `<xsl:apply-templates>` elements, as follows:

```
<xsl:template match="Program" mode="Details">
  <xsl:variable name="programID" as="xs:string"
                select="concat(Series, 'Cast')" />
  <p>
    ...
    <xsl:apply-templates select="Description" />
    <xsl:apply-templates select="$castList" mode="DisplayToggle">
      <xsl:with-param name="divID" select="$programID" />
    </xsl:apply-templates>
  </p>
  <xsl:apply-templates select="$castList">
    <xsl:with-param name="divID" select="$programID" />
  </xsl:apply-templates>
</xsl:template>
```

If you transform `TVGuide.xml` with `TVGuide8.xsl`, which uses these template parameters, to give `TVGuide8.html`, you get the page shown in Figure 6-11, exactly the same as before.

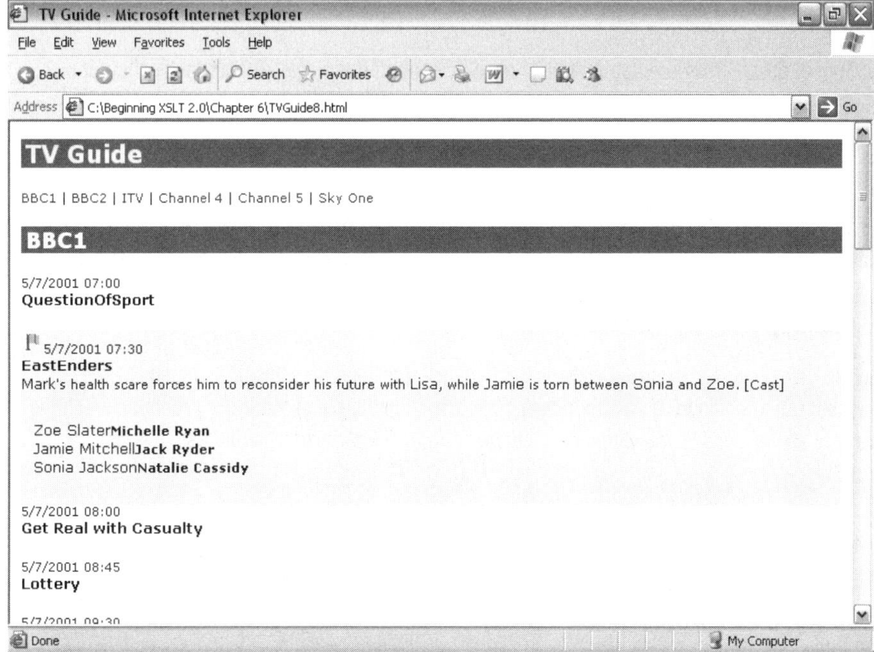

Figure 6-11. *Viewing* `TVGuide8.html` *in Internet Explorer*

The [Cast] "button" hides and reveals the list of cast members as it used to, but the stylesheet is easier to maintain because the way in which you identify the relevant `<div>` element is only defined in one location, rather than in two separate templates.

Tunnel Parameters

Complicated stylesheets can use large numbers of parameters to pass information between templates, and sometimes the template that supplies the value for a parameter can be far removed from the template that needs to use that value. Often that can mean you have to pass a parameter through several templates that don't actually need to use the value of the parameter. Keeping track of all the parameters that might need to be used by templates later on can be very tedious and prone to error.

To get around this problem, XSLT 2.0 introduces the concept of **tunnel parameters**. When you first pass a parameter, you can declare that it's a tunnel parameter using the `tunnel` attribute on `<xsl:with-param>` with a value of `'yes'`. This parameter will be passed on to the templates that are invoked by the `<xsl:apply-templates>` or `<xsl:next-match>` instruction, and to any templates that are invoked by the instructions held in those templates, and so on, without any templates having to actually declare or explicitly pass on the tunnel parameter.

When you want to *use* the tunnel parameter, you declare it in the normal way, but with the `tunnel` attribute on `<xsl:param>` set to `'yes'`. Intermediate templates, which don't use the tunnel parameter, can use parameters with the same name as the tunnel parameter, but they will declare the parameter without a `tunnel` attribute (or with the `tunnel` attribute set to `'no'`), so there is no confusion about which parameter is being used.

Summary Tunnel parameters are automatically passed through templates. To use them, the `tunnel` attribute on `<xsl:param>` and `<xsl:with-param>` is given the value `'yes'`.

Indicating the Program with the Highest Rating

To see how tunnel parameters work, in `TVGuide9.xsl` we'll look at how to add an icon to those programs being shown that have the highest rating in the TV guide.

With the `<TVGuide>` element as our current node, in the template matching the `<TVGuide>` element, we can work out the highest rating given to any of the programs in the TV guide using the `max()` function on all the `rating` attributes of all the `<Program>` elements in all the `<Channel>` elements, as follows:

```
max(Channel/Program/@rating)
```

We'll pass this value as a parameter called `$highestRating` when we process the `<Channel>` elements, as follows:

```
<xsl:template match="TVGuide">
  <xsl:sequence select="$ChannelList" />
  <xsl:apply-templates select="Channel">
    <xsl:with-param name="highestRating"
                    select="max(Channel/Program/@rating)" />
  </xsl:apply-templates>
  <xsl:sequence select="$ChannelList" />
</xsl:template>
```

Later on, when we process a `<Program>` element in `Details` mode, we want to use the value of the `$highestRating` parameter to determine whether or not to add a star icon. We'll declare the parameter called `$highestRating` as a required parameter, and then test whether the `<Program>` element we're looking at has that rating in order to work out whether to add the icon or not:

```
<xsl:template match="Program" mode="Details">
  <xsl:param name="highestRating" as="xs:double" required="yes" />
  ...
  <p>
    <xsl:if test="@rating = $highestRating">
      <img src="star.gif" alt="[Starred]" width="20" height="20" />
    </xsl:if>
    ...
  </p>
  ...
</xsl:template>
```

If you try to transform `TVGuide.xml` using `TVGuide9.xsl`, with just these changes, you will get an error, which is shown in Figure 6-12.

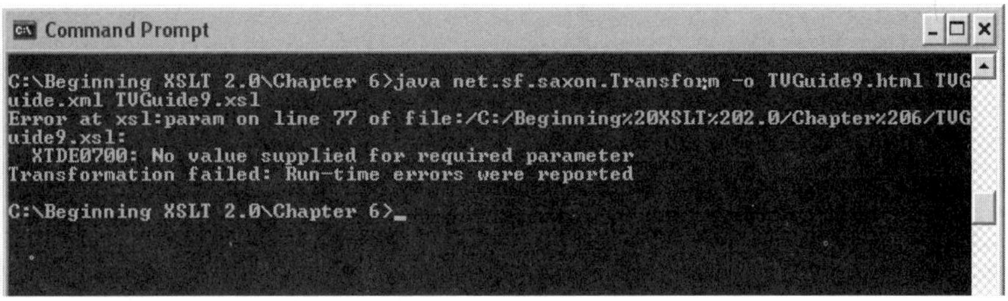

```
Command Prompt
C:\Beginning XSLT 2.0\Chapter 6>java net.sf.saxon.Transform -o TVGuide9.html TVG
uide.xml TVGuide9.xsl
Error at xsl:param on line 77 of file:/C:/Beginning%20XSLT%202.0/Chapter%206/TVG
uide9.xsl:
  XTDE0700: No value supplied for required parameter
Transformation failed: Run-time errors were reported

C:\Beginning XSLT 2.0\Chapter 6>_
```

Figure 6-12. *Error when transforming* `TVGuide.xml` *with* `TVGuide9.xsl`

The error occurs because the required `$highestRating` parameter isn't getting passed into the template that matches `<Program>` elements in `Details` mode. If we look at the flow of templates, we can see why this happens:

1. `<TVGuide>` template applies templates to `<Channel>` elements in default mode, passing the `$highestRating` parameter.
2. `<Channel>` elements are processed by a built-in template, which applies templates to `<Program>` elements in default mode; the `$highestRating` parameter is automatically passed on.
3. `<Program>` elements are processed in default mode, which applies templates to the same element in `Details` mode; the `$highestRating` parameter is *not* passed on.
4. `<Program>` elements are processed in Details mode.

The template that matches the `<Program>` elements in the default mode doesn't declare the `$highestRating` parameter, so it doesn't get passed on when templates are applied to the `<Program>` element in `Details` mode.

We could get around this by declaring the `$highestRating` parameter in the template matching the `<Program>` elements in default mode, as in `TVGuide10.xsl`, which contains the following:

```
<xsl:template match="Program">
  <xsl:param name="highestRating" as="xs:double" required="yes" />
  <xsl:choose>
    <xsl:when
      test="@flag = 'favorite' or @flag = 'interesting' or @rating > 6 or
            contains(lower-case(Series), 'news') or
            contains(lower-case(Title), 'news') or
            contains(lower-case(Description), 'news')">
      <div class="interesting">
        <xsl:apply-templates select="." mode="Details">
          <xsl:with-param name="highestRating" select="$highestRating" />
        </xsl:apply-templates>
      </div>
    </xsl:when>
    <xsl:otherwise>
      <div>
        <xsl:apply-templates select="." mode="Details">
          <xsl:with-param name="highestRating" select="$highestRating" />
```

```
      </xsl:apply-templates>
    </div>
  </xsl:otherwise>
</xsl:choose>
</xsl:template>
```

This works fine, but it's a bit tedious, and it will break again if we add a template that matches `<Channel>` elements in default mode, or if we add another link in the chain of templates between the `<TVGuide>` template and the `<Program>` template.

So a better alternative is to make the `$highestRating` parameter a tunnel parameter, by adding a `tunnel` attribute with the value `'yes'` when it's passed, in the `<TVGuide>` template:

```
<xsl:apply-templates select="Channel">
  <xsl:with-param name="highestRating" tunnel="yes"
                  select="max(Channel/Program/@rating)" />
</xsl:apply-templates>
```

and where it's used, in the template that matches `<Program>` elements in `Details` mode:

```
<xsl:template match="Program" mode="Details">
  <xsl:param name="highestRating" tunnel="yes" as="xs:double" required="yes" />
  ...
</xsl:template>
```

Make these changes, as in `TVGuide11.xsl`, and transform `TVGuide.xml` to create `TVGuide11.html`. In the result, there should only be one program that is starred: the *Star Trek: Voyager* episode "Renaissance Man," as shown in Figure 6-13.

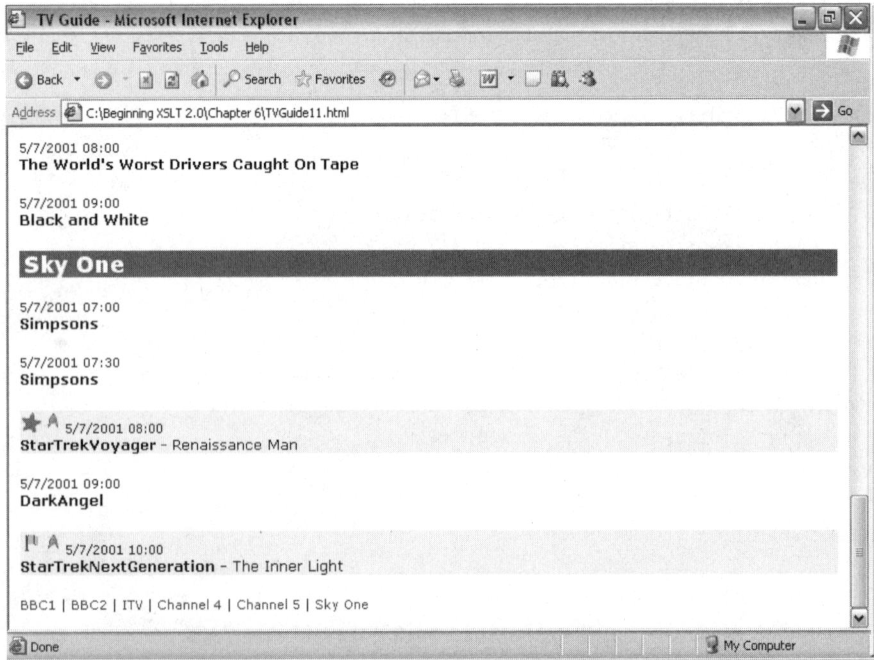

Figure 6-13. *Viewing* `TVGuide11.html` *in Internet Explorer*

The tunnel parameter has allowed us to pass a value through templates that aren't interested in that value, targeting it on the particular template that needs to know the highest rating of the programs in the TV guide. This makes the stylesheet more robust against changes than it would be if we had to pass the parameters explicitly each time.

Summary

This chapter has focused on setting and using variables and parameters. You've learned how to associate a value with variables and parameters using the three new elements:

- `<xsl:variable>`—For setting variables
- `<xsl:param>`—For declaring parameters
- `<xsl:with-param>`—For passing parameters into templates

You've seen the difference between setting variables and parameters using the `select` attribute and the content of these elements. The `select` attribute is used when you can work out the value of a variable using a single XPath expression, whereas the content is used as a sequence constructor when the value needs to be set using XSLT instructions, such as when the value needs to hold new nodes. The `as` attribute plays an important role when you use the content of the variable declaration to set the variable's value, determining whether or not the content is interpreted as a temporary tree or simply as a normal sequence.

You've learned about two new instructions that allow you to insert atomic values and existing nodes within a sequence that's generated with a sequence constructor:

- `<xsl:copy-of>`—Adds a copy of the value that you select to the sequence
- `<xsl:sequence>`—Adds the value itself to the sequence

and you've seen how instructions that you're familiar with, such as `<xsl:value-of>` and literal result elements, are used to create new nodes that get added to the sequence created by a sequence constructor.

You've seen how variables are scoped, to allow you to use the same name for different variables in different templates, with global variables being visible throughout the stylesheet and local variables being visible only by their following siblings and their following siblings' descendants. You've also learned about functions that make it easier to perform operations that you'd normally perform using loops that update variables, namely

- `position()`—To give you the number of an item amongst the others being processed
- `count()`—To count the number of items in a sequence
- `sum()`—To sum the values of the items in a sequence
- `avg()`—To give the average value of the items in a sequence
- `min()`—To give the minimum value of the items in a sequence
- `max()`—To give the maximum value of the items in a sequence

You've found out about the difference between stylesheet parameters and template parameters and how to use them. We'll look at template parameters in more detail in Chapter 11, when we study recursion, and at stylesheet parameters in Chapter 15, when we create dynamic XSLT applications.

As you've seen from this and the previous chapter, XPath expressions are used throughout XSLT to extract information from an XML document and to use that information to perform calculations or reformat it for display. The most useful feature of XPath expressions is their ability to access nodes in the node tree using location paths; in the next chapter, we'll examine how to navigate around the node tree in much more detail.

Review Questions

1. Add as attributes to the following variable declarations so that the type of each variable is correctly declared:

```
<xsl:variable name="price" select="Price" />
<xsl:variable name="keyword">sport</xsl:variable>
<xsl:variable name="good" select="@rating > 6" />
<xsl:variable name="date" select="substring-before(Start, 'T')" />
<xsl:variable name="lineBreak"><br /></xsl:variable>
<xsl:variable name="date" select="xs:date(xs:dateTime(Start))" />
<xsl:variable name="duration"
              select="number(substring(Duration, 3, 1)) * 60" />
```

2. What are the differences between <xsl:value-of>, <xsl:copy-of>, and <xsl:sequence>?

3. Correct the error in the following piece of XSLT:

```
<xsl:choose>
  <xsl:when test="@rating > 6">
    <xsl:variable name="rating" select="'high'" />
  </xsl:when>
  <xsl:when test="@rating < 4">
    <xsl:variable name="rating" select="'low'" />
  </xsl:when>
  <xsl:otherwise>
    <xsl:variable name="rating" select="'medium'" />
  </xsl:otherwise>
</xsl:choose>
<xsl:value-of select="$rating" />
```

4. What are the differences between a global variable and a stylesheet parameter?

5. Write code that calculates the average rating of the programs on a particular channel, and then code that gets the lowest average rating for the entire TV guide.

6. What will the following XSLT stylesheet normally output?

```
<xsl:stylesheet version="2.0"
                xmlns:xsl="http://www.w3.org/1999/XSL/Transform"
                xmlns:xs="http://www.w3.org/2001/XMLSchema">

<xsl:param name="author" as="xs:string" select="$defaultAuthor" />
```

```
<xsl:variable name="defaultAuthor" as="xs:string" select="'A.N.Other'" />
<xsl:template match="/">
  <xsl:param name="by" as="xs:string" />
  <xsl:apply-templates select="." mode="author" />
</xsl:template>
<xsl:template match="/" mode="author">
  <xsl:param name="by" as="xs:string" select="$author" />
  Written by: <xsl:value-of select="$by" />
</xsl:template>
</xsl:stylesheet>
```

7. Under what two circumstances is a parameter automatically passed from one template to another?

CHAPTER 7

Paths and Sequences

As you've learned, the purpose of XSLT is to transform an XML document into something else: text, HTML, or different XML. To do so, XSLT processors accept an XML document as the **input** to the transformation, and output a different document, known as the **result** of the transformation.

XSLT processors regard both the input and the result of the transformation as **node trees**. You've seen what node trees look like in previous chapters; you've used expressions and patterns to select and match nodes within a node tree and constructed new node trees using literal result elements. Over the next couple of chapters, we're going to look at node trees in more detail. In this chapter, we'll examine how to construct paths to walk around input node trees and to match nodes within them. In the next chapter, we'll look at how to construct a new node tree as the result of the transformation.

The first part of this chapter deals with how a node tree is constructed and looks at what information is stored about each node and how whitespace is treated within the node tree. The second part talks about how to construct paths to navigate the node tree. There are two types of paths that we'll look at in this chapter: **paths**, which select nodes for the XSLT processor to process, and **path patterns**, which match nodes so the XSLT processor can tell which template to apply to a particular node. These two types of paths look similar, but they're used in very different ways. We'll look at path patterns first because they're a bit more restricted.

Paths return sequences of nodes, but XPath 2.0 supports sequences of **atomic values** as well. In the last chapter, you saw how to create sequences using **sequence constructors**; in this chapter, you'll see how to create sequences using XPath expressions, and how to manipulate sequences of both nodes and atomic values.

In this chapter, you'll learn

- How to get information about the name and namespace of a node
- How to control the whitespace held in a node tree
- How to test for different kinds of nodes
- How to use predicates when matching nodes
- How to construct patterns that match several nodes

- How to select nodes with various tree relationships
- How to create sequences of atomic values
- How to iterate over and format sequences

Node Trees Revisited

When we first looked at node trees in Chapter 3, we constructed a basic diagram from a simple piece of XML. To remind you, here's the XML again:

```
<?xml version="1.0" encoding="ISO-8859-1"?>
<?xml-stylesheet type="text/xsl" href="TVGuide.xsl"?>
<TVGuide start="2001-07-05" end="2001-07-05">
  <Channel>
    <Name>BBC1</Name>
    ...
    <Program>
      <Start>2001-07-05T19:30:00</Start>
      <Duration>PT30M</Duration>
      <Series>EastEnders</Series>
      ...
    </Program>
    ...
  </Channel>
  ...
</TVGuide>
```

The node tree that we constructed from this XML document is shown in Figure 7-1.

In this section, we're going to revisit this node tree, looking in more detail at how it is constructed. We're going to cover three areas: the information that's stored about each of the nodes within the node tree, how namespaces are handled within the node tree, and finally how to control the whitespace that remains within the node tree.

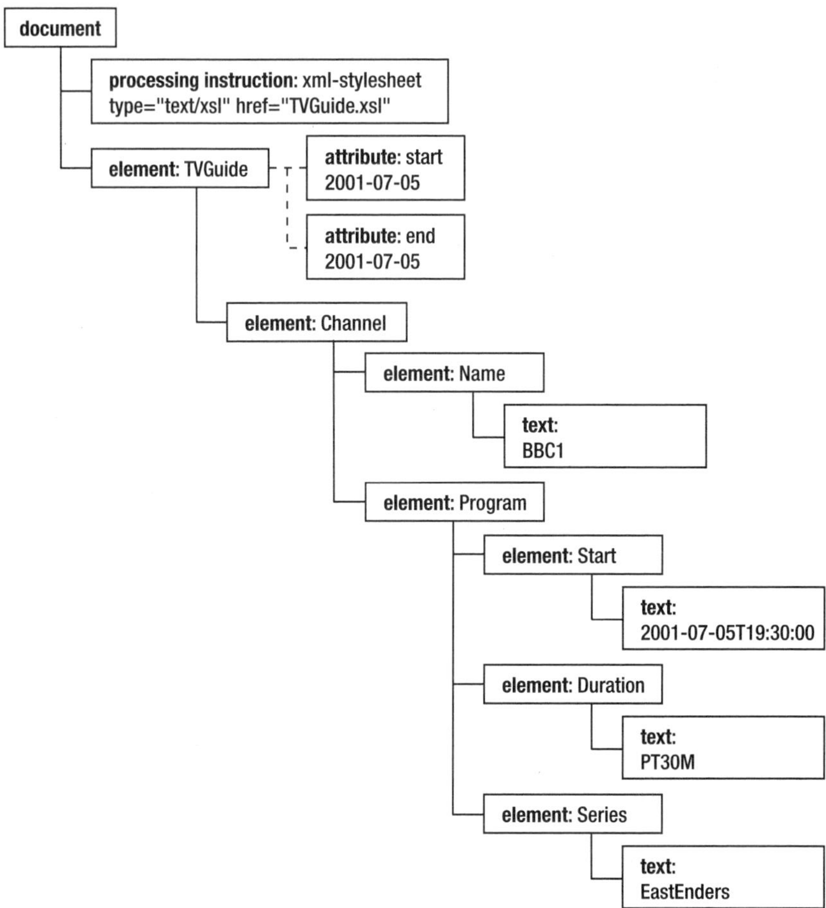

Figure 7-1. *Example node tree*

Accessing Information About Nodes

There are five important aspects of any node in XPath: its **kind**, **name**, **string value**, **type**, and **typed value**.

The kind of a node indicates whether it is an element, attribute, text, or other kind of node. You can't find out the type of a node directly, but you can test whether a node is of a particular kind using a **node test**. Node tests are used in paths, in patterns, and in sequence types to identify nodes of different kinds. Table 7-1 lists the node tests that you can use to select or match the different kinds of nodes.

Table 7-1. *Node Kinds and Node Tests*

Node Kind	Node Test	Description
Nodes	`node()`	
Document nodes	`document-node()`	Matches or selects all document nodes
	`document-node(element(`*name*`))`	Matches or selects document nodes with a single document element with a particular name
	`document-node(element(*, `*type*`))`	Matches or selects document nodes with a single document element with a particular type
	`document-node(element(`*name*`, `*type*`))`	Matches or selects document nodes with a single document element with a particular name and type, as long as it isn't nilled
	`document-node(element(`*name*`, `*type*`?))`	Matches or selects document nodes with a single document element with a particular name and type
	`document-node(schema-element(`*name*`))`	Matches or selects document nodes with a single document element that matches an element declaration within a schema
Text	`text()`	
Elements and attributes	`*`	Matches or selects all elements or attributes
	name	Matches or selects elements or attributes with a particular name
Elements	`element()`	Matches or selects all elements
	`element(`*name*`)`	Matches or selects elements with a particular name
	`element(*, `*type*`)`	Matches or selects elements with a particular type
	`element(`*name*`, `*type*`)`	Matches or selects elements with a particular name and type, as long as it isn't nilled
	`element(`*name*`, `*type*`?)`	Matches or selects elements with a particular name and type
	`schema-element(`*name*`)`	Matches or selects elements based on an element declaration within a schema
Attributes	`attribute()`	Matches or selects all attributes
	`attribute(`*name*`)`	Matches or selects attributes with a particular name
	`attribute(*, `*type*`)`	Matches or selects attributes with a particular type
	`attribute(`*name*`, `*type*`)`	Matches or selects attributes with a particular name and type
	`schema-attribute(`*name*`)`	Matches or selects attributes based on an attribute declaration within a schema
Comments	`comment()`	
Processing instructions	`processing-instruction()`	Matches or selects all processing instructions
	`processing-instruction(target)`	Matches or selects processing instructions with a particular target

Note The node tests that we've been using to match elements, such as `*` and `Program`, are really shorthands for `element()` node tests. The node test `Program`, for example, is a shorthand for `element(Program)`.

Some nodes have names—elements, attributes, processing instructions (a processing instruction node's name is the processing instruction's target), and namespace nodes (which we'll come to in a little while). You can get hold of the name of a node as a string using the `name()` function and as an `xs:QName` using the `node-name()` function, but you can also use the node's name directly when you select or match nodes. Element and attribute names are a little complicated by namespaces, as you'll see shortly.

Another important aspect of a node is its string value, which is what you get when you call the `string()` function on a node. The string value of an attribute is the attribute's value, the string value of a text node is the text itself, and the string value of a comment is the text of the comment. The string value of a processing instruction is the text after the whitespace following the target (or name) of the processing instruction. The string value of an element or a document node is the concatenation of all the text nodes underneath the node.

Elements and attributes also have types and typed values.

A type is associated with a particular element or attribute when the document to which the node belongs is validated against a schema. There is no way to get hold of the name of the type of an element or attribute—you have to test the element or attribute to work out what type it is.

The typed value of an element or attribute is related to the type of the node—for example, if an attribute has a type of `xs:date`, then the typed value of the attribute is an atomic value of type `xs:date`—however, they're not always exactly the same. You can get the typed value of an element or attribute using the `data()` function, but usually you don't have to call this function explicitly, since when you pass a node when an atomic value (or sequence of atomic values) is expected, the typed value for the node gets extracted automatically.

Currently, since we're doing Basic XSLT processing, we're only looking at documents that haven't been validated; in this case, all elements have the type `xdt:untyped` and all attributes have the type `xdt:untypedAtomic`. The typed value of all elements and attributes is the same as their string value, of type `xdt:untypedAtomic`.

Note We'll look at using types to select and match nodes when we see how to use schemas with XSLT in Chapter 13.

Summary Different node kinds are matched or selected by different node tests, such as `node()`, `document-node()`, `element()`, `schema-element()`, `attribute()`, `schema-attribute()`, `text()`, `comment()`, and `processing-instruction()`. Elements, attributes, and processing instructions can be matched or selected by name. Elements and attributes can be matched or selected by type. Document nodes can be matched or selected based on the document element in the document.

Accessing Node Information

You can now build a node tree for an XML document automatically using XSLT. We'll create a stylesheet called NodeTree.xsl that contains the templates for each of the different kinds of nodes and outputs the relevant information about them. NodeTree.xsl is shown in Listing 7-1.

Listing 7-1. NodeTree.xsl

```
<xsl:stylesheet version="2.0"
                xmlns:xsl="http://www.w3.org/1999/XSL/Transform">

<xsl:template match="document-node()">
  document:
    <xsl:apply-templates />
</xsl:template>

<xsl:template match="element()">
  element: <xsl:value-of select="name()" />
  <xsl:apply-templates select="@*" />
  <xsl:apply-templates />
</xsl:template>

<xsl:template match="attribute()">
  attribute: <xsl:value-of select="name()" />:
             <xsl:value-of select="." />
</xsl:template>

<xsl:template match="text()">
  text: <xsl:value-of select="." />
</xsl:template>

<xsl:template match="processing-instruction()">
  processing instruction: <xsl:value-of select="name()" />:
                          <xsl:value-of select="." />
</xsl:template>

<xsl:template match="comment()">
  comment: <xsl:value-of select="." />
</xsl:template>

</xsl:stylesheet>
```

Running this stylesheet over an XML document will give you a text list of the nodes in the document and their node type. If you use NodeTree.xsl with TVGuide.xml to create NodeTree.txt, then you'll get a document that looks something like the following:

```
<?xml version="1.0" encoding="UTF-8"?>
  document:

  processing instruction: xml-stylesheet:
                          type="text/xsl" href="NodeTree.xsl"
  element: TVGuide
  attribute: start:
             2001-07-05
  attribute: end:
             2001-07-05
  text:

  element: Channel
  text:

  element: Name
  text: BBC1
  text:

  element: Program
  text:

  element: Start
  text: 2001-07-05T19:00:00
  text:

  element: Duration
  text: PT30M
  text:

  element: Series
  text: QuestionOfSport
  text:

  element: Title
  text:

  text:
  ...
```

■ **Note** You'll notice that a lot of the lines that start with `text:` just have whitespace in them. Later in this chapter, you'll learn where these text nodes come from and how to get rid of them if you want to.

You can make the result of NodeTree.xsl look prettier by outputting HTML rather than text, using <div> elements to nest and indent the output that you generate. You could also use parameters to keep track of the location of the nodes in the document if you wanted.

Note There are several applications around that give you pretty-printed views of XML documents using XSLT. For example, the Pretty XML Tree Viewer by Mike Brown and myself, available from http://skew.org/xml/stylesheets/treeview/html/, uses XSLT to create a view of a node tree. More sophisticated viewers are interactive, highlighting the nodes selected by the XPaths you enter. See the list available at http://www.xmlsoftware.com/xpath.html.

Namespaces in the Node Tree

Now that we're looking at the node tree in more detail, let's make the XML a bit more complicated by including a couple of namespace declarations on the <TVGuide> element to create TVGuide2.xml, shown in Listing 7-2.

Listing 7-2. TVGuide2.xml

```
<?xml version="1.0" encoding="ISO-8859-1"?>
<?xml-stylesheet type="text/xsl" href="TVGuide.xsl"?>
<TVGuide xmlns="http://www.example.com/TVGuide"
         xmlns:xsi="http://www.w3.org/2001/XMLSchema-instance"
         xsi:schemaLocation="http://www.example.com/TVGuide TVGuide.xsd"
         start="2001-07-05" end="2001-07-05">
  <Channel>
    <Name>BBC1</Name>
    ...
    <Program rating="5" flag="favorite">
      <Start>2001-07-05T19:30:00</Start>
      <Duration>PT30M</Duration>
      <Series>EastEnders</Series>
      ...
    </Program>
    ...
  </Channel>
  ...
</TVGuide>
```

We introduced namespaces in Chapter 2, and you've been using the XSLT namespace in the stylesheets that you've been generating. Adding namespaces to the source document makes life a bit more complicated.

Let's look at what we've added to the <TVGuide> element. First, we've added a **default namespace declaration**:

```
xmlns="http://www.example.com/TVGuide"
```

This sets the **default namespace** for an element and its content. If an element doesn't have a prefix on its name, then it will be in the default namespace; in our document none of the elements have prefixes, so they will all be in the namespace `http://www.example.com/TVGuide`.

The next addition was the **namespace declaration**:

```
xmlns:xsi="http://www.w3.org/2001/XMLSchema-instance"
```

Namespace declarations associate a particular prefix to a namespace URI. This namespace declaration associates the prefix `xsi` with the namespace `http://www.w3.org/2001/XMLSchema-instance` (a namespace used to associate XML documents with XML Schemas). The only node in the document that uses this prefix is the final attribute that we added to the <TVGuide> element:

```
xsi:schemaLocation="http://www.example.com/TVGuide TVGuide.xsd"
```

The name of the attribute is `xsi:schemaLocation`, but the part before the colon is a prefix that indicates the namespace to which the attribute belongs—the `XMLSchema-instance` namespace. XML Schema validators use this attribute to work out where to find the schema for an XML document.

Qualified Names

Introducing namespaces means that we have to look at names a bit more carefully. Elements and attributes have **qualified names**: a **namespace URI** that indicates the markup language that the element or attribute belongs to, and a **local name** that indicates the element or attribute's role within that markup language. There are four functions in XPath that enable you to get at the name of an element or attribute:

- `node-name()`—Returns the qualified name of the element or attribute as an `xs:QName` value
- `name()`—Returns the full name of the element or attribute as given in the source document, including the prefix if there is one, as an `xs:string`
- `namespace-uri()`—Returns the namespace URI of the element's or attribute's namespace as an `xs:anyURI`
- `local-name()`—Returns the element's or attribute's local name as an `xs:string`

Table 7-2 gives some examples of the four functions in action. The left column shows the function call in the stylesheet, and the right shows the result of the function call. I've assumed that the namespace URI `http://www.w3.org/2001/XMLSchema` is associated with the prefix `xsi` in the stylesheet, and that the namespace URI `http://www.example.com/TVGuide` is associated with the prefix `tv` in the stylesheet. I've also assumed that the <TVGuide> element is the current node.

Table 7-2. *Functions That Return a Node's Name*

Function Call	Result
`node-name(@xsi:schemaLocation)`	`QName('http://www.w3.org/2001/XMLSchema-instance', 'schemaLocation')`
`node-name(tv:Channel)`	`QName('http://www.example.com/TVGuide', 'Channel')`
`name(@xsi:schemaLocation)`	`'xsi:schemaLocation'`
`name(tv:Channel)`	`'Channel'`
`namespace-uri(@xsi:schemaLocation)`	`xs:anyURI('http://www.w3.org/2001/XMLSchema-instance')`
`namespace-uri(tv:Channel)`	`xs:anyURI('http://www.example.com/TVGuide')`
`local-name(@xsi:schemaLocation)`	`'schemaLocation'`
`local-name(tv:Channel)`	`'Channel'`

■ **Note** When you locate a node with a path in your stylesheet, such as `tv:Channel`, you need to use the prefixes that are declared in your stylesheet rather than the prefixes that are declared within the input document. We'll look at this in more detail later in the chapter.

The prefix that you associate with a namespace in a particular document (and therefore the prefixes that you use on the elements and attributes in that document) should not matter to your stylesheet. Therefore, in general you should avoid using the `name()` function on elements or attributes so that you don't inadvertently make your stylesheet dependent on the author of a document using particular prefixes in their namespace declarations. You can use the `node-name()` function, or a combination of the `local-name()` function and the `namespace-uri()` function, instead.

In the node tree, we'll illustrate the namespace URI of a particular node by showing it in {}s before the name of the node. Figure 7-2 shows the node tree for the preceding XML document. Note in particular that the namespace declarations themselves aren't included as attributes on the `<TVGuide>` element within the node tree.

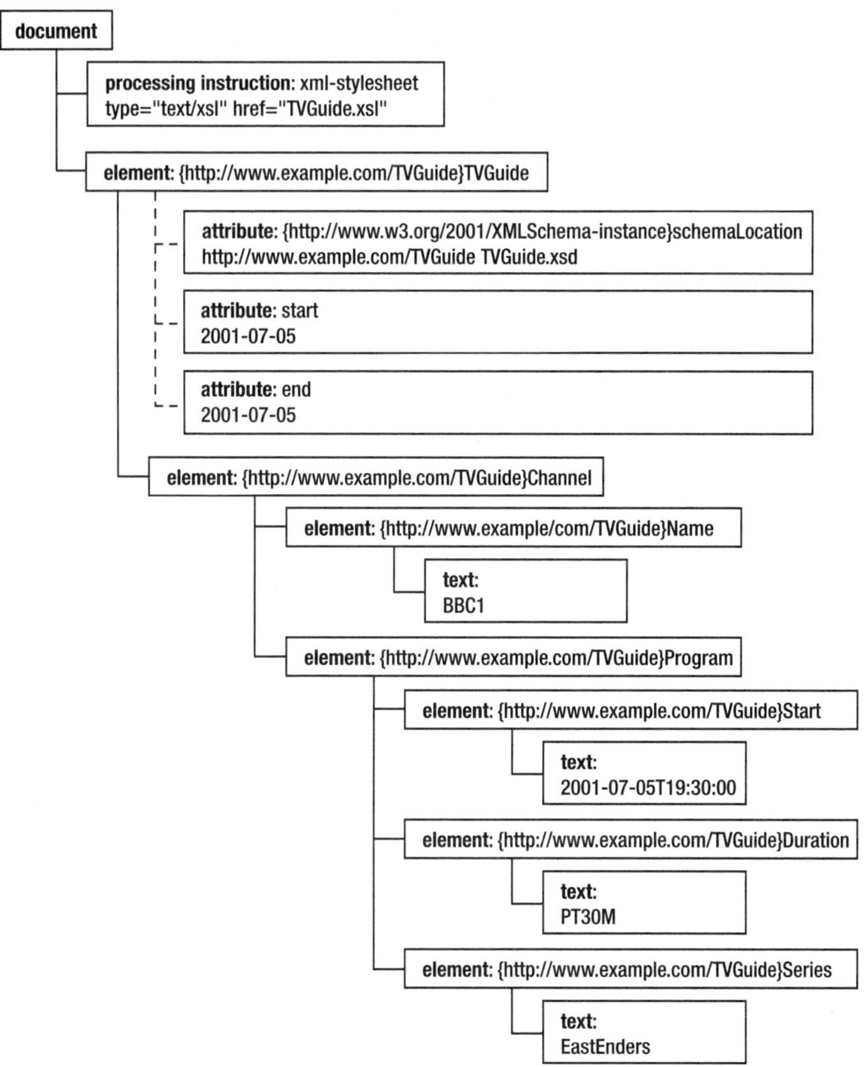

Figure 7-2. *Node tree with namespaces*

Summary The `node-name()` function returns the name of an element or attribute as an `xs:QName`, while the `name()` function returns the name of an element or attribute as an `xs:string`. The `local-name()` function returns the local part of the node's name, and the `namespace-uri()` function returns the URI of the namespace of which the node is a part.

Displaying Namespace Information

We can make a new version of the NodeTree.xsl stylesheet, adding namespace information to the details of elements and attributes. Rather than just giving the name of elements and attributes, it should give their namespace URI and local name. For NodeTree2.xsl, adjust the templates that match elements and attributes to read as follows:

```
<xsl:template match="element()">
  element: {<xsl:value-of select="namespace-uri()" />}
           <xsl:value-of select="local-name()" />
  <xsl:apply-templates select="@*" />
  <xsl:apply-templates />
</xsl:template>

<xsl:template match="attribute()">
  attribute: {<xsl:value-of select="namespace-uri()" />}
             <xsl:value-of select="local-name()" />:
             <xsl:value-of select="." />
</xsl:template>
```

Now try running the stylesheet on a document that uses namespaces, such as TVGuide2.xml, to give NodeTree2.txt, as shown in Listing 7-3.

Listing 7-3. NodeTree2.txt

```
<?xml version="1.0" encoding="UTF-16"?>
  document:

  processing instruction: xml-stylesheet:
                          type="text/xsl" href="NodeTree2.xsl"
  element: {http://www.example.com/TVGuide}
           TVGuide
  attribute: {http://www.w3.org/2001/XMLSchema-instance}
             schemaLocation:
             http://www.example.com/TVGuide TVGuide.xsd
  attribute: {}
             start:
             2001-07-05
  attribute: {}
             end:
             2001-07-05
  text:

  element: {http://www.example.com/TVGuide}
           Channel
  text:
```

```
element: {http://www.example.com/TVGuide}
         Name
text: BBC1
text:

element: {http://www.example.com/TVGuide}
         Program
text:

element: {http://www.example.com/TVGuide}
         Start
text: 2001-07-05T19:00:00
text:

element: {http://www.example.com/TVGuide}
         Duration
text: PT30M
text:

element: {http://www.example.com/TVGuide}
         Series
text: QuestionOfSport
text:

element: {http://www.example.com/TVGuide}
         Title
text:

text:
...
```

The namespace URIs of the elements and attributes are displayed; note that the attributes that don't have a prefix have an empty namespace URI, indicating that they are not in any namespace.

As you learned in Chapter 5, you can also extract a namespace URI and local name from an `xs:QName` value. An alternative approach, which we'll use in `NodeTree3.xsl`, is to use the `node-name()` function to get the name of the node as an `xs:QName`, and then use the `namespace-uri-from-QName()` and `local-name-from-QName()` functions to get hold of the namespace URI and local name, as follows:

```
<xsl:template match="element()">
  <xsl:variable name="name" select="node-name()" as="xs:QName" />
  element: {<xsl:value-of select="namespace-uri-from-QName($name)" />}
           <xsl:value-of select="local-name-from-QName($name)" />
  <xsl:apply-templates select="@*" />
  <xsl:apply-templates />
</xsl:template>
```

```
<xsl:template match="attribute()">
  <xsl:variable name="name" select="node-name()" as="xs:QName" />
  attribute: {<xsl:value-of select="namespace-uri-from-QName($name)" />}
             <xsl:value-of select="local-name-from-QName($name)" />:
             <xsl:value-of select="." />
</xsl:template>
```

Don't forget to add a namespace declaration for the XML Schema namespace (`http://www.w3.org/2001/XMLSchema`), associated with the prefix `xs`, so that the processor can understand the qualified name `xs:QName`, which is used in the `as` attributes of the two variable declarations in the preceding code.

The result of transforming `TVGuide2.xml` with `NodeTree3.xsl` is `NodeTree3.txt`. This looks exactly the same as `NodeTree2.txt`—the only difference between `NodeTree2.xsl` and `NodeTree3.xsl` is how the namespace URI and local name of each node is retrieved.

Namespace Nodes

Namespace declarations each have a scope within which the particular prefix/namespace association holds true. The scope of a namespace declaration is the element that the namespace is declared on and all its contents. In terms of the node tree, a **namespace node** is added to every element in the scope of the namespace declaration. The "name" of the namespace node is the prefix that's used for the namespace (an empty string for the default namespace), and its string value is the namespace URI.

Like attributes, namespace nodes live to one side of the main tree. Figure 7-3 shows the namespace nodes within `TVGuide2.xml`.

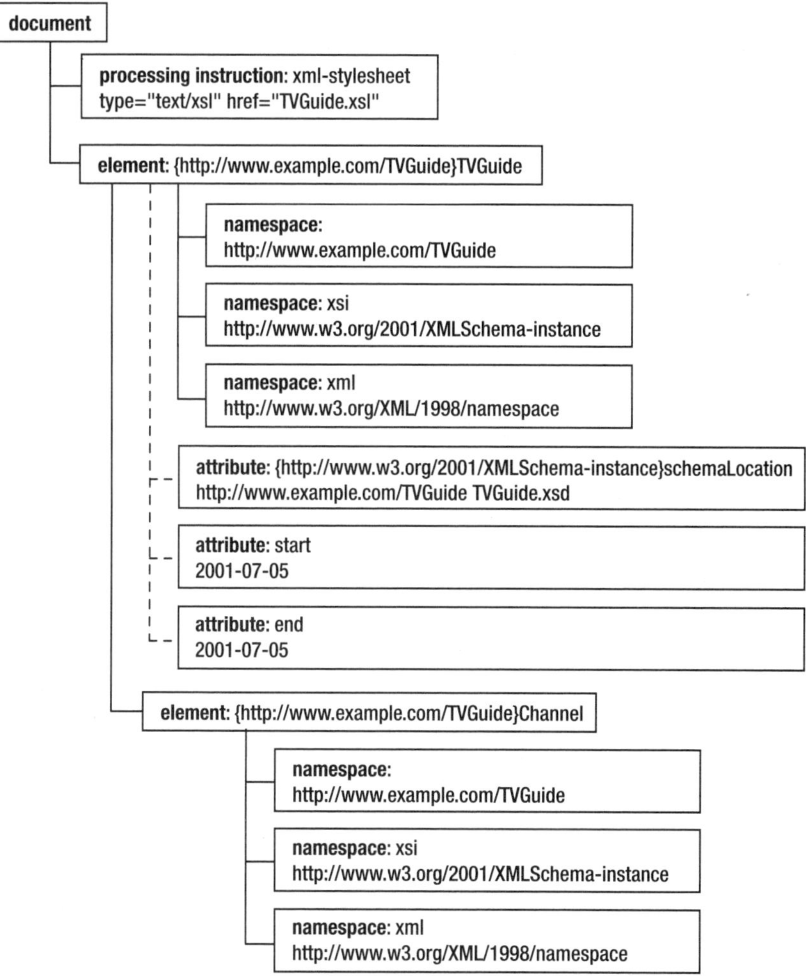

Figure 7-3. *Namespace nodes in* `TVGuide2.xml`

Note Every element in an XML document automatically has a namespace node for the XML namespace `http://www.w3.org/XML/1998/namespace`, associated with the prefix `xml`.

Unlike other nodes, you cannot match namespace nodes, and some processors might not support you selecting them either. However, you can find out about the namespace nodes on a particular element using two functions:

- `in-scope-prefixes()`—Takes an element as an argument and returns a sequence of `xs:strings`, one for the prefix of each namespace node that's in scope for that element.
- `namespace-uri-for-prefix()`—Takes an element as the first argument and a prefix as the second argument, and returns the namespace URI associated with that prefix for that element.

These functions are usually useful only if you have an element or attribute value that contains namespace prefixes for which you want to find out a namespace URI or a namespace URI for which you want to find out a namespace prefix, neither of which happens very often.

Note It's much more common for an element or attribute value to hold a qualified name; in that case, you can use the `resolve-QName()` function, which you learned about in Chapter 5, to work out the namespace URI and local name of the qualified name.

It's useful to know about namespace nodes because when you construct a node tree as the result of a transformation, the locations of the namespace nodes within the node tree determines where namespace declarations will be added when the node tree is serialized into another XML document. We'll look at this in detail in the next chapter.

Summary Every element has a number of namespace nodes, one for each of the namespace declarations that are in scope for that element.

Whitespace in Node Trees

When we used versions of the `NodeTree.xsl` stylesheet in the last couple of sections, we noticed that as well as all the nodes that we expected to find within the tree, we also found a bunch of text nodes that didn't seem to have any content. If you take another look at the XML document, you'll see that in order to format it nicely, we've used new lines between elements and indented elements with tabs and spaces to indicate their level within the node tree. This is good practice because it makes XML documents easier to understand, especially if they have lots of levels, but it also introduces **whitespace** (characters that are displayed as white spaces) to the document that really we want to ignore.

XML regards four characters as whitespace characters:

- Space (` `)
- Tab (`	`)
- Newline (`
`)
- Carriage return (`
`)

Note The code held in brackets is the character reference for the whitespace character.

The whitespace that you use within tags (between the element name and attributes, between attributes, or at the end of the tag) doesn't matter, but whitespace that you use in element content, attribute values, comments, and processing instructions is faithfully reported to the

XSLT processor by the XML parser, and is included in the node tree that the XSLT processor constructs. We can replace the whitespace in element content and attribute values with the character references for the whitespace characters instead, as in TVGuide3.xml, shown in Listing 7-4, and the XSLT processor will build exactly the same node tree.

Listing 7-4. TVGuide3.xml

```
<?xml version="1.0" encoding="ISO-8859-1"?>
<?xml-stylesheet type="text/xsl" href="TVGuide.xsl"?>
<TVGuide start="2001-07-05" end="2001-07-05"
>&#xA;&#x20;&#x20;<Channel
>&#xA;&#x20;&#x20;&#x20;&#x20;<Name>BBC1</Name
>&#xA;&#x20;&#x20;&#x20;&#x20;<Program rating="5" flag="favorite"
>&#xA;&#x20;&#x20;&#x20;&#x20;&#x20;&#x20;<Start>2001-07-05T19:30:00</Start
>&#xA;&#x20;&#x20;&#x20;&#x20;&#x20;&#x20;<Duration>PT30M</Duration
>&#xA;&#x20;&#x20;&#x20;&#x20;&#x20;&#x20;<Series>EastEnders</Series
>&#xA;&#x20;&#x20;&#x20;&#x20;&#x20;&#x20;<Title></Title
>&#xA;&#x20;&#x20;&#x20;&#x20;...</Program
>&#xA;&#x20;&#x20;...</Channel
>&#xA;...</TVGuide>
```

■ **Note** If you replace all the literal line breaks with the character reference
, then you end up with a file that's pretty unreadable because it's all on one line. I've made this file easier to read by adding line breaks within the element start and end tags (where whitespace doesn't matter) instead, which is why most of the lines start with the greater-than signs that signal the end of the tag started on the previous line.

The whitespace that you use to indent elements in your file is included in the node tree as text nodes. Looking at the preceding XML, you can see whitespace between the <TVGuide> and the <Channel> start tags, between the <Channel> start tag and the <Name> element, between the <Name> and the <Program> element, and so on. In fact, the node tree that the XSLT processor constructs for this XML document looks like the one shown in Figure 7-4.

The highlighted nodes in Figure 7-4 are text nodes that consist purely of whitespace, called **whitespace-only text nodes**. We saw these whitespace-only text nodes when we transformed TVGuide.xml with NodeTree.xsl.

Whitespace-only text nodes often cause problems when processing XML documents with XSLT because when you apply templates to all the children of an element using <xsl:apply-templates> without a select attribute, whitespace-only text nodes get included as well. What happens if you apply templates to a text node? The built-in template for text nodes is activated, and the whitespace is output, which means you get a lot of unwanted whitespace in the document you're generating. What's more, if you try to number the nodes using the position() function, then the whitespace-only text nodes are included in the numbering.

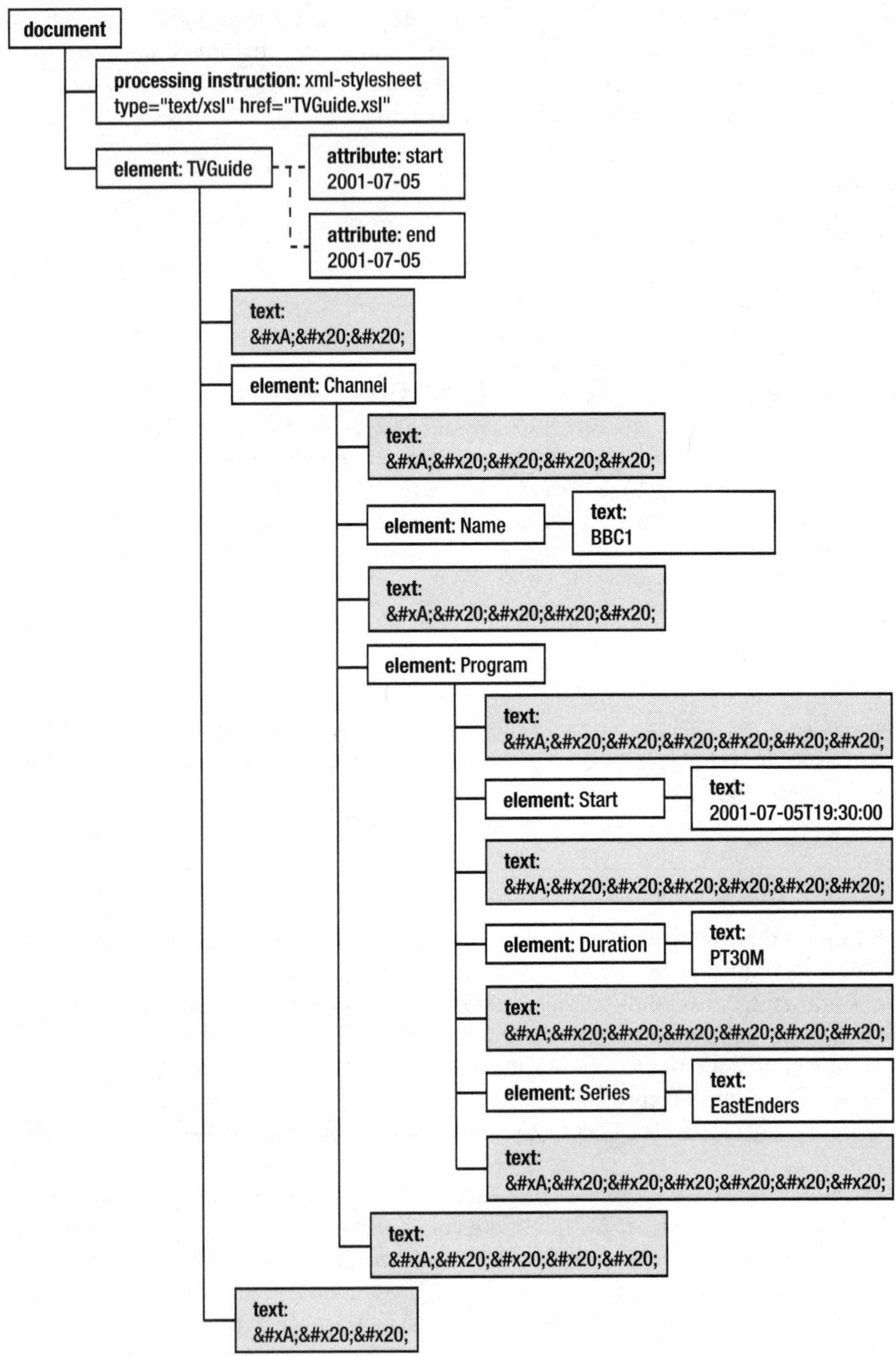

Figure 7-4. *Node tree with whitespace-only text nodes*

Caution What I've said in the preceding paragraph is true for the majority of XSLT processors. However, if you use MSXML through Internet Explorer, you'll find that the node tree actually contains no whitespace-only text nodes. Because Internet Explorer uses the DOM API, which is slightly different from the XSLT view of an XML document, it ignores whitespace-only text nodes by default when it constructs the node tree. If you're running the transformation from code (as in Chapter 14), you can stop this from happening by explicitly setting the property `preserveWhiteSpace` on the `Document` object to `true` when you create the DOM. If you then run MSXML from the command line, whitespace-only text nodes are preserved by default, as they are in other XSLT processors.

Summary Node trees often contain text nodes that contain only whitespace characters (whitespace-only text nodes) due to the indentation used within the XML document.

Stripping Whitespace-only Text Nodes

XSLT provides an element that allows you to tell the XSLT processor to ignore the whitespace-only text nodes. This element is `<xsl:strip-space>` and it's a top-level element, occurring as a direct child of the `<xsl:stylesheet>` document element.

The `<xsl:strip-space>` element has a single attribute, `elements`, whose value is either an asterisk (*) or a whitespace-separated list of element names. If the `elements` attribute holds an asterisk, or if an element's name is one from those listed, then all the whitespace-only text nodes that are children of that element are ignored. Effectively, the named elements are **stripped** of all their whitespace-only text node children.

Note Stripping whitespace-only text nodes has no effect at all on whitespace contained in the values of attributes or whitespace that occurs in text-only elements that contain other characters as well; to control that, you need to use the `normalize-space()` function, which you saw in Chapter 5.

Summary You can get rid of whitespace-only text nodes using the `<xsl:strip-space>` element, whose `elements` attribute lists the elements whose child whitespace-only text nodes are stripped from the node tree.

Ignoring Whitespace-only Text Nodes

Now we'll add an instruction telling the processor to remove all the whitespace-only text nodes from the document. Add an `<xsl:strip-space>` element at the top level of `NodeTree3.xsl` to create a new version, `NodeTree4.xsl`, that strips all the whitespace-only text nodes from the tree, so that the stylesheet reads as follows:

```
<?xml version="1.0" encoding="ISO-8859-1"?>
<xsl:stylesheet version="2.0"
                xmlns:xsl="http://www.w3.org/1999/XSL/Transform"
                xmlns:xs="http://www.w3.org/2001/XMLSchema">
```

```
<xsl:strip-space elements="*" />
...
</xsl:stylesheet>
```

Run NodeTree4.xsl on TVGuide2.xml to give NodeTree4.txt, which should look like the document shown in Listing 7-5.

Listing 7-5. NodeTree4.txt

```
<?xml version="1.0" encoding="UTF-16"?>
  document:

  processing instruction: xml-stylesheet:
                          type="text/xsl" href="TVGuide.xsl"
  element: {http://www.example.com/TVGuide}
           TVGuide
  attribute: {http://www.w3.org/2001/XMLSchema-instance}
             schemaLocation:
             http://www.example.com/TVGuide TVGuide.xsd
  attribute: {}
             start:
             2001-07-05
  attribute: {}
             end:
             2001-07-05
  element: {http://www.example.com/TVGuide}
           Channel
  element: {http://www.example.com/TVGuide}
           Name
  text: BBC1
  element: {http://www.example.com/TVGuide}
           Program
  element: {http://www.example.com/TVGuide}
           Start
  text: 2001-07-05T19:00:00
  element: {http://www.example.com/TVGuide}
           Duration
  text: PT30M
  element: {http://www.example.com/TVGuide}
           Series
  text: QuestionOfSport
  element: {http://www.example.com/TVGuide}
           Title
...
```

The whitespace-only text nodes have been stripped from the tree, so there are no lines that start with `text:` but hold no information.

Preserving Whitespace-only Text Nodes

In data-oriented XML, all whitespace-only text nodes can usually be safely stripped out of the node tree. In document-oriented XML, on the other hand, you often get whitespace-only text nodes that should be **preserved**. For example, look at the following <Description> element:

```
<Description>
  ...
  <Character>Jamie</Character> <Link href="Mitchells.html">Mitchell</Link>
  ...
</Description>
```

The space between the <Character> element and the <Link> element is part of the description; when we read the description in an HTML page, we want to read Jamie Mitchell, not JamieMitchell. But this space occurs without any nonwhitespace characters around it, creating a whitespace-only text node between the <Character> and <Link> elements in the node tree as shown in Figure 7-5.

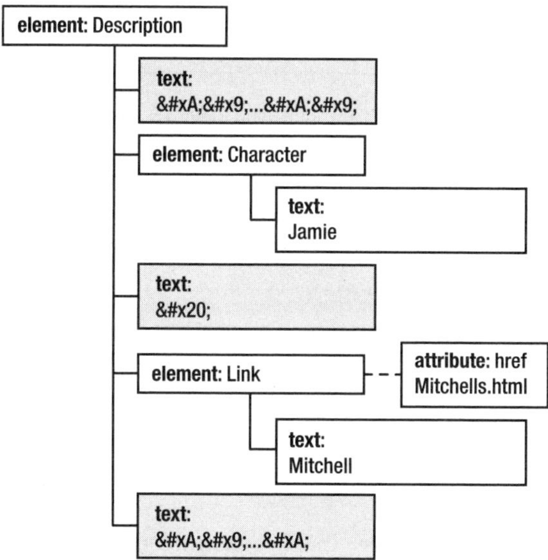

Figure 7-5. *Whitespace-only text nodes in mixed content*

If you used <xsl:strip-space elements="*" /> to strip all the whitespace-only text nodes from the node tree, then this significant whitespace-only text node would be lost as well. On the other hand, if you didn't, then you'd have to be aware of the whitespace-only text nodes that occur in the rest of the document, or list all the element names in the elements attribute of <xsl:strip-space>, which would be tedious.

So there are two facilities for preventing whitespace-only text nodes from being stripped.

The first is <xsl:preserve-space>, which is the opposite of <xsl:strip-space>. The <xsl:preserve-space> element is also a top-level element and has an elements attribute that can take the same kind of values as the elements attribute of <xsl:strip-space>. If an element is listed in the elements attribute of `<xsl:preserve-space>`, then the whitespace-only text nodes that it contains are kept in the node tree. For example, to preserve the whitespace-only text nodes within `<Description>` elements, we can use

```
<xsl:preserve-space elements="Description" />
```

Summary The `<xsl:preserve-space>` element stops whitespace-only text nodes from being stripped from the elements named in its `elements` attribute.

The second method of preventing whitespace-only text nodes from being stripped is to use the attribute `xml:space` with the value `preserve` in the XML document itself. The `xml:space` attribute is defined in the XML Recommendation as the way to indicate how whitespace should be treated within a particular element. If you put an `xml:space` attribute with the value `preserve` on an element in the source XML document, then no matter what `<xsl:strip-space>` instruction you have, all the whitespace-only text nodes that descend from that element will be preserved.

Note You'll notice that the `xml:space` attribute's name includes a colon, indicating that it's a `space` attribute in the XML namespace. Unlike other namespaces, however, you don't have to declare the XML namespace with the prefix `xml`. Namespace-aware applications assume that an element or attribute that has the prefix `xml` is in the XML namespace automatically.

Summary Putting an `xml:space` attribute with the value `preserve` on an element preserves all the whitespace-only text nodes that it contains, at any level.

Matching Nodes

In the first part of this chapter, we've revisited the node tree that is constructed by an XSLT processor when you give it an XML document to process. In this section, we'll look at how to match nodes within that node tree with match patterns.

You've already encountered a number of match patterns, which you've used to create templates that match particular elements in particular contexts. In this section, we'll take a more formal look at the syntax of path patterns, and you'll learn how to construct patterns that match different types of nodes in different contexts and with different values.

Path Patterns

In the patterns that we've looked at in previous chapters, we've seen how to select all elements or particular elements by name and by context. You've seen how a template can match all elements of a particular name in a document by simply naming the elements that it matches. For example, the following template matches all `<Program>` elements:

```
<xsl:template match="Program">
  ...
</xsl:template>
```

You've also seen how you can use path patterns to match elements that occur in specific contexts. For example, the following template matches only those <Program> elements that occur at some level within <Description> elements:

```
<xsl:template match="Description//Program">
  ...
</xsl:template>
```

You can use a single pattern to match several different particular elements by separating their location path patterns with | characters. For example, the following template matches all <Character> and <Actor> elements:

```
<xsl:template match="Character | Actor">
  ...
</xsl:template>
```

Note The character |, when used within a pattern (such as the match attribute of <xsl:template>), separates alternative path patterns. As we'll see later, when you use the character | within an expression (such as in the select attribute of <xsl:apply-templates>), then it acts as the union operator, which creates a sequence of nodes that contains all the nodes from its two operands.

Each one of the path patterns, separated by | characters, can consist of a number of **step patterns**, which can be separated by / or //. Separating step patterns using / indicates a parent-child or element-attribute relationship, while separating steps using // indicates an ancestor-descendant relationship. For example, Description//Program matches <Program> elements that are descendants of <Description> elements at any level, while Description/Program only matches <Program> elements that are direct children of <Description> elements.

Summary Patterns can contain a number of path patterns, separated by | characters. A node matches the pattern as a whole if it matches any of the path patterns.

Step Patterns

Each step pattern is actually made up of three parts, though only one, the node test, is always required. The three parts are an **axis**, which indicates a *tree relationship* between nodes; the **node test**, which specifies the *kind* of node that the step pattern matches; and the **predicates**, which *test* these nodes further to see if they match the pattern. You've already seen node tests, such as node(), text(), and *, in action; here we'll have a closer look at axes and predicates in step patterns.

Axes in Step Patterns

The axis is separated from the node test with a double-colon (`::`). In patterns, the only kinds of axes you can have are the `child::` axis (to match element content) and the `attribute::` axis (to match attributes). If you don't specify an axis, then usually it's just the same as specifying the `child::` axis. For example, the following three patterns all match `<Series>` elements that are children of `<Program>` elements:

```
child::element(Program)/child::element(Series)
child::Program/child::Series
Program/Series
```

You have to use the `attribute::` axis if you want to match attributes, unless you use the `attribute()` node test, in which case the processor guesses you want to use the `attribute::` axis. You can use an `@` instead of `attribute::` as a shorthand. For example, the following patterns match `start` attributes on `<TVGuide>` elements:

```
child::element(TVGuide)/attribute::attribute(start)
child::TVGuide/attribute::start
TVGuide/attribute(start)
TVGuide/@start
```

■ **Note** It's rare to actually specify axes in step patterns, but they are very useful when you start selecting nodes by navigating the node tree via different tree relationships, as you'll see later on.

Predicates in Step Patterns

A step pattern can have one or more predicates to further filter the nodes that are matched by the node test. The predicate contains a test; if the test is `true`, then the node is matched, and if the test is `false`, then the node is not matched. Often a predicate will test the value, children, or attributes of an element. For example, a step pattern that matched `<Program>` elements whose child `<Series>` element started with `'StarTrek'` would be

```
Program[starts-with(Series, 'StarTrek')]
```

If the expression that you use in the predicate evaluates to a number, then the number is tested against the position of the matched node amongst its siblings that are also matched by the portion of the step pattern prior to the predicate. Most frequently you use this to work out whether the matched element is the first child of its type within its parent. For example, the following pattern matches the first `<Program>` element child of the `<Channel>` element:

```
Program[1]
```

You can have as many predicates as you like after specifying the matched node. The second predicate is used on the result of whatever nodes are still matched after the first predicate. If you're using several predicates, including one that indicates the position of a node, you need to make sure that they are in the order that you intend. For example, the following matches the `<Program>` element that is the first `<Program>` element child of its parent element, but only if its `<Series>` element child starts with the string `'StarTrek'`; if the first program is not a *Star Trek* episode, the template will never be used:

```
Program[1][starts-with(Series, 'StarTrek')]
```

On the other hand, the following pattern matches the first <Program> element within its parent whose <Series> child starts with the string 'StarTrek'; even if the first episode of *Star Trek* is the third program shown on the channel, the template with this match pattern will still process it:

```
Program[starts-with(Series, 'StarTrek')][1]
```

Predicates don't always occur at the end of a match pattern. For example, the following pattern matches <Program> element children of <Channel> elements whose <Name> child element starts with the string 'BBC', in other words the programs shown by the BBC:

```
Channel[starts-with(Name, 'BBC')]/Program
```

In general, you can convert templates that only contain an <xsl:if> or <xsl:choose> element into two or more templates, each of which covers one of the possibilities. A template that only contains an <xsl:if> as follows:

```
<xsl:template match="pattern">
  <xsl:if test="test">
    instructions
  </xsl:if>
</xsl:template>
```

can be converted into two templates. One of these does nothing and the other has a match pattern with a predicate that holds the test that was used by the <xsl:if>, as follows:

```
<xsl:template match="pattern" />
<xsl:template match="pattern[test]">
  instructions
</xsl:template>
```

If you use predicates rather than <xsl:choose> or <xsl:if>, you have to beware of two pitfalls:

Templates that have match patterns that include predicates all have a default priority of 0.5, just like those that include information about the parent or ancestors of the node being matched (you learned about the default priorities of different templates in Chapter 3). You need to either construct match patterns that cannot match the same node or add priority attributes to the <xsl:template> elements to make sure that the XSLT processor applies the correct template.

When you test the position of a node, a test within a template relates to its position amongst all the other nodes that are having templates applied to them, in the order in which they are having templates applied (as we'll see when we look at numbering in Chapter 10). On the other hand, a test within a predicate in the step pattern relates to the position of the node amongst other nodes matched by the preceding portion of the step pattern. These two sets of nodes might not be the same.

As an example of this last point, say that you applied templates to only *Star Trek* episodes, with the instruction

```
<xsl:apply-templates select="Program[starts-with(Series, 'StarTrek')]" />
```

and imagine that you had two separate templates—one that matches the first <Program> element (and highlights it), and one that matches other <Program> elements, as follows:

```
<xsl:template match="Program[1]">
  <div class="highlight">
    <xsl:apply-templates select="." mode="Details" />
  </div>
</xsl:template>

<xsl:template match="Program[position() > 1]">
  <div><xsl:apply-templates select="." mode="Details" /></div>
</xsl:template>
```

In this situation, whether or not the first template is ever used depends on whether the first program within the channel is a *Star Trek* episode or not. The first template matches only the first `<Program>` element within the `<Channel>`. If the first program is not a *Star Trek* episode, then even though we're only listing *Star Trek* episodes, the first template will never get used.

What's probably required is a single template that matches all programs, wherever they are, in which you test the position of the program *amongst the selected programs*. This would give the following:

```
<xsl:template match="Program">
  <xsl:choose>
    <xsl:when test="position() = 1">
      <div class="highlight">
        <xsl:apply-templates select="." mode="Details" />
      </div>
    </xsl:when>
    <xsl:otherwise>
      <div><xsl:apply-templates select="." mode="Details" /></div>
    </xsl:otherwise>
  </xsl:choose>
</xsl:template>
```

With this, the first selected program will be highlighted no matter where it occurs in the source document. Using the `position()` function tests the position of the node within the list of nodes to which templates are applied; predicates within match patterns test the position of the node amongst its same-named siblings.

Summary If you include a predicate in a step, then the step only matches nodes for which the predicate is true. The position of a node is assessed within the list of other nodes that match the part of the step prior to the predicate.

Positional Predicates in Match Patterns

Let's return to `TVGuide.xsl` to have a look at how predicates work within match patterns. In `TVGuide2.xsl`, we'll amend the template matching `<Program>` elements so that the first program on each channel (the program that's showing now) is highlighted using the `nowShowing` class, with an additional `<xsl:when>` clause as follows:

```
<xsl:template match="Program">
  <xsl:choose>
    <xsl:when test="position() = 1">
      <div class="nowShowing">
        <xsl:apply-templates select="." mode="Details" />
      </div>
    </xsl:when>
    <xsl:when
      test="@flag = 'favorite' or @flag = 'interesting' or @rating > 6 or
            contains(lower-case(Series), 'news') or
            contains(lower-case(Title), 'news') or
            contains(lower-case(Description), 'news')">
      <div class="interesting">
        <xsl:apply-templates select="." mode="Details" />
      </div>
    </xsl:when>
    <xsl:otherwise>
      <div>
        <xsl:apply-templates select="." mode="Details" />
      </div>
    </xsl:otherwise>
  </xsl:choose>
</xsl:template>
```

We'll add a style to the CSS stylesheet for the TV guide, to create `TVGuide2.css`, so that the details for the first program showing on each channel are shown with a slightly larger font, as follows:

```
div.nowShowing {
    font-size: 120%;
}
```

Remember to change the link that points to the CSS file so that it points to `TVGuide2.css` rather than `TVGuide.css`.

The template matching `<Program>` elements is processed when templates are applied to the children of `<Channel>` elements. At the moment, the XSLT processor applies templates to all the children of the `<Channel>` elements at once, including whitespace-only text nodes and the `<Name>` element, using the built-in template:

```
<xsl:template match="*">
  <xsl:apply-templates />
</xsl:template>
```

When we use `TVGuide2.xsl` to transform `TVGuide.xml`, to give `TVGuide2.html`, we get the page shown in Figure 7-6. Notice that the details of the first program are no larger than the details of the other programs.

Now let's add a template that matches `<Channel>` elements, and change the `<xsl:apply-templates>` instruction so that we explicitly select the `<Program>` elements, as follows, in `TVGuide3.xsl`:

```
<xsl:template match="Channel">
  <xsl:apply-templates select="Name" />
  <xsl:apply-templates select="Program" />
</xsl:template>
```

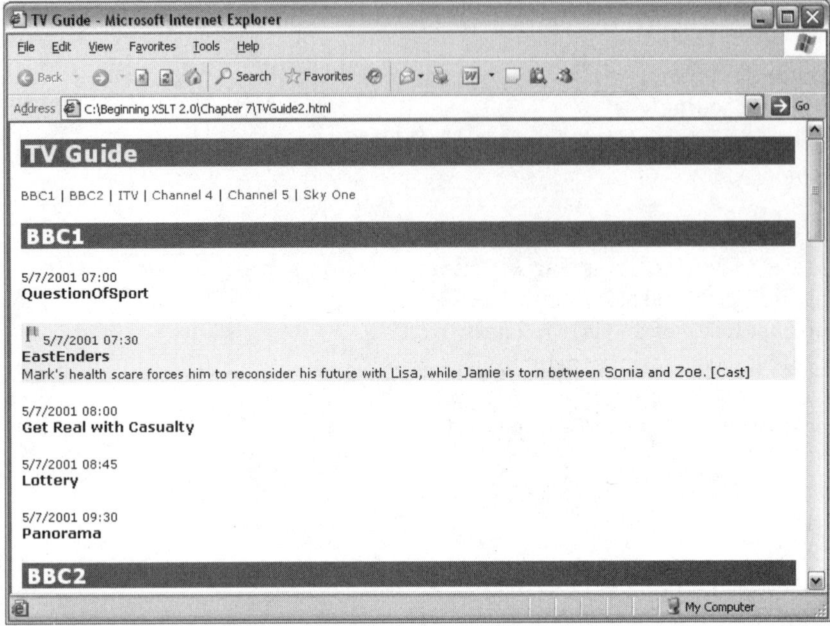

Figure 7-6. *Viewing* `TVGuide2.html` *in Internet Explorer*

When you use `TVGuide3.xsl` with `TVGuide.xml` and look at the result (`TVGuide3.html`), you should see the page shown in Figure 7-7.

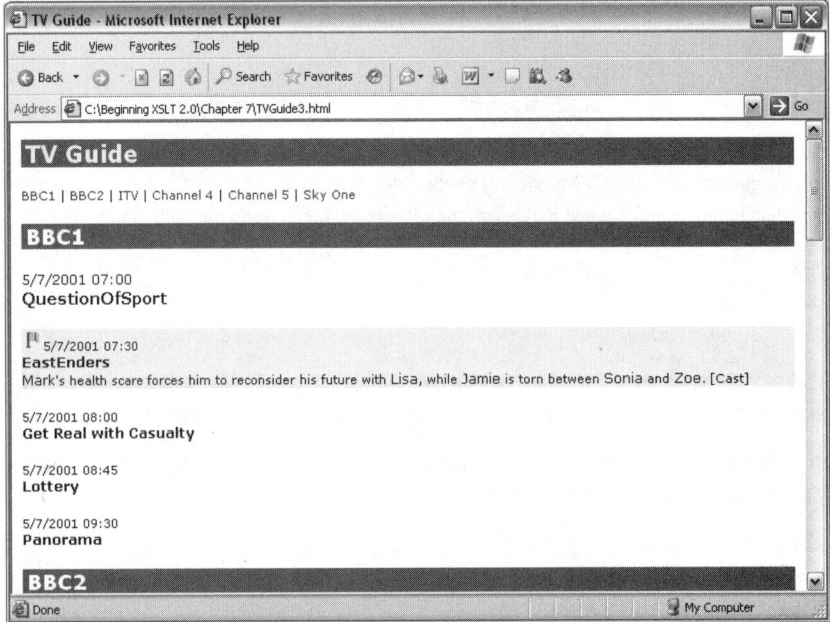

Figure 7-7. *Viewing* `TVGuide3.html` *in Internet Explorer*

The details for *Question of Sport*, and the other programs that are showing "now," one per channel, are larger than the details for the other programs. The position() function, used within the template for the <Program> element, looks at the position of the current node within the current node list, which is now only the <Program> elements for each channel, rather than the <Name> element and any number of whitespace-only text nodes.

Another method of making this work is to split the template into three templates: one for the first program showing on each channel, one for the interesting programs, and one for the rest of the programs. TVGuide4.xsl is based on TVGuide2.xsl (so doesn't have a template for the <Channel> elements, but has three templates that match <Program> elements in default mode):

```
<xsl:template match="Program[1]">
  <div class="nowShowing">
    <xsl:apply-templates select="." mode="Details" />
  </div>
</xsl:template>

<xsl:template match="Program[@flag = 'favorite' or @flag = 'interesting' or
                             @rating > 6 or
                             contains(lower-case(Series), 'news') or
                             contains(lower-case(Title), 'news') or
                             contains(lower-case(Description), 'news')]">
  <div class="interesting">
    <xsl:apply-templates select="." mode="Details" />
  </div>
</xsl:template>

<xsl:template match="Program">
  <div>
    <xsl:apply-templates select="." mode="Details" />
  </div>
</xsl:template>
```

The first template matches the first <Program> elements within each <Channel> element, whether you apply templates to all the children of the <Channel> element (including the <Name> element and whitespace-only text nodes), or just its child <Program> elements.

TVGuide4.html, which is the result of using TVGuide4.xsl (in which templates are applied to all the children of the <Channel> elements) with TVGuide.xml, is almost exactly the same as TVGuide3.html. The only difference occurs because of the different priorities of the conditions in TVGuide4.xsl. In TVGuide3.xsl, the highest priority test is whether the program is the first on the channel; if you look at *Channel 4 News* in TVGuide3.html, shown in Figure 7-8, you'll see that it appears larger than the other programs.

If you look at the same program in TVGuide4.html, as shown in Figure 7-9, you'll see that it is highlighted as an interesting program.

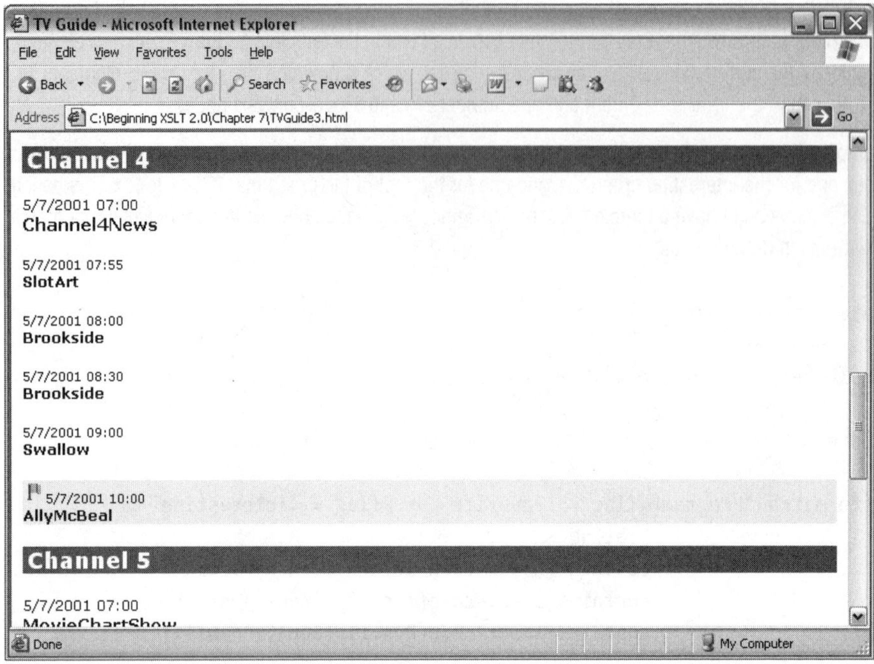

Figure 7-8. *Viewing Channel 4 News in* `TVGuide3.html` *in Internet Explorer*

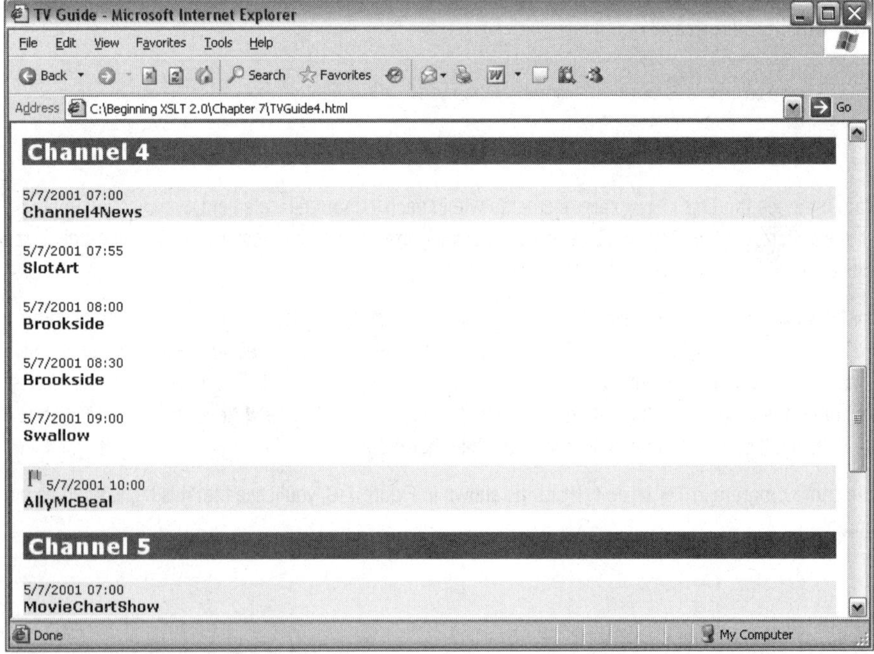

Figure 7-9. *Viewing Channel 4 News in* `TVGuide4.html` *in Internet Explorer*

Why is this? Well, the `<Program>` element for *Channel 4 News* matches both the template that matches the first program on a channel and the template that matches interesting programs. Both these templates have the same priority, and when two templates have the same priority, the one that's later in the stylesheet gets used. Saxon helpfully warns us that this is happening, as shown in Figure 7-10.

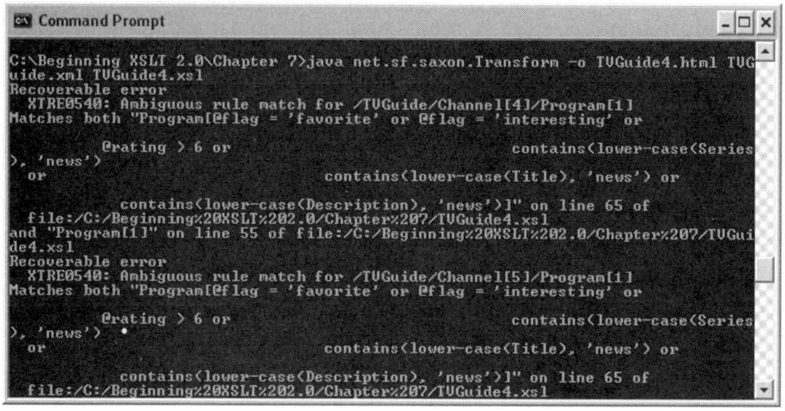

```
Command Prompt
C:\Beginning XSLT 2.0\Chapter 7>java net.sf.saxon.Transform -o TVGuide4.html TVG
uide.xml TVGuide4.xsl
Recoverable error
  XTRE0540: Ambiguous rule match for /TVGuide/Channel[4]/Program[1]
Matches both "Program[@flag = 'favorite' or @flag = 'interesting' or

            @rating > 6 or                              contains(lower-case(Series
), 'news')
  or                          contains(lower-case(Title), 'news') or

          contains(lower-case(Description), 'news')]" on line 65 of
  file:/C:/Beginning%20XSLT%202.0/Chapter%207/TVGuide4.xsl
and "Program[1]" on line 55 of file:/C:/Beginning%20XSLT%202.0/Chapter%207/TVGui
de4.xsl
Recoverable error
  XTRE0540: Ambiguous rule match for /TVGuide/Channel[5]/Program[1]
Matches both "Program[@flag = 'favorite' or @flag = 'interesting' or

            @rating > 6 or                              contains(lower-case(Series
), 'news')
  or                          contains(lower-case(Title), 'news') or

          contains(lower-case(Description), 'news')]" on line 65 of
  file:/C:/Beginning%20XSLT%202.0/Chapter%207/TVGuide4.xsl
```

Figure 7-10. *Saxon warning of ambiguous template match*

You can make the highlighting of the first program on a channel the priority by adding a `priority` attribute to the template that matches the first program on a channel, giving it a value of more than 0.5:

```
<xsl:template match="Program[1]" priority="1">
  <div class="nowShowing">
    <xsl:apply-templates select="." mode="Details" />
  </div>
</xsl:template>
```

This change has been made in `TVGuide5.xsl`; `TVGuide5.html`, which is the result of transforming `TVGuide.xml` with `TVGuide5.xsl`, looks exactly the same as `TVGuide3.html`—*Channel 4 News* is highlighted as the first program on the channel rather than as an interesting program.

Node Tests and Namespaces

When you use a node test to select an element or attribute, then the node test doesn't just test the kind of the node; it also tests its name and sometimes its type. We've seen that node tests that specify the name of an element are shorthands for longer `element()` and `attribute()` node tests. These kinds of tests are termed **name tests**. There are five types of name tests; when applied to elements they work as follows:

- *—Matches any element
- `name`—Matches any element with that local name that is in the default XPath namespace
- `prefix:*`—Matches any element in the namespace indicated by the prefix

- `*:name`—Matches any element with that local name, in any namespace
- `prefix:name`—Matches any element with that local name and that is in the namespace indicated by the prefix

The **default XPath namespace** is used when you give the name of an element without a prefix. Usually, there's no default XPath namespace, which means that if you just have a name test such as `TVGuide`, you will only match `<TVGuide>` elements that are in no namespace. However, you can specify a different default XPath namespace using the `xpath-default-namespace` attribute on the `<xsl:stylesheet>` element.

■ Note The namespaces that are in-scope in the stylesheet and the default XPath namespace are also used to interpret prefixes when you create a qualified name using the `xs:QName()` constructor function, as we saw in Chapter 5.

The preceding name tests work in almost exactly the same way when applied to attributes, except that the default XPath namespace is *not* used when you give an attribute name that doesn't have a prefix.

Matching Elements in Namespaces

The prefixes that you use in paths should be the ones that you use *in the stylesheet*, not the ones that are used in the source XML document. As an example, let's look again at `TVGuide2.xml`, in Listing 7-6, which includes namespaces.

Listing 7-6. `TVGuide2.xml`

```
<?xml version="1.0" encoding="ISO-8859-1"?>
<?xml-stylesheet type="text/xsl" href="TVGuide.xsl"?>
<TVGuide xmlns="http://www.example.com/TVGuide"
         xmlns:xsi="http://www.w3.org/2001/XMLSchema-instance"
         xsi:schemaLocation="http://www.example.com/TVGuide TVGuide.xsd"
         start="2001-07-05" end="2001-07-05">
  <Channel>
    <Name>BBC1</Name>
    ...
    <Program>
      <Start>2001-07-05T19:30:00</Start>
      <Duration>PT30M</Duration>
      <Series>EastEnders</Series>
      ...
    </Program>
    ...
  </Channel>
</TVGuide>
```

All the elements in the XML document are in the TV guide namespace. What happens when we try to process <TVGuide> elements with the following <xsl:apply-templates> instruction?

```
<xsl:apply-templates select="TVGuide" />
```

The name test (TVGuide) doesn't give a prefix, so the XSLT processor will only select the <TVGuide> element if it's in the default XPath namespace, and there's currently no default XPath namespace. The <TVGuide> element in our source XML document are in the http://www.example.com/TVGuide namespace, so it won't get selected. You can see this in action if you try to transform TVGuide2.xml with TVGuide5.xsl to create TVGuide5-2.html. The result of the transformation is shown in Figure 7-11.

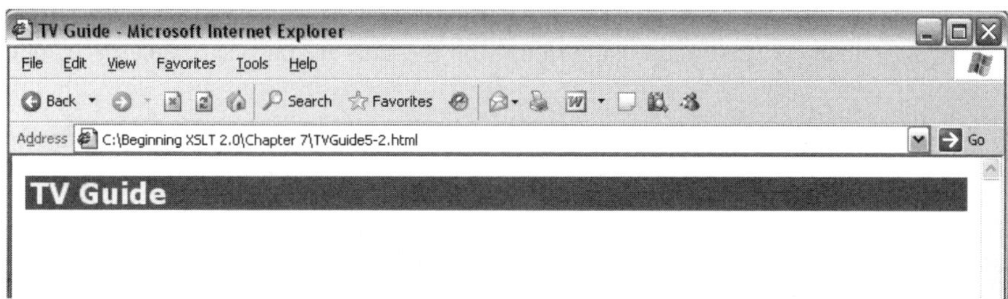

Figure 7-11. *Viewing* TVGuide5-2.html *in Internet Explorer*

We don't get any output from the <xsl:apply-templates> instruction because it hasn't found a node to apply templates to; the page is empty.

As you can see, adding a default namespace declaration to an XML document makes it impossible to use the same stylesheet with it as you used before. There are three ways in which we could change the stylesheet in order to match and select elements in the http://www.example.com/TVGuide namespace.

The simplest change is to change the default XPath namespace to be http://www.example.com/TVGuide, by adding an xpath-default-namespace attribute to the <xsl:stylesheet> element as follows:

```
<xsl:stylesheet version="2.0"
                xmlns:xsl="http://www.w3.org/1999/XSL/Transform"
                xmlns:xs="http://www.w3.org/2001/XMLSchema"
                xmlns:xdt="http://www.w3.org/2005/04/xpath-datatypes"
                xpath-default-namespace="http://www.example.com/TVGuide">
...
</xsl:stylesheet>
```

This is an easy change to make, but you might run into trouble later if you find you want to match or select elements that really are in no namespace; there's no way of doing this if the default XPath namespace is set.

Another change would be to add *: in front of all the element names in the paths and patterns in the stylesheet, so that they match elements in any namespace (but with the particular local name). For example, the name test TVGuide would become *:TVGuide, which would match all elements called TVGuide in any namespace. This would be useful if we wanted to make a stylesheet that could be used with both TVGuide.xml and TVGuide2.xml, but we would have to be careful if we later wanted to process elements that were in a different namespace but that might share the same name.

Finally, we can declare the http://www.example.com/TVGuide namespace in the stylesheet, with a prefix, and then use that prefix in the paths throughout the stylesheet. For example, the name test TVGuide would become tv:TVGuide. You can use the prefix in combination with the wildcard name test as well; for example, the pattern tv:* matches elements in the TV guide namespace, no matter what their local name is.

Note The pattern * still matches elements in any namespace, so in many cases you don't have to prefix wildcard name tests with the relevant prefix. Matching all elements in a particular namespace is really useful, for example, in transformations where you want to strip all the elements in a particular namespace from a document.

Summary If an element you want to select or match is in a namespace, you have to either set the default XPath namespace to that namespace or use a name test that either uses a wildcard prefix or uses the prefix associated with that namespace within the stylesheet.

Adding Namespaces to Stylesheets

We've added a default namespace to the TVGuide2.xml document. Now it's time to make a new version of our stylesheet (TVGuide6.xsl) so that we can display the TV guide in the way we did before. Adding the default namespace to TVGuide2.xml was very easy—we just added an xmlns attribute to the document element, as follows:

```
<TVGuide xmlns="http://www.example.com/TVGuide"
         xmlns:xsi="http://www.w3.org/2001/XMLSchema-instance"
         xsi:schemaLocation="http://www.example.com/TVGuide TVGuide.xsd"
         start="2001-07-05" end="2001-07-05">
  ...
</TVGuide>
```

However, adding this default namespace fundamentally changes the way that the XSLT processor sees the elements in the document. Previously, they've been in no namespace; now they're in the http://www.example.com/TVGuide namespace. The simplest way to match and select the elements is to add an xpath-default-namespace attribute to the <xsl:stylesheet> element, containing the namespace URI for the elements, as in TVGuide6.xsl:

```
<xsl:stylesheet version="2.0"
                xmlns:xsl="http://www.w3.org/1999/XSL/Transform"
                xmlns:xs="http://www.w3.org/2001/XMLSchema"
                xmlns:xdt="http://www.w3.org/2005/04/xpath-datatypes"
                xpath-default-namespace="http://www.example.com/TVGuide">
  ...
</xsl:stylesheet>
```

If you transform TVGuide2.xml with TVGuide6.xsl, the result is TVGuide6.html, which is shown in Figure 7-12. TVGuide6.html looks exactly the same as the result we get when transforming TVGuide.xml (which doesn't have the default namespace declaration) with TVGuide5.xsl (in which there's no xpath-default-namespace attribute).

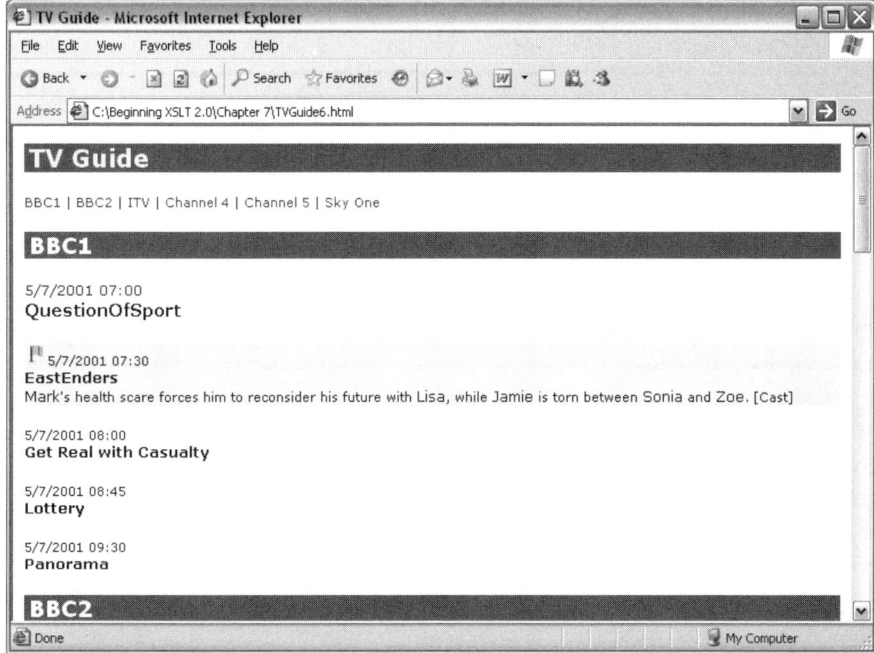

Figure 7-12. *Viewing* TVGuide6.html *in Internet Explorer*

Again, though, if you try transforming TVGuide.xml, in which the elements are in no namespace, with TVGuide6.xsl, which assumes that the elements are in the TV guide namespace, you have the same problem as you did when transforming TVGuide2.xml with TVGuide5.xsl, as shown in Figure 7-11. The namespaces that you use in your input XML document must match the namespaces that you use in your XSLT stylesheet to get the result that you require.

An alternative way of matching and selecting elements in the http://www.example.com/TVGuide namespace is to add a namespace declaration to the <xsl:stylesheet> element, as in TVGuide7.xsl, using the same namespace URI but assigning a prefix to it:

```
<xsl:stylesheet version="1.0"
                xmlns:xsl="http://www.w3.org/1999/XSL/Transform"
                xmlns:xs="http://www.w3.org/2001/XMLSchema"
                xmlns:xdt="http://www.w3.org/2003/05/xpath-datatypes"
                xmlns:tv="http://www.example.com/TVGuide">
  ...
</xsl:stylesheet>
```

and then go through all the patterns and expressions in the stylesheet and add the `tv` prefix to the element names that are used within them. For example, here is a converted version of the template for `<Channel>` elements in `ChannelList` mode. All the element names used in the template are given a `tv` prefix:

```
<xsl:template match="tv:Channel" mode="ChannelList">
  <a href="#{tv:Name}"><xsl:value-of select="tv:Name" /></a>
  <xsl:if test="position() != last()"> | </xsl:if>
</xsl:template>
```

■ **Note** You should *not* add the prefix to the names of attributes. Attributes without prefixes are in no namespace, whatever the default namespace, so you must select them using just their name, without a prefix.

When you have added the `tv` prefix to all the element names in the stylesheet, try transforming `TVGuide2.xml` with `TVGuide7.xsl` to give `TVGuide7.html`. You should see the same result as shown in Figure 7-12.

Template Priorities

You'll remember from Chapter 3 that the default priority of a template, used if you don't give a `priority` attribute, depends on the pattern that you use in the `match` attribute. In Chapter 3, we saw three priority levels; when you start including patterns that match elements in different namespaces and those that match by type, there are five:

- Templates whose match patterns match a particular kind of node, such as `*`, `attribute()`, or `text()`, are assigned a default priority of -0.5.
- Templates whose match patterns match elements or attributes in a particular namespace, such as `tv:*` or `xsi:*`, or match elements or attributes with a particular local name, such as `*:Name`, are assigned a default priority of -0.25.
- Templates whose match patterns match elements or attributes by name only, such as `Channel`, `xsi:schemaLocation`, or `attribute(href)`, or by type only, such as `element(*, xs:dateTime)`, are assigned a default priority of 0.
- Templates whose match patterns match elements or attributes by name and by type, such as `element(Start, xs:dateTime)` or `attribute(start, xs:date)`, or match based on declarations in the schema, such as `schema-element(TVGuide)`, are assigned a default priority of 0.25.
- Templates whose match patterns contain a number of step patterns or include a predicate, such as `Description//Channel` or `Program[1]`, are assigned a default priority of 0.5.

The priority for the `document-node()` node test depends on what it contains. On its own, `document-node()` has a priority of -0.5, like the other node tests that just test the kind of a node. If the `document-node()` node test contains an `element()` or `schema-element()` node test, the priority of the `document-node()` node test is the same as that `element()` or `schema-element()` node test. For example, the priority of `document-node(element(TVGuide))` is 0.

Note We'll be revisiting template priorities once more, when we look at using schema information within a stylesheet, in Chapter 13.

Selecting Nodes

The last section looked at how to indicate what kinds of nodes a template matches, using patterns. In this section, we're going to look at how to select nodes within expressions, using paths.

The paths that you use to select nodes look very similar to the path patterns that you use to match nodes, and it's easy to get confused between them. Remember that patterns are used to test whether a template should be used for a particular node—the processor works *backwards* through the pattern, checking the parents and ancestors of the node that you've told it to process to see if it complies with the pattern. On the other hand, paths are used to gather together a bunch of nodes in order to process or query them—the processor works *forwards* through the expression, starting from whatever node you're currently processing, and traveling step by step through the node tree to locate a sequence of nodes that you want to do something with.

Because they're used to select nodes rather than simply match them, paths have a syntax that's a lot more flexible than that for patterns, as we'll see later.

Sequences of nodes can be constructed by creating a **union** of several other sequences of nodes, using the | or `union` operator. For example, the following expression selects the `<Writer>`, `<Director>`, and `<Producer>` child elements of the current `<Program>` element:

```
Writer | Director union Producer
```

Note The operators | and `union` do exactly the same thing. The | syntax was used in XPath 1.0; the `union` syntax is introduced in XPath 2.0 for consistency with the `intersect` and `except` operators.

You can also combine two sequences of nodes using the `intersect` operator to get their **intersection**: all the nodes that appear in both sequences. For example, the following expression selects all those elements that are in the sequence held by the `$interestingPrograms` variable and that are children of the current `<Channel>` element:

```
$interestingPrograms intersect Program
```

Finally, you can subtract one sequence of nodes from another using the `except` operator. For example, the following expression selects all the child elements of the current `<Program>` element except the `<Series>` and `<Title>` children:

```
* except (Series | Title)
```

Summary In an expression, the | or `union` operators create a union of a number of sequences of nodes. The `intersect` operator returns the intersection of two node sequences, and the `except` operator returns those nodes in the first node sequence that aren't in the second node sequence.

Each path can consist of a number of steps, separated by either a single / or a double //. In fact, the // separator is a shorthand for a more complex step, namely /descendant-or-self::node()/. For example, the following two paths both select the <Link> element descendants of the <Description> child element of the current <Program> element:

```
Description//Link
Description/descendant-or-self::node()/Link
```

There are two kinds of steps that can appear in a path: **general steps** and **axis steps**.

General steps are any expression that returns a sequence of nodes. For example, a general step can contain a union expression. The following expression selects the <Name> children of the <Character> and <Actor> children of the <CastMember> children of the current <CastList> element:

```
CastMember/(Character | Actor)/Name
```

Axis steps comprise the same three components as step patterns in path patterns: an optional axis, a node test, and any number of predicates. Again, if you don't specify an axis, then the processor usually uses the child:: axis (unless the node test is an attribute() node test), and you can use an @ as a shorthand for the attribute:: axis.

You'll recognize that the descendant-or-self:: part of the expanded step earlier is a new axis. Paths can contain a number of axes, which we'll look at in more detail next.

Axes

Axes specify the relationship between the context node and the nodes that each step selects. You've already learned about two axes: the child:: axis, which selects the children of the context node, and the attribute:: axis, which selects its attributes. There are several other axes, and they are all shown in Table 7-3; the example paths all assume that the context node is the <Program> element (node 12) highlighted in Figure 7-13 (note that only the namespace nodes on the <Program> element are shown).

Table 7-3. *Axes*

Axis	Dir	Example	Description
self::	F	self::Program	Selects the node itself (for example, the <Program> element, node 12)
attribute::	F	attribute::*	Selects the node's attributes (for example, any attributes on the <Program> element, node 15)
namespace::	F	namespace::*	Selects the node's namespace nodes (for example, the TVGuide and XMLSchema-instance namespace nodes, 13 and 14)
child::	F	child::Series	Selects immediate children of the node (for example, the <Series> element, node 16)

Axis	Dir	Example	Description
`parent::`	R	`parent::Channel`	Selects the node's parent (for example, the parent `<Channel>` element, node 6)
`descendant::`	F	`descendant::text()`	Selects the node's descendants (for example, all text nodes within the `<Program>` element, node 17)
`descendant-or-self::`	F	`descendant-or-self::node()`	Selects the node's descendants and the node itself (for example, all the nodes within the `<Program>` element, including the `<Program>` element itself, nodes 12, 16, and 17)
`ancestor::`	R	`ancestor::*`	Selects the node's ancestors (for example, the `<Channel>` and `<TVGuide>` elements, nodes 6 and 3)
`ancestor-or-self::`	R	`ancestor-or-self::*`	Selects the node's ancestors and the node itself (for example, the `<Program>`, `<Channel>`, and `<TVGuide>` elements, nodes 12, 6, and 3)
`following-sibling::`	F	`following-sibling::Program`	Selects the node's siblings that occur after the node (for example, the later `<Program>` elements in the same `<Channel>`, node 18)
`preceding-sibling::`	R	`preceding-sibling::Name`	Selects the node's siblings that occur before the node (for example, the earlier `<Name>` element in the same `<Channel>`, node 7)
`following::`	F	`following::Series`	Selects nodes that start after the node ends (for example, the `<Series>` elements within all `<Program>` elements in all `<Channel>` elements after this one, node 19)
`preceding::`	R	`preceding::Series`	Selects nodes that end before the node starts (for example, the `<Series>` elements within all the `<Program>` elements in all the `<Channel>` elements before this one, node 10)

Axes fall into two groups based on the direction in which the XSLT processor goes when it traverses the tree: **forward axes** (indicated by an F in the table) and **reverse axes** (indicated by an R in the table).

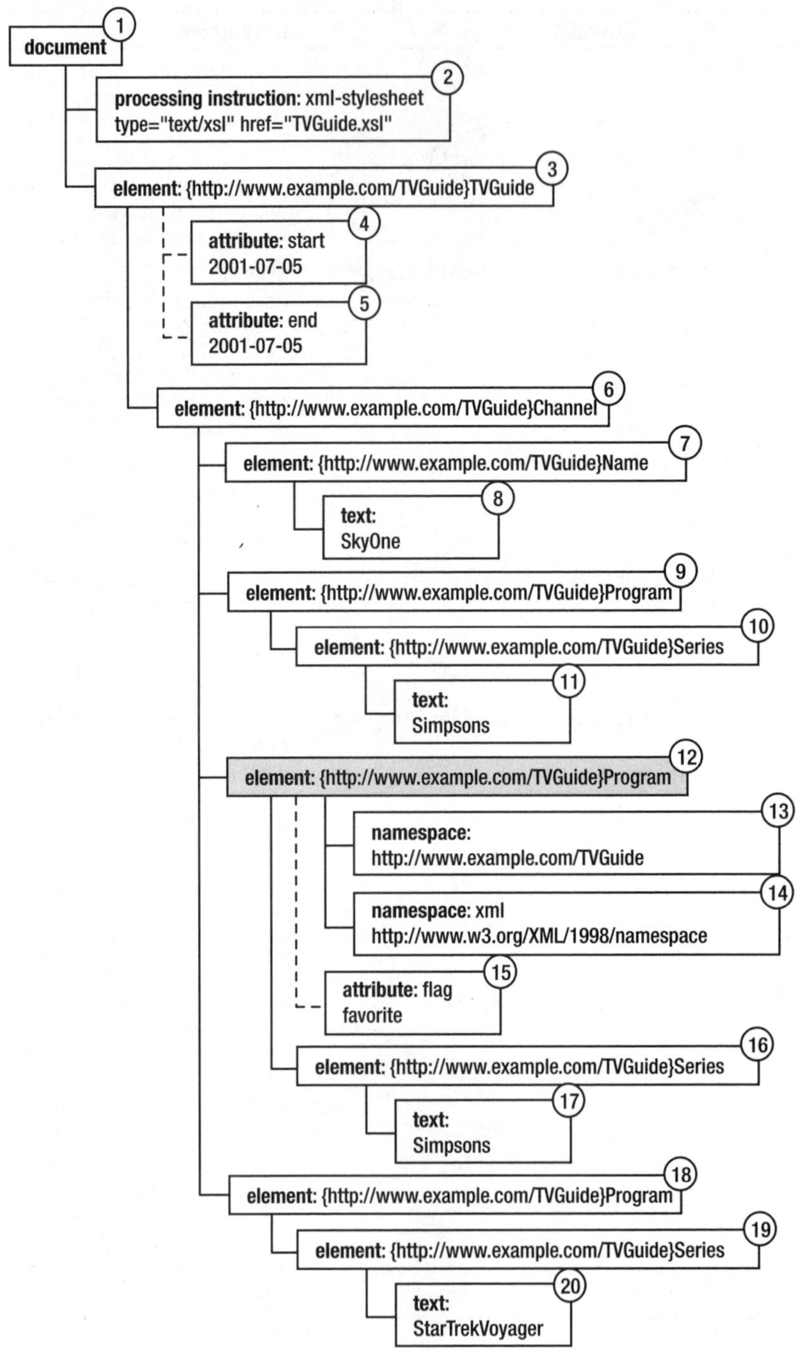

Figure 7-13. *Example node tree*

Caution The `namespace::` axis is deprecated in XPath 2.0, so some XSLT 2.0 processors might not support it. You can use the `in-scope-prefixes()` and `namespace-uri-for-prefix()` functions to get hold of most information you would otherwise get through the `namespace::` axis.

When the XSLT processor collects nodes with a forward axis, then the first node it encounters is the first node in that direction in document order, so `child::Program[1]` gives you the first `<Program>` element child of the context node. On the other hand, when an XSLT processor collects nodes with a reverse axis, then the first node it encounters is the last node in that direction in document order, so `ancestor::*[1]` gives you the immediate ancestor of the context node (its parent).

Note Whether an axis is a forward axis or a reverse axis only affects predicates that are based on the position of the node, not the order of the resulting sequence. If you apply templates to the nodes or iterate over them with `<xsl:for-each>`, they will be processed in document order no matter which axis you used to select them. Likewise, in `(ancestor::*)[1]` the brackets around `ancestor::*` mean that it's evaluated to a sequence (which is in document order) before the positional predicate `[1]` gets applied: you get the document element of the XML document, not the immediate ancestor of the context node.

The path `..`, which we used in earlier chapters, is actually a shorthand for the longer path:

```
parent::node()
```

This selects the parent node, no matter what type it is or what name it has.

Summary Axes indicate the direction in which nodes are collected in a step.

Evaluating Location Paths

Let's now take a more formal look at how an XSLT processor evaluates a location path.

First, the XSLT processor needs to find a starting point for its journey. Usually, paths are relative, and start at the **context node**, the node at which the processor is currently looking. When a path is used in a predicate, the context node is the node selected by the portion of the step prior to the predicate. For example, when the XSLT processor evaluates the path `Series` in the following:

```
Program[Series = 'EastEnders']
```

the context node is the `<Program>` element. You can make the XSLT processor start at other points in the XML document; most notably you can start at the root document node of the document by starting the path with a `/`. The following path starts from the root document node and works from there:

```
/TVGuide/Channel
```

Note If the root node for the node tree isn't a document node, which might happen if you've constructed the node tree in the content of `<xsl:variable>`, you will get an error if you start a path with `/`.

You can also start a path with a variable reference, as long as that variable holds a sequence of nodes. For example, the following sets the `$allPrograms` variable to hold the `<Program>` elements under the current node, and the `$allSeries` variable to hold the `<Series>` children of those `<Program>` elements:

```
<xsl:variable name="allPrograms" select="Program" />
<xsl:variable name="allSeries" select="$allPrograms/Series" />
```

Once it has its starting point, the processor evaluates each step in turn, with each node selected by one step becoming a context node for the next step. It's helpful to view this process step by step; take the following path:

```
/node()
  /Channel
    /Program[Series = 'EastEnders']
      /following-sibling::Program[1]
```

The location path starts with a / so the starting point is the root document node of the node tree, highlighted in Figure 7-14.

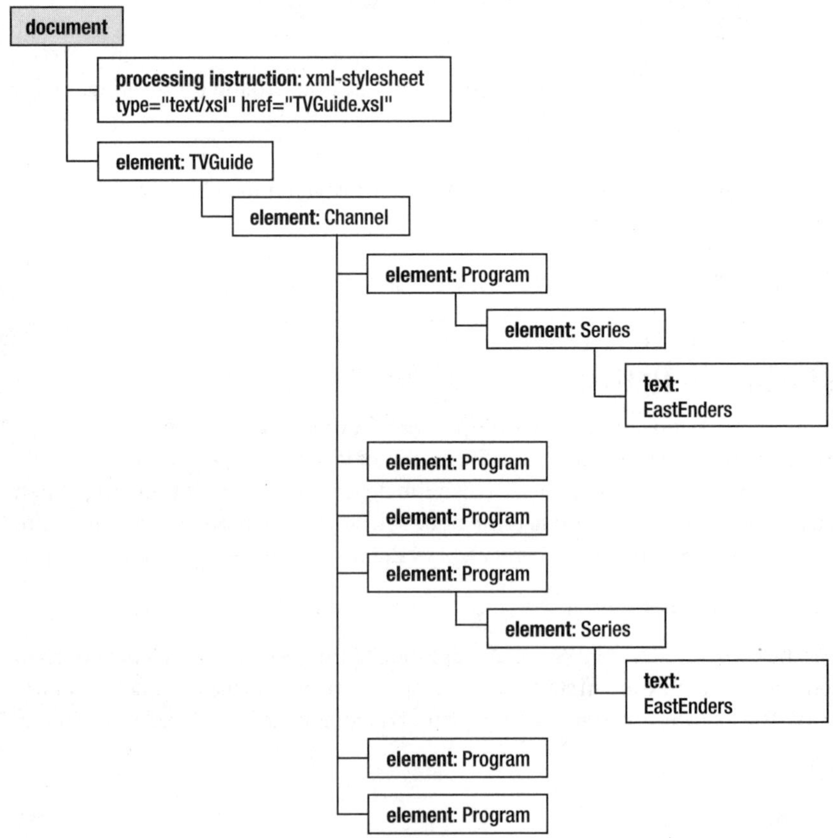

Figure 7-14. *Starting from the root document node*

The first step, highlighted in the following, selects all the children of the context node—the processing instruction and the <TVGuide> element:

```
/node()
  /Channel
    /Program[Series = 'EastEnders']
      /following-sibling::Program[1]
```

The nodes that are selected are highlighted in Figure 7-15.

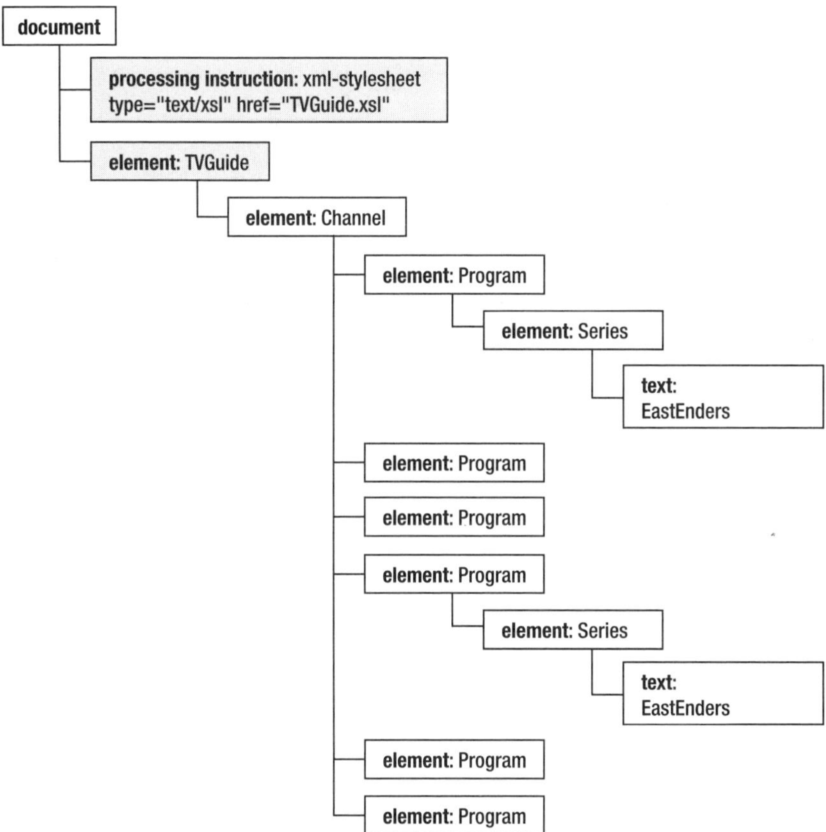

Figure 7-15. *Selecting the Children of the Root Document Node*

The next step selects all <Channel> children of the context node:

```
/node()
  /Channel
    /Program[Series = 'EastEnders']
      /following-sibling::Program[1]
```

The two context nodes are the processing instruction, which doesn't have any children, and the <TVGuide>, which does have <Channel> element children; these are selected as the result of the second step, as shown in Figure 7-16.

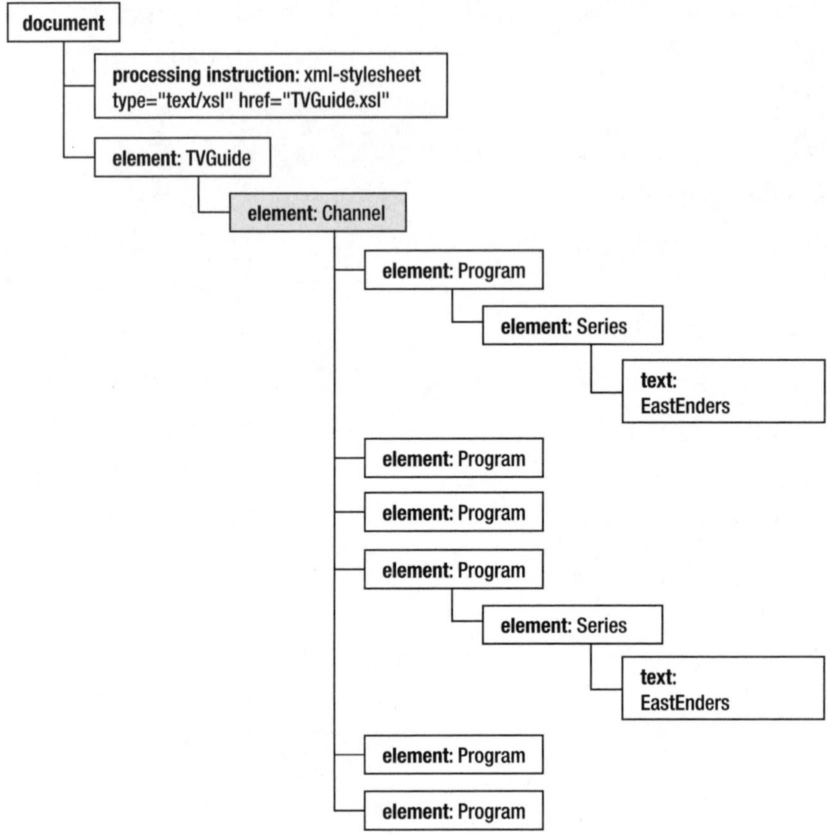

Figure 7-16. *Selecting the* `<Channel>` *elements*

The next step selects the `<Program>` elements whose child `<Series>` element has a string value equal to `'EastEnders'`:

```
/node()
  /Channel
    /Program[Series = 'EastEnders']
      /following-sibling::Program[1]
```

There are two of these `<Program>` elements, so these are selected as the result of the third step, as shown in Figure 7-17.

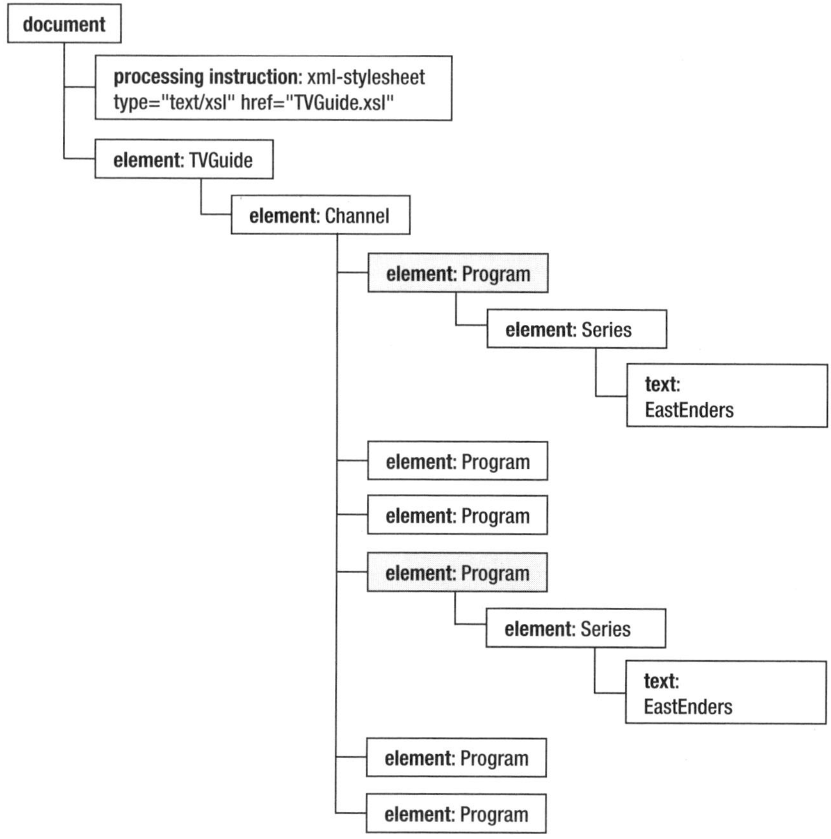

Figure 7-17. *Selecting the* `<Program>` *elements whose* `<Series>` *child has the value* `'EastEnders'`

The final step selects the following sibling `<Program>` elements of the context node, and picks the first of these:

```
/node()
  /Channel
    /Program[Series = 'EastEnders']
      /following-sibling::Program[1]
```

There are two `<Program>` elements that act as context nodes for this step—the two selected by the previous step. So a single `<Program>` element is selected for each of these context nodes, and the result of the path as a whole is a sequence of nodes containing the two `<Program>` elements that immediately follow the `<Program>` elements whose `<Series>` children are equal to `'EastEnders'`, highlighted in Figure 7-18.

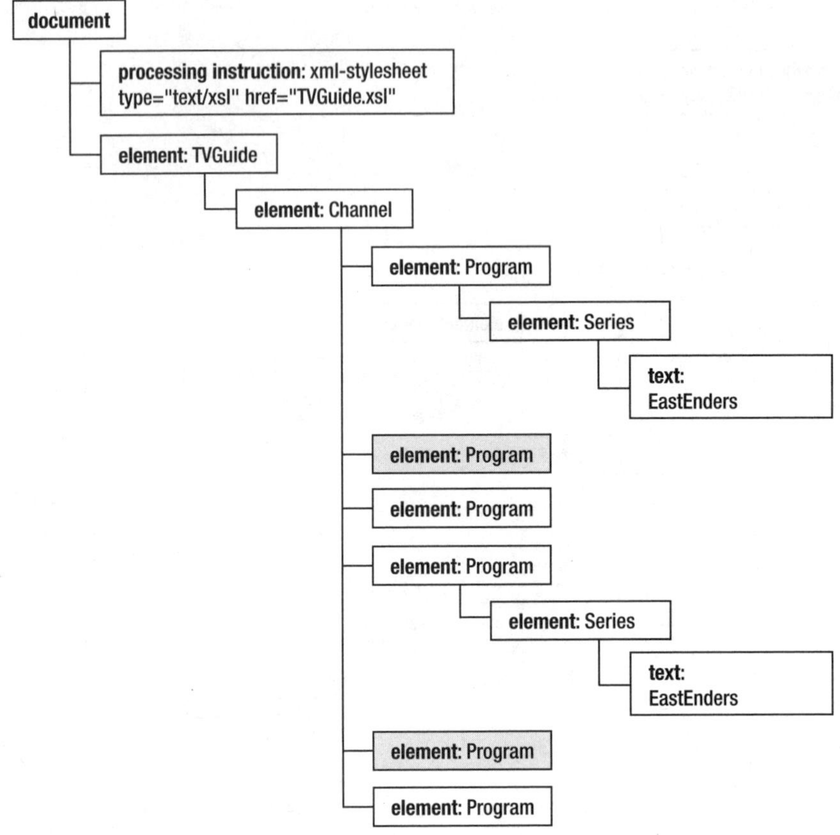

Figure 7-18. *Selecting the immediately following sibling* <Program> *elements*

Accessing the Next Program's Start Time

In Chapter 5, we calculated the end time for a program by adding the start time and duration of a program using

```
xs:dateTime(.) + xdt:dayTimeDuration(../Duration)
```

In fact, the end time of one program is the start time of the next program, so another way of getting hold of that time would be to look at the `<Start>` element child of the following sibling `<Program>` element within the `<Channel>`. We'll do this in the next version of our stylesheet, `TVGuide8.xsl` (and we'll go back to working with `TVGuide.xml` since that means we don't have to worry about namespaces).

The place where we need to work out the end time for a program is within the template that matches the `<Start>` elements, which currently looks like this:

```
<xsl:template match="Start">
  <span class="date">
    <xsl:value-of select="format-dateTime(xs:dateTime(.),
                                          '[M]/[D]/[Y] [H01]:[m]')" />
  </span>
</xsl:template>
```

The current node within this template is the <Start> element child of the <Program> element. We want to find the <Program> immediately after this one in order to find its <Start> time. Our first step has to be up to this <Start> element's parent <Program> element, which you can do with

```
parent::Program
```

■ **Note** You could also do it with the shorthand `..` but sometimes I find that using the `parent::` axis instead helps me keep track of where I am in the document.

Now that we're on the <Program> element, we can get all its following siblings using the `following-sibling::` axis; we're only interested in the <Program> elements that follow this one (not any text nodes), so we can use

```
parent::Program/following-sibling::Program
```

Now we only want the immediately following sibling of the current <Program> element. The `following-sibling::` axis is a forward axis, so if we test the position of the nodes that we're selecting within a predicate, the first will be the earliest <Program> element (after this one) in document order, which is exactly what we want:

```
parent::Program/following-sibling::Program[1]
```

Once we've got hold of this <Program> element, we want to step down to its child <Start> element in order to get its start time:

```
parent::Program/following-sibling::Program[1]/Start
```

We can put this <Start> element in a variable so that we can refer to it later on. Remember when declaring the variable that there might not be a following sibling <Program> element, so the variable might contain an empty sequence, or a single <Start> element.

```
<xsl:variable name="endDateTime" as="element(Start)?"
  select="parent::Program/following-sibling::Program[1]/Start" />
```

If there isn't an end time, we won't include any information about it. We can format this `xs:dateTime` to extract the formatted time using the `format-dateTime()` function again. The new template for the <Start> element looks like this:

```
<xsl:template match="Start">
  <xsl:variable name="endDateTime" as="element(Start)?"
    select="parent::Program/following-sibling::Program[1]/Start" />
  <span class="date">
    <xsl:value-of select="format-dateTime(xs:dateTime(.),
                                          '[M]/[D]/[Y] [H01]:[m]')" />
    <xsl:if test="$endDateTime">
      <xsl:value-of select="format-dateTime(xs:dateTime($endDateTime),
                                            ' - [H01]:[m]')" />
    </xsl:if>
  </span>
</xsl:template>
```

The result of transforming `TVGuide.xml` with `TVGuide8.xsl`, `TVGuide8.html`, is shown in Figure 7-19.

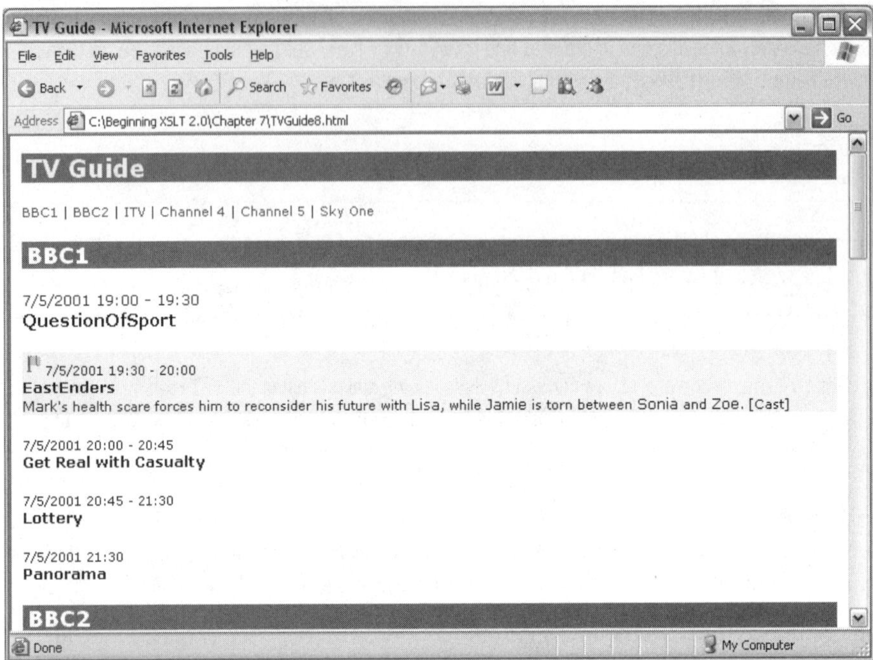

Figure 7-19. *Viewing* `TVGuide8.html` *in Internet Explorer*

Sequences

Paths create sequences of nodes, but XPath 2.0 supports other kinds of sequences as well. The items in a sequence can be atomic values or nodes, and it's possible to have sequences that contain both. In this section, we'll revisit what we've learned about creating and manipulating such sequences so far, and introduce some new ways of generating and processing sequences using XPath.

Sequence Types

As we saw in the last chapter, when you declare a variable or parameter, you should use the `as` attribute to indicate the type of that variable or parameter. The `as` attribute holds a **sequence type**, which is an indication of the kind and number of items that the sequence held by the variable contains.

Sequence types are a bit like patterns: sequence types either match or don't match a particular sequence in the same way that patterns either match or don't match a particular node. Usually, a sequence type specifies the kind of item that the sequence contains using either the name of an atomic type or a node test, and the number of items that it contains using an occurrence indicator (+ for one or more, * for zero or more, ? for zero or one). For example, the sequence type

```
xs:dateTime+
```

matches sequences that contain one or more `xs:dateTime` values, while the sequence type

```
element(Series)
```

matches sequences that contain a single `<Series>` element.

While you probably won't use it elsewhere, the special atomic type `xdt:anyAtomicType` is useful when you want to indicate a sequence that can only contain atomic values (can't contain any nodes). For example, the sequence type

```
xdt:anyAtomicType*
```

matches a sequence of zero or more atomic values. Similarly, you can use the `node()` node test for sequences that only contain nodes.

Within a sequence type, you can use the test `item()` to indicate any item, whether it's an atomic value or a node. For example, the sequence type

```
item()?
```

could be used when declaring a variable that contains either an empty sequence or a single node or a single atomic value.

The special sequence type `void()` matches the empty sequence. You'd probably never use this when declaring the type of a variable or parameter (why would you want a variable or parameter that could only hold an empty sequence?), but you might use it with the `instance of` expression, which we'll look at when we review the testing of sequences later.

Summary A sequence type is a pattern that matches a sequence.

Creating Sequences with XSLT

In the last chapter, we saw that when you use the content of a variable to set the variable's value, and have an `as` attribute on the variable declaration, then you create a sequence. An example was creating a sequence of `xs:dateTime` values holding the end times of the last program on each channel in the TV guide:

```
<xsl:variable name="endTimes" as="xs:dateTime+">
  <xsl:for-each select="Channel">
    <xsl:sequence select="xs:dateTime(Program[last()]/Start) +
                          xdt:dayTimeDuration(Program[last()]/Duration)" />
  </xsl:for-each>
</xsl:variable>
```

The content of the variable declaration holds a **sequence constructor**. The instructions in the sequence constructor contribute items to the sequence. The `<xsl:sequence>` instruction, for example, can be used to add atomic values or existing nodes to the sequence. Literal result elements add new elements to the sequence, while literal text and the `<xsl:value-of>` instruction add new text nodes to the sequence.

In XSLT 2.0, every sequence of instructions is actually a sequence constructor. The sequence of instructions held by a template, for example, determines the sequence that's generated when you apply the template to a node. The sequence of instructions inside a literal result element constructs a sequence that's used to create the content (and attributes) of the element.

Many elements allow you to select a sequence either through a `select` attribute or through their content. This includes `<xsl:variable>`, `<xsl:param>`, `<xsl:with-param>`, and `<xsl:sequence>`, as we saw in the last chapter. It also includes `<xsl:value-of>` and various other instructions that we'll meet in the coming chapters.

■ **Summary** Every sequence of instructions in XSLT is interpreted as a sequence constructor. How the constructed sequence is used depends on the element that encloses the sequence constructor.

Creating Sequences with XPath

Using XSLT to create sequences is very powerful and flexible, but it can also require a lot of typing. XPath, which is designed to be concise, also has mechanisms that you can use for creating sequences: you've seen how to create sequences of nodes using path expressions already. In this section, we'll look at the other kinds of XPath expressions you can use to create sequences.

Concatenating Sequences

The simplest way to create a sequence in XPath is simply to concatenate sequences together using the `,` operator. For example, if you do the following:

```
Title, Description, Series
```

you create a sequence that holds first the `<Title>` element child of the context node, then its `<Description>` element child, and finally its `<Series>` element child.

■ **Note** By comparison, `Title | Description | Series` creates a sequence that contains the `<Title>`, `<Description>`, and `<Series>` elements in the order that they appear in the document. The union operator always reorders the items you select into document order.

Commas are used elsewhere in XPath, most notably to separate arguments to a function, and the comma operator has the lowest priority, so usually when creating a sequence you should use brackets to indicate which items belong to the sequence. For example, say you want to create a sequence that contains a single date if the `start` and `end` attributes of the context `<TVGuide>` element are the same, and contains the `start` attribute followed by the `end` attribute otherwise. You should use

```
if (@start = @end) then @start else (@start, @end)
```

If you didn't use the brackets around `(@start, @end)`, as in

```
if (@start = @end) then @start else @start, @end
```

then the processor interprets the expression as

```
(if (@start = @end) then @start else @start), @end
```

which means that you always get a sequence containing the start attribute followed by the end attribute.

As a corollary, an empty pair of brackets indicates an empty sequence. This can be useful when you want to have an if expression return something only if a particular case is true. For example, we currently have the following code:

```
<xsl:if test="starts-with(tv:Series, 'StarTrek')">
  <xsl:sequence select="$StarTrekLogo" />
</xsl:if>
```

We can turn this into a single <xsl:sequence> element if we use an if expression that returns the $StarTrekLogo if the series starts with 'StarTrek', and an empty sequence otherwise:

```
<xsl:sequence select="if (starts-with(tv:Series, 'StarTrek'))
                      then $StarTrekLogo
                      else ()" />
```

Summary The , operator concatenates items together into a sequence.

Sequences of Integers

One kind of sequence that it turns out to be very useful to be able to create is a sequence of integers. You can create a sequence of integers using the to operator, which returns all the integers between its two operands. For example:

```
1 to 5
```

creates the following sequence:

```
(1, 2, 3, 4, 5)
```

If the second operand is less than the first, then the sequence is in reverse order. For example, 5 to 1 returns (5, 4, 3, 2, 1).

You can use sequences of integers to do the same thing a certain number of times. For example, to create five <br> elements, you can use

```
<xsl:for-each select="1 to 5"><br /></xsl:for-each>
```

Summary The to operator creates a sequence of integers.

Repeating Images to Display Ratings

In the TV guide, each program is given a rating through its rating attribute, which can be any integer from 1 to 10. Rather than displaying this rating as a number, in TVGuide9.xsl we'll rearrange things a bit, so that the icons indicating flagged programs come just before the title, and show a number of stars equal to the rating below the start time for each program.

In the template for the <Program> element in Details mode, we can generate the stars by iterating over a sequence of integers from 1 to the number held in the rating attribute, as follows:

```
<xsl:template match="Program" mode="Details">
  ...
  <p>
    <xsl:apply-templates select="Start" /><br />
    <xsl:for-each select="1 to @rating">
      <img src="star.gif" alt="*" height="15" width="15" />
    </xsl:for-each>
    <br />
    <xsl:if test="@flag">...</xsl:if>
    ...
  </p>
  ...
</xsl:template>
```

The result of transforming TVGuide.xml with TVGuide9.xsl is TVGuide9.html, which is shown in Figure 7-20.

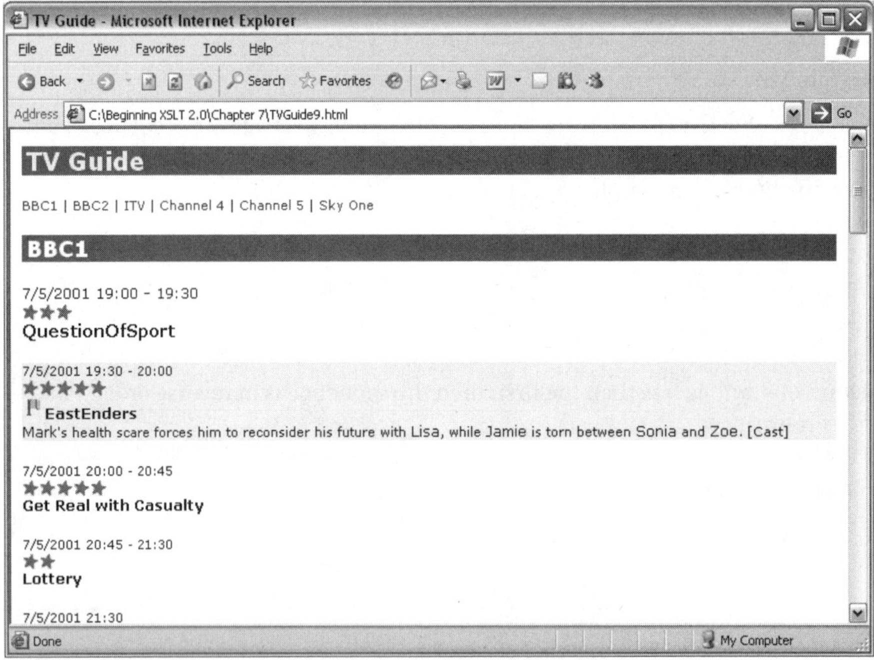

Figure 7-20. *Viewing* TVGuide9.html *in Internet Explorer*

One <img> element is created for each integer in the sequence from 1 to the value of the rating attribute. For example, *EastEnders*, which has a rating of 5, has five stars.

Filtering Sequences

In previous sections, we've seen how you can use predicates to filter sequences of nodes. For example, we saw that

```
Program[Series = 'EastEnders']
```

returns only those `<Program>` elements whose `<Series>` element child has the value `'EastEnders'`.

You can actually use predicates on any kind of sequence, no matter what it contains, to filter that sequence. For example, if you only want to get the *even* numbers between 1 and 100, you can use

```
(1 to 100)[. mod 2 = 0]
```

The subexpression `(1 to 100)` creates a sequence of integers between 1 and 100, and the predicate `[. mod 2 = 0]` then filters them. The test `. mod 2 = 0` is only true for those numbers that have no remainder when divided by 2 (the even numbers).

Summary Predicates can be used to filter any kind of sequence.

A more complex kind of filtering that you might want to do is to remove any duplicates from a sequence. You can do this with the `distinct-values()` function, which takes a sequence of atomic values and removes any duplicate values. For example, to get a list of the series that have episodes showing in the TV guide, you could use

```
distinct-values(Program/Series)
```

A second argument can be provided, giving a collation URI. You'd do this if the sequence contains strings and you want to compare them using a different collation from normal.

Note The main reason for using `distinct-values()` is when grouping, but if you want to do that you should probably use the `<xsl:for-each-group>` instruction, which we'll look at in Chapter 9, instead.

Summary The `distinct-values()` function removes duplicates from a sequence.

Adding and Removing Items

A bunch of functions in XPath 2.0 deal with adding or removing items from a sequence. These functions don't actually change the original sequence, but create a new sequence that's derived from the old one. They're most useful in recursive templates and functions, which we'll look at in Chapter 11.

The insert-before() function inserts items into a sequence at a particular position. The first argument specifies the original sequence, the second gives the position before which they should be inserted, and the third gives the new items. For example, to insert the string "middle" into the middle of the sequence $list, you could use

```
insert-before($list, (count($list) idiv 2) + 1, "middle")
```

If the value of the second argument is greater than the length of the sequence, then the items you give in the third argument get added to the end of the sequence.

Tip If you're adding items at the beginning or end of a sequence, it's usually easier to simply concatenate them together. For example, rather than insert-before($list, 1, 'start'), use ('start', $list).

The remove() function removes an item at a particular position from a sequence. The first argument gives the original sequence and the second argument the index of the item to be removed. For example, to remove the first item from the sequence $list, use

```
remove($list, 1)
```

Note If you prefer using predicates, the other way to get all but the first item in a sequence is to use $list[position() > 1].

The subsequence() function behaves like the substring() function but works on sequences rather than strings. The first argument gives the original sequence, the second argument the position of the first item in the new sequence, and the third, optional, argument the length of the new sequence. If the third argument is missed out, then you get the sequence from the starting item to the end of the original sequence. For example, to get all but the first item in the sequence $list, you can use

```
subsequence($list, 2)
```

To get only the first item in the sequence $list, you could use

```
subsequence($list, 1, 1)
```

Note You could use a predicate here too: $list[1].

Summary The insert-before() function inserts items into a sequence. The remove() function removes an item from a sequence. The subsequence() function extracts a subsequence from a sequence.

Testing Sequences

We looked a bit at testing sequences in Chapter 4. In that chapter, you learned that a test that returns a sequence alone returns false if the sequence is empty, true if the first item is a node, and raises an error if it contains more than one other kind of value. (When the sequence contains a single atomic value, the result of the test depends on the type of the value.)

There are various other kinds of tests that you can perform on a sequence, such as testing the kind of items that it contains, how many items it contains, what values it contains, and so on. We'll look at these kinds of tests in this section.

Testing the Type of a Sequence

It's not always clear what a sequence contains, particularly if you have a parameter or variable that could be passed a range of values.

If you just want to test whether or not a sequence contains any items, you can use the exists() or empty() functions, which are inverses of each other. The exists() function returns true if a sequence contains any items and false if it's empty, while the empty() function returns true if the sequence is empty and false if it contains any items. For example, say that we changed the declaration of the $endDateTime variable we use in the template matching <Start> elements, so that it held either an xs:dateTime value or an empty sequence:

```
<xsl:variable name="endDateTime" as="xs:dateTime?"
  select="parent::Program/following-sibling::Program[1]/Start" />
```

If you wanted to test whether the $endDateTime variable actually contained a value (which it won't do if there's no following program in our TV guide), we could use

```
exists($endDateTime)
not(empty($endDateTime))
```

■ **Tip** If you just want to test whether a sequence contains any items, using exists() or empty() is likely to be more efficient than counting the number of items the sequence contains with the count() function.

For more complex tests, the instance of expression tests whether a sequence is of a particular sequence type. It returns true if the sequence is of the specified sequence type and false otherwise.

For example, if you had a parameter called $numbers, declared to hold zero or more xs:decimal atomic values with

```
<xsl:param name="numbers" as="xs:decimal*" />
```

you could test what $numbers actually contained using the following code:

```
<xsl:choose>
  <xsl:when test="$numbers instance of void()">
    <!-- $numbers is an empty sequence -->
    ...
```

```
  </xsl:when>
  <xsl:when test="$numbers instance of xs:integer*">
    <!-- $numbers contains only integers -->
    ...
  </xsl:when>
  <xsl:when test="$numbers instance of xs:decimal">
    <!-- $numbers contains a single decimal -->
    ...
  </xsl:when>
  <xsl:otherwise>
    ...
  </xsl:otherwise>
</xsl:choose>
```

Note The test `$numbers instance of xs:integer*` tests whether the items in `$numbers` are typed as `xs:integer` values, not whether they're actually integers. For example, if `$numbers` held a sequence of `xs:decimal` values that happened to be integers, such as `(1.0, 2.0, 3.0)`, the test would return `false`.

Summary The `exists()` and `empty()` functions test whether a sequence holds any items. The `instance of` expression tests whether a sequence matches a given sequence type.

Testing Values in a Sequence

As we saw in Chapter 4, the general comparison operators =, !=, <, <=, >, and >= perform **existential comparisons**: if one of the arguments is a sequence, then the other argument is tested against each of the items in that sequence, and if any of the tests are true, then the test as a whole is true.

A corollary of this is that one way in which simple sequences can prove very useful is in allowing you to test several things at once. For example, we currently use the test

```
@flag = 'favorite' or @flag = 'interesting'
```

to test whether the value of the `flag` attribute is `'favorite'` or `'interesting'`. This expression contains two separate tests, combined with an `or`. An alternative is to test the value of the `flag` attribute against the sequence containing the two values `'favorite'` and `'interesting'`:

```
@flag = ('favorite', 'interesting')
```

This test will return true under the same conditions: if the `flag` attribute either has the value `'favorite'` or has the value `'interesting'`.

Another way in which this general method can be useful is for getting hold of a certain subsequence within a sequence. For example, say that we were only interested in the first three programs showing on a channel. One way we could get hold of them would be to use

```
Program[position() = (1 to 3)]
```

The test `position() = (1 to 3)` is true if the position of the program is 1, 2, or 3.

Summary You can often use general comparisons to perform multiple tests at the same time.

Sometimes you might want to know not only whether a sequence contains a particular value, but also where in the sequence the value appears. You can do this with the `index-of()` function, which returns the position of the atomic value given in the second argument within the sequence given as the first argument. For example:

```
index-of(('favorite', 'interesting'), @flag)
```

will return `1` if the value of the `flag` attribute is `'favorite'` and `2` if the value of the `flag` attribute is `'interesting'`.

If the sequence contains multiple instances of the specified value, then `index-of()` returns a sequence containing the positions in which the value appears. If the sequence doesn't contain the given value, then `index-of()` returns an empty sequence.

If you're trying to locate a string within a sequence, you can give a third argument to the `index-of()` function to specify the collation to use. For example, you might use this to do a case-insensitive search. You learned about collations in Chapter 4.

The `index-of()` function is most useful when you're using sequences to hold structured data. Sequences in XPath 2.0 can't contain other sequences, but you can use multiple sequences or fixed-format sequences to get something close.

For example, we're currently using the following code to insert an `<img>` element based on the value of the `flag` attribute:

```
<img src="{if (@flag = 'favorite') then 'favorite' else 'interest'}.gif"
     alt="[{if (@flag = 'favorite') then 'Favorite' else 'Interest'}]"
     width="20" height="20" />
```

There are three sets of values being used here:

- The values of the `flag` attribute in the source document
- The values of the `src` attribute in the new `<img>` element
- The values of the `alt` attribute in the new `<img>` element

We could store these values in separate variables, as follows:

```
<xsl:variable name="flags" as="xs:token+" select="('favorite', 'interesting')" />
<xsl:variable name="srcs" as="xs:token+"  select="('favorite', 'interest')" />
<xsl:variable name="alts" as="xs:token+"  select="('Favorite', 'Interest')" />
```

The position of the value of the `flag` attribute within the `$flags` variable gives us an index that we can use to get the appropriate `src` or `alt` value from the `$srcs` and `$alts` variables:

```
<xsl:variable name="flag-position" as="xs:integer"
              select="index-of($flags, @flag)" />
<img src="{$srcs[$flag-position]}.gif"
     alt="[{$alts[$flag-position]}]"
     width="20" height="20" />
```

Alternatively, we could structure this information within a single sequence that contains sets of three values in which the first value is the value of the flag attribute, the second the value of the src attribute, and the third the value of the alt attribute:

```
<xsl:variable name="flag-data" as="xs:token+"
  select="('favorite',    'favorite', 'Favorite',
           'interesting', 'interest', 'Interest')" />
```

Given this structure, the first instance of the value of the flag attribute within the $flag-data variable gives an index that we can use as the basis for getting the appropriate src and alt values from $flag-data:

```
<xsl:variable name="flag-position" as="xs:integer"
              select="index-of($flag-data, @flag)[1]" />
<img src="{$flag-data[$flag-position + 1]}.gif"
     alt="[{$flag-data[$flag-position + 2]}]"
     width="20" height="20" />
```

■ **Note** Sequences are a lightweight way of holding structured data as an alternative to a temporary tree. Temporary trees are more costly because they require the processor to generate and store nodes, but they are generally easier to use because the data is labelled with the role that it plays.

■ **Summary** The index-of() function returns the positions of a value within a sequence, or an empty sequence if the value doesn't appear in the sequence.

---

some and every Expressions

In our stylesheet, at the same time as testing whether the flag attribute is 'favorite' or 'interesting', we also perform the following tests:

```
contains(lower-case(tv:Series), 'news') or
contains(lower-case(tv:Title), 'news') or
contains(lower-case(tv:Description), 'news')
```

These tests all do basically the same thing—test whether the value of a node, converted to lowercase, contains the substring 'news'. Is there any way of combining them?

Well, we can create a sequence that contains the nodes that we're interested in using

```
(tv:Series, tv:Title, tv:Description)
```

but then we need to test each of them by using them as arguments to a function call. We can't just pass the sequence of nodes to the lower-case() function, as in

```
contains(lower-case((tv:Series, tv:Title, tv:Description)), 'news')
```

because the lower-case() function expects only a single item as its argument. What we need here is a way of testing each of the items in the sequence in turn, and returning true if any of the tests are true.

We can do this with a some expression. The basic some expression looks like this:

```
some $var in sequence satisfies test
```

The test is performed on each item in the sequence in turn, and if any of the tests are true, then the expression as a whole is true. The $var variable is known as a **range variable**; within the test, this variable is bound to the item that's currently being tested.

To test whether any of the series, title, or description contains the substring 'news', for example, we can use

```
some $i in (tv:Series, tv:Title, tv:Description) satisfies
  contains(lower-case($i), 'news')
```

■ Note The astute amongst you will realize that you can also perform this test using a predicate: the expression (tv:Series, tv:Title, tv:Description)[contains(lower-case(.), 'news')] will only return any elements if any of the three elements contains the value 'news'; within a test, a sequence without any elements evaluates as false and a sequence that does contain elements returns true.

XPath 2.0 also has an every expression that tests whether *every* item in a sequence satisfies a particular test. For example, if we were only interested in looking at <Channel> elements in which every <Program> element had a flag attribute, we could use

```
Channel[every $p in Program satisfies $p/@flag]
```

■ Note Again, you can use predicates to achieve the same effect. In this case, an equivalent expression is Channel[not(Program[not(@flag)])], which returns those channels that don't have a program that isn't flagged.

In fact, both the some and every expressions can use any number of range variables to test several sequences in combination. For example, if you wanted to test whether the series, title, or description contained any of the keywords 'news', 'sport', or 'weather', you could use

```
some $text in (tv:Series, tv:Title, tv:Description),
     $keyword in ('news', 'sport', 'weather')
satisfies contains(lower-case($text), $keyword)
```

Every combination of items from the sequences is tested in turn. In the preceding case, there will be nine tests:

```
contains(lower-case(tv:Series), 'news')
contains(lower-case(tv:Series), 'sport')
contains(lower-case(tv:Series), 'weather')
contains(lower-case(tv:Title), 'news')
contains(lower-case(tv:Title), 'sport')
contains(lower-case(tv:Title), 'weather')
contains(lower-case(tv:Description), 'news')
```

```
contains(lower-case(tv:Description), 'sport')
contains(lower-case(tv:Description), 'weather')
```

The range variables that you declare within a `some` or `every` expression are only in-scope within the test for that expression.

Summary The `some` expression performs a test on each item in a sequence and returns true if any of the tests are true. The `every` expression performs a test on each item in a sequence and returns true if all the tests are true.

Simplifying Test Expressions Using Sequences

We've identified two ways in which we could simplify the test expressions that we're using in order to identify which programs are interesting and which are not. In `TVGuide10.xsl`, we'll perform this simplification.

We're currently testing whether a program is interesting or not in the match pattern of the following template:

```
<xsl:template match="Program[@flag = 'favorite' or @flag = 'interesting' or
                             @rating > 6 or
                             contains(lower-case(Series), 'news') or
                             contains(lower-case(Title), 'news') or
                             contains(lower-case(Description), 'news')]">
  <div class="interesting">
    <xsl:apply-templates select="." mode="Details" />
  </div>
</xsl:template>
```

As we've seen, we can combine the two tests of the `flag` attribute into a single test using a general comparison:

```
@flag = ('favorite', 'interesting')
```

Similarly, we can combine the three tests to see whether the keyword `'news'` appears in the series, title, or description of the program using a `some` expression:

```
some $n in (Series, Title, Description)
satisfies contains(lower-case($n), 'news')
```

Putting these together, the new match pattern for the template is

```
<xsl:template match="Program[@flag = ('favorite', 'interesting') or
                             @rating > 6 or
                             (some $n in (Series, Title, Description)
                              satisfies contains(lower-case($n), 'news'))]">
  <div class="interesting">
    <xsl:apply-templates select="." mode="Details" />
  </div>
</xsl:template>
```

Transforming `TVGuide.xml` with `TVGuide10.xsl` gives `TVGuide10.html`, which is shown in Figure 7-21.

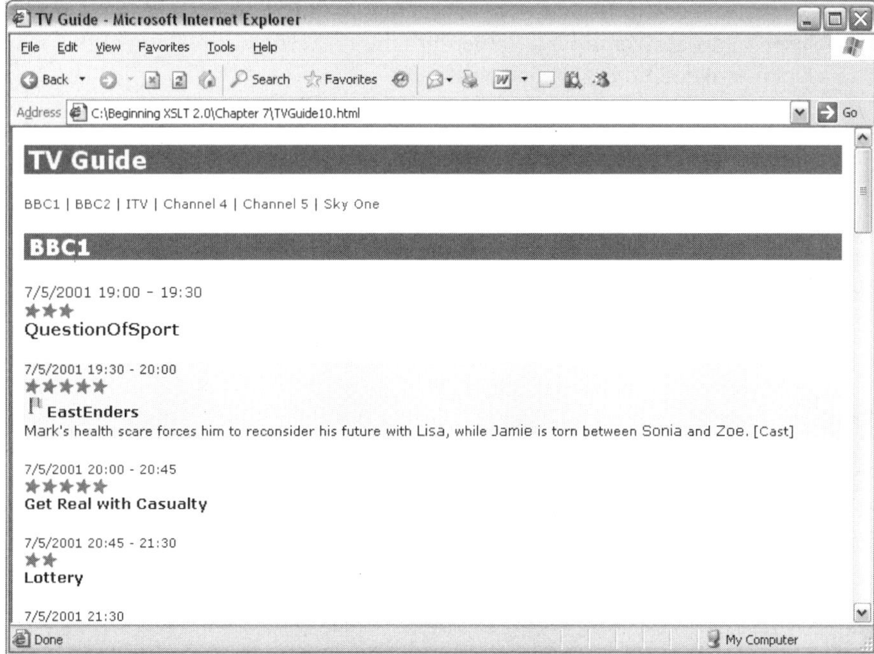

Figure 7-21. *Viewing* `TVGuide10.html` *in Internet Explorer*

The simplification of the tests makes no difference to the result of the transformation, but it makes the stylesheet easier to read and maintain.

Iterating Over Sequences

As you've already seen, you can use the `<xsl:for-each>` element to iterate over the items in a sequence and generate a sequence (using XSLT instructions) as a result. You can also iterate over a sequence to test each item in that sequence using `some` and `every` expressions, which you saw in the last section. Finally, as we'll see in this section, you can use paths and `for` expressions within an XPath to iterate over a sequence.

Paths for Generating Sequences

You can think of paths as a simple method of iterating over a sequence of nodes. Each step is evaluated for each node in a node sequence to give another sequence. In most cases, the resulting sequence is a sequence of nodes, and this sequence of nodes has duplicates removed and is sorted into document order.

For example, the path

```
CastMember/(Character | Actor)/Name
```

iterates over all the `<CastMember>` elements and creates a sequence of their `<Character>` and `<Actor>` children. That sequence of elements is then sorted into document order and iterated over to create a sequence of their `<Name>` element children.

You can also use paths to create sequences of atomic values, but only in the last step, since paths can only be used to iterate over nodes. Remember the <xsl:for-each> element that we used to create a sequence of end times for each channel:

```
<xsl:variable name="endTimes" as="xs:dateTime+">
  <xsl:for-each select="Channel">
    <xsl:sequence select="xs:dateTime(Program[last()]/Start) +
                          xdt:dayTimeDuration(Program[last()]/Duration)" />
  </xsl:for-each>
</xsl:variable>
```

You can also create this sequence of xs:dateTime values using an XPath expression:

```
<xsl:variable name="endTimes" as="xs:dateTime+"
  select="Channel/(xs:dateTime(Program[last()]/Start) +
                   xdt:dayTimeDuration(Program[last()]/Duration))" />
```

The <Channel> elements are iterated over in document order, and an xs:dateTime is created for each one by adding the <Start> of the final <Program> to the <Duration> of the final <Program>.

for Expressions

The for expression has a similar syntax to the some and every expressions, except that instead of a test, the for expression contains an expression that evaluated for each combination of range variables:

```
for $var1 in sequence1, $var2 in sequence2, ... return expression
```

We'll use the same example as the preceding to see the for expression in action. The sequence of xs:dateTime values representing the end time of the last program on each channel can be calculated with

```
<xsl:variable name="endTimes" as="xs:dateTime+"
  select="for $channel in Channel
          return xs:dateTime($channel/Program[last()]/Start) +
                 xdt:dayTimeDuration($channel/Program[last()]/Duration)" />
```

Notice that the paths within the <xsl:for-each> instruction and path expressions are evaluated relative to the item that's currently being processed:

```
xs:dateTime(Program[last()]/Start) +
xdt:dayTimeDuration(Program[last()]/Duration)
```

By contrast, the return expression within a for expression is evaluated relative to the same context item as the expression that selects the items that are iterated over (in this case the <TVGuide> element). So you must use the range variable to refer to the item that's currently being processed, as in

```
xs:dateTime($channel/Program[last()]/Start) +
xdt:dayTimeDuration($channel/Program[last()]/Duration)
```

Forgetting to use the range variable is one of the most common mistakes to make when using the `for` expression, so if you find that it's giving you an error, or isn't giving you the sequence that you expect, then that may well be the reason.

Summary The `for` expression iterates over the items in a sequence and returns a new sequence for each of them.

COMMENTS IN XPATH EXPRESSIONS

As in all code, it's a good idea to use comments to explain what your stylesheet is doing. At the XSLT level, you can use XML comments, for example:

```
<xsl:variable name="endTimes" as="xs:dateTime+">
  <xsl:for-each select="Channel">
    <!-- the end time of the last program showing on the channel -->
    <xsl:sequence select="xs:dateTime(Program[last()]/Start) +
                          xdt:dayTimeDuration(Program[last()]/Duration)" />
  </xsl:for-each>
</xsl:variable>
```

As you start using longer XPath expressions, such as `for`, `some`, and `every` expressions or complicated predicates, comments at the XSLT level are sometimes not able to address particular parts of an expression. Thankfully, XPath 2.0 provides a syntax for comments as well:

```
(: comment :)
```

For example, to include the comment as the preceding in the new version of the `$endTimes` variable declaration, you can use

```
<xsl:variable name="endTimes" as="xs:dateTime+"
  select="for $channel in Channel
          return (: the end time of the last program showing on the channel :)
                 xs:dateTime($channel/Program[last()]/Start) +
                 xdt:dayTimeDuration($channel/Program[last()]/Duration)" />
```

Formatting Sequences

There are many ways of outputting formatted versions of the items in a sequence. The most general method, which we've been using so far, is to use `<xsl:for-each>` or `<xsl:apply-templates>` to process each of the items in the sequence and to generate some output for each item individually. This method has the advantage of making it easy to create HTML formatting around each item. For example, to create a linked list of channel names, with |s separating each name, we can use

```
<xsl:for-each select="Channel">
  <a href="#{Name}"><xsl:value-of select="Name" /></a>
  <xsl:if test="position() != last()"> | </xsl:if>
</xsl:for-each>
```

This gets a bit tedious if you just want to output a simple list of strings. For example, say that you had a variable holding the keywords that you're searching for:

```
<xsl:variable name="keywords" as="xs:string+"
              select="('news', 'weather', 'sport')" />
```

Using `<xsl:for-each>`, you could output a comma-separated list with the following:

```
<xsl:for-each select="$keywords">
  <xsl:value-of select="." />
  <xsl:if test="position() != last()">, </xsl:if>
</xsl:for-each>
```

A simpler alternative, however, is to use the `<xsl:value-of>` instruction. As you'll remember, the `<xsl:value-of>` instruction creates a text node from the value that you select. When you select a sequence with either the `select` attribute or the content of the `<xsl:value-of>` instruction, then first any adjacent text nodes are concatenated together. Then the typed values of the items in the adjusted sequence are cast to strings and concatenated together with a separator. The separator that's used can be supplied by you, via the `separator` attribute; otherwise it defaults to a space if you use the `select` attribute to select the sequence, or to an empty string if you use the content of the `<xsl:value-of>` element.

For example, to create a comma-separated list of keywords, you could just use

```
<xsl:value-of select="$keywords" separator=", " />
```

■ **Note** In many cases, this is just the same as using the `string-join()` function, as in `string-join($keywords, ', ')`, but all the items passed in the first argument to the `string-join()` must be strings. When you use `<xsl:value-of>`, values are cast to strings automatically.

Note that the shortcut provided by the `separator` attribute can't be used to create elements with separators between them. If you tried to create a list of linked channel names, separated by |s with

```
<xsl:value-of separator=" | ">
  <xsl:for-each select="Channel">
    <a href="#{Name}"><xsl:value-of select="Name" /></a>
  </xsl:for-each>
</xsl:value-of>
```

then the HTML elements surrounding each name would be lost: the `<xsl:value-of>` element always extracts the typed values of the items in the sequence you select (in this case the typed values of the new `<a>` elements are simply untyped atomic values), and returns a single text node.

Also note that if you didn't have the <a> elements in the preceding code:

```
<xsl:value-of separator=" | ">
  <xsl:for-each select="Channel">
    <xsl:value-of select="Name" />
  </xsl:for-each>
</xsl:value-of>
```

then you wouldn't get any separators being added at all. The <xsl:value-of> within the <xsl:for-each> creates a text node, the <xsl:for-each> therefore creates a sequence of text nodes, and text nodes are concatenated *without* separators between them. If you want to have separators between items, make sure that they're atomic values or some kind of node other than a text node. In this case, the best alternative is

```
<xsl:value-of select="Channel/Name" separator=" | " />
```

Note As we'll see in the next chapter, other instructions that create nodes with simple values, such as <xsl:attribute> and <xsl:comment>, work in exactly the same way.

Summary You can create a formatted sequence by iterating over them to create HTML, XML, or text output. The <xsl:value-of> element provides a quick way to create a simple list with a separator specified through the separator attribute.

Summary

XSLT is all about querying and constructing node trees, and XPath carries out the querying part of that role. In this chapter, we've looked at node trees in more detail, highlighting some of the aspects that we've glossed over previously, in particular the following:

- The importance of the namespace of elements and attributes
- The existence of namespace nodes on elements within the node tree
- The presence of whitespace-only text nodes due to indentation in the source XML document

You've learned how to manage whitespace-only text nodes within a node tree that you access as the source of your XSLT transformations, using <xsl:strip-space> to get rid of whitespace-only text nodes and <xsl:preserve-space> and xml:space to retain them. Usually, it's easiest to use <xsl:strip-space elements="*" /> to remove all whitespace-only text nodes and override the stripping as necessary with <xsl:preserve-space> and xml:space.

You've also found out more technical details concerning the construction of patterns and expressions. You've seen how to combine several path patterns into a single pattern with the | operator and learned how to use predicates within step patterns. You've learned how to match nodes of different types, and nodes in different namespaces. You've also been taught how to use the node-name(), name(), local-name(), and namespace-uri() functions to access the names and namespaces of nodes.

In terms of expressions, you've been shown how to use the | (or union), intersect, and except operators to combine sequences of nodes. You've been introduced to the full set of axes at your disposal, and we've looked at how the XSLT processor evaluates a path step by step to create a sequence of nodes.

You've also learned about several new expressions that allow you to create and manipulate sequences of other kinds. You've seen how to construct sequences using the , and to operators; how to add and remove items using insert-before(), remove(), and subsequence(); how to test them using the instance of, some, and every expressions; and the exists() and empty() functions, and how to iterate over them within an XPath expression using paths and for expressions.

This chapter has covered all the technical aspects of how you select and match information from an XML document using XPath. In the next chapter, we'll turn our attention to how to generate a new node tree based on this information.

Review Questions

1. Draw a node tree for the following document, including whitespace-only text nodes, whitespace in text nodes, the namespaces of the elements and attributes, and namespace nodes:

```
<Films xmlns="http://www.example.com/Films">
  <Film year="1994">
    <Name>The Shawshank Redemption</Name>
    <per:Director xmlns:per="http://www.example.com/People">
      Frank Darabont
    </per:Director>
  </Film>
</Films>
```

2. What would the node tree from the previous question look like if you included the following in your XSLT stylesheet?

```
<xsl:strip-space elements="Films" />
```

3. What kinds of nodes do the following patterns match? What are the default priorities of templates that use these patterns?

```
text()
text()[normalize-space(.)]
Program//comment()
CastMember[1]
CastMember[position() != last()]
tv:Program
@xsi:*
Actor/Name | Character/Name
```

4. Assuming that the prefix tv is associated with the namespace http://www.example.com/TVGuide within the stylesheet, what kinds of elements do the following expressions select?

```
Program
*:Program
tv:*
tv:Program
*[name(.) = 'Program']
*[starts-with(name(.), 'tv:')]
*[name(.) = 'tv:Program']
*[node-name(.) = expanded-QName('http://www.example.com/TVGuide', 'Program')]
*[local-name(.) = 'Program']
*[namespace-uri(.) = 'http://www.example.com/TVGuide']
*[local-name(.) = 'Program' and
  namespace-uri(.) = 'http://www.example.com/TVGuide']
tv:* intersect *:Program
tv:* except tv:Program
*[not(self::tv:Program)]
```

5. Add XML and XPath comments to the following XSLT extract to explain what it does:

```
<xsl:for-each select="ancestor-or-self::*">
  <xsl:variable name="name" as="xs:string" select="name(.)" />
  /<xsl:value-of select="$name" />
  <xsl:if test="some $s in ../* satisfies node-name($s) = node-name(.)">
    [<xsl:value-of select="count(preceding-sibling::*[name() = $name])" />]
  </xsl:if>
</xsl:for-each>
```

6. Create a path that selects, from a <Program> element, the <Series> children of all the preceding <Program> elements in the same <Channel> element (in other words, siblings of the current <Program> element).

7. Based on the answer to the previous question, create an expression that tests whether the current <Program> element's <Series> child element is the same as the <Series> element child of any preceding <Program> elements in the same <Channel> element.

8. Based on the answer to the previous question, create a path that selects, from a <Channel> element, all those <Program> elements whose <Series> child element is *not* the same as any <Series> element child of the preceding <Program> elements in the same <Channel> element.

9. Create XSLT code to generate an HTML table containing the times tables, up to 12, which should look like that shown in Table 7-4.

Table 7-4. *The Times Tables*

	1	2	3	4	5	6	7	8	9	10	11	12
1	1	-	-	-	-	-	-	-	-	-	-	-
2	2	4	-	-	-	-	-	-	-	-	-	-
3	3	6	9	-	-	-	-	-	-	-	-	-
4	4	8	12	16	-	-	-	-	-	-	-	-
5	5	10	15	20	25	-	-	-	-	-	-	-
6	6	12	18	24	30	36	-	-	-	-	-	-
7	7	14	21	28	35	42	49	-	-	-	-	-
8	8	16	24	32	40	48	56	64	-	-	-	-
9	9	18	27	36	45	54	63	72	81	-	-	-
10	10	20	30	40	50	60	70	80	90	100	-	-
11	11	22	33	44	55	66	77	88	99	110	121	-
12	12	24	36	48	60	72	84	96	108	120	132	144

CHAPTER 8

Result Trees

In the last chapter, we looked in detail at how an XSLT processor views an XML document as a node tree and how to access nodes within that node tree using paths. The source tree isn't the only node tree that the XSLT processor has to deal with, however. During the transformation, a stylesheet generates **temporary trees** when you set a variable using the content of the `<xsl:variable>` element. Most importantly, though, the XSLT processor has to generate at least one **result document** as the output of the transformation as a whole. Both these kinds of node trees are known as **result trees**.

Result trees look very similar to the source tree—they have element and attribute nodes, comments and processing instructions, text nodes (some of which might be whitespace-only text nodes), and namespace nodes. The stylesheet's main job is to build, based on information from the source tree, the result tree that will be the output of the transformation as a whole. To do that, it needs to construct all the different types of nodes and fit them together into a tree. You've already seen how to generate elements, attributes, and text nodes. In this chapter, you'll learn how to generate the other kinds of nodes, how to manage whitespace, and how to dynamically name elements and attributes.

Usually, an XSLT processor doesn't just generate a result document, it also writes the document to a file or displays it in a browser window. To write a result document as output, the XSLT processor needs to know where it should go, and to serialize the result document in some way—it needs to output start and end tags and decide what entity references to use for special characters. As a stylesheet author, you get a fair amount of control about what this serialized output looks like, and in the second part of this chapter we'll look at what you can do to make the output of a transformation readable.

In this chapter, you'll learn

- How to add nodes to a result tree
- How to create attributes conditionally or create attributes with conditional values
- How to add sets of attributes to elements
- How to create elements and attributes when you don't know their names in advance
- How to generate comments, processing instructions, and whitespace

- How to copy parts of the source tree
- How to direct result trees to particular locations
- How to generate text, HTML, and XML output

Generating Nodes

The simplest way of adding a node to the result tree is to include it in the body of a template in the stylesheet. Take the following template from TVGuide.xsl as an example:

```
<xsl:template match="/">
  <html>
    <head>
      <title>TV Guide</title>
      <link rel="stylesheet" href="TVGuide.css" />
      <script type="text/javascript">
        <![CDATA[
        function toggle(element) {
          if (element.style.display == 'none') {
            element.style.display = 'block';
          } else {
            element.style.display = 'none';
          }
        }
        ]]>
      </script>
    </head>
    <body>
      <h1>TV Guide</h1>
      <xsl:apply-templates select="TVGuide" />
    </body>
  </html>
</xsl:template>
```

This template creates the result tree shown in Figure 8-1. The ... at the bottom indicates the part of the result tree that isn't created by this particular template, but rather by the <xsl:apply-templates> instruction.

Within the template, all the elements and attributes that aren't in the XSLT namespace (whether they're in no namespace, such as the <head> element and the href attribute on the <link> element, or in a different namespace, as we'll see later) are added to the result tree, and any text that's included in the element (such as "TV Guide") is added to the result tree as a text node. The dynamic content is added using an <xsl:apply-templates> instruction.

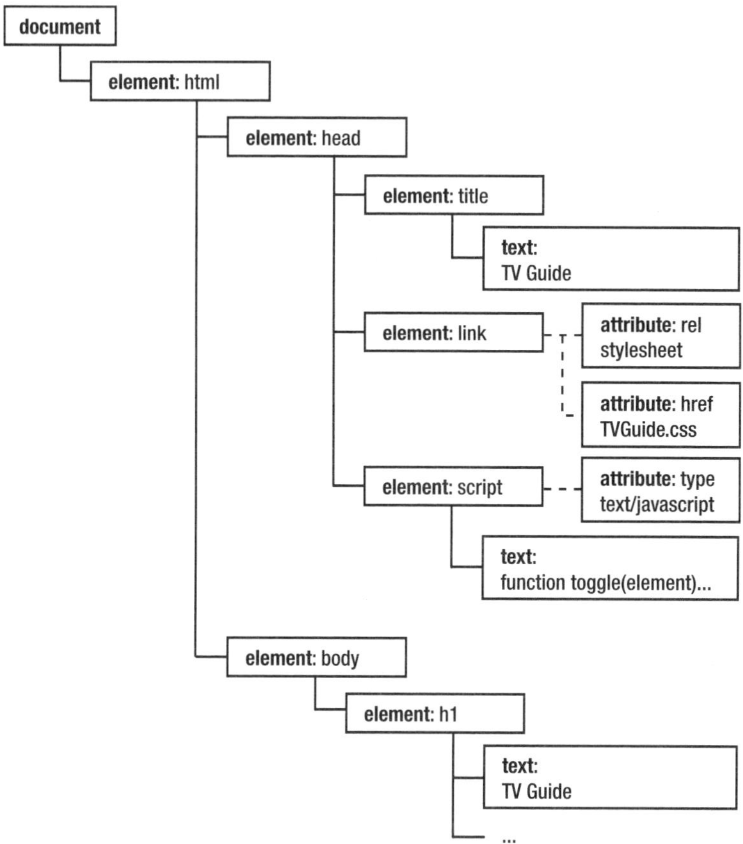

Figure 8-1. *Result tree generated by template matching root document node*

■ Note The CDATA section doesn't become a node in the tree. As described in Chapter 1, unescaped text inside a CDATA section is just the same as escaped text without a CDATA section as far as the XSLT processor is concerned. So the CDATA section becomes a normal text node.

■ Summary The result tree looks a lot like the source tree. The main role of the stylesheet is to construct result trees.

Mostly, all you need to do in a stylesheet is include the result that you want literally. However, XSLT also provides a set of instructions that allow you to create different types of nodes explicitly. These instructions are

- `<xsl:document>`—Creates a document node
- `<xsl:element>`—Creates an element node
- `<xsl:attribute>`—Creates an attribute node

- <xsl:text>—Creates a text node
- <xsl:comment>—Creates a comment node
- <xsl:processing-instruction>—Creates a processing instruction node
- <xsl:namespace>—Creates a namespace node

You saw in Chapter 6 how to use the <xsl:copy-of> instruction to copy nodes that you have stored in variables into the result tree; you can also use this instruction to copy parts of the source tree, and use the <xsl:copy> instruction to create shallow copies, just of the current node.

In this section, we'll look at when and how to use each of these instructions to create nodes in the result tree.

Generating Elements

The simplest way to generate an element is with a **literal result element**. Any element that isn't in the XSLT namespace (whether it's in another namespace or in no namespace at all) is interpreted as a literal result element, and adds an element of that name and namespace to the result tree.

Rather than using a literal result element to generate an element node, you can use the <xsl:element> instruction, specifying the name of the element that you want to create using the instruction's name attribute. Taking the previous example as a starting point, rather than use literal result elements, we could use <xsl:element>, as in TVGuide2.xsl:

```
<xsl:template match="/">
  <xsl:element name="html">
    <xsl:element name="head">
      <xsl:element name="title">TV Guide</xsl:element>
      <xsl:element name="link">
        <xsl:attribute name="rel">stylesheet</xsl:attribute>
        <xsl:attribute name="href">TVGuide.css</xsl:attribute>
      </xsl:element>
      <xsl:element name="script">
        <xsl:attribute name="type">text/javascript</xsl:attribute>
        <![CDATA[
        ...
        ]]>
      </xsl:element>
    </xsl:element>
    <xsl:element name="body">
      <xsl:element name="h1">TV Guide</xsl:element>
      <xsl:apply-templates select="TVGuide" />
    </xsl:element>
  </xsl:element>
</xsl:template>
```

Using <xsl:element> makes no difference to the result that's generated—you still get the same HTML, as you can see from Figure 8-2, which shows TVGuide2.html, the result of using TVGuide2.xsl with TVGuide.xml.

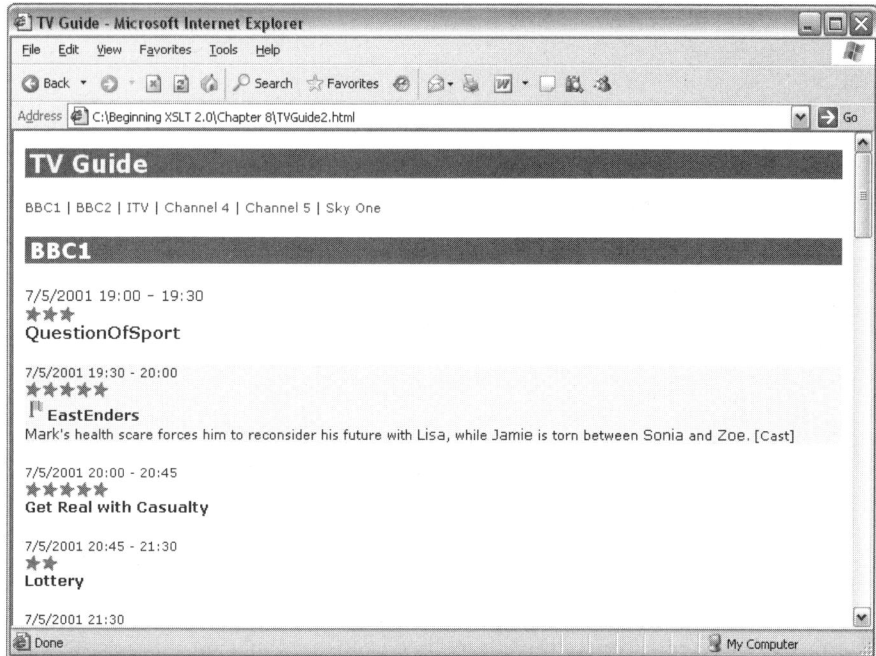

Figure 8-2. *Viewing* `TVGuide2.html` *in Internet Explorer*

If you take a look at `TVGuide2.xsl`, you'll see that using `<xsl:element>` is a lot more verbose than using literal result elements. It also means that you have to use `<xsl:attribute>` (which we'll look at in detail in the next section) to generate attributes, which again adds to the length of the stylesheet. So why use it? Well, the biggest reason is to decide on the name for the element that you're creating dynamically—we'll see how to do that in the next section.

Summary You can use `<xsl:element>` as an alternative to literal result elements, to create element nodes in the result tree.

Dynamic Element Names

In previous chapters, we've seen how to use attribute value templates to set the value of an attribute dynamically. The attributes that we've used attribute value templates with have all been on literal result elements—the attributes were added to the result tree with the value that we specified with the attribute value template.

The `name` attribute of the `<xsl:element>` element is one of several attributes on XSLT instructions that are also attribute value templates. If you use curly brackets, `{}`, within the `name` attribute of `<xsl:element>`, then the content of the brackets is evaluated as an XPath expression and the result is used in the name of the element. For example, in the following the name of the element that's added to the result tree is the value of the `class` attribute on the current node:

```
<xsl:element name="{@class}">
...
</xsl:element>
```

The main situation in which it's handy to have dynamic element names is when you're transforming from one piece of XML to another similar one. One use case is when you're presented with some HTML that is well-formed XML, but uses uppercase element names rather than lowercase element names. One way to approach the problem would be to have separate templates for each of the elements, mapping the uppercase names to the lowercase names, for example:

```
<xsl:template match="UL">
  <ul><xsl:apply-templates /></ul>
</xsl:template>

<xsl:template match="LI">
  <li><xsl:apply-templates /></li>
</xsl:template>
```

However, it's possible to compute the lowercase version of a string using an XPath function that replaces characters within a string: the `lower-case()` function, which we first met in Chapter 5. Just to remind you, the `lower-case()` function translates any uppercase characters in the argument string into lowercase. We can use this method to change the name of an element to lowercase, so we only need one template to deal with all the elements in the original (uppercase) HTML. The argument for the `lower-case()` function is the name of the original element. We can get the name of the current element using the `name()` function, as we saw in the last chapter. Then we can use the new name as the name of the element that we create:

```
<xsl:template match="*">
  <xsl:element name="{lower-case(name(.))}">
    <xsl:apply-templates />
  </xsl:element>
</xsl:template>
```

Summary The `name` attribute on `<xsl:element>` is an attribute value template, so you can use it to dynamically set the name of an element you generate.

Generating XML from XHTML

When we first started looking at XML, we generated a well-formed version of our HTML file, which contained `class` attributes that indicated the purpose of different sections in the HTML document. For example, the cast list looked like the following (see `Castlist.html`):

```
<ul class="castlist">
  <li>
    <span class="character">Zoe Slater</span>
    <span class="actor">Michelle Ryan</span>
  </li>
```

```
  <li>
    <span class="character">Jamie Mitchell</span>
    <span class="actor">Jack Ryder</span>
  </li>
  <li>
    <span class="character">Sonia Jackson</span>
    <span class="actor">Natalie Cassidy</span>
  </li>
</ul>
```

We converted this well-formed HTML to an XML structure by hand, but we could have generated at least some of it automatically using the values of the `class` attributes. The XML structure that we created from `CastList.html` was the following (`CastList.xml`):

```
<CastList>
  <CastMember>
    <Character><Name>Zoe Slater</Name></Character>
    <Actor><Name>Michelle Ryan</Name></Actor>
  </CastMember>
  <CastMember>
    <Character><Name>Jamie Mitchell</Name></Character>
    <Actor><Name>Jack Ryder</Name></Actor>
  </CastMember>
  <CastMember>
    <Character><Name>Sonia Jackson</Name></Character>
    <Actor><Name>Natalie Cassidy</Name></Actor>
  </CastMember>
</CastList>
```

The mapping between the two structures in `CastList.xsl` is fairly straightforward: the `<ul>` element transforms into a `<CastList>` element, the `<li>` element transforms into a `<CastMember>` element, and the `<span>` elements transform into `<Character>` or `<Actor>` elements with `<Name>` elements inside them. We may as well do the mappings for the first two types using separate templates:

```
<xsl:template match="ul">
  <CastList><xsl:apply-templates /></CastList>
</xsl:template>

<xsl:template match="li">
  <CastMember><xsl:apply-templates /></CastMember>
</xsl:template>
```

For the mappings involving the `<span>` elements, on the other hand, the name of the element that you want to create is the same as the value of the `class` attribute, but with the first letter capitalized. You can get hold of the first letter of the value of the `class` attribute using the `substring()` function:

```
substring(@class, 1, 1)
```

And you can then capitalize that letter using the `upper-case()` function:

```
upper-case(substring(@class, 1, 1))
```

You can get the rest of the letters in the value of the class attribute using the substring() function again, extracting from the second character to the end of the string:

```
substring(@class, 2)
```

Concatenating these expressions together gets you the name of the element that you want to create. In a template that matches <span> elements, you can hold that name in a $name variable:

```
<xsl:template match="span">
  <xsl:variable name="name" as="xs:string"
               select="concat(upper-case(substring(@class, 1, 1)),
                              substring(@class, 2))" />
  ...
</xsl:template>
```

You can then insert the value of this variable into the name attribute of an <xsl:element> that you use to create the new element, using an attribute value template:

```
<xsl:template match="span">
  <xsl:variable name="name"
               select="concat(upper-case(substring(@class, 1, 1)),
                              substring(@class, 2))" />
  <xsl:element name="{$name}">
    <Name><xsl:value-of select="." /></Name>
  </xsl:element>
</xsl:template>
```

If you transform CastList.html using CastList.xsl, you should get roughly the same XML structure as that in CastList.xml, as shown in Figure 8-3.

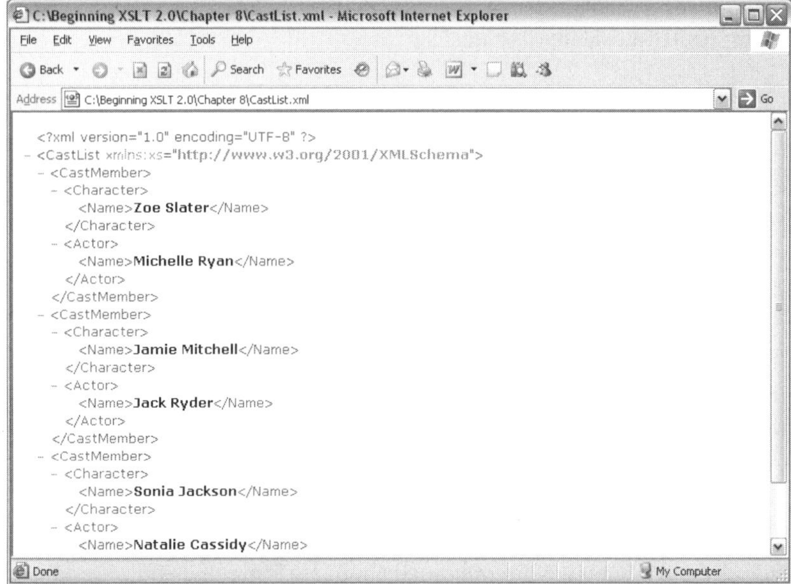

Figure 8-3. *Viewing* `CastList2.xml` *in Internet Explorer*

The only difference is that the XML Schema namespace is declared on the `<CastList>` element. We'll look at why that is next.

Element Namespaces

Just as in a source tree, the elements and attributes in a result tree all have a namespace, and the element nodes that you create with your stylesheet will have namespace nodes associated with them. If and when a result tree is serialized into a file, then the XSLT processor automatically works out where it needs to put namespace declarations to ensure that all the elements are in the desired namespace and have the desired namespace nodes.

In general, any namespace that you declare in the stylesheet will appear in the result of the transformation. If you don't want a namespace to appear, you have to explicitly exclude it using the `exclude-result-prefixes` attribute on the `<xsl:stylesheet>` element. The `exclude-result-prefixes` attribute should hold a whitespace-separated list of the prefixes associated with the namespaces that shouldn't appear in the result of the transformation.

For example, if you want to refer to the XML Schema types in your stylesheet, in order to declare the types of variables or to cast to an appropriate type, you have to declare the XML Schema namespace, and often the XPath datatypes namespace. However, you don't want their namespace declarations to appear in the output because you're creating HTML, which doesn't include elements in those namespaces. To prevent the namespace declarations from appearing, you should include the prefix that you've associated with the XML Schema and XPath datatypes namespaces within the `exclude-result-prefixes` attribute as follows:

```
<xsl:stylesheet version="2.0"
                xmlns:xsl="http://www.w3.org/1999/XSL/Transform"
                xmlns:xs="http://www.w3.org/2001/XMLSchema"
```

```
                  xmlns:xdt="http://www.w3.org/2005/04/xpath-datatypes"
                  exclude-result-prefixes="xs xdt">
...
</xsl:stylesheet>
```

The same goes for any namespaces that you declare because you want to refer to elements from that namespace in the source document. For example, if the elements in the source document are in the http://www.example.com/TVGuide namespace, then you need to exclude that namespace as well:

```
<xsl:stylesheet version="2.0"
                xmlns:xsl="http://www.w3.org/1999/XSL/Transform"
                xmlns:xs="http://www.w3.org/2001/XMLSchema"
                xmlns:xdt="http://www.w3.org/2005/04/xpath-datatypes"
                xmlns:tv="http://www.example.com/TVGuide"
                exclude-result-prefixes="xs xdt tv">
...
</xsl:stylesheet>
```

The other namespaces that you need to be concerned about are those that you want to use in the result. The XSLT processor will take care of declaring the namespaces for the elements that you use; you just have to make sure that the elements that you generate in your stylesheet are in the namespace that you want them to be in. In the rest of this section, we'll look at three ways of creating elements in different namespaces: using literal result elements, using a prefix in the name attribute of <xsl:element>, and using the namespace attribute of <xsl:element>.

Namespaces for Literal Result Elements

When you create an element using a literal result element, then the namespace of the element in the result is the same as the namespace of the element in the stylesheet. In the examples that we've been using so far, none of the literal result elements have had any prefixes—take a look again at the template matching the root node in TVGuide.xsl:

```
<xsl:template match="/">
  <html>
    <head>
      <title>TV Guide</title>
      <link rel="stylesheet" href="TVGuide.css" />
      <script type="text/javascript">
        <![CDATA[
        ...
        ]]>
      </script>
    </head>
    <body>
      <h1>TV Guide</h1>
      <xsl:apply-templates />
    </body>
  </html>
</xsl:template>
```

When an element name doesn't have a prefix, the element is assigned to the default namespace. We can't tell from this one template what the default namespace is—we have to look at the document element of `TVGuide.xsl`, which currently looks like this:

```
<xsl:stylesheet version="2.0"
                xmlns:xsl="http://www.w3.org/1999/XSL/Transform"
                xmlns:xs="http://www.w3.org/2001/XMLSchema"
                xmlns:xdt="http://www.w3.org/2005/04/xpath-datatypes">
...
</xsl:stylesheet>
```

The namespace declarations on the `<xsl:stylesheet>` element are for the XSLT namespace, the XML Schema namespace, and the XPath datatypes namespace. There's no namespace declaration for the default namespace, so all the literal result elements in the previous template have no namespace. However, we can add a default namespace declaration on the `<xsl:stylesheet>` element for the XHTML namespace, as follows:

```
<xsl:stylesheet version="2.0"
                xmlns:xsl="http://www.w3.org/1999/XSL/Transform"
                xmlns:xs="http://www.w3.org/2001/XMLSchema"
                xmlns:xdt="http://www.w3.org/2005/04/xpath-datatypes"
                xmlns="http://www.w3.org/1999/xhtml">
...
</xsl:stylesheet>
```

Now, any literal result elements in the stylesheet that do not have a prefix will be assigned to the XHTML namespace.

■ **Tip** Because the default namespace declaration is on the `<xsl:stylesheet>` element, the default namespace is in scope for the entire stylesheet. This way, it doesn't matter in which template the elements are generated; if you don't use a prefix, they will be in the XHTML namespace. If you put the default namespace declaration on the `<html>` element within the template, on the other hand, it will only be in scope within that element in the template itself, and only the literal result elements in that template will be in the XHTML namespace. Therefore, I always declare all the namespaces that I want to use in an XSLT stylesheet on the `<xsl:stylesheet>` element.

Similarly, if we wanted to, we could add a namespace declaration for another namespace, for example **MathML**, to the `<xsl:stylesheet>` element:

```
<xsl:stylesheet version="2.0"
                xmlns:xsl="http://www.w3.org/1999/XSL/Transform"
                xmlns:xs="http://www.w3.org/2001/XMLSchema"
                xmlns:xdt="http://www.w3.org/2005/04/xpath-datatypes"
                xmlns="http://www.w3.org/1999/xhtml"
                xmlns:math="http://www.w3.org/1998/Math/MathML">
...
</xsl:stylesheet>
```

With that namespace declaration in place, you can use the math prefix on any literal result element, and it will be associated with the MathML namespace.

Note MathML is a markup language for mathematical expressions, developed by the W3C. You can find out more about MathML at http://www.w3.org/Math/.

Summary The namespace of an element in the result tree is the same as the namespace of the literal result element that generates it.

Generating Elements in the XHTML Namespace

Our stylesheet is supposed to generate XHTML, so the elements that we create with it should be in the XHTML namespace (http://www.w3.org/1999/xhtml). The literal result elements that we're using in the stylesheet don't use a prefix, so we can just add a default namespace declaration to the <xsl:stylesheet> document element to place the generated elements in the XHTML namespace:

```
<xsl:stylesheet version="2.0"
                xmlns:xsl="http://www.w3.org/1999/XSL/Transform"
                xmlns:xs="http://www.w3.org/2001/XMLSchema"
                xmlns:xdt="http://www.w3.org/2005/04/xpath-datatypes"
                xmlns="http://www.w3.org/1999/xhtml">
...
</xsl:stylesheet>
```

When you do this, the XSLT processor adds a default namespace declaration to the <html> element that it generates. Take a look at the source of TVGuide3.html, which is the result of transforming TVGuide.xml with TVGuide3.xsl. You should see a namespace declaration for the XHTML namespace in the start tag of the <html> element:

```
<html xmlns:xs="http://www.w3.org/2001/XMLSchema"
      xmlns:xdt="http://www.w3.org/2005/04/xpath-datatypes"
      xmlns="http://www.w3.org/1999/xhtml">
  <head>
  ...
  </head>
  <body>
  ...
  </body>
</html>
```

None of the other elements in the output have a namespace declaration on them because the XSLT processor knows that the namespace declaration it's put on the <html> element remains in scope for the rest of the document.

As you can see, there are also extra namespace declarations for the XML Schema and XPath datatypes namespaces. To get rid of them, we need to use the exclude-result-prefixes attribute on the <xsl:stylesheet> element, listing the prefixes of those namespaces:

```
<xsl:stylesheet version="2.0"
                xmlns:xsl="http://www.w3.org/1999/XSL/Transform"
                xmlns:xs="http://www.w3.org/2001/XMLSchema"
                xmlns:xdt="http://www.w3.org/2005/04/xpath-datatypes"
                exclude-result-prefixes="xs xdt"
                xmlns="http://www.w3.org/1999/xhtml">
...
</xsl:stylesheet>
```

This change has been made in TVGuide4.xsl; look at TVGuide4.html, which is the result of transforming TVGuide.xml with TVGuide4.xsl, and you'll see that the unwanted namespace declarations have been removed:

```
<html xmlns="http://www.w3.org/1999/xhtml">
  <head>
  ...
  </head>
  <body>
  ...
  </body>
</html>
```

Now try removing the default namespace declaration from the <xsl:stylesheet> element and putting it on the <html> element where it's generated within the template matching the root node instead, as in TVGuide5.xsl:

```
<xsl:template match="/">
  <html xmlns="http://www.w3.org/1999/xhtml">
    <head>
      ...
    </head>
    <body>
      <h1>TV Guide</h1>
      <xsl:apply-templates />
    </body>
  </html>
</xsl:template>
```

Transform TVGuide.xml with TVGuide5.xsl and take a look at TVGuide5.html, the result. The only literal result elements for which the default namespace declaration is in scope are those within the preceding template. Elements created in other templates are still in no namespace. The output looks like this:

```
<html xmlns="http://www.w3.org/1999/xhtml">
  <head>
  ...
  </head>
  <body>
    <h1>TV Guide</h1>
    <p xmlns=""><a href="#BBC1">BBC1</a>...</p>
```

```
    <h2 xmlns="" class="channel"><a name="BBC1" id="BBC1">BBC1</a></h2>
    <div xmlns="" class="nowShowing">...</div>
    ...
  </body>
</html>
```

Because the elements that aren't generated in the template matching the root node are in no namespace, the XSLT processor has to add namespace declarations that reset the default namespace back to no namespace on those elements.

Namespaces for Elements Generated with <xsl:element>

When you use <xsl:element> to create an element, the name attribute specifies the name of the element that you generate. The name attribute is treated in exactly the same way as the name of a literal result element—if you specify a prefix in the name attribute, then that prefix is resolved according to the namespace declarations in the stylesheet, to tell the XSLT processor to which namespace the element should be assigned; if you don't specify a prefix in the name attribute, then the processor uses the default namespace, if there is one.

For example, if the prefix math is associated with the MathML namespace within the stylesheet, then the following generates a <matrix> element in the MathML namespace (usually with the prefix math):

```
<xsl:element name="math:matrix">
...
</xsl:element>
```

■ **Note** Technically, XSLT processors are allowed to use whatever prefix they like for the elements that they generate, as long as that prefix is associated with the correct namespace in the result document. In practice, processors use the prefix that you provide for the namespace, though if you declare a namespace twice with different prefixes, it might choose either of the prefixes you provided.

■ **Summary** Including a prefix on the name specified by the <xsl:element> instruction places the generated element in the associated namespace.

Dynamic Element Namespaces

Since the name attribute of <xsl:element> is an attribute value template, you can use {}s to set the name of the element that you create dynamically. This goes for the prefix that you use for the element (and hence its namespace) as well. For example, the following sets the local name of the generated element to the value of the $name variable, and assigns it to the namespace associated with the prefix that's the value of the $prefix variable:

```
<xsl:element name="{$prefix}:{$name}">
...
</xsl:element>
```

You should be careful using this method, however, as you need to make sure that the prefix that you specify for the new element has been declared in the stylesheet. This method also means that you need to know the namespace URI in advance so that you can declare it in your stylesheet, something that isn't always possible in more complex stylesheets. As well as the name attribute, therefore, the <xsl:element> instruction also has a namespace attribute that you can use to set the namespace URI of the element, and which is an attribute value template.

When you create an element using <xsl:element>, then, you can place it in any namespace that you want, even if that namespace can't be hard coded within the stylesheet. The following shows an instruction that generates an element in the namespace specified by the $namespaceURI variable, with a local name held by the $name variable and with a prefix given by the $prefix variable:

```
<xsl:element name="{$prefix}:{$name}" namespace="{$namespaceURI}">
...
</xsl:element>
```

■ **Note** If you specify a prefix in the name attribute as well as a namespace in the namespace attribute, then the prefix is just a hint to the processor about what prefix you'd like it to use. The processor is perfectly free to use whatever prefix it wants, though most honor your intentions and use the prefix that you've specified.

■ **Summary** The namespace of an element generated by the <xsl:element> instruction can be determined on the fly using an attribute value template in the namespace attribute.

Element Content

Whether you generate an element using a literal result element or using the <xsl:element> instruction, the content of the element you generate is specified using a **sequence constructor**. As you've seen in the last couple of chapters, a sequence constructor is any series of XSLT instructions; the result of evaluating that sequence of instructions is a sequence of nodes and/or atomic values. When creating an element, the relevant sequence constructor is the content of the literal result element or the <xsl:element> that's used to generate the element. For example, in the following code:

```
<body>
  <h1>TV Guide</h1>
  <xsl:apply-templates select="TVGuide" />
</body>
```

the sequence constructor that determines the content of the <body> element comprises a literal result element (the <h1> element) and a <xsl:apply-templates> instruction. The sequence constructor that determines the content of the <h1> element contains a piece of literal text.

The sequence that you generate using instructions within a literal result element or `<xsl:element>` instruction usually just contains nodes, but it can contain atomic values as well. The sequence has to be converted into a sequence of nodes that can form the content of the element. This sequence of nodes is generated as follows:

1. All the atomic values in the sequence are converted to `xs:string` values.
2. The `xs:string` values are converted to text nodes; if you have consecutive `xs:string` values, they're converted to a single text node, with a single space between each value.
3. Any document node in the sequence is replaced by its children.
4. If you have consecutive text nodes in the sequence, their values are concatenated to form a new text node.

Usually these rules give you the content that you expect. The one thing that you have to watch out for is that text nodes are treated differently from atomic values. For example, if you create an element using

```
<values>
  <xsl:sequence select="1" />
  <xsl:sequence select="2" />
  <xsl:sequence select="3" />
</values>
```

then the sequence constructor returns a sequence of integers, `(1, 2, 3)`. When these are combined to create element content, their string values are concatenated with spaces in between, and you get

```
<values>1 2 3</values>
```

On the other hand, if you change the `<xsl:sequence>` elements to `<xsl:value-of>` elements, as in

```
<values>
  <xsl:value-of select="1" />
  <xsl:value-of select="2" />
  <xsl:value-of select="3" />
</values>
```

then the sequence constructor returns three text nodes, with the values `1`, `2`, and `3`. When these are combined to create element content, you don't get extra spaces inserted, so the result is

```
<values>123</values>
```

The best way to avoid problems here is to decide whether the element that you're creating holds data or whether it holds text. If the element holds data, then create the sequence of atomic values that it holds, and let the XSLT processor add spaces between the values automatically. If the element holds text, then create a sequence of text nodes and create any spaces that you need within that text yourself.

■ **Summary** The content of a literal result element or <xsl:element> element is a sequence constructor. The sequence that's generated determines the content of the element; consecutive atomic values in that sequence are concatenated together with spaces in between, whereas consecutive text nodes are concatenated without spaces in between.

Generating Namespace Nodes

If you create an element that is in a particular namespace, then the XSLT processor will automatically add namespace nodes to the result tree for that namespace, and the result document will automatically contain the namespace declarations that you need. The same is true if you create an attribute in a particular namespace. In addition, any namespaces that are in-scope for a literal result element (such as those declared on the <xsl:stylesheet> element) will be added to the result document, unless you exclude them using `exclude-result-prefixes`.

On very rare occasions, you might want to include in the result tree a namespace that is used in the *value* of an element or attribute (rather than as the namespace of an element or attribute) and that you don't know in advance (and therefore can't declare within the stylesheet). For example, imagine you were creating a stylesheet that needed to process a schema document that contained a declaration that looked like this:

```
<xs:element name="Name" type="dt:NameType" />
```

The value of the `type` attribute is a qualified name, which should be interpreted based on the namespace declarations that are in place within the schema document. Imagine if you wanted to create, from this schema document, an element like the following:

```
<Name xsi:type="dt:NameType">...</Name>
```

The value of the `xsi:type` attribute here is the same qualified name as that in the `type` attribute in the schema. However, in order for a processor to interpret this latter XML document properly, the namespace associated with the `dt` prefix must be declared in the XML document. If we used this template:

```
<xsl:template match="xs:element">
  <xsl:element name="{@name}" namespace="{/xs:schema/@targetNamespace}">
    <xsl:attribute name="xsi:type" select="@type" />
    ...
  </xsl:element>
</xsl:template>
```

then the only namespace nodes on the generated element would be those required for the namespace of the element itself and for the `xsi` namespace used by the `xsi:type` attribute. We need to add a namespace node for the `dt` namespace. How can we do that?

Well, one way would be to copy the namespace node from the schema. As you saw in the last chapter, you can locate the namespace node using the `namespace::` axis, with a predicate to locate the namespace node whose name is the same as the prefix used in the `type` attribute. You can add the namespace node to the element by including it in the sequence that's constructed for the element, as follows:

```
<xsl:template match="xs:element">
  <xsl:element name="{@name}" namespace="{/xs:schema/@targetNamespace}">
    <xsl:variable name="prefix" as="xs:string"
      select="string(prefix-from-QName(resolve-QName(@type, .)))" />
    <xsl:sequence select="namespace::*[name(.) = $prefix]" />
    <xsl:attribute name="xsi:type" select="@type" />
    ...
  </xsl:element>
</xsl:template>
```

The drawback of this approach is that the `namespace::` axis is deprecated, so you can't guarantee that all XSLT processors will support it.

A more general approach, that's guaranteed to work, is to use the `<xsl:namespace>` instruction to create a namespace node. The `<xsl:namespace>` instruction has a `name` attribute, which holds the prefix of the namespace (and can contain an attribute value template, just like the `name` attribute of the `<xsl:element>` instruction), and can either have a `select` attribute or content, to specify the URI for the namespace.

In this example, you could store the prefix from the `type` attribute in a `$prefix` variable, and use this to specify the prefix for the generated namespace node and to retrieve the URI associated with the prefix on the current `<xs:element>` element:

```
<xsl:template match="xs:element">
  <xsl:element name="{@name}" namespace="{/xs:schema/@targetNamespace}">
    <xsl:variable name="prefix" as="xs:string"
      select="string(prefix-from-QName(resolve-QName(@type, .)))" />
    <xsl:namespace name="{$prefix}"
                   select="namespace-uri-for-prefix($prefix, .)" />
    <xsl:attribute name="xsi:type" select="@type" />
    ...
  </xsl:element>
</xsl:template>
```

■ Summary You can generate a namespace node using the `<xsl:namespace>` element, whose `name` attribute specifies the prefix for the namespace and whose `select` attribute or content specifies the URI for the namespace. Usually this instruction is unnecessary because the XSLT processor will generate any required namespace nodes automatically.

Generating Text Nodes

There are three ways of creating text nodes using a stylesheet, and you've already seen two of them in action. The first, and simplest, method is to include the text that you want within the result tree as text within a template. For example, within a template, the following code:

```
<h1>TV Guide</h1>
```

creates the branch shown in Figure 8-4 within the result tree.

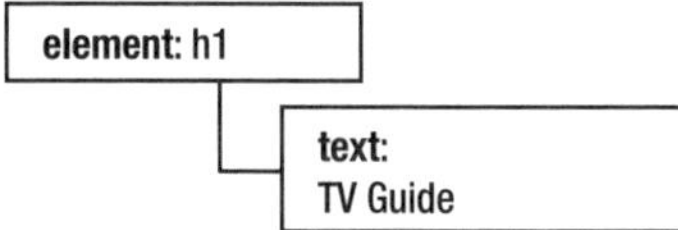

Figure 8-4. *Text node generated using literal text*

The second method is to use `<xsl:value-of>` to insert a text node with a value that's defined through an XPath expression. For example, given that the `<Name>` child of the current `<Channel>` element has the value `BBC1`, the following code:

```
<a href="#{Name}"><xsl:value-of select="Name" /></a>
```

creates the branch shown in Figure 8-5 within the result tree.

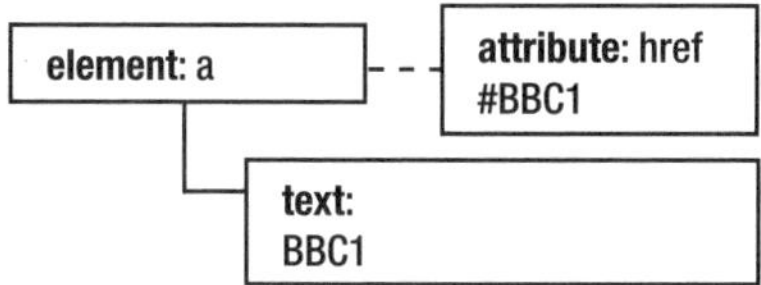

Figure 8-5. *Text node generated using* `<xsl:value-of>`

The third method of creating text nodes is to use `<xsl:text>`. The `<xsl:text>` element can only contain literal text, and whatever you put inside it is added to the result as a text node. For example, the following code:

```
<h1><xsl:text>TV Guide</xsl:text></h1>
```

creates the branch shown in Figure 8-6 within the result tree.

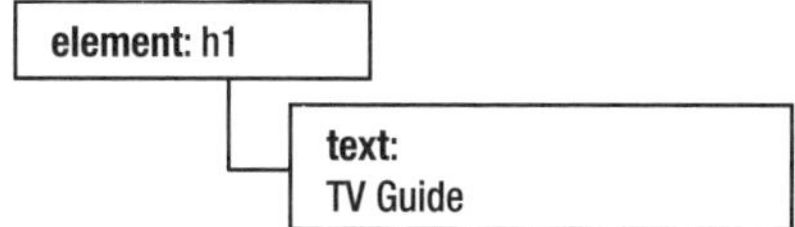

Figure 8-6. *Text node generated using* `<xsl:text>`

But hang on—that's exactly the same as the branch that we got when we used just literal text in the stylesheet. Why bother using `<xsl:text>`? Well, the reason arises from how XSLT processors handle whitespace, which we'll look at next.

■ Summary Text nodes are generated by literal text, `<xsl:value-of>`, and `<xsl:text>`.

Managing Whitespace

In the last chapter, we saw how an XSLT processor builds a node tree from an XML document, and in particular looked at how it treats whitespace within the source document. Of course, stylesheets are XML documents too, and when the XSLT processor is run on a stylesheet, it builds a node tree for the stylesheet as well as the source document. Take the following snippet from a stylesheet as an example:

```
<h1>
  TV Guide:
  <xsl:value-of select="$startDay" />
  <xsl:value-of select="$startMonth" />
</h1>
```

The XSLTprocessor views this stylesheet as the node tree shown in Figure 8-7 (whitespace-only text nodes are highlighted).

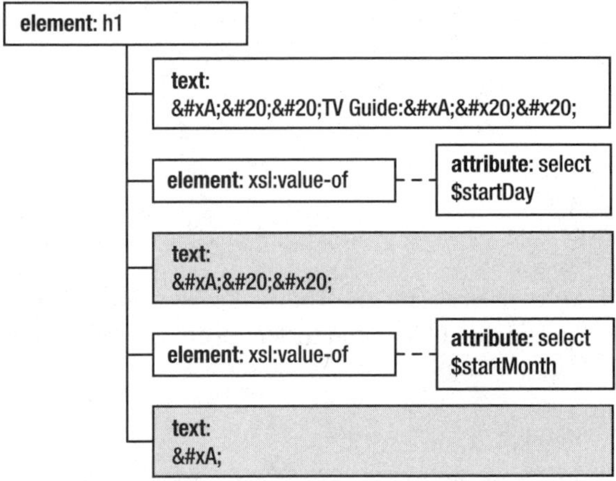

Figure 8-7. *Node tree created from XSLT code*

You'll remember from the last chapter how you could use `<xsl:strip-space>` to get rid of whitespace-only text nodes from the node tree of the source document. When an XSLT processor reads the stylesheet, it automatically ignores any whitespace-only text nodes aside from those within `<xsl:text>` elements, so effectively the node tree for this snippet of the stylesheet is in fact that shown in Figure 8-8.

Now there are two problems with this node tree, which we can see if we look at the result that we get when we use the XSLT snippet. Assuming that the `$startDay` variable has the value `'5'` and the `$startMonth` variable has the value `'July'`, the result is:

```
<h1>
  TV Guide:
  5July</h1>
```

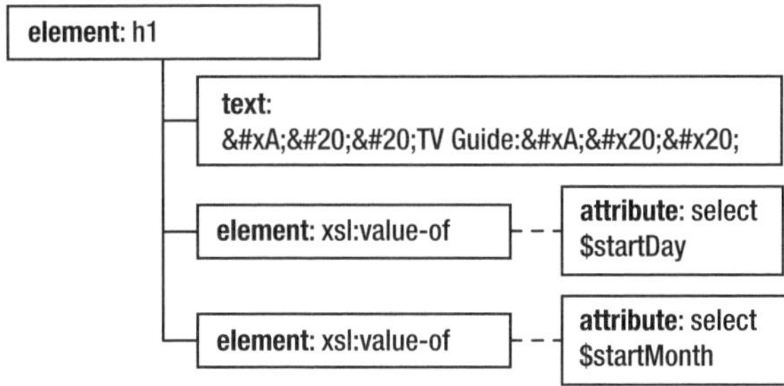

Figure 8-8. *Node tree created from XSLT code after whitespace stripping*

First, we have unnecessary whitespace before the content of the `<h1>` element and between the part that we created with literal text and the part we created with `<xsl:value-of>`. That text comes from the original text node in the stylesheet. Second, there isn't a space between the day and the month because the whitespace-only text node between the `<xsl:value-of>` elements has been stripped away.

We can use `<xsl:text>` to solve both these problems. First, you can use `<xsl:text>` to place boundaries around the text that you actually want to add to the result tree and the whitespace you're just adding to make the stylesheet read better. Second, you can use `<xsl:text>` to add whitespace between the text created by instructions. In the amended code, we use `<xsl:text>` around the "TV Guide: " literal text that we want, and between the two `<xsl:value-of>` instructions to add a space:

```
<h1>
  <xsl:text>TV Guide: </xsl:text>
  <xsl:value-of select="$startDay" />
  <xsl:text> </xsl:text>
  <xsl:value-of select="$startMonth" />
</h1>
```

When the XSLT processor builds a node tree for the stylesheet from this snippet, it sees the tree shown in Figure 8-9.

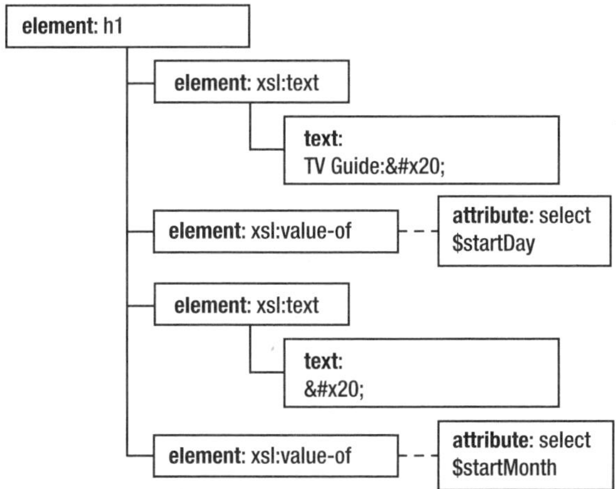

Figure 8-9. *Node tree created from XSLT code with* `<xsl:text>` *instructions*

And the result from running the snippet is the following, with all the whitespace that we need:

```
<h1>TV Guide: 5 July</h1>
```

Summary The <xsl:text> element is useful for delimiting the text that should be added to a tree (to omit whitespace) and for adding whitespace-only text nodes to the result tree.

Managing Whitespace in the Result Tree

There are a couple of places where we could improve the result that we're generating with the next version of our stylesheet by controlling the whitespace that we're generating.

First, when we generate the title of a program that has both a series and a title, we're getting a lot of whitespace before the dash that separates them. This whitespace isn't apparent if you look at the page in a browser (because in HTML consecutive spaces are collapsed into a single space for display), but it shows up if you look at the source code. For example, in TVGuide4.html, you'll see

```
<span class="title">StarTrekVoyager
        - <span class="subtitle">Renaissance Man</span></span><br/>
```

The code that's generating the titles is the following, in the template that matches <Program> elements in Details mode:

```
<span class="title">
  <xsl:choose>
    <xsl:when test="string(Series)">
      <xsl:value-of select="Series" />
      <xsl:if test="string(Title)">
        - <span class="subtitle"><xsl:value-of select="Title" /></span>
      </xsl:if>
    </xsl:when>
    <xsl:otherwise>
      <xsl:value-of select="Title" />
    </xsl:otherwise>
  </xsl:choose>
</span>
```

We're adding a line break and several spaces before the dash. It would make the file smaller (and more readable, in terms of source code) if we got rid of the whitespace that we don't need by wrapping the dash in an <xsl:text> element, as in TVGuide6.xsl:

```
<span class="title">
  <xsl:choose>
    <xsl:when test="string(Series)">
```

```
      <xsl:value-of select="Series" />
      <xsl:if test="string(Title)">
        <xsl:text> - </xsl:text>
        <span class="subtitle"><xsl:value-of select="Title" /></span>
      </xsl:if>
    </xsl:when>
    <xsl:otherwise>
      <xsl:value-of select="Title" />
    </xsl:otherwise>
  </xsl:choose>
</span>
```

Another place where there are problems with whitespace is in the generation of the `<span>` elements in the cast list. The template in `TVGuide4.xsl` is

```
<xsl:template match="CastMember">
  <li>
    <xsl:apply-templates select="Character" />
    <xsl:apply-templates select="Actor" />
  </li>
</xsl:template>
```

But this means that there's no space between the `<span>` element created to hold the character's name and the one created to hold the actor's name, which means the output looks a little strange, as you can see in the screenshot of `TVGuide4.html` shown in Figure 8-10.

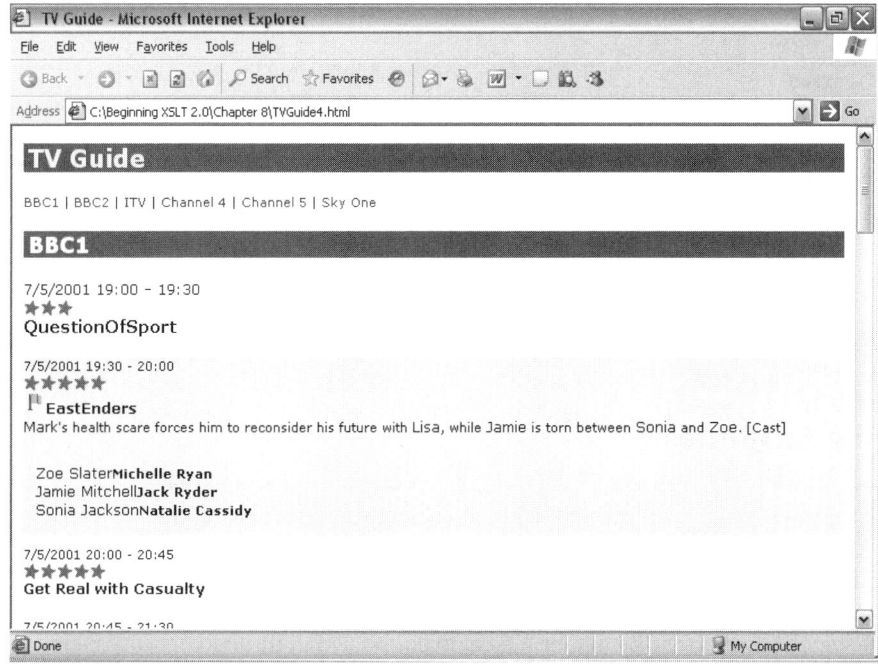

Figure 8-10. *Viewing* `TVGuide4.html` *in Internet Explorer*

Instead, we should add a space between the two <span> elements, using <xsl:text>, as in TVGuide6.xsl:

```
<xsl:template match="CastMember">
  <li>
    <xsl:apply-templates select="Character" />
    <xsl:text> </xsl:text>
    <xsl:apply-templates select="Actor" />
  </li>
</xsl:template>
```

As you can see from Figure 8-11, which shows TVGuide6.html, this makes the cast list a lot more readable.

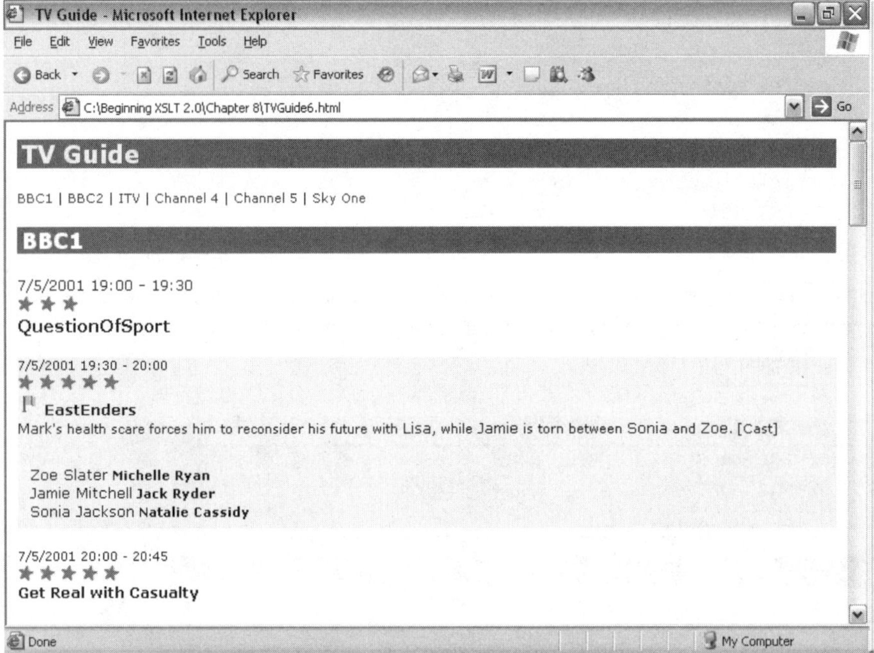

Figure 8-11. *Viewing* TVGuide6.html *in Internet Explorer*

Generating Attributes

You can generate attribute nodes using <xsl:attribute> in much the same way as you can create element nodes using <xsl:element>. Like <xsl:element>, <xsl:attribute> has a name attribute to set the name of the attribute and a namespace attribute to set the namespace of the attribute, both of which are attribute value templates, allowing you to set the name and namespace of an attribute dynamically.

The value of the attribute can be determined in two ways: either through the content of the <xsl:attribute> element, which is a sequence constructor, or through the select attribute. In this way, <xsl:attribute> is a lot like <xsl:value-of>, except that where <xsl:value-of> constructs a text node, <xsl:attribute> constructs an attribute node.

The XSLT processor works out the value of the attribute by first concatenating together any text nodes in the sequence (without any separator between them) and then concatenating the string values of the items in the new sequence with a space separator between each. You can use the separator attribute on <xsl:attribute> to specify an alternative separator. The fact that text nodes are concatenated without separators between them allows you to construct the value of an attribute with literal text, <xsl:text>, or <xsl:value-of> without getting unwanted whitespace added between them. For example, if $divID is 'EastEndersCast', then

```
<xsl:attribute name="onclick">
  <xsl:text>toggle(</xsl:text>
  <xsl:value-of select="$divID" />
  <xsl:text>);</xsl:text>
</xsl:attribute>
```

creates an onclick attribute whose value is 'toggle(EastEndersCast);'.

■**Tip** If you're creating an attribute that contains data, use the select attribute to select the value for the attribute. If you're creating an attribute that holds text, use the content of the <xsl:attribute> element to create the text.

It turns out that <xsl:attribute> is a lot more useful than <xsl:element>. While literal result elements are pretty much equivalent to <xsl:element>, <xsl:attribute> is a very different beast from literal attributes. First, it is an instruction, and therefore can be specified within an <xsl:if> or even within a separate template and still be added to the element you're creating. Second, you can use the content of the <xsl:attribute> element to determine the value of the attribute, and the content of <xsl:attribute> can include any XSLT instructions you like, including calls to other templates, for example.

Attributes can be added to any result element with <xsl:attribute>, whether the result element is generated by a literal result element or using <xsl:element>. In fact, unless you can copy attributes from the original source tree onto the element, you *must* use <xsl:attribute> to specify the attributes of elements generated with <xsl:element>.

■**Note** You can't use <xsl:attribute> to add attributes to XSLT instructions—remember you're adding attribute nodes to the result tree, not to the stylesheet.

Any attributes that you add to an element with <xsl:attribute> instructions have to be added before you add any content to the element that you're generating, so usually <xsl:attribute> instructions come immediately after the start tag of the literal result element or the <xsl:element> instruction that creates the relevant element. You can use <xsl:attribute> to create some attributes, while adding others in the normal way at the same time. For example, the following creates an <img> element with width, height, src, and alt attributes.

```
<img width="20" height="20">
  <xsl:attribute name="src">favorite.gif</xsl:attribute>
  <xsl:attribute name="alt">[Favorite]</xsl:attribute>
</img>
```

Note If an attribute you generate using `<xsl:attribute>` has the same name as an attribute that's already on the literal result element, then the `<xsl:attribute>` instruction overrides the existing attribute.

In this section, we'll look at how to use `<xsl:attribute>` for adding optional attributes, attributes with conditional values, and whole sets of attributes at once.

Summary You can create attribute nodes using the `<xsl:attribute>` instruction, with the name of the attribute given in the `name` attribute and the value of the attribute specified by the content or the `select` attribute of the instruction.

Creating Optional Attributes

When you add an attribute to a literal result element literally, you are forcing the attribute to be present. You can change the value of the literal attribute using an attribute value template, but you can't change whether it's there or not. On the other hand, because the `<xsl:attribute>` element is an instruction, you can put it within `<xsl:if>` or `<xsl:choose>` elements so that an attribute is only added in particular situations, or different attributes are added in different situations. The general patterns are

```
<elementName>
  <xsl:if test="condition">
    <xsl:attribute name="attributeName">attributeValue</xsl:attribute>
  </xsl:if>
  ...
</elementName>
```

and

```
<elementName>
  <xsl:choose>
    <xsl:when test="condition1">
      <xsl:attribute name="attributeName1">attributeValue1</xsl:attribute>
    </xsl:when>
    <xsl:when test="condition2">
      <xsl:attribute name="attributeName2">attributeValue2</xsl:attribute>
    </xsl:when>
    ...
    <xsl:otherwise>
```

```
      <xsl:attribute name="defaultAttributeName">
        <xsl:text>defaultAttributeValue</xsl:text>
      </xsl:attribute>
    </xsl:otherwise>
  </xsl:choose>
</elementName>
```

Summary Wrapping <xsl:attribute> elements in <xsl:if> or <xsl:choose> allows you to control which attributes get added to which elements.

Highlighting Interesting Programs (Again)

To illustrate how <xsl:attribute> is used to create optional attributes, we'll return to a scenario that we first discussed in Chapter 4: highlighting the interesting programs in our TV guide. The interesting programs are highlighted in the HTML using CSS—if the <div> for the program has a `class` attribute with the value `interesting`, then the program is highlighted.

In the solution that we're currently using in `TVGuide6.xsl`, we have separate templates that determine whether or not a `class` attribute is added to the <div> for a program, as follows:

```
<xsl:template match="Program[@flag = ('favorite', 'interesting') or
                             @rating > 6 or
                             (some $n in (Series, Title, Description)
                              satisfies contains(lower-case($n), 'news'))]">
  <div class="interesting">
    <xsl:apply-templates select="." mode="Details" />
  </div>
</xsl:template>

<xsl:template match="Program">
  <div>
    <xsl:apply-templates select="." mode="Details" />
  </div>
</xsl:template>
```

The only difference between these templates is whether the <div> has a `class` attribute. The <div> elements have the same content and occur in the same place. So rather than repeating the same <div> and the same <xsl:apply-templates> to get the content of the <div>, we can use a single literal result element and add the `class` attribute conditionally, as in `TVGuide7.xsl`:

```
<xsl:template match="Program">
  <div>
    <xsl:if test="@flag = ('favorite', 'interesting') or
                  @rating > 6 or
                  (some $n in (Series, Title, Description)
                   satisfies contains(lower-case($n), 'news'))">
```

```
      <xsl:attribute name="class" select="'interesting'" />
    </xsl:if>
    <xsl:apply-templates select="." mode="Details" />
  </div>
</xsl:template>
```

If you transform TVGuide.xml with TVGuide7.xsl to create TVGuide7.html, you'll see the interesting programs highlighted, exactly as they were before, as shown in Figure 8-12.

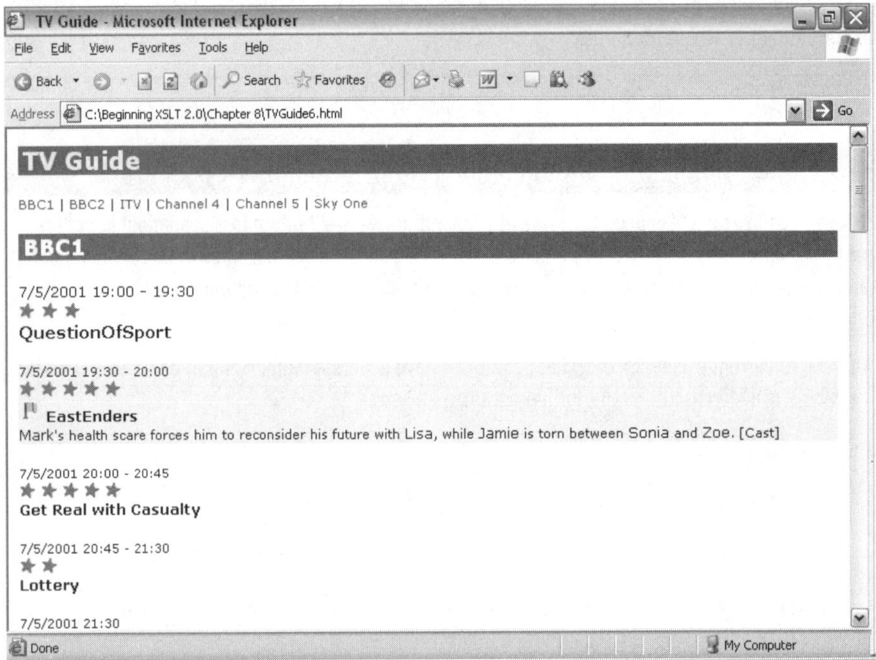

Figure 8-12. *Viewing* TVGuide7.html *in Internet Explorer*

The result of the transformation hasn't changed, but the clarity of the stylesheet has. We could even merge the Details mode template back into the main <Program> template again if we wanted.

Attribute Sets

Another aid to maintenance that is offered by XSLT is the ability to define sets of attributes, which you can then apply to elements in different places within your stylesheet. You can define an attribute set using the <xsl:attribute-set> element, which lives at the top level of your stylesheet as a direct child of the <xsl:stylesheet> document element.

Each <xsl:attribute-set> element has a name attribute, which specifies the name of the attribute set so that you can refer to it later. Within the <xsl:attribute-set> element, you use <xsl:attribute> instructions to define the attributes in the set. For example, the following defines an attribute set called image, which contains the two attributes width and height:

```
<xsl:attribute-set name="image">
  <xsl:attribute name="width">20</xsl:attribute>
  <xsl:attribute name="height">20</xsl:attribute>
</xsl:attribute-set>
```

The `<xsl:attribute-set>` element can only have `<xsl:attribute>` elements as children, so you can't create an attribute set to add optional attributes. However, the values of the attributes in the attribute set can be calculated on the fly, based on the current node at the point where the attribute set is used.

You can use an attribute set to add the attributes that it defines to a particular element with the `xsl:use-attribute-sets` attribute on literal result elements or the `use-attribute-sets` attribute on `<xsl:element>` (or `<xsl:copy>`, which we meet later). Each of these attributes takes a whitespace-separated list of the names of attribute sets. For example, both of the following instructions add attributes defined in the `image` and `highlight` attribute sets to newly created `<img>` elements:

```
<img src="flag.gif" xsl:use-attribute-sets="image highlight" />
<xsl:element name="img" use-attribute-sets="image highlight">
  <xsl:attribute name="src">flag.gif</xsl:attribute>
</xsl:element>
```

■ Note You can also use the `use-attribute-sets` attribute on `<xsl:attribute-set>` to include the attributes that you've defined in one attribute set in another, building a hierarchy of attribute sets.

Attribute sets really come into their own as ways of defining styles when you're generating XSL-FO, because XSL-FO uses attributes a great deal to define the look of a formatting object. They are also useful in other XML-to-XML transformations where several elements share the same set of attributes, but tend not to be as useful when you're just creating HTML—it's fairly rare for an HTML page to have the same attributes repeated on elements that are created in different places.

■ Summary You can define sets of attributes using the `<xsl:attribute-set>` top-level element, and add the attributes that they define to literal result elements with the `xsl:use-attribute-sets` attribute or to elements generated with `<xsl:element>` with the `use-attribute-sets` attribute.

Now you've seen three ways of adding attributes to an element:

- Using attribute sets
- Using literal attributes on literal result elements
- Using `<xsl:attribute>`

It's possible to add an attribute of the same name in all three ways on the same element; if you do so, then the one that you add with <xsl:attribute> overrides the one that you add as a literal attribute on the element, which in turn overrides the one that you add using the attribute set. If you add the same attribute from multiple attribute sets, then the definition in the last attribute set that you use is the one that's added to the element.

Generating Comments and Processing Instructions

Unlike elements, attributes, and text, you can't include comments or processing instructions in the output by including them literally within your stylesheet. Instead, you have to use <xsl:comment> and <xsl:processing-instruction> to create new comment and processing instruction nodes respectively in the result tree.

■ Note Like other nodes, you can always copy comments or processing instructions from the source document using <xsl:copy-of> if they are already around in the correct form.

Both <xsl:comment> and <xsl:processing-instruction> work like <xsl:attribute> and <xsl:value-of> when it comes to determining the value of the generated node. You can use the content or select attribute of the instruction to generate a sequence; text nodes in the sequence are concatenated without any separator, and then the string values of the items in the adjusted sequence are concatenated, with separator spaces, to create the value of the new node. You can control the separator that's inserted between the string values with the separator attribute.

For example, the following adds the comment "Generated automatically using XSLT" to the result tree:

```
<xsl:comment>Generated automatically using XSLT</xsl:comment>
```

When serialized, the comment will look like this:

```
<!--Generated automatically using XSLT-->
```

The <xsl:processing-instruction> instruction must have a name attribute, holding the name (or target) of the processing instruction. Like the name attributes of <xsl:element> and <xsl:attribute>, the name attribute on <xsl:processing-instruction> is an attribute value template, so you can create processing instructions whose names are computed on the fly, if you need to. Unlike the names of elements and attributes, processing instruction names aren't qualified, so the name you give must not include a colon.

The following example creates an xml-stylesheet processing instruction whose value is created from a sequence of strings specified in the select attribute:

```
<xsl:processing-instruction name="xml-stylesheet"
  select="'type=&quot;text/css&quot;',
          'href=&quot;TVGuide.css&quot;'" />
```

When serialized into a file, the processing instruction will look like this:

```
<?xml-stylesheet type="text/css" href="TVGuide.css"?>
```

Note Remember that the content of a processing instruction is just a string as far as an XML application is concerned; the things that look like attributes in the `xml-stylesheet` processing instruction are just part of the string, so you don't create them with `<xsl:attribute>`. Also note that processing instruction targets don't have namespaces, so there's no `namespace` attribute.

Summary You can generate comment nodes using `<xsl:comment>` and processing instruction nodes using `<xsl:processing-instruction>`. The content or `select` attribute of the instruction specifies the value of the node. The `name` attribute of the `<xsl:processing-instruction>` instruction specifies the name or target of the processing instruction.

Creating Documents

The final node-generating instruction that we need to cover is `<xsl:document>` which, surprise, surprise, generates a document node. Probably the only place where you might want to use `<xsl:document>` is when defining a temporary tree using a variable. As we saw in Chapter 6, when you provide content in `<xsl:variable>` and don't specify an `as` attribute, then the processor automatically creates a document node with the content of the `<xsl:variable>` providing the children for the document node. One of the examples we looked at was the following:

```
<xsl:variable name="copyright">
  Copyright <a href="mailto:jeni@jenitennison.com">Jeni Tennison</a>, 2005
</xsl:variable>
```

Now, the `$copyright` variable holds a document node. Since we're good programmers, we'd like to declare the type of the variable using the `as` attribute. The type of the variable is a document node, so we can add an `as` attribute to that effect:

```
<xsl:variable name="copyright" as="document-node()">
  Copyright <a href="mailto:jeni@jenitennison.com">Jeni Tennison</a>, 2005
</xsl:variable>
```

But now we run into problems. If you specify an `as` attribute on the `<xsl:variable>`, then the document node doesn't get created automatically any more, so the value of the variable is actually a sequence of text and element nodes. To make the `as` attribute accurate, and get the `$copyright` variable holding a temporary tree, we need to use the `<xsl:document>` instruction to create the document node:

```
<xsl:variable name="copyright" as="document-node()">
  <xsl:document>
    Copyright <a href="mailto:jeni@jenitennison.com">Jeni Tennison</a>, 2005
  </xsl:document>
</xsl:variable>
```

The `<xsl:document>>` instruction has some other uses when it comes to schema-aware processing, as we'll see in Chapter 13.

■ **Summary** The <xsl:document> instruction creates a document node. The content of the <xsl:document> instruction provides the content of the document.

Copying Nodes and Branches

You've seen how to create new nodes of various descriptions, but what if you have a description already written in XHTML that you just want replicated in the result?

Well, if you cast your mind back to Chapter 6, you'll remember that you can add existing nodes to a sequence with <xsl:sequence>, and create copies of existing nodes using <xsl:copy-of>. If that sequence is used to generate a part of a result tree, then these nodes are copied into that result tree.

■ **Note** Conceptually, this means that if you use <xsl:copy-of> to select nodes you want copied, you actually copy them twice: once to create the copy in the sequence that's being constructed, and once when that copy is added as the child of a document or element in the result tree.

For example, the following adds the content of the <Description> element (without adding the <Description> element itself) to a sequence, which can then be used to create the content of an element:

```
<xsl:sequence select="Description/node()" />
```

While <xsl:sequence> or <xsl:copy-of> are excellent for making copies of entire branches of the source tree, it's often more helpful to use the natural XSLT processing model to traverse the tree, copying the nodes that you encounter as you go, as this enables you to make an exact copy of most of the tree while making small changes at a low level. Rather than using <xsl:sequence> or <xsl:copy-of>, you can use an **identity template**, which matches any kind of node, copies it to the result, and then recurses down the tree. To create a copy of a node, whatever its type, you can use <xsl:copy>, which creates a shallow copy of the node (this doesn't include any attributes or content when you copy an element).

The following identity template matches nodes of any type (including attributes). It uses <xsl:copy> to make a copy of the node. Then it applies templates to the attributes and content of the node—if the node isn't an element, then it won't have any attributes or content, so the <xsl:apply-templates> instruction will do nothing:

```
<xsl:template match="@* | node()">
  <xsl:copy>
    <xsl:apply-templates select="@* | node()" />
  </xsl:copy>
</xsl:template>
```

An identity template is often a useful alternative to the built-in templates—it copies everything exactly as it is by default, and all you have to do is provide templates for the elements and attributes that you want to be treated specially. For example, if you wanted to create a stylesheet that copied most things as is, but changed all the <Description> elements to <Desc> elements, you could use the identity template coupled with the following template:

```
<xsl:template match="Description">
  <Desc><xsl:apply-templates /></Desc>
</xsl:template>
```

The identity template would copy the majority of the source document, with the template for the <Description> element renaming those elements wherever they occurred.

■ **Summary** The <xsl:sequence> and <xsl:copy-of> instructions can be used to copy an entire branch of the source tree to a result tree. The <xsl:copy> instruction is particularly useful within an identity template that copies elements by default.

Creating Result Documents

The previous section dealt with the general topic of how to create nodes within result trees. There are two kinds of result tree that you might generate within a stylesheet:

A **temporary tree**—A result tree that's destined for further processing. In this case, the result tree is held in a variable, and that variable is then processed (usually by applying templates to it or simply by copying it) to create another result tree. This can be useful because it allows you to break down a complex transformation into several steps or store data that you use within your stylesheet using XML.

A **result document**—A result tree that is made available as the result of a transformation. Usually these result trees are written out as files on the local filing system, though some processors might give you greater control over what happens to these documents.

Executing an XSLT transformation usually automatically generates one result document, the main output of the transformation. What's done with this result document depends on the processor.

If you're using Saxon, for example, then you can use the -o option to indicate where you want the result document to be written to. For example, the following command line tells Saxon to write the result document generated by processing TVGuide.xml with TVGuide.xsl as TVGuide.html:

```
java net.sf.saxon.Transform -o TVGuide.html TVGuide.xml TVGuide.xsl
```

If the transformation is being performed by MSXML within Internet Explorer, on the other hand, the result document is automatically displayed as an HTML document in the browser.

You can also create result documents explicitly using the <xsl:result-document> instruction. The content of the <xsl:result-document> is used to generate a result tree (a document node is automatically added at the top of this result tree), and the <xsl:result-document> instruction has an optional href attribute that specifies a URI that the processor will associate with this result tree. For example, to create a document called EastEnders.html, you could use

```
<xsl:result-document href="EastEnders.html">
  ...
</xsl:result-document>
```

The href attribute is an attribute value template, which means that it's possible to determine the URI associated with the result document dynamically, based on something in the source document. If the href attribute is missing, then the URI that's associated with the result document needs to be supplied by the processor itself; this is exactly what the -o option in Saxon does.

As with the main result document, different processors use the href attribute in different ways. If you're performing the transformation from the command line, then the href attribute will probably be used to indicate the locations where the files generated from the result document are written. On the other hand, if you're performing the transformation within a browser, it might just cache the documents internally—allowing you to link between them, but not writing them to disk.

The ability to create multiple result documents in one transformation is particularly useful when doing batch processing, when you take a single XML document and use that document to create multiple HTML files. You could imagine doing it with our TV guide to create separate pages for

- An index of channels
- A program listing for each channel
- A list of series and their episodes

It's also sometimes useful to create multiple documents because the result that you want to create requires that information be held in separate physical documents. For example, if the HTML pages that you're creating use frames, then the contents of the individual frames need to be in separate documents. Similarly, if you generate SVG images with your stylesheet (as we'll do in Chapter 16), they need to be held in separate files from the HTML that points to them.

Of course, you could use separate stylesheets to generate the separate documents, but there are a few advantages to creating all these pages from the same process:

Creating all the pages at once makes it easier to do linking between the pages, because you can make sure that the same identifiers are used across multiple result documents.

Having a single process for creating all the pages means that the source document (TVGuide.xml), which could be very large, only needs to be parsed once rather than multiple times. Parsing big documents and creating node trees for them takes a long time, so being able to do it once rather than hundreds of times can give big savings.

Generating the documents from a single stylesheet means that you don't need to know in advance how many documents need to be generated: that can depend on the information available in the XML document you're processing.

■ Note Stylesheets that support a range of types of result document can get pretty large; you should use the methods that we'll see in Chapter 12 to break them up into separate modules that could be used as standalone stylesheets or within the larger application.

■ Summary The `<xsl:result-document>` instruction creates a result document that's associated with the URI held in its `href` attribute.

Creating a Page per Channel

To try out creating multiple output documents, in `TVGuide8.xsl` we'll create one HTML page per channel listed within `TVGuide.xml`.

To do this, we'll need to have a template that matches `<Channel>` elements. Each `<Channel>` element needs to output an HTML page that looks much like the HTML page that we're currently creating. The URI for the page for each `<Channel>` element can be based on the channel's name, but since these names can contain spaces, we need to escape them with the `escape-uri()` function, with the second argument being `true` so that we escape any other characters that are significant within the name of the channel:

```
<xsl:template match="Channel">
  <xsl:result-document href="{escape-uri(Name, true())}.html">
    <html>
      <head>
        <title><xsl:value-of select="Name" /></title>
        <link rel="stylesheet" href="TVGuide.css" />
        <script type="text/javascript">
          ...
        </script>
      </head>
      <body>
        <xsl:apply-templates />
      </body>
    </html>
  </xsl:result-document>
</xsl:template>
```

This template will be used whenever templates are applied to `<Channel>` elements in the default mode.

The main output for the transformation, which is determined by the template matching the root document node of `TVGuide.xml`, doesn't need to contain a script any more, but it does need to contain links to the pages that are being created for each channel. We'll use a `<ul>` element to hold the list, which means changing the template that matches the `<Channel>` elements in `ChannelList` mode to the following:

```
<xsl:template match="Channel" mode="ChannelList">
  <li>
    <a href="{escape-uri(Name, true())}.html"><xsl:value-of select="Name" /></a>
  </li>
</xsl:template>
```

and changing the template that matches the `<TVGuide>` element to the following:

```
<xsl:template match="TVGuide">
  <ul>
    <xsl:apply-templates select="Channel" mode="ChannelList" />
  </ul>
  <xsl:apply-templates select="Channel" />
</xsl:template>
```

■ **Note** The second `<xsl:apply-templates>` instruction in the preceding template is the one that causes the separate documents for each channel to be created. It doesn't matter whether you do this before or after creating the list of channels.

When you transform `TVGuide.xml` with `TVGuide8.xsl`, you get not only `TVGuide8.html`, but also a bunch of other HTML pages, one per channel in the TV Guide. `TVGuide8.html` is shown in Figure 8-13.

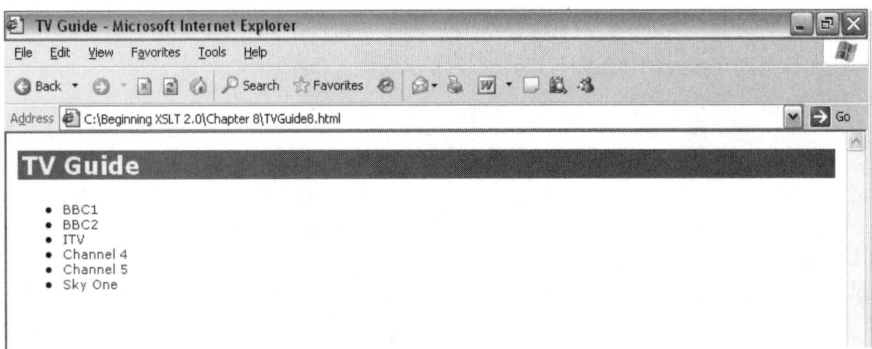

Figure 8-13. *Viewing* `TVGuide8.html` *in Internet Explorer*

Clicking the Sky One link, for example, leads you to `Sky One.html`, which contains the program listing for Sky One, as shown in Figure 8-14.

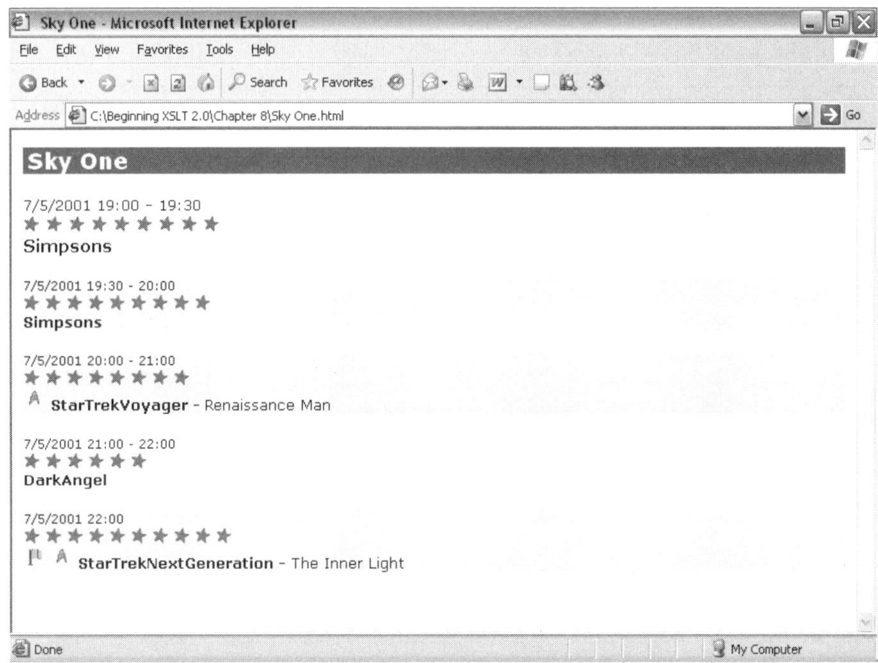

Figure 8-14. *Viewing* `Sky One.html` *in Internet Explorer*

The single stylesheet has generated multiple result documents, and the links between them.

Controlling Output

The first parts of this chapter looked at how to construct a result tree and how to tell a processor which URI to associate with a particular result document. Sometimes, that's all an XSLT processor needs to do—another process then takes the result tree and processes it to create a display or to add information to a database. However, more often than not, and especially when you're debugging a stylesheet, you'll want the result of the XSLT process to be written to a file so that you can view it.

To write the result document to a file, the XSLT processor has to **serialize** the result tree in some way. Serializing involves taking an abstract object (such as a node) that is only held in memory and creating a physical representation of that object (as octets on a disk). For example, when serializing an element node, a processor will write a start and end tag for that element node. When another processor reads that start and end tag, it will create an element node in memory. Thus serializing is the opposite of parsing; and if you serialize a node tree, and then parse the resulting file, then you should get roughly the same node tree as you started with.

Note Not all XSLT processors support serialization: it's an optional part of the XSLT 2.0 specification.

Sometimes an external process might manage this serialization (for example, when using a Cocoon pipeline), but XSLT also gives you some control over the serialization from within the stylesheet, using **output definitions**. An output definition is specified using an <xsl:output> element and the attributes on it. For example:

```
<xsl:output method="xhtml" />
```

is an output definition that specifies that a result tree should be serialized as XHTML.

An <xsl:output> element may have a name attribute, in which case the output definition can be referred to by name; otherwise the <xsl:output> element defines the default output definition. You can have several <xsl:output> elements with the same name (or lack of a name), in which case their attributes are combined (with later <xsl:output> elements overriding earlier ones) when the XSLT processor has to decide what to do. For example, these two <xsl:output> elements:

```
<xsl:output name="xhtml" method="xhtml" />
<xsl:output name="xhtml" encoding="UTF-8" />
```

are combined into a single output definition, which is exactly the same as the one that would be created with

```
<xsl:output name="xhtml" method="xhtml" encoding="UTF-8" />
```

The default output definition is used when serializing the main result tree for the stylesheet (the one that isn't created with the <xsl:result-document> instruction), and when you create a result document with <xsl:result-document> without specifying what format you want it to be output in.

When you create a result document using the <xsl:result-document> instruction, you can tell the processor which output definition to use via the format attribute. The format attribute holds the name of an output definition. For example, to tell the processor to output index.html using the output definition named xhtml, you can use

```
<xsl:result-document href="index.html" format="xhtml">
  ...
</xsl:result-document>
```

All the attributes of the <xsl:output> element are also allowed directly on the <xsl:result-document> element. If you specify an attribute on the <xsl:result-document> instruction, its value overrides the one on the output definition that's being used. For example, if you did

```
<xsl:result-document href="index.html" format="xhtml" encoding="ISO-8859-1">
  ...
</xsl:result-document>
```

then the xhtml output definition would be used but with the encoding ISO-8859-1 rather than UTF-8.

Caution The output-version attribute on <xsl:result-document> is the equivalent of the version attribute on <xsl:output>. The version attribute on <xsl:result-document> actually refers to the version of XSLT being used within that element.

On the <xsl:result-document> instruction, these attributes are actually attribute value templates, which means that you can set their value dynamically. This enables you to, for example, parameterize the encoding used in the result documents. First, you set up a stylesheet parameter to take the encoding:

```
<xsl:param name="encoding" select="'UTF-8'" />
```

and then you refer to the value of the $encoding parameter from the encoding attribute of the <xsl:result-document>:

```
<xsl:result-document href="index.html" method="xhtml" encoding="{$encoding}">
  ...
</xsl:result-document>
```

In the rest of this section, I discuss the attributes that can be used on <xsl:output> and <xsl:result-document> elements to control the serialization of a result tree.

Summary Output definitions, defined using the <xsl:output> top-level element, control how result trees are serialized on output. The <xsl:result-document> instruction can refer to an output definition by name using the format attribute, or control serialization directly.

Output Methods

The first and most important question that you have to answer when serializing the result tree is what **output method** you want to use. The output method determines the syntax that's used for the various different types of nodes in the result document. There are four output methods that are built into XSLT 2.0 processors: xml, html, xhtml, and text. You can tell the XSLT processor to use a particular output method with the method attribute on <xsl:output>. For example, to tell the XSLT processor to use the text output method, you should use

```
<xsl:output method="text" />
```

The xml output method is the default method if the output definition that you use doesn't specify a method explicitly, with two exceptions:

- If the document element of the result document is an <html> element in the XHTML namespace of http://www.w3.org/1999/xhtml, then the default output method is xhtml.
- If the document element of the result document is an <html> element (in any case combination) in no namespace, then the default output method is html.

In this section, we'll use the snippet of a result document shown in Figure 8-15 to illustrate the differences between the different output methods.

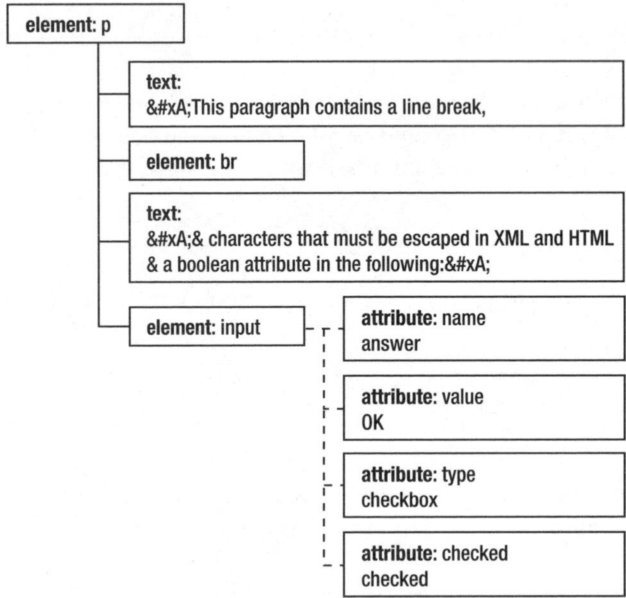

Figure 8-15. *Sample result tree*

The xml Output Method

The most common output method is `xml`, which serializes the result document using the standard XML syntax. For example, given a result tree that looks like the tree shown in Figure 8-15, the `xml` output method creates a section in a document that looks something like this:

```
<p>
This paragraph contains a line break,<br/>
&amp; characters that must be escaped in XML and HTML,
&amp; a boolean attribute in the following:
<input name="answer" value="OK" type="checkbox" checked="checked"/>
</p>
```

As you can see, the resulting output follows the XML rules for well-formedness, with end tags for every element, special characters being escaped, and so on.

By default, if you use the `xml` output method, then you'll get an XML declaration at the start of the document, indicating the version of XML and the encoding that's being used (both of which can be set using attributes on `<xsl:output>`, as we'll see later). You can prevent the XML declaration from being added using the `omit-xml-declaration` attribute on `<xsl:output>` with the value yes. You can determine whether the XML declaration is a standalone XML declaration (includes a `standalone` pseudo-attribute with the value yes) using the `standalone` attribute on `<xsl:output>`.

■Note The XSLT processor won't honor the `omit-xml-declaration` attribute if omitting the XML declaration would mean generating a non-well-formed document. For example, if you're using an encoding other than UTF-8 or UTF-16, an XML declaration is required to indicate the encoding being used.

The `html` Output Method

Under the `html` output method, elements are serialized according to HTML rules—the XSLT processor recognizes certain elements and attributes as being serialized without end tags, for example, and generates output accordingly. For example, taking the same result tree as we used for the `xml` output method, the `html` output method creates a section in a document that looks something like this:

```
<p>
This paragraph contains a line break,<br>
&amp; characters that must be escaped in XML and HTML,
&amp; a boolean attribute in the following:
<input name="answer" value="OK" type="checkbox" checked>
</p>
```

Both the `<br>` and the `<input>` element nodes are serialized without end tags and without the special empty element syntax that's used by XML. The ampersand character is escaped with a character entity reference, as with XML, but the Boolean attribute (`checked`) isn't given a name.

The `html` output method does various other special things during output:

- It usually adds a `<meta>` element to the `<head>` element, specifying the content type of the document, unless you tell it not to by setting the `include-content-type` attribute on the output definition to `no`.
- It usually ensures that URLs, in the `href` attribute of `<a>` elements, for example, are escaped correctly, unless you tell it not to by setting the `escape-uri-attributes` attribute on the output definition to `no`.
- It doesn't escape the special XML characters (for example, less-than signs or ampersands) when they appear within `<script>` or `<style>` elements.
- It uses character entity references, such as ` `, to output those non-ASCII characters for which names are defined in HTML.

All these steps ensure that the output that you generate using the `html` output method adheres to the syntax rules of HTML.

The `xhtml` Output Method

The `xhtml` output method is very similar to the `xml` output method, except that the result is serialized in such a way that normal HTML browsers should display the result as they would the equivalent HTML. Taking the result document snippet in Figure 8-15, the `xhtml` output method creates something like the following:

```
<p>
This paragraph contains a line break,<br />
&amp; characters that must be escaped in XML and HTML,
&amp; a boolean attribute in the following:
<input name="answer" value="OK" type="checkbox" checked="checked" />
</p>
```

As you can see, this is almost exactly the same as the result from the `xml` output method; the only difference is that in the empty element tags for the `<br>` and `<input>` elements, there's a space before the final `"/>"`. This helps to make sure that HTML browsers display the XHTML correctly.

Like the `html` output method, the `xhtml` output method does various other extra things to the output:

- It usually adds a `<meta>` element to the `<head>` element, specifying the content type of the document, unless you tell it not to by setting the `include-content-type` attribute on the output definition to `no`.
- It usually ensures that URLs, in the `href` attribute of `<a>` elements, for example, are escaped correctly, unless you tell it not to by setting the `escape-uri-attributes` attribute on the output definition to `no`.
- The XHTML namespace is declared as the default namespace, rather than with a prefix.
- If an element isn't defined as an empty element in XHTML, it's always serialized with a start and end tag.

These tweaks help make sure that, while the result document is serialized as legal XML, it's also possible to view it in an HTML browser, as HTML.

The `text` Output Method

You can use the `xml`, `html`, or `xhtml` output methods to generate a document that holds only text if the result tree that you generate doesn't contain anything other than text nodes. However, as we've seen, if you use these methods the values of the text nodes are escaped—less-than signs become `<` and ampersands become `&`. The `text` method is therefore essential when you're generating plain text, such as comma-separated files, Java code, or SQL queries, as it prevents the five special XML characters from being escaped with their built-in entity references during serialization.

When you output a result tree using the `text` method, all nodes aside from text nodes are completely ignored. If we take the tree shown in Figure 8-15 as before, the `text` output method would create the following lines of text:

```
This paragraph contains a line break,
& characters that must be escaped in XML and HTML,
& a boolean attribute in the following:
```

As you can see, the elements are ignored, and the ampersand isn't escaped at all.

Summary There are four built-in output methods: `text` for text outputs, `html` for HTML output, `xhtml` for XHTML output, and `xml` for XML-based markup languages. You can tell the processor which output method to use with the `method` attribute.

Bypassing Output Escaping

In very rare cases, you might want to have the ease of the `xml` output method for creating elements and attributes, combined with the ability of the `text` output method to create strings without the special characters (less-than signs and ampersands in particular) being escaped. In other words, you want to bypass the normal output escaping that's done by the `xml` output method for a piece of the document.

Sometimes this happens because you want to generate something that is almost, but not quite, XML. For example, Java Server Pages (JSP) includes a special syntax for directives, such as:

```
<%@ taglib uri="http://java.sun.com/jsp/jstl/core" prefix="c" %>
```

A document that contains one of these directives isn't a legal XML document, but the majority of the rest of the JSP page might look like XML, with normal start and end tags that are used by the JSP to create elements. It would be tedious to create the entire JSP document as text, when the majority of the page could be generated as if it was plain XML.

Another situation where you want to bypass the normal output escaping is when the source XML contains some XML that for one reason or another is double-escaped in the source document. This usually occurs when the XML has been placed inside a CDATA section, such as the following:

```
<content>
  <![CDATA[<p>This is well-formed XML.</p>]]>
</content>
```

As you'll recall from Chapter 1, putting XML within a CDATA section has exactly the same effect as escaping the less-than signs that begin the tags using `<`. To the XSLT processor, the preceding XML is exactly the same as the following:

```
<content>
  &lt;p>This is well-formed XML.&lt;/p>
</content>
```

So if you try to output the value of the `<content>` element with a normal `<xsl:value-of>` instruction, then you will get

```
&lt;p>This is well-formed XML.&lt;/p>
```

Note The best way to solve this problem is to persuade whoever's supplying the XML that they shouldn't hide XML within CDATA sections, but that's not always possible.

XSLT 2.0 has two methods that enable you to bypass the normal output escaping done by the xml output method: by temporarily disabling output escaping using the disable-output-escaping attribute, and by telling the processor to replace certain characters in the result document with other strings in the output using a **character map**.

■ **Summary** If you need to create something that is almost, but not quite, XML, you can use the xml output method and bypass the normal output escaping for the parts of the document that aren't XML.

Disabling Output Escaping

The disable-output-escaping attribute can be placed on <xsl:text> and <xsl:value-of> elements to indicate whether the special characters in the text node that is generated by the instruction should be escaped on output or not. The disable-output-escaping attribute's default value is no, but if you set it to yes, then any less-than signs or ampersands that are included within the text node will be output as less-than signs and ampersands rather than as < and &.

For example, to create a JSP directive, you can use an <xsl:text> element with a disable-output-escaping attribute with the value yes. For example:

```
<xsl:text disable-output-escaping="yes">
  &lt;%@ taglib uri="http://java.sun.com/jsp/jstl/core" prefix="c" %>
</xsl:text>
```

■ **Note** The less-than sign in the stylesheet is still escaped—the stylesheet itself must still be well-formed XML.

If you have an element whose actual value is escaped XML, as in the following:

```
<content>
  <![CDATA[<p>This is well-formed XML.</p>]]>
</content>
```

you can add a disable-output-escaping attribute with the value yes to the <xsl:value-of> instruction, as follows:

```
<xsl:value-of select="content" disable-output-escaping="yes" />
```

When the result tree is serialized, you will see the following in the generated XML file:

```
<p>This is well-formed XML.</p>
```

■ **Summary** Setting the disable-output-escaping attribute on <xsl:text> or <xsl:value-of> to yes turns off the normal output escaping for the piece of text that the instruction generates.

These examples show that disable output escaping seems quite straightforward and easy to use. However, I'm now going to try to persuade you not to use this facility by explaining why disabling output escaping is, in general, a bad idea.

First, and most practically, not all XSLT processors support the disabling of output escaping. According to the XSLT Recommendation, an XSLT processor can ignore the `disable-output-escaping` attribute, and indeed some do ignore it. This is especially the case when an XSLT processor is used to generate a result that is used as a tree rather than being serialized and reparsed. It is also quite restricted even in those XSLT processors that do understand it; for example, you can't use `disable-output-escaping` to prevent the special characters in attribute values from being escaped.

Second, XSLT processors won't necessarily carry through any disabling of output escaping if you use variables to hold the text nodes. For example, if you do the following:

```
<xsl:variable name="content" as="text()">
  <xsl:value-of select="content" disable-output-escaping="yes" />
</xsl:variable>
<xsl:value-of select="$content" />
```

then the XSLT processor might give you an error (using `disable-output-escaping` when creating a node that isn't destined for a result document is technically an error). Alternatively, the processor might ignore the `disable-output-escaping` attribute and give you the escaped XML (the actual value of the `<content>` element), or it might honor the `disable-output-escaping` attribute and output unescaped XML. It's completely up to the processor, which makes it very hard to write portable stylesheets.

Third, the alternative methods for achieving what you want to achieve are almost always more robust and maintainable in the long term than disabling output escaping. This might include refactoring your application so that you're not using XSLT to create JSPs (why not use XSLT to generate whatever the JSP was generating?), or changing the source markup language to use namespaces to distinguish between wrapper elements and the content that you're interested in, so that you have, for example:

```
<content>
  <html:p>This is well-formed XML.</html:p>
</content>
```

Even when these kinds of changes aren't possible, using character maps will give a more robust solution to the problem.

Finally, disabling output escaping often demonstrates underlying misconceptions about how XSLT works. Hopefully, having gone through this book, you understand how to wrap an element around the result of processing a set of elements, that you can output a nonbreaking space by including ` ` in your stylesheet, and so on. People who don't yet have a good grasp of XSLT often try to disable output escaping to get around the problems that they encounter; the XSLT method always ends up being simpler, more effective, and more maintainable.

Summary Don't use `disable-output-escaping`.

Character Maps

Character maps are a new feature in XSLT 2.0. A character map defines mappings between characters (which appear in a result document) and strings (which appear in the serialized output). When a processor serializes a document, it checks each character in every text node and attribute value. If the character appears in a character map, then the character is substituted for the appropriate string.

Character maps are defined using the `<xsl:character-map>` top-level element. Each character map has a name, specified in the `name` attribute of the `<xsl:character-map>` element, so that it can be referred to from an output definition or another character map. The `<xsl:character-map>` element contains any number of `<xsl:output-character>` elements, each of which defines a mapping between a character (held in the `character` attribute) and a string (held in the `string` attribute).

Caution You can't have more than one character map with the same name in the same stylesheet.

Summary Character maps are defined by `<xsl:character-map>` top-level elements, with `<xsl:output-character>` elements inside them describing the mapping of individual characters to strings.

The simplest kind of character map is one that states that particular characters should be escaped using particular entity references. For example, the `xhtml` output method doesn't use entity references such as ` ` or `¡` when outputting characters, even though these entities are declared within the XHTML DTD. You can make a character map that maps the Latin-1 characters to their appropriate entity reference, for example, nonbreaking space characters (` `) to the entity reference ` `, as follows:

```
<xsl:character-map name="lat1.ent">
  <xsl:output-character character=" " string="&amp;nbsp;" />
  <xsl:output-character character="&#161;" string="&amp;iexcl;" />
  ...
</xsl:character-map>
```

When you set up an output definition, you can refer to this character map using the `use-character-maps` attribute. For example, to refer to the preceding character map, you can use

```
<xsl:output use-character-maps="lat1.ent" />
```

You can refer to as many character maps as you like using the `use-character-maps` attribute. They are combined in order, and if there are any characters that appear in more than one character map, then the mapping defined in the last of the character maps is the one that's used. You can also use the `use-character-maps` attribute on the `<xsl:character-map>` element to create collections of character maps. For example, you might define separate character maps for each of the sets of entities defined by XHTML (Latin 1, special characters and symbols), and then combine them into a single `xhtml-entities` character map, as follows:

```
<xsl:character-map name="xhtml-entities"
                   use-character-maps="lat1.ent special.ent symbol.ent" />
```

Summary Character maps can be referred to from output definitions or from other character maps using the use-character-maps attribute.

When it comes to problems like JSP directives and escaped XML, you have to use character maps in conjunction with what I call **placeholder characters**. Placeholder characters are characters that you use in place of whatever significant strings or characters you need to insert in the output but that aren't legal XML. For example, to output a JSP directive such as

```
<%@ taglib uri="http://java.sun.com/jsp/jstl/core" prefix="c" %>
```

you could use placeholder characters for the start of the directive (<%@) and the end of the directive (%>).

Placeholder characters have to be characters that you can guarantee won't appear anywhere else in the document, because character maps work across an entire document. For example, if you used a common character like * as a placeholder character, then every * in the document would get replaced, and that might include characters that really should be *s. The safest thing to do is to use characters from Unicode's **private use area**. These are characters set aside in Unicode that don't represent a fixed character. The main private use area is between #xE000 and #xF8FF, which is over 6,000 characters and is therefore likely to be more than enough!

For example, you might use  as the placeholder character for the start of a JSP directive and  as the placeholder character for the end of a JSP directive. To output a JSP directive, you would declare a character map mapping the placeholder characters onto the relevant strings, as follows:

```
<xsl:character-map name="jsp">
  <xsl:output-character character="&#xE000;" string="&lt;%@" />
  <xsl:output-character character="&#xE001;" string="%>" />
</xsl:character-map>
```

and then use the placeholder characters when creating the JSP directive, for example:

```
&#xE000; taglib uri="http://java.sun.com/jsp/jstl/core" prefix="c" &#xE001;
```

Similarly, you could simply have a placeholder character for the less-than sign:

```
<xsl:character-map name="escaped-xml">
  <xsl:output-character character="&#xF000;" string="&lt;" />
</xsl:character-map>
```

and then translate any less-than signs in escaped XML (such as the content of the <content> element in the example we've been looking at in this section) into that placeholder character:

```
<xsl:value-of select="translate(content, '&lt;', '&#xF000;')" />
```

In the result tree, the text node generated by the preceding <xsl:value-of> instruction will have the following value:

```
&#xF000;p>This is well-formed XML.&#xF000;/p>
```

When this text node is output, the  characters will be replaced by less-than signs, and the result will be unescaped XML:

```
<p>This is well-formed XML.</p>
```

If you use a lot of placeholder characters within a stylesheet, it can be difficult to keep track of which character represents which string, so I find it easiest to define entities within the stylesheet so that I can refer to them by name. For example, in the following, the placeholder character `` is represented by the entity `&jsp-start;` and the placeholder character `` is represented by the entity `&jsp-end;`:

```
<!DOCTYPE xsl:stylesheet [
<!ENTITY jsp-start '&#xE000;'>
<!ENTITY jsp-end '&#xE001;'>
]>
<xsl:stylesheet version="2.0"
                xmlns:xsl="http://www.w3.org/1999/XSL/Transform">
<xsl:character-map name="jsp">
  <xsl:output-character character="&jsp-start;" string="&lt;%@" />
  <xsl:output-character character="&jsp-end;" string="%>" />
</xsl:character-map>
...
</xsl:stylesheet>
```

With these entities defined in the stylesheet, you can create a JSP directive as follows:

```
&jsp-start; taglib uri="http://java.sun.com/jsp/jstl/core" prefix="c" &jsp-end;
```

Placeholder characters can also be used to represent other things that you want to insert in the output, such as external parsed entity references (for example, `&chap1;`) and `<img>` elements that are used to insert glyphs for unusual characters in the output. One advantage of using placeholder characters in these situations is that it's very easy to change what the characters map to later on, should you need to.

Summary To output strings without escaping, define a placeholder character for the string, and then use that placeholder character when you generate text nodes, in place of the string.

Declaring Content Type Information

The `<xsl:output>` element not only determines what kind of output you are creating in general, but also gives you control over a set of features that determine how the content of the output will be interpreted by other applications.

First, and relevant to all output methods, there's the `media-type` attribute, which declares the content type of the output that you're generating. By default, the media type of output produced is `text/xml` with the `xml` output method, `text/html` for the `html` and `xhtml` output methods, and `text/plain` for the `text` output method. However, you might be generating information with different media types—for example, you might be generating SVG using the `xml` output method, and might want to use the media type `image/svg+xml`:

```
<xsl:output method="xml" media-type="image/svg+xml" />
```

Note SVG is a markup language for vector graphics; you can find out more about it in Chapter 16.

Summary The `media-type` attribute indicates the content type of the output.

Second, applicable to the `xml`, `html`, and `xhtml` output methods, you can specify a public and/or system identifier to be used in the `DOCTYPE` declaration of the generated file. In Chapter 1, we saw that XHTML 1.0 documents include a `DOCTYPE` declaration of the form

```
<!DOCTYPE html
     PUBLIC "-//W3C//DTD XHTML 1.0 Strict//EN"
            "DTD/xhtml1-strict.dtd">
```

In this `DOCTYPE` declaration, the public identifier is `-//W3C//DTD XHTML 1.0 Strict//EN` and the system identifier is `DTD/xhtml1-strict.dtd`. These two values can be specified in the `doctype-public` and `doctype-system` attributes on the `<xsl:output>` element, to tell the XSLT processor to include the `DOCTYPE` declaration we need:

```
<xsl:output doctype-public="-//W3C//DTD XHTML 1.0 Strict//EN"
            doctype-system="DTD/xhtml1-strict.dtd" />
```

Note The `DOCTYPE` declaration also gives the name of the document element in the generated document, but the XSLT processor automatically adds this based on the document element in the result tree that you've constructed.

Summary The `doctype-public` and `doctype-system` attributes determine what kind of `DOCTYPE` declaration is added to the output in `xml`, `html`, and `xhtml` output methods.

Thirdly, again only applicable to the `xml`, `html`, and `xhtml` output methods, you can indicate the version of the XML or HTML to be used in the output using the `version` attribute on `<xsl:output>` or `output-version` attribute on `<xsl:result-document>`. The defaults depend on the XSLT processor that you're using. For example, to indicate that you want to use XML 1.1 in the output, you should use

```
<xsl:output method="xml" version="1.1" />
```

Caution When you're using the `xhtml` output method, the version you specify indicates the version of XML being used, not the version of XHTML being used.

Indicating the version of the output doesn't automatically change the DOCTYPE declaration that's used, just might slightly change the way in which the serialization works. For example, XML 1.1 is much the same as XML 1.0, but it has a slightly larger set of acceptable characters, slightly different treatment of line endings, and can support namespace undeclarations.

If you use XML 1.1 as the output method, then you can control whether namespace undeclarations are allowed using the `undeclare-prefixes` attribute. If `undeclare-prefixes` is yes, then if an element doesn't have a namespace node for a particular namespace when its parent does, then that namespace is undeclared. Unless you really need this facility, it's best to leave `undeclare-prefixes` alone, because if you use it you might end up with a document that isn't legal XML 1.0.

■ **Summary** The `version` attribute determines the version of XML or HTML that's used during serialization. The `undeclare-prefixes` attribute controls namespace undeclarations in XML 1.1.

Controlling Output Formats

The final important group of attributes control how the output looks, and tend to be used most when you're debugging your stylesheet because they allow you to view the output easily.

The first, and most important, of these attributes is the `encoding` attribute, which indicates the character encoding that you'd like the XSLT processor to use when writing the output. If you don't include an `encoding` attribute, then the XSLT processor will output UTF-8 or UTF-16, and you may find that this makes the output from your transformations look strange when you view them in simple text editors such as Notepad. Just as it's often easiest to write XML documents in text editors using ISO-8859-1 (or Windows-1252), it's often easiest to *view* XML documents if they're saved in one of these encodings. For example, to save your document in ISO-8859-1, you should use

```
<xsl:output encoding="ISO-8859-1" />
```

■ **Note** The `encoding` attribute applies to all the output methods. If you use it with the `xml` output method, then the XML declaration at the top of the output will specify the encoding; if you use it with the `html` or `xhtml` methods, then the `<meta>` element that the XSLT processor adds will specify this character set. Any characters that aren't available in the encoding that you specify will be replaced with character references when you use the `xml`, `html`, or `xhtml` methods.

■ **Summary** The `encoding` attribute indicates the encoding that the processor should use when saving the output.

The second formatting attribute is the `normalization-form` attribute, which determines whether and how the output is Unicode normalized. We first encountered Unicode normalization in Chapter 5 when looking at the `normalize-unicode()` function. Like the `normalize-unicode()`

function, the `normalization-form` attribute can take the values `'NFC'`, `'NFD'`, `'NKFC'`, `'NKFD'`, or `'fully-normalized'` to indicate the kind of Unicode normalization that should take place. It can also take the value `'none'`, which is the default and indicates that no Unicode normalization should take place, or any other name token for implementation-defined normalization. Usually, if you want Unicode normalization at all, you'll want full normalization:

```
<xsl:output normalization-form="fully-normalized" />
```

You will only need to perform this normalization if the result document contains unusual, un-normalized characters, which will only happen if either the source document or the stylesheet itself contains unusual, un-normalized characters, both of which are very rare.

Summary The `normalization-form` attribute specifies whether the output should be Unicode normalized, and which normalization form should be used.

The third formatting attribute only applies to the `xml`, `html`, and `xhtml` output methods and controls whether extra indentation is added to the document to make it easier to read. If you specify `yes` for the `indent` attribute, then the XSLT processor is free to add whitespace-only text nodes to the document, to put elements on new lines or indent them. The `indent` attribute defaults to `yes` if you use the `html` or `xhtml` output methods, but in this case the processor should only add whitespace if it makes no difference to how the result looks in a browser. Indentation can be very helpful when you need to look at the document that you've just generated, especially if it's highly structured, but of course it adds to the size of the document, so you should only use it if people need to read the document after the transformation. For example:

```
<xsl:output indent="yes" />
```

Summary If the `indent` attribute has the value `yes`, then the XSLT processor can add whitespace to the output of the transformation to make it more readable.

As we've seen, when an XSLT processor outputs an XML document, it will escape all the markup-significant characters, such as < and &, in the document, to create a well-formed XML file. But an alternative method, which is useful when there are a large number of characters that need to be escaped, is to have a CDATA section wrapped around the text. If we go back to the example that we looked at earlier, we can see that an alternative XML serialization of the result tree would be

```
<p><![CDATA[
This paragraph contains a line break,]]><br /><![CDATA[
& characters that must be escaped in XML and HTML,
& a boolean attribute in the following:
]]><input name="answer" value="OK" type="checkbox" checked="checked" />
</p>
```

In the preceding, the text node children of the <p> element are wrapped in CDATA sections, so the ampersands that they contain don't have to be escaped with &. Normally, an XSLT processor will escape the individual special characters rather than use a CDATA section, but you can use the cdata-section-elements attribute to tell it to wrap the text node children of particular elements in CDATA sections instead. The cdata-section-elements attribute lists the elements within which text nodes should be wrapped in CDATA sections, separated by spaces. For example, to tell the XSLT processor to wrap the content of <script> and <style> elements in CDATA sections, you should use

```
<xsl:output cdata-section-elements="script style" />
```

Note If you have multiple <xsl:output> elements with the same name, then all the cdata-section-elements attributes are combined into a single attribute value.

Summary The cdata-section-elements attribute lists the elements whose text node children should be wrapped in CDATA sections.

Generating XHTML

In previous chapters, the XSLT processor has usually been using the html output method when transforming the TV guide because it's detected that the document element of the result tree that we've produced is an <html> element that isn't in a namespace. In this chapter, within TVGuide3.xsl, we changed so that the <html> document element was in the XHTML namespace, and the processor silently switched to using the xhtml output method.

In this example, we'll tweak the XHTML that we're producing to make the XHTML easier to read. TVGuide9.xsl will be based on TVGuide7.xsl (so we don't have to worry about generating multiple result documents as we did with TVGuide8.xsl).

First, it doesn't hurt to add an <xsl:output> element in TVGuide9.xsl to explicitly tell the processor to use the xhtml output method:

```
<xsl:output method="xhtml" />
```

To create a compliant XHTML document, we also need to add a DOCTYPE declaration to the output, using the doctype-public and doctype-system attributes on the <xsl:output> element:

```
<xsl:output method="xhtml"
            doctype-public="-//W3C//DTD XHTML 1.1//EN"
            doctype-system="DTD/xhtml11.dtd" />
```

That's all that you *need* to do to generate XHTML 1.1, but you might also find it helpful to ask the XSLT processor to use ISO-8859-1 as the character encoding, so that you can open the file easily in your text editor. It's also neater if the values of <script> and <style> elements are wrapped in CDATA sections:

```
<xsl:output method="xhtml"
            doctype-public="-//W3C//DTD XHTML 1.1//EN"
            doctype-system="DTD/xhtml11.dtd"
            cdata-section-elements="script style"
            encoding="ISO-8859-1" />
```

Having made these changes, when you transform `TVGuide.xml` with `TVGuide9.xsl` to produce `TVGuide9.html`, the top level of the resulting document should look something like the following:

```
<?xml version="1.0" encoding="ISO-8859-1"?>
<!DOCTYPE html
  PUBLIC "-//W3C//DTD XHTML 1.1//EN" "DTD/xhtml11.dtd">
<html xmlns="http://www.w3.org/1999/xhtml">
   <head>
      <meta http-equiv="Content-Type" content="text/html; charset=ISO-8859-1"/>
      <title>TV Guide</title>
      <link rel="stylesheet" href="TVGuide.css"/>
      <script type="text/javascript"><![CDATA[

        function toggle(element) {
          if (element.style.display == 'none') {
            element.style.display = 'block';
          } else {
            element.style.display = 'none';
          }
        }

      ]]></script></head>
   <body>
      <h1>TV Guide</h1>
      ...
   </body>
</html>
```

Note Your processor might use different numbers of spaces when it indents your result, or choose different places to add indentation.

This XHTML document will look the same as the HTML document that we were generating earlier in most web browsers. Internet Explorer, for example, displays `TVGuide9.html` as shown in Figure 8-16.

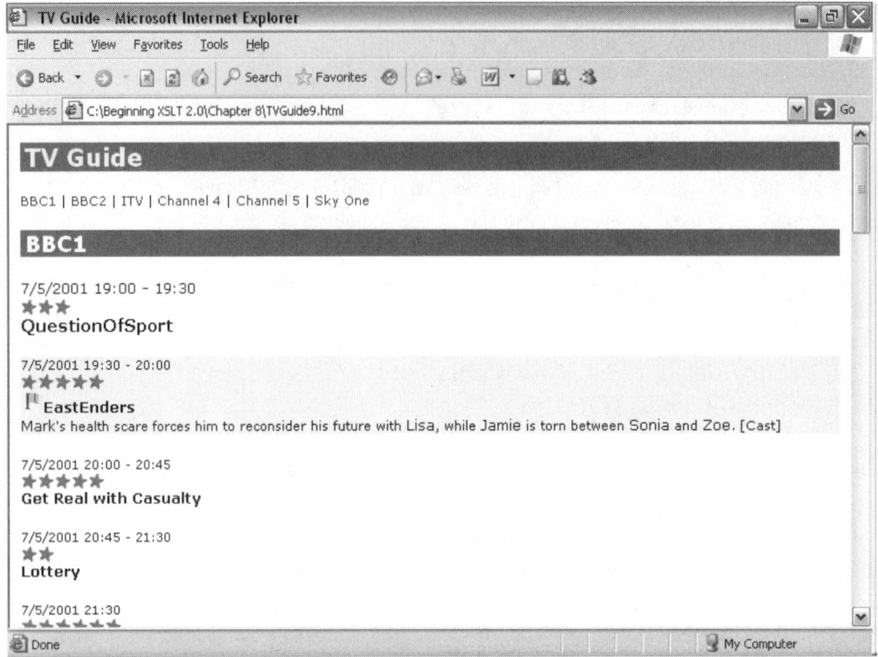

Figure 8-16. *Viewing* `TVGuide9.html` *in Internet Explorer*

Try removing the indentation (by setting the `indent` attribute to `no`) and changing the encoding used to save the file by changing the `encoding` attribute to `UTF-16` to see how this changes the look of the document in your text editor.

Summary

In this chapter, we've looked at the two components of creating some output from an XSLT transformation:

- Creating a result document
- Serializing the result document

You've learned about several new elements that enable you to generate and add nodes to the result tree. Some of the instructions that you've seen in this chapter simply give an extra bit of functionality over and above the methods you've already seen of creating elements, attributes, and text. Using `<xsl:element>`, `<xsl:attribute>`, and `<xsl:text>` when you don't need to can make your stylesheet longer and (arguably) harder to read, so it's worth thinking about whether you really need to use them before you do so.

However, there are no methods for creating comments and processing instructions aside from using `<xsl:comment>` and `<xsl:processing-instruction>` (unless you've got one that you can copy with `<xsl:copy>` or `<xsl:copy-of>`). You've also seen how to use attribute sets, defined by `<xsl:attribute-set>`, to add several attributes to an element at once, whether it's created with a literal result element or using `<xsl:element>`, how to use `<xsl:namespace>` to add a namespace node if it's not being added automatically, and how to create a document node explicitly using `<xsl:document>`.

You can use XSLT 2.0 to generate multiple result documents from a single transformation using the `<xsl:result-document>` instruction. This makes it easy to create whole sets of pages from a single XML document.

Once you've built a result tree, you'll usually need to output it to a file. This serialization process is governed either by an output definition specified with an `<xsl:output>` element or directly on a `<xsl:result-document>` instruction, and you've learned about all of the attributes that control serialization, the most important ones being the following:

- `method`—Determines whether the output is serialized as XML, XHTML, HTML, or text
- `version` (`output-version` on `<xsl:result-document>`)—Sets the version of XML or HTML that's used
- `media-type`—Sets the content type (or mime-type) of the output
- `doctype-public` and `doctype-system`—Add a `DOCTYPE` declaration to the XML, XHTML, or HTML document
- `encoding`—Sets the character encoding of the output
- `indent`—Tells the XSLT processor to produce indented output, which makes it more readable
- `cdata-section-elements`—Tells the XSLT processor which text nodes to wrap in CDATA sections

You've also learned how to use character maps to create documents that use entity references in place of unusual characters, and how to use them with placeholder characters in order to generate output that isn't quite XML.

These first eight chapters have introduced you to XSLT and shown you the basic principles of constructing transformations and the theory behind querying the source tree and generating the result tree. Thus far, we've been going through the concepts gradually, step by step, giving you a good grounding in the fundamentals of XSLT. The rest of the chapters in this book build on what you've learned up till now, and you can feel free to tackle the next five chapters in any order you want—they each deal with a particular aspect of authoring XSLT stylesheets, but there's no need to go through them in order if one strikes you as particularly interesting.

Review Questions

1. What are the two main ways in which you can add a new element node to the result tree? What are the advantages and disadvantages of each?
2. What else do you need to know to work out what namespace the elements generated by the following instructions are in?

```
<html>...</html>
<xsl:element name="html">...</xsl:element>
<xsl:element name="{$prefix}:html">...</xsl:element>
<xsl:element name="html" namespace="{$namespace}">...</xsl:element>
```

3. Write a template that matches any element in the XHTML namespace and generates a copy of that element in no namespace.

4. What are the three main ways in which you can create a text node?

5. What will the value of the generated <value> element be in the following code?

```
<value>
  <xsl:sequence select="(1, 2, 3)" />
  <xsl:text>4</xsl:text>
</value>
```

6. What two reasons might you have for using <xsl:text> rather than literal text within a template?

7. In what situations would you use <xsl:attribute> rather than adding an attribute literally to a literal result element?

8. Look at the following piece of XSLT. What value will the class attribute on the <p> element have?

```
<xsl:template match="Program">
  <p xsl:use-attribute-sets="program show"
     class="{local-name()}">
    <xsl:attribute name="class">episode</xsl:attribute>
  </p>
</xsl:template>
<xsl:attribute-set name="program">
  <xsl:attribute name="class">program</xsl:attribute>
</xsl:attribute-set>
<xsl:attribute-set name="show">
  <xsl:attribute name="class">show</xsl:attribute>
</xsl:attribute-set>
```

9. When would you use an identity template to copy a branch of the source tree rather than <xsl:copy-of>?

10. How would you generate the following ASP directive using XSLT?

```
<%@ Page Language="VB" %>
```

11. Which output method should you use to generate XHTML? What other attributes do you need to set on <xsl:output> to create a conformant XHTML document?

CHAPTER 9

Sorting and Grouping

Now that you've got a good understanding of the fundamentals of processing XML with XSLT, it's time to move on to look at some of the other XSLT elements that support you in getting the output that you want. In this chapter, we're going to be looking at changing the order in which nodes are processed by sorting them and at how to structure the output that you generate into groups.

In this chapter, you'll learn

- How to process sequences in different orders
- How to sort by multiple values
- How to group information by value and by position
- How to add structure to flat XML

Sorting

When you use `<xsl:for-each>` or `<xsl:apply-templates>` to process a sequence, the items are processed in whatever order they appear in the sequence. When you've selected a sequence of nodes using a path, this is **document order**—the order in which the nodes appear in the document. So, for example, when we process `TVGuide.xml` with `TVGuide.xsl`, we create an XHTML page that lists the channels in the TV guide in the order in which the `<Channel>` elements are listed in the XML document, and lists the programs showing on that channel in the order in which the `<Program>` elements are listed in `TVGuide.xml`.

Often document order is precisely the order that you want, particularly in document-oriented XML where the ordering of sections or paragraphs within a document is important rhetorically. However, in data-oriented XML, the ordering of particular items in the source XML document may very well not be the order in which you want to present them, or you might want to be able to present different orders for different situations. For example, we might want to sort the channels alphabetically by name, or by the ratings of the programs that they show, so that the "best" channel comes first.

XPath has a `reverse()` function that you can use to simply reverse a sequence. For example, to apply templates to the `<Channel>` elements in our TV guide in the reverse order from that in which they're given in `TVGuide.xml`, you could use

```
<xsl:apply-templates select="reverse(Channel)" />
```

■ **Summary** The `reverse()` function reverses the order of the items in a sequence.

For more sophisticated sorting, though, XSLT provides the <xsl:sort> element, which can be used within <xsl:for-each> or <xsl:apply-templates> to change the order in which the XSLT processor goes through the items that are selected by the instruction. You can also use <xsl:sort> with a special <xsl:perform-sort> instruction to create a sorted sequence, which is useful if you want to reuse the sorted sequence several times. The <xsl:perform-sort> instruction's `select` attribute selects the sequence to be sorted.

In its basic form (with no attributes), the <xsl:sort> element sorts the items in order based on their type (so strings are ordered alphabetically, numbers are ordered numerically, and so on). Unless you're using Schema-Aware processing, nodes are ordered alphabetically. For example, the following will create a sequence of <Character> elements in alphabetical order:

```
<xsl:perform-sort select="CastMember/Character">
  <xsl:sort />
</xsl:perform-sort>
```

■ **Summary** The <xsl:perform-sort> instruction sorts the items specified in its `select` attribute using the <xsl:sort> elements that it contains.

If you need to sort by something other than the string value of the nodes that you're processing, the <xsl:sort> element can take a `select` attribute, which contains an XPath expression that's evaluated as a string. For example, the following will apply templates to the <CastMember> elements, sorting them in alphabetical order by their child <Character> element's <Name>:

```
<xsl:for-each select="CastMember">
  <xsl:sort select="Character/Name" />
  ...
</xsl:for-each>
```

■ **Note** In <xsl:for-each> instructions, <xsl:sort> elements must come before the body of the <xsl:for-each>, that is, before the part that indicates what should be generated for each of the nodes being processed.

If it's difficult to calculate the value that you want to sort by using a single XPath expression, you can also use the content of the <xsl:sort> element to indicate the value that you want to sort by. The content of the <xsl:sort> element is a sequence constructor, which should return a sequence containing at most a single item. For example, to sort the channels by quality of programming, based on multiplying the rating of each program by the number of minutes it lasts and dividing by the total duration of the programs on the channel, you could use

```
<xsl:apply-templates select="Channel">
  <xsl:sort>
    <!-- create a new set of <Program> elements with a duration attribute
         giving the number of minutes that the program lasts -->
    <xsl:variable name="programInfo" as="element(Program)+">
      <xsl:for-each select="Program">
        <Program rating="{@rating}"
                 duration="{xdt:dayTimeDuration(Duration) div
                            xdt:dayTimeDuration('PT1M')}" />
      </xsl:for-each>
    </xsl:variable>
    <xsl:sequence select="sum(for $p in $programInfo
                              return ($p/@rating * $p/@duration)) div
                          sum($programInfo/@duration)" />
  </xsl:sort>
</xsl:apply-templates>
```

Summary By default, the items in a sequence are processed in the order in which they appear in the sequence. You can process them in a different order using `<xsl:sort>` within `<xsl:for-each>` or `<xsl:apply-templates>`.

When you really don't care about the order in which items are displayed, you can use the `unordered()` function to indicate to the processor that a sequence should be processed in whatever order is most efficient. The `unordered()` function doesn't really change the order of the sequence; rather it tells the processor that it should create that sequence in whatever order it likes. For example, it means the processor doesn't have to sort a sequence of nodes into document order (which can be time-consuming).

It's rare to use the `unordered()` function in XSLT, since usually you *do* care about the order in which items are processed and usually the speed with which the processor creates a sequence isn't critical.

Summary The `unordered()` function indicates to the XSLT processor that the order of the items in a sequence doesn't matter.

Sorting Channels by Name

`TVGuide.xsl` displays the channels within our TV guide in two ways—within a list of channels given at the top and bottom of the page, and within the body of the page itself. As you can see in Figure 9-1, currently the channels are listed in the same order that they're defined in the XML document.

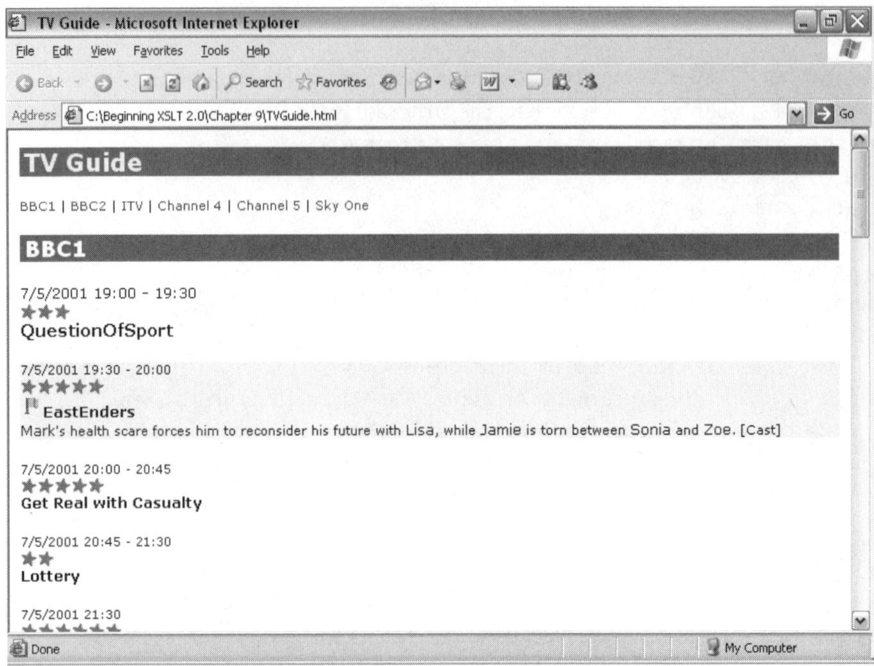

Figure 9-1. *Viewing* TVGuide.html *in Internet Explorer*

To help people find the channel that they're after, it might be handy to have them sorted by name instead, which we'll do in the next version of our stylesheet, TVGuide2.xsl.

The list of <Channel> elements that appears at the top and bottom of the page is generated by applying templates to the <Channel> elements in ChannelList mode, in the definition of the $ChannelList global variable:

```
<xsl:variable name="ChannelList" as="element()+">
  <p><xsl:apply-templates select="/TVGuide/Channel" mode="ChannelList" /></p>
</xsl:variable>
```

The template that tells the processor to apply templates to the <Channel> elements to make up the body of the page is the template matching <TVGuide> elements:

```
<xsl:template match="TVGuide">
  <xsl:sequence select="$ChannelList" />
  <xsl:apply-templates select="Channel" />
  <xsl:sequence select="$ChannelList" />
</xsl:template>
```

Since both these templates should process <Channel> elements in the same order, it would make sense to a sequence of <Channel> elements sorted by name in a global variable. To create this sorted sequence, we should use the <xsl:perform-sort> instruction with an <xsl:sort> that uses the <Name> children of the <Channel> elements to sort the <Channel> elements alphabetically. The variable declaration looks like this:

```
<xsl:variable name="Channels" as="element(Channel)+">
  <xsl:perform-sort select="/TVGuide/Channel">
    <xsl:sort select="Name" />
  </xsl:perform-sort>
</xsl:variable>
```

We can then refer to the sorted sequence held in the `$Channels` variable within the `<xsl:apply-templates>` instructions in the `$ChannelList` global variable and the TVGuide template as follows:

```
<xsl:variable name="ChannelList" as="element()+">
  <p>
    <xsl:apply-templates select="$Channels" mode="ChannelList">
  </p>
</xsl:variable>

<xsl:template match="TVGuide">
  <xsl:sequence select="$ChannelList" />
  <xsl:apply-templates select="$Channels" />
  <xsl:sequence select="$ChannelList" />
</xsl:template>
```

Having made these changes in `TVGuide2.xsl`, the result of the transformation (`TVGuide2.html`) is shown in Figure 9-2.

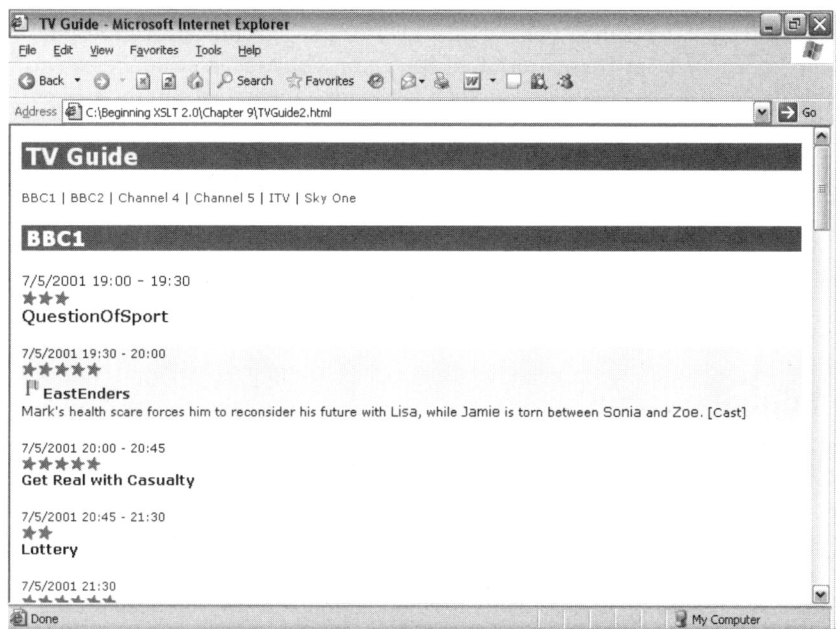

Figure 9-2. *Viewing* `TVGuide2.html` *in Internet Explorer*

You can see that the order of the channels at the top of the page has changed, with ITV coming after Channel 4 and Channel 5 (Figure 9-2 doesn't show it, but so has the ordering of the channels within the body of the page).

Sorting in Different Orders

By default, `<xsl:sort>` sorts in ascending order, first values that begin with `A`, then those that begin with `B`, and so on. There are four attributes on `<xsl:sort>` that give you control over the precise ordering that the XSLT processor uses:

- `order`—Determines whether the values are sorted in `ascending` (the default) or `descending` order.
- `collation`—The URI for the collation that should be used when sorting strings.
- `lang`—The code for the language that should be used to sort the values. This defaults to the language that's being used on the system on which the transformation takes place.
- `case-order`—Determines whether lowercase letters are sorted before uppercase letters (`lower-first`) or vice versa (`upper-first`). The default depends on the language that's being used.

■ **Note** You learned about collations in Chapter 4.

The `collation`, `lang`, and `case-order` attributes are used when the value that's used to sort the items is a string or an untyped value—in other words, when you're doing an alphabetical sort. The `lang` and `case-order` attributes are only used if there's no `collation` attribute to indicate how strings should be sorted; in essence, they enable the processor to choose an appropriate collation based on the language and case order that you want. The processor might give an error if it doesn't recognize the collation that you ask it to use, or it might just sort the strings using the default collation.

■ **Summary** The `order` attribute on `<xsl:sort>` determines whether the nodes are sorted in ascending or descending order. You can fine-tune alphabetical sorts with the `collation`, `lang`, and `case-order` attributes.

Sorting Nonalphabetically

The way in which the `<xsl:sort>` element sorts values is determined by the type of the value that you select using the `select` attribute. Untyped nodes (which are the only kind of nodes you have in Basic XSLT) are sorted alphabetically, so if you sorted elements holding the numbers 1 to 100, you would end up with the order `1`, `10`, `100`, `11`, `12`, ... `2`, `20`, and so on, which isn't the correct numerical order.

If the values that you're sorting by should be sorted nonalphabetically, you need to cast the values to the appropriate type so that they're sorted in the appropriate way. For example, to sort the `<Program>` elements by their duration, you need to cast the value of the `<Duration>` element to an `xdt:dayTimeDuration`:

```
<xsl:apply-templates select="Program">
  <xsl:sort select="xdt:dayTimeDuration(Duration)" />
</xsl:apply-templates>
```

Note The `<xsl:sort>` element has a `data-type` attribute for backwards compatibility with XSLT 1.0, which can hold the special values `text` or `number`, or a qualified name. However, you should use casting to determine the sort order rather than the `data-type` attribute.

Summary The way in which values are sorted depends on their type. Untyped nodes should be cast to an appropriate type for the kind of sorting you want to do.

Sorting by Number

To try out sorting numerically and sorting in different orders, we'll now try to sort the channels in our TV guide according to the ratings of the programs that they show. Each `<Program>` element has a `rating` attribute, ranging from `1` (lousy) to `10` (superb). The channels should be sorted so that the channels that have programs with the highest average rating are sorted first.

Our first problem is working out the average ratings of the programs shown on a particular channel. As you'll recall from Chapter 6, you can get the average value of a sequence using the `avg()` function. In this case, the values are the values of the `rating` attributes of the `<Program>` element children of the context `<Channel>` element:

```
avg(Program/@rating)
```

To sort by the average rating, we just use this expression in the `select` attribute of the `<xsl:sort>`, as in `TVGuide3.xsl`. Since the `avg()` function returns a number, the values will be sorted numerically rather than alphabetically:

```
<xsl:variable name="Channels" as="element(Channel)+">
  <xsl:perform-sort select="/TVGuide/Channel">
    <xsl:sort select="avg(Program/@rating)" />
  </xsl:perform-sort>
</xsl:variable>
```

We want the best channels (the ones with the highest program ratings) to come first in our list, so the `<Channel>` elements should be sorted in *descending* order by adding an `order` attribute with the value `descending` to the `<xsl:sort>`:

```
<xsl:variable name="Channels" as="element(Channel)+">
  <xsl:perform-sort select="/TVGuide/Channel">
    <xsl:sort select="avg(Program/@rating)" order="descending" />
  </xsl:perform-sort>
</xsl:variable>
```

We also want to display the average rating of the channel underneath the channel's name within the main body of the page. The average rating is a number, which might have lots of decimal places (since we're calculating it through division), so we'll format it using `format-number()` to only show one decimal place when we display it. The new template for `<Channel>` elements in `TVGuide3.xsl` is as follows:

```
<xsl:template match="Channel">
  <xsl:apply-templates select="Name" />
  <p class="average">
```

```
    <xsl:text>average rating: </xsl:text>
    <xsl:value-of select="format-number(avg(Program/@rating), '0.0')" />
  </p>
  <xsl:apply-templates select="Program" />
</xsl:template>
```

Note You learned about the `format-number()` function in Chapter 5.

And we'll add some styling information for this new paragraph, in `TVGuide2.css`, as follows:

```
p.average {
  font-size: 0.8em;
  margin: 0;
  text-align: right;
}
```

The result of transforming `TVGuide.xml` with `TVGuide3.xsl` is `TVGuide3.html`, which is shown in Figure 9-3.

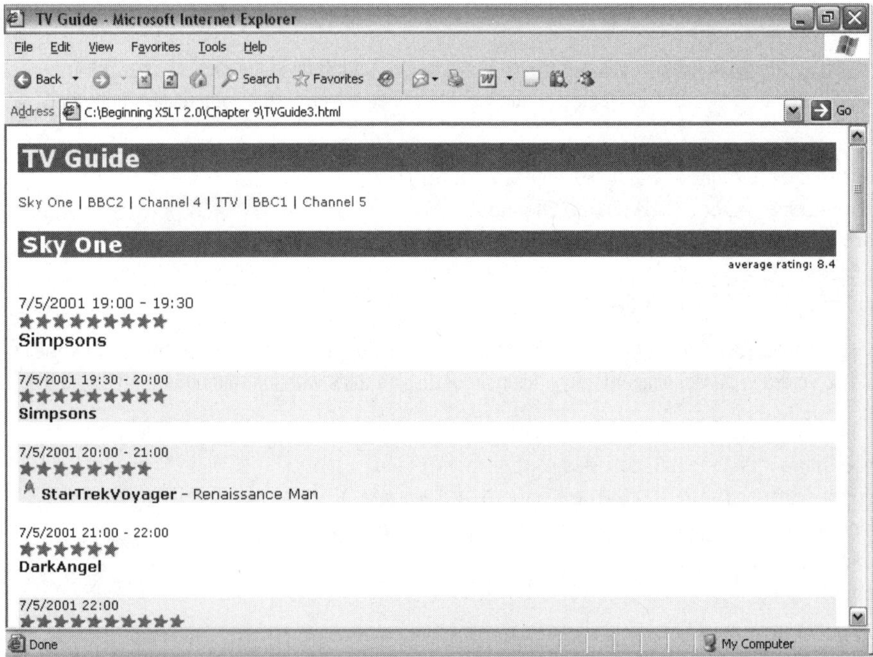

Figure 9-3. *Viewing* `TVGuide3.html` *in Internet Explorer*

As you can see, Sky One tops the listing because it contains the programs with the highest ratings; feel free to change the ratings within `TVGuide.xml` to see how that affects the ordering of the channels.

Multiple Sorts

You can use as many <xsl:sort> elements as you like within an <xsl:for-each>, an <xsl:apply-templates>, or an <xsl:perform-sort> instruction. If two items have the same value for the first <xsl:sort>, then they're sorted in the order specified by the second <xsl:sort>; if they're still the same, they're sorted according to the third <xsl:sort>; and so on.

For example, sorting by character name isn't very helpful in our example because the character names are in the form firstName lastName, so the character whose first name comes first alphabetically is sorted first. Traditionally in English-speaking countries, names are sorted by last name and then by first name. Assuming that all the character names just consist of a first name and a last name (such that none of the characters have middle names), we can access the last name by taking the substring after the space, and the first name by taking the substring before the space. The first sort needs to select the last name, and the second sort selects the first name:

```
<xsl:for-each select="CastMember">
  <xsl:sort select="substring-after(Character/Name, ' ')" />
  <xsl:sort select="substring-before(Character/Name, ' ')" />
  ...
</xsl:for-each>
```

■ **Summary** You can have multiple <xsl:sort> elements—each subsequent <xsl:sort> is a subsort of the previous <xsl:sort>.

Sorting by Average Rating and First Program Rating

Two of the channels in TVGuide.xml turn out to have the same average rating for their programs—Channel 4 and BBC2. As shown in Figure 9-4, in TVGuide3.html, BBC2 is listed first because it appears first in TVGuide.xml.

In TVGuide4.xsl, when two channels have the same average rating, we'll sort them based on the rating of their first <Program> element, in descending order so that the channel whose current program has the highest rating comes first.

This two-level sort needs two <xsl:sort> elements, the first for the average rating for all the programs and the second for the rating of the first program. Remember to cast the rating of the first program to an xs:integer; otherwise, the rating 10 would count as lower than the rating 9:

```
<xsl:variable name="Channels" as="element(Channel)+">
  <xsl:perform-sort select="/TVGuide/Channel">
    <xsl:sort select="avg(Program/@rating)" order="descending" />
    <xsl:sort select="xs:integer(Program[1]/@rating)" order="descending" />
  </xsl:perform-sort>
</xsl:variable>
```

This two-level sort is specified in TVGuide4.xsl. Transform TVGuide.xml with TVGuide4.xsl; the result (TVGuide4.html) is shown in Figure 9-5.

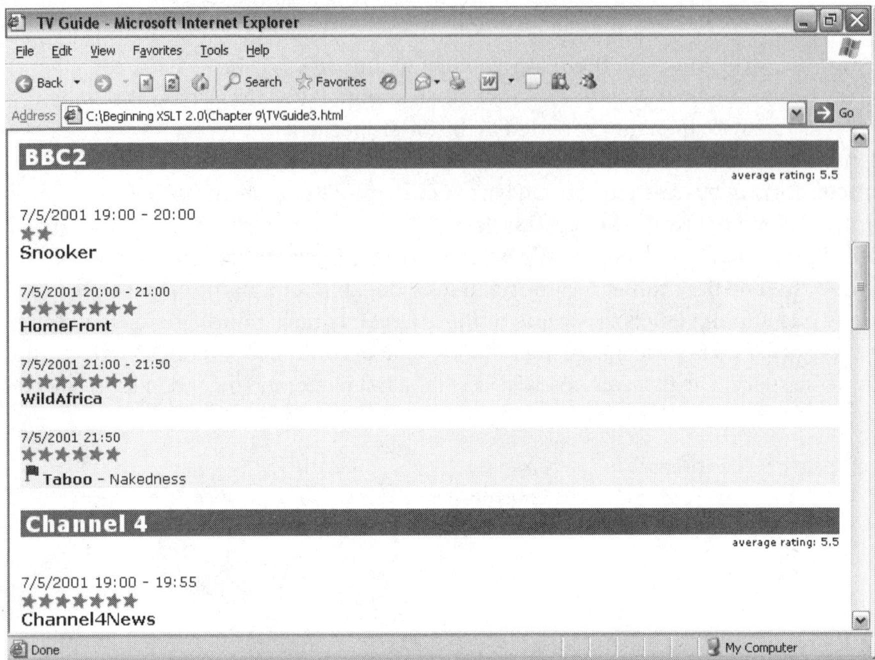

Figure 9-4. *BBC2 and Channel 4 in* `TVGuide3.html`

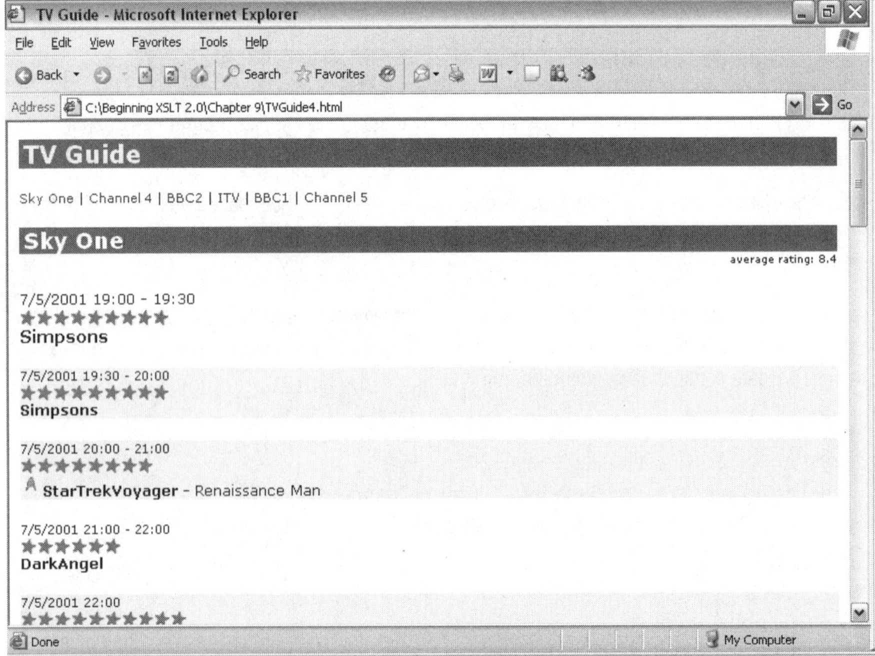

Figure 9-5. *BBC2 and Channel 4 in* `TVGuide4.html`

Channel 4 now appears before BBC2 in the list of channels at the top of the page (and in the main body of the page) because the first program showing on Channel 4 (*Channel 4 News*) has a rating of 7 whereas the first program showing on BBC2 (*Snooker*) has a rating of 2.

Flexible Sorting

Part of the point of using XML and XSLT is that it separates content from presentation. The content part of a page is stored within an XML document, while the stylesheet that you use with that XML document determines the way that the information is presented to the user.

The order in which information is displayed is one of the main ways that you might want to change the presentation of a document. However, while the ordering of the items changes, the way that they're presented and the page around them shouldn't change very much (or at all). In other words, you want to keep the same stylesheet, but use a stylesheet parameter (or other technique) to determine the order in which the items are sorted.

There are two aspects to flexible sorts: changing the **sort order** (for example, whether you sort in ascending or descending order) and changing the **sort value** so that the items are actually sorted on different things.

Flexible Sort Orders

All the attributes that change the order in which an `<xsl:sort>` arranges nodes (aside from the `select` attribute, which chooses the sort value) are attribute value templates. Most importantly, that includes the `order` attribute and the `collation` attribute. Anything that you put within `{}`s in the attribute values is interpreted as an XPath expression and evaluated to give the value of the attribute.

■ **Note** The attribute value templates are evaluated relative to the current node at the point of the `<xsl:for-each>`, `<xsl:apply-templates>`, or `<xsl:perform-sort>` instruction, not relative to the items that are being sorted; this ensures that the same value is used for all the items that are being sorted; otherwise you could end up with some items being sorted in ascending order and others in descending order, which wouldn't make any sense.

You should take care, though, when using attribute value templates within the attributes on XSLT elements, because if the attribute evaluates to a value that isn't allowed, the stylesheet will usually halt with an error. For example, you should make sure that the value of the `order` attribute is set to either `ascending` or `descending`—any other value will cause an error.

■ **Summary** All the attributes on `<xsl:sort>`, aside from the `select` attribute, are attribute value templates, so you can determine their values "on the fly."

Changing Sort Order with a Parameter

In TVGuide5.xsl, we'll aim to use a stylesheet parameter to determine whether the channels should be sorted with the worst channels first (in ascending order on the average rating) or with the best channels first (in descending order on the average rating).

The first step is to declare the stylesheet parameter to hold the sort order, by adding an <xsl:param> element at the top level of the stylesheet. We'll set the parameter to 'descending' by default, so that unless the parameter is specifically given a value, the sort will give the most highly rated channels first:

```
<xsl:param name="sortOrder" as="xs:string" select="'descending'" />
```

In the definition of the $Channels variable, rather than fix the value of the order attribute of the two sorts, you need to calculate it dynamically based on the value of the $sortOrder parameter. You can use an attribute value template in the order attributes of the <xsl:sort> elements to insert the value of the $sortOrder parameter:

```
<xsl:variable name="Channels" as="element(Channel)+">
  <xsl:perform-sort select="/TVGuide/Channel">
    <xsl:sort select="avg(Program/@rating)" order="{$sortOrder}" />
    <xsl:sort select="xs:integer(Program[1]/@rating)" order="{$sortOrder}" />
  </xsl:perform-sort>
</xsl:variable>
```

When you transform TVGuide.xml with TVGuide5.xsl normally, you'll get the channels sorted in descending order by their average rating, exactly as you did in TVGuide4.html. However, you can pass the value ascending for the order attribute instead, using the command line, and the order will be reversed:

```
java net.sf.saxon.Transform -o TVGuide5.html TVGuide.xml TVGuide5.xsl
 sortOrder=ascending
```

The resulting TVGuide5.html is shown in Figure 9-6.

Channel 5 is listed first because it has the lowest average rating; Sky One is listed last because it has the highest average rating.

Now try passing the value 'up' as the value for the $sortOrder parameter. You should get an error from the XSLT processor. For example, with Saxon I get the error shown in Figure 9-7.

To make your stylesheet more robust, you should watch out for a bad value being passed in to the $sortOrder parameter, and make sure that the value that it's set to is either 'ascending' or 'descending'. One way to do this is by shadowing the stylesheet parameter with a local variable that sets itself based on the value of the $sortOrder parameter, as follows:

```
<xsl:variable name="Channels" as="element(Channel)+">
  <xsl:variable name="sortOrder" as="xs:string"
    select="if ($sortOrder = 'ascending') then 'ascending'
                                           else 'descending'" />
  <xsl:perform-sort select="/TVGuide/Channel">
    <xsl:sort select="avg(Program/@rating)" order="{$sortOrder}" />
    <xsl:sort select="xs:integer(Program[1]/@rating)" order="{$sortOrder}" />
  </xsl:perform-sort>
</xsl:variable>
```

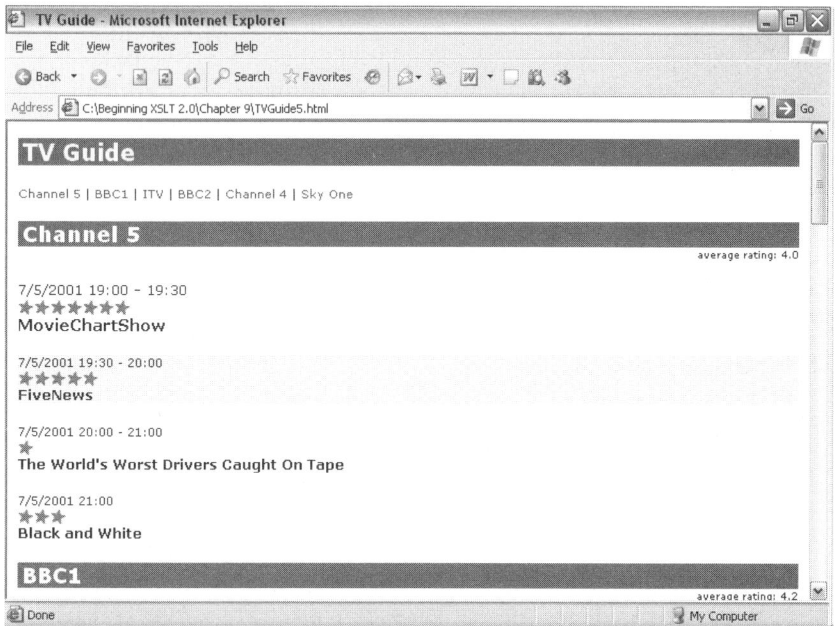

Figure 9-6. *Viewing* `TVGuide5.html` *in Internet Explorer*

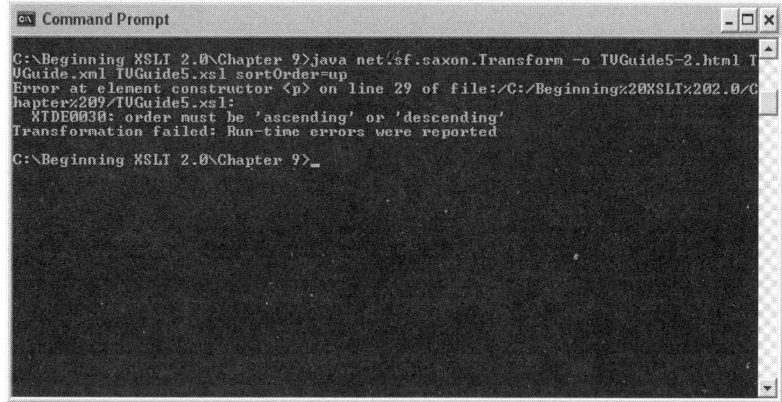

Figure 9-7. *Error when setting parameter to invalid value*

If you try running the same transformation with `$sortOrder` set to `up` (using `TVGuide6.xsl`, in which this change is made), you won't get an error (although the channels will be sorted in descending order, which might not be what's intended by the value `up`!).

Flexible Sort Values

It's more complicated to change *what* you want to sort on the fly than it is to change *how* that value should be sorted (as demonstrated previously). The select attribute isn't an attribute value template, so you can't pass a path into the stylesheet using a parameter and then use that path to choose what to sort.

However, the select attribute does take an XPath expression, which gives you a certain amount of flexibility in choosing what to sort by, and you can use the content of the <xsl:sort> element instead, which gives you a lot more. The easiest situations are where the parameter can hold the name of the child element that you want to sort by. In these cases, you can select the child element whose name has the same value as the parameter with

```
<xsl:sort select="*[name(.) = $sortBy]" />
```

■ **Caution** The usual issues surrounding qualified names apply; it would be better to test the local name of the element and its namespace URI, rather than testing its name as a string.

Sometimes the different sort values might come from several locations (rather than all being children of the nodes that are being sorted). For example, if we're sorting <Program> elements from TVGuide.xml, then $sortBy might be 'start' to get the start time (held in the <Start> element child), 'series' to get the series (held in the <Series> element child), or 'channel' to get the name of the channel it's on (held in its parent <Channel> element's child <Name> element). In these cases, you can use an if expression to select the correct node, as follows:

```
<xsl:sort select="if ($sortBy = 'start') then Start
                  else if ($sortBy = 'series') then Series
                  else if ($sortBy = 'channel') then ../Name
                  else ()" />
```

If you want to give even more flexibility, and provide a path to the relevant value, then you need to use either a user-defined function or a recursive template, called from the content of the <xsl:sort> element. We'll learn about user-defined functions and recursive templates in Chapter 11.

■ **Note** Some processors have an extension function that enables you to evaluate XPath expressions on the fly, which can help in situations like these. We'll be looking at extension functions in Chapter 14.

■ **Summary** You can choose what to sort by on the fly using predicates and if expressions within the select attribute of <xsl:sort>.

Grouping

Sorting and grouping are similar kinds of activities: in each you have a sequence of items that need to be arranged based on some value derived from the item. In XSLT 2.0, grouping is carried out using the <xsl:for-each-group> instruction, which is fairly similar to the <xsl:for-each>

instruction. You select the sequence of items that you want to group with the `select` attribute of `<xsl:for-each-group>`, and the content of the `<xsl:for-each-group>` instruction determines what's done for each group that's identified in the selected sequence.

Note The `distinct-values()` function, which you encountered in Chapter 7, can give you the unique items within a sequence, which you can then use to group a sequence, but `<xsl:for-each-group>` is a lot more sophisticated and efficient.

The details of the grouping itself is carried out by one of four attributes, which can be classified in two categories:

Grouping by value—The `group-by` and `group-adjacent` attributes hold XPath expressions that are evaluated for each item in the sequence to give a **grouping key**. With the `group-by` attribute, all the items with the same value for the grouping key are grouped together (effectively reordering the sequence). With the `group-adjacent` attribute, any consecutive items that have the same value for their grouping key are grouped together (the order of the sequence is retained).

Grouping in sequence—The `group-starting-with` and `group-ending-with` attributes hold patterns. The XSLT processor runs through the nodes in the sequence in turn. With the `group-starting-with` attribute, each time it comes across a node that matches the pattern, it starts a new group. With the `group-ending-with` attribute, it ends each group with a node that matches the pattern.

Note When calculating a grouping key, the expression held in the `group-by` or `group-adjacent` attribute is evaluated with the item as the context item and its position within the sequence as the context position. The type of the grouping key determines how values are compared when grouping the items (for example, whether it's done numerically or alphabetically).

For example, to group all the programs in the TV guide by the series that they belong to, you can use the following. The `select` attribute selects the programs that you want to group. The `group-by` attribute selects the value that you want to group by, namely the series that each program belongs to.

```
<xsl:for-each-group select="/TVGuide/Channel/Program" group-by="Series">
  ...
</xsl:for-each-group>
```

Summary The `<xsl:for-each-group>` instruction groups the items in the sequence selected by its `select` attribute based on either the value selected by the expression in its `group-by` or `group-adjacent` attributes, or into groups that start or end with nodes matching the pattern held in the `group-starting-with` or `group-ending-with` attributes.

The instructions within the <xsl:for-each-group> instruction are executed once per group. Usually, the groups will be ordered based on the position of their first item within the sequence that's being grouped. So in this example:

```
<xsl:for-each-group select="/TVGuide/Channel/Program" group-by="Series">
  ...
</xsl:for-each-group>
```

the first series listed will be the series specified by the first <Program> element in the TV guide. You can alter this default ordering using <xsl:sort> elements within the <xsl:for-each-group> instruction.

Tip Most commonly, when grouping by value using group-by, you want to sort the groups based on their grouping key. You can do this with <xsl:sort select="current-grouping-key()" />.

Within the <xsl:for-each-group> instruction, the current item is the first item in the group. Any expression within the <xsl:for-each-group> instruction is evaluated relative to the first <Program> element in a particular series. So, for example, you can give the title of the series using

```
<xsl:for-each-group select="/TVGuide/Channel/Program" group-by="Series">
  <h3><xsl:value-of select="Series" /></h3>
  ...
</xsl:for-each-group>
```

Usually it's useful to be able to know which items from the selected sequence belong to the group. You can get this sequence of items using the current-group() function. For example, to apply templates to the episodes in the series (the programs in the current group), you can use

```
<xsl:for-each-group select="/TVGuide/Channel/Program" group-by="Series">
  <h3><xsl:value-of select="Series" /></h3>
  <xsl:apply-templates select="current-group()" />
</xsl:for-each-group>
```

Summary Within an <xsl:for-each-group> instruction, the current-group() function returns the items in the current group.

When grouping by value with the group-by attribute, it's possible for an item to be placed in more than one group. For example, each program might star multiple actors. If you grouped programs based on the actors that appeared in them with

```
<xsl:for-each-group select="/TVGuide/Channel/Program"
                    group-by="CastList/CastMember/Actor/Name">
  ...
</xsl:for-each-group>
```

then each <Program> element could appear in several different groups. In this case, you need to be able to work out the name of the actor for the particular group; you can't work that out based on the current <Program> element because the current <Program> element might appear in several groups. Instead, you need the current-grouping-key() function, which gives you the grouping key common to all the items in the current group. For example, to sort the groups by the actor's name, give a heading providing the actor's name, and then apply templates to the programs the actor stars in, you could use

```
<xsl:for-each-group select="/TVGuide/Channel/Program"
                    group-by="CastList/CastMember/Actor/Name">
  <xsl:sort select="current-grouping-key()" />
  <h3><xsl:value-of select="current-grouping-key()" /></h3>
  <xsl:apply-templates select="current-group()" />
</xsl:for-each-group>
```

Summary Within an <xsl:for-each-group> instruction that uses group-by or group-adjacent, the current-grouping-key() function returns the grouping key common to the items in the current group.

Grouping Programs by Hour

In TVGuide.xml, all the programs showing on a particular channel are grouped together. It would make it easier to see what was on at a particular time if the programs were grouped by the hour at which they are being shown and sorted by the precise time at which they're shown.

To achieve this presentation, we need to group the programs (all the <Program> elements, whatever channel they're on) according to the hour at which they are shown. Currently, the programs are grouped by channel (because that's how the TV guide XML is structured): we apply templates to the sorted <Channel> elements, and processing the <Channel> elements entails processing the <Program> elements:

```
<xsl:template match="TVGuide">
  <xsl:sequence select="$ChannelList" />
  <xsl:apply-templates select="$Channels" />
  <xsl:sequence select="$ChannelList" />
</xsl:template>

<xsl:template match="Channel">
  ...
  <xsl:apply-templates select="Program" />
</xsl:template>
```

In TVGuide7.xsl, in the template matching the <TVGuide> element, we want to group all the programs based on the hour in which they're shown. We can do this by selecting all the <Program> element children of the <Channel> elements and grouping by the hour (as provided by the hours-from-dateTime() function):

```
<xsl:template match="TVGuide">
  <xsl:for-each-group select="Channel/Program"
                      group-by="hours-from-dateTime(Start)">
```

```
    ...
  </xsl:for-each-group>
</xsl:template>
```

We need to sort these groups based on the hour. Otherwise, if the first program that starts between 20:00 and 21:00 occurs in a channel listed before the channel showing the first program that starts between 19:00 and 20:00, then the first group will be from 20:00 rather than from 19:00. So we need to add an `<xsl:sort>` element that uses the current grouping key (the hour) to sort the programs:

```
<xsl:template match="TVGuide">
  <xsl:for-each-group select="Channel/Program"
                      group-by="hours-from-dateTime(Start)">
    <xsl:sort select="current-grouping-key()" />
    ...
  </xsl:for-each-group>
</xsl:template>
```

For each group, we want to create a heading that indicates the hour on which the programs in that group are shown. This is the same as the value that's being used to group the items, so we can use the `current-grouping-key()` function to get it:

```
<xsl:template match="TVGuide">
  <xsl:for-each-group select="Channel/Program"
                      group-by="hours-from-dateTime(Start)">
    <xsl:sort select="current-grouping-key()" />
    <h2>Showing from <xsl:value-of select="current-grouping-key()" />:00</h2>
    ...
  </xsl:for-each-group>
</xsl:template>
```

To give the details of the programs showing during that hour, we need to apply templates to the `<Program>` elements that are part of the current group, which we get at using the `current-group()` function:

```
<xsl:template match="TVGuide">
  <xsl:for-each-group select="Channel/Program"
                      group-by="hours-from-dateTime(Start)">
    <xsl:sort select="current-grouping-key()" />
    <h2>Showing from <xsl:value-of select="current-grouping-key()" />:00</h2>
    <xsl:apply-templates select="current-group()" />
  </xsl:for-each-group>
</xsl:template>
```

We actually want these `<Program>` elements to be sorted based on the time at which they start, which means sorting them by their `<Start>` child element (cast to an `xs:dateTime`). We can also sort them by their duration, so that the shorter programs appear earlier in the list:

```
<xsl:template match="TVGuide">
  <xsl:for-each-group select="Channel/Program"
                      group-by="hours-from-dateTime(Start)">
    <xsl:sort select="current-grouping-key()" />
    <h2>Showing from <xsl:value-of select="current-grouping-key()" />:00</h2>
```

```
    <xsl:apply-templates select="current-group()">
      <xsl:sort select="xs:dateTime(Start)" />
      <xsl:sort select="xdt:dayTimeDuration(Duration)" />
    </xsl:apply-templates>
  </xsl:for-each-group>
</xsl:template>
```

Transforming `TVGuide.xml` with `TVGuide7.xsl` gives `TVGuide7.html`, which is shown in Figure 9-8.

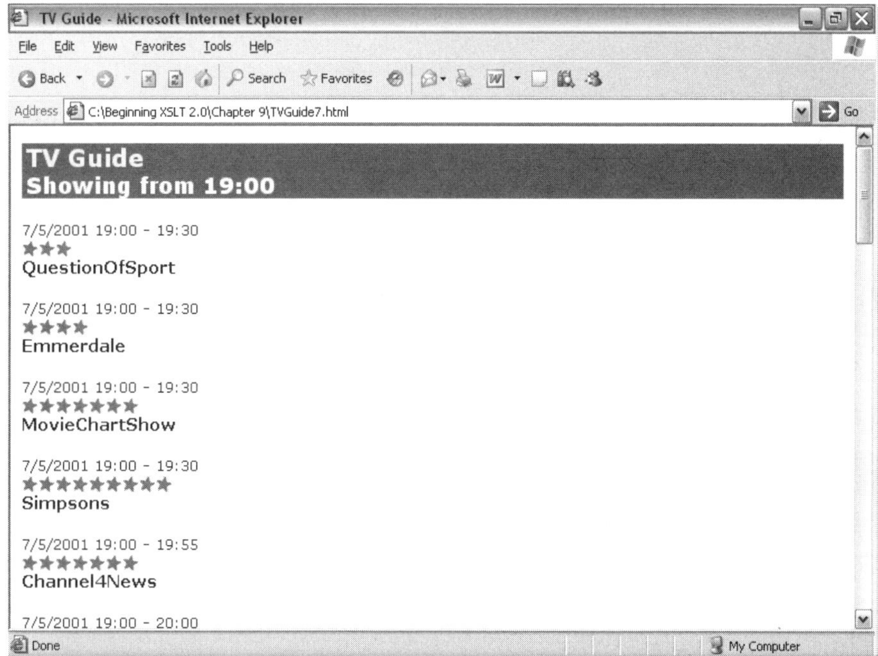

Figure 9-8. *Viewing* `TVGuide7.html` *in Internet Explorer*

The programs are now sorted according to their start time and duration, with headings indicating each hour.

Grouping by Position

One of the ways in which grouping is often used is to split up large amounts of data onto separate pages, so that each page lists up to ten items, for example. This kind of grouping can be achieved using either the `group-by` or the `group-adjacent` attributes on `<xsl:for-each-group>`.

Here, you need to define a grouping key such that the first ten items have the same value, as do the next ten items, and the next. The easiest such grouping key uses the `position()` function as follows:

```
(position() - 1) idiv 10
```

Tip Of course, you can use any number you like rather than `10` in the preceding example, to get groups of different sizes; you might even pass in that group size as a parameter to the stylesheet.

Either the `group-by` or `group-adjacent` attribute can be used with this grouping key, since the items must be in the desired order for the grouping key to work at all. For example:

```
<xsl:for-each-group select="$items"
                    group-adjacent="(position() - 1) idiv 10">
  ...
</xsl:for-each-group>
```

Note To get separate pages for each group, use the `<xsl:result-document>` instruction, which you met in the last chapter.

Summary You can group a sequence into items of a particular size using a grouping key like `(position() - 1) idiv` *N* where *N* is the size of the groups that you want.

Grouping Programs into Pages Alphabetically

To try out grouping by position, in `TVGuide8.xsl` we'll arrange programs alphabetically (based on their series and title), and then create pages such that each page contains no more than five programs.

Our first task is to create a sorted list of the programs in the TV guide, based on their series and title. We can do this with the `<xsl:perform-sort>` instruction:

```
<xsl:variable name="SortedPrograms" as="element(Program)+">
  <xsl:perform-sort select="/TVGuide/Channel/Program">
    <xsl:sort select="..." />
  </xsl:perform-sort>
</xsl:variable>
```

As the basis of the sort, we'll use a string that looks like *`Series`*`:` *`Title`* for programs that have a value for their `<Series>` element child, and just *`Title`* for those that don't:

```
<xsl:variable name="SortedPrograms" as="element(Program)+">
  <xsl:perform-sort select="/TVGuide/Channel/Program">
    <xsl:sort select="if (string(Series)) then concat(Series, ': ', Title)
                                          else string(Title)" />
  </xsl:perform-sort>
</xsl:variable>
```

Once we have this sorted list of programs, we can group the programs based on their position within the sequence. To group into groups of five, we need to use the following:

```
<xsl:for-each-group select="$SortedPrograms"
                    group-adjacent="(position() - 1) idiv 5">
  ...
</xsl:for-each-group>
```

For each of these groups, we want to create a new document using the `<xsl:result-document>` element. We'll name the documents `Programs1.html`, `Programs2.html`, and so on, using the `position()` function (which here returns the position of the group amongst the other groups) to give the appropriate number:

```
<xsl:for-each-group select="$SortedPrograms"
                    group-adjacent="(position() - 1) idiv 5">
  <xsl:result-document href="Programs{position()}.html">
    ...
  </xsl:result-document>
</xsl:for-each-group>
```

Inside the `<xsl:result-document>` instruction, we need to create the HTML page for the programs in the current group. This is much the same as the HTML page that we're currently creating for the TV guide as a whole, except that rather than applying templates to the `<TVGuide>` element, we want to apply templates to the `<Program>` elements in the current group (returned by the `current-group()` function). The template in `TVGuide8.xsl` that matches the root node looks like this:

```
<xsl:template match="/">
  <xsl:variable name="SortedPrograms" as="element(Program)+">
    ...
  </xsl:variable>
  <xsl:for-each-group select="$sortedPrograms"
                      group-adjacent="(position() - 1) idiv 5">
    <xsl:result-document href="Programs{position()}.html">
      <html>
        <head>
          ...
        </head>
        <body>
          <xsl:apply-templates select="current-group()" />
        </body>
      </html>
    </xsl:result-document>
  </xsl:for-each-group>
</xsl:template>
```

When you transform `TVGuide.xml` with `TVGuide8.xsl`, you get six documents created, each of which hold the details of up to five programs. For example, Figure 9-9 shows the five programs listed in `Programs3.html`.

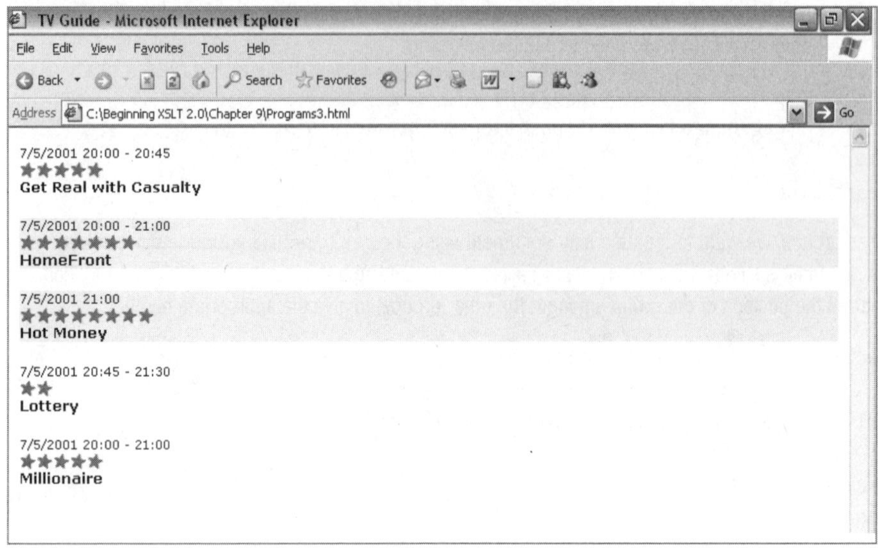

Figure 9-9. *Viewing* `Programs3.html` *in Internet Explorer*

To make these pages easier to navigate, you should add links between the generated pages, as in `TVGuide9.xsl`. You can add one to the value returned by the `position()` function to work out the number for the next page, and subtract one from the value returned by the `position()` function to work out the number for the previous page. The code for generating the links looks like the following:

```
<p>
  <xsl:choose>
    <xsl:when test="position() = 1">Previous</xsl:when>
    <xsl:otherwise>
      <a href="Programs{position() - 1}.html">Previous</a>
    </xsl:otherwise>
  </xsl:choose>
  <xsl:text> | </xsl:text>
  <xsl:choose>
    <xsl:when test="position() = last()">Next</xsl:when>
    <xsl:otherwise>
      <a href="Programs{position() + 1}.html">Next</a>
    </xsl:otherwise>
  </xsl:choose>
</p>
```

Putting this at the top and/or bottom of each page enables users to flip through the programs in alphabetical order, viewing up to five programs on each page.

Grouping in Sequence

Grouping by value is probably the most common kind of grouping that you'll need to do in data-oriented XML, but it's also sometimes useful to be able to group the elements in a document based on the order in which they appear. This is especially true when you have "flat" XML to which you want to add structure.

For example, CastList.xml, shown in Listing 9-1, contains a <CastList> element whose children are alternate <Character> and <Actor> elements.

Listing 9-1. CastList.xml

```
<CastList>
  <Character><Name>Zoe Slater</Name></Character>
  <Actor><Name>Michelle Ryan</Name></Actor>
  <Character><Name>Jamie Mitchell</Name></Character>
  <Actor><Name>Jack Ryder</Name></Actor>
  <Character><Name>Sonia Jackson</Name></Character>
  <Actor><Name>Natalie Cassidy</Name></Actor>
</CastList>
```

Say that you wanted to process CastList.xml to generate a cast list containing <CastMember> elements, as in TVGuide.xml:

```
<CastList>
  <CastMember>
    <Character><Name>Zoe Slater</Name></Character>
    <Actor><Name>Michelle Ryan</Name></Actor>
  </CastMember>
  <CastMember>
    <Character><Name>Jamie Mitchell</Name></Character>
    <Actor><Name>Jack Ryder</Name></Actor>
  </CastMember>
  <CastMember>
    <Character><Name>Sonia Jackson</Name></Character>
    <Actor><Name>Natalie Cassidy</Name></Actor>
  </CastMember>
</CastList>
```

To do this you need to go through the children of the <CastList> element in turn, creating <CastMember> elements; each <Character> element you come across signals the start of another <CastMember> element. This is what the group-starting-with attribute is used for.

The <xsl:for-each-group> instruction that does the grouping needs to select all the element children of the <CastList> element for grouping. The group-starting-with attribute needs to hold a pattern that matches <Character> elements (the pattern Character is the simplest one):

```
<xsl:template match="CastList">
  <CastList>
    <xsl:for-each-group select="*" group-starting-with="Character">
      ...
    </xsl:for-each-group>
  </CastList>
</xsl:template>
```

Each time you find a <Character> element, you want to create a new <CastMember> element, and inside it place the elements in the group: the <Character> and <Actor> elements.

```
<xsl:template match="CastList">
  <CastList>
    <xsl:for-each-group select="*" group-starting-with="Character">
      <CastMember>
        <xsl:sequence select="current-group()" />
      </CastMember>
    </xsl:for-each-group>
  </CastList>
</xsl:template>
```

Note You could also use group-ending-with, matching <Actor> elements, to create the same set of groups.

The group-adjacent attribute is sometimes useful when transforming from flat to structured XML. For example, if you have a document that contains <p> elements and a sequence of <li> elements at the same level, as in the following:

```
<p>Here is a paragraph...</p>
<li>First list item</li>
<li>Second list item</li>
<li>Third list item</li>
<p>Another paragraph...</p>
```

then you can wrap the <li> elements in a <ul> element by grouping adjacent items based on their names, and then, if a group is a group of <li> elements, wrapping the group in a <ul> element:

```
<xsl:for-each-group select="*"
                    group-adjacent="name(.)">
  <xsl:choose>
    <xsl:when test="current-grouping-key() = 'li'">
      <ul><xsl:sequence select="current-group()" /></ul>
    </xsl:when>
    <xsl:otherwise>
      <xsl:sequence select="current-group()" />
    </xsl:otherwise>
  </xsl:choose>
</xsl:for-each-group>
```

■ **Summary** The `group-starting-with` and `group-ending-with` attributes are useful for adding structure to XML. The `group-adjacent` attribute, using a grouping key based on element names, can often be useful here as well.

Multilevel Grouping

The previous sections have focused on single-level grouping. If you want to group by more than one thing at once, there are two techniques that are open to you.

First, you can nest one level of grouping inside another level of grouping. The inner `<xsl:for-each-group>` selects the current group from the outer `<xsl:for-each-group>` as the sequence to group. For example, to group all the programs in the TV guide first by their series and then by channel, you can do

```
<xsl:for-each-group select="/TVGuide/Channel/Program"
                    group-by="Series">
  <xsl:variable name="Series" as="xs:string" select="current-grouping-key()" />
  <h2><xsl:value-of select="$Series" /></h2>
  <xsl:for-each-group select="current-group()"
                      group-by="../Name">
    <xsl:variable name="Name" as="xs:string" select="current-grouping-key()" />
    <h3><xsl:value-of select="$Name" /></h3>
    <xsl:apply-templates select="current-group()" />
  </xsl:for-each-group>
</xsl:for-each-group>
```

■ **Tip** I've made this code clearer by assigning the value returned by `current-grouping-key()` to an appropriately named variable within each `<xsl:for-each-group>`.

There is no requirement for the two levels of grouping to use the same kind of grouping mechanism. For example, you could first group adjacent items using `group-starting-with`, and then group the items in that group using `group-by`.

The other technique is to construct a grouping key that combines the things that you want to group by, usually by concatenating them into a single string with a unique separator between them. This technique is most useful if you want all the groups to be at the same level (rather than nested, as in the preceding example), and particularly if you want to number the groups in sequence. For example, to group programs by both series and channel at the same time, you could use

```
<xsl:for-each-group select="/TVGuide/Channel/Program"
                    group-by="concat(Series, ' on ', ../Name)">
  <h2><xsl:value-of select="current-grouping-key()" /></h2>
  <xsl:apply-templates select="current-group()" />
</xsl:for-each-group>
```

Summary You can do multilevel grouping by nesting an `<xsl:for-each-group>` that selects the current group within another `<xsl:for-each-group>`, or by using a grouping key that uses `concat()` to create a value combining the values by which you want to group.

Grouping Programs by Hour and Minute

In `TVGuide7.xsl`, we grouped programs by the hour at which they started. Now we'll add a second-level group to the stylesheet, so that the programs are grouped both by the hour and the minute at which they are shown.

The current grouping is done by the following template, which matches the `<TVGuide>` element:

```
<xsl:template match="TVGuide">
  <xsl:for-each-group select="Channel/Program"
                      group-by="hours-from-dateTime(Start)">
    <xsl:sort select="current-grouping-key()" />
    <h2>Showing from <xsl:value-of select="current-grouping-key()" />:00</h2>
    <xsl:apply-templates select="current-group()">
      <xsl:sort select="xs:dateTime(Start)" />
      <xsl:sort select="xdt:dayTimeDuration(Duration)" />
    </xsl:apply-templates>
  </xsl:for-each-group>
</xsl:template>
```

Rather than applying templates to the programs that start within the same hour, in `TVGuide10.xsl` we want to group these programs again, based on the minute when the program starts. So we need another `<xsl:for-each-group>`, this one selecting the members of the current group and grouping them by the minute, as retrieved by `minutes-from-dateTime()`:

```
<xsl:template match="TVGuide">
  <xsl:for-each-group select="Channel/Program"
                      group-by="hours-from-dateTime(Start)">
    <xsl:sort select="current-grouping-key()" />
    <h2>Showing from <xsl:value-of select="current-grouping-key()" />:00</h2>
    <xsl:for-each-group select="current-group()"
                        group-by="minutes-from-dateTime(Start)">
      <h3><xsl:value-of select="format-dateTime(Start, '[H01]:[m]')" /></h3>
      <xsl:apply-templates select="current-group()">
        <xsl:sort select="xs:dateTime(Start)" />
        <xsl:sort select="xdt:dayTimeDuration(Duration)" />
      </xsl:apply-templates>
    </xsl:for-each-group>
  </xsl:for-each-group>
</xsl:template>
```

We need to pay a bit of attention to ordering here. The hour-level groups are being sorted based on the hour, but we also need to sort the minute-level groups based on the minute. There's then no need to sort the programs by their start time, since all the members of the group will have the same start time, so we can remove the first `<xsl:sort>` from within the `<xsl:apply-templates>` instruction, and add one within the nested `<xsl:for-each-group>` instruction, as follows:

```
<xsl:template match="TVGuide">
  <xsl:for-each-group select="Channel/Program"
                      group-by="hours-from-dateTime(Start)">
    <xsl:sort select="current-grouping-key()" />
    <h2>Showing from <xsl:value-of select="current-grouping-key()" />:00</h2>
    <xsl:for-each-group select="current-group()"
                        group-by="minutes-from-dateTime(Start)">
      <xsl:sort select="current-grouping-key()" />
      <h3><xsl:value-of select="format-dateTime(Start, '[H01]:[m]')" /></h3>
      <xsl:apply-templates select="current-group()">
        <xsl:sort select="xdt:dayTimeDuration(Duration)" />
      </xsl:apply-templates>
    </xsl:for-each-group>
  </xsl:for-each-group>
</xsl:template>
```

The result of applying this stylesheet, `TVGuide10.xsl`, to `TVGuide.xml`, is `TVGuide10.html`, which is shown in Figure 9-10.

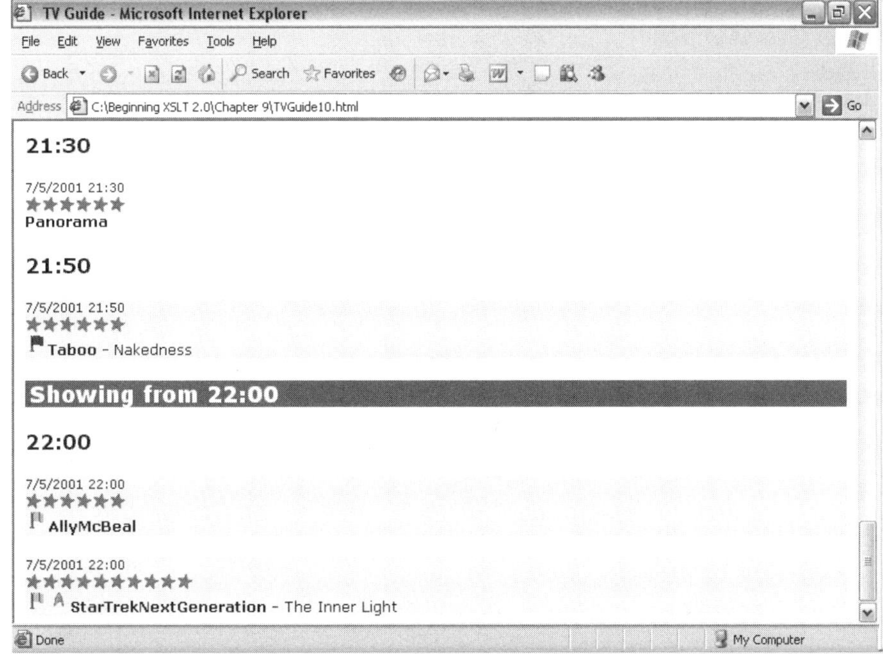

Figure 9-10. *Viewing* `TVGuide10.html` *in Internet Explorer*

Summary

In this chapter, we've looked at two methods of enhancing the presentation of a set of items—by sorting them and by grouping them.

You've learned about how to use the <xsl:sort> element with <xsl:for-each> and <xsl:apply-templates> to change the order in which nodes and other items are processed, and within <xsl:perform-sort> to create a sorted sequence. You've seen how to sort in ascending and descending order, how to do nonalphabetical sorts by casting the sort key to the appropriate type, and how to get finer control over alphabetical sorts using the `collation`, `lang`, and `letter-value` attributes.

You've also discovered how to do more sophisticated sorts, either by combining several sorts or by deciding dynamically what to sort a set of items on and in which order. These techniques often come in handy when you're designing dynamic applications such as those that we'll be looking at in Chapter 15.

We then looked at performing grouping of various kinds using the <xsl:for-each-group> element. You've seen how to group using a grouping key selected with `group-by` or `group-adjacent` and how to add structure to a flat document by grouping in sequence using `group-starting-with` or `group-ending-with`. You've learned how to group items into groups of a particular size, using the `position()` function, and how to create multiple levels of groups by nesting <xsl:for-each-group> instructions inside each other. Within <xsl:for-each-group>, you've seen how to retrieve the value of the grouping key that's used to identify the individual groups with `current-grouping-key()` and how to get the items that belong to the group using `current-group()`.

Review Questions

1. Which XSLT elements can be parents of <xsl:sort> elements?

2. What language is used when you sort alphabetically?

3. What does the following piece of code do? Is the sort alphabetical or numerical? How else could you do it?

```
<xsl:apply-templates select="Program">
  <xsl:sort select="position()" order="descending" />
</xsl:apply-templates>
```

4. What order will the <Program> elements be sorted in with the following code? How can you fix the code to make it do what was probably intended?

```
<xsl:variable name="series" as="xs:string" select="'Series'" />
<xsl:apply-templates select="Program">
  <xsl:sort select="$series" />
  <xsl:sort select="Title" />
</xsl:apply-templates>
```

5. What does the following piece of code do?

```
<xsl:apply-templates select="Program">
  <xsl:sort select="if ($sortBy = 'rating') then xs:integer(@rating)
                    else if ($sortBy = 'series') then Series
                    else if ($sortBy = 'title') then Title
                    else ()" />
</xsl:apply-templates>
```

6. What are the differences between using the group-by, group-adjacent, group-starting-with, and group-ending-with attributes on <xsl:for-each-group>?

7. What does the following piece of code do?

```
<xsl:for-each-group select="/Films/Film"
                    group-adjacent="(position() - 1) idiv 15">
  <xsl:variable name="start" as="xs:string"
                select="current-group()[1]/Title" />
  <xsl:variable name="end" as="xs:string"
                select="current-group()[last()]/Title" />
  <xsl:result-document href="{$start}-{$end}.html">
    <xsl:apply-templates select="current-group()" />
  </xsl:result-document>
</xsl:for-each-group>
```

8. Construct a stylesheet that groups <Film> elements by their <Year> children and then by their rating attributes.

CHAPTER 10

IDs, Keys, and Numbering

One of the big advantages of using XML to hold information is that it is a lot easier to **search** for specific information than it is when that information is stored in HTML. In the TV guide example, a simple search on the HTML page might reveal that a particular actor appears in a program that week, but a search on the XML would give you easy access to find which program that was, when it was showing, on which channel, and who else appeared in it.

This chapter discusses how to search XML documents for information using IDs that are built into the source XML structure, or those that you generate yourself. You can search an XML document quickly based on any combination of information by constructing keys, and doing so often makes for more efficient stylesheets.

The flip-side of using identifiers in an XML document is creating identifiers in the result that you generate from that document. So we'll also look at creating IDs that you can use as anchors in HTML documents, for example, and at adding numbers to the output that you generate, which can help identify items for both users and other processes.

In this chapter, you'll learn

- How to define and use `ID` attributes
- How to create keys to quickly access information
- How to generate IDs to cross-reference in the HTML that you generate
- How to number the items in a list (sorted and unsorted)
- How to number nodes across an entire document
- How to create hierarchical numbers

Searching

We've already seen some searches in action in previous chapters where we tried to get hold of all *Star Trek* programs being shown on a channel with

```
Program[starts-with(Series, 'StarTrek')]
```

When an XSLT processor evaluates this path, it looks at all the `<Program>` elements in the current channel and filters that set to include only those whose child `<Series>` element starts with the string `'StarTrek'`. The first part of the path indicates the type of node that we're searching for, while the predicate (the part within the `[]`s) indicates what constraints there are on that value.

There are lots of types of conditions that you can place in a predicate. You can check whether an attribute or element value starts with a particular string using the `starts-with()` function, matches a particular regular expression using the `matches()` function, is equal to something with the equals operator, and so on. You can even combine these tests together using `and` and `or`. So, searching for information within an XML document using predicates is very flexible and very powerful.

However, searching using predicates can also be pretty inefficient. In the preceding example, the XSLT processor visits every `<Program>` element within a particular `<Channel>` element, and checks each one's `<Series>` element. If there are 100 `<Program>` elements, then the XSLT processor visits 200 nodes (100 `<Program>` elements and 100 `<Series>` elements). If there was another similar path in the same stylesheet:

```
Program[starts-with(Series, 'EastEnders')]
```

then the XSLT processor would visit those 200 nodes again, despite the fact that it has already had to find out what `<Program>` elements there are and to which series they belong. In this section, we'll examine two ways of increasing the efficiency of searches for specific information within an XML document: using IDs and using keys.

■ **Note** Most processors offer an option that allows you to time how long a transformation takes as a whole. For example, you can use the `-t` options in Saxon and MSXML and the `-DIAG` command-line option with Xalan. There is also software available that helps you isolate inefficient parts of your stylesheet, such as CatchXSL! from `http://www.xslprofiler.org`, which you can use with Saxon or Xalan.

■ **Summary** You can search an XML document using predicates, which are powerful and flexible, but which can be inefficient.

IDs

The first type of search that we'll look at is when a particular piece of information can be uniquely identified within a larger set using a **unique identifier**. For example, customers have customer IDs, books have ISBN numbers, and streets have postcodes or zip codes. If you want to reference or retrieve information about a particular customer, book, or street, you can use this unique identifier to do so.

XML offers two levels of support for identifiers: **ID attributes** and **identity constraints**. `ID` attributes are attributes whose type is `xs:ID`; no element can have more than one `ID` attribute, and all the `ID` attributes in a document must have different values. The special attribute `xml:id` is recognized as an `ID` attribute automatically, but otherwise a document has to be validated for `ID` attributes to be recognized as such. Identity constraints are more sophisticated identifiers that are defined in an XML Schema using `<xs:key>` or `<xs:unique>` elements. XPath 2.0 doesn't provide any support for using identity constraints to access elements quickly, but it does offer some support for accessing elements by their `ID` attribute.

Note If you define ID attributes using XML Schema rather than a DTD, you must use a Schema-Aware XSLT processor to have them recognized. On the other hand, some Basic XSLT 2.0 processors will recognize ID attributes declared in DTDs, and all will recognize the special name xml:id. If you do validate a document that has xml:id attributes in it, they do need to be declared in the DTD or schema just like any other attribute.

The values of ID attributes are fairly tightly constrained—they must be "names" in XML terms. In effect they have to follow the same rules as element and attribute names (starting with a letter, not containing any whitespace, and only holding a restricted set of punctuation characters).

Summary Elements in an XML document can each be assigned a unique identifier within ID attributes. The values of ID attributes have to follow the same rules as element and attribute names.

Declaring ID Attributes

The easiest way to declare an ID attribute is within a DTD, using an **ATTLIST declaration**. You cannot specify a default (or fixed) value for an ID attribute—it can be either required, in which case it is declared with

```
<!ATTLIST elementName attributeName ID #REQUIRED>
```

or optional, in which case it is declared with

```
<!ATTLIST elementName attributeName ID #IMPLIED>
```

Note Most processors will recognize these ATTLIST declarations even if you don't have a corresponding element declaration for that element. However, to work with MSXML, you must have an element declaration as well; <!ELEMENT elementName (ANY)> is the simplest of these.

In XML Schema, you declare an ID attribute by assigning the attribute the type xs:ID. For example, an attribute declaration might look like this:

```
<xs:attribute name="attributeName" type="xs:ID" />
```

You can also declare that an element itself is of type xs:ID, in an element declaration such as the following:

```
<xs:element name="elementName" type="xs:ID" />
```

Summary ID attributes are declared within an ATTLIST declaration in a DTD or through assigning the type xs:ID to an attribute declared in an XML Schema schema.

Uniquely Identifying Series

When we developed the markup language for our TV guide in Chapter 1, we decided to keep information that applied to all episodes in a series separate from the description of the series and other information about it, such as who its writers, directors, and producers were. We haven't used this information so far, but now we'll include it in the same file as the rest of the TV guide, after the <Channel> elements, as in TVGuide.xml, shown in Listing 10-1.

Listing 10-1. TVGuide.xml

```
<?xml version="1.0" encoding="ISO-8859-1"?>
<TVGuide start="2001-07-05" end="2001-07-05">
  <Channel>
    <Name>BBC1</Name>
    ...
    <Program rating="5" flag="favorite">
      <Start>2001-07-05T19:30:00</Start>
      <Duration>PT30M</Duration>
      <Series>EastEnders</Series>
      <Title></Title>
      ...
    </Program>
    ...
  </Channel>
  ...
  <Series type="soap">
    <Title>EastEnders</Title>
    <Description>Soap set in the East End of London.</Description>
  </Series>
  ...
</TVGuide>
```

To make sure that each series is only described once, each should have its own identifier, which we'll put in an ID attribute. Lacking imagination, we'll call this attribute id. At the top of TVGuide2.xml, we can declare that the id attributes of the <Series> elements are ID attributes with a DOCTYPE declaration, as shown in Listing 10-2.

Listing 10-2. TVGuide2.xml

```
<?xml version="1.0" encoding="ISO-8859-1"?>
<!DOCTYPE TVGuide [
<!ELEMENT Series (Title, Description)>
<!ATTLIST Series id ID #IMPLIED>
]>
<TVGuide start="2001-07-05" end="2001-07-05">
  <Channel>
    <Name>BBC1</Name>
    ...
    <Program rating="5" flag="favorite">
      <Start>2001-07-05T19:30:00</Start>
```

```
      <Duration>PT30M</Duration>
      <Series>EastEnders</Series>
      <Title></Title>
      ...
    </Program>
    ...
  </Channel>
  ...
  <Series id="EastEnders" type="soap">
    <Title>EastEnders</Title>
    <Description>Soap set in the East End of London.</Description>
  </Series>
  ...
</TVGuide>
```

Note The element declaration is included so that this will work with MSXML; other processors don't need it.

Doing this doesn't make the document valid (since the DTD doesn't declare every element in the document), but it does allow an XSLT processor to recognize `ID` attributes.

An alternative that doesn't rely on DTD processing at all is just to use the `xml:id` attribute instead of the `id` attribute. The XML namespace doesn't need to be declared. `TVGuide3.xml` in Listing 10-3 shows what this looks like.

Listing 10-3. `TVGuide3.xml`

```
<?xml version="1.0" encoding="ISO-8859-1"?>
<TVGuide start="2001-07-05" end="2001-07-05">
  <Channel>
    <Name>BBC1</Name>
    ...
    <Program rating="5" flag="favorite">
      <Start>2001-07-05T19:30:00</Start>
      <Duration>PT30M</Duration>
      <Series>EastEnders</Series>
      <Title></Title>
      ...
    </Program>
    ...
  </Channel>
  ...
  <Series xml:id="EastEnders" type="soap">
    <Title>EastEnders</Title>
    <Description>Soap set in the East End of London.</Description>
  </Series>
  ...
</TVGuide>
```

As we'll see in the next section, either declaring an `ID` attribute or using `xml:id` enables us to locate the details of a series if we know its ID.

Accessing Elements by ID

`ID` attributes can be treated just like any other attribute, and you can find an element that has a particular value in an attribute you know to be an `ID` attribute using a predicate. For example, to find the description of *EastEnders* as a series, you can search for the `<Series>` element that has been assigned the value `EastEnders` for its `id` attribute, and go from that `<Series>` element to its child `<Description>` element with

```
Series[@id = 'EastEnders']/Description
```

However, if you declare that the `id` attribute is an `ID` attribute or you use `xml:id` attributes, then XSLT offers another method of getting hold of the `<Series>` element, using the `id()` function. This function takes a single argument, the `ID` of the element that you want to access, and returns the element node that has that particular `ID`:

```
id('EastEnders')/Description
```

■ **Note** If you're using elements rather than attributes to hold IDs (in which case you must be declaring them using an XML Schema schema), the `id()` function returns the element that contains the ID.

The string `'EastEnders'` could come from anywhere, and typically it would come from an attribute or element elsewhere. In the TV guide XML, the `<Series>` element within the `<Program>` element holds a reference to the series of which the program is an episode. Within the template for the `<Program>`, you could retrieve and apply templates to the description of the series with the following:

```
<xsl:template match="Program" mode="Details">
  ...
  <xsl:apply-templates select="id(Series)/Description" />
  ...
</xsl:template>
```

The big advantage of using an `ID` attribute and the `id()` function rather than a predicate is that it is more efficient. When an XSLT processor first looks at an XML document, it can build up a table of each element and their unique `ID`s, which it can then use to retrieve the element with a particular `ID`. Whereas with a predicate those elements would have to be visited again and again every time you wanted to find them, with `ID` attributes the elements are visited just once, and the processor generates a table that can retrieve them a lot faster.

■ **Summary** The `id()` function retrieves the element that has a particular unique identifier within a document.

Getting Information About TV Series

In our TV guide, each program may belong to a particular series. The details about each series are held in `<Series>` elements below the TV listings for each channel, each of which has an `xml:id` attribute that holds a unique identifier for the series. The `<Program>` elements refer to this information with their own child `<Series>` element, whose value is one of these unique identifiers.

In anticipation of using `ID` attributes to refer to the series information, the values of the `<Series>` elements within the `<Program>` elements conform to the rules about the names of IDs; in particular, they don't contain any spaces. So far, we've just presented the value of the `<Series>` element for a `<Program>`, but then the presented information doesn't look very good: rather than "Star Trek: Voyager," we see "StarTrekVoyager" in `TVGuide.html`, for example, as shown in Figure 10-1.

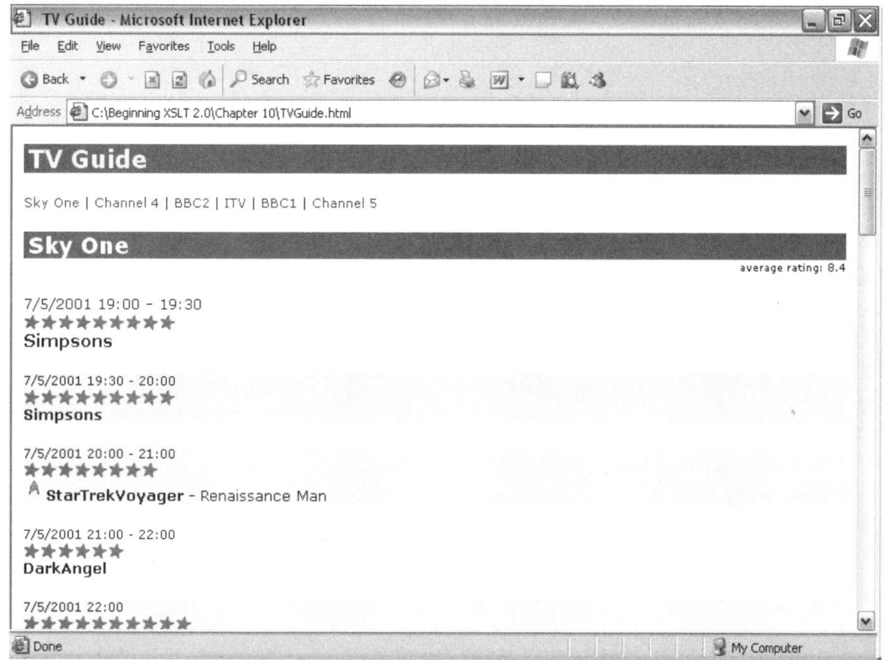

Figure 10-1. *Viewing* `TVGuide.html` *in Internet Explorer*

To get a readable name for the series, we need to access the series information that's being pointed to from the `<Program>` and from there find the `<Title>` under the referenced `<Series>` element. Currently, in `TVGuide.xsl`, the template providing the HTML giving details of the series looks as follows:

```
<xsl:template match="Program" mode="Details">
  ...
  <span class="title">
    <xsl:choose>
      <xsl:when test="string(Series)">
        <xsl:value-of select="Series" />
```

```
        <xsl:if test="string(Title)">
          <xsl:text> - </xsl:text>
          <span class="subtitle"><xsl:value-of select="Title" /></span>
        </xsl:if>
      </xsl:when>
      <xsl:otherwise>
        <xsl:value-of select="Title" />
      </xsl:otherwise>
    </xsl:choose>
  </span>
  ...
</xsl:template>
```

Rather than giving the value of that `<Series>` element, we need to retrieve the `<Series>` element that has that `ID` (using the `id()` function) and get its child `<Title>` element:

```
<xsl:template match="Program" mode="Details">
  ...
  <span class="title">
    <xsl:choose>
      <xsl:when test="string(Series)">
        <xsl:value-of select="id(Series)/Title" />
        <xsl:if test="string(Title)">
          <xsl:text> - </xsl:text>
          <span class="subtitle"><xsl:value-of select="Title" /></span>
        </xsl:if>
      </xsl:when>
      <xsl:otherwise>
        <xsl:value-of select="Title" />
      </xsl:otherwise>
    </xsl:choose>
  </span>
  ...
</xsl:template>
```

With this change made in `TVGuide2.xsl`, the result of transforming `TVGuide3.xml` is `TVGuide2.html`, shown in Figure 10-2.

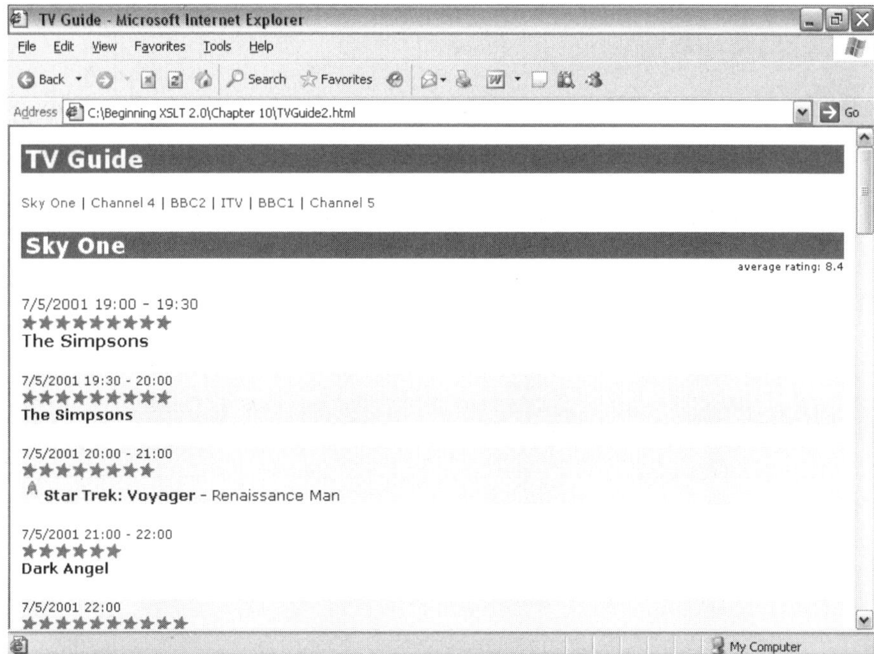

Figure 10-2. *Viewing* `TVGuide2.html` *in Internet Explorer*

The title of each series is retrieved from the information further down in `TVGuide3.xml`, using the ID given as the value of the `<Series>` element within each program and as the value of the `xml:id` attribute in the series details.

Resolving Multiple References

In the last section, you saw the `id()` function being passed a single `ID` and retrieving the single element that had that `ID`. If you have lots of references, you can also use the `id()` function to return more than one element at a time. For example, each program and series can have several writers, some of which may work on more than one program or series within the TV guide. Rather than repeating information about each of the writers, we could also separate the information about writers and store that further down in the TV guide:

```
<Writer xml:id="NickSaltrese">
  <Name>Nick Saltrese</Name>
  <Bio>...</Bio>
</Writer>
<Writer xml:id="JulieWassmer">
  <Name>Julie Wassmer</Name>
  <Bio>...</Bio>
</Writer>
```

There are two ways to refer to this information from within the `<Program>` element. First, we could use a space-separated list of IDs, as follows:

```
<Writers>NickSaltrese JulieWassmer</Writers>
```

When you use a space-separated list of IDs as the argument to the `id()` function, it returns a sequence of the elements that have those IDs. So, to list the names of the writers (with commas separating them), we could retrieve the `<Writer>` elements with a call to the `id()` function and use `<xsl:value-of>` with a comma as the separator, as follows:

```
<xsl:value-of select="id(Writers)/Name" separator=", " />
```

Summary If the argument to the `id()` function is a space-separated list of IDs, it returns the elements with those IDs.

The second way to refer to the information from within the `<Program>` element would be to use separate `<Writer>` elements to refer to each writer, as follows:

```
<Writers>
  <Writer>NickSaltrese</Writer>
  <Writer>JulieWassmer</Writer>
</Writers>
```

You can also use this structure with the `id()` function. If the argument to the `id()` function is a sequence, then the `id()` function takes the items in that sequence and creates a sequence of elements comprising the result of using the `id()` function on each of the items. In essence, you get the element(s) referred to by each of the items in the sequence. With this second representation, the comma-separated list of writer's names could then be generated with the following:

```
<xsl:value-of select="id(Writers/Writer)/Name" separator=", " />
```

Summary If the argument to the `id()` function is a sequence, it returns the elements with the IDs given by the items in the sequence.

Locating References to IDs

Just as you can declare, in a DTD or schema, that an attribute contains an ID, you can also declare that an attribute contains one or more *references* to an ID by assigning to it the type `xs:IDREF` or `xs:IDREFS`.

Using a DTD, you can only state that attributes are references to IDs: you can't declare the types of elements (such as the `<Series>` element in the XML we're using). For example, if we had XML such as

```
<Program rating="5" flag="favorite" series="EastEnders">
  <Start>2001-07-05T19:30:00</Start>
  <Duration>PT30M</Duration>
  ...
</Program>
```

then we could declare that the `series` attribute on the `<Program>` element was a reference to an identifier using the following:

```
<!ATTLIST Program series IDREF #IMPLIED>
```

Similarly, if we were referring to a number of writers from a `<Writers>` element that looked like this:

```
<Writers idrefs="NickSaltrese JulieWassmer" />
```

we could declare that the `idrefs` attribute contained a whitespace-separated list of references to IDs elsewhere in the document using the `ATTLIST` declaration:

```
<!ATTLIST Writers idrefs IDREFS #IMPLIED>
```

If you're using a Schema-Aware XSLT processor, you can declare that an element contains a reference to an ID by declaring it to be of type `xs:IDREF`; for example, the `<Series>` element in our TV guide XML should be declared as being of type `xs:IDREF`:

```
<xs:element name="Series" type="xs:IDREF" />
```

■ **Summary** You can declare that an attribute (or element, if you're using a schema) contains one or more references to identifiers used elsewhere in the document by assigning it the type `xs:IDREF` or `xs:IDREFS`.

Just as you can use the `id()` function to return the elements that have particular IDs, you can use the `idref()` function to return those elements that reference those IDs. For example, given that the `series` attribute on the `<Program>` element has been declared as being of type `IDREF`, you could get all of the `<Program>` elements associated with the current `<Series>` element using

```
idref(@id)
```

Like the `id()` function, the `idref()` function can take a sequence of IDs as an argument, in which case it returns all the elements in the document that reference any of those IDs. But unlike `id()`, it can't take a space-separated string as an argument: if you have such a list, you need to use `tokenize()` to split it up into separate strings.

■ **Summary** The `idref()` function retrieves those elements that reference a particular ID through an `IDREF` or `IDREFS` attribute.

Keys

As we've seen, the big benefit of using the `id()` and `idref()` functions over using predicates to search a document is the fact that the XSLT processor doesn't have to search through the entire document again and again to find elements with particular identifiers. However, using `ID` or `IDREF` attributes can be problematic for the following reasons:

- The `ID` or `IDREF` attributes have to be declared within a DTD or schema, but you can't guarantee that a document will reference a DTD or schema, that the DTD or schema will be accessible, or that an XSLT processor will access the DTD or schema. Placing the DTD within the instance document helps, but that is impractical if your markup language contains lots of `ID` or `IDREF` attributes on lots of different elements. Using `xml:id` is an option for `ID` attributes, but you might want to use a more descriptive name for the identifier.
- You have to add an ID to all the elements to which you want to refer, which adds to the size of the document and means that you have to think of a unique ID for every element in your document.
- When using a DTD, the IDs and ID references must be specified in attributes, but this might not fit in with your preferences when designing your markup language.
- When using a schema, you must use a Schema-Aware XSLT processor, but other people using your stylesheet might not have access to such a processor.
- The IDs have to follow the rules for XML names, but some IDs don't naturally fit with this pattern (for example, ISBNs start with a number, and the names of TV series often contain spaces).
- The IDs have to be unique within a document, but sometimes you might want to have them scoped to particular element types or to particular sections within a document.

These constraints can make it impractical or inadvisable to rely on `ID` attributes and the `id()` function. XSLT therefore offers an alternative method of assigning identifiers to elements and of accessing elements by those identifiers: **keys**.

■ **Summary** Using `ID` or `IDREF` attributes and the `id()` or `idref()` functions can be very limiting. Keys offer a more flexible way of identifying and referencing elements.

Using Keys Instead of IDs

The first step in using keys is roughly equivalent to declaring an `ID` attribute—you need to tell the XSLT processor that a particular set of elements can be identified by a particular attribute value. It's in declaring keys that we come across the first difference between keys and IDs: you declare keys within the XSLT stylesheet rather than within an XML document. This means you don't have to worry about whether the person authoring the source XML for your transformation has made all the declarations that you need them to have made for the stylesheet to work.

Keys are declared with the `<xsl:key>` element, which is placed at the top level of your stylesheet (the same level as `<xsl:template>` and global variables). As we'll see later in this chapter, you can have several keys within the same document, indexing different elements in different ways, using key values that are arbitrary strings, all while allowing several elements to share the same key value.

Note Don't confuse XSLT keys with XML Schema keys, since the capabilities are somewhat different. First, XML Schema key values are sequences of node values rather than arbitrary strings. Secondly, keys are scoped so that they only operate within a certain type of element, rather than across the entire document. Finally, every element within the scope of a key must have a different value for that key (although elements in different scopes can have the same value for the key). XPath 2.0 doesn't support accessing information via keys defined in XML Schema.

The simplest keys are those that are directly equivalent to an `ATTLIST` declaration for an `ID` attribute. These kinds of keys have the following pattern:

```
<xsl:key name="IDs" match="elementName" use="@attributeName" />
```

For example, to declare a key that says that `<Series>` elements can be identified using their `id` attribute, you would use the following key definition:

```
<xsl:key name="IDs" match="Series" use="@id" />
```

Tip If you define one of these keys for each `ID` attribute in your DTD, you'll end up with one key that indexes all the ID'ed elements in your document by their `ID` attribute.

If `<xsl:key>` is equivalent to the `ATTLIST` declaration for `ID` attributes, then you also need something equivalent to the `id()` function to retrieve the element that has a particular ID. The equivalent of the `id()` function is the `key()` function, which usually takes two arguments—the name of the key (as given in the `name` attribute of `<xsl:key>`) and the identifier that's assigned to the element that you want to retrieve. For example, having defined the `IDs` key, to get hold of the `<Series>` element that has the ID `'EastEnders'`, you would use

```
key('IDs', 'EastEnders')
```

The second argument to the `key()` function isn't quite as flexible as the argument to the `id()` function, in that it can't take a space-separated list of IDs to return the elements with those IDs (because, unlike with the `id()` function, the identifier itself could have spaces in it), but the second argument can be a sequence. For example, if you've set up a key for the `<Writer>` elements:

```
<xsl:key name="IDs" match="Writer" use="@id" />
```

then the references to the <Writer> elements must either be held in separate elements, as follows:

```
<Writers>
  <Writer>NickSaltrese</Writer>
  <Writer>JulieWassmer</Writer>
</Writers>
```

in which case you could then use the key() function to retrieve all the <Writer> elements with those IDs with

```
key('IDs', Writers/Writer)
```

or, if the XML contained a space-separated list of writers, as in the following:

```
<Writers>NickSaltrese JulieWassmer</Writers>
```

you would have to tokenize this string based on whitespace, to give a sequence of strings, as follows:

```
key('IDs', tokenize(Writers, '\s+'))
```

Caution This will also return any <Series> elements whose ID is the same as a writer's ID. In the next section, we'll see how key spaces can be used to focus the search onto particular types of elements.

Summary You can declare a key with the <xsl:key> element at the top level of the stylesheet, and access elements indexed by the key using the key() function.

Using Keys Instead of IDs

When we looked at IDs, we wrote a template that would insert the name of a series in the details of a program by accessing the relevant <Series> element through its ID. The id attribute of the <Series> element was declared as an ID attribute with the following ATTLIST declaration within the DTD:

```
<!ATTLIST Series id ID #IMPLIED>
```

Try removing the DOCTYPE declaration from TVGuide2.xml so that the XML document no longer references the DTD, to give TVGuide4.xml. Transforming TVGuide4.xml with TVGuide2.xsl gives TVGuide2-2.html, which is shown in Figure 10-3.

When you remove the DTD, the XSLT processor no longer has access to the fact that the id attribute on the <Series> element is an ID attribute, so it can't retrieve the name of the series for presentation on the page.

This might well happen if an author forgets to include a DOCTYPE declaration in the XML document, or if for some reason the DTD for the XML document is unavailable. To make the stylesheet more robust, you can use a key with the same effect instead. Add an <xsl:key> element to the top level of TVGuide3.xsl to tell the XSLT processor to index all the <Series> elements according to their id attribute, as follows:

```
<xsl:key name="IDs" match="Series" use="@id" />
```

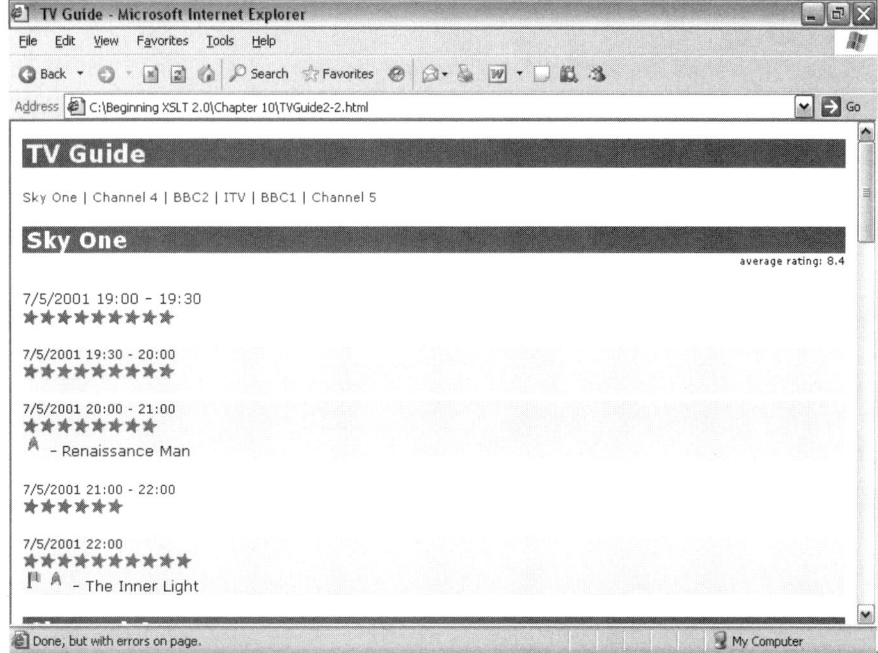

Figure 10-3. *Viewing* TVGuide2-2.html *in Internet Explorer*

Now change the call to the id() function so that you use the key instead. The first argument to the key() function is the name of the key ('IDs'), and the second argument is the same as the argument you used for the id() function—the ID that you want to use to retrieve the element:

```
<xsl:template match="Program" mode="Details">
  ...
  <span class="title">
    <xsl:choose>
      <xsl:when test="string(Series)">
        <xsl:value-of select="key('IDs', Series)/Title" />
        <xsl:if test="string(Title)">
          <xsl:text> - </xsl:text>
          <span class="subtitle"><xsl:value-of select="Title" /></span>
        </xsl:if>
      </xsl:when>
      <xsl:otherwise>
        <xsl:value-of select="Title" />
      </xsl:otherwise>
    </xsl:choose>
  </span>
  ...
</xsl:template>
```

When you run the transformation of TVGuide4.xml with TVGuide3.xsl, you get TVGuide3.html, as shown in Figure 10-4.

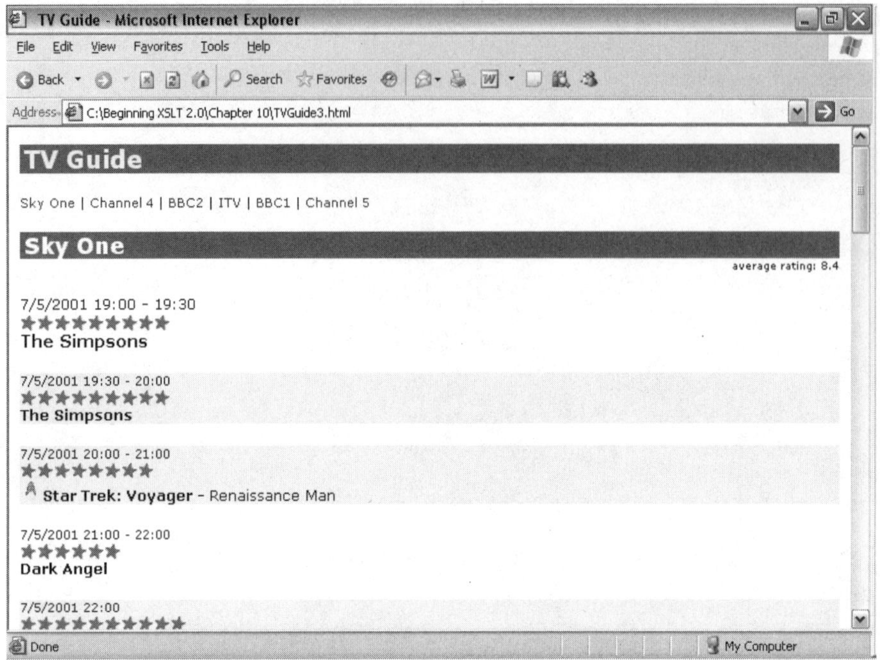

Figure 10-4. *Viewing* TVGuide3.html *in Internet Explorer*

The names of the series appear as they did before you removed the DTD, because keys do not rely on information held within the DTD, only the key definitions in the stylesheet.

Key Spaces

Defining keys rather than ID attributes grants you independence from a DTD, but that's just one of its advantages. As you might guess from the fact that keys have names, you can have several **key spaces**.

With IDs, you could only have one set of IDs throughout the document, so even if you knew that an ID could only refer to a <Series> element, you still had to make sure that it wasn't the same as an ID that you used for a <Writer> element. With keys, you can have separate keys for separate sets of IDs. You can have one key for series:

```
<xsl:key name="series" match="Series" use="@id" />
```

and another key for writers:

```
<xsl:key name="writers" match="Writer" use="@id" />
```

■ **Note** You can have two <xsl:key> elements with the same name attribute, in which case the two indexes created by the <xsl:key> elements are merged into one.

There are two advantages to using different key spaces for different indexes.

First, having several key spaces means two elements can use the same identifier, but you can still retrieve the one that you want. For example, if a series and a writer happened to have the same name, not only could they use the same value for their id attributes, but also you would be able to retrieve the <Series> element when you wanted to retrieve the series, and the <Writer> element when you needed the writer.

Second, the indexes that are built by keys can be much smaller and much more focused than the ones for IDs, which have to cover every element with an ID attribute in the entire document. Using an index is a big advantage over searching through the document multiple times, but likewise the smaller the index, the quicker it is to build and the faster the XSLT processor can retrieve nodes within it.

Summary The name attribute of <xsl:key> defines a key space, which allows several elements to have the same identifier and assists you in focusing the search for them more effectively.

Choosing What to Index

The match attribute on <xsl:key> determines the kinds of nodes that are indexed by the key. As you might expect from its name, the match attribute on <xsl:key> holds the same kinds of values as the match attribute on <xsl:template>—a pattern. The XSLT processor searches through the entire XML document to find all the nodes that match the pattern given in the match attribute, and the index that it creates holds an entry for each of them.

You can tell the XSLT processor to index only text nodes or particular attributes, but most often the kinds of nodes that you want to retrieve using a key are elements. The main purpose of the match attribute, then, is to limit the kinds of elements that are indexed by the key so that it doesn't hold unnecessary information.

For example, the only <Series> elements that we're really interested in indexing are those that are children of the <TVGuide> element that is a child of the root node, and not those that are children of the <Program> element. So we could change the match pattern to only match these kinds of <Series> elements, and not those that are held within <Program> elements, with

```
<xsl:key name="series" match="/TVGuide/Series" use="@id" />
```

You can also use the fact that the match attribute takes a pattern to create keys that index several different kinds of elements within the same key space. For example, to create a key that indexes <Writer>, <Director>, and <Producer> children of the <TVGuide> element by their id attributes, you could use

```
<xsl:key name="productionStaff"
         match="/TVGuide/Writer | /TVGuide/Director | /TVGuide/Producer"
         use="@id" />
```

Using a match pattern of multiple parts has exactly the same effect as if you had several <xsl:key> elements, all with the same name, as follows:

```
<xsl:key name="productionStaff" match="/TVGuide/Writer" use="@id" />
<xsl:key name="productionStaff" match="/TVGuide/Director" use="@id" />
<xsl:key name="productionStaff" match="/TVGuide/Producer" use="@id" />
```

■ **Summary** The `match` attribute of `<xsl:key>` specifies the types of nodes that are indexed by the key. The key indexes all the nodes in a document that match the pattern held in the `match` attribute.

Indexing by XPaths

With IDs, the ID of an element has to be stored within an attribute, and has to conform to the rules for XML names. The **key values** used to identify elements indexed by a key are a lot more flexible—they can come from child elements, or any other calculated value, as well as from attributes, and can be of any type at all.

The value that's used to index a particular element is specified with either an XPath expression held in the `use` attribute on `<xsl:key>` or the content of the `<xsl:key>` element, which is a sequence constructor. You can use long and convoluted location paths or call functions to get an identifier for an element, or create an identifier using XSLT code.

When the XSLT processor creates an index for a key, it evaluates the XPath held in the `use` attribute, or the sequence constructor held in the content of the `<xsl:key>` element, with the node that it's indexing as the current node, to give the key value by which the node is indexed. For example, you could use the `<Name>` elements to identify the `<Actor>` elements that contain them as follows:

```
<xsl:key name="actors" match="Actor" use="Name" />
```

Alternatively, you could identify each program based on a combination of the channel on which it's shown (the `<Name>` child of the `<Program>` element's parent `<Channel>`) and the date and time at which it starts (the `<Program>` element's child `<Start>` element), by concatenating them together with the `concat()` function:

```
<xsl:key name="programs" match="Program"
         use="concat(../Name, ' at ', Start)" />
```

With the preceding key, you could retrieve the program on BBC1 starting at 19:30 on 5 July 2001 with the following call to the `key()` function:

```
key('programs', 'BBC1 at 2001-07-05T19:30:00')
```

■ **Note** The fact that key values can contain spaces is the reason that you can't use space-separated lists of IDs as the second argument to the `key()` function, whereas you can use them as the argument for the `id()` function.

When it comes to retrieving nodes using the key, the type of the key value is important, as this determines how values are compared, just as it does in `<xsl:sort>`, for example. If you index programs by their start time, which is an `xs:dateTime` value, you could use

```
<xsl:key name="programs" match="Program" use="xs:dateTime(Start)" />
```

If the key value is an `xs:dateTime`, then only other `xs:dateTime` values can possibly match it. If the second argument to the `key()` function isn't an `xs:dateTime`, then you won't get anything back. For example:

```
key('programs', xs:dateTime('2001-07-05T19:30:00'))
```

will return all the programs that start at 19:30 on 5 July 2001, but

```
key('programs', '2001-07-05T19:30:00')
```

will return nothing.

The fact that the types have to match is particularly relevant if you pass a node as the second argument of the key() function. In this case, the untyped value of the node is implicitly cast to a string, and thus you will only get back values if the key value is a string as well. So

```
key('programs', Start)
```

(which would otherwise give you all the programs that started at the same time as this one) won't give you anything either. You need to explicitly cast the value of the <Start> element, as in the following:

```
key('programs', xs:dateTime(Start))
```

Tip If a key value is anything other than a string, remember to cast the second argument of the key() function to the relevant type.

As you'll remember from Chapter 4, when we looked at comparing strings, and from the last chapter, when we looked at sorting, there's no fixed way of comparing two strings: for example, you might want to compare them in a case-insensitive way or based on a particular language. If you need to, you can specify the collation used for comparing strings used as key values using the collation attribute on <xsl:key>.

Summary You can specify the key value used to index an element either with the use attribute (which contains an XPath expression) or with the sequence constructor content of the <xsl:key> element. The types of key values are significant. The collation used to compare key values that are strings is specified with the collation attribute.

Multiple Key Values

Keys are not bound by the limitation on IDs that states there can only be one element with a particular identifier. The same key value can be used to access multiple elements. This is particularly useful when you want to look at reverse relationships (such as those used by the idref() function), from an element to all the elements that refer to it.

For example, you could set up a key that would allow you to find all the programs that belong to a particular series. The elements that you want to retrieve are <Program> elements, so the match pattern needs to match them, and the key values that they need to be indexed by are the values of their <Series> elements. The key definition looks like this:

```
<xsl:key name="programsBySeries" match="Program" use="Series" />
```

It doesn't matter that several programs belong to the same series—all of them are returned by the call to the key() function. For example, the following returns all <Program> elements that are part of the *EastEnders* series:

```
key('programsBySeries', 'EastEnders')
```

Note When you use the key() function, the second argument must match the key value exactly. There's no way to retrieve all the *Star Trek* episodes (those programs whose series starts with 'StarTrek') using this key, for example, because the programs are indexed by the entirety of their series name.

What's more, while usually the key value is a single item, you can also use an expression that evaluates to a sequence. If you do, then the indexed node can be retrieved using the value of *any* of the items in the sequence, essentially giving the element multiple identifiers. This is particularly useful when you want to access the same element in many different ways.

For example, to enable us to retrieve all the <Program> elements that star a particular actor, we could set up a key that again matches <Program> elements but this time using the <Name> child of the <Actor> child of the <CastMember> child of the <CastList> element, as follows:

```
<xsl:key name="programsByActors" match="Program"
         use="CastList/CastMember/Actor/Name" />
```

When it's evaluated from the context of a <Program> element, the path CastList/CastMember/Actor/Name returns a sequence containing several <Name> elements (one for each actor in the program). The values of these <Name> elements are used to index the <Program> element within the programsByActors key. Whichever actor is named by the call to the key, the <Program> element will be returned by it. For example, given the following cast list as in TVGuide4.xml:

```
<Program>
  ...
  <CastList>
    <CastMember>
      <Character><Name>Zoe Slater</Name>...</Character>
      <Actor><Name>Michelle Ryan</Name>...</Actor>
    </CastMember>
    <CastMember>
      <Character><Name>Jamie Mitchell</Name>...</Character>
      <Actor><Name>Jack Ryder</Name>...</Actor>
    </CastMember>
    <CastMember>
      <Character><Name>Sonia Jackson</Name>...</Character>
      <Actor><Name>Natalie Cassidy</Name>...</Actor>
    </CastMember>
    ...
  </CastList>
  ...
</Program>
```

the following calls to the key() function will all return the preceding <Program> element (possibly along with others, if several programs star the same actors):

```
key('programsByActors', 'Michelle Ryan')
key('programsByActors', 'Jack Ryder')
key('programsByActors', 'Natalie Cassidy')
```

Summary A key can assign the same key value to multiple elements (in which case the key() function returns all the elements) and can assign multiple key values to the same element (in which case the key() function will return the element no matter which value is used).

Creating Lists of Programs in Each Series

It's easy to tell which series a particular program is an episode of using the XML structure that we've put together, but it's not clear from the XML which episodes of a particular series are being shown. In TVGuide4.xsl, we'll add lists of the episodes showing in each series to the bottom of our TV guide.

As a first step, we need to add a template that matches the <Series> elements that are direct children of the <TVGuide> element so that we can create sections that describe each series. The basic template just gives the name of the series as a heading, followed by its description:

```
<xsl:template match="TVGuide/Series">
  <div>
    <h3><xsl:value-of select="Title" /></h3>
    <p>
      <xsl:apply-templates select="Description" />
    </p>
  </div>
</xsl:template>
```

We'll use this template to add information about the series being shown at the bottom of our page, by modifying the template that matches the <TVGuide> element. We'll apply templates to the <Series> elements in alphabetical order, based on their IDs:

```
<xsl:template match="TVGuide">
  <xsl:sequence select="$ChannelList" />
  <xsl:apply-templates select="$Channels" />
  <xsl:sequence select="$ChannelList" />
  <h2>Series</h2>
  <xsl:apply-templates select="Series">
    <xsl:sort select="@id" />
  </xsl:apply-templates>
</xsl:template>
```

These two changes have been made in TVGuide4.xsl. When you transform TVGuide4.xml with TVGuide4.xsl to create TVGuide4.html, you should see a list of the series at the bottom of the page, as shown in Figure 10-5.

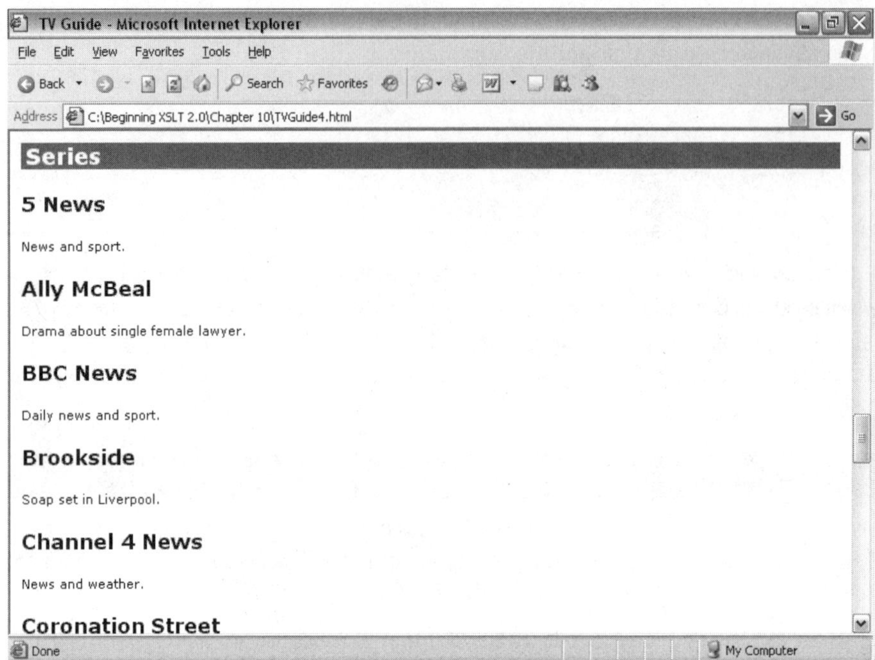

Figure 10-5. *Viewing* TVGuide4.html *in Internet Explorer*

One of the things to add to this description of the series is a list of the programs being shown from the series. To retrieve these programs efficiently, we should set up a key that indexes all the <Program> elements within TVGuide4.xml by the value of their <Series> child element, as follows:

```
<xsl:key name="programsBySeries" match="Program" use="Series" />
```

The values of the <Series> element children of the <Program> elements tie up with the values of the id attributes on the <Series> element children of the <TVGuide> element. In the template for the latter <Series> elements, we can therefore retrieve all the <Program> elements that refer to the series using the following:

```
key('programsBySeries', @id)
```

Once we've got hold of the <Program> elements using the key, we can iterate over them with an <xsl:for-each> as follows:

```
<xsl:template match="TVGuide/Series">
  <div>
    <h3><xsl:value-of select="Title" /></h3>
    <p>
      <xsl:apply-templates select="Description" />
    </p>
    <h4>Episodes</h4>
    <ul>
      <xsl:for-each select="key('programsBySeries', @id)">
        <li>
```

```
        <xsl:value-of select="parent::Channel/Name" />
        <xsl:text> at </xsl:text>
        <xsl:value-of select="format-dateTime(Start,
                                              '[H01]:[m] on [M]/[D]/[Y]')" />
        <xsl:if test="string(Title)">
          <xsl:text>: </xsl:text>
          <xsl:value-of select="Title" />
        </xsl:if>
      </li>
    </xsl:for-each>
  </ul>
</div>
</xsl:template>
```

Making these changes in `TVGuide5.xsl` creates `TVGuide5.html` when used with `TVGuide4.xml`. `TVGuide5.html` is shown in Figure 10-6.

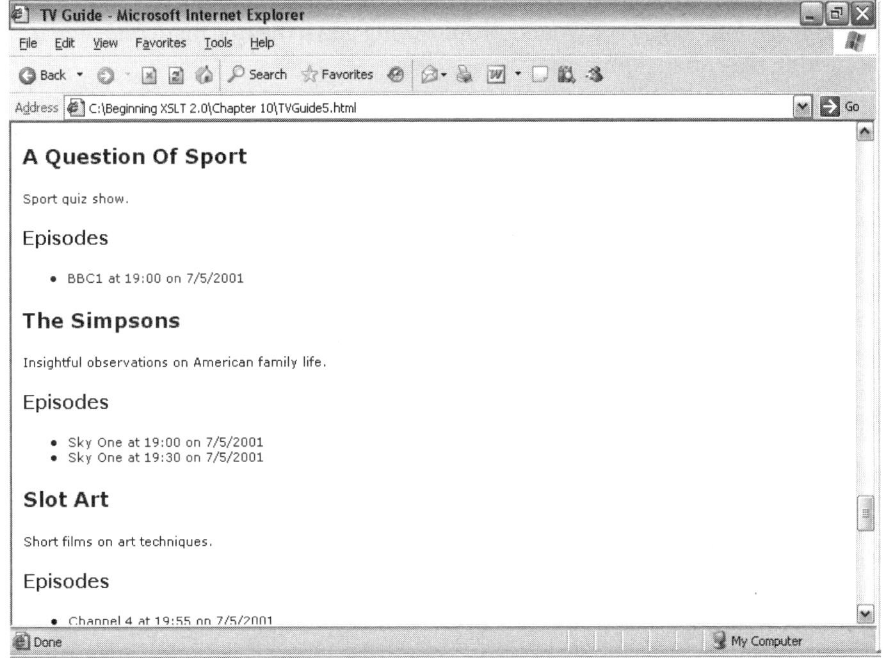

Figure 10-6. *Viewing* `TVGuide5.html` *in Internet Explorer*

A Question Of Sport has one episode, on BBC1 at 19:00, whereas there are two episodes of *The Simpsons* showing, at 19:00 and 19:30 on Sky One. The key has indexed each program by its series, and it's used to retrieve all the programs of a particular series.

Searching a Subtree

The final feature of keys that differentiates them from IDs is that you can search within a subtree of your XML document. When you use the id() or idref() function, and when you use the key() function with two arguments, you always search the entirety of the document that contains the context node. But if you give a node as the third argument of the key() function, then you search only that node and its descendants.

For example, say you'd indexed all the <CastMember> elements by the name of the actor, with

```
<xsl:key name="CastMemberByActor" match="CastMember" use="Actor/Name" />
```

and you're currently on a <Program> element for which you know that one of the actors is Jack Ryder. If you try to find out the character played by the actor Jack Ryder using the two-argument version of key(), as in

```
key('CastMemberByActor', 'Jack Ryder')/Character/Name
```

then you'll get *all* the characters played by Jack Ryder, throughout the TV guide.

To find only the character played by Jack Ryder in this particular program, you should use the three-argument version of the key() function, narrowing down the tree that's searched to the <CastList> within the current <Program>:

```
key('CastMemberByActor', 'Jack Ryder', CastList)/Character/Name
```

■ **Note** The three-argument version of the key() function is also useful if you need to search a different document from the one you're on currently; just give the document node of that document as the third argument.

The third argument to the key() function must be a single node, so you can't use it to search several subtrees at once. For example, if you wanted to search all flagged programs in the current channel for Jack Ryder, you couldn't use the following:

```
key('CastMemberByActor', 'Jack Ryder', Program[@flag]/CastList)/Character/Name
```

If you tried this with most channels, you'd get an error because you'd pass more than one <CastList> element as the third argument.

However, you can use paths to search several subtrees. In this example, you could use

```
Program[@flag]/key('CastMemberByActor', 'Jack Ryder', CastList)/Character/Name
```

The first step in this path creates a sequence of <Program> elements. These are considered one by one, and for each one the key is used to identify, within their <CastList> child, the <CastMember> elements that contain an <Actor> element whose <Name> is equal to 'Jack Ryder'. From those <CastMember> elements, a sequence of character names is constructed.

■ **Summary** You can specify a node as a third argument to the key() function. Only that node and its descendants are searched for nodes that match the key.

Generating IDs

If you have an XML structure that contains a lot of cross-references, then you're likely to find it useful to have a presentation format that does the same kind of thing. As an example, the XML for the TV guide separates the details of TV series off into separate elements, and the HTML presentation follows this format as well, with the descriptions of the series presented after the channel listings.

When you have references within an HTML page, it's helpful to make the references into **hypertext links** so that someone reading the document can jump from place to place. To enable local HTML links, you have to create **anchors** within the HTML document that you generate with the XSLT, and create links that reference these anchors. As you know, you can do this with the <a> element in HTML, using the name and id attributes to create anchors and the href attribute to create a link.

For example, it would be good to link from each program to the series of which it's an episode. To do this, we need to create an anchor when we generate the HTML that describes each series, within the template for the <Series> elements within the <TVGuide> element, and a link to the anchor from the name of the series when we generate it in the template matching <Series> elements within <Program> elements. We can use the ID assigned to the series as the basis of the links, as the value of the name and id attributes in the anchor:

```
<xsl:template match="TVGuide/Series">
  <div>
    <h3><a name="{@id}" id="{@id}"><xsl:value-of select="Title" /></a></h3>
    ...
  </div>
</xsl:template>
```

and as the fragment identifier in the href attribute in the link:

```
<xsl:template match="Program" mode="Details">
  ...
  <span class="title">
    <xsl:choose>
      <xsl:when test="string(Series)">
        <a href="#{Series}">
          <xsl:value-of select="key('IDs', Series)/Title" />
        </a>
        <xsl:if test="string(Title)">
          <xsl:text> - </xsl:text>
          <span class="subtitle"><xsl:value-of select="Title" /></span>
        </xsl:if>
      </xsl:when>
      <xsl:otherwise>
        <xsl:value-of select="Title" />
      </xsl:otherwise>
    </xsl:choose>
  </span>
  ...
</xsl:template>
```

These changes, in TVGuide6.xsl, generate a page in which you can navigate from a program to its series by clicking the name of the series.

Likewise, it would be useful to have links to the programs that are listed in the episode lists for each series. Here, we need an anchor in the result generated from each <Program> element and a link in the episode lists generated when we get a description of the series. However, unlike the series, there's no ready-made ID that we can use for the anchors.

There are several ways to create unique IDs for elements in an XML document—using their name and position within the XML document, a path-like ID generated from looking at their ancestors, or information specific to the area that you're looking at (such as the combination of the channel name and the time)—but by far the easiest is to use the generate-id() function. The generate-id() function generates a valid XML ID (starting with a letter, not containing any spaces) and is guaranteed to return the same ID for any particular node no matter how many times you call it within a particular run of a stylesheet. If you use the generate-id() function without an argument, you get the ID of the context node; if you pass an argument, then it must be a single node, and the generate-id() function will return an ID for that node.

The thing to watch out for when using the generate-id() function is that it is *not* guaranteed to give the same ID on different runs of the same stylesheet, or with different stylesheets operating over the same XML document, let alone across different processors. So, while you can use it to generate IDs that you use locally within a page, you can't use it to generate IDs that take you between pages.

■ **Note** Even within a page, it's a little risky, since sometimes people record URLs that include the IDs you use. If you were to then regenerate the page, the IDs would change completely.

■ **Summary** The generate-id() function generates a unique ID for a node.

Linking from Series to Programs

The <Program> elements don't have any ready-made IDs, so we need to use the generate-id() function to give us anchors, which we can then refer to from within the episode lists for each series. We can use the generate-id() function in attribute value templates for the name and id attributes on an anchor in the template for <Program> elements (and, in fact, this generated ID is much better than the name of the series as a source of the identifier for the cast list):

```
<xsl:template match="Program" mode="Details">
  <xsl:variable name="castList" as="element()?" select="CastList" />
  <xsl:variable name="programID" as="xs:string"
                select="concat(generate-id(), 'Cast')" />
  <p>
    <a name="{generate-id()}" id="{generate-id()}">
      <xsl:apply-templates select="Start" />
    </a>
    ...
```

```
    <xsl:apply-templates select="$castList" mode="DisplayToggle">
      <xsl:with-param name="divID" select="$programID" />
    </xsl:apply-templates>
  </p>
  <xsl:apply-templates select="$castList">
    <xsl:with-param name="divID" select="$programID" />
  </xsl:apply-templates>
</xsl:template>
```

And we can use the same function to give an ID to use in the link within the episode lists for each series:

```
<xsl:template match="TVGuide/Series">
  <div>
    <h3><a name="{@id}" id="{@id}"><xsl:value-of select="Title" /></a></h3>
    <p>
      <xsl:apply-templates select="Description" />
    </p>
    <h4>Episodes</h4>
    <ul>
      <xsl:for-each select="key('programsBySeries', @id)">
        <li>
          <a href="#{generate-id()}">
            <xsl:value-of select="parent::Channel/Name" />
            <xsl:text> at </xsl:text>
            <xsl:value-of select="format-dateTime(Start,
                                                   '[H01]:[m] on [M]/[D]/[Y]')" />
            <xsl:if test="string(Title)">
              <xsl:text>: </xsl:text>
              <xsl:value-of select="Title" />
            </xsl:if>
          </a>
        </li>
      </xsl:for-each>
    </ul>
  </div>
</xsl:template>
```

The ID that you generate with the `generate-id()` function when you process the `<Program>` element to create its details in the main schedule is guaranteed to be the same ID as you get when you process the `<Program>` element in order to describe it in the episode listing. If you use `TVGuide7.xsl`, which uses `generate-id()` in this way, to transform `TVGuide4.xml` into `TVGuide7.html`, you should find that the episode lists are linked to the program descriptions. For example, if I click the only *EastEnders* episode listed, I jump to the *EastEnders* episode shown in Figure 10-7.

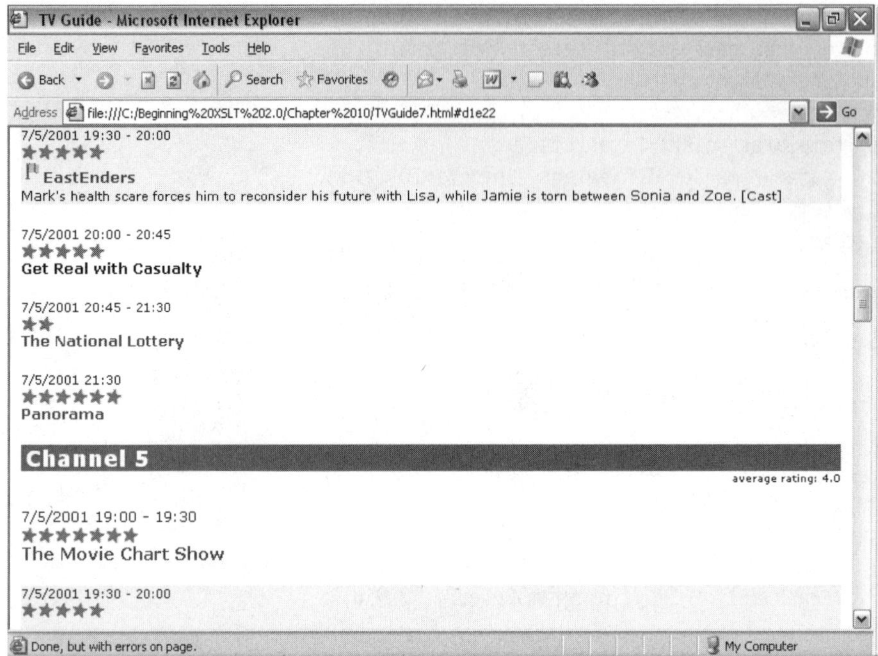

Figure 10-7. *Viewing* `TVGuide7.html` *in Internet Explorer*

The precise ID that you get (shown after the # in the `Address` bar) will probably be different, but you should be able to navigate from the program to the series description and back again without any difficulties.

Numbering

The `generate-id()` function gives a computer-generated ID that is guaranteed to work, but doesn't look particularly pretty and doesn't have any permanence: each time you run the transformation the generated ID might change. Another way of producing IDs that are both easier on the eye and more long-lasting and consistent across processors is to create numbers for nodes.

Numbering items is primarily useful in document-oriented XML, particularly when generating XSL-FO: for example, to sequentially number items in a list, to create footnotes, or to give numbers to section headings. In terms of the construction of the result tree, when you generate a number, you're actually generating a text node in the result tree in the same way as you would be with `<xsl:value-of>`.

There are two stages to numbering items:

- Working out the number for the item
- Formatting the number for different numbering schemas

In this section, we'll look first at three ways of getting the number of an item in a simple list (and introduce <xsl:number>), and then you'll learn how to use <xsl:number> to format the numbers that you get. Then we'll look at two other types of numbering schemes—numbering across an entire document (such as for numbering footnotes) and hierarchical numbering (such as for numbering sections).

Getting the Number of an Item

The most explicit method of getting a number for an item in XSLT is to use the <xsl:number> instruction to generate it for you. The basic form of the <xsl:number> instruction, without any attributes, gives you the number of the current node within the set of similar siblings, counting in document order and starting from 1. So you can number the channels in the TV guide by adding an empty <xsl:number> element to the template for the <Channel> elements in ChannelList mode:

```
<xsl:template match="Channel" mode="ChannelList">
  <a href="#{Name}">
    <xsl:number />
    <xsl:text> </xsl:text>
    <xsl:value-of select="Name" />
  </a>
  <xsl:if test="position() != last()"> | </xsl:if>
</xsl:template>
```

For example, the result of this template for BBC2, which is the second <Channel> element in the document, would be

```
<a href="#BBC2">2 BBC2</a> |
```

Summary The <xsl:number> instruction creates a number based on the position of the current node in the source tree.

If you want, you can explicitly state what node is being numbered using the select attribute. The select attribute holds an expression that selects the node to be numbered. For example, you could number the channels within the template matching their <Name> elements, as follows:

```
<xsl:template match="Channel/Name">
  <h2 class="channel">
    <a name="{.}" id="{.}">
      <xsl:number select="parent::Channel" />
      <xsl:text> </xsl:text>
      <xsl:value-of select="." />
    </a>
  </h2>
</xsl:template>
```

You can also state what kind of nodes you want to number using the count attribute. The count attribute holds a pattern (so shares the same syntax as the match attribute of <xsl:template>); the processor only counts nodes that match that pattern. The default for the count attribute is to match all nodes that are the same kind and have the same name as the node that you're numbering. So the <xsl:number> instruction in the preceding template is equivalent to the following:

```
<xsl:number select="parent::Channel" count="Channel" />
```

If the node that you're generating a number for doesn't match the count pattern, then the processor tries to find an ancestor of the current node that *does* match the pattern, and counts *its* preceding siblings instead. So selecting the parent <Channel> element in the preceding template gives the same result as only counting <Channel> elements in the first place, with

```
<xsl:number count="Channel" />
```

The count attribute is useful when you need to count all the siblings of an element, no matter what kind of node they are, which you can do with

```
<xsl:number count="node()" />
```

The count attribute is also handy if you have different types of elements in a list and want to number them sequentially. For example, if you want to number both <Program> and <Film> elements in a list in which the two are intermingled, you could use

```
<xsl:number count="Program | Film" />
```

Summary The select attribute on <xsl:number> is used to select the node to number. The count attribute holds a pattern that matches the nodes that you want to count when creating the number. It defaults to a pattern that matches nodes of the same type and name as the current node.

There are two disadvantages with using <xsl:number> to give you the number of an item, however. It calculates the number of a node based on the source tree rather than what you're generating in the output, and it always starts counting from 1. In the next couple of sections, we'll see ways around these two limitations.

Numbering Cast Members Based on Document Order

To try out numbering with <xsl:number>, we'll add numbers to the cast member list that we generate. Of course, because we're generating HTML, the first and easiest method is just to change the numbering scheme used for the <li> element using the list-style-type property as in TVGuide2.css:

```
.castlist li {
  display: list-item;
  list-style-type: decimal;
}
```

When transformed with TVGuide8.xsl, which generates XHTML that refers to TVGuide2.css, TVGuide4.xml generates TVGuide8.html, with decimal numbering of the cast members, as shown in Figure 10-8.

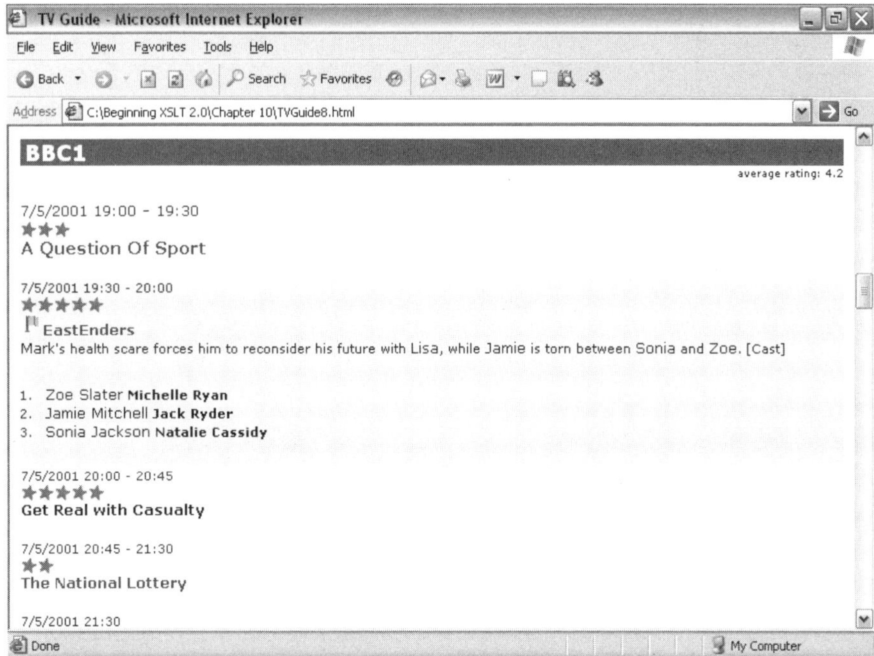

Figure 10-8. *Viewing* `TVGuide8.html` *in Internet Explorer*

However, CSS does not give full control over the item numbers—for example, you can't make them italic. To do that, you must create the list numbers by hand with XSLT. So, in `TVGuide9.xsl`, we'll change the template for the `<CastList>` element so that it just creates a `<div>` with a class of `castlist`:

```
<xsl:template match="CastList">
  <xsl:param name="divID" as="xs:string" required="yes" />
  <div id="{$divID}" style="display: none;" class="castlist">
    <xsl:apply-templates />
  </div>
</xsl:template>
```

We'll also change the template for the `<CastMember>` elements to create `<div>` elements in `castmember` style that contain a number (in `number` style) before the content. To begin with, let's number the characters using the basic form of `<xsl:number>`. We'll add a space between the number and the character's name, so that it's more readable:

```
<xsl:template match="CastMember">
  <div class="castmember">
    <span class="number"><xsl:number /></span>
    <xsl:text> </xsl:text>
    <xsl:apply-templates select="Character" />
    <xsl:text> </xsl:text>
    <xsl:apply-templates select="Actor" />
  </div>
</xsl:template>
```

In TVGuide3.css, we'll add a style for the number class, so that the numbers are italic:

```
.number {
  font-style: italic;
}
```

TVGuide9.xsl makes these changes and creates XHTML that refers to TVGuide3.css. When you use TVGuide9.xsl on the source file TVGuide4.xml to create TVGuide9.html, you see the page shown in Figure 10-9.

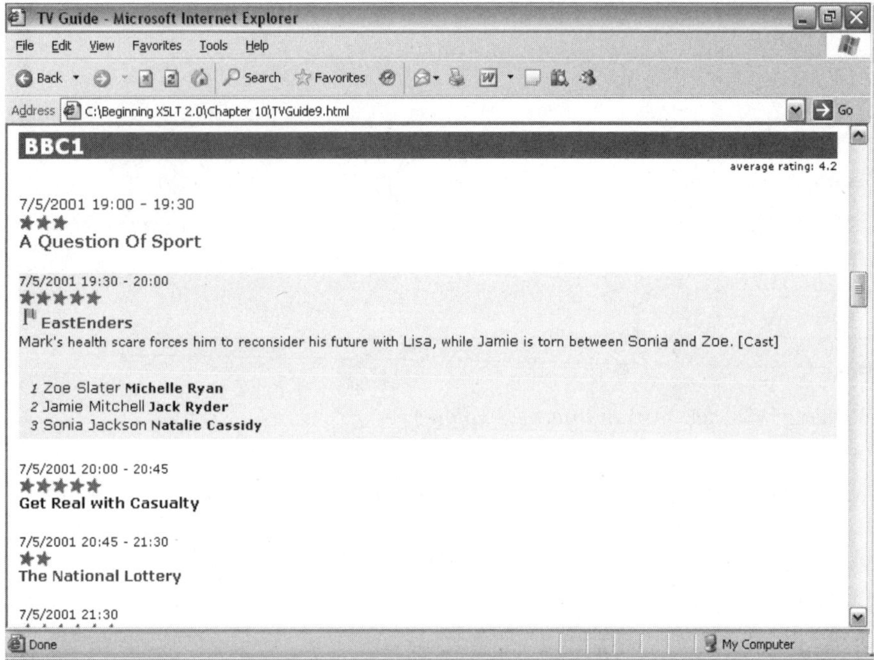

Figure 10-9. *Viewing* TVGuide9.html *in Internet Explorer*

The cast members are numbered in sequence, based on their order in the source XML document.

Numbering Sorted and Filtered Items

The <xsl:number> instruction always gives you the same number for the node, based on its position in the source node tree, and not the position of the node in terms of how and when it's processed. For example, TVGuide4.xml holds details about the following six channels:

1. BBC1
2. BBC2
3. ITV

4. Channel 4

5. Channel 5

6. Sky One

Say that you only want to present information about the channels that show flagged programs, and you want to display them sorted by average rating and rating of the first program as before. The template for the channel name can provide the number with <xsl:number>, and the $Channels variable holds the relevant channels sorted in the desired order:

```
<xsl:variable name="Channels" as="element(Channel)+">
  <xsl:perform-sort select="/TVGuide/Channel[Program[@flag]]">
    <xsl:sort select="avg(Program/@rating)" order="descending" />
    <xsl:sort select="xs:integer(Program[1]/@rating)" order="descending" />
  </xsl:perform-sort>
</xsl:variable>
```

Only some of the channels are displayed, and in a different order from the order in which they appear in the XML document, but the numbers generated by the <xsl:number> element for a particular <Channel> element are exactly the same as they would be if all the channels were being viewed in document order:

6. Sky One

2. BBC2

4. Channel 4

1. BBC1

Sometimes this behavior is exactly what you want—in this example, you might want the channels to retain their original numbering if those are the numbers that your TV set uses. But more often than not, you want the numbers that you generate to be sequential based on the *result* that you're generating rather than the *source* that holds the original information.

The closest that you can get to numbering based on the result is to number nodes in the order that they're processed. When you tell an XSLT processor to process a bunch of nodes with <xsl:for-each> or <xsl:apply-templates>, those nodes become the current node list and each node that gets processed has a position within it. When you process a particular node, you can get its position in the current node list using the position() function. So if you swap the <xsl:number> instruction for an <xsl:value-of> instruction that selects the current node's position, then the channels will be numbered in the order that they're processed in once more:

```
<xsl:template match="Channel">
  <h2 class="channel">
    <a name="{Name}" id="{Name}">
      <xsl:value-of select="position()" />
      <xsl:text> </xsl:text>
      <xsl:value-of select="Name" />
    </a>
  </h2>
</xsl:template>
```

Note Using the position of the current node to number nodes is also more efficient than using `<xsl:number>` because the position of the current node is immediately available to the XSLT processor, whereas each time you use `<xsl:number>` the processor has to check all the preceding siblings of the node that you're processing.

Something that you have to be careful of when you use the `position()` function to number nodes is that the numbering that you get totally depends on the way in which you apply templates to the nodes. A common trap here is that if you apply templates to all the child nodes of an element, then you often include whitespace-only text nodes in the list, between each of the elements you're actually interested in. This can lead to a sequence of even numbers in the result.

Stripping whitespace-only text nodes using `<xsl:strip-space>` (as we have seen in Chapter 7) can help prevent you getting the wrong numbering in your result. More generally, you should take care to only select the nodes that you're actually interested in when you create a numbered sequence.

Summary If nodes are filtered or sorted, you should use the `position()` function to number according to the position of an item in the result.

Numbering Cast Members Based on Processing Order

In the last example, we saw how to generate numbers for the members of our cast list using `<xsl:number>`. But what happens when you change the template for the `<CastList>` element, as in `TVGuide10.xsl`, so that the cast is listed in alphabetical order by character name, sorted first on surname then on first name?

```
<xsl:template match="CastList">
  <xsl:param name="divID" />
  <div id="{$divID}" style="display: none;" class="castlist">
    <xsl:apply-templates select="CastMember">
      <xsl:sort select="substring-after(Character/Name, ' ')" />
      <xsl:sort select="substring-before(Character/Name, ' ')" />
    </xsl:apply-templates>
  </div>
</xsl:template>
```

When you transform `TVGuide4.xml` with `TVGuide10.xsl` to create `TVGuide10.html`, you get the cast list shown in Figure 10-10.

Each cast member is allotted the same number as they were originally, so the numbers in the result are not in sequential order.

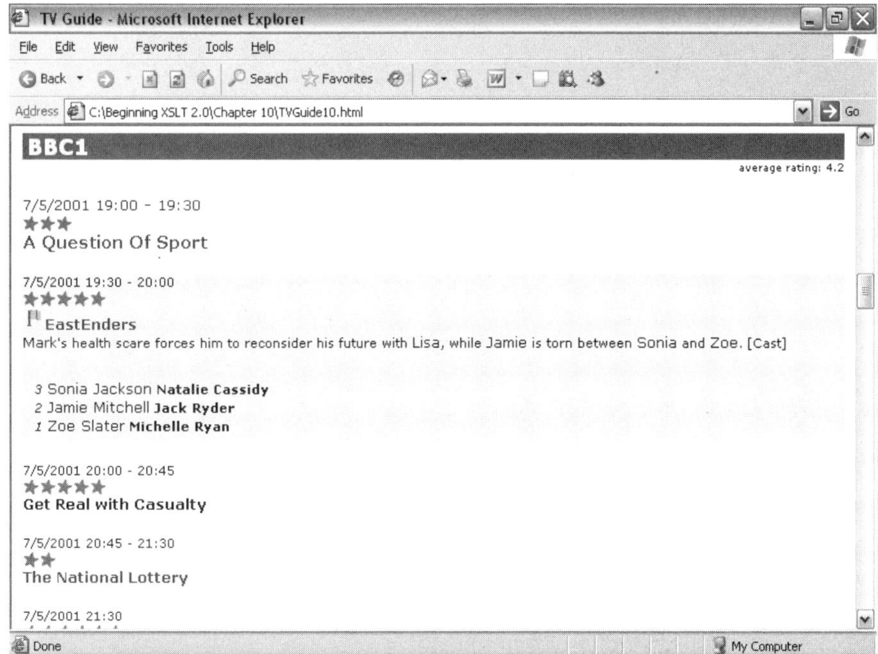

Figure 10-10. *Viewing* `TVGuide10.html` *in Internet Explorer*

To make the numbers sequential, you have to change the way in which the number is generated so that it uses the order in which the nodes are processed rather than the order in which they appear in the source node tree, using `position()`, as in `TVGuide11.xsl`:

```
<xsl:template match="CastMember">
  <div class="castmember">
    <span class="number"><xsl:value-of select="position()" /></span>
    <xsl:text> </xsl:text>
    <xsl:apply-templates select="Character" />
    <xsl:text> </xsl:text>
    <xsl:apply-templates select="Actor" />
  </div>
</xsl:template>
```

When you use `TVGuide11.xsl` with `TVGuide4.xml` to produce `TVGuide11.html`, you get the page shown in Figure 10-11.

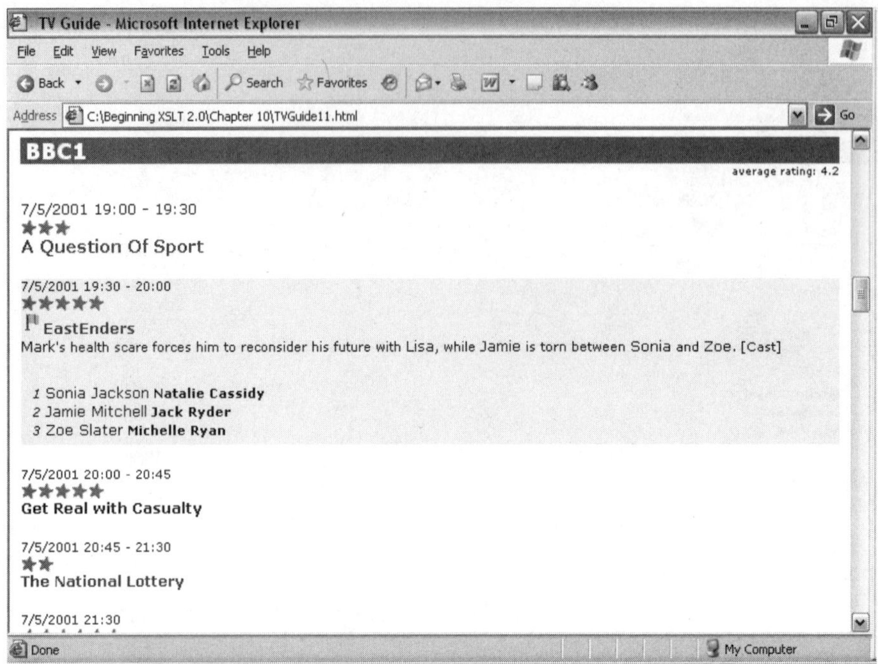

Figure 10-11. *Viewing* TVGuide11.html *in Internet Explorer*

The numbers are sequential again, as they should be. You may also want to compare using <xsl:number> with using the position() function while timing the transformation, to see whether it has any impact with your XSLT processor.

Changing the Starting Number

The <xsl:number> instruction always numbers nodes starting from 1. On digital boxes, the first channel (BBC1) is numbered 101, the second 102, and so on—the numbering starts from 101 and proceeds from there. Assuming that the channels should be numbered according to this scheme (but we don't want them numbered in the order they're processed in), we need to use something other than <xsl:number> to give us the number of each channel.

The solution to this problem is to write an XPath expression that does exactly the same thing as the equivalent <xsl:number> instruction in order to calculate the number to use. The number of a channel in this case is the number of sibling <Channel> elements that come before it, plus 101 (which is the number we want to get for the first channel). You can get all the <Channel> elements that precede the one you're looking at using the preceding-sibling:: axis:

```
preceding-sibling::Channel
```

This returns an empty sequence for the first channel; a sequence containing the first <Channel> element for the second channel; a sequence containing the first two <Channel> elements for the third channel; and so on. You can find out how many <Channel> elements the sequence contains using the count() function:

```
count(preceding-sibling::Channel)
```

This returns 0 for the first channel, 1 for the second channel, 2 for the third channel, and so on. To get the number that we want to display, add 101:

```
<xsl:template match="Channel">
  <h2 class="channel">
    <a name="{Name}" id="{Name}">
      <xsl:value-of select="count(preceding-sibling::Channel) + 101" />
      <xsl:text> </xsl:text>
      <xsl:value-of select="Name" />
    </a>
  </h2>
</xsl:template>
```

■ **Summary** You can count the preceding siblings of a node by hand, using the `count()` function and the `preceding-sibling::` axis, to start numbering from something other than 1.

Formatting Numbers

The `<xsl:number>` instruction's second role is to **format** numbers using different numbering schemes. All XSLT processors support eight different numbering schemes:

Format Token	Numbering Scheme	Example
1	Decimal numbering	1, 2, 3, ...
01	Decimal numbering with leading zeros	01, 02, 03, ...
a	Lowercase alphabetical numbering	a, b, c, ..., aa, ab, ac, ...
A	Uppercase alphabetical numbering	A, B, C, ..., AA, AB, AC, ...
i	Lowercase Roman numbering	i, ii, iii, iv, v, vi, ...
I	Uppercase Roman numbering	I, II, III, IV, V, VI, ...
w	Lowercase words	one, two, three, ...
W	Uppercase words	ONE, TWO, THREE, ...
Ww	Titlecase words	One, Two, Three, ...

■ **Note** These numbering schemes are the same as those used by the `format-dateTime()`, `format-date()`, and `format-time()` functions that you learned about in Chapter 5.

You can tell the XSLT processor which format to use for a particular number using the `format` attribute on `<xsl:number>`. Including the format token for a numbering scheme in the `format` attribute tells the XSLT processor to use that numbering scheme, but you can also add spaces or punctuation characters to the numbers. For example, to generate numbers consisting of lowercase Roman numerals in brackets, with a space after the close bracket, you should use

```
<xsl:number format="(i) " />
```

■ **Summary** The `format` attribute on `<xsl:number>` holds a pattern for the number, which must include a number token to give decimal (1, 2, 3), alphabetical (a, b, c), Roman (i, ii, iii), or spelled-out (one, two, three) numbering.

You can use the formatting controls offered by `<xsl:number>` on numbers that aren't generated by `<xsl:number>` using the `value` attribute, which takes an XPath expression that's interpreted as a number. For example, if you're generating numbers using the `position()` function, so that items are numbered according to the order in which the nodes are processed rather than the order in which they appear in the source, then you can use `<xsl:number>` to format and output the number instead of `<xsl:value-of>`:

```
<xsl:number value="position()" format="A." />
```

■ **Summary** The `value` attribute on `<xsl:number>` can specify any XPath expression that evaluates as a number, to be formatted according to the `format` attribute.

The `format` attribute is an attribute value template, so you can decide on the numbering scheme to use on the fly if you want, for example, to use different numbering schemes depending on the depth of a list.

Formatting Large Numbers

If you're numbering lots of items, you may wish to start grouping the digits that make up those numbers so that the numbers can be read more easily. The `<xsl:number>` instruction takes two attributes that allow you to control the grouping of digits in the numbers that you format:

- `grouping-size`—The number of digits in a group (defaults to 3)
- `grouping-separator`—The character used to separate groups of digits (defaults to a comma)

For example, to generate numbers that have pairs of digits separated by spaces, all within square brackets, you could use

```
<xsl:number format="[1]" grouping-size="2" grouping-separator=" " />
```

Both the attributes are attribute value templates, so again you can decide on their values on the fly to give different types of numbering in different situations or on user request.

■ **Summary** The `grouping-size` and `grouping-separator` attributes on `<xsl:number>` specify how the digits in large numbers are grouped together.

Formatting Numbers with Different Alphabets

Some XSLT processors support extra numbering schemes as well as the eight that are built in, such as numbering using different languages (α, β, γ, ...). However, while numbering schemes in some languages (such as Greek) use totally different scripts, those in other languages (such as Finnish) start with the same character as is used in English (a). More obviously, if you use spelled-out numbering, you care about the language in which the numbers are spelled out. To allow you to generate numbers in different languages, `<xsl:number>` has two attributes:

- `lang`—The language code for the language used by the numbering scheme
- `letter-value`—Whether to use the normal `alphabetic` numbering scheme of the language or the `traditional` numbering scheme

You should check your XSLT processor's documentation to see which languages it supports and whether there is a traditional variant for that particular language. If you don't specify a language, XSLT processors can use whatever language they want as a default, though most use English, with a traditional numbering scheme if you use the letter `i` and an alphabetical numbering scheme if you use the letter `a`.

■ **Summary** The `lang` and `letter-value` attributes on `<xsl:number>` give extra control with alphabetical and spelled-out numbering schemes.

Formatting the Numbers for Cast Members

The template that we're currently using, in `TVGuide11.xsl`, for `<CastMember>` elements looks as follows:

```
<xsl:template match="CastMember">
  <div class="castmember">
    <span class="number"><xsl:value-of select="position()" /></span>
    <xsl:text> </xsl:text>
    <xsl:apply-templates select="Character" />
    <xsl:text> </xsl:text>
    <xsl:apply-templates select="Actor" />
  </div>
</xsl:template>
```

The number that you get with this template is just the decimal number showing the position of the `<CastMember>` element amongst its siblings. You can use `<xsl:number>` and its `format` attribute to create a decimal number with curly brackets, but remember that curly brackets are special within attribute value templates, so you have to double them up to get them to appear in the result:

```
<xsl:template match="CastMember">
  <div class="castmember">
    <span class="number">
      <xsl:number value="position()" format="{{1}}" />
    </span>
```

```
    <xsl:text> </xsl:text>
    <xsl:apply-templates select="Character" />
    <xsl:text> </xsl:text>
    <xsl:apply-templates select="Actor" />
  </div>
</xsl:template>
```

This change is made in TVGuide12.xsl. When you use TVGuide12.xsl to transform TVGuide4.xml into TVGuide12.html, you should see the page shown in Figure 10-12.

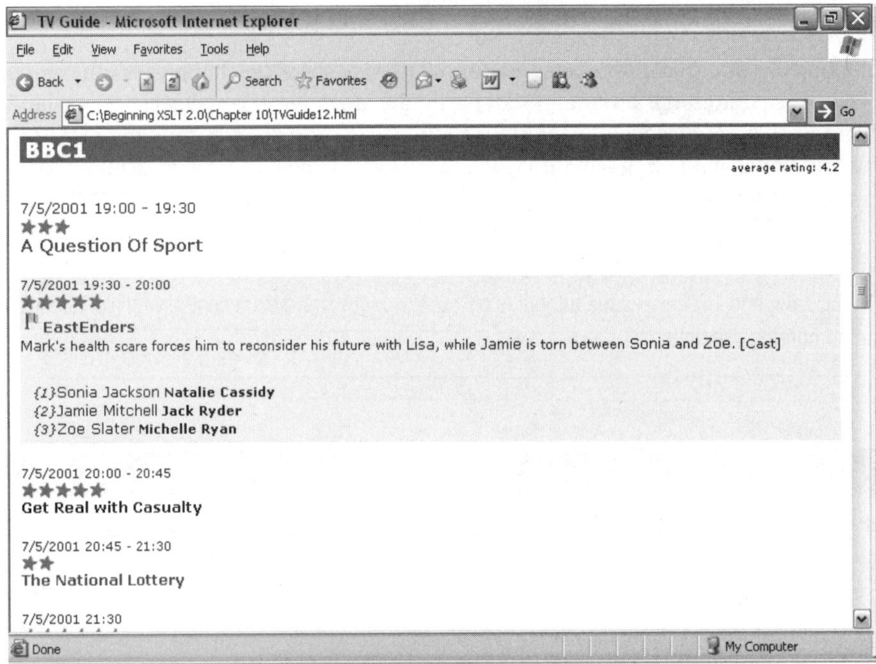

Figure 10-12. *Viewing* TVGuide12.html *in Internet Explorer*

The format attribute tells the XSLT processor to format the number that it gets from the position() function with curly brackets around it.

Look up the documentation about the numbering schemes supported by the XSLT processor that you're using and try out a few other numbering schemes to experiment with the grouping-size, grouping-separator, lang, and letter-value attributes to see their effect.

Numbering Across a Document

The numbering with <xsl:number> that we've looked at so far is limited to numbering simple lists where the items that you want to number are all children of the same parent. If you imagine creating numbers for <ol> lists, then this simple form of <xsl:number> is precisely what you want. On the other hand, imagine that you're trying to number footnotes that are included in paragraphs spread across many sections. The footnotes aren't siblings, but they should still be numbered sequentially.

To do numbering across a document, or any time the items that you want to number are not siblings of each other, you need to use the <xsl:number> instruction, adding a `level` attribute with the value `any`:

```
<xsl:number level="any" />
```

With this instruction, the XSLT processor doesn't just count the preceding *siblings* that are similar to the current node, it looks at all the ancestors and preceding nodes in the document that are of the same type and have the same name as the current node, and counts how many there are. You can specify exactly the kinds of nodes that you want to count using the `count` attribute as normal, and the number can be formatted with the `format` and other attributes in just the same way as described previously for simple lists.

Note The `level` attribute has the value `single` by default, which gives numbering of simple lists where all the items are siblings of each other.

Summary If the `level` attribute of <xsl:number> is given the value `any`, it numbers nodes amongst similar nodes across the entire document.

If you only want to number the items within a particular section (for example, to restart the numbering of footnotes with each new chapter in a book), then you should combine the `level` attribute with the `from` attribute. The `from` attribute on <xsl:number> is a pattern; the XSLT processor finds the nearest ancestor or preceding node that matches the pattern and starts counting nodes from there. For example, to number <Link> elements (which aren't siblings), but only within a particular <Channel>, the template matching the <Link> element should contain the following:

```
<xsl:number level="any" from="Channel" />
```

Summary The `from` attribute of <xsl:number> matches the types of nodes at which counting should restart from 1.

Generating Hierarchical Numbers

The final type of numbering supported by <xsl:number> is the numbering of nodes arranged in hierarchies. Hierarchical numbering is often seen in technical documentation, where each part, chapter, section, subsection, or even paragraph, is numbered, with numbers like `B.3.5.iv` indicating the fourth paragraph of the fifth section of the third chapter of the second part of a report.

Hierarchical numbers are supported in XSLT by setting the `level` attribute of `<xsl:number>` to `multiple`. The `count` attribute is particularly useful with hierarchical numbers, since the elements at different levels of the hierarchy tend to be named different things. You should set the `count` attribute to a pattern that matches the types of elements that are significant within the hierarchy. For example, to create a hierarchical number that numbered each `<CastMember>` within each `<Program>` within each `<Channel>`, you could use

```
<xsl:number level="multiple" count="Channel | Program | CastMember" />
```

Tip The order in which you put the patterns in the `count` attribute has no effect on the way the hierarchical number is constructed, but I find it most intuitive to put them in the order in which they will be used within the number, from the highest to the lowest.

Summary If the `level` attribute of `<xsl:number>` is given the value `multiple`, it generates hierarchical numbers. The `count` attribute is a pattern that matches the elements that should be counted at each level.

When formatting hierarchical numbers, you need a format pattern that is made up of multiple tokens, one for each of the levels in the numbering scheme. If you set the `format` attribute to the number that you'd expect the first item to have, as a kind of template for the others, then you'll get the numbering scheme that you want. So to number the `<CastMember>` elements `1-1.A`, `1-1.B`, ... `1-2.A`, `1-2.B`, ... `2-1.A`, `2-1.B`, and so on, you need to use the following `<xsl:number>` instruction:

```
<xsl:number level="multiple" count="Channel | Program | CastMember"
            format="1-1.A" />
```

The tokens that you can use in these hierarchical numbers are exactly the same as the tokens that you can use in the normal simple lists (for example, `1` for decimal numbering, `I` for uppercase Roman numbering).

Summary

In this chapter, we started off by looking at the ways in which you could search for elements from an XML document that have particular values for their attributes or child elements. While you can use predicates to search for practically anything within an XML document, they can be very inefficient, particularly if you perform the same type of search several times.

To help with this efficiency problem, XPath and XSLT offer two techniques that tell the XSLT processor to index elements within an XML document so that they can be accessed quickly by some value. The first technique is to use `ID` attributes and the `id()` function, but this has several disadvantages such as forcing the identifier to be held within an attribute, constraining the format of the identifier, and allowing only one-to-one mappings between identifiers and elements.

The second technique gets around these problems by giving you full flexibility in the way in which elements, or other nodes, are indexed. With a key, you can state that particular elements should be accessible quickly by key values; these values can be in any format and can come from anywhere. Keys also have the advantage of not making the stylesheet dependent on a DTD or schema being specified for the source XML document, which means that you can rely on the stylesheet having access to the elements through the key in a way that you can't with an ID. Keys also support many-to-many mappings where the same key value can be used to access many elements and the same element can be accessed with many key values.

We've also introduced `<xsl:number>` in this chapter as a method of generating and formatting numbers. The `<xsl:number>` instruction is arguably less useful in the data-oriented XML that we're primarily working with here than it is in document-oriented XML, where you often need to number lists, footnotes, and sections. However, numbering can sometimes come in handy, especially when you're generating IDs for items that will remain the same over transformations (unlike those generated with the `generate-id()` function).

You've seen how `<xsl:number>` can be used for three different kinds of numbering: single-level simple lists, numbering items across entire documents or within particular sections, and generating multilevel numbers for hierarchical structures. The `format` attribute controls how these numbers are displayed, allowing you to create numbers from many different numbering schemes. Again, the `format` attribute and the other attributes that control the presentation of the numbers that you generate are all attribute value templates, which means that they can all be set dynamically based on parameters passed into the stylesheet or the individual template.

We've also touched on a couple of other methods of numbering, which you can use to generate numbers even if you still use `<xsl:number>` to format them, namely using `position()` and counting the preceding siblings of the node that you're interested in. The `<xsl:number>` instruction tends to be quite inefficient when it comes to generating numbers, and it always gives you numbers based on the source tree, so it's often better to use the `position()` function to create numbers if you can.

Review Questions

1. What is the advantage of using `ID` attributes and the `id()` function over using predicates to search for elements?

2. What format can the values of `ID` attributes take?

3. Create a DTD in which the required `custNo` attribute of the `<Customer>` element is an `ID` attribute.

4. What three types of arguments can the `id()` function take and what does it return from each?

5. What advantages are there for using keys rather than IDs?

6. In what situations might you use the keys defined as follows?

```
<xsl:key name="films" match="Film" use="@id" />
<xsl:key name="filmsByCharacters" match="Film"
         use="CastList/CastMember/Character/Name" />
<xsl:key name="filmsByYear" match="Film" use="Year" />
<xsl:key name="filmsByDirector" match="Film" use="Director/Name" />
<xsl:key name="filmsByYearAndDirector" match="Film"
         use="concat(Year, '::', Director/Name)" />
```

7. What two ways can you use to generate a number giving the position of a node within the source tree?

8. What's the biggest difference between using `position()` and using `<xsl:number>` to number items?

9. What does the following piece of code generate?

```
<xsl:for-each select="Program">
  <xsl:variable name="format">
    <xsl:choose>
      <xsl:when test="position() mod 3 = 1">{1}</xsl:when>
      <xsl:when test="position() mod 3 = 2">[A]</xsl:when>
      <xsl:otherwise>(i)</xsl:when>
    </xsl:choose>
  </xsl:variable>
  <xsl:number format="{$format}" />
  ...
</xsl:for-each>
```

10. What different values can the `level` attribute on `<xsl:number>` take and how does its value change the numbering of a node?

CHAPTER 11

Named Templates, Stylesheet Functions, and Recursion

Previous chapters have introduced you to the concept of **templates**: blocks of code that break up a stylesheet to make it more manageable and more reusable. So far, we've only looked at **matching templates**, which are invoked when you apply templates to a particular type of node. In this chapter, we'll look at **named templates**, which are templates that you invoke by calling them by name.

We'll also introduce **stylesheet functions**. Like named templates, stylesheet functions are reusable blocks of code that are invoked by name, but whereas named templates are called using an instruction (`<xsl:call-template>`) within a sequence constructor, stylesheet functions are called using a standard function call from within an XPath expression or a pattern.

Named templates and stylesheet functions are very powerful: they enable you to use XSLT to perform just about every computation you might want to, making XSLT a true programming language. But as we've already seen, XSLT is different from most programming languages. In **procedural** programming languages, you can use iteration to perform calculations: you can initialize a variable and update it each time you loop. XSLT, on the other hand, is a **functional** programming language, which means that the same instruction in the same context will always produce the same thing, no matter how many times it's run. XSLT doesn't have `while` loops, for example, because a variable's value can't change (if it did, the number of times you assigned a new value to a variable would determine what value the variable took).

Therefore, when you're programming with XSLT, you need to use **recursion** to give the same effect as you would get from `while` loops in procedural languages. In this chapter, you'll learn how to construct recursive templates and functions to carry out common tasks.

In this chapter, you'll learn

- How to create and call a named template
- How to create and call a stylesheet function
- The principles of recursion
- How to write a recursive template or function
- Recursing with numbers, strings, and sequences

Named Templates

Thus far, the templates that you've been writing have all matched a particular node and done something with it. Some of these templates have been templates with modes, which enable you to get a different result from the same node, and some of them have used parameters to pass in extra information about how the node should be processed. These templates are the main component of your stylesheets because the main goal of XSLT is to process nodes from a source node tree.

Splitting up your stylesheet into templates actually helps you in two ways. First, it allows you to use the processor's node-matching capabilities to work out what piece of code to use to process a particular node. This is particularly useful when you're processing document-oriented XML or XML whose structure might evolve over time. Second, it enables you to break up a stylesheet into reusable portions. This cuts down on the length of the stylesheet (because you don't have to repeat the same code in different places) and makes it easier to author and maintain (because it helps you focus on a particular bit of code at a time). We've used both these aspects of templates in previous chapters, taking advantage of the latter feature when we apply templates to a node in a particular mode to process that node in a particular way.

However, some pieces of processing aren't dependent on what node you're processing, or might need to be carried out when there is no node available on which to hang the process. For example, say that we wanted to provide different images according to the value of the `flag` attribute on the `<Program>` element. We can use a template that matches the `flag` attribute to provide the image, as follows:

```
<xsl:template match="@flag">
  <img src="{if (. = 'favorite') then 'favorite' else 'interest'}.gif"
       alt="[{if (. = 'favorite') then 'Favorite' else 'Interest'}]"
       width="20" height="20" />
</xsl:template>
```

But say that we want to provide a spacer image if the `flag` attribute is missing. There's no `flag` attribute node to match on in this case, so the code has to be embedded in the template for the `<Program>` element instead:

```
<xsl:template match="Program" mode="Details">
  ...
  <img src="{if (@flag) then
               (if (@flag = 'favorite') then 'favorite' else 'interest')
             else 'spacer'}.gif"
       alt="[{if (@flag) then
                (if (@flag = 'favorite') then 'Favorite' else 'Interest')
              else ' '}]"
       width="20" height="20" />
  ...
</xsl:template>
```

While there's nothing wrong with that in terms of the functionality of the code, it does use seven lines in the template processing the `<Program>` element, rather than one line applying the template to the `flag` attribute, and these seven lines would have to be repeated if the same code were required elsewhere.

What's required in such situations is a way to create a template and call it without applying templates to a particular node. You can do this in XSLT using **named templates**. Every template can be assigned a name with its `name` attribute (including those templates that are already matching templates). Each must have its own distinct name, though it can be the same as the name of a mode. Named templates can take parameters, just like any other template, and indeed since they have no other source of information about what they're supposed to do, it's a rare named template that doesn't have any. In this example, a template named `image` could take a `$flag` parameter, as follows:

```
<xsl:template name="image">
  <xsl:param name="flag" as="xs:string" required="yes" />
  <img src="{if ($flag) then
               (if ($flag = 'favorite') then 'favorite' else 'interest')
             else 'spacer'}.gif"
       alt="[{if ($flag) then
                (if ($flag = 'favorite') then 'Favorite' else 'Interest')
              else ' '}]"
       width="20" height="20" />
</xsl:template>
```

Summary Named templates are useful when you want to reuse code that doesn't use the current node. A template is given a name with the `<xsl:template>` element's `name` attribute.

You can invoke named templates by calling them with `<xsl:call-template>`. The `<xsl:call-template>` instruction takes a `name` attribute that names the called template. Like `<xsl:apply-templates>`, `<xsl:call-template>` can contain `<xsl:with-param>` elements in order to pass in values for the parameters of the template that it calls.

Tip The current node within a called template is the same as the current node at the point where the template is called. I think that it's bad practice to use the current node within a named template (for example, by using relative location paths), because you have no way of knowing what kind of node it might be. If the current node is important, I use a matching template (which might also be named).

So in the template for the `<Program>` element, you need an `<xsl:call-template>` instruction calling the `image` template. The `$flag` parameter is assigned the value of the `flag` attribute of the `<Program>` element, as follows:

```
<xsl:template match="Program" mode="Details">
  ...
  <xsl:call-template name="image">
    <xsl:with-param name="flag" select="@flag" as="xs:string" />
  </xsl:call-template>
  ...
</xsl:template>
```

Summary You can call a named template, with parameters if necessary, using the <xsl:call-template> instruction.

Named templates are a lot like methods in object-oriented programming languages—you call them by name, often passing arguments (parameters) to them, and they return a result. You can declare the type of the result of a template using the as attribute on <xsl:template>, which holds a sequence type, just like the as attribute on <xsl:variable>. Often this will be a sequence of nodes, but it could be an atomic value instead. For example, to declare that our image template returns a single <img> element, we can use

```
<xsl:template name="image" as="element(img)">
  <xsl:param name="flag" as="xs:string" required="yes" />
  <img src="{if ($flag) then
              (if ($flag = 'favorite') then 'favorite' else 'interest')
            else 'spacer'}.gif"
       alt="[{if ($flag) then
               (if ($flag = 'favorite') then 'Favorite' else 'Interest')
             else ' '}]"
       width="20" height="20" />
</xsl:template>
```

Note You can also declare the type of the result of a matching template using the as attribute.

Summary You can declare the type of the result of invoking a template using the as attribute on <xsl:template>.

Creating Links with a Named Template

There are several places within TVGuide.xsl where we need to create a link from a string to a URL. To make the user experience more enthralling, all the <a> elements generated by TVGuide2.xsl need to include attributes to change the style of links when you hover over the link with a mouse. To make it easy to add the attributes, we'll store them in a linkEvents attribute set, which needs to be included on each of the <a> elements that creates a link. The linkEvents attribute set is as follows:

```
<xsl:attribute-set name="linkEvents">
  <xsl:attribute name="style">
    <xsl:text>color: black; border-bottom: 1pt groove #CCC</xsl:text>
  </xsl:attribute>
  <xsl:attribute name="onmouseover">
    <xsl:text>javascript:this.style.background = '#CCC';</xsl:text>
  </xsl:attribute>
```

```
  <xsl:attribute name="onmouseout">
    <xsl:text>javascript:this.style.background = 'transparent';</xsl:text>
  </xsl:attribute>
</xsl:attribute-set>
```

Most of the links are generated around the value of nodes, but on occasion the linked text and the URL being linked to can also be partial values or newly generated text. Each `<a>` element that's generated needs to have the `linkEvents` attribute set added to it using the `xsl:use-attribute-sets` attribute. The links are generated in several templates, for example:

```
<xsl:template match="Channel" mode="ChannelList">
  <a xsl:use-attribute-sets="linkEvents" href="#{Name}">
    <xsl:value-of select="Name" />
  </a>
  <xsl:if test="position() != last()"> | </xsl:if>
</xsl:template>
```

The result of transforming `TVGuide.xml` with `TVGuide2.xsl`, which contains this code, is `TVGuide2.html`, on which the links are underlined and where, when you hover over a link with the mouse, the link background turns gray. For example, in Figure 11-1 the mouse is hovering over the link to BBC2 at the top of the page.

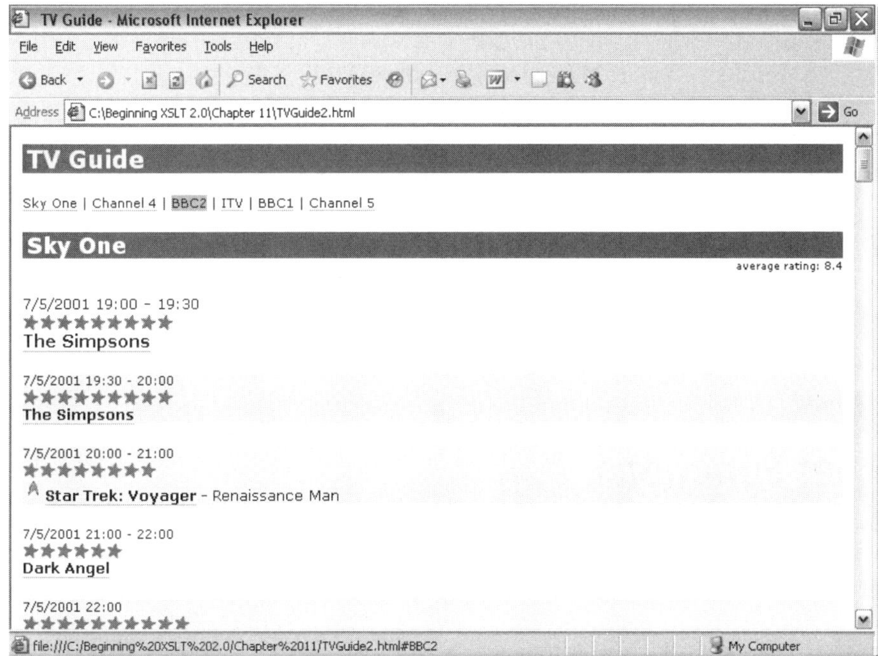

Figure 11-1. *Viewing* `TVGuide2.html` *in Internet Explorer*

In `TVGuide2.xsl`, roughly the same code is used in multiple different templates to create the same kind of link. In fact, the only things that vary in each place are the URL to which the link is made and the content of the `<a>` element.

However, if you changed your mind about the name of the attribute set, for example, you wanted to add a new attribute set to the <a> elements or wanted to add an icon after each link, then you would have to search through the stylesheet to find each instance and change it.

To make it more maintainable, you can put the link-generating code into a named template that you call on demand. In TVGuide3.xsl, the link template takes a URL to link to and a value for the content of the <a> element, and creates the required <a> element. Both the $href and $content parameters are required; $href is a string while $content can be any sequence of items (as long as there's one or more of them). The result of the template is a single element:

```
<xsl:template name="link" as="element()">
  <xsl:param name="href" as="xs:anyURI" required="yes" />
  <xsl:param name="content" as="item()+" required="yes" />
  <a href="{$href}" xsl:use-attribute-sets="linkEvents">
    <xsl:sequence select="$content" />
  </a>
</xsl:template>
```

The templates that create the <a> elements then need to be changed so that they call this template instead. For example:

```
<xsl:template match="Channel" mode="ChannelList">
  <xsl:call-template name="link">
    <xsl:with-param name="href" as="xs:anyURI"
                    select="xs:anyURI(concat('#', Name))" />
    <xsl:with-param name="content" as="xs:string" select="Name" />
  </xsl:call-template>
  <xsl:if test="position() != last()"> | </xsl:if>
</xsl:template>
```

The result of TVGuide3.xsl, which uses the link template, is exactly the same as TVGuide2.xsl. Using the named template has unified the way in which links are created throughout the stylesheet, which makes it easier to target changes that need to be made to all the links that get created.

Stylesheet Functions

We've now seen how to call a block of XSLT code by name using named templates. There is another way to call a block of code in XSLT 2.0: using a **stylesheet function**. Stylesheet functions are functions that are defined within the stylesheet rather than being built into the XSLT processor.

Note As well as stylesheet functions and built-in functions, there is a third class of function: extension functions. We'll look at extension functions in Chapter 14.

Like other functions, stylesheet functions can be called from within an XPath expression using the syntax *functionName(arguments)*, which is shorter than the equivalent `<xsl:call-template>` instruction and can be used in places where an `<xsl:call-template>` instruction can't, such as in a predicate.

Stylesheet functions can be useful just as a replacement for long XPath expressions, especially if the same expression is used in several places. For example, we might want to replace this test:

```
<xsl:if test="@flag = ('favorite', 'interesting') or @rating > 6 or
             (some $n in (Series, Title, Description)
              satisfies contains(lower-case($n), 'news'))">
  ...
</xsl:if>
```

with a call to a function called something like `is-interesting-program()`. This would make it more apparent that the code was testing whether the program is interesting or not.

Another way in which stylesheet functions are sometimes useful is that they can wrap around XSLT code to make it callable from an XPath expression. There are some things that you can do with XSLT code that you can't do within an XPath expression. For example, the following XSLT elements offer functionality that isn't otherwise available in XPath:

- The `<xsl:variable>` element enables you to hold values in variables to simplify your code; the only variables supported in XPath are range variables, which can't hold sequences.
- The `<xsl:perform-sort>` instruction enables you to sort sequences, and in particular do sorts based on calculated values.
- The `<xsl:for-each-group>` instruction enables you to create sequences of distinct items based on calculated values (such as the number of children a node has).
- The `<xsl:analyze-string>` instruction enables you to do much more complex string manipulation than that supported by the functions available in XPath.

Stylesheet functions can help if you want to do any of these things in a context where it's difficult or impossible to use XSLT code directly, such as within the match pattern of a template.

Finally, stylesheet functions can simply be used instead of templates, depending on your coding style. It's a good idea to take advantage of templates with different match patterns if you need to generate different results for different nodes, so if the result of a block of code depended on the type or kind of a node, then I'd use templates—one for each different kind of node. Otherwise, I'd usually use a template if the result included newly generated nodes (as in the `link` template that we looked at in the last section) and a function if the result was a sequence of atomic values or existing nodes (such as for the `is-interesting-program()` function, which would return a Boolean value).

Now that we've seen why stylesheet functions might be useful, we'll turn to looking at how to declare them.

Summary Stylesheet functions are functions that are defined within the stylesheet.

Declaring Stylesheet Functions

A declaration for a stylesheet function looks a lot like the declaration for a named template, except that it uses the <xsl:function> element rather than the <xsl:template> element. The basic syntax for a stylesheet function is as follows:

```
<xsl:function name="functionName" as="resultType">
  <xsl:param name="argument1" as="argument1Type" />
  ... other parameters ...
  ... code generating function result ...
</xsl:function>
```

Function declarations go at the top-level of the stylesheet, at the same level as template declarations.

■ **Summary** Stylesheet functions are declared using an <xsl:function> element at the top level of the stylesheet.

Naming the Function

The name attribute of the <xsl:function> element specifies the name of the function. Stylesheet functions differ from normal functions in that they must be in a namespace, which entails that their name must have a prefix. For example, you can't define a function that's just called is-interesting-program(); instead, it must be called something like tv:is-interesting-program().

■ **Note** The fact that stylesheet functions are all in namespaces ensures that they don't get confused with built-in functions.

It doesn't particularly matter what namespace you use, though it's good practice to use a namespace that you have control over, such as a URI that includes a domain name that you own. Usually, you won't want to have this namespace be included in the output of the stylesheet, so as well as declaring the namespace, you should list its prefix in the exclude-result-prefixes attribute on the <xsl:stylesheet>. For example, to put the stylesheet functions that we'll use in the http://www.example.com/TVGuide namespace (associated with the prefix tv), the <xsl:stylesheet> element needs to look something like this:

```
<xsl:stylesheet version="2.0"
                xmlns:xsl="http://www.w3.org/1999/XSL/Transform"
                xmlns:xs="http://www.w3.org/2001/XMLSchema"
                xmlns:xdt="http://www.w3.org/2005/04/xpath-datatypes"
                xmlns:tv="http://www.example.com/TVGuide"
                exclude-result-prefixes="xs xdt tv"
                xmlns="http://www.w3.org/1999/xhtml">
  ...
</xsl:stylesheet>
```

Tip You can actually use namespaces for the names of most things in an XSLT stylesheet, such as template names, mode names, and key names; doing so helps to prevent clashes between definitions with the same name, particularly when combining stylesheets, which we'll be looking at in the next chapter.

Summary The `name` attribute of `<xsl:function>` specifies the name of the function. Stylesheet functions must be in a namespace, which entails that their names must be given a prefix.

Declaring Arguments

As with templates, you declare the arguments to a stylesheet function with `<xsl:param>` elements. However, there are several differences between template parameters and function parameters, which partly arise from the different ways in which templates and functions are called.

When you call a template or apply templates to a sequence of nodes, you pass parameters to the template using the `<xsl:with-param>` element. Each `<xsl:with-param>` element specifies the name of the parameter for which it's supplying a value: parameter values are passed *by name*. It therefore doesn't matter if you change the order of the `<xsl:with-param>` elements, and if you miss out a parameter when you call a template then; as long as that parameter's not required, the parameter's default value will be used.

On the other hand, when you call a function, there's no opportunity to specify a name for each argument. Instead, argument values are passed *by position*: the first argument corresponds to the first parameter declared in the function declaration, the second argument to the second parameter, and so on.

The fact that function arguments are passed by position opens the question of what happens when the number of arguments doesn't match the number of parameters declared for the function. The answer is that it's an error: all function parameters are required (and thus the `<xsl:param>` elements in function definitions cannot have a `required` attribute or specify a default value).

However, XSLT 2.0 allows you to have several `<xsl:function>` elements, all with the same name but with different numbers of arguments, and this allows you to support functions with optional arguments.

For example, say that you wanted to declare a `tv:is-interesting-program()` function, and wanted it to take two arguments: the `<Program>` element that may or may not be interesting, and a keyword that you want to search for in its series, title, or description. The keyword part is optional: if you don't supply it, then you want to search for the keyword `'news'`. To define this function, you need two `<xsl:function>` elements, one for the function in its two-argument form:

```
<xsl:function name="tv:is-interesting-program" as="xs:boolean">
  <xsl:param name="program" as="element(Program)" />
  <xsl:param name="keyword" as="xs:string" />
  <xsl:sequence select="$program/@flag = ('favorite', 'interesting') or
                        $program/@rating > 6 or
                        (some $n in $program/(Series, Title, Description)
                         satisfies contains(lower-case($n), $keyword))" />
</xsl:function>
```

and another for the function in its single-argument form, which simply calls the two-argument function of the same name, but with the string 'news' as the second argument:

```
<xsl:function name="tv:is-interesting-program" as="xs:boolean">
  <xsl:param name="program" as="element(Program)" />
  <xsl:sequence select="tv:is-interesting-program($program, 'news')" />
</xsl:function>
```

The different function declarations could have completely different arguments if you wanted, and do completely different things, but it's good practice for functions with the same name to perform the same operation, with the arguments in the same order (which means that the "optional" arguments come after those that are required).

■ **Note** You cannot have two function declarations that have the same name and the same number of parameters. In particular, you can't have two function declarations that differ only in the declared types of the parameters (polymorphic functions). If you want a function to work differently for arguments of different types, you need to test the type of the argument using the `instance of` expression in an `<xsl:choose>` or by applying templates to the argument, if it's a node.

■ **Summary** Function arguments are passed by position rather than by name. Within a function declaration, all parameters are required (so they can't have default values), but you can have two function declarations with the same name and different numbers of arguments.

Defining the Result

As you might expect, the result of the function is defined by a sequence constructor in the content of the `<xsl:function>` element, following the parameter declarations. The `as` attribute of `<xsl:function>` tells the XSLT processor what kind of sequence the function should return; you don't have to specify it, but it's a good idea to do so. The XSLT processor will try to cast the value generated by the sequence constructor to that type, and will raise an error if it can't do so.

If a function is simply replacing a long and complicated XPath expression, then the body of the function declaration will usually just contain an `<xsl:sequence>` element whose `select` attribute holds the XPath expression. The declaration of the `tv:is-interesting-program()` function is an example:

```
<xsl:function name="tv:is-interesting-program" as="xs:boolean">
  <xsl:param name="program" as="element(Program)" />
  <xsl:param name="keyword" as="xs:string" />
  <xsl:sequence select="$program/@flag = ('favorite', 'interesting') or
                        $program/@rating > 6 or
                        (some $n in $program/(Series, Title, Description)
                         satisfies contains(lower-case($n), $keyword))" />
</xsl:function>
```

One thing is worth noting here: unlike with named templates, the sequence constructor for a function is evaluated without a context item. That means you can't declare stylesheet functions that default to operating on the context node in the way that some of the built-in functions (such as `name()` and `string()`) do. If you try to refer to the context item or the context position (using `position()`), you will get an error.

Note Thus, a function without parameters must always return the same value.

Summary After any `<xsl:param>` elements, the `<xsl:function>` element holds a sequence constructor that generates the result of the function. You can specify the type of this result using the `as` attribute on `<xsl:function>`.

Defining a Function to Test Programs

Let's add the `tv:is-interesting-program()` function to `TVGuide3.xsl`, to create `TVGuide4.xsl`. There are three changes that we need to make in this stylesheet. First, we need to declare a namespace that the function can live in, and specify that this namespace shouldn't be included in the result document:

```
<xsl:stylesheet version="2.0"
                xmlns:xsl="http://www.w3.org/1999/XSL/Transform"
                xmlns:xs="http://www.w3.org/2001/XMLSchema"
                xmlns:xdt="http://www.w3.org/2005/04/xpath-datatypes"
                xmlns:tv="http://www.example.com/TVGuide"
                exclude-result-prefixes="xs xdt tv"
                xmlns="http://www.w3.org/1999/xhtml">
  ...
</xsl:stylesheet>
```

Second, we need to add the function declarations that we've looked at previously. We have two function declarations, both with the same name but with different numbers of parameters:

```
<xsl:function name="tv:is-interesting-program" as="xs:boolean">
  <xsl:param name="program" as="element()" />
  <xsl:param name="keyword" as="xs:string" />
  <xsl:sequence select="$program/@flag = ('favorite', 'interesting') or
                        $program/@rating > 6 or
                        (some $n in $program/(Series, Title, Description)
                         satisfies contains(lower-case($n), $keyword))" />
</xsl:function>

<xsl:function name="tv:is-interesting-program" as="xs:boolean">
  <xsl:param name="program" as="element()" />
  <xsl:sequence select="tv:is-interesting-program($program, 'news')" />
</xsl:function>
```

Finally, we need to call this function when we test whether to add a `class` attribute with a value of `interesting` to the `<div>` element generated for a `<Program>` element. We'll just use the one-argument version of the function as follows:

```
<xsl:template match="Program">
  <div>
    <xsl:if test="tv:is-interesting-program(.)">
      <xsl:attribute name="class">interesting</xsl:attribute>
    </xsl:if>
    <xsl:apply-templates select="." mode="Details" />
  </div>
</xsl:template>
```

The result of transforming TVGuide.xml with TVGuide4.xsl is TVGuide4.html, which looks exactly the same as TVGuide3.html. The result hasn't changed, but it's now clearer what's going on in the template that matches the <Program> element.

Recursion

When we looked at variables and parameters in Chapter 6, we noted that variables are not available outside their scope, which means that you can't change a variable's value. We looked at how that meant you couldn't use iteration to do things like counting how many items there are in a sequence. In procedural programming languages, you'd count the items in a sequence by iterating over the sequence, and keeping a running total in a variable. But because you can't update a variable in XSLT, you can't use iteration.

There are lots of places that you use iteration in procedural programming languages. You use iteration for summing values, for processing strings and numbers, and for doing the same thing a fixed number of times. In XSLT, some of those tasks are supported with purpose-built functions such as count() and sum(). But in general, rather than using iteration to solve the problem, you have to use **recursion** instead.

■ **Note** Recursion used to be a very important technique in XSLT 1.0; in XSLT 2.0 it's less often necessary both because there are more aggregate functions (such as min() and avg()), and because it's now easy to split a complex calculation into smaller steps by creating sequences of values.

■ **Summary** Because variables can't vary in XSLT, you need to use recursion rather than iteration to do most processing.

In this section, we're going to look at how to do recursion in XSLT to solve some of the common problems encountered when transforming XML documents. We'll start off with a general description of recursion, and then look at specific types of recursion for processing values of different types.

Recursive Principles

Recursion is a pattern in which a labeled block of code calls itself with different starting conditions. In XSLT, that means having a named template or a stylesheet function that calls itself with different values for its parameters. These templates and functions are known as **recursive templates** and **recursive functions**.

The result of a recursive template or function is some combination of (usually just part of) the values that have been passed through its parameters and the result of calling itself with different values in the parameters. The values passed for these parameters are usually based on the initial parameter value in some way, for example, a substring or the result of subtracting one from the initial parameter value.

Of course, if the template or function keeps calling itself, and the result of that call is another call to the same template or function, and so on, the process keeps going forever. This is known as **infinite recursion**, and is something to be avoided! To prevent infinite recursion, the template or function also has to test whether it's time to stop the recursion, and it should only call itself under certain conditions. The condition that tests when it's time to stop recursing is known as the **stopping condition**, and it involves testing the parameters, usually to see whether they're empty strings or zero or something along those lines.

Recursive templates generally use either `<xsl:if>`, as follows:

```
<xsl:template name="templateName" as="returnType">
  <xsl:param name="paramName" as="paramType" select="defaultValue" />
  ...
  <xsl:if test="condition">
    ...
    <xsl:call-template name="templateName">
      <xsl:with-param name="paramName" as="paramType"
                      select="differentValue" />
    </xsl:call-template>
    ...
  </xsl:if>
</xsl:template>
```

or `<xsl:choose>`, as follows:

```
<xsl:template name="templateName" as="returnType">
  <xsl:param name="paramName" as="paramType" select="defaultValue" />
  ...
  <xsl:choose>
    <xsl:when test="condition">
      ...
    </xsl:when>
    <xsl:otherwise>
      ...
      <xsl:call-template name="templateName">
        <xsl:with-param name="paramName" as="paramType"
                        select="differentValue" />
      </xsl:call-template>
      ...
```

```
    </xsl:otherwise>
  </xsl:choose>
</xsl:template>
```

Recursive functions are similar, except that, as we've seen, they can't have default values for their parameters, and the call to the function is made using a function call rather than an `<xsl:call-template>` instruction. The fact that the recursive call can be made in an XPath expression rather than an XSLT instruction means that you can use an `if` expression to test the stopping condition instead of an `<xsl:choose>`:

```
<xsl:function name="functionName" as="returnType">
  <xsl:param name="paramName" as="paramType" />
  ...
  <xsl:sequence select="if (condition) then
                          ...
                        else
                          ... functionName(differentValue) ..." />
</xsl:template>
```

Summary A recursive template or function is a named template or stylesheet function that calls itself.

Numeric Calculations Using Recursion

The first type of recursion we'll look at in detail is recursion to perform a numeric calculation. XPath provides operators and functions for some numeric calculations, but not all of them. For example, XPath doesn't offer functions for getting the square root of a number or getting the power of a number.

Note Writing stylesheet functions for these functions can be quite tricky; usually you can use an extension function instead, as you'll see in Chapter 14, or you can reuse utility functions such as those from EXSLT (`http://www.exslt.org/math`). I'm really only including these functions here as examples of recursion in use.

In these kinds of functions, you use a parameter to keep track of the value attained so far, and only emit that value when you come to the end of the recursion. This parameter is only ever used within the recursion, so there are usually two function declarations that support the function: one that provides the user interface to the function (without the extra parameter) and another that actually carries out the recursion.

Tip When a function parameter should never actually be used by a user, I usually put the function that accepts the extra parameter in a different namespace. For example, the `math:squareRoot()` function would be the one that the user calls (without the extra parameter), with the `private-math:squareRoot()` function being the one that actually does the work (with the extra parameter).

For example, the following `math:squareRoot()` stylesheet function (provided in `squareRoot.xsl`), or rather its helper function `private-math:squareRoot()`, gives the square root of a number by repeatedly adjusting an estimate of the square root by half of the difference between the square of the estimate and the number of which you're attempting to find the square root. We prevent infinite recursion by only using a certain precision, passed in as a parameter. The `$precision` parameter is used to round the number to a certain number of decimal places in conjunction with the `round-half-to-even()` function. If the current estimate is the same as the next estimate, to the specified precision, then you've found the square root of the number, at least to the desired precision:

```
<xsl:function name="math:squareRoot" as="xs:double">
  <xsl:param name="number" as="xs:double" />
  <xsl:sequence select="math:squareRoot($number, 4)" />
</xsl:function>

<xsl:function name="math:squareRoot" as="xs:double">
  <xsl:param name="number" as="xs:double" />
  <xsl:param name="precision" as="xs:integer" />
  <xsl:sequence select="private-math:squareRoot($number, $precision, 1)" />
</xsl:function>

<xsl:function name="private-math:squareRoot" as="xs:double">
  <xsl:param name="number" as="xs:double" />
  <xsl:param name="precision" as="xs:integer" />
  <xsl:param name="estimate" as="xs:double" />
  <xsl:variable name="nextEstimate" as="xs:double"
    select="$estimate + (($number - $estimate * $estimate) div
                         (2 * $estimate))" />
  <xsl:variable name="roundedEstimate" as="xs:double"
    select="round-half-to-even($nextEstimate, $precision) " />
  <xsl:sequence
    select="if ($estimate = $roundedEstimate) then $estimate
            else private-math:squareRoot($number, $precision, $roundedEstimate)" />
</xsl:function>
```

For example, you could call the `math:squareRoot()` function with the following call:

```
math:squareRoot(10)
```

and it would return the square root of 10 to 4 decimal places (since that's the precision supplied by the version of the function with a single argument)—3.1623.

In other calculating functions, the solution is adjusted a particular number of times. In a function to work out the power of a number, for example, the number needs to be multiplied by itself a certain number of times. In the `math:power()` function (provided in `power.xsl`), the `$result` parameter keeps track of the result and is adjusted by being multiplied by the same number (held in the `$number` parameter) the number of times specified by the `$power` parameter:

```
<xsl:function name="math:power" as="xs:double">
  <xsl:param name="number" as="xs:double" />
```

```
  <xsl:param name="power" as="xs:integer" />
  <xsl:sequence select="private-math:power($number, $power, 1)" />
</xsl:function>

<xsl:function name="private-math:power" as="xs:double">
  <xsl:param name="number" as="xs:double" />
  <xsl:param name="power" as="xs:integer" />
  <xsl:param name="result" as="xs:double" />
  <xsl:sequence
    select="if ($power = 0) then $result
            else private-math:power($number, $power - 1, $result * $number)" />
</xsl:function>
```

For example, you could call the `math:power()` function with the following call:

```
math:power(2, 8)
```

This would return 2 to the power of 8—256.

These functions give surprisingly good performance, even with quite large numbers, and especially with processors that optimize tail-recursive functions (which we'll talk about in more detail later in this chapter). However, they will never be as fast as built-in functions, so if your processor supports extension functions for performing these calculations, and performance is an issue, you should use the extensions.

Note You'll learn how to use extension functions in Chapter 14.

Summary To perform calculations with recursive templates, you need a parameter that is only used for the recursion, to keep track of the result so far.

Recursing Over Strings

Recursive templates that deal with strings usually perform some function on the first part of a string and then move on to the rest of the string. There are two common ways of splitting a string into the "first" and the "rest":

- Use `substring-before()` to get the first part before a particular character or substring, and `substring-after()` to get the rest, after the same character or substring.
- Use `substring()` to get the first character(s) in the string and to get the remaining characters in the string.

Let's look at an example of the second kind of recursion. XPath 2.0 provides a very useful `tokenize()` function for splitting up a string at a particular delimiter to give a sequence of strings, but doesn't give a way of breaking a string down into a sequence of characters. For example, say that you want to iterate over the letters of the English alphabet; it's much easier, in a stylesheet to write the alphabet as a single string:

```
'ABCDEFGHIJKLMNOPQRSTUVWXYZ'
```

than it is to write a sequence that holds each character individually:

```
('A', 'B', 'C', ..., 'X', 'Y', 'Z')
```

To create a sequence of characters from a string, you need to take the first letter from the string and add it to the sequence, then, if there are any letters left, move on to the rest of the string (the string from the second character on). `characters.xsl` contains a `str:characters()` function that does just this:

```
<xsl:function name="str:characters" as="xs:string*">
  <xsl:param name="string" as="xs:string" />
  <xsl:if test="$string">
    <xsl:sequence select="substring($string, 1, 1)" />
    <xsl:variable name="remainder" select="substring($string, 2)" as="xs:string" />
    <xsl:if test="$remainder">
      <xsl:sequence select="str:characters($remainder)" />
    </xsl:if>
  </xsl:if>
</xsl:function>
```

■ **Summary** You can split a string into characters by returning the first character (as revealed by the `substring()` function) followed by the result of recursing on the rest of the string (again using the `substring()` function).

Iterating Over the Alphabet to Create Alphabetical Indexes

One common reason for iterating over the alphabet is to construct alphabetical indexes where each letter has its own section; for example, alphabetical indexes of programs and series. In this example, we'll create an alphabetical index of the series in our TV guide, as in `TVGuide5.xsl`.

As you learned in the previous chapter, you can use keys to collect together all the series with the same starting letter. First, you need a key that indexes `<Series>` elements by the first letter in their `id` attribute (we'll use the series' ID because that's likely not to include irrelevant words like "A" or "The"):

```
<xsl:key name="seriesByFirstLetter" match="Series"
         use="substring(@id, 1, 1)" />
```

Now, you could find the letters of the alphabet by grouping the `<Series>` elements by their first letter using `<xsl:for-each-group>`. However, since you know what letters these can be, it's a lot easier to iterate over the letters of the alphabet.

We'll store the alphabet in a `$alphabet` stylesheet parameter, so that future users of the stylesheet can change the alphabet that's used if they need to; we'll default it to the English alphabet:

```
<xsl:param name="alphabet" as="xs:string"
           select="'ABCDEFGHIJKLMNOPQRSTUVWXYZ'" />
```

To create a sequence of the letters of the alphabet, we need to use the `str:characters()` function that we just looked at:

```
<xsl:function name="str:characters" as="xs:string*">
  <xsl:param name="string" as="xs:string" />
  <xsl:if test="$string">
    <xsl:sequence select="substring($string, 1, 1)" />
    <xsl:variable name="remainder" select="substring($string, 2)" as="xs:string" />
    <xsl:if test="$remainder">
      <xsl:sequence select="str:characters($remainder)" />
    </xsl:if>
  </xsl:if>
</xsl:function>
```

Don't forget to declare the `str` prefix; I've used the namespace `http://www.example.com/string` for it, though it doesn't really matter what you use. You should also make sure that namespace doesn't appear in the output by including the `str` prefix in the `exclude-result-prefixes` attribute on the `<xsl:stylesheet>` element.

In the template matching the `<TVGuide>` element, we'll store the sequence of characters that results from calling this template on the `$alphabet` stylesheet parameter in a local `$alphabet` variable:

```
<xsl:template match="TVGuide">
  ...
  <h2>Series</h2>
  <xsl:variable name="alphabet" as="xs:string+"
                select="str:characters($alphabet)" />
  ...
</xsl:template>
```

And the `<TVGuide>` element itself, which we'll otherwise lose track of when we iterate over the alphabet, within a `$TVGuide` variable:

```
<xsl:template match="TVGuide">
  ...
  <h2>Series</h2>
  <xsl:variable name="alphabet" as="xs:string+"
                select="str:characters($alphabet)" />
  <xsl:variable name="TVGuide" as="element()" select="." />
  ...
</xsl:template>
```

We can then iterate over this sequence of characters twice using `<xsl:for-each>`, first to create a line that provides links to each alphabetical section:

```
<xsl:template match="TVGuide">
  ...
  <h2>Series</h2>
  <xsl:variable name="alphabet" as="xs:string+"
                select="str:characters($alphabet)" />
  <xsl:variable name="TVGuide" as="element()" select="." />
  <xsl:for-each select="$alphabet">
    <xsl:variable name="series" as="element()*"
                  select="key('seriesByFirstLetter', ., $TVGuide)" />
```

```
    <xsl:choose>
      <xsl:when test="$series">
        <xsl:call-template name="link">
          <xsl:with-param name="href" as="xs:anyURI"
                          select="xs:anyURI(concat('#series', .))" />
          <xsl:with-param name="content" as="xs:string" select="." />
        </xsl:call-template>
      </xsl:when>
      <xsl:otherwise>
        <xsl:value-of select="." />
      </xsl:otherwise>
    </xsl:choose>
    <xsl:if test="position() != last()"> . </xsl:if>
  </xsl:for-each>
  ...
</xsl:template>
```

and then to create each alphabetical section by accessing all the <Series> elements whose IDs start with that letter (using the key defined previously) and, if there are any, creating a heading (which includes an anchor point for the heading, so that you can link to it) and applying templates to <Series> elements:

```
<xsl:template match="TVGuide">
  ...
  <h2>Series</h2>
  <xsl:variable name="alphabet" as="xs:string+"
                select="str:characters($alphabet)" />
  <xsl:variable name="TVGuide" as="element()" select="." />
  <xsl:for-each select="$alphabet">
    ...
  </xsl:for-each>
  <xsl:for-each select="$alphabet">
    <xsl:variable name="series" as="element()*"
                  select="key('seriesByFirstLetter', ., $TVGuide)" />
    <xsl:if test="$series">
      <h3>
        <a id="series{.}" name="series{.}">
          <xsl:value-of select="." />
        </a>
      </h3>
      <xsl:apply-templates select="$series">
        <xsl:sort select="@id" />
      </xsl:apply-templates>
    </xsl:if>
  </xsl:for-each>
</xsl:template>
```

TVGuide5.xsl contains these changes, and also changes the level of the headings produced by the <Series> elements, so that the structure of the document is clearer. The result of transforming TVGuide.xml with TVGuide5.xsl is TVGuide5.html, which is shown in Figure 11-2.

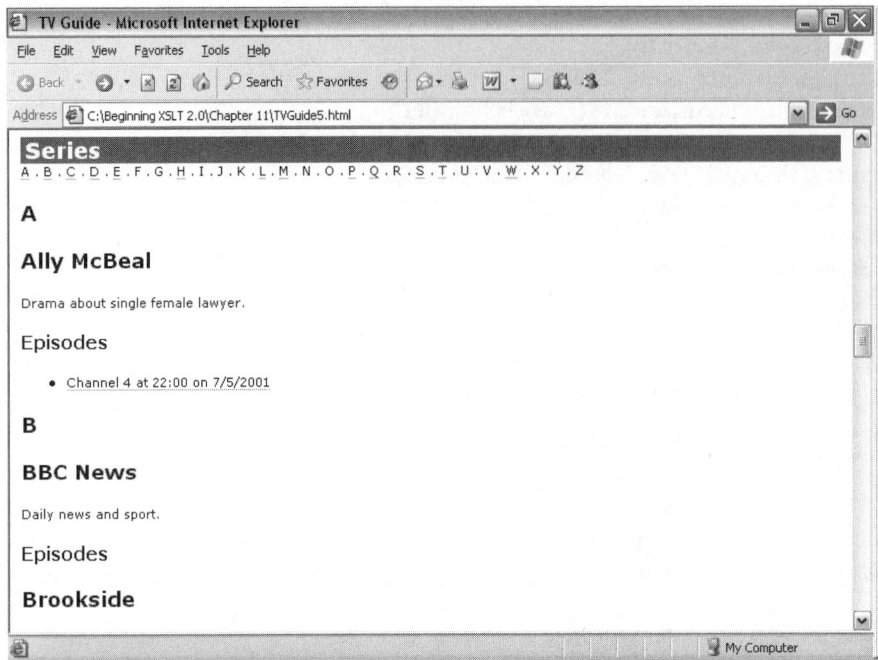

Figure 11-2. *Viewing* TVGuide5.html *in Internet Explorer*

The alphabet just underneath the `Series` heading gives links to the alphabetically ordered series further down the page. Both of the alphabetical orderings have been created by iterating through the characters of the alphabet, rather than by looking to see what the first letters of each series are.

Recursing with Sequences

Unlike strings or numbers, XSLT has built-in support for iterating over sequences using `<xsl:for-each>`, `<xsl:apply-templates>`, and the XPath expressions `for`, `some`, and `every`. If you need to iterate over a sequence, you should use one of these instructions rather than create a complicated recursive template. XPath also offers support for the kinds of things that you would otherwise need to do using recursion with a variety of aggregate functions. The following functions in particular are helpful in reducing the requirement for recursive templates:

- `position()`—Gives you a counter
- `count()`—Counts how many items there are in a sequence
- `string-join()`—Concatenates the strings in a sequence
- `sum()`—Sums the values of all the items in a sequence
- `min()`—Returns the minimum value of the items in a sequence
- `max()`—Returns the maximum value of the items in a sequence
- `distinct-values()`—Returns the distinct values in a sequence

Even if you can't use these aggregate functions with the sequence you have, you can usually avoid the requirement for recursion by creating a sequence from the sequence you have that you *can* use with the appropriate aggregate function.

However, there are still times when you do need to use recursion with sequences, in particular when you need to combine the items in a sequence in some way that isn't supported by one of the supplied aggregate functions.

A function that works over a sequence using recursion, then, will usually have at least two parameters: one to hold the sequence that is being recursed over and another, used purely within the recursion itself, to hold the result thus far. Because the user should never have to supply a value for the second of these parameters, I usually create a helper function to perform the recursion itself, and call that function from a more user-friendly function that only includes the required parameters.

Within the helper function, the first item of the sequence to be processed can be accessed using a numeric predicate, while the "rest" of the items are those whose position in the sequence is more than one. If you prefer, you can use the `subsequence()` or `remove()` functions to get these subsequences rather than using predicates. The recursion should stop when the sequence is empty and there are no more items to process. Thus, the basic outline for one of these functions is the following:

```
<xsl:function name="pref:nodeRecursionFunction" as="...">
  <xsl:param name="seq" as="item()*" />
  <xsl:sequence select="private-pref:nodeRecursionFunction($seq, defaultValue)" />
</xsl:function>

<xsl:function name="private-pref:nodeRecursionFunction" as="...">
  <xsl:param name="seq" as="item()*" />
  <xsl:param name="current" as="..." />
  <xsl:choose>
    <xsl:when test="exists($seq)">
      ... do something with $seq[1] ...
      ... private-pref:nodeRecursionFunction($seq[position() > 1], newValue) ...
    </xsl:when>
    <xsl:otherwise>
      <xsl:sequence select="$current" />
    </xsl:otherwise>
  </xsl:choose>
</xsl:template>
```

An example of such a function is a function that multiplies together the items in a sequence of numbers, `math:product()` in `product.xsl`, which could be used to apply a number of discounts to a price, for example. The helper template, which actually does the recursion, needs to accept two parameters: a sequence of numbers and the product so far. If there are numbers left in the sequence, then the new product for the next recursion needs to be the result of multiplying the current product with the first of the numbers in the sequence; the result of the function is the result of calling the function recursively, with the first argument being the rest of the sequence and the second argument being the new product. If there aren't any numbers left in the sequence, then we've come to the end of the list and can return the product that we've found:

```
<xsl:function name="private-math:product" as="xs:double">
  <xsl:param name="numbers" as="xs:double*" />
  <xsl:param name="product" as="xs:double" />
  <xsl:sequence
    select="if (exists($numbers))
            then private-math:product($numbers[position() > 1],
                                      $product * $numbers[1])
            else $product" />
</xsl:function>
```

The user-interface function that wraps this helper function needs to accept a sequence of numbers and, as long as that sequence actually contains some numbers, return the result of calling the helper template with

```
<xsl:function name="math:product" as="xs:double">
  <xsl:param name="numbers" as="xs:double*" />
  <xsl:sequence select="if (exists($numbers))
                        then private-math:product($numbers, 1)
                        else ()" />
</xsl:function>
```

For example, you could call the `math:product()` function with the following call:

```
math:product((2, 3, 4))
```

This would return 2 * 3 * 4—24.

■ **Summary** XSLT and XPath have good support for operations that would usually involve iteration over a sequence. Where an operation is not supported, you can use a recursive template or function that uses the predicates to pull out the first item on which to operate and the rest of the items on which to recurse.

Tail Recursion

Recursion can be computationally expensive. When a processor comes across a loop in procedural programming languages, it can assign a particular set of resources to hold the values of the variables that are updated within the loop. However, with a recursive process, the processor may have to assign different resources to hold the values of the parameters each time the template is called.

For example, when working through a string containing the alphabet, the processor might have to assign one byte for every letter in the alphabet, so 26 bytes for the alphabet to start with. With a loop, those same 26 bytes can be reused again and again. However, with a recursive template or function, the parameter has different resources assigned to it each time the template or function is called, so the total memory consumption is more like 26 + 25 + 24 + ... + 3 + 2 + 1 = 351 bytes.

The fact that a processor has to assign new resources on each recursion means that it has to keep track of where it is within the program by recording which function called this function, and which function called that function, and so on up to the very first call that started the program running. This record of functions calling other functions is known as the **stack**. When you use recursive templates or functions, the stack can get very large; each time a template or function calls itself, it adds another level to the stack. So in the example of working through the alphabet letter by letter, on the last recursion you're 26 levels deeper than you were in the first recursion.

All processors have a limit to the size of the stack, and therefore a limit to the depth that the recursion can reach. If you have a template that has to call itself a lot of times, you might reach the stack limit; at that point the process stops altogether, and the stylesheet generates an error.

Fortunately, most processors are clever enough to recognize when they can reuse the resources that are assigned to a recursive template or function and so don't need to add another level to the stack. In particular, if you write a template or function so that it only calls itself once, and the recursive call is the last thing that's done by a template or function, then the processor can interpret the recursive instructions exactly as if they were specified in a loop. Templates or functions that call themselves as the very last thing they do are known as **tail recursive**.

■ Note Different processors are built in different ways and optimize different aspects of XSLT and XPath. If you need to improve the speed of your stylesheet, then you should try out different ways of solving the same problem to see which one gives you the best performance with your data and your processor.

■ Summary Tail recursive templates are more efficient than recursive templates that are not tail recursive.

When you are writing a recursive template or function that will need to call itself lots of times, then it is worthwhile trying to make it tail recursive. The two things that you need to ensure are

- Within every branch of the instructions inside the template or function, the template or function only calls itself once.
- Within every branch of the instructions inside the template or function, the recursive call is the last thing the processor needs to do.

We'll look at an alternative design for a template working out the product of a sequence of numbers to illustrate these issues. First, look at the `private-math:product()` helper function from the last section (the recursive call is highlighted):

```
<xsl:function name="private-math:product" as="xs:double">
  <xsl:param name="numbers" as="xs:double*" />
  <xsl:param name="product" as="xs:double" />
  <xsl:sequence
    select="if (exists($numbers))
            then private-math:product($numbers[position() > 1],
                                      $product * $numbers[1])
            else $product" />
</xsl:function>
```

There's only one recursive call within this function (the one that's highlighted) and it occurs as the last thing within an if expression in a <xsl:sequence> that is the last instruction in the function. If the recursive call happens at all, then it's the last thing that happens.

Now consider the following definition of the function, which performs the same calculation, but this time by getting the product of the "rest" of the items, and then multiplying that by the value of the first item:

```
<xsl:function name="private-math:product" as="xs:double">
  <xsl:param name="numbers" as="xs:double*" />
  <xsl:sequence
    select="if (exists($numbers))
            then $numbers[1] * private-math:product($numbers[position() > 1])
            else 1" />
</xsl:function>
```

In this version, there's still only one recursive call to the private-math:product() function, but it is not the last thing that happens when the function is processed. After getting the product of the rest of the numbers, the template goes on to use that product to work out what value to give as the result (by multiplying it by the first number in the sequence). So the preceding template is not tail recursive.

Summary A tail recursive template is a template that only calls itself once, as the last thing it does during its instantiation.

Summary

This chapter has introduced you to named templates and stylesheet functions as a way of splitting up a stylesheet to make it more manageable, and to perform calculations that require recursion.

You can name any template (including those that match nodes) using the name attribute on <xsl:template>. Every template's name must be different, so that the processor can identify it when you call it with the <xsl:call-template> instruction. Like normal templates, you can pass parameters into named templates with <xsl:with-param> elements within <xsl:call-template>. You can declare the type of the result of a template using the as attribute on the <xsl:template> element.

You can define a stylesheet function using the <xsl:function> element, which is very similar in structure to a template. Parameters are passed to functions by position rather than by name, so all function parameters are therefore required (and none can have a default value). You can define two functions with the same name and different numbers of parameters in order to support functions with "optional" arguments. Also, unlike templates, the function body is always evaluated without a context item, so you need to pass any information that you want to use in the function via arguments, explicitly.

XSLT and XPath 2.0 have a lot more support for sequences than XSLT 1.0 did, in particular because they allow sequences of atomic values. XSLT supports iteration over a sequence with <xsl:for-each> and <xsl:apply-templates>, and you can iterate over a sequence in XPath with for, some, and every expressions. XPath supports counters with the position() function and has several aggregating functions such as count(), sum(), min() and string-join(). However, to perform certain calculations, you still need recursive templates or functions.

Recursive templates and functions call themselves, and you should design them so that they're tail recursive, as this allows processors to execute them without assigning lots of unnecessary resources to them. A tail-recursive template or function calls itself once only, and it's the last thing that it does during a single instantiation of the template or function. We've seen how to use recursive templates and functions to perform numeric calculations and to split up a string into characters.

There are many different ways of using XSLT. At the beginning of this book, you learned how to use XSLT as a designer—creating a template of a page and then populating it with information from an XML document. In the previous several chapters, you've become an XSLT author, which has enabled you to create more sophisticated pages. Now, knowing how to design and use recursive templates and functions, you are on your way to becoming an XSLT programmer, someone who can use XSLT to perform just about any task that involves manipulating XML.

Review Questions

1. How do you assign a name to a template?
2. What are the two situations in which the instructions held in a template might be enacted?
3. What restrictions are there on the names that you can use for functions?
4. Create a `str:substring-after-last()` function that returns the substring after the last occurrence of a particular delimiter (which should be a regular expression). The default delimiter should be any whitespace character. For example, the following function call:

   ```
   str:substring-after-last('Some sequence of words.')
   ```

   should result in the string `'words.'`.
5. When should you use named templates rather than matching templates, and when a function rather than a template?
6. What is the defining feature of a recursive template or function? What's special about a tail recursive template or function?
7. In general, how many parameters are different in a recursive call than in the call to the original template or function?
8. Create a tail-recursive template that performs line wrapping. The template should insert `<br>` elements into a string such that lines always end with a whitespace character (so you don't get words broken over lines). You will probably find the `str:substring-after-last()` function that you created earlier useful. For example:

   ```
   <xsl:call-template name="line-wrap" as="node()*">
     <xsl:with-param name="string" as="xs:string"
       select="'This is a long string with over 70 characters in it. It should
   have &lt;br> elements inserted at least every 70 characters so that it's
   displayed wrapped over several lines within an XML page.'" />
     <xsl:with-param name="line-length" as="xs:integer" select="70" />
   </xsl:call-template>
   ```

should result in the following XHTML:

```
This is a long string with over 70 characters in it. It should have<br />
&lt;br> elements inserted at least every 70 characters so that it's<br />
displayed wrapped over several lines within an XML page.
```

CHAPTER 12

Building XSLT Applications

In all the transformations that you've carried out so far, there's been a single stylesheet operating on a single source document. In this chapter, you'll see how to split a single stylesheet into multiple physical files, and how to access multiple XML documents to get hold of extra information.

There are two reasons why you might want to split up your stylesheet into separate physical documents. First, it helps with **maintenance** if you can focus on a particular file to find the code that you need, rather than searching through one big stylesheet. Second, if templates or other declarations are housed in a separate file, you can **reuse** them in multiple XSLT applications.

There are also two ways in which being able to access other source documents is useful. First, external documents can hold extra data that the stylesheet can use, for example, lookup tables to hold multilingual dictionaries or search and replace strings. Second, the source document for the transformation might not hold all the information that you need to be present; if this information is spread over several separate files, then you need to be able to access them as well—for example, the information about TV series could be kept in a separate document from the main TV listing.

In this chapter, you'll learn

- How to split and then include stylesheets with `<xsl:include>`
- How to import stylesheets with `<xsl:import>`
- How to override components from an imported stylesheet
- How to access external documents
- How to hold data within the stylesheet itself
- How to retrieve referenced information

Splitting Up Stylesheets

The first aspect of larger XSLT applications that we'll look at is how to divide or split up a stylesheet into several separate files using `<xsl:include>`. As your XSLT applications get larger, the files start to become unwieldy—you have to scroll through lots of templates and other declarations to find the piece of code that you want. While authoring tools can help with managing stylesheets, they can also suffer with poor performance when trying to cope with large documents. Therefore, it helps you manage and maintain your XSLT applications if you can split up your stylesheet into multiple parts.

XSLT allows you to split up your stylesheet into multiple files and then **include** the information from one stylesheet in another with the `<xsl:include>` element. The `<xsl:include>` element sits at the top level of the stylesheet, as a child of the `<xsl:stylesheet>` document element. It takes a single attribute—`href`—which holds the URL of the stylesheet that you want to include, relative to the including stylesheet. For example, the following `<xsl:include>` element includes the `descriptions.xsl` stylesheet:

```
<xsl:include href="descriptions.xsl" />
```

When an XSLT processor comes across an `<xsl:include>` element, it accesses the referenced stylesheet and essentially copies all the contents of that stylesheet (all the components declared within the `<xsl:stylesheet>` element) into the including stylesheet.

■ **Note** The inclusion process isn't a textual copy. Instead, it copies the logical components from the included stylesheet. In particular, it's a namespace-aware copy, so you can use different prefixes for different namespaces in the separate stylesheets if you want to.

To the XSLT processor, the resulting stylesheet is just the same as a stylesheet where all the components from the included stylesheet were defined within the including stylesheet at the point where the `<xsl:include>` element appears. This process is shown in Figure 12-1.

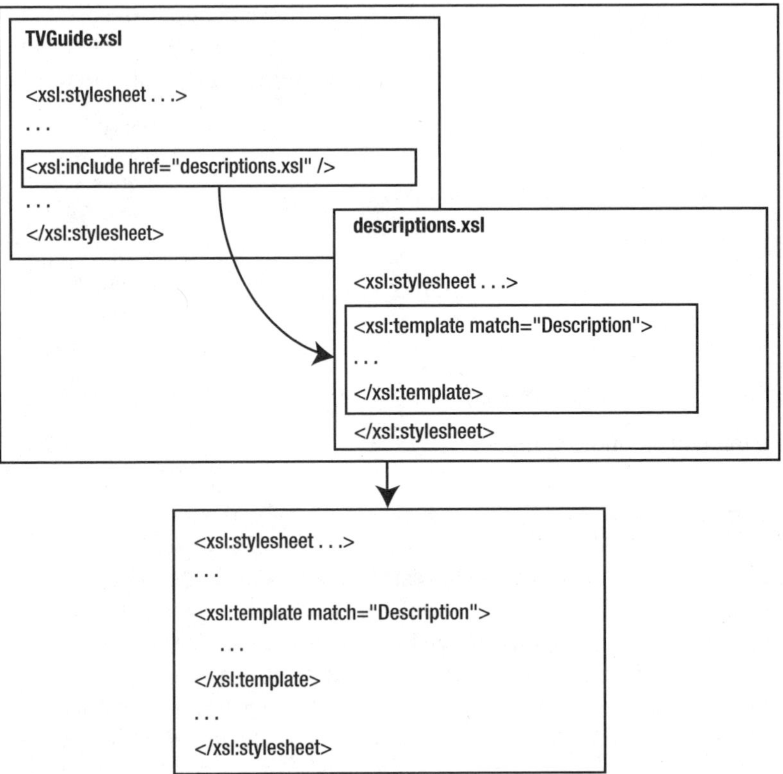

Figure 12-1. *Including* `descriptions.xsl` *in* `TVGuide.xsl`

The fact that the contents of the included template are in effect included at the location of the `<xsl:include>` element has two implications:

The names of components in the included and including stylesheet can clash. So, for example, the included stylesheet must not contain any named templates that have the same name as a named template in the including stylesheet.

When an XSLT processor needs to decide between two components, it uses the last one in the stylesheet (as long as it doesn't halt with an error), so the position of the `<xsl:include>` matters. For example, consider the situation where you have two templates that match the same element in the same mode with the same priority, one in the included stylesheet and one in the including stylesheet. If the `<xsl:include>` is placed *after* the template in the including stylesheet, then the template from the included stylesheet will be used; whereas if the `<xsl:include>` is placed *before* the template in the including stylesheet, then the template from the included stylesheet will not be used.

You therefore have to be careful when you're using `<xsl:include>` to include stylesheets. In particular, if a stylesheet contains named templates or stylesheet functions, then you have to make sure that you don't include them twice.

Tip As you'll see in the next section, you're usually safer using `<xsl:import>` to use a stylesheet that holds named templates or stylesheet functions.

You're perfectly free to include a stylesheet that itself includes another stylesheet. However, you do have to watch out for circular inclusions, where stylesheet A includes stylesheet B, which includes stylesheet C, which includes stylesheet A. Circular inclusion will cause an error.

Summary You can include the components from another stylesheet with the `<xsl:include>` element, which goes at the top level of the stylesheet and whose `href` attribute holds a URL pointing to the included stylesheet.

Separating Templates for the Contents of Descriptions

The `TVGuide.xsl` stylesheet is beginning to get a little bulky, so to ease maintenance we'll split it into two files: `TVGuide2.xsl` as the main stylesheet, and a number of supplementary stylesheets, roughly divided up into functional units:

- `utils.xsl` to hold the named templates and stylesheet functions—the `link` template (along with the `linkEvents` attribute set), and the definitions of `tv:is-interesting-program()`, and `str:characters()`
- `description.xsl` to hold the templates that deal with elements in `<Description>` elements
- `channelList.xsl` to hold the templates that create the channel listing at the top and bottom of the page (in `ChannelList` mode) and the `$ChannelList` global variable
- `series.xsl` to hold templates, parameter definitions, and key declarations that deal with generating the series listings, which we've put at the bottom of the page

Each of these stylesheets looks just like a normal stylesheet—you don't have to put any special declarations in it to state that it's going to be included elsewhere. For example, description.xsl holds all the templates that match elements within <Description> elements. The descriptions.xsl stylesheet looks as follows:

```
<xsl:stylesheet version="2.0"
                xmlns:xsl="http://www.w3.org/1999/XSL/Transform"
                xmlns:xs="http://www.w3.org/2001/XMLSchema"
                exclude-result-prefixes="xs"
                xmlns="http://www.w3.org/1999/xhtml">
  <xsl:template match="Description//Link">...</xsl:template>
  <xsl:template match="Description//Program">...</xsl:template>
  <xsl:template match="Description//Series">...</xsl:template>
  <xsl:template match="Description//Channel">...</xsl:template>
</xsl:stylesheet>
```

■Caution Don't forget the namespace declaration for the XHTML namespace; otherwise the literal result elements that you generate in the included stylesheets will be in no namespace, rather than the XHTML namespace. Otherwise, the stylesheets only have to contain the namespaces that they actually refer to.

Once you've moved the various templates, attribute sets, keys, and global variables to their separate stylesheets, you can remove them from TVGuide2.xsl. In their place, add <xsl:include> elements whose href attributes point to the stylesheet modules:

```
<xsl:stylesheet version="2.0"
                xmlns:xsl="http://www.w3.org/1999/XSL/Transform"
                xmlns:xs="http://www.w3.org/2001/XMLSchema"
                xmlns:xdt="http://www.w3.org/2005/04/xpath-datatypes"
                xmlns:tv="http://www.example.com/TVGuide"
                exclude-result-prefixes="xs xdt tv"
                xmlns="http://www.w3.org/1999/xhtml">
...
<xsl:include href="utils.xsl" />
<xsl:include href="description.xsl" />
<xsl:include href="channelList.xsl" />
<xsl:include href="series.xsl" />
...
</xsl:stylesheet>
```

Now transform TVGuide.xml with TVGuide2.xsl to create TVGuide2.html. You should get just the same result as you have previously, shown in Figure 12-2.

The global variable and templates that create the channel listing are located in channelList.xsl; the templates that create the series listing at the bottom of the page are located in series.xsl; the templates that provide the main listing are in the stylesheet that's actually referenced, TVGuide2.xsl. It doesn't matter where the components come from; they are all combined when the processor uses TVGuide2.xsl to transform TVGuide.xml.

To see the conflicts that can occur when including stylesheets, we'll try a couple of variations.

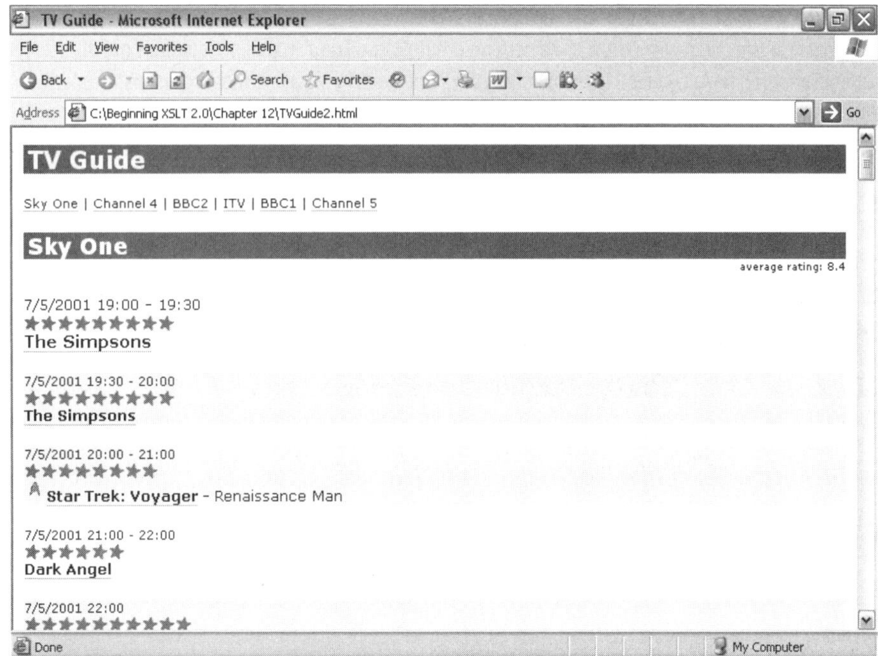

Figure 12-2. *Viewing* `TVGuide2.html` *in Internet Explorer*

First, we'll copy the `link` template from `utils.xsl` into `TVGuide3.xsl`, so that there's one copy in each stylesheet. If you try transforming `TVGuide.xml` with `TVGuide3.xsl`, you should see something like the error shown in Figure 12-3.

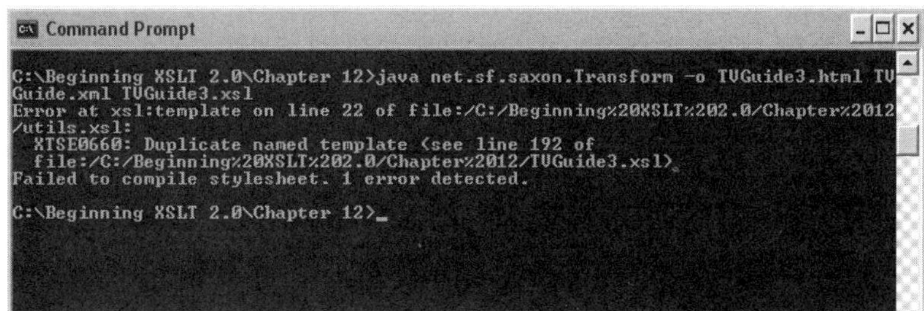

Figure 12-3. *Error due to duplicate named template*

The XSLT processor reports an error because there are two templates with the same name, even though they are in different stylesheets. The same kind of error will occur if you try copying the definition of the global variable `$ChannelList` into `TVGuide3.xsl` because you can't have two global variables that have the same name.

Now try adding a template to the main stylesheet that matches `<Channel>` elements in `ChannelList` mode but does nothing with them:

```
<xsl:template match="Channel" mode="ChannelList" />
```

Place this template *after* the `<xsl:include>` element that includes `channelList.xsl`, as in `TVGuide4.xsl`, and try transforming `TVGuide.xml` with `TVGuide4.xsl` to create `TVGuide4.html`. If you don't get an error (processors can complain if you have two templates matching the same node in the same mode at the same priority), you should get the page shown in Figure 12-4.

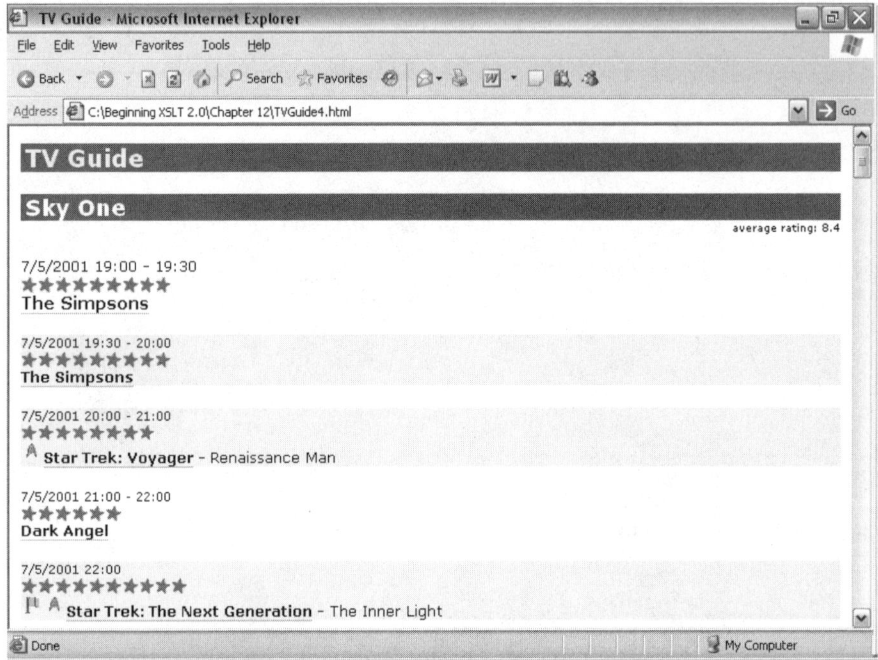

Figure 12-4. *Viewing* `TVGuide4.html` *in Internet Explorer*

The channel list is omitted, because the empty template in `TVGuide4.xsl` has been used in preference to the template in `channelList.xsl`.

If you move the template so that it is placed *before* the `<xsl:include>` element that includes `channelList.xsl`, then the template from `channelList.xsl` will be used and you'll get the same result as you did with `TVGuide2.xsl` originally.

Reusing Stylesheets

Dividing a stylesheet for manageability is helpful, but the real win of splitting up a stylesheet is that it allows you to reuse code in multiple XSLT applications. This is particularly helpful when you create stylesheet functions or named templates to perform utilities such as getting the square root of a number, splitting a string into its characters, or something that's more specific to your application domain. However, often some of the stylesheet functions or named templates in the reusable stylesheet don't do *exactly* what you want them to do, because they've been designed with different applications in mind, and you need to override them to get precisely the behavior that you desire.

Note There are a number of resources on the Web that provide utility templates for XSLT 1.0 to do things like finding the maximum or minimum from a set of nodes or formatting dates. In particular, have a look at `http://xsltsl.sourceforge.net`, `http://www.exslt.org`, and `http://www.topxml.com/xsl/articles/fp/`. Many of these can be done a lot more easily in XSLT 2.0, but you can expect a growing number of utility functions to be made available in similar libraries as XSLT 2.0 grows.

To reuse most of the templates in another stylesheet, but override some of them, you need to **import** the stylesheet rather than include it. You can import a stylesheet using the `<xsl:import>` element, which is very similar to the `<xsl:include>` element in that it occurs at the top level of the stylesheet, and it takes an `href` attribute that points to the stylesheet you want to import. The major difference is that any `<xsl:import>` elements in your stylesheet must be the very first elements in the stylesheet, the first children of the `<xsl:stylesheet>` document element.

For example, the following `<xsl:import>` element imports the `utils.xsl` stylesheet:

```
<xsl:import href="utils.xsl" />
```

If there aren't any conflicts between the importing and imported stylesheet, importing a stylesheet has much the same effect in terms of what the processor does as including that stylesheet would. If `TVGuide.xsl` imports `utils.xsl`, this makes the `link` template that it contains accessible within the effective stylesheet, as illustrated in Figure 12-5.

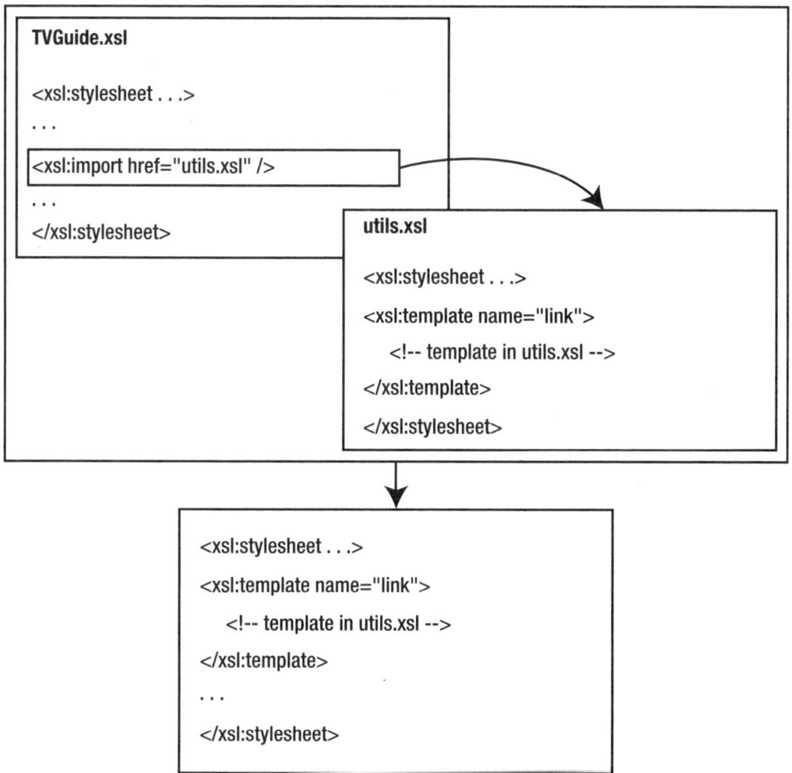

Figure 12-5. *Importing* `utils.xsl` *into* `TVGuide.xsl` *with no override*

However, when you import a stylesheet, any templates or other components that are defined within the imported stylesheet can be **overridden** by their equivalents in the importing stylesheet. This is handy because it allows you to customize the behavior of the components in the imported stylesheet to the requirements of your particular application, for example, to change the way that the imported stylesheet calculates the value for a node when finding the minimum. In a way, this is similar to creating a subclass (your stylesheet) that overrides methods (templates and functions) on its superclass (the imported stylesheet). This overriding behavior is illustrated in Figure 12-6; this time `TVGuide.xsl` and `utils.xsl` both have a `link` template; it's the `link` template from `TVGuide.xsl` that gets used.

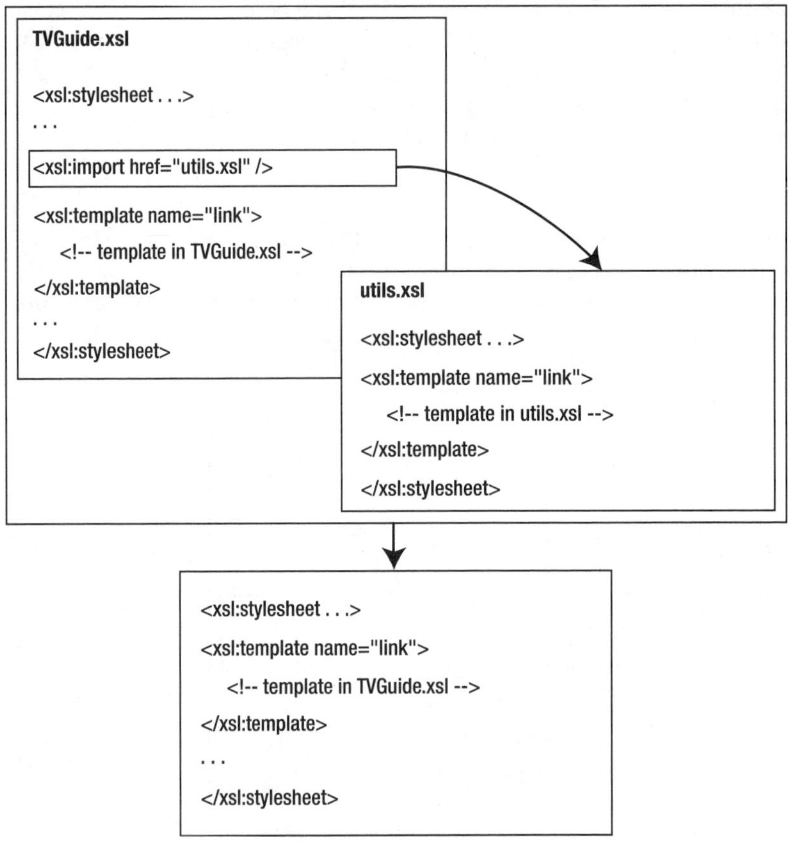

Figure 12-6. *Importing* `utils.xsl` *into* `TVGuide.xsl` *with overriding template*

The reason that the components in the importing stylesheet override those in the imported stylesheet is that they have higher **import precedence**. The import precedence of a stylesheet comes into effect when the processor has multiple components to choose from, either because they have the same name or because they match the same node. The kinds of things that you can override in an importing stylesheet are

- Global variable and parameter definitions
- Key definitions
- Named templates
- Matching templates
- Stylesheet functions

If you import several stylesheets, then the one that's imported last will have a higher import precedence than the ones that were imported earlier. So if you import two stylesheets that contain definitions for the same named template (and your importing stylesheet doesn't contain a template of that name), then the template from the last stylesheet that you import will have precedence over the template from the first stylesheet you import. Figure 12-7 illustrates what happens when you have two stylesheets imported one after another; `description.xsl` is imported after `utils.xsl`, so the `link` template from `description.xsl` is used in preference to the one from `utils.xsl`.

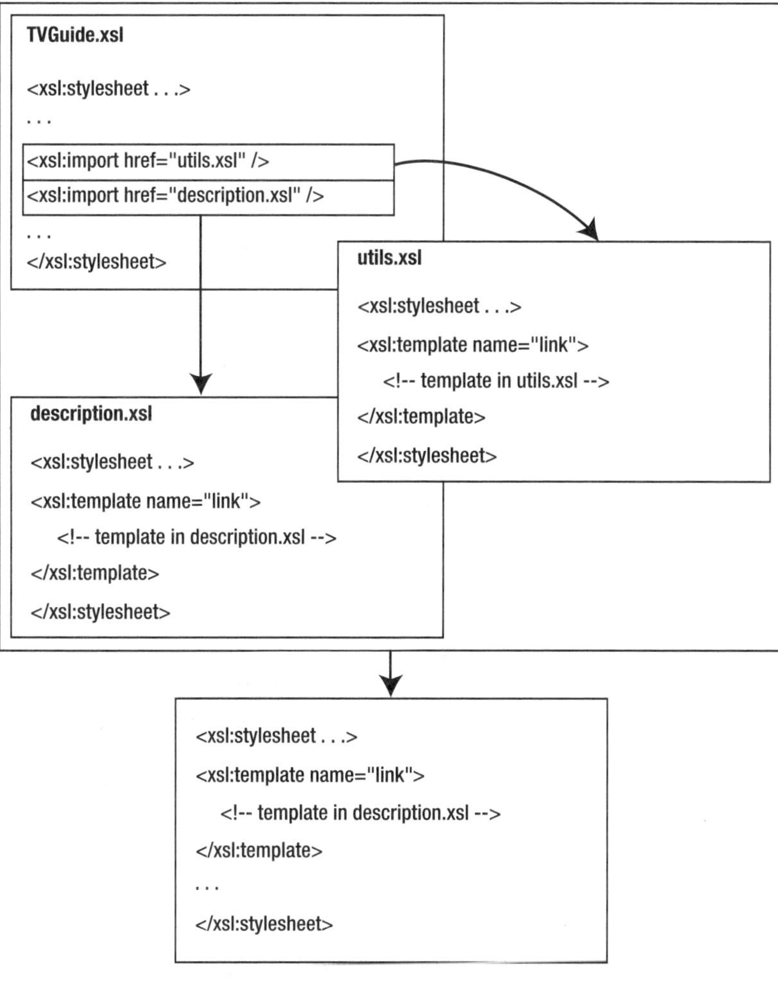

Figure 12-7. *Importing* `utils.xsl` *and* `description.xsl` *into* `TVGuide.xsl`

Summary When you import a stylesheet, you can override the declarations that it contains from within your stylesheet. You can import stylesheets with <xsl:import> elements, which must be the first elements in a stylesheet and which take href attributes to indicate the imported stylesheet.

The way matching templates are overridden deserves a bit of explanation. Basically, if a template in an importing template can match a node, then it will. It doesn't matter how high a priority a template in an imported stylesheet has, it won't be used if there's a template in the importing stylesheet that can be applied to the node.

This feature can be used to advantage if your stylesheet needs to adjust the behavior of the stylesheet that it's importing. If you cast your mind back to Chapter 3, you'll remember the <xsl:next-match> instruction, which applies the next best matching template to the current node. It doesn't matter where the next best matching template is (and that includes imported stylesheets), the <xsl:next-match> instruction will use it.

A similar instruction is <xsl:apply-imports>, which doesn't have any attributes but can contain any number of <xsl:with-param> elements. Like <xsl:next-match>, this applies another template to the current node, but it only looks at a subset of the possible templates, namely those in stylesheets that are imported into the one that contains the <xsl:apply-imports> instruction.

This distinction makes the <xsl:apply-imports> instruction useful if you're building complex hierarchies of imported stylesheets. For example, say stylesheet A imports stylesheets B and C (in that order, such that stylesheet C has a higher import precedence than stylesheet B), stylesheet B imports stylesheets D and E, and stylesheet C imports stylesheets F and G. An <xsl:next-match> instruction in stylesheet C would look at other templates in stylesheets C and templates in B, D, and E as well as those in stylesheets F and G. On the other hand, an <xsl:apply-imports> instruction in stylesheet C will only look at templates in stylesheets F and G. Using <xsl:apply-imports> means the behavior of a stylesheet doesn't change when it's imported into a stylesheet that itself imports another stylesheet.

Summary You can use <xsl:next-match> or <xsl:apply-imports> to apply templates to the next best matching template. The <xsl:apply-imports> instruction will only use templates that are imported into the stylesheet that the <xsl:apply-imports> instruction occurs in.

Overriding Named Templates

The utils.xsl stylesheet is quite useful for other stylesheets that we might develop, such as those showing only interesting programs or programs in particular series. All these stylesheets would benefit from having a simple template named link that generates a link as follows:

```
<xsl:template name="link" as="element()">
  <xsl:param name="href" as="xs:string" required="yes" />
  <xsl:param name="content" as="item()+" required="yes" />
  <a href="{$href}"><xsl:sequence select="$content" /></a>
</xsl:template>
```

However, in the main TV guide, the links are a bit more exotic—the style of the links changes when you move the mouse over them. This is controlled by three attributes on the <a> elements, which are held in the linkEvents attribute set so that they can be reused in several situations:

```
<xsl:attribute-set name="linkEvents">
  <xsl:attribute name="style">
    <xsl:text>color: black; border-bottom: 1pt groove #CCC</xsl:text>
  </xsl:attribute>
  <xsl:attribute name="onmouseover">
    <xsl:text>javascript:this.style.background = '#CCC';</xsl:text>
  </xsl:attribute>
  <xsl:attribute name="onmouseout">
    <xsl:text>javascript:this.style.background = 'transparent';</xsl:text>
  </xsl:attribute>
</xsl:attribute-set>
```

So the more general-purpose link template isn't quite right because it doesn't add the linkEvents attribute set. Since the stylesheet we're working on is the exception to the general rule, it makes sense to change the link template in utils2.xsl to the simple version just shown. But then we need to override the link template in TVGuide5.xsl, so that it produces the links including the linkEvents attributes there (and move the linkEvents attribute set back into TVGuide5.xsl).

As you've seen, you can't override the link template if you *include* utils2.xsl, so you have to import it by removing the <xsl:include> that's currently including utils.xsl and adding an <xsl:import> element instead, right at the top of the stylesheet, just under the start tag for the <xsl:stylesheet> element, as in TVGuide5.xsl:

```
<xsl:stylesheet version="2.0"
                xmlns:xsl="http://www.w3.org/1999/XSL/Transform"
                xmlns:xs="http://www.w3.org/2001/XMLSchema"
                xmlns:xdt="http://www.w3.org/2005/04/xpath-datatypes"
                xmlns:tv="http://www.example.com/TVGuide"
                exclude-result-prefixes="xs xdt tv"
                xmlns="http://www.w3.org/1999/xhtml">
<xsl:import href="utils2.xsl" />
...
</xsl:stylesheet>
```

Now, to override the link template from the utils.xsl stylesheet, all you need to do is add a link template to TVGuide5.xsl that does what you want it to do, along with the linkEvents attributes that it's referring to:

```
<xsl:template name="link" as="element()">
  <xsl:param name="href" as="xs:string" required="yes" />
  <xsl:param name="content" as="item()+" required="yes" />
  <a href="{$href}" xsl:use-attribute-sets="linkEvents">
    <xsl:sequence select="$content" />
  </a>
</xsl:template>
```

When you transform TVGuide.xml with TVGuide5.xsl to create TVGuide5.html, you should see the page shown in Figure 12-8.

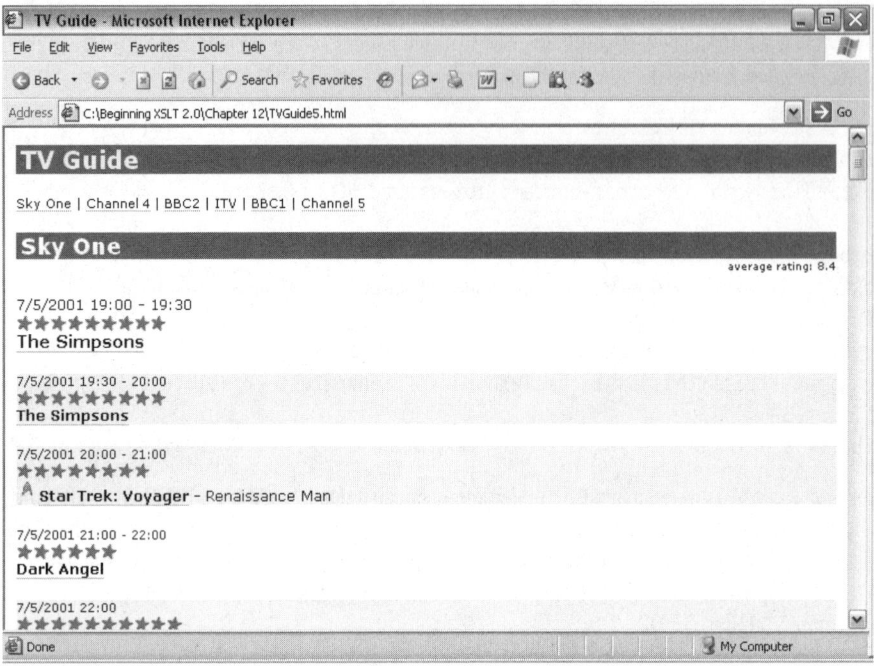

Figure 12-8. *Viewing* `TVGuide5.html` *in Internet Explorer*

The links are still in the original style, with a gray underline, and react when you place the mouse over them. The `link` template in `TVGuide5.xsl` is used instead of the `link` template in `utils2.xsl`, even if it's called from templates within `utils2.xsl` or any of the stylesheets included in `TVGuide5.xsl`.

Accessing Data

A good way to increase the maintainability, extensibility, and reusability of stylesheets (as with any program) is to move the information that the program uses from being embedded in code to being stored separately as data. For example, we've been using the following code to determine what kind of flag graphic should be added to each of the programs in the TV guide:

```
<img src="{if (@flag = 'favorite') then 'favorite' else 'interest'}.gif"
     alt="[{if (@flag = 'favorite') then 'Favorite' else 'Interest'}]"
     width="20" height="20" />
```

While this code does the job, it's not very easy to change or extend. If we wanted to change it to incorporate other possible values for the `flag` attribute, or to change the names or location of the graphics that are used for the flags, then we have to go into the stylesheet and edit the code itself. Given how large our stylesheet is getting, remembering where the code that generates the flag graphic actually is might be a problem in six months' time. We'll reap the benefits in the future from anything that we can do to make it easier to change the things in our stylesheet that are likely to change.

Really, we want to be able to define somewhere that a flag called "favorite" should point to the graphic favorite.gif and have the alternative text [Favorite], and similarly that a flag called "interesting" should point to the graphic interest.gif and have the alternative text [Interest]. Since we know that XML is a good way of representing information, we could store the mappings in an XML structure, and then use that XML to determine what the <img> element should look like:

```
<flags>
  <flag name="favorite" src="favorite.gif" alt="Favorite" />
  <flag name="interesting" src="interest.gif" alt="Interest" />
</flags>
```

We could place this XML within the source document for the stylesheet, TVGuide.xml, but that would mix the content (the programs and so on) and the presentation of the content in the same document, which is precisely what we moved to XML to avoid.

We could also use a global variable to hold the data:

```
<xsl:variable name="flags" as="element(flag)+">
  <flag name="favorite" src="favorite.gif" alt="Favorite" />
  <flag name="interesting" src="interest.gif" alt="Interest" />
</xsl:variable>
```

This is fairly easy to manage for small amounts of data, but it still means editing the stylesheet itself (and locating the relevant variable declaration within it) every time we want to make changes.

The final alternative is to put the information in a separate document (flags.xml). Holding information in a separate document is useful because it means that you don't have to edit the stylesheet itself in order to change the way the stylesheet works. Separate documents are usually used in conjunction with stylesheets to provide configuration information to the stylesheet, such as the following:

- Lookup tables, such as dictionaries
- User preferences
- Output templates
- Filtering and sorting specifications
- Snippet libraries

To access information from the stylesheet to use it in these ways, we need some functions . . .

Accessing External Documents

There are three ways of accessing external documents in XSLT 2.0:

- doc() function—Used to access the document node of a single XML document
- document() function—Used to access nodes in one or more XML documents
- unparsed-text() function—Used to access the content of a file as a string

Accessing XML Data

The easiest way to access an external XML document is with the `doc()` or `document()` function. Using a single string as the argument, both these functions retrieve the document located at the URL specified by the string (which is resolved relative to the location of the stylesheet itself). They return the document node of the node tree from that document, which is built in just the same way as the node tree for the source document (which you learned about in Chapter 7).

Tip A side-effect of the fact that the URL is resolved relative to the stylesheet itself is that you can access the stylesheet itself using an empty string as the URL. For example, `document('')` returns the document node of the node tree for the stylesheet itself, and `document('')/xsl:stylesheet/xsl:template[@name]` returns the `<xsl:template>` elements in the stylesheet that have `name` attributes.

For example, to get hold of the document node of `flags.xml`, you can use either of the following expressions:

```
doc('flags.xml')
document('flags.xml')
```

Note There is no requirement for the strings specifying the filename to be literals in the stylesheet: you could create them automatically based on a parameter, for example.

The first argument is a URL rather than a file path. This means that you should use forward slashes to separate directories, if you want to access a file on your local machine you should prefix the filename with `file:///`, and any spaces or URI-significant characters in the directory or file names should be escaped. For example, if I wanted to use an absolute path to `flags.xml`, which is held in the directory `C:\Beginning XSLT 2.0\Chapter 12\` on my local Windows machine, I would have to use the URL `file:///C:/Beginning%20XSLT%202.0/Chapter%2012/flags.xml`.

Note You could use any URL that returns an XML document. For example, the document could be generated on the fly on the server (from a database, say). If you use the `document()` function rather than the `doc()` function, you can use fragment identifiers to retrieve a particular node within the external document (as long as your processor supports the fragment identifier scheme that you use, such as the element scheme within the XPointer framework).

Because the `doc()` and `document()` functions return nodes, you can use them at the beginning of a path and then step down further into the document. For example, to find the `<flag>` element in the `flags.xml` document whose `name` attribute has the value `'interesting'`, you could use

```
document('flags.xml')/flags/flag[@name = 'interesting']
```

Once you get hold of a node from an external document, you can do anything with it that you could do with a node from the source document: you can extract information from it, copy it, apply templates to it, and so on.

When you access external documents within your stylesheet, it's good practice to create global variables that hold the document nodes of both the external documents and the original source document, so that you can easily switch between the documents if necessary. For example, if I were using flags.xml, I would usually include the following variable definitions in my stylesheet:

```
<xsl:variable name="TVGuide" select="/" />
<xsl:variable name="flags" select="document('flags.xml')" />
```

Summary You can use the doc() and document() functions to access information from an external XML document as if it were the source document for the stylesheet. The first argument is the location of the XML document.

Accessing Text Files

The documents that you access with the doc() or document() function must be well-formed XML documents, just the same as the source XML document, and have to have a single document element. You cannot use the doc() or document() function to access plain text documents, for example: for that you need the unparsed-text() function.

The unparsed-text() function can be used to access any text document, and it returns the content of the text document as a string. Like the doc() and document() functions, the first argument is a URL that points to the text document's location relative to the stylesheet.

This function is useful for accessing data that's stored in documents in non-XML formats, such as comma-delimited files. Once you get hold of the string content of the text file, you can process it using regular expressions, with the <xsl:analyze-string> instruction. For example, to access data.properties and parse each line as a *property=value* pair, you could use

```
<xsl:analyze-string select="unparsed-text('data.properties')"
                    regex="([^=]+)=(.*)" flags="m">
  <xsl:matching-substring>
    <property name="{regex-group(1)}" value="{regex-group(2)}" />
  </xsl:matching-substring>
</xsl:analyze-string>
```

Another way in which the unparsed-text() function might be used is to access the content of an HTML file to insert it into the output, or even to access the content of an XML file as a string (a useful way of inserting examples into XML documents).

As we saw in Chapter 1, text files use different encodings to map the character content of the document to bytes for storage on disk or transmission over the network. The XSLT processor will attempt to work out what encoding a text file is using, based on information passed from "elsewhere" (the web server the file comes from, for example) or, if the file is an XML document, from the XML declaration in the file.

If the XSLT processor can't work out the encoding of the text file, it will fall back on the optional second argument of the unparsed-text() function, which is the name of an encoding.

If you haven't provided a second argument, then the XSLT processor will assume that the file is encoded as UTF-8 and interpret it accordingly. For example, to access the content of `disclaimer.html` as a string, with a default encoding of ISO-8859-1, you would use

```
unparsed-text('disclaimer.html', 'ISO-8859-1')
```

■ **Summary** You can use the `unparsed-text()` function to access external text documents as a string. The first argument is the location of the text file, and the optional second argument is the default encoding for the file, used if no other information is available about its encoding.

Unavailable Documents

If the processor has any problems locating the document that you've specified when using the `document()` or `unparsed-text()` functions, then the processor can either return an empty sequence (or string for the `unparsed-text()` function) or halt the transformation altogether. The same thing happens if the document you point to with the `document()` functions turns out not to be an XML document. Most processors halt the transformation in these circumstances. Processors will also halt if the file you refer to with the `doc()` function isn't available or isn't an XML document.

All this means you have to be quite careful that the file paths that you use do actually point to an existing document. You can test whether an XML document is actually available at a particular location using the `doc-available()` function. This takes a string URI as an argument and returns `true` if there's an XML document at that location and `false` if not.

Usually, then, you would wrap a call to `doc()` or `document()` within an `if` statement that tested for the presence of an XML document before accessing it, and returned something useful (such as an empty sequence) if the document itself isn't available. For example:

```
if (doc-available('flags.xml')) then doc('flags.xml') else ()
```

The `doc-available()` function isn't suitable for testing for the presence of documents you're going to open with `unparsed-text()`, since these documents usually aren't *XML* documents and therefore `doc-available()` will return `false` for them. Instead, the `unparsed-text-available()` function has a similar purpose: it takes a URI and, optionally, an encoding, and tests whether the document specified by the URI is readable. For example:

```
if (unparsed-text-available('disclaimer.html', 'ISO-8859-1'))
then unparsed-text('disclaimer.html', 'ISO-8859-1')
else ''
```

■ **Summary** The transformation will usually halt if the external document that you've indicated cannot be opened. The `doc-available()` and `unparsed-text-available()` functions allow you to test whether `doc()`, `document()`, or `unparsed-text()` will actually work.

Using Information from an External XML Document

To test out using information from external XML documents, we'll try to use the information from flags.xml to create the <img> element shown next to a program. The flags.xml document looks like

```
<flags>
  <flag name="favorite" src="favorite.gif" alt="Favorite" />
  <flag name="interesting" src="interest.gif" alt="Interest" />
</flags>
```

In TVGuide5.xsl, when we process a program using the template matching <Program> elements in Details mode, we use the following code:

```
<xsl:if test="@flag">
  <img src="{if (@flag = 'favorite') then 'favorite' else 'interest'}.gif"
       alt="[{if (@flag = 'favorite') then 'Favorite' else 'Interest'}]"
       width="20" height="20" />
</xsl:if>
```

Instead, in TVGuide6.xsl, we can try to retrieve the relevant <flag> element from the flags.xml document, and then process it to produce the flag graphic. The relevant <flag> element is the one whose name attribute has the same value as the value of the flag attribute of the current <Program> element:

```
document('flags.xml')/flags/flag[@name = current()/@flag]
```

If we simply apply templates to this <flag> element, then we won't get a graphic if no <flag> element was found, which is precisely what we want. So rather than testing whether a flag attribute is present, we can just apply templates to the <flag> element from the flags.xml document:

```
<xsl:apply-templates
  select="document('flags.xml')/flags/flag[@name = current()/@flag]" />
```

Then we need a template that matches the <flag> element and produces the relevant <img> element. The value of the src attribute comes from the src attribute on the <flag> element, and the value of the alt attribute comes from the alt attribute on the <flag> element (you could simply copy them if you prefer):

```
<xsl:template match="flag">
  <img src="{@src}" alt="{@alt}" width="20" height="20" />
</xsl:template>
```

The result of transforming TVGuide.xml with TVGuide6.xsl is TVGuide6.html, which is shown in Figure 12-9.

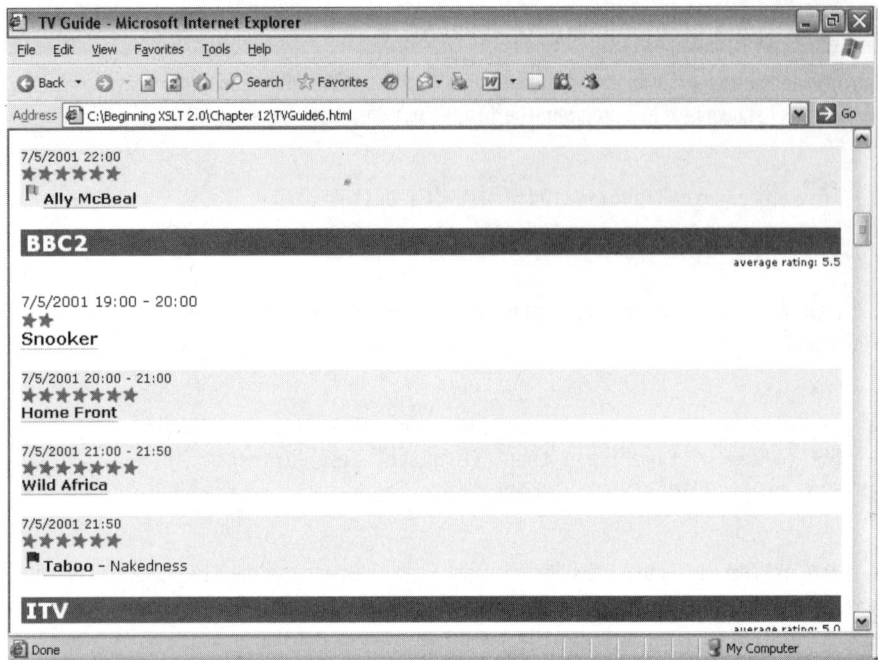

Figure 12-9. *Viewing* `TVGuide6.html` *in Internet Explorer*

The flags on *Ally McBeal* and *Taboo* are being generated based on data held in `flags.xml`. If you wanted to add different kinds of flags, or change the location of the flags that the document is using, then you could edit `flags.xml` without touching the stylesheet.

Using Keys in External Documents

One of the main ways in which you can use external documents to augment your stylesheet is to provide **lookup tables**. Lookup tables encode the mapping between an identifier and a piece of information, as in `flags.xml`. They are used to do things like the following:

- Give translations for a term in different languages.
- Provide the labels used for different codes.
- Hold the mapping between abbreviations and full names.
- Specify the ordering of a set of strings (the position of the node acts as its identifier).

Often the set of mappings held in the XML lookup table will be quite large, or you will want to access it many times. As you learned in Chapter 10, the quickest way of accessing information by the value of one of its attributes or descendants is using a key, defined with an `<xsl:key>` element and accessed using the `key()` function.

However, the `key()` function (and the `id()` and `idref()` functions) usually only searches for the relevant element within the document that holds the context node. As we've seen, the lookup tables are often held in external documents. If you try to use the key while processing an element in the source document, then the XSLT processor will only look in the source document for the elements that match the key.

There are two ways to use a key on an external document. The first is to use the optional third argument of the key() function, specifying a node in the external document. If you use the document node of the external document, then the entire document will be searched; otherwise you'll just search the descendants of the node you specify. For example:

```
key('keyName', keyValue, doc('externalDocument.xml'))
```

Alternatively, you can change the context node from the source document to the document in which the lookup table is located. The easiest way to do this is to use the key() function in a step within a path whose earlier steps access the external document. For example:

```
doc('externalDocument.xml')/key('keyName', keyValue)
```

This second option is easiest to use if you have several external documents to search. But remember that the expression you use to select the key value will be evaluated relative to the node(s) selected by the previous step. If the key value comes from the original document, you should store it in a variable so that you can get hold of the value easily.

Summary You can use the third argument of the key() function to search an external document, or change the context node to a node in the external document and then use the key(), id(), or idref() functions as normal.

Centralizing Series Information

The data in TVGuide.xml is made up of two main sections: the channels and their program listings, and information about series. In the original plan for the XML TV guide, back in Chapter 1, we wanted the information about series to be held in a separate document from the program listing. In this example, we'll separate out this series information into another file, series.xml, and access information from that file using keys.

Our first task is to separate the information from TVGuide.xml into two documents: TVGuide2.xml for the program listing and series.xml for the series information. TVGuide2.xml looks like this:

```
<?xml version="1.0" encoding="ISO-8859-1"?>
<TVGuide>
  <Channel>...</Channel>
  <Channel>...</Channel>
  ... more <Channel> elements ...
</TVGuide>
```

while series.xml looks like this:

```
<?xml version="1.0" encoding="ISO-8859-1"?>
<SeriesList>
```

```
  <Series>...</Series>
  <Series>...</Series>
  ... more <Series> elements ...
</SeriesList>
```

Now, in TVGuide7.xsl (and in series2.xsl, which it includes) we need to access the series.xml document for the series information that we need.

The first thing we'll do is create a global variable in series2.xsl that holds the document node of the series.xml document:

```
<xsl:variable name="series" as="document-node()" select="doc('series.xml')" />
```

and a global variable in TVGuide7.xsl that holds the document node of the source document:

```
<xsl:variable name="TVGuide" as="document-node()" select="/" />
```

Now, when we retrieve information about series (which we always do using keys), we need to switch context to that document before using the key. For example, in the template matching <Program> elements in Details mode in TVGuide6.xsl, we currently create a link whose content is the title of the series using

```
<xsl:call-template name="link">
  <xsl:with-param name="href" as="xs:string" select="concat('#', Series)" />
  <xsl:with-param name="content" as="xs:string"
                  select="key('IDs', Series)/Title" />
</xsl:call-template>
```

The context node needs to be a node in series.xml when the call to the key() function is evaluated; one way to do that is to add another step in the path, switching to the document node of series.xml (as held in the $series variable) before calling the key() function. We also need to make sure that the second argument to the key() function references the <Series> element within the current <Program> element (rather than trying to access a <Series> element under the document node held in the $series variable, which will only lead to disappointment):

```
<xsl:call-template name="link">
  <xsl:with-param name="href" as="xs:anyURI"
                  select="xs:anyURI(concat('#', Series))" />
  <xsl:with-param name="content" as="xs:string"
                  select="$series/key('IDs', current()/Series)/Title" />
</xsl:call-template>
```

Similar changes need to be made in the template in series.xsl matching the <TVGuide> element in Series mode. In this template, the series that start with a particular first letter are held in $series variables using the following code:

```
<xsl:for-each select="$alphabet">
  <xsl:variable name="series" as="element()*"
                select="key('seriesByFirstLetter', ., $TVGuide)" />
  ...
</xsl:for-each>
```

Here, we're using the third argument of the key() function to look in the <TVGuide> element. Instead, we need to switch context to series.xml, held in the $series global variable:

```
<xsl:for-each select="$alphabet">
  <xsl:variable name="series" as="element()*"
                select="key('seriesByFirstLetter', ., $series)" />
  ...
</xsl:for-each>
```

The final thing that we need to change is the template, again in `series2.xsl`, that currently matches `<Series>` elements within a `<TVGuide>` element. The relevant `<Series>` elements now live within a `<SeriesList>` element, so we need to change the match pattern for the template:

```
<xsl:template match="SeriesList/Series">
  ...
</xsl:template>
```

We also need to change the way in which this template gets hold of the episodes in the series. Currently, it uses the `'programsBySeries'` key as follows:

```
<xsl:for-each select="key('programsBySeries', @id)">
  ...
</xsl:for-each>
```

Within this template, the context node is a `<Series>` element from `series.xml`. To find the relevant programs, we need to look in the `TVGuide2.xml` document, the document node of which is held in the `$TVGuide` global variable. So again, we can add a third argument to the `key()` function call to refer to the document node of `TVGuide2.xml`:

```
<xsl:for-each select="key('programsBySeries', @id, $TVGuide)">
  ...
</xsl:for-each>
```

Transforming `TVGuide2.xml` with `TVGuide7.xsl` results in `TVGuide7.html`. `TVGuide7.html` doesn't look any different from `TVGuide6.html`, but it's generated using information from two files, `TVGuide2.xml` and `series.xml`, rather than all the information coming from a single XML document.

Retrieving Referenced Information

In the last section you saw how to use the `doc()`, `document()`, and `unparsed-text()` functions to access documents holding additional information that can be used by the stylesheet as lookup tables, as user preferences, and so on. All these kinds of documents give further information about how the source XML document should be *presented*. Whatever XML document is accessed, and wherever that XML document is, the same presentation information should be used. Therefore these types of documents are accessed relative to the stylesheet itself.

A second class of document is one that provides additional *content*. The source information for the stylesheet might be split over several XML documents, to make the authoring of the XML document more manageable (for example, splitting the XML for a book into one file per chapter) or to allow the reuse of information from several XML documents (for example, holding the descriptions of TV series in a separate file from the weekly TV guides).

Whatever XSLT stylesheet accesses the source XML document, and wherever that stylesheet is, the same content should be used. Therefore these types of documents usually need to be accessed relative to the source document rather than relative to the stylesheet.

Resolving Relative URLs

Say that our site houses TV guides for several different countries. Each set of TV guides is stored in its own directory—`usa` for the USA TV guides, `uk` for the UK TV guides, and so on. Each set of TV guides has its own `series.xml` document that lists the series that are shown in that country and a description of each of them. There's one `series.xml` document in the `usa` directory, another in the `uk` directory, and so on.

When the stylesheet comes to display a particular TV guide, it needs to look at the `series.xml` document that's in the same directory as the TV guide at which it's looking. If the `TVGuide.xml` document is in the `usa` directory, then it needs to look at `usa/series.xml`, and if it's in the `uk` directory the processor needs to access `uk/series.xml`.

By default, as we've seen, the `doc()` and `document()` functions access documents based on their location relative to the stylesheet. If you want to access a document relative to the location of the source document, you can do one of two things: either provide an absolute URL for the document you want to access, or use the second argument of the `document()` function.

To provide an absolute URL for the document you want to access, you first need the base URI of the source document. You can get this using the `base-uri()` function, which takes a single node as an argument and returns the base URI for that node. The base URI of a node is usually the location of the document containing the node, though that can be overridden using the `xml:base` attribute. For example, to get the base URI of the document that you're currently looking at, you can use

```
base-uri(/)
```

Once you have that base URI for the document, you can use the `resolve-uri()` function, which you met in Chapter 5, to resolve the relative URI based on this base URI. For example, to access the `series.xml` document in the same directory as the current `TVGuide.xml` document, you can use

```
doc(resolve-uri('series.xml', base-uri(/)))
```

You can use absolute URIs when accessing files relative to the stylesheet as well, if you want. The `static-base-uri()` function (which has no arguments) gives you the URI of the stylesheet, so in fact, the following calls to the `doc()` function are equivalent:

```
doc('flags.xml')
doc(resolve-uri('flags.xml', static-base-uri()))
```

■ **Summary** You can create an absolute URI for a document by resolving the relative URI to the document using a base URI, with the `resolve-uri()` function. You can get the base URI of a node (and hence a document) using the `base-uri()` function. You can get the base URI of the stylesheet using the `static-base-uri()` function.

Alternatively, when you use the document() function, you can tell the XSLT processor to resolve a relative URL based on the base URI of a particular node by passing that node as a second argument. So an alternative way to get hold of the series.xml document in the same directory as the current TVGuide.xml document is

```
document('series.xml', /)
```

Summary The URL passed as the first argument to the document() function is resolved relative to the base URI of the node passed as the optional second argument. By default, it is resolved relative to the stylesheet itself.

Accessing Multiple Documents

A TV listing is likely to be quite a large document, especially when you have lots of channels. Having a big source document is both unwieldy for an author and unwieldy for a stylesheet—the larger a source document, the more information the XSLT processor has to hold. Therefore, it's a good idea to split large XML documents into several smaller ones, such as one per channel. For example BBC1.xml is shown in Listing 12-1.

Listing 12-1. BBC1.xml

```
<Channel>
  <Name>BBC1</Name>
  <Program>
    <Start>2001-07-05T19:30:00</Start>
    <Duration>PT30M</Duration>
    <Series>EastEnders</Series>
    <Title></Title>
    <Description>
      Mark's health scare forces him to reconsider his future with Lisa,
      while Jamie is torn between Sonia and Zoe.
    </Description>
    ...
  </Program>
  ...
</Channel>
```

To include a particular channel within a TV listing, the TVGuide3.xml document, shown in Listing 12-2, could refer to them with <Channel> elements whose href attribute points to the XML document for the channel.

Listing 12-2. TVGuide3.xml

```
<TVGuide start="2001-07-05" end="2001-07-05">
  <Channel href="BBC1.xml" />
```

```
  <Channel href="BBC2.xml" />
  <Channel href="ITV.xml" />
  ...
</TVGuide>
```

You already know one way to process all the <Channel> elements from these files: access all the <Channel> elements in TVGuide3.xml and apply templates to the document referenced in the href attribute (remembering to resolve the URL based on the location of the source document):

```
<xsl:template match="TVGuide">
  ...
  <xsl:apply-templates
    select="Channel/doc(resolve-uri(@href, base-uri(.))/Channel" />
  ...
</xsl:template>
```

■ **Note** If you prefer, you can use the document() function to do this, with the path Channel/document(@href, .)/Channel.

There's another way to do this. Rather than being a string, the first argument to the document() function can be a sequence. If it is a sequence, then the document() function returns a sequence of the nodes retrieved from *all* the documents referred to by the URLs in the sequence. What's more, if you don't have a second argument, then if the sequence contains a node, the URL specified by that node is resolved relative to the node itself. So another way of getting the documents referred to by the <Channel> elements is to select the sequence of href attributes as the only argument:

```
<xsl:template match="TVGuide">
  ...
  <xsl:apply-templates select="document(Channel/@href)/Channel" />
  ...
</xsl:template>
```

The XSLT processor takes each href attribute in turn, resolves the URL based on the base URI of the href attribute, and accesses the XML document at that location.

■ **Note** Remember, though, that the more documents you have, the more you have to worry about which document you are in if you use things like keys.

■ **Summary** If the first argument to the document() function is a sequence, it returns the nodes referenced by all the items in the sequence. If an item is a node, and you don't have a second argument, the URL is resolved relative to the base URI of the node itself.

Summary

As you create bigger XSLT applications, both the stylesheet and the source document can become very large and unwieldy. This chapter looked at two main ways of making XSLT applications more modular.

In the first part of the chapter, you saw how to use `<xsl:include>` and `<xsl:import>` to split up a stylesheet into several stylesheets. There are two main advantages of splitting up a stylesheet:

- It makes the stylesheet easier to maintain.
- It allows you to reuse the same templates and other components in several stylesheets.

Importing stylesheets into each other is often more useful than including them, particularly when it comes to reusing the same utility stylesheet in several XSLT applications, because it allows you to override the templates, global variables and parameters, keys, and so on that the imported stylesheet contains.

In the second part of this chapter, you learned how to use the `doc()`, `document()`, and `unparsed-text()` functions to access information from documents other than the source of the transformation. The documents retrieved by the `doc()` and `document()` functions must be well-formed XML documents, but the documents retrieved by the `unparsed-text()` function can contain any text at all. These documents can hold information that supplements either the stylesheet or the main source document, for example:

- Data for performing operations like searching and replacing
- Lookup tables of various sorts
- User preferences and customization information
- Snippets of XHTML to be included in the result
- Additional information referenced by the source document

The `doc()` and `unparsed-text()` functions simply retrieve documents based on a URL. If you want to retrieve a document whose URL is relative to the source document, you have to resolve the URL, using `resolve-uri()`, based on the base URL of a node in the source document, which you can get using the `base-uri()` function.

The `document()` function has more sophisticated behavior than the `doc()` function, in several ways. First, the first argument to the `document()` function can be a sequence, in which case the result of the function call is a sequence of nodes, one for each URL in the sequence. Second, a second argument to the `document()` function can provide a node whose base URI is used to resolve any relative URLs from the first argument. Finally, the `document()` function allows you to use fragment identifiers within a URL in order to access specific nodes within a document, rather than always getting the document node.

Review Questions

1. What difference does it make if you move an `<xsl:include>` up or down a stylesheet?
2. Name two things that, if they occur within an including stylesheet, an included stylesheet must not contain.

3. Can you use `<xsl:include>` within templates?

4. What differences are there between `<xsl:include>` and `<xsl:import>`?

5. Where must you place `<xsl:import>` within a stylesheet?

6. How does the XSLT processor decide which template to use if the main stylesheet and an imported stylesheet both contain templates that match the same node?

7. What is the difference between `<xsl:next-match>` and `<xsl:apply-imports>`?

8. Is it possible to include or import different stylesheets based on the value of a parameter?

9. What functions can you use to access external documents from the stylesheet? What are the differences between them?

10. Given that the stylesheet is in the `xslt` directory and the current node comes from the source document, which is in the `xml` directory, what documents do the following calls access?

```
doc('extra.xml')
document('extra.xml', /)
doc(resolve-uri('extra.xml', base-uri(/)))
document('extra.xml', .)
doc(resolve-uri('extra.xml', static-base-uri()))
document('extra.xml', document(''))
```

11. Create some XSLT to search `films.xml` for `<Film>` elements whose `<Director>` element child has the value `'James Cameron'`. (The current document is `TVGuide.xml`.)

12. Given that the current node has several `<Reference>` element children, each of whose values is a URL, what do the following calls access?

```
document(Reference)
document(Reference, .)
document(concat('http://www.example.com/', Reference))
document(resolve-uri(Reference, 'http://www.example.com/'))
```

CHAPTER 13

Schemas

One of the largest changes between XSLT 1.0 and XSLT 2.0 is the introduction of **schema-awareness**. For the most part, the only information about an XML document that you have access to in XSLT 1.0 is that available in well-formed XML documents: information about the elements and attributes that are actually present in the XML document and how they are arranged. In XSLT 2.0, this information can be supplemented by information from a schema, including defaulted and fixed elements and attributes and, most importantly, the **type** of each node.

As we saw in Chapter 2, there are two levels of conformance in XSLT 2.0: **Basic XSLT processors** are like XSLT 1.0 processors in that they don't have access to information from a schema; **Schema-Aware XSLT processors**, on the other hand, support node trees that have been annotated during schema validation. All the stylesheets that we've looked at so far have been written with a Basic XSLT processor in mind, and as we've seen, you can do a lot with just that information. However, using information from a schema within your stylesheet can make the stylesheet easier to write initially and to maintain if the markup language changes.

In this chapter, you'll learn

- How to import schema information into a stylesheet
- How to match nodes by their type
- How to match elements by their substitution group
- How to add type annotations to generated nodes

Validation, Schemas, and Types

Before we dive into the details about how to use a schema within a stylesheet, it's worth having a quick overview of how schemas and stylesheets fit together.

Schemas and Type Annotations

As we saw in Chapter 1, a **schema** defines a markup language by specifying what elements and attributes are allowed where and what kind of text they can contain. There are several different schema languages around, including

- **DTDs**—The schema language that's built into XML
- **XML Schema**—The official W3C schema language
- **RELAX NG**—A schema language originally from OASIS, now an ISO standard
- **Schematron**—A very flexible rule-based schema language, also an ISO standard

Conceptually, at least for the purposes of XSLT 2.0, a schema contains three interesting kinds of information:

- **Element declarations**, which specify the expected type of an element of a particular name in a particular context, and the substitution group to which an element belongs
- **Attribute declarations**, which specify the expected type of an attribute of a particular name in a particular context
- **Type definitions**, which define the allowed content of an element or attribute and are related to other types in a **type hierarchy**

The main purpose of a schema is to enable **validation** of an XML document. Validation checks whether the XML document adheres to the rules of the markup language, giving either a list of the validity errors that the XML document contains or success (indicating a valid document).

When a processor validates a particular element or attribute, it identifies the appropriate element or attribute declaration within the schema and checks whether the content of the element or attribute conforms to the type that's been declared. If it does, the element or attribute node is given a **type annotation**: it is labeled with the type against which it has been validated. An XSLT processor can then use the type annotation to select or match elements or attributes that have a particular kind of content.

■ **Note** Elements that haven't been validated have a type annotation of `xdt:untyped`, while attributes that haven't been validated have a type annotation of `xdt:untypedAtomic`. Invalid elements and elements that have only been partially validated (since they have invalid descendants, for example) have a type annotation of `xs:anyType`. Invalid or partially validated attributes have a type annotation of `xdt:untypedAtomic`.

■ **Summary** The result of validating a document against a schema is a node tree in which elements and attributes are annotated with their type.

Typed Values

The most important thing about a type annotation is that it means a processor can tell what type of value a node contains, and therefore how to treat that value when you use a polymorphic operator. For example, if you cast your mind back to Chapter 5, you'll remember that in order to get the `xs:dateTime` at which a program ended, you had to explicitly cast the value of the `<Start>` element to an `xs:dateTime` and explicitly cast the value of the `<Duration>` element to an `xdt:dayTimeDuration`, as follows:

```
xs:dateTime(Start) + xdt:dayTimeDuration(Duration)
```

The explicit casting was needed because the + operator can be used with many different types of values, most commonly with numbers. Without the casts, the XSLT processor would assume that, since you were trying to add them, the values of the <Start> and <Duration> elements were numbers, and it would raise an error because the values can't be converted to numbers.

Now consider what happens when the <Start> and <Duration> elements are annotated with a type. The declarations for these elements in the TVGuide.xsd schema are as follows:

```
<xs:element name="Start" type="xs:dateTime" />
<xs:element name="Duration" type="xdt:dayTimeDuration" />
```

After validation, the <Start> element is annotated with the type xs:dateTime, while the <Duration> element is annotated with the type xdt:dayTimeDuration. Because these elements have a type annotation, the **typed values** of the elements have appropriate types: the typed value of the <Start> element has the type xs:dateTime, and the typed value of the <Duration> element has the type xdt:dayTimeDuration.

This means we no longer have to explicitly cast the typed value of the <Start> element to an xs:dateTime or the typed value of the <Duration> element to an xdt:dayTimeDuration because the XSLT processor already knows that the <Start> and <Duration> elements' values are of those types. So the expression becomes

```
Start + Duration
```

■ **Note** The schema TVGuide.xsd has to import a schema containing the declaration for the xdt:dayTimeDuration type, since unlike the XML Schema types, the XPath datatypes aren't built into XML Schema validators.

This can cut both ways. Although it's easier to manipulate the value of the <Start> element as an xs:dateTime, it's correspondingly harder to manipulate it as a string. For example, you might want to test whether a program started in July 2001, which corresponds to the <Start> element beginning with '2001-07'. But since the value of the <Start> element is now recognized as an xs:dateTime, you couldn't use the starts-with() function directly on the value of the <Start> element, as in

```
starts-with(Start, '2001-07')
```

To use the starts-with() function to perform the comparison, you have to explicitly access the string value of the <Start> element using the string() function:

```
starts-with(string(Start), '2001-07')
```

Alternatively, of course, you can use the various functions that enable you to access information about an xs:dateTime:

```
year-from-dateTime(Start) = 2001 and month-from-dateTime(Start) = 07
```

or convert it to an xs:gYearMonth and do a comparison with that:

```
xs:gYearMonth(Start) = xs:gYearMonth('2001-07')
```

Elements that are declared with mixed content in the schema have an `xdt:untyped` typed value, which means their values will be converted to the type required by a function or operator. For example, the `<Description>` element is declared as having mixed content, and therefore will be automatically converted to a string when it's used in the `contains()` function, so the following will still work:

```
contains(Description, 'news')
```

On the other hand, trying to access the typed value of an element that's declared with element-only content in the schema will give you an error. For example, trying to test whether a `<Program>` element contains the string `'news'` as in the following:

```
contains(Program, 'news')
```

will give an error. You must access the string value of the `<Program>` element using the `string()` function if you need to test its contents:

```
contains(string(Program), 'news')
```

■ **Caution** The `string()` function gives you the string value of an element, which is the string that results from concatenating the values of all its text node descendants. The `xs:string()` function, on the other hand, converts the typed value of an element to a string; since accessing the typed value of an element that has element-only content raises an error, using the `xs:string()` function rather than the `string()` function will give you an error.

■ **Summary** Type annotations usually make it unnecessary to use explicit casts to indicate the type of a value.

Using Schemas Within Stylesheets

There are three ways in which schemas might be used with a stylesheet:

- To validate source documents in order to annotate the elements and attributes they contain with type information
- To validate elements and attributes generated by the stylesheet in order to annotate them with type information
- To provide element and attribute declarations and type definitions that can be referred to when matching or selecting nodes.

The source documents that are accessed by a Schema-Aware XSLT processor may include type annotations that indicate the types of the elements and attributes in the document. Which schema is used to provide these type annotations, or indeed whether a schema is used at all, isn't something that you can specify from within a stylesheet. Instead, an XSLT processor might use information within the XML document itself (such as the `DOCTYPE` declaration or an `xsi:schemaLocation` attribute) to work out which schema to use, or might let you specify which schema to use via a command-line option or through the API that you use to run the transformation.

■ **Note** In Saxon-SA, the only Schema-Aware XSLT 2.0 processor around as I write this, you have to use the command-line option `-val` to request validation of the source document. Saxon-SA then uses the `xsi:schemaLocation` or `xsi:noNamespaceSchemaLocation` attributes in the source document to identify the schema to use to validate the document.

You can, however, automatically strip out all the type annotations that are added to source documents using the `input-type-annotations` attribute on the `<xsl:stylesheet>` element. If you set the `input-type-annotations` attribute to `strip`, then any type annotations on source documents are replaced by `xdt:untyped` for elements and `xdt:untypedAtomic` for attributes. This is useful when you have a stylesheet that you want to work in the same way for both validated and unvalidated documents or a stylesheet that is only designed to work under Basic XSLT.

For example, `TVGuide.xsl` is designed to work with unvalidated XML documents. To make writing it easier, and to prevent us from accidentally relying on typing information that wouldn't be available if `TVGuide.xsl` were used with a Basic XSLT processor, we should add an `input-type-annotations` attribute to the `<xsl:stylesheet>` element, as in `TVGuide2.xsl`:

```
<xsl:stylesheet version="2.0"
                xmlns:xsl="http://www.w3.org/1999/XSL/Transform"
                xmlns:xs="http://www.w3.org/2001/XMLSchema"
                xmlns:xdt="http://www.w3.org/2005/04/xpath-datatypes"
                xmlns:tv="http://www.example.com/TVGuide"
                exclude-result-prefixes="xs xdt tv"
                input-type-annotations="strip"
                xmlns="http://www.w3.org/1999/xhtml">
  ...
</xsl:stylesheet>
```

Now, if you use Saxon-SA to process `TVGuide2.xml` with validation using `TVGuide2.xsl`, `TVGuide2.xml` is parsed and validated against `TVGuide.xsd`, but any type annotations on the nodes that it contains are removed prior to processing with the stylesheet.

■ **Note** Stripping type annotations does not necessarily leave you with exactly the same document as you had originally: validation can add defaulted or fixed attributes and add values to defaulted or fixed elements, and these attributes and element values will still be present in the source node tree.

The `input-type-annotations` attribute can also take the values `preserve` or `unspecified`, which is the default value. When an XSLT application is made up of several stylesheet modules, type annotations will be stripped if *any* of them specify `input-type-annotations="strip"`. It's an error if you have one stylesheet module that states that type annotations should be stripped and another that says that they should be preserved, so setting `input-type-annotations="preserve"` in a stylesheet module guarantees that they will be present (assuming the document is actually validated, of course).

■Summary When the `input-type-annotations` attribute on `<xsl:stylesheet>` is set to `strip`, all type annotations from validated source documents are removed.

To validate the elements and attributes that you generate, or to match elements and attributes based on their type, you must import the schema that contains the relevant declarations and definitions into your stylesheet. We'll look at how to do this in the next section before moving on to looking at how to select and match nodes by their type and substitution group, and then how to validate and annotate the nodes that you generate in your stylesheet.

Using Annotated Source Documents

To start preparing for the changes to our stylesheets that we'll be carrying out in this chapter, we'll first make those changes that we can make simply by using source documents that have been annotated with type information.

■Caution If you make changes to the stylesheet that rely on type annotations, then you might not be able to use the stylesheet with a Basic XSLT processor.

Our first task is to ensure that the XSLT processor annotates the source documents that we're using with the appropriate types. To do this, we have to associate the source documents `TVGuide.xml` and `series.xml` with the `TVGuide.xsd` schema, which we do using the `xsi:noNamespaceSchemaLocation` attribute on the document element of each XML document.

■Note We need to use the `xsi:noNamespaceSchemaLocation` attribute because the elements in the documents we're using aren't in any namespace. If they were in a namespace, `TVGuide.xsd` would need to have a `targetNamespace` attribute on its `<xs:schema>` element, and we would use the `xs:schemaLocation` attribute in the XML documents.

Adding the `xsi:noNamespaceSchemaLocation` attribute and the namespace declaration for the XML Schema instance namespace, `TVGuide2.xml` looks like this:

```
<TVGuide start="2001-07-05" end="2001-07-05"
         xmlns:xsi="http://www.w3.org/2001/XMLSchema-instance"
         xsi:noNamespaceSchemaLocation="TVGuide.xsd">
  <Channel>...</Channel>
  <Channel>...</Channel>
  ... more channels ...
</TVGuide>
```

and series2.xml looks like this:

```
<SeriesList xmlns:xsi="http://www.w3.org/2001/XMLSchema-instance"
            xsi:noNamespaceSchemaLocation="TVGuide.xsd">
  <Series>...</Series>
  <Series>...</Series>
  ... more series ...
</Series>
```

Now, when a Schema-Aware XSLT processor accesses these XML documents, each element and attribute will be assigned a type as specified in the schema. Already, this means we can make certain changes in our stylesheets. For example, in TVGuide3.xsl, there's no need to explicitly cast the value of the rating attribute of the <Program> element to an integer in order to get numeric sorting, as in the following:

```
<xsl:variable name="Channels" as="element(Channel)+">
  <xsl:perform-sort select="/TVGuide/Channel">
    <xsl:sort select="avg(Program/@rating)" order="descending" />
    <xsl:sort select="xs:integer(Program[1]/@rating)" order="descending" />
  </xsl:perform-sort>
</xsl:variable>
```

because, to the Schema-Aware XSLT processor, the rating attribute already has a type that is derived from xs:integer:

```
<xs:simpleType name="Rating">
  <xs:restriction base="xs:integer">
    <xs:minInclusive value="1" />
    <xs:maxInclusive value="10" />
  </xs:restriction>
</xs:simpleType>
```

Similarly, there's no need to explicitly cast the value of the <Start> element into an xs:dateTime, because it's already declared with this type in the schema.

On the other hand, we have to take care about what we do with elements that are declared in the schema as having element-only content, because we can no longer access their values directly as strings—we have to use the string() function to get their string value explicitly. We also have to watch out for attributes and elements that are given a different type in the schema from the type that we want to use in the stylesheet, such as values typed as date/time types being processed as if they are strings. Fortunately, we don't have any instances of these in our stylesheets.

With these changes made, try transforming TVGuide2.xml with TVGuide3.xsl to create TVGuide3.html, shown in Figure 13-1. To use Schema-Aware Saxon, you need to use this command-line:

```
java com.saxonica.Transform -val -o TVGuide3.html TVGuide2.xml TVGuide3.xsl
```

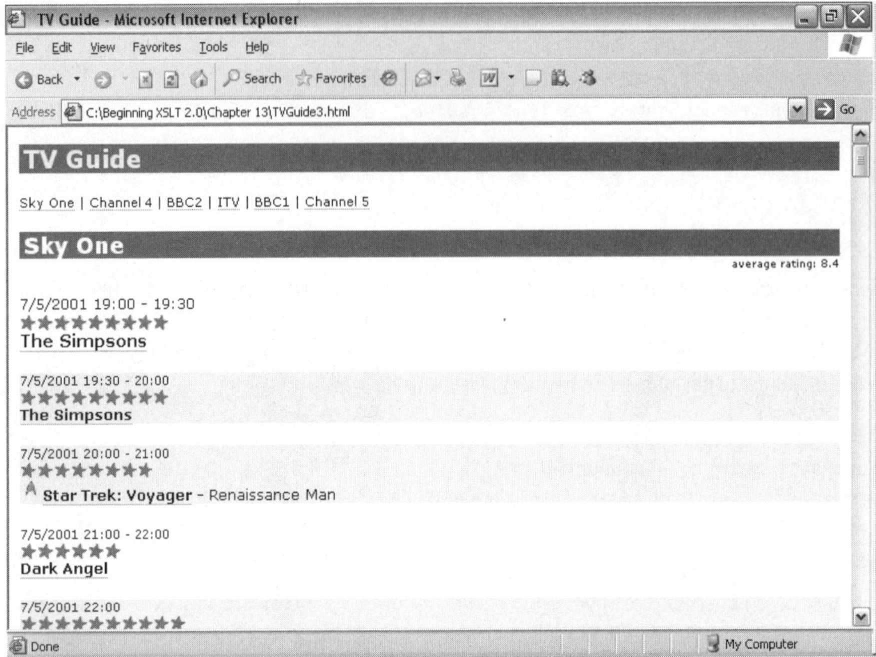

Figure 13-1. *Viewing* `TVGuide3.html` *in Internet Explorer*

The changes that we made in `TVGuide3.xsl` to take advantage of the Schema-Aware processing haven't actually rendered it unusable with a Basic XSLT processor or when the XML document isn't validated. Try using Schema-Aware Saxon without the `-val` command-line option: without this option, `TVGuide2.xml` isn't validated, so its element and attribute nodes aren't annotated with type information, but the only change this actually incurs is that if two channels have the same average rating, they will be arranged in *alphabetical* order of the rating of their first programs rather than in *numeric* order.

Importing Schemas

XSLT processors have built-in knowledge about certain type definitions. Most of these are the atomic types that we looked at in Chapter 5: the built-in types defined in XML Schema plus those defined to fill in the gaps for XPath 2.0. While Basic XSLT processors only know about the primitive types, `xs:integer`, and the XPath 2.0 datatypes, Schema-Aware XSLT processors know about all the XML Schema built-in types (which includes derived types such as `xs:NMTOKEN` and `xs:language`) as well as the XPath 2.0 datatypes.

Note Some XSLT processors may give you other built-in types, or provide mechanisms for specifying your own types. For example, XSLT processors written in Java might have built-in definitions for the Java primitive types.

You can use and refer to these type definitions to your heart's content, but if you want to refer to your own type definitions, or to element and attribute declarations, you need to import a schema that contains them.

Schemas are imported into a stylesheet using the `<xsl:import-schema>` element, which lives at the top level of a stylesheet, at the same level as the templates, key declarations, and so on. The `<xsl:import-schema>` element has two attributes:

- `schema-location` is a URI that specifies the location of the schema to be imported.
- `namespace` specifies a namespace URI, which is either used by the processor to locate an appropriate schema or used to check that the schema identified by the `schema-location` attribute contains declarations and definitions for the appropriate namespace.

Caution XSLT 2.0 follows XML Schema's guidelines for locating schemas, which are very loose. An XSLT 2.0 processor can have built-in schema information for particular namespaces, or might support you specifying the locations of schema via the command line or API to the processor. In this case, the `schema-location` attribute might be ignored.

The schema identified by the `schema-location` attribute needs to be in a format that's recognizable by the XSLT processor that you're using. In most cases, this will be an XML Schema schema; the `namespace` attribute should give the target namespace for the schema (or be omitted if the schema doesn't have a target namespace), and the `schema-location` attribute should give the location of the schema.

Note An XSLT processor will give an error if it doesn't recognize the schema that you specify: you can't provide different schemas for processors that support different schema languages.

Rather than referring to a separate schema, you can use the content of the `<xsl:import-schema>` element to specify a schema. The `<xsl:import-schema>` element can contain an `<xs:schema>` element; if it does, the `schema-location` attribute must be absent, and if you specify a `namespace` attribute, then its value must be the same as the value of the `targetNamespace` attribute on the `<xs:schema>` element.

A local schema embedded in the stylesheet is obviously only useful within the stylesheet itself. You can't validate the source document against it, so its main purpose is for declaring elements and attributes and defining types that are used solely within the stylesheet. For example, if you create a temporary tree in your stylesheet, you might provide an embedded schema for that temporary tree, so that you can take advantage of the type annotations that this will give you.

You can have as many `<xsl:import-schema>` elements as you like within a stylesheet, as long as they specify different namespaces. All the schemas are combined to provide element and attribute declarations and type definitions that you can use in your stylesheet.

■ **Caution** A Basic XSLT processor will halt with an error if it sees an `<xsl:import-schema>` element in a stylesheet, although you can "hide" them using the `use-when` attribute, which we'll meet in the next chapter.

A consequence of only allowing one schema document per namespace is that if documents require different schemas, then they must have different namespaces. For example, neither `TVGuide.xml` nor `flags.xml` has a namespace. If we import the schema that's appropriate for `TVGuide.xml` using

```
<xsl:import-schema schema-location="TVGuide.xsd" />
```

then we can't import a schema for `flags.xml` because it would also be associated with no namespace. Similarly, if our stylesheet generated HTML, which has no namespace, then we wouldn't be able to import both a schema for HTML (to check the result of the stylesheet) and a schema for the TV guide markup language (to help select elements and attributes by type).

This limitation makes it all the more important to use namespaces throughout your applications. In our case, we should use `TVGuide3.xml`, which uses the following namespace:

```
http://www.example.com/TVGuide
```

and update our stylesheet accordingly, as in `TVGuide4.xsl`, by adding prefixes on all references to elements in the document.

■ **Summary** You can import the element and attribute declarations and type definitions from a schema using the `<xsl:import-schema>` top-level element. Its `schema-location` attribute specifies the location of the schema, and its `namespace` attribute specifies the namespace of the schema components that are made available. Alternatively, a local schema can be embedded within the `<xsl:import-schema>` element.

Matching by Type

As we saw in Chapter 7, every element and attribute has a **type** and a **typed value**. In the documents accessed by and created by Basic XSLT processors, all elements must have a type of `xdt:untyped`, and all attributes must have a type of `xdt:untypedAtomic`. It's only if you're using a Schema-Aware processor (and have validated the nodes that you're looking at) that an element or attribute can have a different type.

In this section, we'll look at how matching and selecting nodes based on their type can help simplify your stylesheets.

Matching by Named Type

You can match an element or attribute by its type by specifying the type as the second argument of the `element()` or `attribute()` node test. The type that you specify needs to be a type that the XSLT processor knows about—it must be a built-in XML Schema type, an XPath type, or a type in a schema imported into the stylesheet using the `<xsl:import-schema>` element.

Note Remember that `element()` and `attribute()` node tests can be used in paths as well as in patterns. When used in a path, they select the nodes that they match along whatever axis is used in a step.

If you use the name of a type as the second argument of the `element()` or `attribute()` node test, then it will only match elements or attributes with the name and type specified. The name must match exactly, but the node test will match nodes whose type is derived from the type named. For example:

```
element(tv:Character, tv:Inline)
```

will only match `<tv:Character>` elements whose type is `tv:Inline` or a type derived (by extension or restriction) from `tv:Inline`.

Caution Types will only match if they have exactly the same definition as well as having the same name. For example, if `TVGuide3.xml` was validated against `TVGuide2.xsd`, then the `<tv:Character>` element would be assigned the type called `tv:Inline`. If, rather than importing `TVGuide3.xsd` to the stylesheet, you imported a schema by embedding it within `<xs:import-schema>`, and defined the type `tv:Inline` within that embedded schema, then the `<tv:Character>` elements would not match the preceding element node test because the type definition used when the element was validated would not be exactly the same as the type definition imported into the schema.

Matching by name and type is useful when you have an element that can be of several possible types, as it enables you to choose what to do based on the type. In our TV guide, for example, `<tv:Character>` elements can either be of the type `tv:Inline` (when they appear within a `<tv:Description>` element), in which case they contain text, or of the type `tv:Person` (when they appear within a `<tv:CastList>` element), in which case they contain a `<tv:Name>` element. We can have separate templates that deal with the two types of `<tv:Character>` element:

```
<xsl:template match="element(tv:Character, tv:Inline)">
  <span class="character"><xsl:apply-templates /></span>
</xsl:template>

<xsl:template match="element(tv:Character, tv:Person)">
  <span class="character"><xsl:apply-templates select="Name" /></span>
</xsl:template>
```

Summary If you name a type in the second argument of the `element()` or `attribute()` node tests, the node test will only match nodes of that type.

You can also use a * as the first argument of the `element()` or `attribute()` node tests in order to match any element or attribute with a particular type. One way in which this is useful is to provide a standard way of formatting values of a particular type. For example, if you always wanted all dates to be formatted using the US date format of MM/DD/YYYY, then you could create a template in format mode that matched all elements and attributes of the type xs:date, and formatted the dates accordingly:

```
<xsl:template match="element(*, xs:date) | attribute(*, xs:date)"
              mode="format">
  <xsl:sequence select="format-date(., '[M,2]/[D,2]/[Y,4]')" />
</xsl:template>
```

and similarly, you could create another template in format mode that would format numbers using two decimal places and commas as grouping separators every three digits:

```
<xsl:template match="element(*, xs:double)  | attribute(*, xs:double) |
                     element(*, xs:float)   | attribute(*, xs:float)  |
                     element(*, xs:decimal) | attribute(*, xs:decimal)"
              mode="format">
  <xsl:sequence select="format-number(., '#,##0.00')" />
</xsl:template>
```

■ **Note** To capture elements and attributes of all the numeric types, you have to test for xs:double, xs:float, and xs:decimal, as these three are primitive types and don't have a common numeric supertype.

In other templates, then, whenever you want to give the value of an element or attribute, you should apply templates to it in format mode and the appropriate formatting will be used.

■ **Note** Node tests that test only the type of a node have the same priority as node tests that test only the name of a node (0). Node tests that test both the name and type of a node have a higher priority than either (0.25).

■ **Summary** If you use an asterisk as the first argument of the element() or attribute() node test, it will match an element or attribute of any name with the specified type.

Consolidating Templates Using Common Types

The schema that we're using uses a common type called tv:Person for all the elements that can hold details about a person, such as <tv:Actor>, <tv:Character>, <tv:Writer>, <tv:Director>, and <tv:Producer> elements. Each of these elements contains a <tv:Name> child and an optional <tv:Description> child, as specified in the type definition:

```
<xs:complexType name="Person">
  <xs:sequence>
    <xs:element name="Name" type="xs:token" />
    <xs:element name="Description" type="Inline" minOccurs="0" />
  </xs:sequence>
</xs:complexType>
```

In the TV guide display that we have, we're not interested in the descriptions of these people, only in their names. We can make sure that all of these elements are treated in the same way, by creating a `<span>` element with a `class` attribute that's the lowercase version of the element name and whose value is the result of applying templates to the `<Name>` element child, with a template that matches all elements with the type `Person`, as follows:

```
<xsl:template match="element(*, tv:Person)">
  <span class="{lower-case(local-name(.))}">
    <xsl:apply-templates select="tv:Name" />
  </span>
</xsl:template>
```

To refer to the `Person` type, we need to import the schema into our stylesheet with an `<xsl:import-schema>` element at the top level of the stylesheet. The declarations and definitions in the schema belong to the `http://www.example.com/TVGuide` namespace, so the `namespace` attribute of `<xsl:import-schema>` needs to be set to that URI, and we can specify where the schema lives using the `schema-location` attribute:

```
<xsl:import-schema namespace="http://www.example.com/TVGuide"
                   schema-location="TVGuide2.xsd" />
```

The template that matches all elements of type `tv:Person` has the same priority as the templates that match all `<tv:Character>` and `<tv:Actor>` elements. If the XSLT processor encounters a `<tv:Character>` or `<tv:Actor>` element of type `tv:Person`, it won't know which template to use. For now, we'll change the templates that match `<tv:Character>` and `<tv:Actor>` elements so that they only match those elements within `<tv:Description>` elements (where they're of type `tv:Inline` rather than of type `tv:Person`), and place these templates in `description4.xsl`:

```
<xsl:template match="tv:Description//tv:Character">
  <span class="character"><xsl:apply-templates /></span>
</xsl:template>

<xsl:template match="tv:Description//tv:Actor">
  <span class="actor"><xsl:apply-templates /></span>
</xsl:template>
```

These changes have been made in `TVGuide5.xsl`. Transforming `TVGuide3.xml` with `TVGuide5.xsl` creates `TVGuide5.html`, which looks exactly the same as previous versions of the TV guide. However, if you try to use `TVGuide5.xsl` with an XSLT processor that isn't Schema-Aware, you will get an error, shown in Figure 13-2.

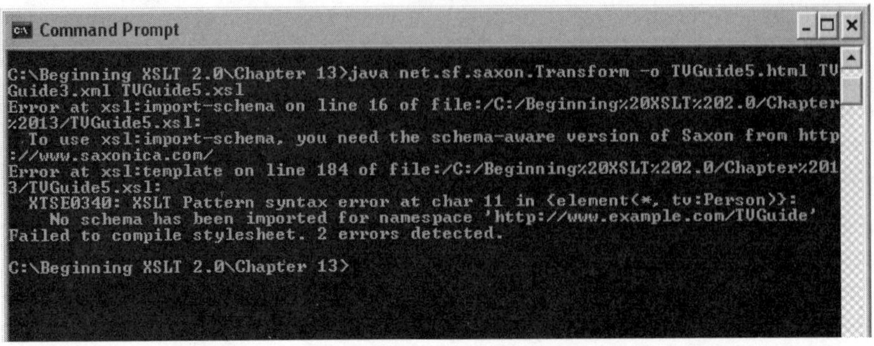

```
Command Prompt

C:\Beginning XSLT 2.0\Chapter 13>java net.sf.saxon.Transform -o TVGuide5.html TV
Guide3.xml TVGuide5.xsl
Error at xsl:import-schema on line 16 of file:/C:/Beginning%20XSLT%202.0/Chapter
%2013/TVGuide5.xsl:
  To use xsl:import-schema, you need the schema-aware version of Saxon from http
://www.saxonica.com/
Error at xsl:template on line 184 of file:/C:/Beginning%20XSLT%202.0/Chapter%201
3/TVGuide5.xsl:
  XTSE0340: XSLT Pattern syntax error at char 11 in {element(*, tv:Person)}:
    No schema has been imported for namespace 'http://www.example.com/TVGuide'
Failed to compile stylesheet. 2 errors detected.

C:\Beginning XSLT 2.0\Chapter 13>
```

Figure 13-2. *Error transforming* TVGuide3.xml *with* TVGuide5.xsl *using Basic Saxon*

Matching by Declared Type

There are several ways in which schemas can be designed. Using named types, as described earlier, makes it easy for elements of different names to share the same kind of content, and makes it easy for you to design stylesheets that use those types in order to get common behavior in different situations.

However, not all schemas are designed with named types. When declaring an element or attribute, it's also possible to nest the definition of an **anonymous type** inside the element or attribute declaration. In TVGuide2.xsd, this is done for the <tv:TVGuide> element, for example:

```
<xs:element name="TVGuide">
  <xs:complexType>
    <xs:sequence>
      <xs:element name="Channel" type="Channel" maxOccurs="unbounded" />
    </xs:sequence>
    <xs:attribute name="start" type="xs:date" use="required" />
    <xs:attribute name="end" type="xs:date" use="required" />
  </xs:complexType>
</xs:element>
```

In these cases, and in cases where you don't care what the type of the element or attribute is, but it must be the same as (or derived from) that declared in the schema, you can use the schema-element() and schema-attribute() node tests.

In the schema-element() and schema-attribute() node tests, the argument is the name of a top-level element or attribute declaration. For example, the node test

```
schema-element(tv:TVGuide)
```

points to the global element declaration for the <tv:TVGuide> element.

The schema-element() and schema-attribute() node tests match elements or attributes that are consistent with the element or attribute declaration that they point to. What this means is

- The element or attribute must have the same name as that given in the declaration (or be part of the element substitution group, as we'll see in the next section).
- The element or attribute must have the same type as that given in the declaration (or a type derived from the declared type).

■ **Note** Templates that match elements or attributes based on a declaration have a default priority of 0.25.

This does *not* necessarily mean that the element or attribute that's matched by the node test has been validated against the global element or attribute declaration. Any element with the given name and the type specified in the declaration will match. For example, in `TVGuide2.xsd` there's a global element declaration for a `<tv:Title>` element, declaring it to have the type `xs:string`:

```
<xs:element name="Title" type="xs:string" />
```

and local declarations for `<tv:Title>` elements within the `tv:Program` and `tv:Series` type definitions in which the `<tv:Title>` element is declared to have the type `xs:token`. The `tv:Series` type definition is

```
<xs:complexType name="Series">
  <xs:sequence>
    <xs:element name="Title" type="xs:token" />
    <xs:element name="Description" type="Inline" />
  </xs:sequence>
  <xs:attribute name="id" type="xs:NCName" use="required" />
  <xs:attribute name="type" type="ProgramType" use="required" />
</xs:complexType>
```

Say we create a template that matches `<tv:Title>` elements using the global element declaration for the `<tv:Title>` element, as in

```
<xsl:template match="schema-element(tv:Title)">
  ...
</xsl:template>
```

This template will match all `<tv:Title>` elements that have the name `tv:Title` and the type `xs:string` or a type derived from `xs:string` (which includes `xs:token`). Despite the fact that they're not actually validated against the global element declaration for the `<tv:Title>` element, `<tv:Title>` elements that appear within both `<tv:Program>` and `<tv:Series>` elements will match the preceding template.

If we want to match only those `<tv:Title>` elements that appear within an element whose type is `tv:Series`, we need to use a path pattern that matches `<tv:Title>` elements whose parent element is of the type `tv:Series`, as in

```
<xsl:template match="element(*, tv:Series)/tv:Title">
  ...
</xsl:template>
```

This template will not match <tv:Title> elements that appear within <tv:Program> elements because the type of <tv:Program> elements is tv:Program, not tv:Series.

Summary In the schema-element() and schema-attribute() node tests, the element or attribute must match the global element or attribute declaration: it must have the same name and the same type as that declaration, but there's no requirement for it to have been validated against that declaration.

Matching by Substitution Group

In the previous section, I've said that the argument to the schema-element() node test specifies the name of the element that it matches. This isn't entirely true; the name of the element does not always have to be exactly the same as the name specified, if you take into account **substitution groups**.

Substitution groups are a mechanism provided in XML Schema to define groups of elements that can substitute for each other. Each substitution group has a **head element**, which is usually abstract (and thus can't actually appear within a document), and a number of **member elements**. Whenever the head element is referenced in a content model, one of the member elements of the substitution group can appear instead. In addition, the types of the member elements of the substitution group must be the same as, or derived from, the type of the head element.

Note Members of a substitution group may themselves be the head elements of another substitution group, such that the substitution groups form a hierarchy.

There are two substitution groups used in the schema in TVGuide2.xsd, which illustrate two ways in which substitution groups are commonly used in schemas.

First, substitution groups are used to identify elements that can appear in the same context, usually in document-oriented XML. In TVGuide2.xsd, there is a substitution group for the elements that can appear inline within a <tv:Description> element. The head element is the abstract <tv:_Inline> element:

```
<xs:element name="_Inline" type="Inline" abstract="true" />
```

The member elements are those elements that can appear inline, such as the <tv:Character>, <tv:Actor>, and <tv:Link> elements, which are declared globally with

```
<xs:element name="Character" substitutionGroup="_Inline" />
<xs:element name="Actor" substitutionGroup="_Inline" />
<xs:element name="Link" type="Link" substitutionGroup="_Inline" />
```

Note In XML Schema, if you don't specify a type for an element that belongs to a substitution group, then it takes the type of the head element of that substitution group. So in the preceding, the <tv:Character> and <tv:Actor> elements automatically get the type tv:Inline.

The <tv:_Inline> abstract element is referenced within the tv:Inline type, as follows:

```
<xs:complexType name="Inline" mixed="true">
  <xs:sequence>
    <xs:element ref="_Inline" minOccurs="0" maxOccurs="unbounded" />
  </xs:sequence>
</xs:complexType>
```

This says that any element with the type tv:Inline (which includes the <tv:Description> element, for example) can contain mixed content with any number of elements that belong to the tv:_Inline substitution group. The equivalent type definition would be

```
<xs:complexType name="Inline" mixed="true">
  <xs:sequence>
    <xs:choice minOccurs="0" maxOccurs="unbounded">
      <xs:element ref="_Inline" />
      <xs:element ref="Character" />
      <xs:element ref="Actor" />
      <xs:element ref="Link" />
    </xs:choice>
  </xs:sequence>
</xs:complexType>
```

Using substitution groups in this way simplifies the content models used in a schema, and allows other users to extend a schema to add elements to a substitution group.

The second common use for substitution groups in schemas is to create a substitution group hierarchy that supports the type hierarchy. This is commonly used in data-oriented markup languages. The example in TVGuide2.xsd is the substitution group that's headed by the <tv:_Person> abstract element:

```
<xs:element name="_Person" type="Person" abstract="true" />
```

which has as its members the <tv:Writer>, <tv:Director>, and <tv:Producer> elements:

```
<xs:element name="Writer" substitutionGroup="_Person" />
<xs:element name="Director" substitutionGroup="_Person" />
<xs:element name="Producer" substitutionGroup="_Person" />
```

The <tv:_Person> element is referenced from within the tv:PersonList type:

```
<xs:complexType name="PersonList">
  <xs:sequence maxOccurs="unbounded">
    <xs:element ref="_Person" />
  </xs:sequence>
</xs:complexType>
```

This definition enables the tv:Writers, tv:Directors, and tv:Producers types to be derived from the tv:PersonList type by restricting the elements that are allowed within each. For example, the tv:Writers type is defined as follows:

```
<xs:complexType name="Writers">
  <xs:complexContent>
```

```
    <xs:restriction base="PersonList">
      <xs:sequence maxOccurs="unbounded">
        <xs:element ref="Writer" />
      </xs:sequence>
    </xs:restriction>
  </xs:complexContent>
</xs:complexType>
```

The end result is that the `<tv:Writers>`, `<tv:Directors>`, and `<tv:Producers>` elements have a common type of `tv:PersonList`, and that the `<tv:Writer>`, `<tv:Director>`, and `<tv:Producer>` elements have a common type of `tv:Person` and belong to the `tv:_Person` substitution group. Each of these commonalities is a hook that you can use within a stylesheet to produce common behavior for these elements.

Summary Substitution groups are groups of elements that can appear in the same context and that have the same type.

In the `schema-element()` node test, the name that you specify may be the name of the head element of a substitution group. In this case, the node test will match any element whose name is the same as any of the members of that substitution group. For example, the node test

```
schema-element(tv:_Person)
```

will match any element called `<tv:Writer>`, `<tv:Director>`, or `<tv:Producer>`, whose type is (or is derived from) `tv:Person` (the declared type of the `<tv:_Person>` element).

Substitution groups are very useful for simplifying your stylesheet, because they enable you to treat all elements in the particular substitution group in the same way. For example, if we wanted to process all lists of people in the same way (by creating an HTML unordered list, say), we could select all the people within those lists very simply:

```
<xsl:template match="element(*, tv:PersonList)">
  <ul>
    <xsl:for-each select="schema-element(tv:_Person)">
      <li><xsl:apply-templates select="tv:Name" /></li>
    </xsl:for-each>
  </ul>
</xsl:template>
```

Matching or selecting using a substitution group ensures that if the markup changes, such as the addition of other kinds of lists of people, the stylesheet will probably be able to handle the extra elements correctly.

Summary The `schema-element()` node test matches by substitution group: if you specify the name of the head element of a substitution group, then elements whose name is the same as a member element of that substitution group will be matched as well.

Consolidating Templates Using Substitution Groups

In this example, we'll look at how to use substitution groups to get common behavior for a bunch of elements. The substitution group we'll concentrate on is the tv:_Inline substitution group, which has as members all the elements that can appear inline within a <tv:Description> element.

Currently, in description4.xsl, we have separate templates for each of the elements that can appear within the <tv:Description> element. Most of these templates do almost exactly the same thing: create a <span> element whose class attribute is the lowercase version of the element name, and apply templates to the content of the element.

For example, the templates that match <tv:Character> and <tv:Actor> elements within <tv:Description> elements are as follows:

```
<xsl:template match="Description//Character">
  <span class="character"><xsl:apply-templates /></span>
</xsl:template>

<xsl:template match="Description//Actor">
  <span class="actor"><xsl:apply-templates /></span>
</xsl:template>
```

Rather than having separate templates for each of these elements, we can have one template that matches all elements in the tv:_Inline substitution group, as follows:

```
<xsl:template match="schema-element(tv:_Inline)">
  <span class="{lower-case(local-name(.))}"><xsl:apply-templates /></span>
</xsl:template>
```

The only element that shouldn't be treated in this way is the <tv:Link> element, which needs to be turned into a link. The original template, which matches <tv:Link> elements appearing within <tv:Description> elements, can be retained:

```
<xsl:template match="tv:Description//tv:Link">
  <xsl:variable name="content" as="item()+">
    <xsl:apply-templates />
  </xsl:variable>
  <xsl:call-template name="link">
    <xsl:with-param name="href" as="xs:anyURI" select="@href" />
    <xsl:with-param name="content" select="$content" />
  </xsl:call-template>
</xsl:template>
```

This template has a higher priority (0.5) than the template that matches all elements in the tv:_Inline substitution group, which has a priority of 0.25.

TVGuide6.xsl includes description5.xsl, in which these changes are made. Transforming TVGuide3.xml with TVGuide6.xsl, with validation of TVGuide3.xml, results in TVGuide6.html, which looks exactly the same as before.

However, we're now reliant on validation of TVGuide3.xml to get the look we're after. Look at the *EastEnders* cast list in TVGuide6.html, shown in Figure 13-3. This is the look that we're after, with the names of characters in the description of the program shown in a slightly larger font, and a list of characters and actors without the descriptions of either.

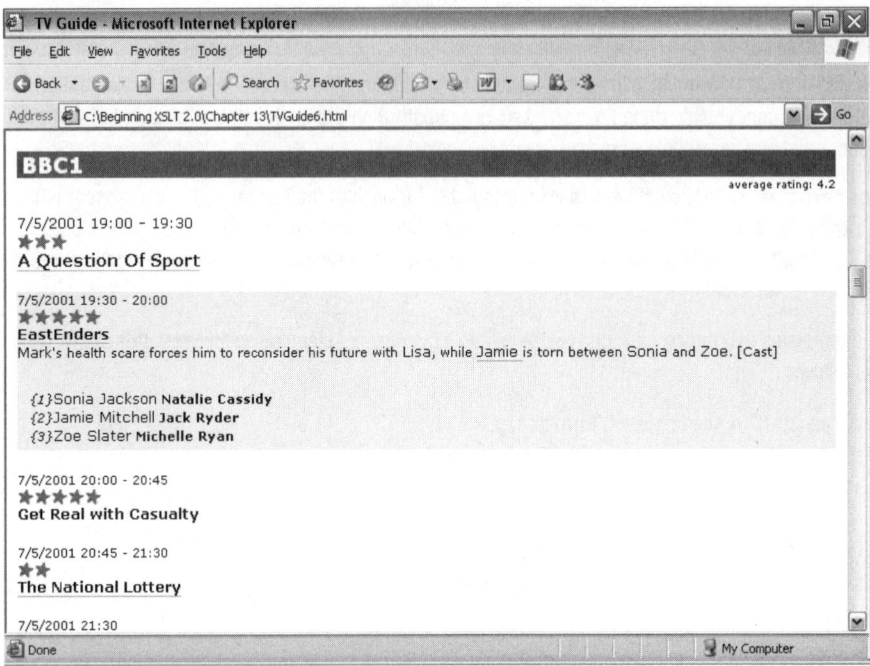

Figure 13-3. *Viewing* `TVGuide6.html` *in Internet Explorer*

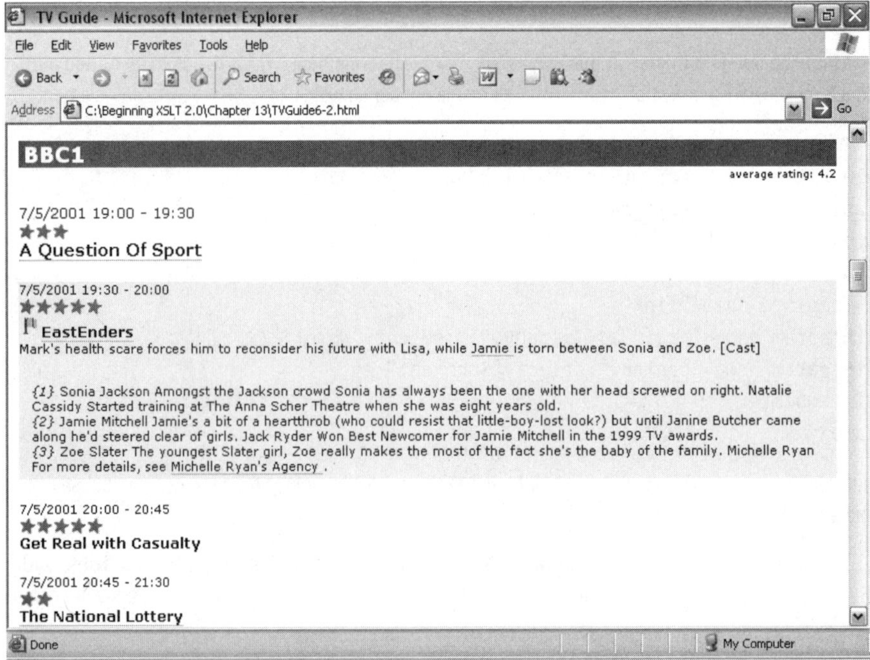

Figure 13-4. *Viewing* `TVGuide6-2.html` *in Internet Explorer*

Now try transforming TVGuide3.xml with TVGuide6.xsl without validation, to give TVGuide6-2.html. As shown in Figure 13-4, the details of the *EastEnders* episode are no longer styled correctly. The <tv:Character> elements within the program description aren't recognized as being part of the tv:_Inline substitution group, so the names of characters no longer appear in a larger font; and the <tv:Character> and <tv:Actor> element children of <tv:CastMember> are no longer annotated with the type tv:Person, so we get the full description as well.

In the new XSLT application, description5.xsl is a lot shorter, and you probably won't have to change it if you want to add new inline elements to descriptions later on. But we're increasingly reliant on validation of the TV guide against the schema that we reference within the stylesheet to get the look we're after.

Annotating Node Trees

As we've seen earlier in this chapter, type annotations on nodes mean that you don't have to explicitly cast their values when using polymorphic operators and that you can use templates that match elements and attributes by their type in order to get common behavior for groups of elements and attributes, thus simplifying your stylesheet.

Nodes in source trees may be annotated before they are passed into the stylesheet, but how that annotation is done depends on the XSLT processor that you use. If you want more control over the type annotations that are added to a node, or if you are creating temporary trees that you want to process later, you may want to add annotations to the nodes that you create.

Adding a type annotation also validates the node against the particular type (otherwise you would be able to end up with a node that claimed to be of a type that it wasn't), so adding type annotations can also be used to guarantee that either the result of your stylesheet is valid, or the stylesheet generates an error. This is useful in situations where invalid output is more costly than no output at all.

■ **Note** The result of a transformation is a node tree, which may include type annotations. If you serialize that node tree, as we saw in Chapter 8, those type annotations will be lost (though they may be reconstructed by revalidating the output against the schema). XSLT processors don't automatically add xsi:type attributes to elements with type annotations, for example.

Several XSLT instructions can be used to generate element and attribute nodes:

- Literal result elements generate element nodes.
- xsl:element generates an element node.
- xsl:attribute generates an attribute node.
- xsl:copy generates a copy of the context node, which might be an element or attribute node.
- xsl:copy-of generates a copy of whatever nodes you select, which might be element or attribute nodes.

Each of these instructions has two attributes that control the type annotation added to the node—the `type` attribute and the `validation` attribute—only one of which can be present on a particular instruction.

■ **Note** On literal result elements, these attributes must be in the XSLT namespace: `xsl:type` and `xsl:validation`.

In this section, we'll look at how to add type annotations to nodes using these two attributes.

Specifying Node Types Explicitly

The `type` attribute specifies the type of the node generated by the XSLT instruction on which it's specified. This needs to be a type that the XSLT processor knows about, either because it is a built-in type or because it's in a schema that you've imported using the `<xsl:import-schema>` element.

For example, to generate a `<tv:End>` element whose type is `xs:dateTime`, based on the `<tv:Start>` and `<tv:Duration>` child elements of the current `<tv:Program>` element, you could use the `<xsl:element>` instruction with a `type` attribute:

```
<xsl:element name="tv:End" type="xs:dateTime">
  <xsl:sequence select="tv:Start + tv:Duration" />
</xsl:element>
```

or you could use a literal result element with an `xsl:type` attribute:

```
<tv:End xsl:type="xs:dateTime">
  <xsl:sequence select="tv:Start + tv:Duration" />
</tv:End>
```

The content of the element or attribute is validated against the type that you specify. If the content isn't valid, then a type error gets raised and the XSLT processor stops the transformation. Otherwise, the element or attribute is annotated with the specified type.

■ **Summary** The `type` attribute (or the `xsl:type` attribute on a literal result element) specifies the type of the element or attribute that's generated by the instruction.

Validating Against a Schema

If you don't know the name of the type that an element or attribute should be validated against, or if the type is anonymous such that you can't point to it by name, you can use the `validation` attribute to annotate the node. The `validation` attribute has four possible values:

- `strip` indicates that all type annotations on the node (and its attributes and descendants) should be cleared, leaving elements with the type `xdt:untyped` and attributes with the type `xdt:untypedAtomic`.
- `preserve` indicates that type annotations on the node's attributes and descendants should be kept. If the node's copied using `<xsl:copy-of>`, then that node's type is also retained; otherwise, it's assigned the type `xs:anyType` if it's an element and `xdt:untypedAtomic` if it's an attribute.
- `strict` indicates that the node should be validated against the global element or attribute declaration with the relevant name. The transformation halts with an error if there isn't such a declaration, or the node isn't valid against the declaration.
- `lax` indicates that the node should be validated against the global element or attribute declaration with the relevant name, if there is one; if there isn't, the node (and its attributes and descendants) are untyped (elements have the type `xdt:untyped`, attributes the type `xdt:untypedAtomic`). The transformation halts with an error if a declaration is found but the node isn't valid against it.

As well as being able to specify the `validation` attribute on individual XSLT instructions, you can specify a `default-validation` attribute on the `<xsl:stylesheet>` element. If neither a `type` attribute nor a `validation` attribute is specified, the value of the `default-validation` attribute is used to determine how the element or attribute is validated. If that isn't specified, then the default is that type annotations are stripped.

■ **Tip** If you do any type annotating at all, whether with the `type` attribute or the `validation` attribute, you should set the default validation for the stylesheet to `preserve` so that these type annotations aren't unwittingly lost.

■ **Summary** The `validation` attribute can be used to validate a generated element or attribute against a global element or attribute declaration, or can be used to strip or preserve type annotations from the attributes and descendants of the element. The default for the `validation` attribute is the value of the `default-validation` attribute on the `<xsl:stylesheet>` element, which is `strip` by default.

As well as being present on the instructions that are used to generate elements and attributes, the `validation` and `type` attributes are allowed on the `<xsl:document>` and `<xsl:result-document>` instructions. The effect is the same as if the `validation` or `type` attribute had been present on the instruction generating the element child (or children) of the generated document node, with two extra constraints:

- If you specify a type with the `type` attribute, or specify `strict` or `lax` validation, the document node must only have one element child and no text node children (it may have as many comment or processing instruction children as you like). In other words, it must represent a well-formed document.
- Identity constraints, such as the uniqueness of `ID` attributes within the document, are checked.

For example, if you just want to make sure that a document generated by your stylesheet is a well-formed XML document, you can apply lax validation (and make sure that there aren't any imported element declarations for elements within the document you're generating):

```
<xsl:result-document validation="lax">
  ...
</xsl:result-document>
```

If you want to make sure that the result document complies with one of the schemas that you've imported into the stylesheet, you can apply strict validation. This doesn't specify the name of the document element, or even its namespace, but it does ensure that the document is valid against one of the imported schemas:

```
<xsl:result-document validation="strict">
  ...
</xsl:result-document>
```

Going one step further, you can make sure that the document element is valid against a particular type specified in the schema. For example, if the XHTML schema specifies that the `<xhtml:html>` element has the type `xhtml:htmlType` then you could use

```
<xsl:result-document type="xhtml:htmlType">
  ...
</xsl:result-document>
```

If you're working with a schema in which the document element is declared with an anonymous type, or in which there are several elements that have the same type as the type of the document element that you're after, you need to carry out validation in two steps: validate the document strictly and then assign it to a variable that's declared to be a document with a particular document element. For example, to have the XSLT processor check that you're creating valid XHTML, with an `<xhtml:html>` element as the document element, you need to do the following:

```
<xsl:variable name="document" as="document-node(schema-element(xhtml:html))">
  <xsl:document validation="strict">
    <xsl:apply-templates />
  </xsl:document>
</xsl:variable>
<xsl:copy-of select="$document" validation="preserve" />
```

If you generate a result document implicitly (without the `<xsl:result-document>` instruction), it's validated based on the value of the `default-validation` attribute on the `<xsl:stylesheet>` element of the main stylesheet.

■ **Summary** On the `<xsl:result-document>` and `<xsl:document>` instructions, the `validation` attribute can be used to validate the document as a whole, including identity constraints. The `type` attribute specifies the type for the document element.

Annotating Source Trees Within the Stylesheet

Relying on the validation of a source document before it is passed into the stylesheet can be a little dangerous, since you, as the stylesheet author, have no control over what schema is used to validate the document and therefore what types the source document might contain. One way to gain control over the schema that's actually used to validate your source documents is to perform the validation in the stylesheet itself.

Currently, the source documents that we're using are held in the two global variables `$TVGuide` and `$series` (declared in the `series4.xsl` stylesheet).

We want to make sure that the document node held by the `$TVGuide` variable is a valid document whose document element is a `<tv:TVGuide>` element. We can do this by copying the document while invoking strict validation, as follows:

```
<xsl:variable name="TVGuide" as="document-node(schema-element(tv:TVGuide))">
  <xsl:copy-of select="/" validation="strict" />
</xsl:variable>
```

Similarly, we can copy the document node of `series4.xml` and invoke strict validation in order to get a validated copy of the node:

```
<xsl:variable name="series" as="document-node(schema-element(tv:SeriesList))">
  <xsl:copy-of select="doc('series4.xml')" validation="strict" />
</xsl:variable>
```

To ensure that the stylesheet operates on the validated version of the TV guide document, we need to rejig the template that currently matches the root document node of the source document. This template will currently activate whenever the stylesheet is used, no matter what the source document for the stylesheet looks like. To prevent this from happening, we can change its pattern so that it only matches document nodes whose document element is a `<tv:TVGuide>` element valid against the declaration for `<tv:TVGuide>` elements within the imported schema:

```
<xsl:template match="document-node(schema-element(tv:TVGuide))">
  <html>
    ...
  </html>
</xsl:template>
```

If the source document hasn't been validated yet (and therefore doesn't match this template), we want to apply templates to the validated copy of the source document held in the `$TVGuide` variable:

```
<xsl:template match="/">
  <xsl:apply-templates select="$TVGuide" />
</xsl:template>
```

Finally, we need to adjust the `$Channels` variable so that it contains `<tv:Channel>` elements in the validated version of the source document rather than the original unvalidated version:

```
<xsl:variable name="Channels" as="element(tv:Channel)+">
  <xsl:perform-sort select="$TVGuide/tv:TVGuide/tv:Channel">
    <xsl:sort select="avg(tv:Program/@rating)" order="descending" />
    <xsl:sort select="tv:Program[1]/@rating" order="descending" />
  </xsl:perform-sort>
</xsl:variable>
```

These changes have been made to `TVGuide7.xsl`, which includes `series5.xsl`. Transforming `TVGuide4.xml`, which doesn't itself reference the schema `TVGuide2.xsd`, without validation using `TVGuide7.xsl` results in `TVGuide7.html`. As you can see in Figure 13-5, despite the fact that the source document isn't validated externally, the elements end up with the type annotations they should have, and we get the correct output for the description and cast list of the *EastEnders* episode.

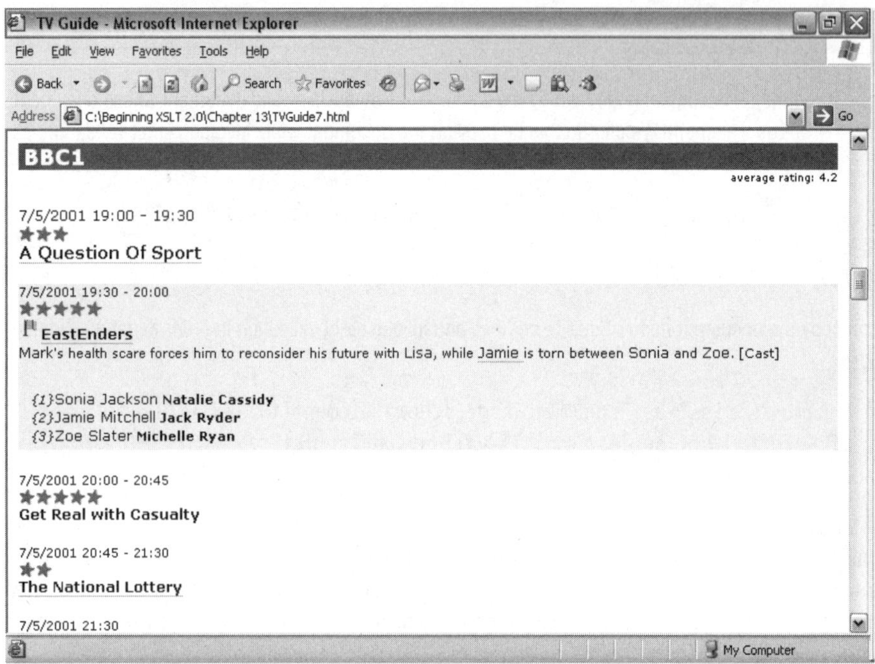

Figure 13-5. *Viewing* `TVGuide7.html` *in Internet Explorer*

The source document is validated based on the schema imported into the stylesheet rather than based on any references to schemas that it includes itself, making the stylesheet more robust and able to handle documents that don't point to schemas themselves.

Managing Type Annotations

It's worth highlighting a few gotchas that arise when using type annotations.

First, just because an element's content or attribute's value is generated from an atomic value does not mean that the element or attribute is assigned the type of that atomic value. For example, if you have the following:

```
<a href="{xs:anyURI('http://www.w3.org/')}">
  <xsl:attribute name="class" select="xs:NMTOKEN('link')" />
  <xsl:sequence select="xs:NMTOKEN('W3C')" />
</a>
```

then the `href` and `class` attributes both have the type `xdt:untypedAtomic`, and the `<a>` element has the type `xdt:untyped`. Only the `[xsl:]type` and `[xsl:]validation` attributes have the power to assign types to elements and attributes.

Summary The types of the atomic values that are used to create the content of an element or the value of an attribute play no part in the types assigned to elements or attributes.

Second, declaring the type of a variable or parameter using the as attribute does not automatically validate the content of the variable or parameter. For example, we know how to declare that a variable holds an `<xhtml:a>` element:

```
<xsl:variable name="link" as="element(xhtml:a)">
  <a href="{...}">...</a>
</xsl:variable>
```

Let's say that we want to declare that the `$link` variable holds a *valid* `<xhtml:a>` element. In the XML Schema for XHTML, the `<xhtml:a>` element is declared with the type `xhtml:a.type` as follows:

```
<xs:element name="a" type="a.type"/>
```

Note The XML Schema for XHTML used here is available from `http://www.w3.org/TR/2004/WD-xhtml-modularization-20040218/`.

Assuming that the default validation for the stylesheet is `preserve`, just changing the declared type of the variable, as in

```
<xsl:variable name="link" as="element(xhtml:a, xhtml:a.type)">
  <a href="{...}">...</a>
</xsl:variable>
```

will give an error because the generated `<xhtml:a>` element hasn't been validated, so it has the type `xdt:untyped` and not the type `xhtml:a.type` and therefore doesn't match the type declared for the variable.

To make the variable's type declaration accurate, we have to validate the `<xhtml:a>` element against the `xhtml:a.type` type using the `xsl:type` attribute:

```
<xsl:variable name="link" as="element(xhtml:a, xhtml:a.type)">
  <a xsl:type="xhtml:a.type" href="{...}">...</a>
</xsl:variable>
```

The same considerations apply when you declare the return type of a function or template using the as attribute: just because you say that a template returns an element with a particular type does not guarantee that the element will be validated.

Summary Declaring the type of a variable or parameter does not invoke validation of the nodes held by the variable or parameter. Similarly, declaring the return type of a function or template does not invoke validation of the nodes returned by that function or template.

Finally, if you assign a type to a generated element, through either the `type` attribute or the `validation` attribute, and that element contains other elements or has attributes, then those elements and attributes are validated as well; the types that they're validated against depend on the types that they're declared with in the schema.

For example, in the XHTML schema, the `href` attribute on the `<xhtml:a>` element is declared with the type `xhtml:URI`:

```
<xs:attribute name="href" type="URI"/>
```

Say we generate an `<xhtml:a>` element, with an `href` attribute, and state that its type is `xhtml:a.type`:

```
<a xsl:type="xhtml:a.type" href="{...}">...</a>
```

Assuming the content is valid, the new `<xhtml:a>` element is annotated with the type of `xhtml:a.type`. But what's more, the `href` attribute is annotated with the type of `xhtml:URI`, because that's the type specified for the `href` attribute in the schema.

Now say that the `href` attribute was generated using an `<xsl:attribute>` instruction, with the `type` attribute specifying the type `xs:anyURI`:

```
<a xsl:type="xhtml:a.type">
  <xsl:attribute name="href" type="xs:anyURI" select="..." />
  ...
</a>
```

In this case, the `href` attribute's value is first validated against the type that's being given to the `href` attribute, namely `xs:anyURI`. Assuming that the value of the `href` attribute is a valid URI, the `href` attribute is annotated with the type `xs:anyURI`. However, when the `<xhtml:a>` element is generated, and the `href` attribute added to it, the `href` attribute is validated again, this time against the `xhtml:URI` type, and the `href` attribute is assigned the type `xhtml:URI`. If the `<xhtml:a>` element's parent also had a type specified for it, the `href` attribute might end up with another type entirely.

The upshot of all this is that the more types you specify in your stylesheet, the more validation the XSLT processor has to do. A single element or attribute might be validated against several different types.

Summary The validation of a parent element determines the ultimate type annotation given to its attributes and children.

There are two different strategies that can help you manage type annotations without burdening the XSLT processor with repeated validation or yourself with repeated type declarations:

Annotate only the very top of the node tree—the document element or document node—so that the node tree is validated only once, with the types of the nodes lower down the tree being assigned based on the schema. This way you get types throughout the node tree and you're guaranteed a valid document, but the XSLT processor might not notice that you've created invalid nodes until right at the end of the process, when the node tree is eventually validated.

Annotate only the very bottom of the node tree—the attributes and the elements that have text content and no attributes—so that you don't get repeated validation of the same elements and attributes. Set the default validation for the stylesheet to `preserve`. The elements and attributes at the bottom of the tree end up annotated with types, but the elements higher up the node tree will simply be assigned the general type `xs:anyType`. This strategy is particularly useful for temporary trees because it enables you to access correctly typed element and attribute values (useful for avoiding explicit casting) without having to create an entire schema for the temporary tree.

Ensuring Valid Output

Validation of the result of a stylesheet can be a useful first step in testing that the stylesheet is working OK. Adding validation of the result is pretty simple: all you need to do is validate the result document(s) that the stylesheet generates, by adding a `type` or `validation` attribute to the `<xsl:result-document>` element if you have one, or an `[xsl:]type` or `[xsl:]validation` attribute to the literal result element or `<xsl:element>` instruction that creates the document element of the result.

`TVGuide7.xsl` is supposed to generate valid XHTML. To check that this is happening, in `TVGuide8.xsl` we'll import the schema for XHTML 1.1 and validate the document generated by the stylesheet against it.

You can import the XHTML 1.1 schema using the `<xsl:import-schema>` element, with the `namespace` attribute giving the XHTML namespace and the `schema-location` attribute pointing to the location of the XHTML schema:

```
<xsl:import-schema namespace="http://www.w3.org/1999/xhtml"
                   schema-location="xhtml/xhtml11.xsd" />
```

To validate the document that we generate against the XHTML schema, we simply tell the XSLT processor to strictly validate the `<xhtml:html>` element that's the document element of the result, using the `xsl:validation` attribute:

```
<xsl:template match="document-node(schema-element(tv:TVGuide))">
  <html xsl:validation="strict">
    ...
  </html>
</xsl:template>
```

When you transform `TVGuide4.xml` with `TVGuide8.xsl`, you get the error shown in Figure 13-6. It turns out that the XHTML we've been generating has been invalid according to the XHTML schema all along!

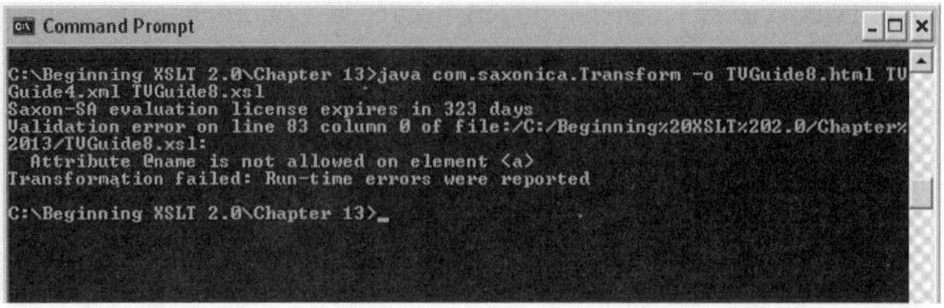

```
Command Prompt
C:\Beginning XSLT 2.0\Chapter 13>java com.saxonica.Transform -o TVGuide8.html TV
Guide4.xml TVGuide8.xsl
Saxon-SA evaluation license expires in 323 days
Validation error on line 83 column 0 of file:/C:/Beginning%20XSLT%202.0/Chapter%
2013/TVGuide8.xsl:
  Attribute @name is not allowed on element <a>
Transformation failed: Run-time errors were reported

C:\Beginning XSLT 2.0\Chapter 13>_
```

Figure 13-6. *Errors when transforming* TVGuide4.xml *with* TVGuide8.xsl *using Saxon-SA*

You can fix the problems that Saxon-SA reports with the XHTML generated by TVGuide8.xsl to create TVGuide9.xsl. The main problems are

- name attributes aren't allowed on <xhtml:a> elements in XHTML 1.1 (they were in XHTML 1.0).
- Identifiers used in id attributes must be valid ID values. We've been taking the name of a channel as an identifier, but the channel Sky One has a space in its name, which isn't allowed in an ID. Removing the space using the translate() function solves this problem, though remember to change the link to the channel as well as the value of the id attribute.
- The alphabetical links to series were being generated directly within the <body> element. They need to be generated within a <p> element to give valid XHTML.

Transforming TVGuide4.xml with TVGuide9.xsl generates TVGuide9.html without any validity errors being reported.

Summary

This chapter has looked at the kinds of changes that you can (or have to!) make to your schema if you use a Schema-Aware XSLT processor.

The first set of changes to your stylesheets arises from using node trees in which nodes have been annotated with their type via validation against a schema. Having type annotations in a node tree often alleviates the requirement for explicit casting because the XSLT processor already knows that an element or attribute is of a particular type. On the other hand, you have to explicitly get the string value of an element, using the string() function, if it's got element-only content, and you have to be careful that the type assigned by the schema is appropriate for the way that you use the node's value in the stylesheet.

Perhaps more usefully, using schemas with your stylesheets can help you simplify the stylesheets by consolidating templates that do similar things to elements or attributes that share a type, or to elements that belong to the same substitution group. Having a template that matches on the type of a node enables you to treat elements and attributes that have the same kind of content in the same way; templates that match on substitution group enable you to treat elements that appear in the same place in the same way. Both mechanisms help you to make stylesheets more maintainable, particularly in the face of changes to the markup language.

Finally, we've looked at how you can use the type and validation attributes on the <xsl:element>, <xsl:attribute>, <xsl:copy>, <xsl:copy-of>, <xsl:document>, and <xsl:result-document> instructions to add type annotations to the elements and attributes that you generate. Doing this is useful as it enables you to check whether the result of your stylesheet is actually valid, and because it lets you take advantage of type annotations on the temporary nodes that you use within your stylesheet.

Whether you're validating and annotating new nodes or matching nodes based on their type or substitution group, the XSLT processor needs to be aware of the schema that should be used. As we've seen in this chapter, you can tell the XSLT processor to use declarations and definitions from a particular schema using the <xsl:import-schema> top-level element.

While useful, using any of these Schema-Aware features restricts the use of your stylesheet to Schema-Aware XSLT processors, and in particular to those XSLT processors that recognize the schema language that your schema is written in. If you want to create a portable XSLT stylesheet, you're better off avoiding these features in your stylesheets.

Review Questions

1. What are the differences between a node tree that has been validated against a schema and a node tree that has not been validated against a schema?

2. The <comments> element is declared as being of element-only content. Correct the following XSLT code:

```
<xsl:template match="comments" mode="summary">
  <xsl:value-of select="concat(substring(., 1, 20), '...')" />
</xsl:template>
```

3. Write an <xsl:import-schema> element that imports a schema for the XHTML namespace (http://www.w3.org/1999/xhtml) that you have in xhtml.xsd.

4. Given the <xsl:import-schema> element that you created in answer to the last question, where will a Schema-Aware XSLT processor look for a schema document? What restrictions are there on the schema document that it finds?

5. What kind of nodes do the following patterns match?

```
attribute(*, xs:ID)
@xml:space
schema-attribute(xml:space)
TVGuide/@start
schema-element(TVGuide)/@start
schema-element(TVGuide)/schema-attribute(start)
element(Year, xs:gYear)
schema-element(_block)
document-node(schema-element(TVGuide))
document-node()[schema-element(TVGuide)]
```

6. What types of nodes do the following instructions create? What information do you need to know about the context in which they're used in order to answer the question fully?

```
<xsl:attribute name="id" type="xs:ID" select="generate-id()" />
```

```
<a xsl:type="a.type" href="{$href}"><xsl:apply-templates /></a>
```

```
<Year>1969</Year>
```

```
<xsl:element name="Year" type="xs:gYear">1969</xsl:element>
```

```
<Year xsl:validation="strict">1969</Year>
```

```
<xsl:copy-of select="/TVGuide" validation="strip" />
```

```
<a xsl:validation="preserve">
  <xsl:attribute name="href" type="xs:anyURI" select="$href" />
  <xsl:apply-templates />
</a>
```

```
<xsl:document validation="lax">
  <html>...</html>
</xsl:document>
```

CHAPTER 14

Backwards Compatibility and Extensions

XSLT 2.0 and XPath 2.0 have added a lot of capabilities to XSLT 1.0 and XPath 1.0. XPath 2.0 introduces new functions, such as `current-dateTime()` and `lower-case()`, as well as new datatypes. XSLT 2.0 introduces new instructions, such as `<xsl:for-each-group>` and `<xsl:analyze-string>`, as well as additional attributes on XSLT 1.0 instructions. If you want to write stylesheets that work with both XSLT 1.0 and XSLT 2.0 processors, you need to be able to detect what version of XSLT a processor supports and provide alternative code to be used if an XSLT 1.0 processor is used with your stylesheet.

Conversely, it's never possible for a programming language to include features that do everything that every user might ever want to do, and there are still some tasks that are difficult or impossible to do with XSLT 2.0. For example, XPath 2.0 isn't particularly strong on mathematics— in particular it lacks any trigonometric functions— and there's no way to dynamically evaluate an XPath expression that you have stored in a string.

Naturally, as XSLT and XPath develop, they will come to include instructions and functions that enable users to do the things that they need to do quickly and easily. However, in the meantime, implementers are bound to respond to pressure from users for additional features, just as Netscape and Microsoft did within their respective web browsers during the development of HTML. In these situations, with different applications supporting different features, it can be hard to recognize when a particular feature is part of the standard language and when it is something defined in a particular implementation. Eventually, as with HTML, this leads to the implementations leading the standardization process rather than the other way around.

To prevent the confusion that could arise from implementers extending XSLT and XPath, both languages have a standard way of dealing with extensions, so that you can easily tell which instructions and functions are part of the XSLT and XPath standards and which are implementer-defined extensions. In this chapter, you'll see how to use the extensions that are offered by your XSLT processor and learn about a few extensions that are offered by particular XSLT processors.

In this chapter, you'll learn

- What to avoid when writing a stylesheet to run in an XSLT 1.0 processor
- What to update when moving from XSLT 1.0 to XSLT 2.0
- How to use different code based on an XSLT processor's capabilities
- How to detect what version of XSLT a processor supports

- How to detect whether a particular function or instruction is available
- How to recover when an extension instruction is not available
- How to issue warnings to people running your stylesheet with the wrong processor
- What different types of extensions implementations can make to XSLT and XPath

Backwards Compatibility

A large number of the functions, and several of the instructions, that we've looked at in previous chapters were introduced in XPath 2.0 and XSLT 2.0 and so aren't supported in XSLT 1.0 processors. What's more, the whole way in which an XSLT processor sees an XML document—the data model that it uses—has changed between XSLT 1.0 and XSLT 2.0, so an XSLT 2.0 processor will regard a stylesheet written in XSLT 1.0 in a slightly different light.

In this section, we'll look at making the transition from using XSLT 1.0 to using XSLT 2.0, first in terms of how an XSLT 2.0 processor will react to an XSLT 1.0 stylesheet, and then in terms of what you have to do to make a stylesheet work with both versions of XSLT processor. Before we do so, we'll take a quick look at how to test the capabilities of an XSLT processor so that you can tell what version of XSLT they support.

Testing XSLT Processors

You can access information about the XSLT processor that's being used from within the stylesheet itself using the `system-property()` function. The `system-property()` function takes a single argument, which is a string in the format of a qualified name, and returns a string providing a value for that property.

The most important property for our purpose here is the `xsl:version` property, which tells you the version of XSLT that's supported by the processor that you're using. It returns the string `'2.0'` in XSLT 2.0 processors and the number `1.0` in XSLT 1.0 processors.

■ **Caution** In XSLT 1.0, the `system-property()` function didn't always return a string; for example, it returned the number `1.0` when you asked for the `xsl:version` property. Make sure that you explicitly cast the result of `system-property('xsl:version')` to either a string or a number before you use it, so that the code works the same way in both XSLT 1.0 and XSLT 2.0 processors.

For example, to test whether the processor being used is an XSLT 1.0 processor, you can use

```
<xsl:choose>
  <xsl:when test="number(system-property('xsl:version')) = 1.0">
    ... code used by XSLT 1.0 processor ...
  </xsl:when>
  <xsl:otherwise>
    ... code used by other XSLT processors ...
  </xsl:otherwise>
</xsl:choose>
```

Caution XSLT processors that support the XSLT 1.1 Working Draft will return `1.1` as the result of `system-property('xsl:version')`. Similarly, XSLT processors that don't quite support XSLT 2.0 completely will probably return a number between `1.0` and `2.0`.

The full list of arguments that you can give to the `system-property()` function appears in Table 14-1. Note that XSLT 1.0 processors only recognize some of these arguments, as indicated by a check mark.

Table 14-1. *System Properties*

Property	Description	XSLT 1.0
`xsl:version`	The version of XSLT supported by the processor	✓
`xsl:vendor`	A string identifying the XSLT processor being used	✓
`xsl:vendor-url`	A URL for the XSLT processor	✓
`xsl:product-name`	The name of the XSLT processor being used	
`xsl:product-version`	The version of the XSLT processor being used	
`xsl:is-schema-aware`	Gives `'yes'` if the XSLT processor is schema-aware, `'no'` otherwise	
`xsl:supports-serialization`	Gives `'yes'` if the XSLT processor can be used to serialize a result tree, `'no'` otherwise	
`xsl:supports-backwards-compatibility`	Gives `'yes'` if the XSLT processor can behave in a backwards-compatible fashion, `'no'` otherwise	

Note We'll look at the effect of support for backwards compatibility in the next section.

XSLT processors can return values for other properties as well; look at your XSLT processor's documentation to see what properties it supports. If you try to get the value of a property that the XSLT processor doesn't understand (for example, if you're using an XSLT 1.0 processor and you try to access the value of the `xsl:is-schema-aware` property), you will get an empty string as a result.

Summary You can test the capabilities of an XSLT processor using the `system-property()` function.

Getting Information About Your XSLT Processor

When it comes to debugging a stylesheet, it's often useful to be able to tell which XSLT processor you're using. This is particularly true if you're operating with a system where the XSLT processor is determined based on the environment, such as when using Java-based XSLT processors.

In this example, we'll create a simple stylesheet, `info.xsl`, which will generate a text file that lists the important information about the XSLT processor you're using, accessing it using the `system-property()` function.

The stylesheet itself is an XSLT 2.0 stylesheet that uses the following text output method:

```
<xsl:stylesheet version="2.0"
                xmlns:xsl="http://www.w3.org/1999/XSL/Transform">
<xsl:output method="text" />
...
</xsl:stylesheet>
```

The stylesheet only needs one template, which may as well match the root document node of whatever XML is used as the input to the stylesheet (the input doesn't matter at all, since we won't be using any information from it). Within this template, we'll test the version of XSLT that's being supported, and use that information to determine which other properties are worth looking at, since XSLT 1.0 processors don't support properties such as `xsl:product-name` and `xsl:product-version`. To get the basic information about the XSLT processor, we'll use the following template:

```
<xsl:template match="/">
  <xsl:choose>
    <xsl:when test="number(system-property('xsl:version')) > 1.0">
      <xsl:text>XSLT version </xsl:text>
      <xsl:value-of select="system-property('xsl:version')" />
      <xsl:text> processor</xsl:text>
      <xsl:text>&#xA;Processor: </xsl:text>
      <xsl:value-of select="system-property('xsl:product-name')" />
      <xsl:text>&#xA;Version:   </xsl:text>
      <xsl:value-of select="system-property('xsl:product-version')" />
      <xsl:text>&#xA;Vendor:    </xsl:text>
      <xsl:value-of select="system-property('xsl:vendor-url')" />
    </xsl:when>
    <xsl:otherwise>
      <xsl:text>XSLT version 1.0 processor</xsl:text>
      <xsl:text>&#xA;Processor: </xsl:text>
      <xsl:value-of select="system-property('xsl:vendor')" />
      <xsl:text>&#xA;Vendor:    </xsl:text>
      <xsl:value-of select="system-property('xsl:vendor-url')" />
    </xsl:otherwise>
  </xsl:choose>
</xsl:template>
```

Running this stylesheet with itself as the input using Saxon 8.4B gives `info.saxon.txt`, shown in Listing 14-1.

Listing 14-1. `info.saxon.txt`

```
XSLT version 2.0 processor
Processor: SAXON
Version:   8.4
Vendor:    http://www.saxonica.com/
```

On the other hand, running the stylesheet with itself as the input using MSXML3 gives `info.msxml.txt`, shown in Listing 14-2.

Listing 14-2. `info.msxml.txt`

```
XSLT version 1.0 processor
Processor: Microsoft
Vendor:    http://www.microsoft.com
```

You can add to this stylesheet to get additional information about the XSLT processor that's being used, either using the `system-property()` function or using the `function-available()` and `element-available()` functions that we'll be looking at later in this chapter.

Upgrading XSLT 1.0 Stylesheets to XSLT 2.0

If you already have XSLT 1.0 stylesheets, you may want to gradually upgrade to XSLT 2.0. There are two stages in this upgrade: starting to run your XSLT 1.0 stylesheets in an XSLT 2.0 processor, and updating your XSLT 1.0 to use XSLT 2.0.

Running XSLT 1.0 Stylesheets in XSLT 2.0 Processors

The first step in upgrading an XSLT 1.0 stylesheet is to start using it with an XSLT 2.0 processor.

XSLT processors work out what version of XSLT is being used in a stylesheet through the `version` attribute. Usually the only `version` attribute that you'll have in your stylesheet is on the `<xsl:stylesheet>` document element, but you can put it on any XSLT element, or on literal result elements (in which case you should name the attribute `xsl:version`). The `version` attribute indicates the version of XSLT being used within whichever element you put it on, so you can have portions of your stylesheet that use XSLT 1.0 and other portions that use XSLT 2.0.

When XSLT 2.0 processors encounter a section of a stylesheet that uses XSLT 1.0, they try to behave in a **backwards-compatible** way, such that the XSLT works in the same way as it would with an XSLT 1.0 processor. However, there are two caveats that you should bear in mind.

First, there's no requirement for all XSLT 2.0 to support backwards-compatible behavior. At the time of writing, most XSLT 2.0 processors are upgrades of existing XSLT 1.0 processors, so probably do support backwards compatibility, but it's unlikely that new processors written for XSLT 2.0 will add code in order to support features that are out of date.

Second, even when trying to behave in a backwards-compatible way, there are a few things that work differently in an XSLT 2.0 processor than in an XSLT 1.0 processor. These differences arise for two reasons:

There are fundamental differences in the data models that the two versions of XSLT use. The XSLT 2.0 processor can't just switch between the two data models, so it does its best to emulate XSLT 1.0 behavior given the XSLT 2.0 data model. Sometimes this emulation isn't absolutely right, but the cases where it isn't are usually rare and pretty minor.

XSLT 2.0 processors tend to be stricter than XSLT 1.0 processors in places where something doesn't actually make sense. For example, an XSLT 1.0 processor will accept an `<xsl:template>` element that doesn't have a `match` attribute but does have a `mode` attribute or a `priority` attribute, despite the fact that the mode and priority of the template are never relevant if there's no pattern that tells the processor what kind of node the template matches; an XSLT 2.0 processor will give you an error if it encounters such a template.

A lot of effort has gone into making sure that there aren't subtle differences between an XSLT 1.0 processor and an XSLT 2.0 processor using backwards-compatible behavior. In most cases, if there's a difference in behavior, it will be that the XSLT 2.0 processor will throw an error, whereas the XSLT 1.0 processor won't.

The only thing you have to scan your stylesheet for is places where you cast a number to a string. The rules for turning numbers into strings have changed for very big (over 1,000,000) and very small (under 0.000001) `xs:double` values (where scientific notation is now used) and for infinity and negative infinity. Rather than relying on the default formatting of numbers as strings, you should use the `format-number()` function to specify the kind of format that you want to use.

Otherwise, do a test run of your XSLT 1.0 stylesheet using an XSLT 2.0 processor on a sample document. If you get errors, then they're likely to arise from places where you're doing strange things anyway, and probably indicate something wrong with your stylesheet that an XSLT 1.0 processor wouldn't pick up on.

Summary As long as your XSLT 2.0 processor supports backwards-compatible behavior, you should be able to use it to run XSLT 1.0 stylesheets with minimal changes.

Switching to XSLT 2.0

If you've got an XSLT 1.0 stylesheet that works in an XSLT 2.0 processor (using backwards-compatible behavior), the next stage is usually to start using XSLT 2.0 in that stylesheet instead, simply by changing the `version` attribute on `<xsl:stylesheet>` to `2.0`. As we'll see, this can involve changing your stylesheet quite significantly.

The first changes that you'll need to make are type-related changes. XPath 1.0 supported implicit casting between values, whereas in XPath 2.0, you usually need to cast values to a particular type explicitly. For example, the arguments to the `concat()` function are supposed to be strings; if you pass a number to the `concat()` function in XPath 1.0, it will be automatically turned into a string, whereas in XPath 2.0 you will get a type error for passing the wrong kind of argument.

These type-related changes are mostly limited to XPath: the only change of this kind that you really need to watch out for in XSLT is if you select more than one node using the `select` attribute of `<xsl:sort>`: in XSLT 1.0, the value of the first of the nodes is used to sort the sequence; in XSLT 2.0, you will get an error.

The easiest way to detect where you need to add explicit casts is to simply try running the stylesheet, and fix the errors as they turn up. The kinds of changes that you'll need to make are as follows:

- Explicitly take the first item of a sequence of nodes, using a `[1]` predicate.
- Turn numbers and Boolean values into strings using the `string()` function.
- Turn strings and numbers into Booleans using the `boolean()` function.
- Turn strings and Boolean values into numbers using the `number()` function.

Next, you should turn your attention to the more subtle changes in the behavior of the stylesheet. These all revolve around the behavior you get when you select a sequence of nodes. In XSLT 1.0, instructions that expect a single node usually take the first of the nodes if you provide more than one, whereas in XSLT 2.0 they usually try to use all the items in the sequence. So:

- If you select a sequence of nodes using `<xsl:value-of>`, you will get their space-separated values in XSLT 2.0, rather than the value of the first of the nodes as in XSLT 1.0.
- If you select a sequence of nodes in an expression within an attribute value template, you will again get their space-separated values in XSLT 2.0, rather than the value of the first of the nodes in XSLT 1.0.
- If you select a sequence of nodes using the `value` attribute of `<xsl:number>`, you will get a multilevel number in XSLT 2.0 (such as 2.5.1), whereas in XSLT 1.0 you will get the number for the first of the nodes.

In each of these cases, adding a `[1]` predicate at the end of the expression that you're using to select the nodes will give you the XSLT 1.0 behavior. For example, if you have the following `<xsl:value-of>` element:

```
<xsl:value-of select="Writer | Producer | Director" />
```

then you should turn this into

```
<xsl:value-of select="(Writer | Producer | Director)[1]" />
```

The other kind of subtle change you need to look out for arises from how empty sequences are treated in XPath 2.0. In XPath 1.0, providing an empty sequence when a number is expected is the same as providing `NaN`. In XPath 2.0, on the other hand, providing an empty sequence to a numeric function or operator usually results in an empty sequence. For example, if there's no `rating` attribute, then

```
floor(@rating)
```

returns `NaN` in XPath 1.0, but returns an empty sequence in XPath 2.0. If you convert the result to a string and test if it's the string `'NaN'`, as in the following:

```
string(floor(@string)) = 'NaN'
```

then you will get `true` in XPath 1.0, but `false` in XPath 2.0.

The solution to this incompatibility is to convert the sequence to a number explicitly, using the `number()` function. In this case, use

```
floor(number(@rating)) = 'NaN'
```

Summary Changing the version of a stylesheet from 1.0 to 2.0 will probably require you to add explicit casts. You should also check places where sequences of nodes are passed around to make sure they are interpreted in the expected way, particularly if they might be empty.

Running XSLT 2.0 Stylesheets in XSLT 1.0 Processors

We've seen what changes are needed in order to run an XSLT 1.0 stylesheet with an XSLT 2.0 processor. Now we'll look at the reverse situation, where you (or someone to whom you pass your stylesheet) run your XSLT 2.0 stylesheet with an XSLT 1.0 processor.

Just as XSLT processors can run in backwards-compatible mode in order to accommodate stylesheets from an earlier version of XSLT, they can also run in forwards-compatible mode to accommodate stylesheets from a later version of XSLT. In forwards-compatible mode, XSLT processors will ignore syntactic problems with the stylesheet, such as the following:

- Top-level XSLT elements that it doesn't recognize
- Attributes that it doesn't recognize on XSLT elements
- Attributes on XSLT elements with values that it doesn't recognize (if the attribute can be ignored)

An XSLT processor in forwards-compatible mode will also ignore any function calls or XPath syntax that it doesn't recognize, as long as it isn't expected to try to execute the expression. This means you can use conditional logic to determine what to output. For example, the following code uses the `lower-case()` function in an XSLT 2.0 (or above) processor, and the less powerful `translate()` function in an XSLT 1.0 processor:

```
<xsl:choose>
  <xsl:when test="number(system-property('xsl:version')) >= 2.0">
    <xsl:value-of select="lower-case(.)" />
  </xsl:when>
  <xsl:otherwise>
    <xsl:value-of select="translate(., 'ABCDEFGHIJKLMNOPQRSTUVWXYZ',
                                       'abcdefghijklmnopqrstuvwxyz')" />
  </xsl:otherwise>
</xsl:choose>
```

The fact that an XSLT 1.0 processor doesn't recognize the `lower-case()` function doesn't stop it from attempting to run the XSLT 2.0 stylesheet. If it had to execute the `lower-case()` function, it would give an error, because it wouldn't know what to do, but with the preceding code, it has an alternative set of code that can be used instead.

Similarly, an XSLT processor will ignore any XSLT instructions that it doesn't recognize, as long as it isn't expected to try to carry out the instruction. So you can use conditional logic to provide nongrouped output rather than grouped output in earlier XSLT processors:

```
<xsl:choose>
  <xsl:when test="number(system-property('xsl:version')) >= 2.0">
    <xsl:for-each-group select="/TVGuide/Channel/Program"
                        group-by="Series">
      ...
```

```
    </xsl:for-each-group>
  </xsl:when>
  <xsl:otherwise>
    <xsl:apply-templates select="/TVGuide/Channel/Program" />
  </xsl:otherwise>
</xsl:choose>
```

Again, the fact that an XSLT 1.0 processor doesn't recognize the `<xsl:for-each-group>` instruction doesn't stop it from trying to run the stylesheet.

Summary In forwards-compatible mode, XSLT processors ignore what they don't understand, as long as they don't have to try to execute it.

Providing Fallbacks

The preceding examples have shown how to stop an XSLT 1.0 processor from complaining about an unsupported instruction using `<xsl:choose>`. An alternative method of dealing with this situation is to provide a **fallback** set of code using the `<xsl:fallback>` element. The `<xsl:fallback>` element can go inside any instruction; if an XSLT processor comes across an instruction but doesn't know what to do with it, it will process the content of the `<xsl:fallback>` elements within the instruction rather than giving an error.

For example, rather than testing whether an XSLT processor supports the `<xsl:for-each-group>` element by testing the version of XSLT the processor supports, and providing alternative code if so, you can just slot the alternative code into the `<xsl:fallback>` element when you use the `<xsl:for-each-group>` element. For example, rather than using

```
<xsl:choose>
  <xsl:when test="number(system-property('xsl:version')) >= 2.0">
    <xsl:for-each-group select="/TVGuide/Channel/Program"
                        group-by="Series">
      ...
    </xsl:for-each-group>
  </xsl:when>
  <xsl:otherwise>
    <xsl:apply-templates select="/TVGuide/Channel/Program" />
  </xsl:otherwise>
</xsl:choose>
```

you can use

```
<xsl:for-each-group select="/TVGuide/Channel/Program"
                    group-by="Series">
  ...
  <xsl:fallback>
    <xsl:apply-templates select="/TVGuide/Channel/Program" />
  </xsl:fallback>
</xsl:for-each-group>
```

Whether you use `<xsl:choose>` or `<xsl:fallback>` is up to you. Generally, using `<xsl:choose>` is more useful than `<xsl:fallback>` if you want to test for the availability of a number of instructions—you can use lots of `<xsl:when>`s rather than having very deep nesting of elements inside `<xsl:fallback>`. Using `<xsl:choose>` is also handy if you want to test whether an instruction is available early on in the stylesheet rather than waiting until you need to use the instruction.

■ **Summary** An XSLT processor will process the contents of an `<xsl:fallback>` element within an instruction if the processor doesn't understand the instruction.

Sending Messages to the User

Of course you might *want* the processing to stop if the processor doesn't support XSLT 2.0—the fact that it doesn't might mean that the stylesheet simply can't be used with that particular processor. In that case, you can use `<xsl:message>` to stop the process.

The `<xsl:message>` element sends a message to the user. The way the message is presented depends on the processor you use and the way in which you call the processor, but usually if you use a command-line processor, you'll see the message appear on the command line, and if you use a processor embedded in a browser, you won't see the message at all.

The message that's sent to the user usually goes in the content of the `<xsl:message>` element. You can put anything you like in there, including literal result elements and XSLT instructions, so you're not just limited to textual messages.

If you want processing to stop under a particular condition, such as when the stylesheet is called with an XSLT 1.0 processor, then you should set the `terminate` attribute to yes. The content of the `<xsl:message>` can give a more user-friendly error than the one the processor is likely to give on its own.

For example, the following template matches the root node and generates an error if the processor used with the stylesheet isn't an XSLT 2.0 processor or above:

```
<xsl:template match="/">
  <xsl:if test="number(system-property('xsl:version')) &lt; 2.0">
    <xsl:message terminate="yes">
      <xsl:text>This stylesheet requires an XSLT 2.0 processor.</xsl:text>
    </xsl:message>
  </xsl:if>
  <html>
    ...
  </html>
</xsl:template>
```

The `<xsl:message>` element can also be useful for debugging, or simply sending messages to the user to report on progress, especially if the stylesheet takes a long time to run. In these cases, you don't want the transformation to stop, so you should omit the `terminate` attribute or give it the value `"no"`.

■ **Note** As we'll see in the next section, the `error()` and `trace()` functions are alternative methods of halting the transformation or getting debugging messages, but these only work with XSLT 2.0 processors.

If you know that the processor is an XSLT 2.0 processor, you can use the `select` attribute rather than the content of the `<xsl:message>` element to provide the content of the message. However, this attribute wasn't allowed in XSLT 1.0, so there's no point using it if the message is intended for XSLT 1.0 processors.

Summary The `<xsl:message>` element sends a message to the user. If the `terminate` attribute is set to `yes`, the transformation halts.

Same-Version Compatibility

The previous section focused on providing alternative code for XSLT 1.0 and XSLT 2.0 processors. The techniques outlined there can also be used to provide alternative code for XSLT 2.0 processors that need to run stylesheets in a future version of XSLT, because if a stylesheet is labeled as using version 3.0 (say), an XSLT 2.0 processor will operate in forwards-compatible mode and ignore any unknown functions or instructions as long as it doesn't have to execute them.

But if you run an XSLT 2.0 stylesheet with an XSLT 2.0 processor that is incomplete, or run a Schema-Aware XSLT 2.0 stylesheet with a Basic XSLT 2.0 processor, the processor won't operate in forwards-compatible mode. In this case, the processor will report an error if you use a function or instruction that it doesn't support (even if that function or instruction is in the spec), or use syntax that relies on schema-awareness (such as the `schema-element()` node test).

In this section, we'll look at how you can test the capabilities of your XSLT 2.0 processor and provide alternative code when it doesn't support particular parts of XSLT 2.0.

Testing Function Availability

As we've seen, XSLT 1.0 and XSLT 2.0 processors support different sets of functions, and XSLT processors that haven't yet reached full XSLT 2.0 compliance might only support a subset of the functions that they're supposed to. What's more, implementations can add support for their own **extension functions**, going beyond those specified in the standard languages.

So how do you work out whether the processor that's being used to run the stylesheet supports the function that you want to use? Well, you can use the `function-available()` function to find out. The `function-available()` function takes the name of a function as an argument and returns `true` if the processor supports the function and `false` if the processor doesn't support the function. So, for example, you could work out whether the processor that's being used with the stylesheet supports the `avg()` function with

```
function-available('avg')
```

Tip Using the `function-available()` function is more accurate than determining what functions might be supported based on the version of XSLT the processor claims to support using the `system-property()` function, because processors that don't have full conformance with XSLT 2.0 might still support the function. It's also less work for you than trying to work out what functions are supported based on the name and version of the processor.

Functions sometimes have optional arguments, and sometimes a processor might only support the function with (or without) those optional arguments. For example, the third argument to the key() function was only introduced in XSLT 2.0, so XSLT 1.0 processors won't understand it. The function-available() function can take a second argument, specifying the number of arguments for the function. For example, you could work out whether a processor supported the three-argument version of the key() function with

```
function-available('key', 3)
```

Caution The two-argument version of function-available() was only introduced in XSLT 2.0, so you shouldn't use it in code that might be executed by an XSLT 1.0 processor.

Summary You can use the function-available() function to test whether the XSLT processor being used supports a particular function.

Testing Instruction Availability

Just as the function-available() function tests whether a particular function is available, the element-available() function tests whether a particular instruction is available. Again, this can be used to accurately work out what a processor supports, and to test for support for **extension instructions**.

Note Despite its name, the element-available() function only tests the availability of *instructions* (elements that appear within a template). For example, element-available('xsl:template') will return false because the <xsl:template> element is not an instruction.

The element-available() function takes a single argument—the name of the extension element that you are interested in. If the processor supports the extension element, then it returns true; if it doesn't support the extension element, then it returns false. For example, to test whether the processor supports the <xsl:for-each-group> instruction from XSLT 2.0, you could use

```
element-available('xsl:for-each-group')
```

Note The element-available() function tests what instructions an XSLT processor supports; it doesn't test whether an element is present within an XML document or stylesheet.

Summary The element-available() function returns true if the element whose name is passed as the argument to the function is supported by the XSLT processor.

Excluding Portions of a Stylesheet

In XSLT 2.0, a new attribute called `use-when` has been introduced that provides an alternative mechanism for including or excluding code.

The `use-when` attribute can be present on any XSLT element, and there's an `xsl:use-when` attribute that you can use on literal result elements to the same effect. If the XPath expression that it contains evaluates to `false`, then the element on which the `use-when` attribute is found and all its contents are completely ignored by the XSLT processor.

The evaluation of `use-when` attributes happens very early on in the process, when the stylesheet is first parsed and interpreted by the XSLT processor. Because this happens so early, `use-when` is a very efficient mechanism for getting the processor to ignore code that it should never use. However, it does mean that the XPath expressions you can use within the `use-when` attribute are restricted. These expressions can't refer to information in source documents used by the stylesheet; they can't refer to global variables or parameters; they can't use stylesheet functions, keys, decimal formats, and so on; they can't refer to element or attribute declarations or type definitions that have been imported into the stylesheet with `<xsl:import-schema>`.

What `use-when` *can* do is test whether the processor supports particular functions or elements, or optional features. To reuse the example that we've been looking at, rather than

```
<xsl:choose>
  <xsl:when test="number(system-property('xsl:version')) >= 2.0">
    <xsl:for-each-group select="/TVGuide/Channel/Program"
                        group-by="Series">
      ...
    </xsl:for-each-group>
  </xsl:when>
  <xsl:otherwise>
    <xsl:apply-templates select="/TVGuide/Channel/Program" />
  </xsl:otherwise>
</xsl:choose>
```

which won't work if the processor is an XSLT 2.0 processor that doesn't yet support `<xsl:for-each-group>`, you could use

```
<xsl:for-each-group select="/TVGuide/Channel/Program"
                    group-by="Series"
                    use-when="element-available('xsl:for-each-group')">
  ...
</xsl:for-each-group>
<xsl:apply-templates select="/TVGuide/Channel/Program"
                     use-when="not(element-available('xsl:for-each-group'))" />
```

There's actually not much point in using `use-when` to test whether XSLT 2.0 instructions are supported, since XSLT 1.0 processors won't understand `use-when` attributes. If you run the preceding code on an XSLT 1.0 processor, you'll get an error because the `<xsl:for-each-group>` instruction isn't supported and no fallback has been provided. It's better in this situation to use `<xsl:fallback>`, as in

```
<xsl:for-each-group select="/TVGuide/Channel/Program"
                    group-by="Series">
  ...
```

```
  <xsl:fallback>
    <xsl:apply-templates select="/TVGuide/Channel/Program" />
  </xsl:fallback>
</xsl:for-each-group>
```

since this will work with every version of processor.

A common use for use-when is to test whether an XSLT processor is Schema-Aware or not, and import different stylesheets based on the outcome:

```
<xsl:import href="schema-aware.xsl"
            use-when="system-property('xsl:is-schema-aware') = 'yes'" />
<xsl:import href="basic.xsl"
            use-when="system-property('xsl:is-schema-aware') = 'no'" />
```

With the preceding code, a Schema-Aware XSLT processor will import schema-aware.xsl, while a Basic XSLT processor will import basic.xsl. (XSLT 1.0 processors will import both stylesheets.)

Another way of using use-when is to temporarily exclude some code from your stylesheet while debugging. Setting use-when to false() effectively "comments out" the code. (This is more useful than using XML comments since XML comments can't nest inside each other, which means you can't easily comment out documented code.)

Dealing with Incomplete Implementations

The version of Saxon I'm using, 8.4, supports nearly all the XPath functions, but it doesn't support the normalize-unicode() function. In TVGuide2.xsl, we'll add a template that matches text nodes and outputs their Unicode-normalized values:

```
<xsl:template match="text()">
  <xsl:value-of select="normalize-unicode(.)" />
</xsl:template>
```

When I try transforming TVGuide.xml with TVGuide2.xsl using Saxon 8.4, I get the error message shown in Figure 14-1.

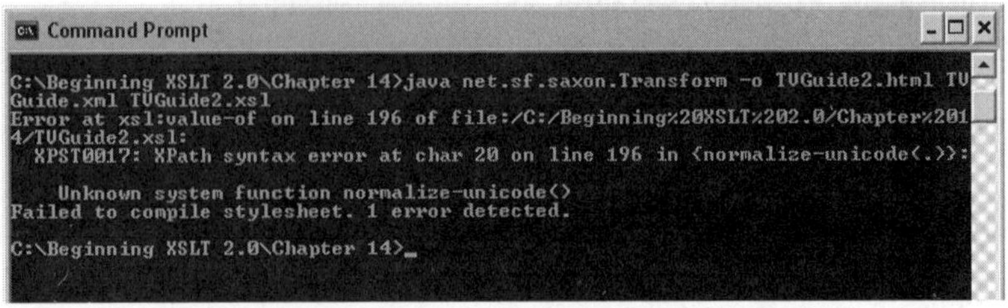

```
Command Prompt
C:\Beginning XSLT 2.0\Chapter 14>java net.sf.saxon.Transform -o TVGuide2.html TV
Guide.xml TVGuide2.xsl
Error at xsl:value-of on line 196 of file:/C:/Beginning%20XSLT%202.0/Chapter%201
4/TVGuide2.xsl:
  XPST0017: XPath syntax error at char 20 on line 196 in {normalize-unicode(.)}:

    Unknown system function normalize-unicode()
Failed to compile stylesheet. 1 error detected.

C:\Beginning XSLT 2.0\Chapter 14>_
```

Figure 14-1. *Error message due to unsupported function in Saxon 8.4*

Although we'd prefer to, Unicode-normalizing the text that appears in the result isn't critical to the stylesheet, so it's worth supplying an alternative set of code that can be used when the `normalize-unicode()` function isn't available. In `TVGuide3.xsl`, we can use the `function-available()` function to test whether the `normalize-unicode()` function is available, and the `use-when` attribute to choose which `<xsl:value-of>` instruction to use in each case, as follows:

```
<xsl:template match="text()">
  <xsl:value-of select="normalize-unicode(.)"
                use-when="function-available('normalize-unicode')" />
  <xsl:value-of select="."
                use-when="not(function-available('normalize-unicode'))" />
</xsl:template>
```

Using Saxon 8.4 to transform `TVGuide.xml` with `TVGuide3.xsl` produces `TVGuide3.html`, as shown in Figure 14-2, rather than an error.

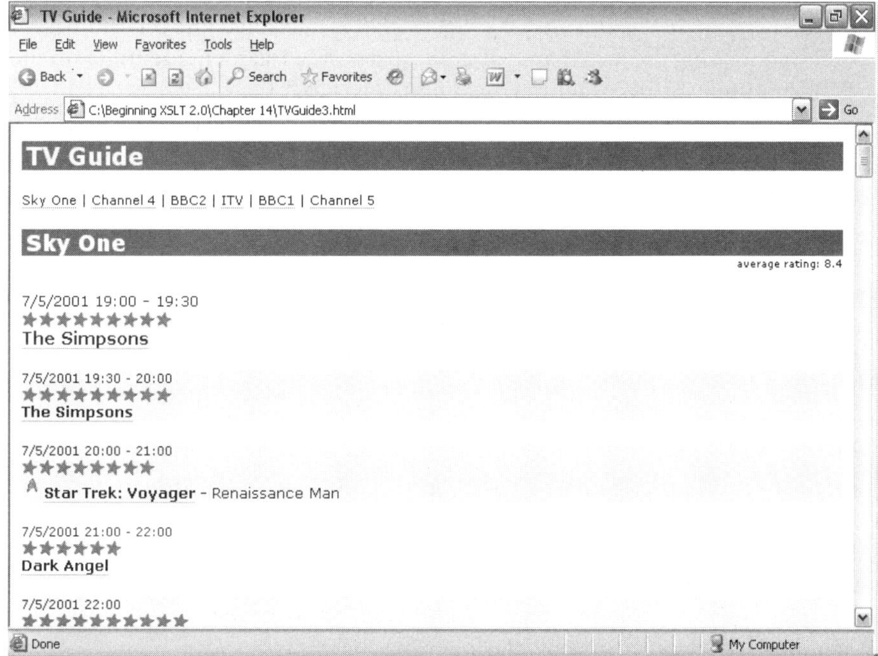

Figure 14-2. *Viewing* `TVGuide3.html` *in Internet Explorer*

It's hard to tell that the text isn't Unicode-normalized, because with the simple English text we're using it doesn't make any difference, but at least the stylesheet runs without an error now.

Sending Messages to the User in XSLT 2.0

As you learned in the last section, the `<xsl:message>` instruction can be used in either XSLT 1.0 or XSLT 2.0 processors to send messages to the user about error conditions or simply the progress of the transformation. XPath 2.0 has two new functions, `error()` and `trace()`, that provide similar capabilities.

The `error()` function halts the transformation and provides the processor with a URI that identifies the error. In its most basic form, with no arguments, a generic error URI is reported, namely:

```
http://www.w3.org/2004/07/xqt-errors#FOER0000
```

■Caution Like the other XPath URLs, this one will change as successive Working Drafts come out.

The optional first argument can provide an `xs:QName` that is translated into the URI passed to the processor by appending the local name of the `xs:QName` as a fragment identifier on the namespace URI. For example, if you call the `error()` function with

```
error(QName('http://www.example.com/tv/error', 'flag-file-missing'))
```

then the URI passed to the processor will be

```
http://www.example.com/tv/error#flag-file-missing
```

■Note Saxon 8.4 ignores the URI part of the error, so you just get the local name of the `xs:QName` reported.

There are two other optional arguments to the `error()` function: a string description of the error and a sequence that provides additional information. There are no constraints about how the processor deals with this information: Saxon 8.4 reports the description and ignores the third argument.

For example, you could test whether `flags.xml` was available using the `doc-available()` function and, if it wasn't, issue an error using the following code:

```
<xsl:apply-templates
  select="if (doc-available('flags.xml'))
          then document('flags.xml')/flags/flag[@name = current()/@flag]
          else error(QName('http://www.example.com/tv/error', 'flag-file-missing'),
                     'Unable to locate flags.xml')" />
```

■Summary The `error()` function halts processing with an error identified by an `xs:QName` with an optional description and sequence providing extra information.

The `trace()` function takes two arguments: a sequence and a message. When the processor evaluates the `trace()` function, it reports the message and the value of the sequence to the user and returns the sequence.

The `trace()` function is most useful when you want to debug a particular piece of an XPath expression to see why it isn't giving you the value that you expect. For example, in `TVGuide4.xsl`, I use the following variable declaration for `$Channels`:

```
<xsl:variable name="Channels" as="element(Channel)+">
  <xsl:perform-sort select="trace(/TVGuide/Channel, 'sorting channels')">
    <xsl:sort select="trace(avg(Program/@rating),
                            '  average rating')"
              order="descending" />
    <xsl:sort select="trace(xs:integer(Program[1]/@rating),
                            '  first program rating')"
              order="descending" />
  </xsl:perform-sort>
</xsl:variable>
```

Transforming `TVGuide.xml` with `TVGuide4.xsl` gives the messages shown in Figure 14-3. For each channel, I'm told the element that's being sorted (via a path to that element) and the values of the sort keys that are used to sort them. Perhaps most valuably, I'm also told the *type* of each of the values and of the elements that are being sorted, something which I can't get at with normal XSLT code.

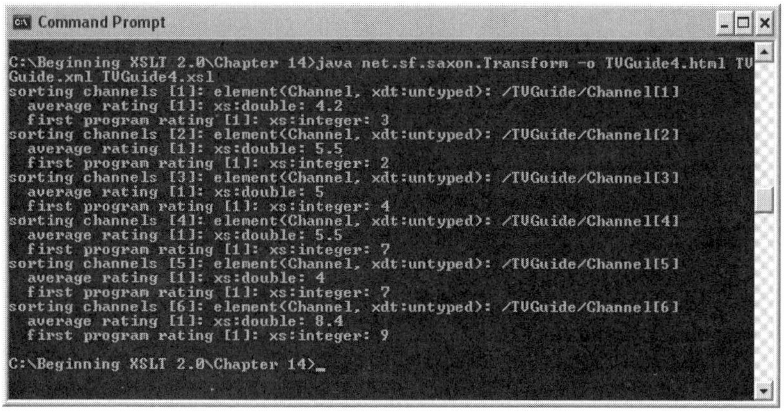

```
Command Prompt
C:\Beginning XSLT 2.0\Chapter 14>java net.sf.saxon.Transform -o TVGuide4.html TV
Guide.xml TVGuide4.xsl
sorting channels [1]: element(Channel, xdt:untyped): /TVGuide/Channel[1]
  average rating [1]: xs:double: 4.2
  first program rating [1]: xs:integer: 3
sorting channels [2]: element(Channel, xdt:untyped): /TVGuide/Channel[2]
  average rating [1]: xs:double: 5.5
  first program rating [1]: xs:integer: 2
sorting channels [3]: element(Channel, xdt:untyped): /TVGuide/Channel[3]
  average rating [1]: xs:double: 5
  first program rating [1]: xs:integer: 4
sorting channels [4]: element(Channel, xdt:untyped): /TVGuide/Channel[4]
  average rating [1]: xs:double: 5.5
  first program rating [1]: xs:integer: 7
sorting channels [5]: element(Channel, xdt:untyped): /TVGuide/Channel[5]
  average rating [1]: xs:double: 4
  first program rating [1]: xs:integer: 7
sorting channels [6]: element(Channel, xdt:untyped): /TVGuide/Channel[6]
  average rating [1]: xs:double: 8.4
  first program rating [1]: xs:integer: 9

C:\Beginning XSLT 2.0\Chapter 14>_
```

Figure 14-3. *Messages from* `trace()` *in Saxon*

It's harder to use the `trace()` function to report values that you don't use, or don't use in the form you want reported. For example, you couldn't use the `trace()` function in the `$Channels` variable declaration to provide the *names* of the channels (which would make the message easier to interpret) rather than a path to the channel. So while `trace()` is useful for quick debugging, `<xsl:message>` is more useful for user-oriented messages.

Summary The `trace()` function reports the value given in the first argument with the message given in the second argument.

Extensions to XSLT and XPath

The XSLT Recommendation defines precisely what kinds of extensions implementers are allowed to make to XSLT and XPath. In this section, we'll look at the kinds of things that extensions are allowed to do, before going on to look at how to use them. The five kinds of extensions that we'll look at are

- Extension functions
- Extension instructions
- Extension attribute values
- Extension attributes
- Data elements

Extension Functions

The first, and most common, way in which implementers can extend the utility of XSLT and XPath is by adding to the functionality of expressions and patterns. The only way in which implementers are allowed to extend XPath is by adding **extension functions**—they can't, for example, add a new operator or change the way in which their processor "sees" XML documents.

Note More drastic changes are reserved for changes to the XPath standard itself. For example, the set of expressions and the data model used by XPath changed substantially between XPath 1.0 and XPath 2.0.

Most extension functions enable you to do things with expressions that you can't normally do in XPath. Even with the extra capabilities introduced in XPath 2.0, there are still lots of things that XPath can't do, many of which can be done using XSLT templates or stylesheet functions instead. The majority of extension functions enable you to do things that you could do with stylesheet functions, but that would be tedious to implement, such as the following:

- Evaluating strings as XPath expressions
- Calculating the square root of a number
- Generating a sequence of random numbers

Other functions are simply impossible to do from within XSLT at all, because of the limited access that a stylesheet has to its environment or because of the data model that XPath and XSLT use, for example:

- Getting the name of the type of a node or atomic value as an `xs:QName`
- Accessing locale information, such as the language in use on the system on which the transformation takes place

The third class of extension functions is simply shortcuts for things that are already fairly easy to do within XPath. For example, an `eg:node-kind()` extension function that returns the kind of a node as a string is just a shortcut for testing whether the node is an instance of each possible kind of node and returning the name of the relevant node kind.

■ Note This third kind of extension function can be implemented as stylesheet functions, but an XSLT processor might offer them as extension functions since functions that are built into the processor are likely to be more efficient.

Different XSLT processors support different extension functions; indeed, different versions of the *same processor* often support different functions. In general, therefore, you should only use extension functions when you really need to, as the more you use, the harder it becomes to swap to another XSLT processor should you need to in the future. If you do use an extension function and can't provide an alternative implementation, you should test for support for the function using `function-available()` and use the `use-when` attribute to provide alternative code (which might be a message that halts the stylesheet) if the function isn't supported.

■ Note The EXSLT initiative (`http://www.exslt.org/`) tries to standardize extension functions that are common across processors, to increase portability. However, not all processors implement EXSLT functions, so portability is always an issue, whoever defines the extension function.

Identifying Extension Functions

Extension functions must have qualified names, which means they must have a prefix (just as stylesheet functions must). The namespace URI associated with the prefix usually indicates which implementer came up with the function and which XSLT processors support the function. For example, the extension functions supported by MSXML all have the namespace `urn:schemas-microsoft-com:xslt`, whereas most of the extension functions supported by Xalan have the namespace `http://xml.apache.org/xalan`.

To use an extension function, you must first declare the namespace for the extension function within the stylesheet, usually in the `<xsl:stylesheet>` document element. This means that you can use the extension function with a particular prefix throughout the stylesheet. For example, you could use the extension functions in the EXSLT Math module if you declared the Math module namespace within your stylesheet as follows:

```
<xsl:stylesheet version="2.0"
                xmlns:xsl="http://www.w3.org/1999/XSL/Transform"
                xmlns:math="http://exslt.org/math"
                exclude-result-prefixes="math">
  ...
</xsl:stylesheet>
```

Tip I've added an `exclude-result-prefixes` attribute to the `<xsl:stylesheet>` element so that the EXSLT Math namespace doesn't get added to the result document that we're generating. The `exclude-result-prefixes` attribute stops the namespaces with the listed prefixes from being declared in the result document unless it's necessary. As you'll see later in this chapter, you can also use `extension-element-prefixes` to achieve the same effect.

Once you've declared the prefix `math` as being associated with the namespace `http://exslt.org/math` in your stylesheet, you can use it when calling functions. An XSLT processor that recognizes the EXSLT Math namespace and the particular function that you're using will evaluate the function accordingly. For example, you could use the `math:sqrt()` function to calculate the square root of a number. Extension functions are called in just the same way as other functions.

Summary Extension functions have a prefix that indicates the namespace to which they belong. You must declare the namespace to use the extension functions in that namespace.

Providing Alternative Implementations

If an extension function does something that can be done using XSLT, you may want to provide an alternative implementation as a stylesheet function, so that XSLT processors that don't support the particular extension function you're using can still execute the stylesheet.

As we saw in Chapter 11, you can create a stylesheet function using the `<xsl:function>` top-level element. If the name that you specify for a stylesheet function is the same as the name of an extension function that is supported by the XSLT processor that you're using, then the XSLT processor looks at the `override` attribute to work out what to do.

If the `override` attribute is missing, or if it has the value yes, then the XSLT implementation of the function, as specified by the `<xsl:function>` element, will be used instead of the built-in extension function. This is useful if you want to guarantee that all XSLT processors will use exactly the same code to perform a function.

If the `override` attribute has the value `no`, on the other hand, then the implementation that you've provided using the stylesheet function will only be used if the XSLT processor doesn't provide an implementation of the function itself. For example, we could define the `math:sqrt()` function using the code from Chapter 11, and specify `override="no"` as follows:

```
<xsl:function name="math:sqrt" as="xs:double" override="no">
  <xsl:param name="number" as="xs:double" />
  <xsl:sequence select="private-math:squareRoot($number, 4, 1)" />
</xsl:function>
```

```
<xsl:function name="private-math:squareRoot" as="xs:double">
  <xsl:param name="number" as="xs:double" />
  <xsl:param name="precision" as="xs:integer" />
  <xsl:param name="estimate" as="xs:double" />
  <xsl:variable name="nextEstimate" as="xs:double"
    select="$estimate + (($number - $estimate * $estimate) div
                        (2 * $estimate))" />
   <xsl:variable name="roundedEstimate" as="xs:double"
     select="round-half-to-even($nextEstimate, $precision) " />
  <xsl:sequence
     select="if ($estimate = $roundedEstimate) then $estimate
             else private-math:squareRoot($number, $precision, $roundedEstimate)" />
</xsl:function>
```

Doing this means that XSLT processors that have built-in support for the `math:sqrt()` function will use that built-in support, while those that don't will use the preceding stylesheet implementation. Any built-in support for the `math:sqrt()` function is likely to be more efficient and will undoubtedly be more precise (in the preceding implementation, the result is only reported to four decimal places), so this definition takes advantage of the capabilities of the XSLT processors that support the `math:sqrt()` function while retaining portability to different XSLT processors.

Summary You can use the `override` attribute of the `<xsl:function>` element to tell an XSLT processor to use the built-in implementation of an extension function rather than a stylesheet function of the same name.

Extensions to Attribute Values

As well as XPath, implementers also have a fair degree of control over the functionality of XSLT. The first set of extensions that an implementer can make is to define the set of acceptable values of certain attributes in XSLT instructions. There are two examples of this which we will look at briefly:

- The `method` attribute of `<xsl:output>`
- The `collation` attribute of `<xsl:sort>`, `<xsl:for-each-group>`, and `<xsl:key>`

Note The `data-type` attribute of `<xsl:sort>` also allows an implementer to change how a sort is done, but the attribute is deprecated in favor of using the datatype of the selected value.

Additional Output Methods

As you'll remember from Chapter 8, the `method` attribute of `<xsl:output>` determines the serialization method that's used when the result tree is output by the stylesheet to file or to another application. XSLT defines four specific values that are allowed for the `method` attribute of `<xsl:output>`—`html`, `xhtml`, `xml`, and `text`—but allows a processor to accept other values, as long as they are qualified names with a prefix.

The output method that you use controls things like the following:

- The syntax for elements, especially empty elements
- Which characters are represented as entity references, if any, and how
- Whether extra information is added to indicate the encoding of the document
- How Boolean attributes are output
- What defaults are used for other attributes on `<xsl:output>`

The HTML output method in particular does a lot behind the scenes because the processor is aware of some of the semantics of HTML elements and attributes, for example:

- The `href` attribute on the `<a>` element is a URI, and non-ASCII characters within it should therefore be escaped.
- The `<br>` element cannot take any content and should be output without an end tag.
- The character `é` can be represented with the character entity reference `é`.

Often other XML-based markup languages, such as MathML or SVG, assign special semantics to particular element or attribute values. Some elements should contain CDATA sections, for example, or some attributes should have their values normalized when they are output. Many markup languages have their own sets of character entity references that should be used in the place of numeric character references to aid the readability of the resulting document. However, an XSLT processor is unable to take advantage of that knowledge because it has no way of knowing which markup language you are generating with the XSLT stylesheet.

The way in which the result tree is written to a file is known as its **serialization**. Different processors support different types of serialization by extending the set of values that they accept in the `method` attribute of `<xsl:output>`. The additional acceptable values must be qualified names; usually the namespace of these qualified names will be one based on the implementation itself.

For example, Saxon would define its own set of output methods using the Saxon namespace (`http://saxon.sf.net/`). In fact, in Saxon you can use whatever namespace you like as long as the local part of the name is the name of a Java class that implements either the `org.xml.sax.ContentHandler` or the `net.sf.saxon.event.Receiver` interface. Whatever class you name is passed the result tree generated by Saxon under the assumption that it will serialize it. This can be very useful if you need to write certain characters using entity references, or if you want to generate files in a non-XML format, such as CSS or comma-delimited files, but take advantage of the ease with which an XSLT stylesheet generates elements and attributes compared to the difficulties with managing text output.

The result tree could even be written using a completely different syntax from XML, including being written as a binary file. For example, a `fo:pdf` output method might generate PDF documents from a result tree written in XSL-FO. Similarly, a `svg:jpeg` output method might generate a JPEG image from an SVG result tree.

Different XSLT processors support different output methods; as with all extensions, you should check the documentation of the processor that you're using to see which ones it supports.

Alternatively, you can take control of the serialization yourself by managing the transformation through code or within a pipelining framework such as that supported by Cocoon (which we'll look at in the next chapter).

Note There's no way to work out what output methods a processor supports from within an XSLT stylesheet.

Summary There are lots of ways to serialize a result tree. The `method` attribute of `<xsl:output>` can be given a qualified name to allow you to use an extension output method supported by the XSLT processor you're using.

Additional Collations

As we saw in Chapter 5, collations are used when comparing two strings to work out which one is first. Usually collations determine some kind of alphabetical ordering, perhaps based on a particular language or tweaked such that uppercase or lowercase characters come first.

In XPath and XSLT, collations are referred to using a URI. The only collation that is specified in XPath or XSLT is the Unicode codepoint collation, which simply compares the Unicode codepoints of the characters being compared to work out which one comes first. The URL for this collation is currently `http://www.w3.org/2005/04/xpath-functions/collation/codepoint`. However, XSLT implementations are free to recognize other URLs for collations.

Saxon, for example, recognizes collation URIs of the form

```
http://saxon.sf.net/collation?keyword=value;keyword=value;...
```

where the keywords and possible values are shown in Table 14-2.

Table 14-2. *Keywords Used in Collation URIs in Saxon*

Keyword	Description
`class`	A Java class that implements the interface `java.util.Comparator`; this should implement code that compares two strings. The `class` keyword cannot be used with any other keyword.
`lang`	The language that should be used when comparing the strings.
`strength`	Identifies the level of difference between two characters for them to be considered different. The possible values are `primary`, which identifies that `A` and `B` are different characters, but doesn't recognize case or accent differences; `secondary`, which recognizes differences in case but not accents; and `tertiary`, which recognizes differences in case and in accents.
`decomposition`	Determines whether composed characters are decomposed prior to comparison. The value `none` does no decomposition; `standard` decomposes canonical variants; `full` decomposes canonical and compatibility variants.

Note The `decomposition` keyword is only relevant if the strings are not already Unicode normalized.

Collation URIs are used in the collation attributes of <xsl:sort>, <xsl:for-each-group>, and <xsl:key>, as well as the possible values for the final argument in many of the string manipulation functions, such as compare(), starts-with(), and contains(). The default collation used in a particular part of the stylesheet can be set with the default-collation attribute (or xsl:default-collation, if you set it on a literal result element). For example, to index a set of <maincourse> elements case-insensitively based on the value of their <name> child element, which is in French, you could use the following key definition in Saxon:

```
<xsl:key name="maincourses" match="maincourse" use="name"
         collation="http://saxon.sf.net/collation?lang=fr;strength=primary" />
```

As with other extensions, different processors will recognize different collation URIs, so you should check your XSLT processor's documentation to find out what you can use. It's likely that libraries of collation URIs will develop to support standard collations. In addition, some XSLT processors will provide mechanisms for defining your own collations through external code (as Saxon does through a Java class), or perhaps through internal code within a top-level data element within the stylesheet.

Note There's no way to work out what collations a processor supports from within an XSLT stylesheet.

Summary Collation URIs are used to determine how to compare two strings. Different XSLT processors support different sets of collation URIs.

Extension Attributes

The attributes of XSLT elements give fine control over the way in which the element operates. To allow XSLT implementers to give you more control over the behavior of an element, every XSLT element can take **extension attributes**. Extension attributes are attributes that are in a namespace (and therefore must have a prefix), but not in the XSLT namespace (and therefore must not have the prefix that you've associated with the XSLT namespace, which is usually xsl).

Each XSLT processor has its own set of extension attributes, some of which might be allowed on any element and others that are permitted on specific elements. One set of extension attributes that's particularly useful is the set allowed on <xsl:output> for giving you finer control over the way in which the result of the XSLT transformation is serialized on output. For example, Saxon offers the extension attributes described in Table 14-3.

Table 14-3. *Extension Attributes on* <xsl:output> *in Saxon*

Attribute	Description
saxon:indent-spaces	Determines the number of spaces used to indent elements in the output when indent is yes.
saxon:character-representation	Gives you control over the way that characters are output: as character entity references or as numeric character references, with decimal or hexadecimal numbers.
saxon:byte-order-mark	If yes, outputs a byte-order mark at the start of the output; otherwise does not.

Attribute	Description
saxon:next-in-chain	Gives the URL of a stylesheet that should be used to further transform the result tree.
saxon:require-well-formed	If yes, and you provide your own code for serializing the result tree (using a qualified name in the method attribute), then Saxon will generate an error if the result of the stylesheet is not a well-formed XML document, for example, if it contains more than one document element.

■ **Note** To use the Saxon extension attributes, you have to declare the Saxon namespace of `http://saxon.sf.net/` within the XSLT stylesheet.

There's nothing stopping you from using several extension attributes from different namespaces—a processor will ignore extension attributes that aren't in a namespace that it recognizes. If two implementations offer similar extension attributes, for example, you might end up with two sets of extension attributes on a particular element. For example, both Saxon and Xalan support extension attributes that determine how many spaces should be used when indenting output; a portable stylesheet would include both, as follows:

```
<xsl:stylesheet version="2.0"
                xmlns:xsl="http://www.w3.org/1999/XSL/Transform"
                xmlns:saxon="http://saxon.sf.net/"
                xmlns:xalan="http://xml.apache.org/xalan"
                exclude-result-prefixes="saxon xalan">

<xsl:output indent="yes" saxon:indent-spaces="2" xalan:indent-amount="2" />
...
</xsl:stylesheet>
```

■ **Summary** XSLT processors can define their own extension attributes to alter the behavior of XSLT elements.

Extension Instructions

As well as changing the fine detail of how an XSLT element works, XSLT processors are also able to define their own new XSLT instructions, known as **extension instructions**. Like extension attributes, extension instructions have to be in a namespace, and the namespace that they're in cannot be the XSLT namespace.

There's one aspect of using extension elements that's a bit more complex than using extension attributes. To illustrate it, consider the following XSLT stylesheet:

```
<xsl:stylesheet version="2.0"
                xmlns:xsl="http://www.w3.org/1999/XSL/Transform"
                xmlns:ext="http://www.example.com/XSLT/extensions">
```

```
<xsl:template match="Channel">
  <ext:for variable="program" in="Program">...</ext:for>
</xsl:template>

</xsl:stylesheet>
```

When an XSLT processor comes across an element that isn't in the XSLT namespace (such as the <ext:for> element), what does it do? It thinks that the element is a literal result element, so it adds the element to the result tree. In the preceding, however, we intend the processor to try to follow the instruction, to look at the <ext:for> element and iterate over the <Program> elements that it's selecting.

The XSLT processor needs some way of telling the difference between an element that isn't in the XSLT namespace and that's intended to be added to the result tree as a literal result element, and an element that isn't in the XSLT namespace and that's intended to be understood by the XSLT processor as an instruction.

To enable the XSLT processor to make that distinction, you need to declare that the namespace used for the extension element (in this case `http://www.example.com/XSLT/extensions`) is a namespace for extension elements. You can do this by giving the prefix associated with that namespace within the `extension-element-prefixes` attribute on the <xsl:stylesheet> document element, as follows:

```
<xsl:stylesheet version="2.0"
                xmlns:xsl="http://www.w3.org/1999/XSL/Transform"
                xmlns:ext="http://www.example.com/XSLT/extensions"
                extension-element-prefixes="ext">

<xsl:template match="Channel">
  <ext:for variable="program" in="Program">...</ext:for>
</xsl:template>

</xsl:stylesheet>
```

Now, when the XSLT processor comes across the <ext:for> element, it knows that it needs to do something with that element, that it's an extension instruction rather than a literal result element.

The `extension-element-prefixes` attribute can have as many prefixes listed within it as you like, separated by spaces, and if you have several namespaces that you use for extension instructions, you'll have to list them all here. This happens particularly when you have different extension instructions doing the same kind of thing in different XSLT processors.

You can also use the `extension-element-prefixes` attribute to exclude the namespaces that you use for extensions from the result document. The elements in the result tree won't have namespace nodes for the namespaces listed in the `extension-element-prefixes` attribute unless they have to (because one of their attributes is in that namespace), which means that they won't have namespace declarations in the output. Therefore, it's good practice to include all the namespaces that you're using for extensions (whether they're extension attribute values, extension attributes, extension instructions, extension functions, or extension data elements) in the `extension-element-prefixes` list.

- Providing an alternative to an instruction within a nested `<xsl:fallback>` element
- Using the `use-when` attribute to use alternative XSLT for different processors
- Providing an alternative implementation of an extension function using an `<xsl:function>` element with an `override` attribute with the value `yes`

We've also looked at three ways of letting the user know what's happening by providing more user-friendly error messages or simply supplying arbitrary information, which is particularly useful when debugging:

- Issuing a message with `<xsl:message>`, and either halting the process or carrying on
- Halting the transformation with an error using the `error()` function
- Reporting the value of an XPath expression using the `trace()` function

This chapter is the last of the ones covering the details of XSLT. You've learned about pretty much all the elements and attributes that are available in XSLT, and the functions and operators that are available in XPath, and in this chapter you've learned how to add to what XSLT and XPath offer as standard. In the next chapters, we'll turn our attention to some practical uses of XSLT and XPath so that you can see how it all fits together in the real world.

Review Questions

1. What kinds of changes do you need to make when upgrading an XSLT 1.0 stylesheet to XSLT 2.0?
2. Write some portable XSLT that identifies the highest-rated program within the TV guide. You can do this using the `max()` function in XSLT 2.0, if it's supported by the XSLT 2.0 processor; the `math:max()` extension function, if it's supported by the XSLT processor; a stylesheet function, if it's supported by the XSLT 2.0 processor; and otherwise have to use a recursive template. Use appropriate techniques to work out which method the XSLT processor can use and provide alternative code or messages to the user.
3. Which extension attributes does your XSLT processor support and what do they do?
4. How does an XSLT processor tell the difference between a literal result element and an extension instruction?
5. What two ways are there of detecting when an XSLT processor doesn't support an extension instruction, and when is it appropriate to use them?

CHAPTER 15

Dynamic XSLT

So far, we have been transforming XML in a batch process from the command line. Using a command-line processor is very useful when first developing a stylesheet for several reasons. First, it tends to be easier and quicker to debug stylesheets when using a processor from the command line rather than using it in a more dynamic environment. Second, there are lots of processors that you can use from the command line, so you can often work out what's going wrong by trying to use several different ones on the same transformation. Third, command lines often give you access to additional information about the performance of the stylesheet, such as timing information or trace reports that you can use to perfect the stylesheet.

However, batch processing is seldom the best approach in real-world systems. The result of a transformation can change for several reasons—amendments to the stylesheet, changes to the source document (perhaps because it is itself generated dynamically), alterations to the supplementary documents that you're using, and so on—and with batch processing you need to run the transformation each time one of these documents changes. This can easily lead to the transformed documents being out of step with the original documents.

If you can use a dynamic process to perform the transformation and display the results, then you don't have to worry about the source document changing later on—any changes will be automatically reflected in the newly transformed result. In this chapter, we'll look at how to carry out transformations dynamically and at two applications that support dynamic XSLT.

In this chapter, you'll learn

- How to run dynamic transformations
- The advantages and disadvantages of client-side and server-side transformations
- How to set up and use Cocoon 2
- How to manage client-side transformations using Sarissa
- How to pass parameters to create dynamic applications

Dynamic Transformations

Dynamic XSLT transformations can take place in two locations—**server side** or **client side**. Server-side transformations are run on the server in response to the client's request for a particular page. Client-side transformations are run on the client when it receives a particular page.

Note This chapter focuses on transforming XML for presentation, but the same distinction between server-side and client-side transformations can be made for XML-to-XML transformations as well—the XML is transformed into the desired format either in the application that is the source of the XML or in the application that receives the XML.

Server-Side Transformations

With server-side transformations, the client makes a single request for a page, and the server returns a single page to the client. When the server receives a request, it identifies the XML that holds the data for the page to use and what XSLT stylesheet to use with it. The server then performs the transformation and returns the result of the transformation to the client. This process is illustrated in Figure 15-1.

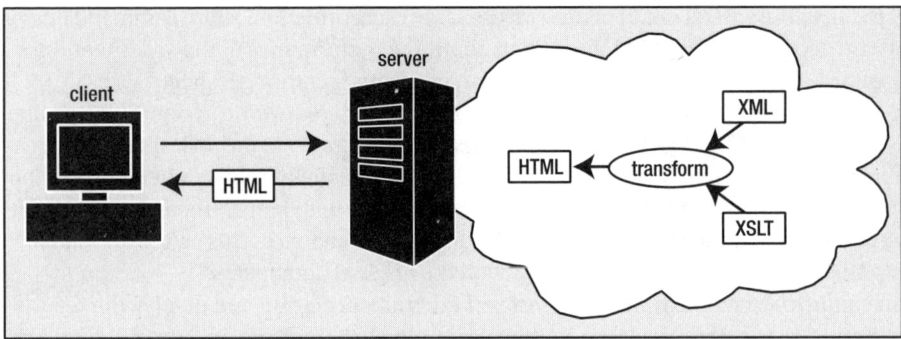

Figure 15-1. *Server-side transformations*

Assuming that the standard web protocol (HTTP) is being used, the server can work out what information the client should receive by looking at the **headers** of the request, which include the URL that's being requested and information about the client that's making the request. Based on this, the server can deliver different information according to the client—different HTML or XHTML for different web browsers, even XML if the client is one that can carry out client-side transformations. The server, and therefore the developer of the application, is in control of what stylesheet is used and what kind of result the client sees. As far as the client is concerned, the server is just like any other—the client can't tell what's going on behind the scenes and doesn't know that the page is automatically generated.

Server-side transformations have a disadvantage in that they place a heavy load on the server. If 100 clients request XML pages in a minute, then the server has to perform those 100 transformations itself, and deliver the results, within a reasonable timeframe. While each individual transformation might be manageable, 100 transformations might not be, especially if those transformations take a long time or, more importantly, involve high memory use.

On the plus side, server-side transformations can make sensible use of caches, to enable the server to store the results of common transformations so that it doesn't have to run them afresh each time a particular XML document is requested. However, this is only beneficial when you have XML pages that are relatively long lived (and that are requested more than once before being changed) and if the transformations that you carry out with them don't rely on changeable information such as user preferences or other display information.

You can write server-side scripts (in Perl or ASP, for example) to support server-side transformations yourself, or you can often use XSLT processors as Java servlets with your HTTP server. However, there are several sophisticated XML frameworks that incorporate server-side transformations, and it's worth having a look at them before you launch into your own. For example:

- AxKit—An Apache module, implemented in Perl, that uses libxslt, Sablotron, or XML::XSLT for its transformations (`http://www.axkit.org/`)
- Cocoon—A Java servlet that uses Xalan (by default) to transform XML documents that may be generated on the fly (`http://cocoon.apache.org/`)
- XSQL—A Java servlet that generates XML from a database and uses Oracle's XSLT processor to transform it (`http://technet.oracle.com/`)

Of these three, Cocoon is arguably the most advanced, and is the one that we will look at in detail later on in this chapter.

Client-Side Transformations

With client-side transformations, the page that the client requests from the server includes instructions that tell the client how to transform the XML. The client performs the transformation, and displays the results.

There are two main models for client-side transformations. The first and simplest is when the client requests an XML document and you tell the client what XSLT stylesheet to use with that XML document using the `xml-stylesheet` processing instruction. This approach is illustrated in Figure 15-2.

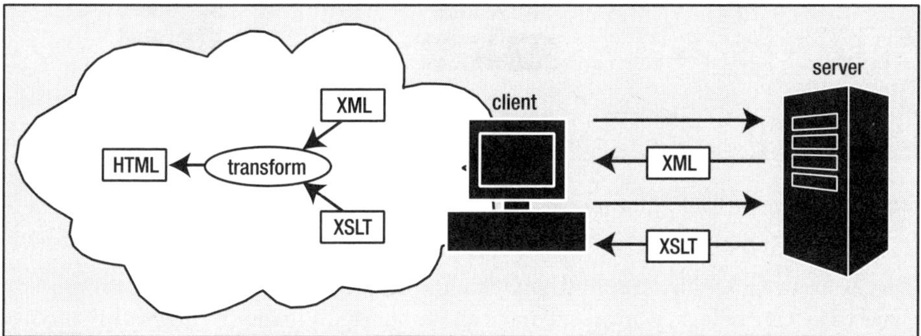

Figure 15-2. *Client-side transformation using* `xml-stylesheet` *processing instruction*

The `xml-stylesheet` processing instruction has two main pseudo-attributes: `href`, which points to the stylesheet that should be used with the XML document, and `type`, which states the content type of the stylesheet (`application/xslt+xml` for XSLT documents).

Tip XSLT 2.0 specifies that the correct content type for XSLT stylesheets is `application/xslt+xml`, but standard practice before XSLT 2.0 has been to use the content type `text/xsl`. Including several `xml-stylesheet` processing instructions with different `type` pseudo-attributes is the best way to ensure that the client will locate the stylesheet.

You can have multiple `xml-stylesheet` processing instructions within a document, in which case the client should choose which one to use based on the other pseudo-attributes. In particular, the `media` pseudo-attribute should contain the type of client that the stylesheet should be used with—for example, `screen`, `handheld`, or `print`. However, these additional pseudo-attributes are not well supported in current clients.

The simple automatic transformation using the `xml-stylesheet` processing instruction is often all that you need. However, if you want to do more sophisticated things on the client, such as cache the XML or XSLT documents or pass parameters into the stylesheet, then you need to control the client-side transformation somehow. These kinds of dynamic transformations are essential when creating pages that provide different views of the same XML document, such as tables that you can sort dynamically or applications where you can page through information.

Most usually you control the transformation with a script within an HTML page—it is this HTML page that the client first requests, and this HTML page that contains the instructions about which XML document and which XSLT stylesheet to use. This pattern is illustrated in Figure 15-3.

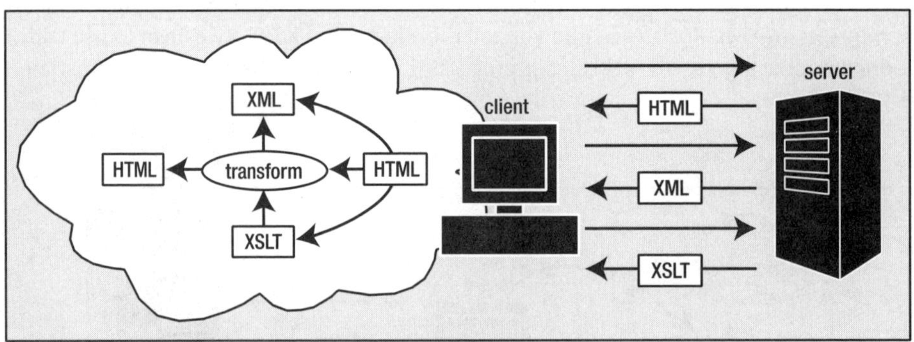

Figure 15-3. *Client-side transformation using script within HTML page*

The biggest drawback with designing applications around client-side transformations is that you have to beware of legacy browsers that don't support XSLT. The six browsers that currently support client-side transformations are listed here:

- Internet Explorer 5+—Supports client-side transformation to HTML using MSXML; versions 5 and 5.5 require MSXML3 to be installed in replace mode (`http://www.microsoft.com/ie`), but Internet Explorer 6+ runs out of the box
- Firefox—Supports client-side transformation to HTML using TransforMiiX (`http://www.getfirefox.com`)

- Netscape 6.1+—Supports client-side transformation to HTML using TransforMiiX (`http://www.netscape.com`)
- Mozilla—Supports client-side transformation to HTML using TransforMiiX (`http://www.mozilla.org`)
- Antenna House Formatter—Supports client-side transformations to XSL-FO using MSXML3 (`http://www.antennahouse.com`)
- XSmiles—Supports client-side transformations to XSL-FO using Xalan (`http://www.xsmiles.org`)

Several of these provide good support for running transformations using scripts, as we will see later on, but no existing client has any support for XSLT 2.0.

The advantage of using client-side transformations is in the lighter load that it places on the server. Rather than having to transform every file that's requested itself, the server can offload this processing onto the client, where it's much more likely that there will be sufficient resources for the processing to be carried out quickly.

In some applications, client-side transformations can be particularly beneficial in reducing the number of requests that are made to the server as well. For example, imagine an application that involves transforming the same XML page with the same XSLT stylesheet again and again using different parameters each time, perhaps to sort the same table in different ways each time. With a server-side transformation, the XML page would be requested, and the resulting HTML file returned to the client each time a change was made to a parameter. With a client-side transformation, the XML and XSLT files are requested just once, and can then be reused again and again, just with different parameters. This can make XSLT applications involving client-side transformations very responsive.

Client Side or Server Side?

XSLT is now a fairly stable technology, and there are a number of good XSLT 1.0 processor implementations (though very few XSLT 2.0 implementations as yet). However, neither client-side nor server-side transformations are particularly mature. Aside from the basic method of associating a set of stylesheets to an XML document, there is no standard API for running either type of transformation. Whichever method you use, it will involve configuring your application with implementation-specific details. Hopefully, this situation will improve as time goes on, and projects that provide cross-browser code, such as Sarissa, are a useful stopgap.

Whether you should use client-side or server-side transformations generally comes down to whether you can guarantee that the users accessing your site will be using browsers that can carry out client-side transformations, particularly if those transformations require the use of XSLT 2.0. If you can't, then delivering XML rather than HTML will exclude a significant number of people from your site. On the other hand, if you're limited in the control you have over your web server, then you might not have a choice.

However, the decision between client-side or server-side transformation is not necessarily an either/or selection. Even if you opt for a server-side transformation for the majority of browsers, you can still use client-side transformations on those clients that can manage it, sending them the XML that you want them to use and letting them identify the XSLT to use with it. This gives you the benefits of offloading as much work as possible to the clients, while retaining the ability to supply usable content to other browsers.

Server-Side Transformations Using Cocoon

In this section, we'll look at how to use Cocoon 2 to automatically transform XML pages into various formats using XSLT. First, we'll go through how to install Cocoon 2 with Jakarta Tomcat as the Java servlet engine, then look at how Cocoon works, and finally see how to configure Cocoon to carry out various dynamic transformations, including the following:

- Simple transformations of an XML document with an XSLT stylesheet
- Providing different results depending on which browser is being used
- Providing different results based on parameters passed to the stylesheet

Installing Cocoon

Cocoon runs as a Java servlet. To use it, you must first install a Java Software Development Kit (SDK). To get Cocoon working with my setup, I installed the SDK for Java 2 Standard Edition (J2SE) version 1.4.2. You can get hold of J2SE version 1.4.2 from `http://java.sun.com/j2se/1.4.2/`. I installed my copy in the directory `C:\j2sdk1.4.2_07`.

■ **Caution** Cocoon 2.1 doesn't work with Java 1.5.0.

Once you have installed the Java SDK, you need to set the `JAVA_HOME` environment variable to the directory in which you've installed it, in my case `C:\j2sdk1.4.2_07`. You can set the `JAVA_HOME` environment variable through the `System` control panel in Windows.

Next, download the latest distribution of Cocoon from `http://cocoon.apache.org/mirror.cgi`. In my case, this version was Cocoon 2.1. Unzip the contents of the distribution; I put my copy into `C:\cocoon`. Since Cocoon 2.1 is only distributed as source code, it needs to be compiled. To do so, run the `build` program in Cocoon's directory:

```
C:\cocoon>build
```

■ **Note** This takes some time, so go and get the beverage of your choice. You can modify what actually gets built into Cocoon by copying the `blocks.properties` file to `local.blocks.properties`, copying `build.properties` to `local.build.properties`, and modifying the local versions of the files.

Once Cocoon has been compiled, you can start up the servlet by running the `cocoon` batch file with the argument `servlet` as follows:

```
C:\cocoon>cocoon servlet
```

When you've done this, try navigating to `http://localhost:8888/`. The page will take a little time to load because Cocoon has to do a few things behind the scenes as it's the first time it's being used, but you should eventually see the page shown in Figure 15-4.

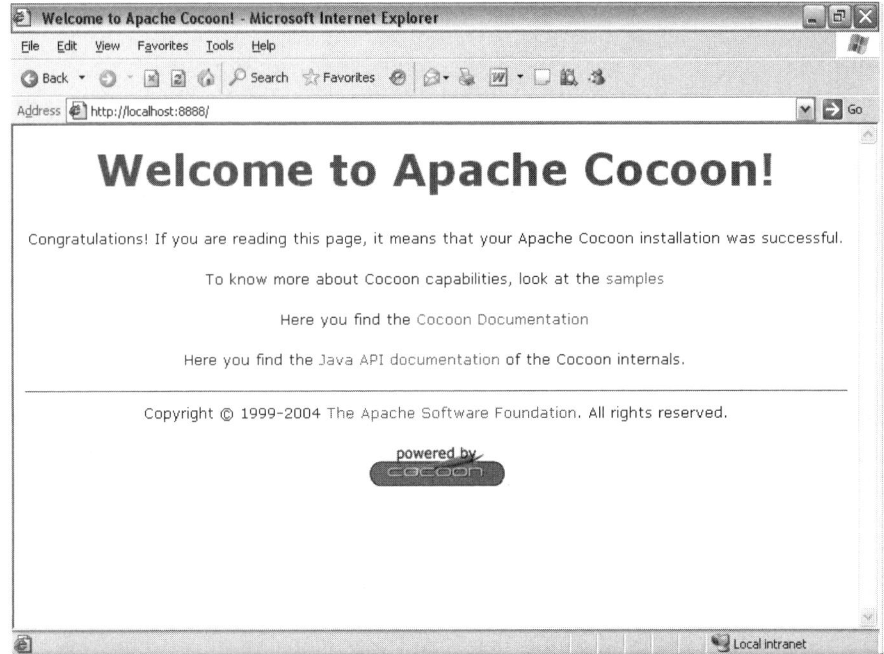

Figure 15-4. *Cocoon home page*

This page, like the rest of the pages accessible through `http://localhost:8888`, is generated dynamically by transforming some XML with XSLT. You can view the source for the welcome page at `C:\cocoon\build\webapp\welcome.xml` and the stylesheet at `C:\cocoon\build\webapp\welcome.xslt`.

You can read more about Cocoon and how it works by following the `Cocoon Documentation` link to `http://localhost:8888/docs/index.html`, which gives you the same information as can be found on the main Cocoon site at `http://cocoon.apache.org/2.1/`.

Note We're just going to be trying things out with Cocoon on a local server, so all the URLs that we'll be using will start with `http://localhost:8888/`. If you want your application to appear under a different URL, you need to configure your web server to redirect URLs so that requests to your web server are redirected to Cocoon. See the Cocoon FAQ at `http://localhost:8888/docs/faq/faq-configure-environment.html` for more details.

Pipelines

Conceptually, all the pages that you access using Cocoon go through a **pipeline**, which is a three-stage process:

- Generating
- Transforming
- Serializing

Pipelines are called pipelines because they are like pipes that you fit together in order to route water (information) from one place to another. The generating process creates some information—it's like the faucet at the beginning of a pipe. The transforming process transforms that information into another format. There can be several transformations, each working on the result of the previous one—they're like the pieces of pipe that can be fitted together. Finally, the serializing process takes the result of the last transformation and writes it out into a series of bytes—that's the faucet right at the end of the pipe.

The details of an individual pipeline—what gets generated, how it's transformed, and how it's serialized (or in plumbing terms, which faucet to attach the pipe to, what pipes to use, and what kind of faucet to fit at the end)—depend on the request that's made to Cocoon. Cocoon works out what you want to do by matching and selecting various aspects of the request, most importantly the URL. The processes that do the matching and selecting are like robots that fit the pipeline together—it's up to you, as the plumber, to make sure that those robots create the correct pipeline for the job.

Before we leap into using Cocoon, we'll take a little time to look at the components of the pipeline that are available to you in a bit more detail, and how matching and selecting works within Cocoon.

Generating

The generation step generates the XML content of a page. The simplest and most useful kind of **generator** is the File Generator, which just accesses an XML file that exists within the file system on your computer. For example, when you access `http://localhost:8888/`, the generator is a File Generator that accesses the file at `C:\cocoon\build\webapp\welcome.xml`.

Cocoon also supports many other types of generators, for example:

- Directory Generator—Generates an XML page that describes the content of a directory
- Request Generator—Generates an XML page that represents the information held in the original page request
- HTML Generator—Generates an XHTML page from an HTML page

With these generators, you can create pages for navigating through your directory structure, or use information about the browser that requested the page.

Transforming

The transformation step transforms the XML that's been generated by applying a series of **transformers**. The most common kind of transformer, and the kind that we'll be using, is an XSLT Transformer, which transforms the generated XML using an XSLT stylesheet. For example, when you access `http://localhost:8888/`, the transformer is an XSLT Transformer that uses the XSLT stylesheet at `C:\cocoon\build\webapp\welcome.xslt`.

Other useful transformers are XInclude Transformers, which resolve XInclude elements within the generated XML, and Filter Transformers, which group a set of records in the generated XML according to their position.

You can have several transformers in a pipeline, each of them providing the input to the next transformer or (in the case of the last one) to the serializer. This enables you to split transformations into multiple steps, which makes each individual transformation easier to write and means that you can reuse them as necessary.

Serializing

The final step in a pipeline is serialization, which is carried out by a **serializer**. The default kind of serializer is the HTML Serializer, which serializes the result of the transformations as HTML.

Other useful serializers are listed here:

- XML Serializer—Serializes the result as XML
- XHTML Serializer—Serializes the result as XHTML
- Text Serializer—Serializes the result as text
- PDF Serializer—Serializes the XSL-FO result as PDF
- SVG Serializer—Converts the SVG result to JPEG or PNG graphics

The page `http://localhost:8888/` uses the XHTML serializer; if you view the source of the page, you'll see that an XHTML DOCTYPE has been added to the page, for example.

Note that the fact that serializers are a distinct step within the pipeline means that it doesn't matter what output instructions you include within your XSLT stylesheet using `<xsl:output>`; these will be overridden by the instructions supplied by the serializer that you use within the pipeline.

Reading

For some resources, such as images and CSS files, going through the whole generate, transform, serialize process would be overkill: all you want to do is deliver the content of the file to the browser. **Readers** compress the generate/transform/serialize pipeline into a single step.

The default reader is the Resource Reader, which delivers content without altering the files in any way, and is useful for images, CSS files, and static HTML pages. Another reader that you might find useful is the JSP Reader, which uses the instructions in a JSP page to create content, bypassing the normal Cocoon pipeline.

Matching and Selecting Pipelines

The generator, transformer, and serializer that are to be used to give the result of a particular request are determined by **matchers** and **selectors**. Matchers try to match a particular aspect of the request against a pattern string, which might contain wildcards or a regular expression. Selectors choose between multiple distinct possibilities.

The most frequently used matcher in Cocoon is the Wildcard URI Matcher, which matches the URI requested by the client against a pattern that can contain the wildcards * (which means any individual part of a URI, any characters not including the / character) or ** (which means any path within a URI, any characters including the / character).

For example, when you access the image `http://localhost:8888/images/powered.gif`, it gets picked up by a matcher that matches `images/*.gif`. The * matches the name of the image (`'powered'`, in this case), and this name is used to identify the appropriate graphic within `C:\cocoon\build\webapp\resources\images`. This graphic is delivered using the Resource Reader, configured to indicate the mime type of the graphic as being `image/gif`.

You can also match URIs against regular expressions with the Regular Expression URI Matcher, or you can match against the presence and values of request parameters with the Request Parameter Matcher and the Wildcard Request Parameter Matcher.

Selectors tend to be used to test other aspects of the request. The most common kind of selector is the Browser Selector, which determines what to do based on the identity of the browser that's being used to access the page. You can also use selectors to determine what to do based on the values of request headers and parameters, the host of the page, or the referring page.

Summary Cocoon serves information by activating a pipeline in response to a request. The pipeline generates, transforms, and serializes XML, or delivers binary content directly using a reader. Cocoon comes with a set of generators, transformers, serializers, readers, matchers, and selectors built in.

Configuring Cocoon

Cocoon is configured using **sitemaps** that describe the way the web site is arranged, just like a sitemap on a web site. You can change what Cocoon does when it receives a particular request by editing the sitemap. The main sitemap for the Cocoon site as a whole is the `sitemap.xmap` file within the `webapp` directory (in my setup, at `C:\cocoon\build\webapp\sitemap.xmap`).

Sitemaps are XML documents; the document element is a `<map:sitemap>` element (where the prefix `map` is associated with the namespace URI `http://apache.org/cocoon/sitemap/1.0`). You can describe the whole site within that one sitemap or, as we'll see later in this section, you can define sitemaps for subdirectories individually.

Sitemaps have two roles: defining the various generators, transformers, serializers, readers, matchers, and selectors that you can use, and defining the pipelines that are used for the various requests you might make. In terms of the plumbing analogy, they describe what kind of faucets and pipes you have available and the rules used by the robots to fit the pipes to faucets and to each other.

The structure of the sitemap XML document has two main parts, following this division. Within the `<map:sitemap>` document element are two important child elements: `<map:components>`, in which the various components are defined, and `<map:pipelines>`, in which the pipelines are defined by bringing together those components. Thus the basic outline of a sitemap file is as follows:

```
<map:sitemap xmlns:map="http://apache.org/cocoon/sitemap/1.0">
<map:components>
  <map:generators default="file">...</map:generators>
  <map:transformers default="xslt">...</map:transformers>
  <map:serializers default="html">...</map:serializers>
  <map:readers default="resource">...</map:readers>
  <map:selectors default="browser">...</map:selectors>
```

```
  <map:matchers default="wildcard">...</map:matchers>
  ...
</map:components>
...
<map:pipelines>
  <map:pipeline>...</map:pipeline>
  ...
</map:pipelines>
</map:sitemap>
```

Defining Components

Since we're going to have to use Saxon to carry out the transformations we're interested in, we're going to have to do a bit of editing of the component definitions in our sitemaps. In general, though, you shouldn't have to touch the component definitions, because Cocoon comes with them all set up nicely.

Each of the children of the `<map:components>` element is a wrapper for a series of component definitions. For example, the `<map:components>` element holds a `<map:transformers>` child that contains any number of `<map:transformer>` elements, each of which defines a type of transformer that you can use.

Each of the component definitions follows the same basic format: it has a `name` attribute that gives the name of the component and a `src` attribute that points to the Java class that implements that component type, and it may have a number of child elements, each of which configures the component in some way. This basic outline for a component definition is shown here:

```
<map:component name="name" src="javaClass">
  <parameter>parameterValue</parameter>
  ...
</map:component>
```

As an example, the `sitemap.xmap` that comes with Cocoon uses the following component definition to define the XSLT Transformer:

```
<map:transformer name="xslt"
                 src="org.apache.cocoon.transformation.TraxTransformer"
                 ...>
  <use-request-parameters>false</use-request-parameters>
  <use-session-parameters>false</use-session-parameters>
  <use-cookie-parameters>false</use-cookie-parameters>
  <xslt-processor-role>xalan</xslt-processor-role>
  <check-includes>true</check-includes>
</map:transformer>
```

This means that you can use the name `xslt` to refer to a **TraxTransformer** (TrAX is an API for running XML transformations, used by Xalan and Saxon among others). Request parameters, session parameters, and cookie parameters are not passed into the stylesheet by default, and by default the XSLT processor that gets used is Xalan.

When you define pipelines, you can choose which generator, transformer, serializer, matcher, or selector to use by referring to them by the name that's used to define them in this section of the sitemap. To make life easier, you can also set up a default component that will be used if you don't refer to one specifically by name. You state what component should be used by default using the default attribute on the wrapper element that contains the component definitions.

For example, the following XML is used in the root sitemap.xmap file that comes with Cocoon to define the matchers that you can use:

```
<map:matchers default="wildcard">
  <map:matcher name="wildcard"
               src="org.apache.cocoon.matching.WildcardURIMatcher" .../>
  <map:matcher name="regexp"
               src="org.apache.cocoon.matching.RegexpURIMatcher" .../>
  <map:matcher name="request"
               src="org.apache.cocoon.matching.RequestParamMatcher" .../>
  ...
</map:matchers>
```

This allows you to explicitly use the Wildcard URI Matcher by referring to it by the name wildcard, the Regular Expression URI Matcher using the name regexp, the Request Parameter Matcher using the name request, and so on. If you don't explicitly say which matcher you want to use when you match within a pipeline, Cocoon will assume that you're matching the URI using a wildcard pattern, because the default value on the <map:matchers> element is wildcard.

Using Saxon in Cocoon

The default setup for Cocoon uses Xalan as the XSLT processor. This isn't any good for us because we're using XSLT 2.0 transformations, which are only supported by Saxon. So we need to change the default configuration so that we can use Saxon instead.

First, let's modify welcome.xslt so that we can tell which XSLT processor is being used to perform the transformation. As you saw in Chapter 14, you can use the system-property() function with the argument 'xsl:vendor' to identify the XSLT processor that's being used, in both XSLT 1.0 and XSLT 2.0. We'll simply add a paragraph to the welcome page to indicate the processor, as follows:

```
<xsl:template match="welcome">
  <html xmlns="http://www.w3.org/1999/xhtml" xml:lang="en" lang="en">
    <head>
      ...
    </head>
    <body>
      <h1>Welcome to Apache Cocoon!</h1>
      <xsl:apply-templates/>
      <p>
        This page generated by
        <xsl:value-of select="system-property('xsl:vendor')" />.
      </p>
      ...
    </body>
```

```
  </html>
</xsl:template>
```

If you view `http://localhost:8888/` after making this change, you should see the extra paragraph appear just above the horizontal rule, as shown in Figure 15-5.

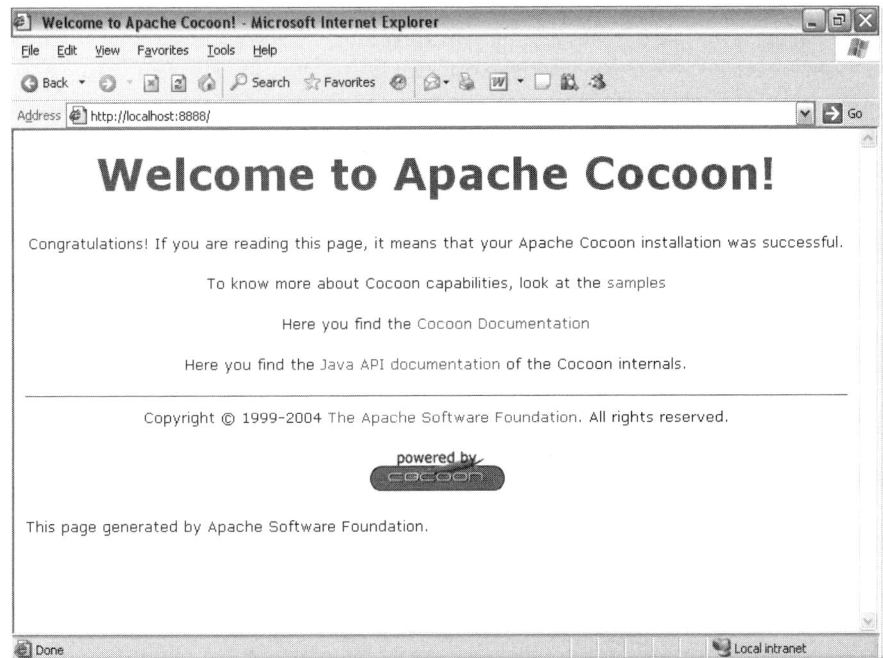

Figure 15-5. *Viewing* `http://localhost:8888/` *with Xalan as XSLT processor*

As you can see, the vendor of the XSLT processor being used is the "Apache Software Foundation," which is the implementer of Xalan.

To use Saxon instead, we need to make two changes to Cocoon's configuration, and copy a file.

First, we need to change the default transformer that Cocoon uses so that it refers to Saxon rather than Xalan. The default transformer is the transformer named `xslt`, and it's configured in `sitemap.xmap`. The current specification is as follows:

```
<map:transformer name="xslt"
                 src="org.apache.cocoon.transformation.TraxTransformer"
                 ...>
  <use-request-parameters>false</use-request-parameters>
  <use-session-parameters>false</use-session-parameters>
  <use-cookie-parameters>false</use-cookie-parameters>
  <xslt-processor-role>xalan</xslt-processor-role>
  <check-includes>true</check-includes>
</map:transformer>
```

All we need to do here is change the xslt-processor-role parameter to refer to saxon rather than xalan, as in sitemap2.xmap:

```
<map:transformer name="xslt"
                 src="org.apache.cocoon.transformation.TraxTransformer"
                 ...>
  <use-request-parameters>false</use-request-parameters>
  <use-session-parameters>false</use-session-parameters>
  <use-cookie-parameters>false</use-cookie-parameters>
  <xslt-processor-role>saxon</xslt-processor-role>
  <check-includes>true</check-includes>
</map:transformer>
```

The value of the xslt-processor-role parameter is used by Cocoon to locate the appropriate Java class for the XSLT processor. The name that you use in this parameter is matched with a name defined in cocoon.xconf, which lives in the C:\cocoon\build\webapp\WEB-INF directory in my setup, so the next thing you need to do is to edit this file. Look for the <xslt-processor> element in this file. Below it are a number of <component> elements that define XSLT processors that you might want to use, including (commented out) a <component> element that can be used for Saxon. Uncomment this <component> element, and edit the value of the transformer-factory parameter it so that it reads as follows:

```
<component logger="core.xslt-processor"
           role="org.apache.excalibur.xml.xslt.XSLTProcessor/saxon"
           class="org.apache.excalibur.xml.xslt.XSLTProcessorImpl">
  <parameter name="use-store" value="true"/>
  <parameter name="transformer-factory"
             value="net.sf.saxon.TransformerFactoryImpl"/>
</component>
```

Finally, you need to make sure that the net.sf.saxon.TransformerFactoryImpl class is accessible to Cocoon. To do this, you need to copy saxon8.jar into C:\cocoon\lib\endorsed; Cocoon doesn't use your classpath to work out which Java classes are available.

Once you've made these changes, you need to shut down and restart Cocoon to make them come into effect. After doing so, try viewing http://localhost:8888/. You should see the page shown in Figure 15-6.

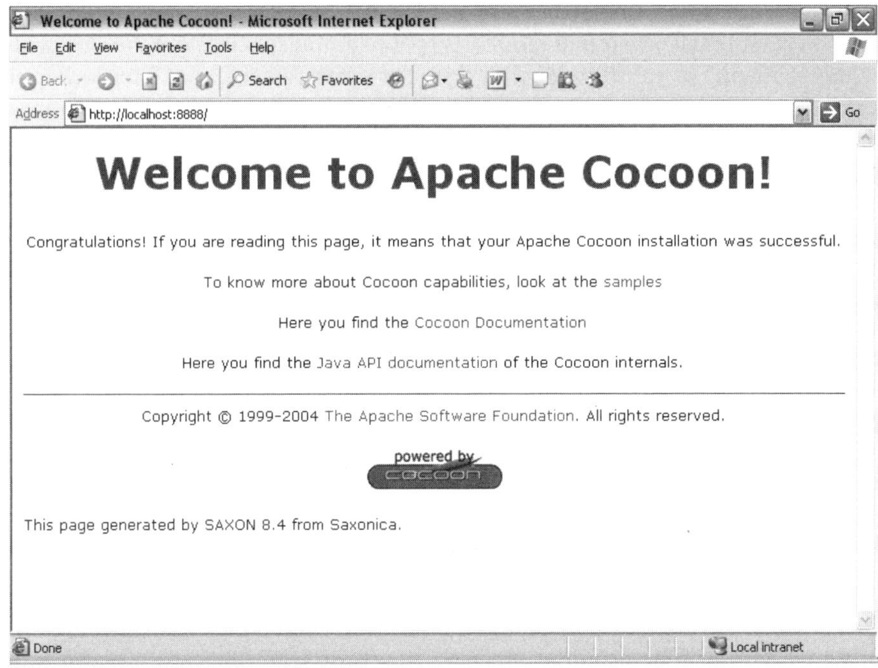

Figure 15-6. *Viewing* `http://localhost:8888/` *with Saxon as XSLT processor*

The paragraph that states which XSLT processor is being used now states that the XSLT processor is "SAXON 8.4 from Saxonica."

Defining Pipelines

The main part of configuring Cocoon to serve web pages is defining the pipelines that should be used. Each pipeline is defined within the `<map:pipelines>` element with its own `<map:pipeline>` element. You can use separate `<map:pipeline>` elements to have different error handling in different cases, but mainly you just need to have one `<map:pipeline>` element containing several `<map:match>` elements, each of which specifies a different request or class of requests and how to deal with it.

Each `<map:match>` element has an optional `type` attribute, which specifies the kind of matcher that should be used. If you don't give the `type` attribute specifically, then you'll use the default matcher, which is set when you define the matchers (in the `default` attribute of the `<map:matchers>` element). The URI (or whatever the matcher tests against) is matched against the pattern held in the `pattern` attribute. For example, to define a pipeline that should be used when someone requests `TVGuide.html`, you can use the following:

```
<map:pipeline>
  <map:match pattern="TVGuide.html">
    ...
  </map:match>
</map:pipeline>
```

Within the <map:match> element you put the definition of the generator, transformers, and serializer that you want to use when that request is received. You specify the generator with a <map:generate> element, the transformers with <map:transform> elements, and the serializer with a <map:serialize> element. Each of these elements can take a type attribute if you want to specifically select a particular generator, transformer, or serializer for the content.

When we receive a request for TVGuide.html, for example, we want to use the XML from TVGuide.xml, transformed with the stylesheet from TVGuide.xsl, and serialized as HTML. The File Generator, XSLT Transformer, and HTML Serializer are the defaults in the basic Cocoon setup, so you can simply use

```
<map:pipeline>
  <map:match pattern="TVGuide.html">
    <map:generate src="TVGuide.xml" />
    <map:transform src="TVGuide.xsl" />
    <map:serialize />
  </map:match>
</map:pipeline>
```

Creating Subsitemaps

The main sitemap, found in the webapp directory, contains the definitions of many of the components that are available within Cocoon, as described previously. Each directory can also have its own subsitemap, which deals with the requests for that directory and its subdirectories (unless they too have their own subsitemap). These can provide their own component definitions, but often will just contain some pipeline definitions dealing with the requests that are made for files in that directory.

To use one of these subsitemaps, you must **mount** the sitemap within the parent sitemap. You do this by defining a simple pipeline that matches paths that start with the directory name. For example, to create a user subdirectory, you need a pipeline that matches paths starting with user/, as follows:

```
<map:pipeline>
  <map:match pattern="user/**">
    ...
  </map:match>
</map:pipeline>
```

■ **Note** The ** ensures that requests made for files or directories at whatever level below the user subdirectory are passed on to the sitemap for the user subdirectory.

Within the pipeline for the subdirectory, you need to mount the subsitemap using a <map:mount> element. The <map:mount> element has two important attributes: the src attribute that specifies the subdirectory (don't forget to end it with a trailing /), and the uri-prefix that specifies the string that's taken off the beginning of the URI when it is passed through to the sitemap in that directory (which again is usually the same as the name of the directory). So, to mount the user subdirectory, which contains its own sitemap in sitemap.xmap, you can use the following:

```
<map:pipeline>
  <map:match pattern="user/**">
    <map:mount src="user/" uri-prefix="user/" />
  </map:match>
</map:pipeline>
```

Summary You can configure Cocoon through sitemaps. You can set up components and define pipelines within a sitemap. Each sitemap can mount other sitemaps, usually from other directories.

Creating a Sitemap for a Subdirectory

To try out what you've learned about sitemaps in Cocoon, we'll create a directory called `TVGuide` that holds the various XML and XSLT files that we've been using and configure Cocoon so that the URL `http://localhost:8888/TVGuide/listing` returns the result of applying the `TVGuide.xsl` stylesheet to the `TVGuide.xml` file.

First, create a subdirectory of the `C:\cocoon\build\webapp` directory, called `TVGuide`, and put all the files that we've been using, such as `TVGuide.xml`, `series.xml`, `TVGuide.xsl`, and the various graphic files, into this directory.

If you try accessing these files directly at the URL `http://localhost:8888/TVGuide/TVGuide.xml`, you'll get a 404 error, as shown in Figure 15-7, because Cocoon hasn't been configured yet to accept that as a URL.

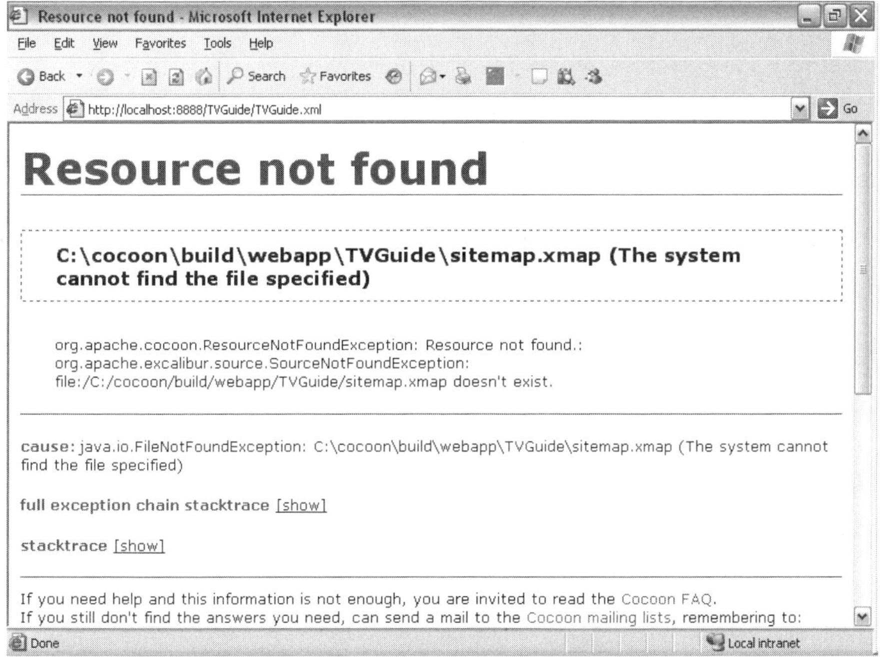

Figure 15-7. *Error when trying to view* `TVGuide.xml` *without configuring Cocoon*

Next, we'll make a sitemap for the TVGuide directory. This sitemap is really just the bare bones of a sitemap—it will use the components that are defined in the root sitemap that comes with Cocoon. For now it will just contain one pipeline—when the client requests the URL http://localhost:8888/TVGuide/listing, it will "generate" XML from TVGuide.xml (which actually just involves reading that file), transform it using TVGuide.xsl, and serialize the result as HTML. The sitemap for the TVGuide directory, sitemap3.xmap, shown in Listing 15-1, needs to be saved as C:\cocoon\webapp\TVGuide\sitemap.xmap.

Listing 15-1. sitemap3.xmap

```
<map:sitemap xmlns:map="http://apache.org/cocoon/sitemap/1.0">
<map:pipelines>
  <map:pipeline>
    <map:match pattern="listing">
      <map:generate src="TVGuide.xml" />
      <map:transform src="TVGuide.xsl" />
      <map:serialize />
    </map:match>
  </map:pipeline>
</map:pipelines>
</map:sitemap>
```

Finally, we need to mount this subsitemap within the main sitemap for Cocoon: C:\cocoon\build\webapp\sitemap.xmap in my setup. You need to add a pipeline that mounts the subsitemap we've just created for use when people request a URI that begins with TVGuide, as in sitemap4.xmap. The pipeline that you need to add within the <map:pipelines> element is as follows:

```
<map:pipeline>
  <map:match pattern="TVGuide/**">
    <map:mount src="TVGuide/" uri-prefix="TVGuide/" />
  </map:match>
</map:pipeline>
```

Now try accessing the URL http://localhost:8888/TVGuide/listing. You should see the results of transforming TVGuide.xml with TVGuide.xsl, as shown in Figure 15-8.

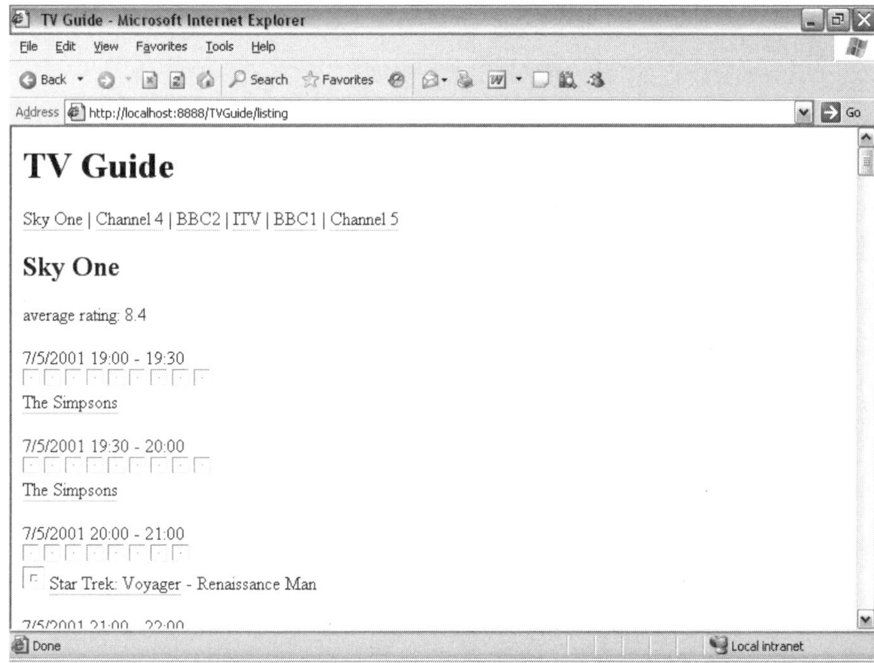

Figure 15-8. *Viewing* `http://localhost:8888/TVGuide/listing` *with simple sitemap*

The result doesn't look quite right because the generated HTML page includes references to various other files (the CSS stylesheet and various images). You need to configure Cocoon so that requests for CSS files and GIFs within the `TVGuide` subdirectory simply result in returning those files by adding a couple more `<map:match>` elements to the `sitemap.xmap` for the `TVGuide` subdirectory, as in `sitemap5.xmap`:

```
<map:pipelines>
  <map:pipeline>
    <map:match pattern="listing">
      <map:generate src="TVGuide.xml" />
      <map:transform src="TVGuide.xsl" />
      <map:serialize />
    </map:match>
    <map:match pattern="**.css">
      <map:read src="{1}.css" mime-type="text/css" />
    </map:match>
    <map:match pattern="**.gif">
      <map:read src="{1}.gif" mime-type="image/gif" />
    </map:match>
  </map:pipeline>
</map:pipelines>
```

If you make these changes, viewing `http://localhost:8888/TVGuide/listing` should give you the familiar, properly formatted page, as shown in Figure 15-9.

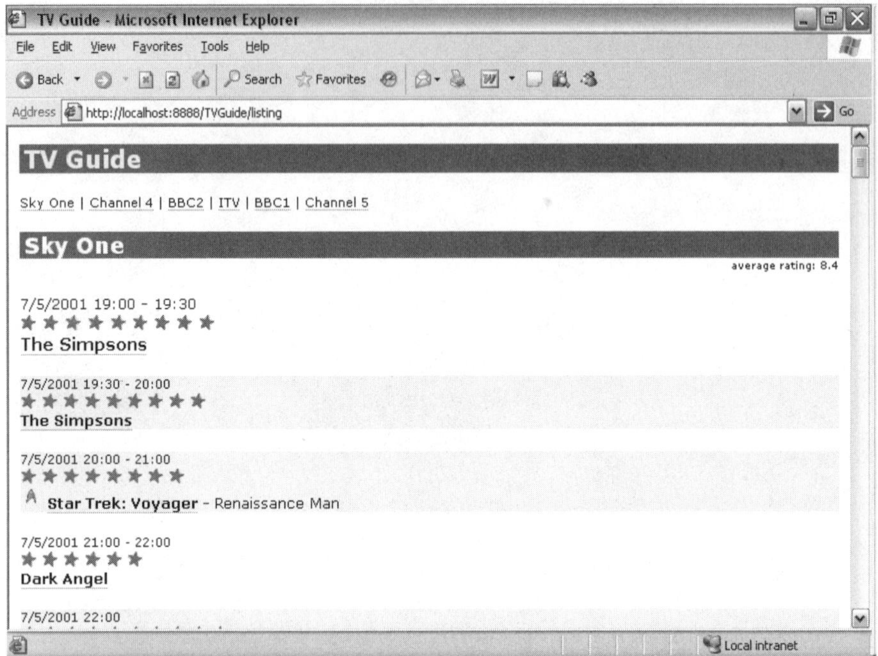

Figure 15-9. *Viewing* `http://localhost:8888/TVGuide/listing` *with complete sitemap*

Different Stylesheets for Different Browsers

You can configure Cocoon to use different stylesheets for different browsers using a Browser Selector. These give the same kind of effect as HTML pages containing "sniffer" scripts that test what kind of browser you're using and create different pages as a result.

The Browser Selector named `browser` is the default selector in the usual Cocoon setup, and it defines the identifiers for the browsers that can be discriminated within the sitemap. The selector named `browser` is set up as follows in the main `sitemap.xmap`:

```
<map:selector name="browser"
              src="org.apache.cocoon.selection.BrowserSelector">
  <!-- # NOTE: The appearance indicates the search order. This is very
       # important since some words may be found in more than one browser
       # description. (MSIE is presented as "Mozilla/4.0 (Compatible; MSIE
       # 4.01; ...")
  -->
  <browser name="explorer" useragent="MSIE"/>
  <browser name="pocketexplorer" useragent="MSPIE"/>
  <browser name="handweb" useragent="HandHTTP"/>
  <browser name="avantgo" useragent="AvantGo"/>
  <browser name="imode" useragent="DoCoMo"/>
  <browser name="opera" useragent="Opera"/>
```

```
  <browser name="lynx" useragent="Lynx"/>
  <browser name="java" useragent="Java"/>
  <browser name="wap" useragent="Nokia"/>
  <browser name="wap" useragent="UP"/>
  <browser name="wap" useragent="Wapalizer"/>
  <browser name="mozilla5" useragent="Mozilla/5"/>
  <browser name="mozilla5" useragent="Netscape6/"/>
  <browser name="netscape" useragent="Mozilla"/>
</map:selector>
```

You can set up your own Browser Selectors if you want to, with different names, for example, to group all the desktop browsers together or to distinguish more precisely between different versions of browsers. The Browser Selector is set up using `<browser>` child elements, each of which gives the identifier for a browser in the `name` attribute and the string that appears within the **User-Agent** HTTP header when that browser is used to request a file in the `useragent` attribute.

Once a selector has been set up, you can use it within a pipeline with the `<map:select>` element. The `<map:select>` element takes an optional `type` attribute, which specifies the name of the selector component that you want to use (and usually defaults to `browser`, the Browser Selector as shown previously).

The content of the `<map:select>` element is similar to the content of the `<xsl:choose>` element and works in roughly the same way. Within the `<map:select>` element are a number of `<map:when>` elements, each with a `test` attribute. The content of a `<map:when>` element is used if its `test` attribute holds the selected value (in this case, the name of the browser). The `<map:select>` element may also have a `<map:otherwise>` child, which is used if none of the `<map:when>` elements hold the relevant value.

For example, to use `TVGuide.ie.xsl` to transform `TVGuide.xml` if the browser is Internet Explorer or Pocket Internet Explorer, and the normal `TVGuide.xsl` otherwise, you could use the following:

```
<map:pipeline>
  <map:match pattern="listing">
    <map:generate src="TVGuide.xml" />
    <map:select>
      <map:when test="explorer">
        <map:transform src="TVGuide.ie.xsl" />
      </map:when>
      <map:when test="pocketexplorer">
        <map:transform src="TVGuide.ie.xsl" />
      </map:when>
      <map:otherwise>
        <map:transform src="TVGuide.xsl" />
      </map:otherwise>
    </map:select>
    <map:serialize />
  </map:match>
</map:pipeline>
```

Sometimes the serialization of the transformed XML should vary according to the browser that's used, perhaps at the same time as the method of transformation. For example, if you have TVGuide.wap.xsl that transforms to WML for WAP phones, then you should have the <map:serialize> element within the <map:select> as well, this time using an XML Serializer configured so that it outputs WML properly:

```
<map:pipeline>
  <map:match pattern="listing">
    <map:generate src="TVGuide.xml" />
    <map:select>
      <map:when test="wap">
        <map:transform src="TVGuide.wap.xsl" />
        <map:serialize type="wap" />
      </map:when>
      <map:otherwise>
        <map:transform src="TVGuide.xsl" />
        <map:serialize />
      </map:otherwise>
    </map:select>
  </map:match>
</map:pipeline>
```

You can nest selectors and matches inside each other as much as you like in order to configure the pipeline.

■ **Summary** You can change the stylesheet that you use according to the client requesting the file using the browser selector.

Using Parameters

The great advantage of using dynamic transformations rather than static batch transformations is that you can create HTML pages that rely on user input, passed into the stylesheet using parameters. As you'll recall from Chapter 6, you can make a stylesheet accept a parameter by declaring the parameter at the top level of the stylesheet.

You can pass parameters into a stylesheet that you access using Cocoon in two main ways: by setting the parameter from within the sitemap or by passing through parameters from the URL of the request. These two methods can be combined for any particular request, but we'll look at how to use them individually in the next two sections.

Setting Parameters in the Sitemap

The first way of passing parameters into a transformation is to use <map:parameter> within the <map:transform> element that runs the transformation in the sitemap. This technique is most useful if you want to pass in a parameter that's fixed based on one of the headers used in the request or the path of the request URL itself—for example, if you wanted to pass a different value for a parameter based on the web browser that's being used or based on the "directory" named in the URL.

■ Caution One of the things about Cocoon that can take some getting used to is the fact that the URL used to access a page can bear little or no relation to the actual location of the documents used to generate the page.

You pass parameters in to the transformation using the `<map:parameter>` element, with a `name` attribute giving the name of the parameter (the name that's used in the `<xsl:param>` definition within the stylesheet) and a `value` attribute specifying the string value of the parameter, as follows:

```
<map:transform src="stylesheet.xsl">
  <map:parameter name="parameterName" value="parameterValue" />
</map:transform>
```

For example, you could use the same stylesheet, `TVGuide.xsl`, to transform `TVGuide.xml` to either produce a listing of the programs grouped by what channel they're on or produce a listing based on what time the programs are showing. The grouping that was used could depend on the `$group` parameter, which takes a value of either `'channels'` or `'startTimes'`, with a default of `'channels'`. The parameter would be declared in `TVGuide.xsl` as follows:

```
<xsl:param name="group" as="xs:string" select="'channels'" />
```

In the sitemap, the group that's used depends on the URL that's used to access the information. The URL `http://localhost:8888/TVGuide/listing/channels` shows the listings by channel, whereas the URL `http://localhost:8888/TVGuide/listing/startTimes` shows the listings by start time. To define the different treatment of the two URLs, we could use two separate pipelines:

```
<map:pipeline>
  <map:match pattern="listing">
    <map:generate src="TVGuide.xml" />
    <map:match pattern="listing/channels">
      <map:transform src="TVGuide.xsl">
        <map:parameter name="group" value="channels" />
      </map:transform>
    </map:match>
    <map:match pattern="listing/startTimes">
      <map:transform src="TVGuide.xsl">
        <map:parameter name="group" value="startTimes" />
      </map:transform>
    </map:match>
    <map:serialize />
  </map:match>
</map:pipeline>
```

If the value of the parameter links up with the value used in the URL, as it does here, it's also possible to use wildcards to set the value of the parameter. Any * or ** used in the pattern of a `<map:match>` within the sitemap is assigned to implicit variables, named 1, 2, 3, and so on. You can refer to these variables within the `value` attribute of `<map:parameter>` using {}s around the number. So, for example, to insert the value matched by the first * in the pattern, you would use `{1}`.

In this case, the string after the listing/ part of the URL is the value that we want to pass as the parameter. So we can use a wildcard as follows:

```
<map:pipeline>
  <map:match pattern="listing/*">
    <map:generate src="TVGuide.xml" />
    <map:transform src="TVGuide.xsl">
      <map:parameter name="group" value="{1}" />
    </map:transform>
    <map:serialize />
  </map:match>
</map:pipeline>
```

Note You can also use parameters from the match pattern in various other places, including the src attributes of <map:generate> and <map:transform>. We used them earlier in this section when we configured Cocoon to return CSS and GIF files that were requested explicitly.

Summary You can pass parameters in to stylesheets using the <map:parameter> element within a <map:transform> in the sitemap. The value of the parameter can be based on the URL using wildcards.

Passing Parameters in to the Stylesheet

The parameter that we'll pass in to the stylesheet is the $sortOrder parameter, which determines whether the channels are sorted in ascending or descending order. We'll try to set up Cocoon so that the URL http://localhost:8888/TVGuide/listing/ascending uses the TVGuide2.xsl stylesheet on TVGuide.xml with the $sortOrder parameter set to 'ascending', and the URL http://localhost:8888/TVGuide/listing/descending performs a transformation with the same source and stylesheet, but this time with the $sortOrder parameter set to 'descending'.

The $sortOrder parameter is declared in TVGuide2.xsl as follows:

```
<xsl:param name="sortOrder" as="xs:string" select="'descending'" />
```

It's used when creating the sorted list of <Channel> elements held in the $Channels variable:

```
<xsl:variable name="Channels" as="element(Channel)+">
  <xsl:perform-sort select="/TVGuide/Channel">
    <xsl:sort select="avg(Program/@rating)" order="{$sortOrder}" />
    <xsl:sort select="xs:integer(Program[1]/@rating)" order="{$sortOrder}" />
  </xsl:perform-sort>
</xsl:variable>
```

The general pattern for the URLs is `listing/*`, where the * represents the sort order and the value for the `$sortOrder` parameter. URLs of this form should cause `TVGuide.xml` to be transformed using `TVGuide2.xsl` and then serialized using the default HTML Serializer. You can therefore include the following `<map:match>` within the pipeline for the site:

```
<map:match pattern="listing/*">
  <map:generate src="TVGuide.xml" />
  <map:transform src="TVGuide2.xsl" />
  <map:serialize />
</map:match>
```

Now we can add the passing of a value for the `$sortOrder` parameter in to the stylesheet. The `<map:transform>` element needs a `<map:parameter>` child element whose `name` attribute has the value `sortOrder` and whose `value` attribute refers to the part of the URL matching the first * in the pattern, as follows:

```
<map:match pattern="listing/*">
  <map:generate src="TVGuide.xml" />
  <map:transform src="TVGuide2.xsl">
    <map:parameter name="sortOrder" value="{1}" />
  </map:transform>
  <map:serialize />
</map:match>
```

Since the URL used to access the listing is different, the browser will also request CSS files and GIFs with the same base URI. Therefore, you also need to include some `<map:match>` elements to deal with these requests. These need to come before the preceding `<map:match>` element; otherwise Cocoon will try to pass the filename `TVGuide.css` as the value of the `$sortOrder` parameter.

```
<map:match pattern="listing/**.css">
  <map:read src="{1}.css" mime-type="text/css" />
</map:match>
<map:match pattern="listing/**.gif">
  <map:read src="{1}.gif" mime-type="image/gif" />
</map:match>
```

With these changes, your `sitemap.xmap` should look the same as `sitemap6.xmap`.

Now try accessing `http://localhost:8888/TVGuide/listing/ascending`. The result of the transformation should show the channels listed in ascending order of average rating, as shown in Figure 15-10.

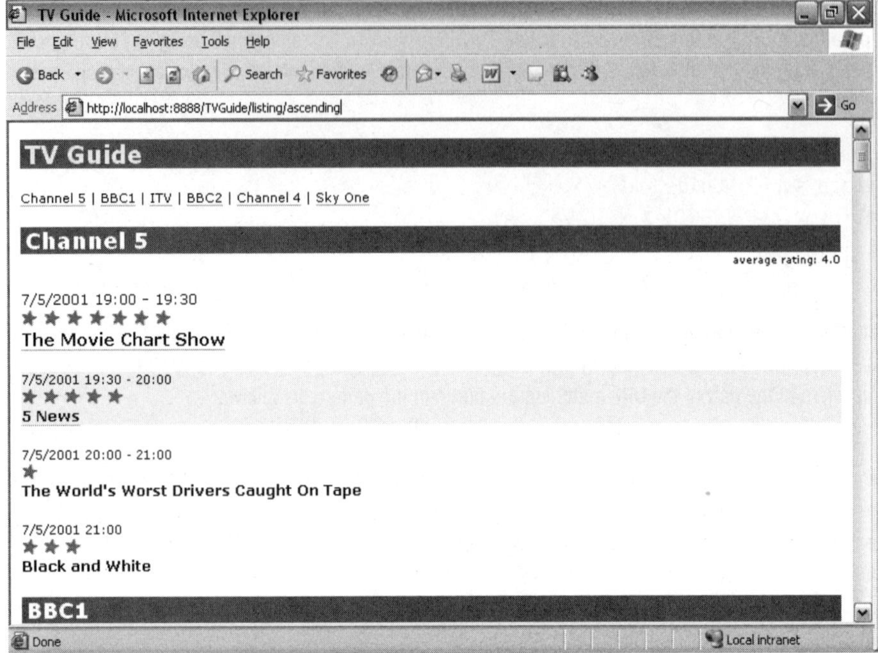

Figure 15-10. *Viewing* `http://localhost:8888/TVGuide/listing/ascending`

The order has changed because the `$sortOrder` parameter is being set to `'ascending'` rather than the default `'descending'`. Viewing either `http://localhost:8888/TVGuide/listing/descending` or `http://localhost:8888/TVGuide/listing` will show the channels in descending order, the first because the `$sortOrder` parameter is explicitly set to `'descending'` by Cocoon, and the second because the `$sortOrder` parameter is defaulted to `'descending'` within the stylesheet.

Passing Parameters from the URL

Using a part of the main URL as the value for a parameter is often very handy, but when you want more flexibility, you should use **request parameters**. The request parameters of a URL are the name-value pairs that are placed in the URL after the ?. For example, in the following URL, there are two request parameters: `user` with the value `JeniT`, and `sortOrder` with the value `descending`:

```
http://localhost:8888/cocoon/TVGuide/listing?user=JeniT&sortOrder=descending
```

Request parameters can be added to a URL manually by the user or automatically by submitting a form, as well as being hard coded into a particular link. This is more flexible than using the main part of the URL because the user could type anything into an input field in a form and see the result of the transformation with that value being used.

In the default setup of Cocoon, request parameters do not get passed through to the stylesheet, so to get the `user` and `sortOrder` parameters to be passed through to `TVGuide2.xsl`, we need to explicitly tell Cocoon to use the request parameters. This is simple to do using

<map:parameter> inside the <map:transform>, this time with the special name use-request-parameters and the value set to true as follows:

```
<map:match pattern="listing">
  <map:generate src="TVGuide.xml" />
  <map:transform src="TVGuide2.xsl">
    <map:parameter name="use-request-parameters" value="true" />
  </map:transform>
  <map:serialize />
</map:match>
```

All the request parameters are now passed through to TVGuide2.xsl as stylesheet parameters of the same name, with the string value specified within the URL.

Summary Request parameters are passed through to the stylesheet if you set the use-request-parameters parameter for a particular <map:transform> to true within the sitemap.

Passing Request Parameters in to the Stylesheet

To test out the request parameters, we'll make a very simple HTML page that invites users to enter a sort order, and uses the value that they type as the value of the $sortOrder parameter when the form is submitted. The HTML page, sortOrder.html, is shown in Listing 15-2.

Listing 15-2. sortOrder.html

```
<html>
  <head><title>Choose Sort Order</title></head>
  <body>
    <form action="listing">
      <p>
        Enter the order in which the channels should be sorted:
        <input name="sortOrder" />
      </p>
    </form>
  </body>
</html>
```

We have to set up the sitemap to deliver sortOrder.html as an HTML page, when it is requested using the URL http://localhost:8888/TVGuide/sortOrder.html, with the following <map:match> element:

```
<map:match pattern="sortOrder.html">
  <map:read src="sortOrder.html" mime-type="text/html" />
</map:match>
```

Note Since this is a static HTML page, there's no need to go through a lengthy generate/transform/serialize process; instead, Cocoon can just deliver the file as-is.

The existing `<map:match>` for viewing the listing needs to be modified slightly. The `<map:parameter>` within the `<map:transform>` needs to set the value of the `use-request-parameters` special parameter to `true`, as follows:

```
<map:match pattern="listing">
  <map:generate src="TVGuide.xml" />
  <map:transform src="TVGuide2.xsl">
    <map:parameter name="use-request-parameters" value="true" />
  </map:transform>
  <map:serialize />
</map:match>
```

Once you've made these changes, your `sitemap.xmap` should look the same as `sitemap7.xmap`.

Try requesting the HTML file at `http://localhost:8888/TVGuide/sortOrder.html`. You should see the page shown in Figure 15-11.

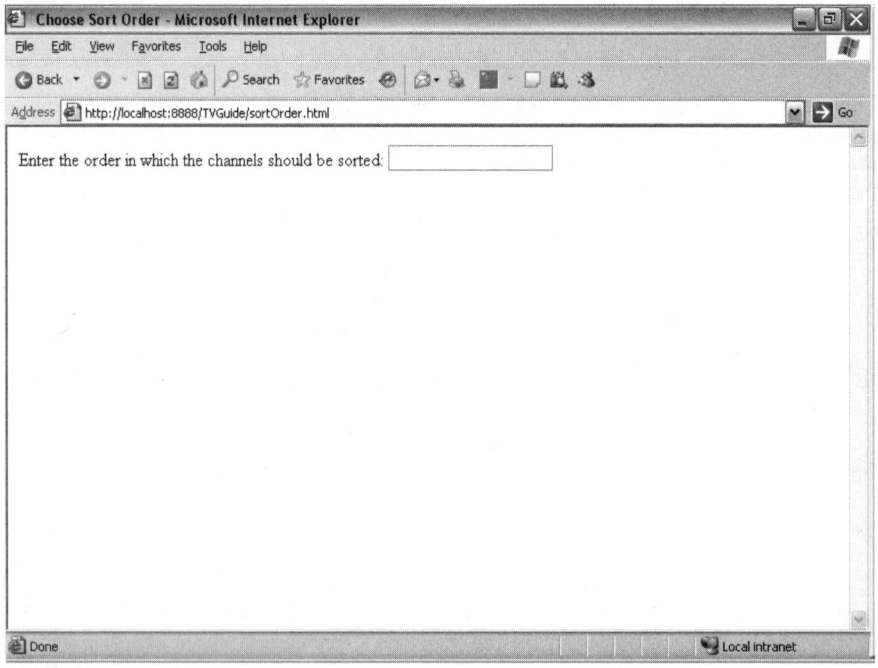

Figure 15-11. *Viewing* `http://localhost:8888/TVGuide/sortOrder.html`

Fill in the order that you want to view the channels in, and submit the form by pressing Return. The request URL is in the form `http://localhost:8888/TVGuide/listing?sortOrder=ascending`, and the `sortOrder` request parameter gets passed through to `TVGuide2.xsl` as the `$sortOrder` stylesheet parameter. The resulting page should contain the channels listed in ascending order, as in Figure 15-10.

Client-Side Transformations Using Sarissa

We'll now turn our attention to transformations managed on the client side using Sarissa. Sarissa is an ECMAScript library that provides a scripting interface for XSLT transformations in both Internet Explorer and Mozilla/Firefox, which makes it easy to write cross-browser code. The latest version of Sarissa can be downloaded from `http://sourceforge.net/projects/sarissa/`. Documentation can be found at `http://sarissa.sourceforge.net/doc/`.

Caution There is no client-side support for XSLT 2.0 at time of writing. Therefore, you can only use client-side transformations if an XSLT 1.0 processor can execute your stylesheet. See Chapter 14 to learn how to make stylesheets that can run in both kinds of processor. The stylesheets we've been using can't run with XSLT 1.0 processors, so there aren't any long examples in this section.

The easiest way of using a client-side transformation is to let the browser pick up on which stylesheet to use from the `xml-stylesheet` processing instruction at the top of the XML document. For example, including the following `xml-stylesheet` processing instruction at the top of `TVGuide.xml` tells the browser to use `TVGuide.xsl` to transform the XML document:

```
<?xml-stylesheet type="text/xsl" href="TVGuide.xsl"?>
```

When a browser that supports client-side transformations sees the `xml-stylesheet` processing instruction, it tries to locate the referenced stylesheet and applies it using its built-in XSLT processor (MSXML for Internet Explorer, TransforMiiX for Mozilla/Firefox) automatically, displaying the result of the transformation viewed as an HTML page.

As we saw earlier, there is another method of managing client-side transformations: using a script within an HTML page. Using a script gives you much greater control over the execution of the transformation, in particular allowing you to pass in parameters to the stylesheet. In this section, we'll look at how to perform transformations using scripted client-side transformations.

Loading Sarissa

The first step in using Sarissa is to load the ECMAScript library into your HTML page. This is as easy as pointing at the `sarissa.js` file that comes with the Sarissa distribution using a `<script>` element:

```
<script type="text/javascript" src="sarissa.js">
</script>
```

Caution Both Internet Explorer and Mozilla/Firefox require the closing `</script>` tag to load the script.

The `sarissa.js` file contains all the functions that you really need to load and transform XML documents. Three other ECMAScript libraries come with Sarissa:

- `sarissa_dhtml.js` contains utility code for loading XML or the results of transforming XML into an existing node. This is particularly useful when replacing part of the page with the results of a transformation, as we'll see later.
- `sarissa_ieemu_xpath.js` contains implementations of the `selectSingleNode()` and `selectNodes()` methods that allow you to select nodes using an XPath expression. This can be useful if you want to extract information from an XML document for use within your JavaScript code.
- `sarissa_ieemu_xslt.js` contains deprecated code for performing XSLT transformations, which you shouldn't use.

■ **Summary** Load Sarissa by importing `sarissa.js` into your HTML page with the `<script>` element.

Creating DOMs

The first step in scripting a client-side transformation is to parse the source XML document and the stylesheet to create a **document object model** (DOM) of each. DOMs are abstract representations of the node trees for documents, held in memory. You create a DOM to hold information from an XML document or XSLT stylesheet in three stages:

- Create a Document object.
- Load the XML document into the Document object.
- Check that the XML document has loaded properly.

Creating Document Objects

The `Sarissa.getDomDocument()` method creates a new Document object. For example, you would use

```
var xmlDOM = Sarissa.getDomDocument();
```

■ **Summary** You create a Document object with `Sarissa.getDomDocument()`.

Loading the XML Document or Stylesheet

Loading an XML document or stylesheet into the Document object that you've created for it is simply a matter of calling the `load()` method on the Document object. The `load()` method takes a single argument—the location of the file that you want to load into the Document object.

For example, to load the file `TVGuide.xml` into the new Document object (assuming that `TVGuide.xml` was in the same directory as the script), you would use the following JavaScript:

```
xmlDOM.load('TVGuide.xml');
```

You can load a document asynchronously or synchronously, determined by the `async` property, which you can set before loading the file. The default is asynchronously, which means that the code after the call on the `load()` method is executed while the file is loaded, and you have to set up a handler function that detects when the loading is finished. I usually use synchronous loading, such as the following:

```
var xmlDOM = Sarissa.getDomDocument();
xmlDOM.async = false;
xmlDOM.load('TVGuide.xml');
```

■ **Summary** You can load a document into the Document object using the `load()` method. Setting the `async` flag to `false` ensures that the rest of the code is only executed once the file has been loaded.

Checking for Parse Errors

There are several things that can go wrong during loading. For example, the document might not be accessible, it might not be well-formed, or, if you're validating the document, it might not be valid.

■ **Caution** XML documents will automatically be validated by Internet Explorer if you supply either a DTD or point to a schema (via the `xsi:noNamespaceSchemaLocation` or `xsi:schemaLocation` attributes), and there's no way of preventing this validation from occurring. If you do point to a DTD or schema from your document, make sure that it's accessible and that the document is valid against it, or you won't be able to work with the document.

Errors in the loading of an XML document or stylesheet don't generate exceptions—instead, you need to look at the `parseError` property of the Document object to see if the document has been loaded properly. The `parseError` property returns an integer; anything other than `0` means that there's been an error of some kind.

If there has been an error, then you can use the `Sarissa.getParseErrorText()` method on the Document object to get an error message:

```
if (xmlDOM.parseError != 0) {
  /* parse error */
  alert(Sarissa.getParseErrorText(xmlDOM));
}
```

■ **Summary** You can see whether there's been an error loading a document by checking the `parseError` property of the Document object, and get a detailed error message using `Sarissa.getParseErrorText()`.

Performing Transformations

Having a Document object for the stylesheet does not immediately enable you to transform the XML document using the stylesheet. Creating the Document object for the stylesheet reads in the stylesheet as an XML document like any other. Now you need to tell the XSLT processor to consider the stylesheet as an XSLT stylesheet, to compile it to create some runnable code that can be used against the XML document to create a result.

Creating a Compiled Stylesheet

In Sarissa, **XSLTProcessor objects** hold the result of compiling a stylesheet DOM, which can be used to perform multiple transformations. You need to create an XSLTProcessor object:

```
var xslProcessor = new XSLTProcessor();
```

There's only one thing you need to do to configure the XSLTProcessor object, and that's to import the stylesheet DOM:

```
xslProcessor.importStylesheet(xslDOM);
```

When you import the stylesheet into the XSLTProcessor object, the processor checks the stylesheet to make sure that it's valid. For example, it checks that all the XSLT elements are arranged in the way that they should be and that the XPaths that you use follow the XPath syntax. If there's anything wrong with the way that your stylesheet is constructed, importing the stylesheet raises an exception, which will be displayed to the user as a JavaScript error if it's not caught.

■ **Note** In Firefox, the error is raised when you actually try to perform a transformation using the invalid stylesheet; either way, you need to catch it.

You can catch this error using a `try-catch` statement around the part of your code where you import the stylesheet into the XSLTProcessor object. If you wish, you can display the cause of the exception using the `description` property of the exception. For example:

```
try {
  var xslProcessor = new XSLTProcessor();
  xslProcessor.importStylesheet(xslDOM);
  ...
} catch (exception) {
  alert(exception.description);
}
```

■ **Summary** To run a stylesheet, you need to create an XSLTProcessor object and import the stylesheet with its `importStylesheet()` method.

Doing the Transformation

Once you've created the XSLTProcessor object, you need to transform the source document into a result document with the transformToDocument() method, with

```
var resultDOM = xslProcessor.transformToDocument(xmlDOM);
```

Caution To work in Internet Explorer, the result of the transformation must be a well-formed document. Most importantly, that means it can only have one document element.

Running the transformation can also cause exceptions to be raised, if, for example, you try within the stylesheet to treat a string as a node set or to access an inaccessible document using the document() function. Again, then, you should wrap the code enacting the transformation within a try-catch statement, which could be the same as the one that you use when importing the stylesheet into the XSLTProcessor object:

```
try {
  var xslProcessor = new XSLTProcessor();
  xslProcessor.importStylesheet(xslDOM);
  var resultDOM = xslProcessor.transformToDocument(xmlDOM);
  ...
} catch (exception) {
  alert(exception.description);
}
```

Summary To run a transformation, call the transformToDocument() method on the XSLTProcessor object, which results in a new Document object.

Handling Output

You can simply serialize the result of your transformation (or indeed any Document object) with the Sarissa.serialize() method. This results in a string that you can then put in an alert box or write to the document:

```
document.write(Sarissa.serialize(resultDOM));
```

However, there are a couple of other ways of handling the output of the transformation that make better use of the fact you're doing the transformation dynamically and on the client side.

Replacing Part of the Page

It's often handy to only replace a part of the HTML with the result of the transformation, in particular because this allows you to reuse the same Document and XSLTProcessor objects multiple times.

You can replace the content of a particular element with the content of a document using the Sarissa.updateContentFromNode() method that's included in the sarissa_dhtml.js library. This normally takes two arguments: the Document object whose content you want to use and the element in which you want to put it. For example, if you have the following HTML document containing the script that's performing the transformation:

```
<html>
  <head>
    <title>TV Listing</title>
    <script type="text/javascript" href="sarissa.js">
    </script>
    <script type="text/javascript" href="sarissa_dhtml.js">
    </script>
    <script type="text/javascript">
      ... your code ...
    </script>
  </head>
  <body id="result">
  </body>
</html>
```

then you can load the result of the transformation into the <body> element with

```
Sarissa.updateContentFromNode(resultDOM, result);
```

Sarissa also offers a slight shortcut, in that you can give an optional third argument that specifies an XSLTProcessor object that's used to transform the Document object given as the first argument. So you can also do the following:

```
Sarissa.updateContentFromNode(xmlDOM, result, xslProcessor);
```

Even quicker, the Sarissa.updateContentFromURI() method accepts a URI for an XML document as the first argument, but otherwise works in the same way:

```
Sarissa.updateContentFromURI('TVGuide.xml', result, xslProcessor);
```

though note that this method doesn't allow you to reuse the XML document in different transformations as efficiently as reusing the Document object.

If you use this method, remember to make sure that the stylesheet generates something that can be placed in the content of the element that you're using. For example, the stylesheet shouldn't generate an <html> element if you're replacing the content of the <body> element.

Summary You can replace the content of an element in your HTML page with a Document object using the Sarissa.updateContentFromNode() method.

Continuing Processing

When we looked at Cocoon, we saw that multiple transformations could be joined together in a pipeline, with each transformation using the result of the previous transformation as the source for its own transformation, until finally the result of the last transformation was serialized.

You can pipeline the results of a transformation to another stylesheet using code by passing the Document object that was the result of the transformation as the argument to the `transformToDocument()` function, or even importing it into an XSLTProcessor object as a stylesheet. For example, to use `resultDOM` as the source of another transformation, and display the result of that, you could simply do the following:

```
var secondXSLProcessor = new XSLTProcessor();
secondXSLProcessor.importStylesheet(secondStylesheetDOM);
var secondResultDOM = secondXSLProcessor.transformToDocument(resultDOM);
Sarissa.updateContentFromNode(secondResultDOM, result);
```

Summary Since it's just another Document object, you can use the result of one transformation as the source (or stylesheet) for another.

Passing Parameters

The fact that you're running the transformation from code rather than letting the browser do it automatically hasn't gained you much so far, since all you're doing is exactly what the browser would do—displaying the results of the basic transformation of `TVGuide.xml` with `TVGuide.xsl`.

One of the benefits of using code, however, is the fact that you can pass parameters in to the stylesheet. Once you've generated an XSLTProcessor object and imported the stylesheet, and before you run the transformation, you can set the values of parameters using the `setParameter()` method. The `setParameter()` method takes three arguments: the namespace of the parameter (usually an empty string), the name of the parameter, and the value of the parameter. For example, to set the `$userID` parameter to `'JeniT'`, you could use

```
xslProcessor.setParameter('', 'userID', 'JeniT');
```

You can reset the parameters on a particular XSLTProcessor multiple times to provide different transformations based on the same stylesheet and source document, for example, to re-sort the rows of a table in different ways according to which column is clicked. If you want to check what values were last used for a particular parameter, use the `getParameter()` method. This takes two arguments, the namespace and local name of the parameter, and returns the value for the parameter that was previously passed to the XSLTProcessor object.

Summary You can pass a parameter in to the stylesheet using the `setParameter()` method on the XSLTProcessor object.

Summary

Although it's useful to run transformations from the command line while developing XSLT stylesheets, most XSLT applications use either server-side or client-side processing (or both). Client-side and server-side processing allow you to create dynamic applications that react to updates in the source XML or in the stylesheet, and also allow the user to pass in parameters to stylesheets to create different pages in different circumstances.

You've learned in this chapter about two applications that support dynamic transformations: Cocoon for server-side transformations and Sarissa for client-side transformations. These aren't the only applications that are available to you—there are other servlets that you can use on the server side, such as AxKit and XSQL, and other browsers that you can use on the client side that aren't supported by Sarissa, such as the Antenna House Formatter and XSmiles—but they are the two that are best developed and most widely used.

You've learned the principles underlying Cocoon's treatment of HTTP requests, and seen how to configure it for common tasks, such as delivering HTML documents, automatically transforming XML, delivering different results to different browsers, and using parameters. If you continue working with Cocoon, you will learn about the different types of generators, transformers, serializers, matchers, and selectors that you can use with it. The user documentation on Cocoon, at `http://cocoon.apache.org/2.1/userdocs/index.html`, contains further details about each of these, and if you get into the details, you'll probably find the API documentation at `http://cocoon.apache.org/2.1/apidocs/` handy.

You have also been shown how to script transformations using Sarissa. We've looked at the necessary objects, properties, and methods for running transformations, how to pass parameters in to those transformations, and a couple of ways of using the result of the transformations. If you continue working with Sarissa and client-side processing in general, you will come to be familiar with manipulating DOMs. You can find details about the standard DOM API at `http://www.w3.org/TR/DOM-Level-3-Core/`.

Review Questions

1. What are the advantages and disadvantages of using server-side or client-side transformations?

2. Which three steps are involved in a pipeline in Cocoon?

3. What file do you have to edit to configure Cocoon?

4. How does Cocoon choose which pipeline to use given a particular HTTP request?

5. Introduce a new subdirectory called `Films`, with its own sitemap, to your local version of Cocoon.

6. Add directives such that when you view `http://localhost:8888/Films/index`, you get a list of the films held in `Films.xml`, transformed using `Films.xsl`.

7. Add instructions so that when Internet Explorer 6 requests `http://localhost:8888/Films/index`, Cocoon delivers the raw XML of `Films.xml` rather than running the transformation on the server side.

8. Edit `Films.xsl` so that it accepts a `$film` parameter and displays only those films that start with the string held by the `$film` parameter. Use Cocoon to enable users to pass in the parameter in two ways:

   - Using part of the URL: `http://localhost:8888/Films/Leon`
   - Using a request parameter: `http://localhost:8888/Films?film=Leon`

9. Using Sarissa, write a utility function called `parseXMLDocument()` that returns a Document object for an XML file when passed a filename. If the file is inaccessible or not well formed, the function should create an alert giving details of the error and return null.

10. Using Sarissa, write a utility function called `createXSLTProcessor()` that returns an XSLTProcessor object for an XSLT stylesheet. If the stylesheet isn't a valid stylesheet, then the function should create an alert giving details of the error and return null.

11. Write a utility function called `performTransformation()` that returns the result of a transformation run with a particular XSLTProcessor and source document given an array of pairs of parameter names and values.

12. Use your utility functions in an HTML page where you enter the start of a name of a film in an input field and it displays a list of all the films in `Films.xml` that start with that string, by transforming using a suitably modified `Films.xsl`. Remember to do as much as you can at a global level in the script, so that you cache the Document and XSLTProcessor objects.

CHAPTER 16

Creating SVG

SVG, which stands for **Scalable Vector Graphics**, is a markup language for describing images. SVG is an important markup language for use with XSLT because it allows you to use XSLT to create graphics from XML data—something that XSLT would normally struggle to do since most graphic formats are binary formats.

In most uses of SVG, graphics are embedded within an HTML page. You might create a menu list, a graph, a pie chart, a tree, animations, or buttons using SVG. In some cases, where you need a great amount of control over the look of a page, you could even create the entire page using SVG. SVG can be used in many cases where you include graphics in your page, as well as those that use Flash to create dynamic and reactive graphics.

In this chapter, you'll learn

- How to write a simple SVG document
- How to create simple graphics
- How to link from SVG to other documents
- How to use XSLT to generate SVG
- How to embed SVG within an HTML page

Introducing SVG

SVG is a markup language dedicated to expressing the appearance, animation, and interactivity of images. SVG documents define graphics as **vector graphics** rather than bitmaps, for example, which means that you can scale and zoom in and out of SVG graphics without losing detail.

Note For further information about SVG, the SVG 1.1 Recommendation is available at `http://www.w3.org/TR/SVG11/`.

To view SVG, you need to download an application that understands and renders SVG. A good application for Windows is the SVG Viewer from Adobe, which can act as a browser plug-in and is available at `http://www.adobe.com/svg/viewer/install/main.html`. When you open an SVG document, your browser should activate the SVG Viewer, so that the SVG is displayed within the browser window.

■ Note A full list of SVG implementations is available from the W3C pages at `http://www.w3.org/Graphics/SVG/SVG-Implementations.htm8`.

For example, try viewing the simple SVG graphic in Listing 16-1 (`circle.svg`) after installing SVG Viewer.

Listing 16-1. `circle.svg`

```
<svg width="12cm" height="4cm" viewBox="0 0 1200 400"
     xmlns="http://www.w3.org/2000/svg">
  <circle r="100" cx="600" cy="200"
          fill="#C00" stroke="black" stroke-width="10"  />
</svg>
```

You should see a red circle with a black border in the browser window, as shown in Figure 16-1.

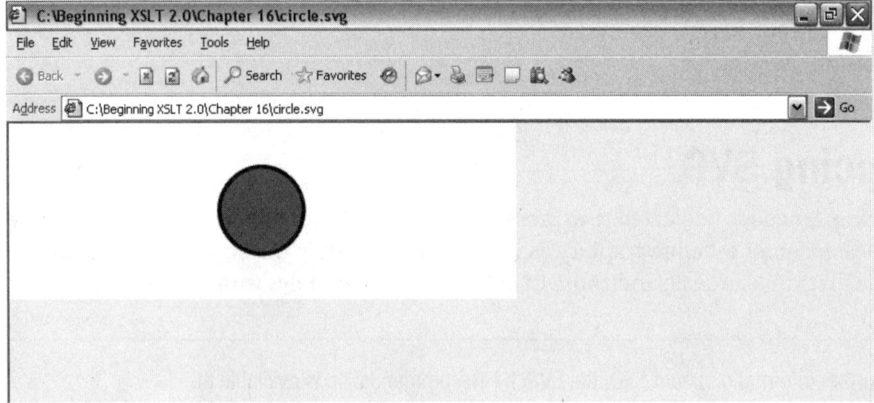

Figure 16-1. *Viewing* `circle.svg` *in Internet Explorer*

This looks just the same as a bitmap image. For example, Figure 16-2 shows `circle.bmp` in Microsoft Paint at a normal zoom.

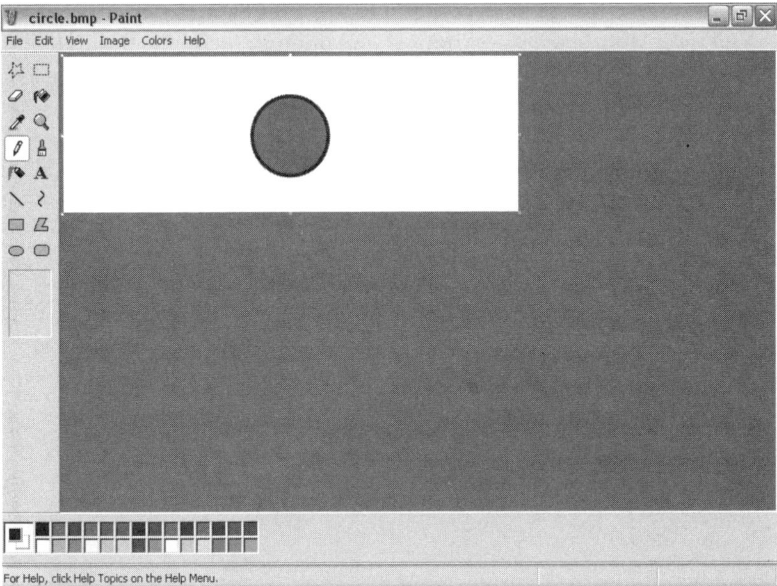

Figure 16-2. *Viewing* `circle.bmp` *in Paint at normal zoom*

The bitmap circle looks smooth at this resolution, but when you zoom in to the circle's edge, you start to see the pixels that make up the picture, as shown in Figure 16-3.

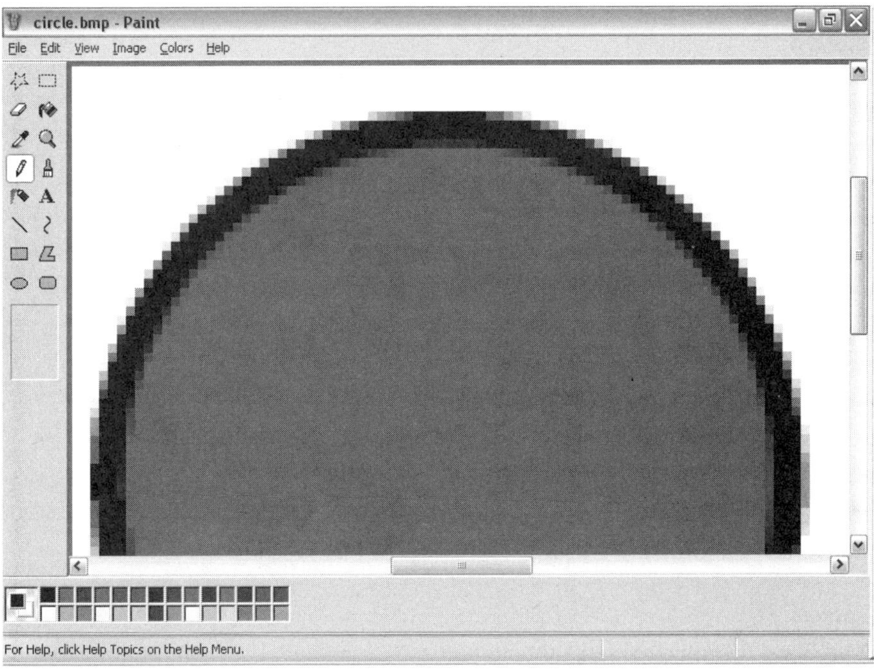

Figure 16-3. *Viewing* `circle.bmp` *in Paint at 8x zoom*

If, using Adobe's SVG Viewer, you bring up the context menu for the SVG graphic in Internet Explorer (right-click the picture), then you'll see various useful options, including the ability to zoom in to the image. You can use this context menu to zoom in to the edge of the circle, as shown in Figure 16-4.

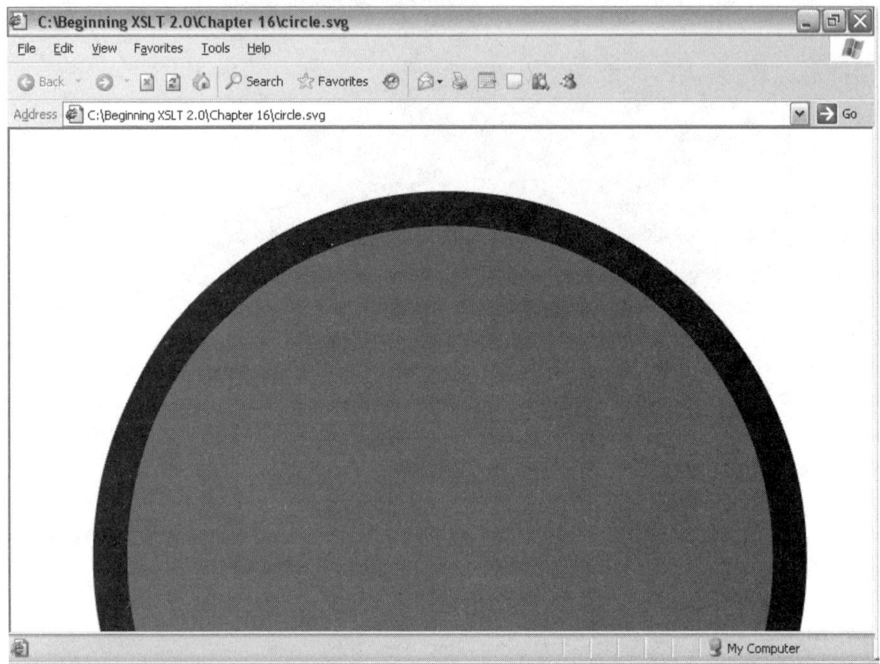

Figure 16-4. *Viewing* `circle.svg` *in Internet Explorer at 8x zoom*

Notice that no matter how closely you zoom in to the image, the edge never becomes pixilated. This demonstrates the advantage of vector graphics over bitmaps.

Like any other markup language, SVG uses namespaces to distinguish between elements that are part of SVG and elements that are part of other markup languages (which might be included in the SVG graphic, such as XHTML or XLink). The namespace for SVG elements is

```
http://www.w3.org/2000/svg
```

■ **Tip** You may notice that some SVG graphics don't include a namespace declaration for this namespace. That's because the DTD for SVG includes an attribute declaration for an attribute named `xmlns` that effectively declares the default namespace. I recommend that you always include the namespace declaration explicitly, so that the SVG graphic is readable even if the DTD isn't available for some reason.

The document element of an SVG document is an `<svg>` element. Inside the `<svg>` element are the elements used to construct the image. But before we start looking at how graphics are drawn, it's worth having a quick look at how coordinates work within SVG.

Lengths and Coordinates

Aside from the namespace declaration, the `<svg>` element can define the size of the SVG graphic using the `height` and `width` attributes. These attributes describe the default size of the **canvas**, which is the area in which the graphic is displayed. These values may be overridden when the SVG graphic is embedded within an HTML page (or even within another SVG graphic).

You can also specify a `viewBox` attribute on the `<svg>` element, which holds four numbers separated by spaces: minimum x-coordinate, minimum y-coordinate, width, and height. The `viewBox` attribute defines a coordinate system used when defining lengths within the graphic and defines the size of a **user unit**. For example, in `circle.svg` the `viewBox` attribute defined a coordinate system starting at (0, 0), spanning 1200 user units in width and 400 user units in height. This sets up a grid as shown in Figure 16-5.

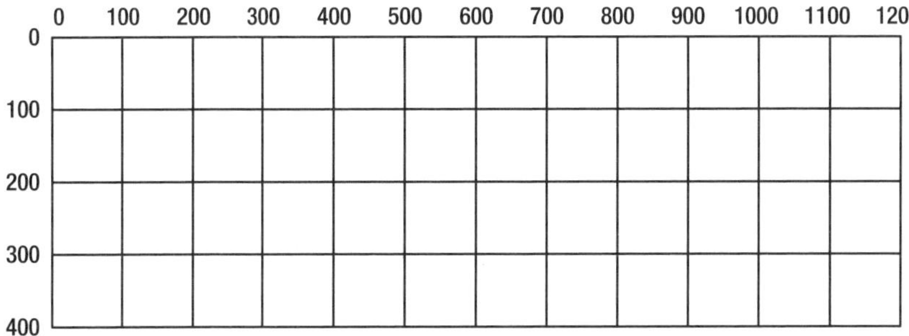

Figure 16-5. *A 1200×400 view box*

The graphic as a whole has a width of 12 cm and a height of 4 cm, corresponding to the width of 1200 user units and the height of 400 user units. Thus 100 user units on the grid correspond to 1 cm in the page. If the width had instead been set to 24 cm and the height to 8 cm, then 100 user units on the grid would correspond to 2 cm in the page; if the width had been set to 600 mm and the height to 200 mm, then 100 user units would correspond to 50 mm.

In the rest of the image, most lengths and coordinates are described relative to this grid. For example, take another look at the definition of the circle:

```
<circle r="100" cx="600" cy="200"
        fill="#C00" stroke="black" stroke-width="10" />
```

The radius of the circle (specified with the `r` attribute) is defined as 100 user units and the center of the circle (specified with the `cx` and `cy` attributes) is at the coordinate (600, 200), which is the center of the grid. When displayed in the page, the circle should have a 1 cm radius and be placed 6 cm across and 2 cm down the page, because 100 user units is equivalent to 1 cm.

If the width of the image is 12 cm and the height 8 cm (such that the ratio of units to length on the width is different from the ratio of units to length on the height), then the `preserveAspectRatio` attribute comes into play. Usually, one user unit will be the same distance horizontally and vertically, with the grid aligned in the center of the image, as in Figure 16-6, which shows `circle2.svg`.

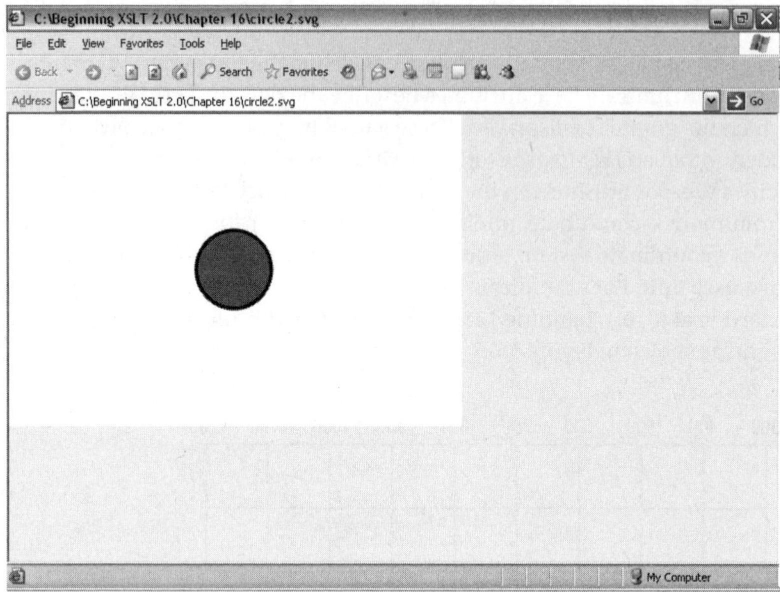

Figure 16-6. *Viewing* `circle2.svg` *in Internet Explorer*

However, if you set `preserveAspectRatio` on the `<svg>` element to `none`, then the actual size of the horizontal and vertical user units can be different, and the circle will be stretched as required to fill the image area on the page, as in Figure 16-7, which shows `circle3.svg`.

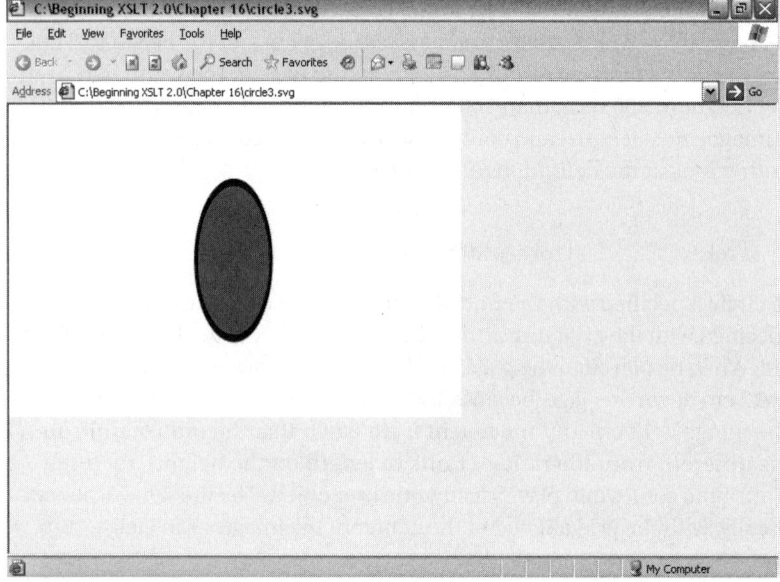

Figure 16-7. *Viewing* `circle3.svg` *in Internet Explorer*

You can use other units of length within SVG. One useful type of length is a percentage length, which calculates a length based on the width or height of the image. For example, the radius and center of the circle could be specified with the following:

```
<svg width="12cm" height="4cm" viewBox="0 0 1200 400"
     xmlns="http://www.w3.org/2000/svg">
  <circle r="11.18%" cx="50%" cy="50%"
          fill="#C00" stroke="black" stroke-width="1.118%"  />
</svg>
```

Note Percentages other than for x, y coordinates are worked out relative to a combination of the number of user units making up the height and width of the image, which is why 100 user units corresponds to 11.18%.

Other units look like absolute units, but when they are used within the SVG graphic (rather than being used to set the height and width of the SVG graphic), they are actually calculated based on user units. These units are

- `px`—1 px is equivalent to 1 user unit.
- `pt`—1 pt is equivalent to 1.25 user units.
- `pc`—1 pc is equivalent to 15 user units.
- `in`—1 in is equivalent to 90 user units.
- `mm`—1 mm is equivalent to 3.543307 user units.
- `cm`—1 cm is equivalent to 35.43307 user units.

When you use text within an SVG graphic, it's also handy to be able to specify lengths relative to the size of the text that you're using. You can do this with the following units:

- `em`—1 em is equivalent to the size of the current font.
- `ex`—1 ex is equivalent to the x-height of the current font.

Graphic Elements

The most important elements held within an SVG document are **graphic elements**, which draw shapes on the screen. The graphic elements in SVG are

- `<line>`—Draws a straight line
- `<polyline>`—Draws a line made up of multiple straight segments
- `<rect>`—Draws a rectangle (or square)
- `<circle>`—Draws a circle
- `<ellipse>`—Draws an ellipse

- <polygon>—Draws a shape whose outline can be described by multiple contiguous straight lines, such as triangles or stars
- <path>—Draws any line or the outline of any shape, including shapes with holes in the middle, for example
- <text>—Adds some text to the graphic
- <image>—Adds a PNG, JPEG, or SVG image to the graphic
- <use>—Refers to and includes other elements from the SVG document

---

■ **Note** The <use> graphic element reuses graphic elements that you've used elsewhere. We're not going to go into the <use> element here, but you can read more about it in the SVG 1.1 Recommendation at http://www.w3.org/TR/SVG11/struct.html#UseElement.

The order in which you include graphic elements is important, as later graphics are overlaid on earlier graphics. For example, the SVG graphic in Listing 16-2 (2circles.svg) contains two <circle> elements.

Listing 16-2. 2circles.svg

```
<svg width="12cm" height="4cm" viewBox="0 0 1200 400"
     xmlns="http://www.w3.org/2000/svg">
  <circle r="100" cx="550" cy="200"
          fill="#C00" stroke="black" stroke-width="10"  />
  <circle r="100" cx="650" cy="200"
          fill="#C00" stroke="black" stroke-width="10"  />
</svg>
```

The second circle is displayed over the first circle, giving the graphic shown in Figure 16-8.

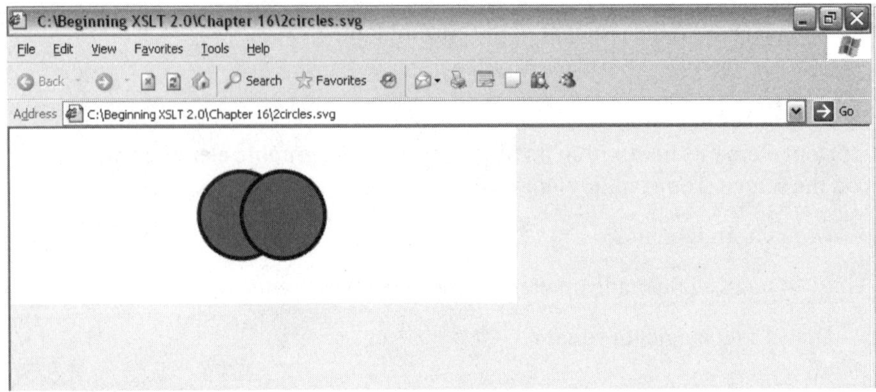

Figure 16-8. *Viewing* 2circles.svg *in Internet Explorer*

Each of the graphic elements has attributes that position the graphic and control its precise size, shape, and color. Now we'll quickly go through each of the graphic elements to describe how their position, size, shape, and appearance are determined.

Lines

Lines are the simplest of the graphical elements. They start at one point on the canvas and end up at another point. The `<line>` element has two pairs of attributes to describe the start point and the end point of the line:

- `x1` and `y1` specify the coordinate of the start of the line.
- `x2` and `y2` specify the coordinate of the end of the line.

All these attributes default to 0 (the top left of the image) if you don't specify them explicitly.

The style of the line is determined by the **stroke properties** of the line, which are a set of attributes as follows:

- `stroke`—The color of the line, which can be a keyword, a color specification (as in CSS or a reference to a color), or a gradient defined earlier in the graphic or in a separate file
- `stroke-opacity`—The opacity of the line; a number between 0 (transparent) and 1 (opaque)
- `stroke-width`—The width of the line
- `stroke-linecap`—How the end of the line is drawn; one of `butt` (square, stopping at the end of the line, the default), `round`, or `square` (square, stopping half the `stroke-width` over the end of the line)
- `stroke-dasharray`—The pattern of dashes and spaces that are used to draw the line as a series of comma-separated values giving, alternately, the length of dashes and spaces
- `stroke-dashoffset`—The point within the dash array at which the line starts

To demonstrate these attributes in action, look at the `<line>` element in `line.svg`, as in Listing 16-3.

Listing 16-3. `line.svg`

```
<svg width="12cm" height="4cm" viewBox="0 0 1200 400"
     xmlns="http://www.w3.org/2000/svg">
  <line x1="400" y1="200" x2="800" y2="200"
        stroke="red" stroke-opacity="0.25"
        stroke-width="25" stroke-linecap="round"
        stroke-dasharray="25,50,75,50" stroke-dashoffset="50" />
</svg>
```

The line starts at (400, 200) and ends at (800, 200) within the image. It's red, but has an opacity of 0.25, which means it's fairly transparent. The width of the line is 25 user units, and its ends are rounded, which means that the end of the line actually extends 12.5 user units (half the width of the line) past the end coordinate. The line is dashed, the pattern being a dash 25 user units long followed by a space 50 user units long, followed by a dash 75 user units long, followed by a space 50 user units long (this pattern is repeated for the length of the line). The line starts 50 user units into this dash pattern—halfway through the first space—so it begins with the rest of the space (25 user units), and the first dash that's drawn is 75 user units long. The line looks as shown in Figure 16-9.

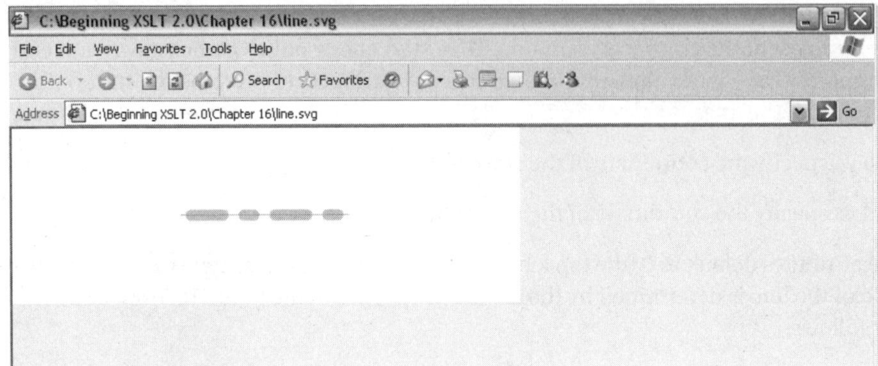

Figure 16-9. *Viewing* `line.svg` *in Internet Explorer*

The stroke properties are used with other elements (including polylines and paths) specifically when drawing the outlines of shapes like rectangles and circles.

Polylines

The `<polyline>` element gives a line made up of multiple straight lines. The coordinates of the points along the line are specified within the `points` attribute, which holds space-separated pairs of numbers representing x, y coordinates.

All the stroke properties that can be used with `<line>` can also be used with the `<polyline>` element to give different colors, widths, dash patterns, and so on in the line. Another stroke property is applicable to polylines, specifically the `stroke-linejoin` property, which determines how corners are drawn. The default value is `miter`, which means that the corner is drawn as an angle; the other permissible values are `round`, which rounds the corners, and `bevel`, which chops off the corners.

To see polylines in practice and the difference between the different `stroke-linejoin` attributes, try the SVG elements in Listing 16-4, `polyline.svg`.

Listing 16-4. `polyline.svg`

```
<svg width="12cm" height="4cm" viewBox="0 0 1200 400"
     xmlns="http://www.w3.org/2000/svg">
  <polyline points="200,300 300,100 400,300" fill="none"
            stroke="black" stroke-width="25"
            stroke-linecap="butt" stroke-linejoin="miter" />
  <polyline points="500,300 600,100 700,300" fill="none"
            stroke="black" stroke-width="25"
            stroke-linecap="round" stroke-linejoin="round" />
  <polyline points="800,300 900,100 1000,300" fill="none"
```

```
            stroke="black" stroke-width="25"
            stroke-linecap="square" stroke-linejoin="bevel" />
</svg>
```

All the lines are stroked in black, 25 user units in width. The first polyline goes from the coordinate (200, 300) to (300, 100) to (400, 300), and the other polylines follow the same kind of pattern, but offset across the image. The first polyline uses the default line cap and line join values of `butt` and `miter`, giving square ends at the point where the line ends and an angular join. The second polyline has rounded line ends and a rounded corner. The third polyline has square ends (if you look carefully, you can see that they extend a little further than the `butt` ends of the first polyline) and a cut-off (`bevel`) corner. The lines look as shown in Figure 16-10.

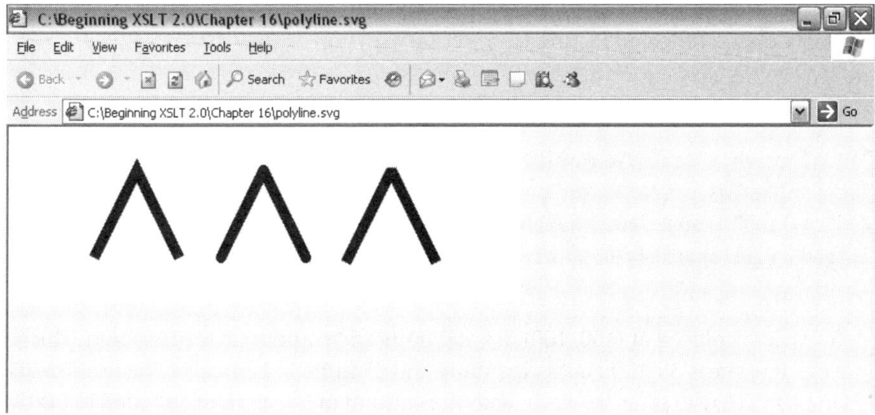

Figure 16-10. *Viewing* `polyline.svg` *in Internet Explorer*

■ **Note** You'll note that each of the `<line>` elements given in the preceding text have a `fill` attribute with a value of `none`. A polyline can be used like a polygon (see "Polygons," later) to give any shape whose outline can be described by straight lines; but it is not automatically closed, so it is generally used for open lines, and usually the `fill` attribute should take the value `none`.

Rectangles

Rectangles (and squares) are drawn using the `<rect>` element. The size and shape of the rectangle are determined by three pairs of attributes:

- `x` and `y` specify the coordinate of the top-left corner of the rectangle.
- `width` and `height` specify the width and height of the rectangle and are required.
- For rounded rectangles, `rx` and `ry` specify the horizontal and vertical radii of the ellipse used on the corners.

If you don't give coordinates for x or y, the rectangle is placed in the top-left corner of the canvas. A rectangle will only have rounded corners if you specify one of rx or ry; if you only specify one of this pair, then the other of the pair defaults to the value of the first, and you get circular corners.

As well as the stroke properties (including stroke-linejoin) that we've already seen, rectangles and other similar graphics all have **fill properties** that describe the color of the content of the shape. There are two fill properties:

- fill—Specifies the color of the body of the shape, which again can be a keyword, a hexadecimal color, or a reference to a color or gradient defined elsewhere
- fill-opacity—Indicates the opacity of the fill; can be a number between 0 (transparent) and 1 (opaque)

For example, try the rectangle in Listing 16-5, rectangle.svg.

Listing 16-5. rectangle.svg

```
<svg width="12cm" height="4cm" viewBox="0 0 1200 400"
     xmlns="http://www.w3.org/2000/svg">
  <rect x="400" y="100" width="400" height="200" rx="50" ry="25"
        fill="red" fill-opacity="0.5" stroke="black" stroke-width="10" />
</svg>
```

The top-left corner is placed at (400, 100), it's 400 units wide, and it's 200 units high. The rounding of the corners starts 50 units in horizontally and 25 units in vertically. The outline of the rectangle is in black, 10 user units in width, with the content of the rectangle shaded in partly transparent red. The resulting rectangle looks as shown in Figure 16-11.

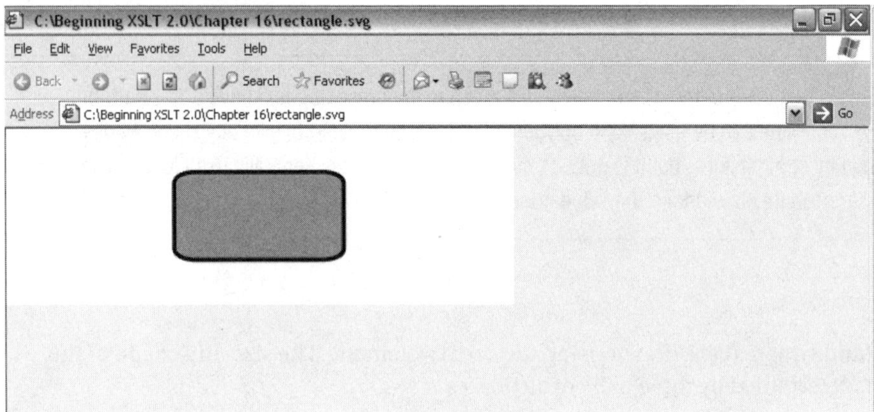

Figure 16-11. *Viewing* rectangle.svg *in Internet Explorer*

Circles

You've already seen circles in action in circle.svg and 2circles.svg. The <circle> element has three attributes that determine its location:

- cx and cy give the coordinates for the center of the circle.
- r specifies the radius of the circle and is required.

If you don't give an x, y coordinate for the center of the circle, then it will be drawn with its center being the top-left corner of the canvas. As with rectangles, you can specify stroke and fill properties to determine the look of the circle.

Ellipses

Ellipses are very similar to circles aside from the fact that you need two radii to describe them—a horizontal radius and a vertical radius. The <ellipse> element therefore has two pairs of attributes to determine its location and size:

- cx and cy give the coordinates for the center of the ellipse.
- rx and ry specify the horizontal and vertical radius of the ellipse respectively and are required.

Again, if you don't specify an x, y coordinate for the center of the ellipse, then it is drawn with its center in the top-left corner of the canvas. For example, try the SVG ellipse in Listing 16-6, ellipse.svg.

Listing 16-6. ellipse.svg

```
<svg width="12cm" height="4cm" viewBox="0 0 1200 400"
     xmlns="http://www.w3.org/2000/svg">
  <ellipse cx="600" cy="200" rx="200" ry="100"
           fill="#C00" stroke="black" stroke-width="10" />
</svg>
```

This ellipse is centered within the canvas and has a radius of 200 units horizontally, a radius of 100 units vertically, a black outline, and a red body. It is rendered as shown in Figure 16-12.

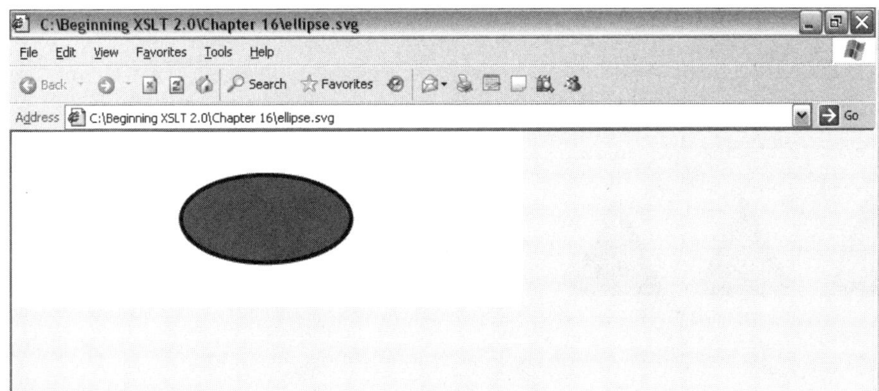

Figure 16-12. *Viewing* ellipse.svg *in Internet Explorer*

Polygons

Polygons are much like polylines, except that they are automatically closed to create a shape. They have a `points` attribute to specify the corners of the shape as pairs of coordinates, and they can take stroke properties to describe the line and fill properties to describe the interior of the shape.

■ **Note** Automatically closing the polygon means that the lines link up properly. You can make a polyline end at the same place that it begins, so that it describes the same shape as a polygon, but the start/end corner will be rendered in the end-of-line style rather than the corner style.

We can amend the `<polyline>` elements that we used earlier to give red triangles, for example, as in Listing 16-7, `polygon.svg`.

Listing 16-7. `polygon.svg`

```
<svg width="12cm" height="4cm" viewBox="0 0 1200 400"
     xmlns="http://www.w3.org/2000/svg">
  <polygon points="200,300 300,100 400,300" fill="red"
           stroke="black" stroke-width="25"
           stroke-linecap="butt" stroke-linejoin="miter" />
  <polygon points="500,300 600,100 700,300" fill="red"
           stroke="black" stroke-width="25"
           stroke-linecap="round" stroke-linejoin="round" />
  <polygon points="800,300 900,100 1000,300" fill="red"
           stroke="black" stroke-width="25"
           stroke-linecap="square" stroke-linejoin="bevel" />
</svg>
```

These three `<polygon>` elements are rendered as shown in Figure 16-13.

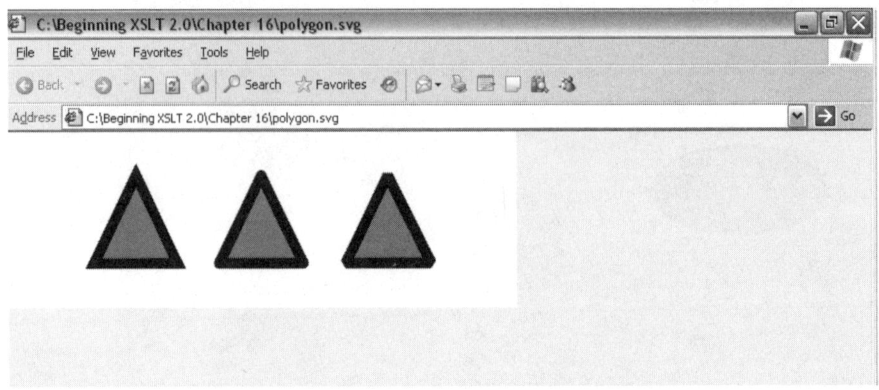

Figure 16-13. *Viewing* `polygon.svg` *in Internet Explorer*

Paths

Paths are a little like polylines, except that the segments in a path are not necessarily straight and are not necessarily stroked when the path is drawn. The description of a path is known as **path data** and is given in the d (data) attribute of the <path> element. Path data has a special syntax that is also used elsewhere in SVG.

Each SVG path consists of a number of **subpaths**, each describing a line. Each subpath consists of a number of **commands**, each of which is identified by a letter, often followed by parameters for the command. The letters that are used for the commands can be either uppercase or lowercase; uppercase indicates that absolute coordinates are used within the parameters for the command, while lowercase indicates that the coordinates are relative to the current location within the path. The basic commands available in SVG are as follows:

M (absolute) or m (relative)	Move to	"Lifts the pen off the paper" and moves to the specified point on the canvas without drawing a line
Z or z	Close path	Draws a line from the current point to the point at which the path started, closing the path
L (absolute) or l (relative)	Line to	Draws to the point specified
H (absolute) or h (relative)	Horizontal line to	Draws a horizontal line to the x-coordinate specified
V (absolute) or v (relative)	Vertical line to	Draws a vertical line to the y-coordinate specified

Each subpath starts with a move to command, and they often end with a close path command. For example, the following path consists of two subpaths. The first subpath starts at (600, 50), draws a line to a point 200 units right and 300 units down from there (which is (800, 350)), then draws a line 400 units left horizontally (in other words to (400, 350)), before closing the path (drawing a line back to (600, 50)). The second subpath begins at (600, 150), draws a line to the point (700, 300), and then draws a line to (500, 300) using the horizontal line to command, before closing the path:

```
M 600,50  l 200,300 h -400 Z
M 600,150 L 700,300 H  500 Z
```

The result of this path is two triangles set inside each other—one from the first subpath and one from the second subpath. The stroke and fill of the two triangles are the same, because they're both specified with the same path. However, you can make the "interior" of the shape include only the part between the two triangles by setting the fill-rule attribute to evenodd (which means that a point is "inside" the shape if drawing a line from that point to a point outside the canvas involves crossing an odd number of lines), as follows, from paths.svg:

```
<path d="M 600,50  l 200,300 h -400 Z
         M 600,150 L 700,300 H 500 Z"
      fill="red" fill-rule="evenodd"
      stroke="black" stroke-width="25"
      stroke-linecap="round" stroke-linejoin="round" />
```

When you view the SVG containing this path, you see the graphic shown in Figure 16-14.

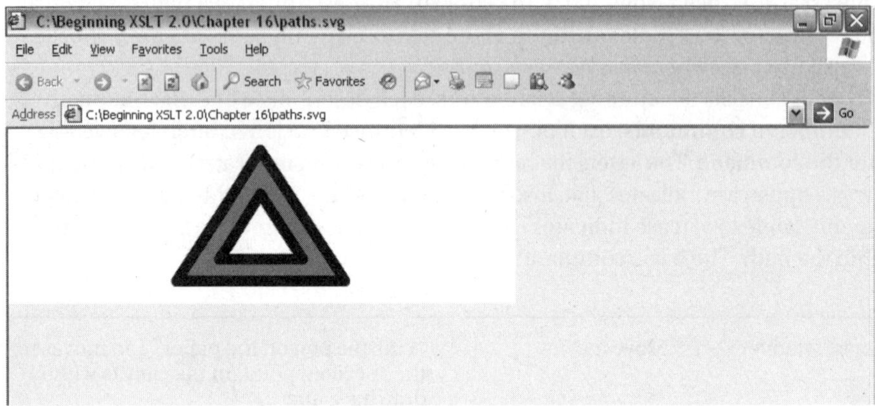

Figure 16-14. *Viewing* `paths.svg` *in Internet Explorer*

Being able to draw "hollow" shapes is one of the main advantages of paths over polygons. The other advantage that paths have over polygons and polylines is the ability to have some or all segments in the path curved. There are three types of curve that are supported by SVG:

- Cubic Bézier curves, defined by a start point, an end point, and two control points
- Quadratic Bézier curves, defined by a start point, an end point, and a control point
- Elliptical arcs, defined by a start point, an end point, x and y radii, rotation, and flags indicating whether to use a long or short arc that proceeds with a positive or negative angle

These commands are beyond the scope of this book, but the SVG Recommendation has a detailed description of each of them at `http://www.w3.org/TR/SVG11/paths.html#PathDataCurveCommands`.

Text

You can include text within an SVG image using the `<text>` element. The text itself is the content of the `<text>` element. The `x` and `y` attributes of the `<text>` element indicate the point at which the text is anchored. The `text-anchor` property determines how that point affects the position of the text; `start` (the default) indicates that the text starts at that point (giving left alignment), `end` that the text ends at that point (giving right alignment), and `middle` that the middle of the text is aligned at that point (giving center alignment).

The fill properties that you've already seen determine the color and opacity of the letters, while the stroke properties add an outline around the letters.

Selecting Fonts

As you might expect, `<text>` elements can also specify the kind of font that's used for the text using **font selection properties**. These properties mirror the properties that are available in CSS, but are represented as separate attributes on `<text>` elements:

- font-family—The name of the font that should be used, or the generic font family such as serif, sans-serif, or monospace
- font-size—An absolute or relative size, based on user units as usual
- font-weight—A keyword (normal, the default, or bold), a relative weight (bolder or lighter), or a number (one of 100, 200, 300, 400, 500, 600, 700, 800, or 900)
- font-style—One of normal (the default), italic, or oblique
- font-variant—One of normal (the default) or small-caps
- font-stretch—A keyword (ultra-condensed, extra-condensed, condensed, semi-condensed, normal [the default], semi-expanded, expanded, extra-expanded, or ultra-expanded) or a relative stretch (narrower or wider)

Many of these properties can be summarized in a single font attribute comprising any definitions of style, variant, or weight, followed by the font size, optionally followed by the font family. Alternatively, the font attribute can be used to derive font specifications from the viewer's environment by specifying the keywords caption, small-caption, menu, icon, message-box, or status-bar.

Highlighting Phrases

Text often contains phrases, words, or characters that should be rendered differently from the rest of the text. To support this in SVG, the <text> element can contain <tspan> elements, each of which has its own set of font selection properties. Each <tspan> element can have an explicit start point, specified through its x and y attributes, or be offset from the surrounding text using dx and dy attributes.

For example, Listing 16-8 (text.svg) includes a <text> element with an internal <tspan> element.

Listing 16-8. text.svg

```
<svg width="12cm" height="4cm" viewBox="0 0 1200 400"
     xmlns="http://www.w3.org/2000/svg">
  <text x="600" y="250" text-anchor="middle" font-size="150" fill="black">
    Learning
    <tspan stroke-width="5" font-weight="bold" fill="red"
           stroke="black" stroke-linejoin="round">SVG</tspan>
  </text>
</svg>
```

The <text> element contains the text "Learning SVG". The text is anchored with its middle at the point (600, 250). Note that the glyphs are rendered above this point vertically, so the value 250 indicates the vertical position of the baseline of the text. The "Learning" part of the text is in black, and the "SVG" part of the text is bold and in red with a black outline. When rendered, the SVG looks as shown in Figure 16-15.

One of the benefits of using SVG to render text rather than a binary image format like JPEG or GIF is that you can actually select the text in the image. Try selecting the string "Learning SVG" from the SVG image. To copy it in Adobe's SVG Viewer, you need to use the context menu and select the option Copy Selected Text; you can then paste it into other applications.

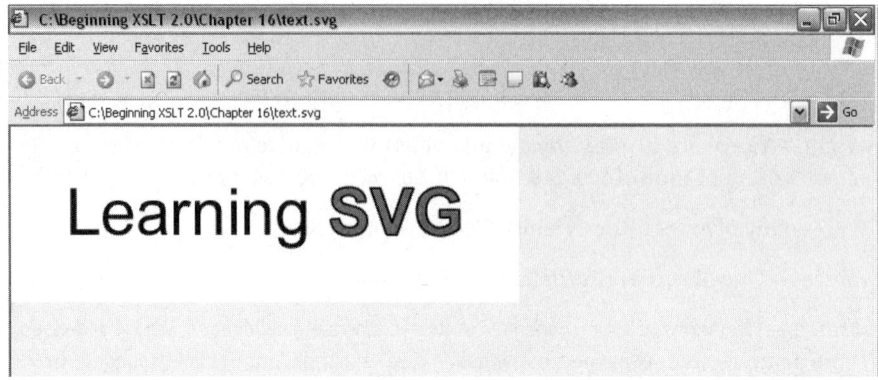

Figure 16-15. *Viewing* `text.svg` *in Internet Explorer*

Creating Lines

You have to be careful using text within SVG because SVG 1.1 does not include any automated word wrapping—it assumes that each `<text>` element represents a separate line of text, and clips any text that goes over the boundary. If you want a single `<text>` element to contain several lines of text, you can use `<tspan>` elements to represent each line.

■ Note SVG 1.2, which is under development at time of writing, includes methods for automatic text wrapping. See `http://www.w3.org/TR/SVG12/` for details.

For example, in Listing 16-9 (`textlines.svg`), the `<text>` element contains three `<tspan>` elements. The first `<tspan>` element starts at the coordinate (50, 120), the second `<tspan>` has the same x-coordinate but starts 100 user units below the first `<tspan>`, and the third `<tspan>` starts 100 user units below the second.

Listing 16-9. `textlines.svg`

```
<svg width="12cm" height="4cm" viewBox="0 0 1200 400"
     xmlns="http://www.w3.org/2000/svg">
  <text fill="black" font-size="70">
    <tspan x="50" y="120">First line of text.</tspan>
    <tspan x="50" dy="100">Second line of text.</tspan>
    <tspan x="50" dy="100">Third line of text.</tspan>
  </text>
</svg>
```

When you view `textlines.svg`, you should see the graphic shown in Figure 16-16.

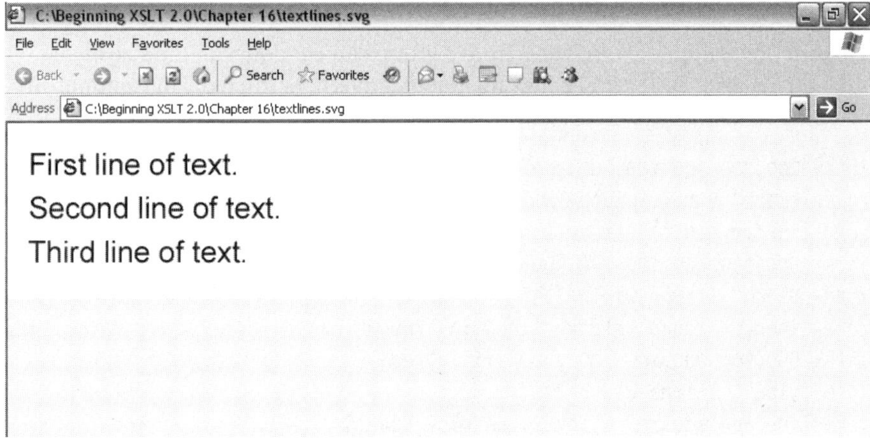

Figure 16-16. *Viewing* `textlines.svg` *in Internet Explorer*

Images

While geometric shapes are easy to draw using SVG, sometimes you want to include a picture in a graphic. You can include images in PNG or JPEG formats using the `<image>` element. Positioning the `<image>` element is similar to positioning a rectangle:

- `x` and `y` specify the coordinate of the top-left corner.
- `width` and `height` specify the width and height of the image.

The location of the image is indicated with the `xlink:href` attribute, where `xlink` is the prefix associated with the namespace `http://www.w3.org/1999/xlink`.

Container Elements

As well as graphic elements, SVG defines a number of elements that are used as containers for other elements, either grouping them together so that they can be referenced and used as a single graphic or bestowing a common behavior on all the elements in the container.

We'll have a quick look at two useful container elements: `<g>`, which groups graphics together, and `<a>`, which creates links from a graphic.

Grouping Graphics

You can group sets of graphics together by placing them within a `<g>` element. The `<g>` element can hold any graphic elements and/or other container elements (you can nest `<g>` elements inside each other).

The `<g>` element is useful in two primary ways: it enables you to apply the same presentational graphics to a set of graphics, and it enables you to move, rotate, and skew a set of graphics together.

Inheriting Presentational Attributes

Being able to inherit presentational attributes from a group can cut down on the size of an SVG document, and makes it easier to see how the document is constructed. For example, in polygon.svg we used three <polygon> elements to generate three triangles:

```
<polygon points="200,300 300,100 400,300" fill="red"
         stroke="black" stroke-width="25"
         stroke-linecap="butt" stroke-linejoin="miter" />
<polygon points="500,300 600,100 700,300" fill="red"
         stroke="black" stroke-width="25"
         stroke-linecap="round" stroke-linejoin="round" />
<polygon points="800,300 900,100 1000,300" fill="red"
         stroke="black" stroke-width="25"
         stroke-linecap="square" stroke-linejoin="bevel" />
```

All these <polygon> elements have the same values for the fill, stroke, and stroke-width attributes. Rather than repeating them on each <polygon>, we can use a <g> element to hold these attributes and they will be inherited by the polygons, as in polygongroup.svg:

```
<g fill="red" stroke="black" stroke-width="25">
  <polygon points="200,300 300,100 400,300"
           stroke-linecap="butt" stroke-linejoin="miter" />
  <polygon points="500,300 600,100 700,300"
           stroke-linecap="round" stroke-linejoin="round" />
  <polygon points="800,300 900,100 1000,300"
           stroke-linecap="square" stroke-linejoin="bevel" />
</g>
```

Each of the polygons are filled in red and have a black border 25 user units thick because each <polygon> inherits the fill, stroke, and stroke-width attributes from the surrounding group. polygongroup.svg will be rendered in exactly the same way as polygon.svg, shown in Figure 16-13.

Transforming

The second helpful feature of <g> elements is that they enable you to move, rotate, or skew a set of graphic elements together through the transform attribute. You can use the transform attribute on any of the graphic elements individually, but it's generally more useful on the <g> element, where it can be applied to a set of graphic elements together.

The transform attribute is a space-separated list of **transform definitions**. Each transform definition looks like a function—a name followed by a comma-separated list of arguments in brackets. The principal transformation definitions are

- translate(tx, ty?)—Moves the graphic tx right and ty down (ty is assumed to be 0 if it is not specified)
- scale(sx, sy?)—Multiplies the width of the graphic by sx and the height of the graphic by sy (sy is assumed to be the same as sx if it is not specified)

- `rotate(angle, [cx, cy]?)`—Rotates the graphic by `angle` degrees around the coordinate specified by `(cx, cy)` (the center of the rotation is assumed to be the origin `(0, 0)` if `cx` and `cy` are not specified)
- `skewX(angle)`—Skews the graphic by `angle` degrees, such that y-coordinates stay the same but x-coordinates are changed
- `skewY(angle)`—Skews the graphic by `angle` degrees, such that x-coordinates stay the same but y-coordinates are changed

Each transformation is applied in turn on the result of running the rest of the transformations on the graphic. For example, in Listing 16-10, `transform.svg`, a rectangle and some text are both first rotated through 90° about the center of the rectangle, and then moved 450 user units right and 100 user units down to position them in the center of the canvas.

Listing 16-10. `transform.svg`

```
<svg width="12cm" height="4cm" viewBox="0 0 1200 400"
     xmlns="http://www.w3.org/2000/svg">
  <g transform="translate(450, 100) rotate(90, 150, 100)">
    <rect width="300" height="200" fill="#C00"
          stroke="black" stroke-width="20" />
    <text x="150" y="150" text-anchor="middle"
          font-size="120" fill="yellow">SVG</text>
  </g>
</svg>
```

The resulting graphic is shown in Figure 16-17.

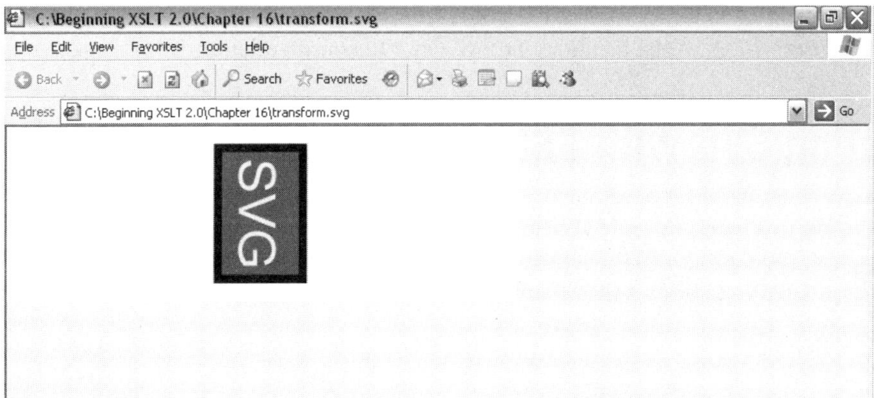

Figure 16-17. *Viewing* `transform.svg` *in Internet Explorer*

Linking from SVG

You can link from graphics within an SVG image using the <a> element. The <a> element works much like the <g> element; it groups together a bunch of graphic elements so that you can apply common presentational attributes to them, and so that you can move, scale, rotate, and skew them.

The <a> element also adds a behavior to the graphics that it contains, namely that if you click them, then the browser opens up the page that's linked to with the xlink:href attribute—the href attribute in the XLink namespace of http://www.w3.org/1999/xlink. The <a> element in SVG therefore works like the <a> element in HTML, except that it contains graphics rather than text (usually).

For example, you could change the <g> element from the last example into an <a> element and add an xlink:href attribute, not forgetting to add the namespace declaration for XLink, as in Listing 16-11 (linking.svg).

Listing 16-11. linking.svg

```
<svg width="12cm" height="4cm" viewBox="0 0 1200 400"
     xmlns="http://www.w3.org/2000/svg"
     xmlns:xlink="http://www.w3.org/1999/xlink">
  <a xlink:href="http://www.w3.org/TR/SVG11/"
     transform="translate(450, 100) rotate(90, 150, 100)">
    <rect width="300" height="200" fill="#C00"
          stroke="black" stroke-width="20" />
    <text x="150" y="150" text-anchor="middle"
          font-size="120" fill="yellow">SVG</text>
  </a>
</svg>
```

Now, when you view linking.svg and click the rectangle, the browser should take you to http://www.w3.org/TR/SVG11/, the location of the SVG 1.1 Recommendation.

Generating SVG with XSLT

Now that you have a rough idea of what you can achieve with SVG and how to achieve it, it's time to start trying to generate some SVG using XSLT. Our task will be to generate a graphical TV guide, displaying the programs that are showing between 7 p.m. and 10 p.m. on a particular day, looking something like that shown in Figure 16-18.

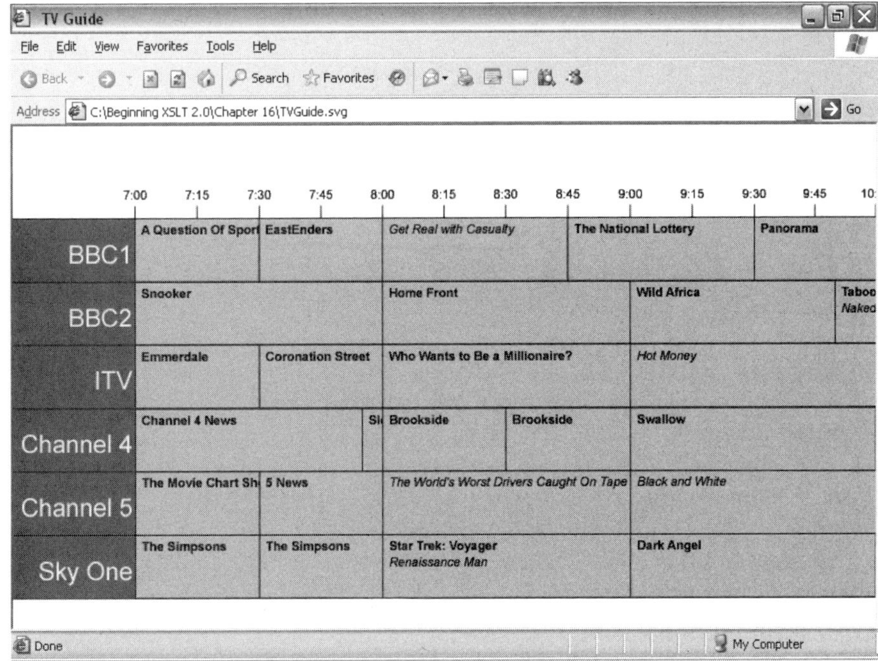

Figure 16-18. *Graphical SVG TV guide*

SVG Design

Our first task to create this image is to work out what SVG to use. The SVG given in Listing 16-12 (TVGuide.svg) generates this image.

Listing 16-12. TVGuide.svg

```
<svg xmlns="http://www.w3.org/2000/svg"
     xmlns:xlink="http://www.w3.org/1999/xlink"
     viewBox="0 0 1400 700">
  <title>TV Guide</title>
  <g text-anchor="middle" font-size="20" fill="black">
    <desc>Timeline markers</desc>
    <text x="200" y="70">7:00</text>
    <text x="300" y="70">7:15</text>
    ...
  </g>
  <g stroke="black" stroke-width="2">
    <desc>Vertical grid lines</desc>
    <line x1="200" y1="80" x2="200" y2="700"/>
    <line x1="300" y1="80" x2="300" y2="700"/>
    ...
  </g>
```

```
  <g transform="translate(0, 100)">
    <desc>BBC1</desc>
    <g>
      <desc>Channel Label</desc>
      <rect x="0" y="0" height="100" width="200" fill="#C00"/>
      <text x="195" y="70" text-anchor="end" font-size="40"
            fill="yellow">BBC1</text>
    </g>
    <g>
      <desc>Programs</desc>
      ...
      <g transform="translate(400)">
        <rect x="0" y="0" fill="#CCC" height="100" stroke="black"
              stroke-width="2" width="200"/>
        <text y="0" font-size="20" fill="black">
          <tspan font-weight="bold" x="0.5em" dy="25">EastEnders</tspan>
        </text>
      </g>
      ...
    </g>
  </g>
  ...
  <g stroke="black" stroke-width="2">
    <desc>Horizontal grid lines</desc>
    <line x1="0" y1="100" x2="1400" y2="100"/>
    <line x1="0" y1="200" x2="1400" y2="200"/>
    ...
  </g>
</svg>
```

The SVG is split into a number of <g> elements that demonstrate the structure of the graphic and allow groups of graphics to be positioned within the image and to share the same presentational attributes. There are four kinds of groups at the top level:

- A group holding the timeline markers displaying 15-minute intervals; these timeline markers cover the topmost 100 user units of the graphic.
- A group holding vertical gridlines that start just below the timeline markers and continue to the bottom of the graphic, every 100 user units across the image, starting 200 user units from the left.
- Groups holding the information about a particular channel, each displayed in a single row within the graphic. Each channel takes up 100 user units vertically, with the label taking up 200 user units at the left. The more channels there are, the greater the height of the graphic.
- A group holding the horizontal gridlines that separate the information from each channel, every 100 user units down the image.

The groups are arranged in this order so that the vertical gridlines are painted over by programs (if there is a program at a particular time), whereas the horizontal gridlines are painted over the graphics for each channel.

The group for each channel contains two groups: a group giving the label for the channel, and a group holding the programs showing on that channel. The details for each program are displayed in their own group as well.

Constructing the Stylesheet

You're familiar by now with the content of the `TVGuide.xml` and `series.xml` documents that will form the source document for our transformation, and we've just looked at the `TVGuide.svg` document that we want to generate. Our task now is to create the stylesheet, `TVGuide.svg.xsl`, which will carry out the transformation from one to the other.

In the rest of this section, we'll build up the stylesheet bit by bit, first constructing the outline of the stylesheet and then adding the templates that we need to generate the result we want.

Basic Stylesheet

Our first step is to construct the document element, which controls namespaces, to work out how we're going to handle whitespace in our source document, and to decide what kind of output we're generating with this stylesheet.

Namespace Declarations and Management

Let's start at the beginning and consider what our `<xsl:stylesheet>` document element should look like. We certainly need to include the XSLT namespace declaration and a `version` attribute with the value `2.0`.

We also need namespace declarations for the namespaces that we'll use in the stylesheet. We don't have to worry about any namespaces on the source document because we're not using any. However, the SVG that we're generating does use a couple of namespaces:

- `http://www.w3.org/2000/svg` for the SVG elements
- `http://www.w3.org/1999/xlink` for the XLink attributes that are used to refer to elsewhere

We'll also be using the namespaces for the datatypes that we'll use in our stylesheet, which includes some from XML Schema (such as `xs:integer`) and some from XPath (such as `xdt:dayTimeDuration`). These two namespaces are

- `http://www.w3.org/2001/XMLSchema` for the XML Schema datatypes
- `http://www.w3.org/2005/02/xpath-datatypes` for the XPath datatypes

We don't really want either of these namespaces to show up in the final SVG document, so we need to exclude them using the `exclude-result-prefixes` attribute.

Because most of the stylesheet will be concerned with generating SVG elements, we'll make the SVG namespace the default namespace. We'll use the standard prefixes `xlink` for XLink attributes, `xs` for the XML Schema datatypes, and `xdt` for the XPath datatypes. The `<xsl:stylesheet>` document element for the stylesheet therefore looks as follows:

```
<xsl:stylesheet version="2.0"
                xmlns:xsl="http://www.w3.org/1999/XSL/Transform"
                xmlns="http://www.w3.org/2000/svg"
                xmlns:xlink="http://www.w3.org/1999/xlink"
                xmlns:xs="http://www.w3.org/2001/XMLSchema"
                xmlns:xdt="http://www.w3.org/2005/02/xpath-datatypes"
                exclude-result-prefixes="xs xdt"
...
</xsl:stylesheet>
```

Whitespace Stripping

Next up is managing the whitespace in our source document. The source document for this transformation is mainly data-oriented, so most of the whitespace that we have in `TVGuide.xml` is just there to make it easier to read. We should therefore strip the whitespace-only text nodes from the source node tree using the `<xsl:strip-space>` element, as follows:

```
<xsl:strip-space elements="*" />
```

There are a few document-oriented elements in `TVGuide.xml` in which whitespace matters, namely the `<Description>` element and the various styling elements that it contains. However, this SVG document isn't going to be including the content of the `<Description>` elements, so we don't have to worry about the fact that whitespace within them will be stripped from the tree.

Output Control

Our final job in setting up the stylesheet is to describe the result of the transformation using the `<xsl:output>` element. This stylesheet generates SVG, which is XML, so we need to use the `xml` output method. The media type for SVG is `image/svg+xml`, so we'll use that in the `media-type` attribute. We'll indent the output so that we can view it easily later on and set the encoding to `ISO-8859-1` so that we can open it in normal text editors without having to worry about special characters. The `<xsl:output>` element is as follows:

```
<xsl:output method="xml" media-type="image/svg+xml"
            indent="yes" encoding="ISO-8859-1" />
```

Creating the SVG Element

The first element that we need to generate with our stylesheet is the `<svg>` element that holds the specification of the graphic. We can generate this element with a literal result element, without using a prefix, because the default namespace for the stylesheet is the SVG namespace. We'll create this element in the template for the document element, the `<TVGuide>` element, as follows:

```
<xsl:template match="TVGuide">
  <svg ...>
    ...
  </svg>
</xsl:template>
```

The namespace declarations that are specified on the <svg> element in TVGuide.svg will be automatically generated when the result tree is serialized, because the <svg> element in the stylesheet is in the SVG namespace and has a namespace node for the other namespace we need to use, XLink. As you'll remember from Chapter 8, the XSLT processor will add the namespace declarations automatically where necessary, so we don't have to add them explicitly. However, we do have to add the viewBox attribute.

Calculating the Height of the Coordinate System

In TVGuide.svg, the viewBox attribute has the value 0 0 1400 600. The coordinate system should always begin at (0, 0), so the first two numbers are fixed. But we might want it to be something other than 1400 user units in width—it depends on the start and end times we're showing—and the height of the graphic should change depending on how many channels we have.

First, let's define some variables to hold the start and end time that we want to use in our timeline. We should make these global variables since they'll be useful throughout the stylesheet:

```
<xsl:variable name="startTime" as="xs:time" select="xs:time('19:00:00')" />
<xsl:variable name="endTime" as="xs:time" select="xs:time('22:00:00')" />
```

The width of the SVG depends on the number of 15-minute intervals between these two times. In fact, the width is 200 user units for the labels, plus 100 for every quarter hour between the two times: in this case, 200 + (100 * 12), giving 1400.

The number of intervals that we're interested in will be useful later on, when we come to creating the timeline and associated vertical gridlines, so we'll keep that number in a global variable called $intervals. We can calculate it by subtracting the $startTime from the $endTime to give an xdt:dayTimeDuration and dividing that xdt:dayTimeDuration by the xdt:dayTimeDuration PT15M:

```
<xsl:variable name="intervals" as="xs:integer"
              select="xs:integer(($endTime - $startTime) div
                                 xdt:dayTimeDuration('PT15M'))" />
```

The width that we want is then the value of the $intervals variable, multiplied by 100, plus 200. Again, we'll store this in a global variable so that we can use it in other templates:

```
<xsl:variable name="width" as="xs:integer" select="($intervals * 100) + 200" />
```

The height, on the other hand, should be 100 user units for each channel, plus the 100 user units needed to display the timeline markers. Therefore the fourth value in the viewBox attribute (which gives the height of the graphic in user units) should be dependent on the number of channels that are specified within the source document. Again, this number is useful in several places in our stylesheet, so we'll store it in a global variable:

```
<xsl:variable name="nChannels" as="xs:integer"
              select="count(/TVGuide/Channel)" />
```

We'll also assign the total height to a global variable so that we can refer to it from elsewhere, as follows:

```
<xsl:variable name="height" as="xs:integer"
              select="($nChannels * 100) + 100" />
```

We can use an attribute value template to insert the values of the width and height into the viewBox attribute, as follows:

```
<xsl:template match="TVGuide">
  <svg viewBox="0 0 {$width} {$height}">
    ...
  </svg>
</xsl:template>
```

Now let's look at the content of the <svg> element. As we saw earlier, the content is broken up into four groups: one for the timeline markers, one for the vertical gridlines, one for each of the channels, and one for the horizontal gridlines. We'll get the <g> elements for each channel by applying templates to them and create the other groups with named templates. The content of the <svg> element in the stylesheet is therefore as follows:

```
<xsl:template match="TVGuide">
  <svg viewBox="0 0 {$width} {$height}">
    <title>TV Guide</title>
    <xsl:call-template name="timelineMarkers" />
    <xsl:call-template name="verticalGridlines" />
    <xsl:apply-templates select="Channel"/>
    <xsl:call-template name="horizontalGridlines" />
  </svg>
</xsl:template>
```

Creating Timeline Markers

The timeline markers are a series of <text> elements displaying times specifying every quarter hour between 19:00 and 22:00. All these <text> elements have some things in common—the way they're anchored, the size of the font, and the color of the text, for example—so they're collected into a group. This also helps identify the timeline markers separate from the other graphic elements.

In the stylesheet, the timeline markers need to be constructed with a template called timelineMarkers, which is called from the template that matches the <TVGuide> element. The template generates the <g> element, as follows:

```
<xsl:template name="timelineMarkers">
  <g text-anchor="middle" font-size="20" fill="black">
    <desc>Timeline markers</desc>
    ...
  </g>
</xsl:template>
```

The timeline markers are always going to be the same for this stylesheet, so we could just fill in the timelineMarkers template with the <text> elements directly, as follows:

```
<xsl:template name="timelineMarkers">
  <g text-anchor="middle" font-size="20" fill="black">
    <desc>Timeline markers</desc>
    <text x="200" y="70">7:00</text>
```

```
    <text x="300" y="70">7:15</text>
    <text x="400" y="70">7:30</text>
    <text x="500" y="70">7:45</text>
    <text x="600" y="70">8:00</text>
    <text x="700" y="70">8:15</text>
    <text x="800" y="70">8:30</text>
    <text x="900" y="70">8:45</text>
    <text x="1000" y="70">9:00</text>
    <text x="1100" y="70">9:15</text>
    <text x="1200" y="70">9:30</text>
    <text x="1300" y="70">9:45</text>
    <text x="1400" y="70">10:00</text>
  </g>
</xsl:template>
```

However, this is fairly long and error-prone, and it won't scale up well if we decide to make the stylesheet more flexible and show more of the evening's programs. Therefore, we'll use a loop to generate the timeline based on a sequence of integers.

To create the timeline markers, we can iterate over a sequence of integers ranging from 0 to the number of 15-minute intervals that we've got in the `$intervals` variable:

```
<xsl:for-each select="0 to $intervals">
  ...
</xsl:for-each>
```

Now, we need to create a `<text>` element on each iteration. The two things that change in each `<text>` element are the value of its `x` attribute and its content, both of which can be calculated based on the current integer. The value of the `x` attribute is the integer multiplied by 100, plus 200:

```
<xsl:for-each select="0 to $intervals">
  <text x="{(. * 100) + 200}" y="70">
    ...
  </text>
</xsl:for-each>
```

The content of the `<text>` element is the start time, plus the integer multiplied by an `xdt:dayTimeDuration` of 15 minutes. This time needs to be formatted using `format-time()` as follows:

```
<xsl:for-each select="0 to $intervals">
  <text x="{(. * 100) + 200}" y="70">
    <xsl:variable name="time" as="xs:time"
                  select="$startTime + (. * xdt:dayTimeDuration('PT15M'))" />
    <xsl:value-of select="format-time($time, '[h,1]:[m]')" />
  </text>
</xsl:for-each>
```

Slotting this into the `timelineMarkers` template, we get the following:

```
<xsl:template name="timelineMarkers">
  <g text-anchor="middle" font-size="20" fill="black">
    <desc>Timeline markers</desc>
    <xsl:for-each select="0 to $intervals">
      <text x="{(. * 100) + 200}" y="70">
        <xsl:variable name="time" as="xs:time"
          select="$startTime + (. * xdt:dayTimeDuration('PT15M'))" />
        <xsl:value-of select="format-time($time, '[h,1]:[m]')" />
      </text>
    </xsl:for-each>
  </g>
</xsl:template>
```

Creating Vertical Gridlines

The next group is the group of vertical gridlines. The vertical gridlines are generated by the template named `verticalGridlines`, which looks like the following:

```
<xsl:template name="verticalGridlines">
  <g stroke="black" stroke-width="2">
    <desc>Vertical grid lines</desc>
    ...
  </g>
</xsl:template>
```

The method of generating the vertical gridlines is much the same as that for creating the timeline markers. We could generate them simply by adding the `<line>` elements explicitly to the group, but this would not be very flexible in the long run. Therefore, we'll generate them automatically using a loop from 0 to the number of intervals held in the `$intervals` variable:

```
<xsl:template name="verticalGridlines">
  <g stroke="black" stroke-width="2">
    <desc>Vertical grid lines</desc>
    <xsl:for-each select="0 to $intervals">
      ...
    </xsl:for-each>
  </g>
</xsl:template>
```

Each line is created with a `<line>` element, starts 70 user units from the top of the graphic, and goes down to the bottom of the graphic. As you'll remember from when we created the coordinate system for this image, the height of the image might change depending on how many channels there are. We need to get the value of the maximum y-coordinate from the `$height` global variable that we used in the `viewBox` attribute when creating the `<svg>` element. The x-coordinate of the start and end of the line is the same: equal to 200 plus the integer multiplied by 100:

```
<xsl:template name="verticalGridlines">
  <g stroke="black" stroke-width="2">
    <desc>Vertical grid lines</desc>
```

```
    <xsl:for-each select="0 to $intervals">
      <line x1="{(. * 100) + 200}" y1="80"
            x2="{(. * 100) + 200}" y2="{$height}" />
    </xsl:for-each>
  </g>
</xsl:template>
```

Creating Horizontal Gridlines

Before we go on and look at how to generate the content for the grid, we'll just add the final group in the <svg> element—the group for the horizontal gridlines. The horizontal gridlines separate the channels from each other: there's a line across the image above the row for each channel, plus a line at the bottom of the image.

These horizontal gridlines are generated by the horizontalGridlines template, which is called from the template that matches the <TVGuide> element. The horizontalGridlines template needs to create the <g> element, like the other named templates have done:

```
<xsl:template name="horizontalGridlines">
  <g stroke="black" stroke-width="2">
    <desc>Horizontal grid lines</desc>
    ...
  </g>
</xsl:template>
```

The horizontal gridlines need to be constructed slightly differently from the vertical gridlines and the timeline markers because the number of horizontal gridlines is dependent on the number of channels that are held in the source TV guide. For this, you need to iterate over the integers from 0 to the number of <Channel> elements in the document, which we have stored in the $nChannels global variable. You can then use the integer to tell you how far down to place the gridline—the first at 100 user units, the second at 200 user units, and so on, so 100 plus the integer multiplied by 100. The value of the x2 attribute is the width of the graphic, which we can get from the $width global variable. So the template looks like this:

```
<xsl:template name="horizontalGridlines">
  <g stroke="black" stroke-width="2">
    <desc>Horizontal grid lines</desc>
    <xsl:for-each select="0 to $nChannels">
      <line x1="0"        y1="{(. * 100) + 100}"
            x2="{$width}" y2="{(. * 100) + 100}" />
    </xsl:for-each>
  </g>
</xsl:template>
```

Creating Groups for Channels

At last we're on to the most important information that's displayed in the graphic—what's actually showing on each of the channels. Back in the template for the <TVGuide> element, we applied templates to the <Channel> elements to generate the groups for each channel. So we need a template that matches <Channel> elements to generate these groups:

```
<xsl:template match="Channel">
  <g ...>
    <desc><xsl:value-of select="Name"/></desc>
    ...
  </g>
</xsl:template>
```

If you look back at the source of TVGuide.svg, you'll see that each of the <g> elements for the channels uses a transform attribute to move its contents down the graphic. The amount that the group is moved down the graphic depends on the position of the channel—the first channel is moved down 100 user units, the second 200 user units, and so on. We can therefore use the position() attribute to work out how much the group should be translated by, as shown here:

```
<xsl:template match="Channel">
  <g transform="translate(0, {position() * 100})">
    <desc><xsl:value-of select="Name"/></desc>
    ...
  </g>
</xsl:template>
```

The content of the channel group is made up of two more groups: the label for the channel and the programs that are shown on the channel. These groups are purely there to add structure to the SVG document—the <g> elements don't provide default values for presentational attributes, nor do they move their contents anywhere:

```
<xsl:template match="Channel">
  <g transform="translate(0, {position() * 100})">
    <desc><xsl:value-of select="Name"/></desc>
    <g>
      <desc>Channel Label</desc>
      ...
    </g>
    <g>
      <desc>Programs</desc>
      ...
    </g>
  </g>
</xsl:template>
```

The channel label consists of a rectangle in red that is 200 user units wide and 100 user units in height, with some right-aligned yellow text on top giving the name of the channel. You can right-align the text by using the text-anchor attribute, set to end, so that the x, y anchor coordinate for the text specifies the coordinate of the end of the text, as follows:

```
<xsl:template match="Channel">
  <g transform="translate(0, {position() * 100})">
    <desc><xsl:value-of select="Name"/></desc>
    <g>
      <desc>Channel Label</desc>
```

```
      <rect x="0" y="0" height="100" width="200" fill="#C00"/>
      <text x="195" y="70" text-anchor="end" font-size="40" fill="yellow">
        <xsl:value-of select="Name"/>
      </text>
    </g>
    <g>
      <desc>Programs</desc>
      ...
    </g>
  </g>
</xsl:template>
```

Last but not least, we need to apply templates to generate the rectangles that display the details of each program. We'll do this simply by applying templates to all the <Program> elements within the <Channel> and let the template for the <Program> elements figure out whether they should be displayed or not:

```
<xsl:template match="Channel">
  <g transform="translate(0, {position() * 100})">
    <desc><xsl:value-of select="Name"/></desc>
    <g>
      <desc>Channel Label</desc>
      <rect x="0" y="0" height="100" width="200" fill="#C00"/>
      <text x="195" y="70" text-anchor="end" font-size="40" fill="yellow">
        <xsl:value-of select="Name"/>
      </text>
    </g>
    <g>
      <desc>Programs</desc>
      <xsl:apply-templates select="Program"/>
    </g>
  </g>
</xsl:template>
```

Creating Groups for Programs

Our last task is to generate the rectangles that display the details of each program. We'll do this in a template that matches <Program> elements:

```
<xsl:template match="Program">
  ...
</xsl:template>
```

The first task is to figure out whether the program should be displayed at all. We're only displaying programs that start between the `$startTime` and the `$endTime` (and assuming that all the programs listed are on the same day). The start time of a program is stored in the <Start> child element of the <Program> element, as an `xs:dateTime`. If we cast the value of the <Start> element to an `xs:dateTime`, and then cast that to an `xs:time`, we will have a time that we can compare with the `$startTime` and `$endTime` to work out whether to show the program:

```
<xsl:template match="Program">
  <xsl:variable name="time" as="xs:time"
                select="xs:time(xs:dateTime(Start))" />
  ...
</xsl:template>
```

We only want to show the program if the value of the $time variable is greater than or equal to the $startTime, and less than the $endTime:

```
<xsl:template match="Program">
  <xsl:variable name="time" as="xs:time"
                select="xs:time(xs:dateTime(Start))" />
  <xsl:if test="$time >= $startTime and $time &lt; $endTime">
    ...
  </xsl:if>
</xsl:template>
```

The <Start> element also gives us the location of the group for the program—it needs to be indented according to the start time, with a program starting at 19:00 indented 200 user units, one at 19:15 indented 300 user units, and so on. The actual formula is 200 user units (for the channel labels) plus 100 user units for every quarter hour after the $startTime. So first, we need to work out the difference between the $time and the $startTime:

```
$time - $startTime
```

then divide that by an xdt:dayTimeDuration of 15 minutes:

```
($time - $startTime) div xdt:dayTimeDuration('PT15M')
```

We'll store this in a $start variable:

```
<xsl:variable name="start" as="xs:double"
  select="($time - $startTime) div xdt:dayTimeDuration('PT15M')" />
```

We need to multiply this by 100 and add 200 to give the indent. In some cases, this will give us a fraction (for example, a program that starts at 19:05 should start 233.333333333 user units in from the side). We don't really need a high level of accuracy, though—two decimal places will be more than enough—so we'll format the number that we get to fix it to a maximum of two decimal places with the format-number() function:

```
<xsl:variable name="indent" as="xs:string"
  select="format-number(($start * 100) + 200, '0.##')"/>
```

Now that we've got the start x-coordinate for the rectangle for the program, we need to work out how wide the rectangle needs to be. The width of the rectangle depends on its duration—it should cover 100 user units for every quarter hour that it lasts. To work this out, we need to look at the <Duration> child of the <Program> element, and divide its value by the xdt:dayTimeDuration PT15M:

```
<xsl:variable name="duration" as="xs:double"
  select="xdt:dayTimeDuration(Duration) div xdt:dayTimeDuration('PT15M')" />
```

When we translate this to a number of user units, we again want to format to two decimal places:

```
<xsl:variable name="width" as="xs:string"
  select="format-number($duration * 100, '0.##')"/>
```

We've now gathered together all the information that we need to position the group containing the program information, and to draw the rectangle that forms the background to the text describing the program. The group needs to be moved right by the amount held in the $indent variable, and the background rectangle's width is held in the $width variable. The template looks as follows:

```
<xsl:template match="Program">
  <xsl:variable name="hour" select="substring(Start, 12, 2)"/>
  <xsl:if test="$hour &gt;= 19 and $hour &lt; 22">
    <xsl:variable name="start" as="xs:double"
       select="($time - $startTime) div xdt:dayTimeDuration('PT15M')" />
    <xsl:variable name="indent" as="xs:string"
      select="format-number(($start * 100) + 200, '0.##')"/>
    <xsl:variable name="duration" as="xs:double"
                  select="xdt:dayTimeDuration(Duration) div
                          xdt:dayTimeDuration('PT15M')" />
    <xsl:variable name="width" as="xs:string"
      select="format-number($duration * 100, '0.##')"/>
    <g transform="translate({$indent})">
      <rect x="0" y="0" height="100" width="{$width}"
            fill="#CCC" stroke="black" stroke-width="2" />
      ...
    </g>
  </xsl:if>
</xsl:template>
```

Now let's look at the text content of the program. We want to display the series name of the program, if it has one, followed on a new line by the series title of the program, if it has one. If we place both these pieces of text within the same <text> element, then they can be selected at the same time. It will also help us to position the text. So we'll create a <text> element in this template and use templates for the <Series> and <Title> templates to generate the <tspan> elements that contain the text itself.

■ **Note** Using <tspan> elements also helps us design the stylesheet because we can take advantage of the fact that you can position a <tspan> element relative to the previous <tspan> element, using the dx and dy attributes.

We'll generate the <tspan> elements using separate templates for the <Series> and <Title> elements, but we only want to apply these templates, and generate the <tspan> elements, if there's something to generate information about. All the <Program> elements in TVGuide.xml have <Series> and <Title> child elements, but not all the <Series> and <Title> elements have any content— if a program doesn't belong to a series, then its <Series> element is empty, for example. Rather than using a test within the templates, we'll only apply templates to the <Series> and <Title> elements if they contain some text, using a predicate as shown in the following:

```
<xsl:template match="Program">
  <xsl:variable name="hour" select="substring(Start, 12, 2)"/>
  <xsl:if test="$hour &gt;= 19 and $hour &lt; 22">
    <xsl:variable name="start" as="xs:double"
       select="($time - $startTime) div xdt:dayTimeDuration('PT15M')" />
    <xsl:variable name="indent" as="xs:string"
      select="format-number(($start * 100) + 200, '0.##')"/>
    <xsl:variable name="duration" as="xs:double"
                select="xdt:dayTimeDuration(Duration) div
                        xdt:dayTimeDuration('PT15M')" />
    <xsl:variable name="width" as="xs:string"
      select="format-number($duration * 100, '0.##')"/>
    <g transform="translate({$indent})">
      <rect x="0" y="0" height="100" width="{$width}"
            fill="#CCC" stroke="black" stroke-width="2" />
      <text y="0" font-size="20" fill="black">
        <xsl:apply-templates select="Series[string(.)]"/>
        <xsl:apply-templates select="Title[string(.)]"/>
      </text>
    </g>
  </xsl:if>
</xsl:template>
```

Displaying the Series Title

We're applying templates to the <Series> element within a <Program> to display the name of the series that the program belongs to. However, the <Series> element contains the series ID, not the full title of the series. To get hold of the full title of the series, we need to look in series.xml, which lists each series and gives its full title.

Because we'll be querying information from series.xml several times during the course of the transformation, we'll store the root node for the document in a global variable called $seriesDocument, as follows:

```
<xsl:variable name="seriesDocument" as="document-node()"
              select="document('series.xml')" />
```

The second preparatory step to take is to create a key that gives us quick access to the information about a series, given the ID for that series. To create this key, we need an <xsl:key> element whose match attribute holds a pattern that matches the <Series> elements (in series.xml) and whose use attribute leads from the <Series> element to its id attribute:

```
<xsl:key name="series" match="Series" use="@id" />
```

Now let's see the template that matches <Series> element children of <Program> elements and generates a <tspan> holding the series title. To make it clear that the <Series> element that we're matching is a child of the <Program> element, we'll use a more specific match pattern than usual:

```
<xsl:template match="Program/Series">
  ...
</xsl:template>
```

The <tspan> element will make its content bold, using the font-weight attribute. To get hold of the text, we need to query series.xml (whose root node is held in $seriesDocument) using the series key with the value of the <Series> element that we're looking at. Remember that keys usually only search in the document that holds the context node. To use the key on a different document, we can supply it as the third argument to the key() function. Once we have the <Series> element from series.xml, we can find its <Title> element child and display its content as the value of the <tspan> element, as follows:

```
<xsl:template match="Program/Series">
  <tspan x="0.5em" dy="25" font-weight="bold">
    <xsl:value-of select="key('series', ., $seriesDocument)/Title"/>
  </tspan>
</xsl:template>
```

Displaying the Program Title

Displaying the program's title is easier than displaying the series title because the program's title is right there in the <Program> element's child <Title> element. The template is simply the following:

```
<xsl:template match="Title">
  <tspan x="0.5em" dy="25" font-style="italic">
    <xsl:value-of select="."/>
  </tspan>
</xsl:template>
```

Completed Stylesheet

The complete XSLT stylesheet is shown in Listing 16-13.

Listing 16-13. TVGuide.svg.xsl

```
<?xml version="1.0"?>
<xsl:stylesheet version="2.0"
                xmlns:xsl="http://www.w3.org/1999/XSL/Transform"
                xmlns="http://www.w3.org/2000/svg"
                xmlns:xlink="http://www.w3.org/1999/xlink"
                xmlns:xs="http://www.w3.org/2001/XMLSchema"
                xmlns:xdt="http://www.w3.org/2003/05/xpath-datatypes"
                exclude-result-prefixes="xs xdt">

<xsl:strip-space elements="*" />

<xsl:output method="xml" media-type="image/svg+xml"
            indent="yes" encoding="ISO-8859-1" />

<xsl:variable name="startTime" as="xs:time" select="xs:time('19:00:00')" />
<xsl:variable name="endTime" as="xs:time" select="xs:time('22:00:00')" />
```

```
<xsl:variable name="intervals" as="xs:integer"
  select="xs:integer(($endTime - $startTime) div
                     xdt:dayTimeDuration('PT15M'))" />
<xsl:variable name="nChannels" as="xs:integer"
              select="count(/TVGuide/Channel)" />

<xsl:variable name="width" as="xs:integer"
              select="($intervals * 100) + 200" />
<xsl:variable name="height" as="xs:integer"
              select="($nChannels * 100) + 100" />

<xsl:variable name="seriesDocument" as="document-node()"
              select="document('series.xml')" />

<xsl:key name="series" match="Series" use="@id" />

<xsl:template match="TVGuide">
  <svg viewBox="0 0 {$width} {$height}">
    <title>TV Guide</title>
    <xsl:call-template name="timelineMarkers" />
    <xsl:call-template name="verticalGridlines" />
    <xsl:apply-templates select="Channel" />
    <xsl:call-template name="horizontalGridlines" />
  </svg>
</xsl:template>

<xsl:template name="timelineMarkers">
  <g text-anchor="middle" font-size="20" fill="black">
    <desc>Timeline markers</desc>
    <xsl:for-each select="0 to $intervals">
      <text x="{(. * 100) + 200}" y="70">
        <xsl:variable name="time" as="xs:time"
          select="$startTime + . * xdt:dayTimeDuration('PT15M'))" />
        <xsl:value-of select="format-time($time, '[h,1]:[m]')" />
      </text>
    </xsl:for-each>
  </g>
</xsl:template>

<xsl:template name="verticalGridlines">
  <g stroke="black" stroke-width="2">
    <desc>Vertical grid lines</desc>
    <xsl:for-each select="0 to $intervals">
      <line x1="{(. * 100) + 200}" y1="80"
            x2="{(. * 100) + 200}" y2="{$height}" />
    </xsl:for-each>
  </g>
</xsl:template>
```

```
<xsl:template name="horizontalGridlines">
  <g stroke="black" stroke-width="2">
    <desc>Horizontal grid lines</desc>
    <xsl:for-each select="0 to $nChannels">
      <line x1="0"         y1="{(. * 100) + 100}"
            x2="{$width}" y2="{(. * 100) + 100}" />
    </xsl:for-each>
  </g>
</xsl:template>

<xsl:template match="Channel">
  <g transform="translate(0, {position() * 100})">
    <desc><xsl:value-of select="Name" /></desc>
    <g>
      <desc>Channel Label</desc>
      <rect x="0" y="0" height="100" width="200" fill="#C00" />
      <text x="195" y="70" text-anchor="end" font-size="40" fill="yellow">
        <xsl:value-of select="Name" />
      </text>
    </g>
    <g>
      <desc>Programs</desc>
      <xsl:apply-templates select="Program" />
    </g>
  </g>
</xsl:template>

<xsl:template match="Program">
  <xsl:variable name="time" as="xs:time"
                select="xs:time(xs:dateTime(Start))" />
  <xsl:if test="$time >= $startTime and $time &lt; $endTime">
    <xsl:variable name="start" as="xs:double"
      select="($time - $startTime) div xdt:dayTimeDuration('PT15M')" />
    <xsl:variable name="indent" as="xs:string"
      select="format-number(($start * 100) + 200, '0.##')" />
    <xsl:variable name="duration" as="xs:double"
      select="xdt:dayTimeDuration(Duration) div
              xdt:dayTimeDuration('PT15M'))" />
    <xsl:variable name="width" as="xs:string"
      select="format-number($duration * 100, '0.##')" />
    <g transform="translate({$indent})">
      <rect x="0" y="0" height="100" width="{$width}"
            fill="#CCC" stroke="black" stroke-width="2" />
      <text y="0" font-size="20" fill="black">
        <xsl:apply-templates select="Series[string(.)]" />
        <xsl:apply-templates select="Title[string(.)]" />
      </text>
```

```
    </g>
  </xsl:if>
</xsl:template>

<xsl:template match="Program/Series">
  <tspan x="0.5em" dy="25" font-weight="bold">
    <xsl:value-of select="key('series', ., $seriesDocument)/Title" />
  </tspan>
</xsl:template>

<xsl:template match="Program/Title">
  <tspan x="0.5em" dy="25" font-style="italic">
    <xsl:value-of select="." />
  </tspan>
</xsl:template>

</xsl:stylesheet>
```

Transforming `TVGuide.xml` with `TVGuide.svg.xsl` gives you the SVG graphic that you saw at the beginning of this section.

Embedding SVG in HTML Pages

The SVG graphics that we've looked at thus far in this chapter have been stand-alone files, created with a batch or server-side process that we've opened individually. We haven't discussed either embedding the SVG within an HTML page or displaying SVG that is generated on the client side.

Different browsers support different methods of embedding SVG graphics within HTML pages. Some browsers, such as Mozilla or XSmiles, allow you to embed SVG directly within an XHTML page. This enables you to generate SVG in the same process as generating other information from the same XML source.

Most browsers, however, require you to embed an SVG graphic within an HTML page using the `<object>` and/or `<embed>` elements. For example, `TVGuide.html` embeds `TVGuide.svg` as follows:

```
<object data="TVGuide.svg" type="image/svg+xml"
        width="700" height="350">
  <embed src="TVGuide.svg" type="image/svg+xml"
         width="700" height="350"
         pluginspage="http://www.adobe.com/svg/viewer/install/" />
</object>
```

The `<object>` element is the W3C-sanctioned method of embedding non-HTML formats within HTML pages. The `data` attribute specifies the source of the SVG graphic, the `type` attribute gives the content type of the graphic, and the `width` and `height` attributes determine the width and height of the graphic within the page, here set to `700` pixels by `350` pixels (such that each user unit is half a pixel wide).

The <embed> element is provided for legacy browsers that don't support HTML 4.01. The attributes have the same kind of effect—`src` is used rather than `data` to indicate the source of the graphic, with the `pluginspage` attribute directing people who don't have Adobe's SVG Viewer installed to Adobe's site. The semantics of the <object> element and HTML mean that the <embed> element will be ignored unless the browser doesn't support the <object> element or can't provide a viewer for the SVG graphic.

When you view `TVGuide.html`, if you have Adobe's SVG Viewer installed, you should see the page shown in Figure 16-19.

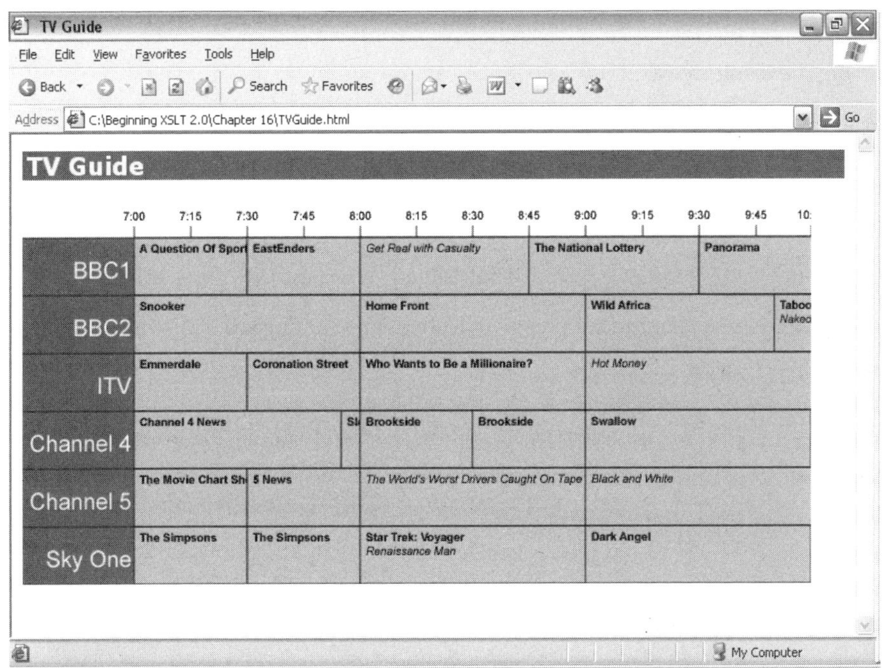

Figure 16-19. *Viewing* `TVGuide.html` *in Internet Explorer*

This can be a bit of a constraint because it makes it harder to create SVG and the rest of the page in one process. If you are processing the document in batch mode, from the command line, you can use <xsl:result-document> to create multiple output documents, as we saw in Chapter 8. If you are processing the document server side, you can make sure that the request for the SVG graphic causes the server to generate the SVG dynamically from the XML source.

Embedding SVG within HTML pages when the transformation is carried out on the client side is a lot harder, particularly because the XSLT processors that are used client side don't support XSLT 2.0 and therefore can't use the <xsl:result-document> instruction to create multiple output documents. In Internet Explorer and Mozilla/Firefox, it has to be done through scripts that perform DOM manipulation. For details and tools that support client-side transformation involving SVG, see Chris Bayes's `domtodom.js` utility at `http://www.bayes.co.uk/xml/index.xml?/xml/utils/domtodom.xml`.

Summary

This chapter has introduced you to the basics of SVG and shown you how you can create nice-looking, interactive graphics using XSLT to transform your XML data to SVG. You've learned about how to draw graphics and text on the screen using SVG; how to control their presentation; how to move, rotate, stretch, and skew those graphics; and how to link to other documents.

In creating the stylesheet transforming XML to SVG, you've seen many of the techniques that were discussed theoretically in the first part of this book being used in practice:

- Declaring namespaces for use in the result tree
- Stripping whitespace from data-oriented XML
- Serializing the result tree as XML
- Counting the number of nodes in a document
- Performing numeric and date/time calculations using XPath
- Creating and using global variables
- Using attribute value templates to insert calculated values into attribute values
- Using named templates to break up your stylesheet into manageable portions of code
- Using the `position()` function as a counter
- Formatting numbers to certain numbers of decimal places
- Selecting subsets of nodes to apply templates to
- Using keys, in particular with external documents

Review Questions

1. Add stars to the programs to indicate how highly rated they are (the number of stars is held in the `rating` attribute on the `<Program>` element). A good polygon to use for a star is

   ```
   <polygon points="12,0 15,9 24,9 17,14 20,25 12,18 4,25 7,14 0,9 9,9" />
   ```

   You can wrap all the stars in a `<g>` element to use the same presentational attributes with each, and use the `transform` attribute on the `<polygon>` elements to move them to the right so that you don't have to come up with a new set of x-coordinates each time.

2. Highlight the `<Program>` elements with `flag` attributes by coloring them differently from the other programs. Use blue for programs with an "interesting" flag and green for programs with a "favorite" flag.

3. Some `<Series>` elements in `series.xml` have an `xlink:href` attribute that points to a home page for the series. When there is such an attribute, use an `<a>` element in the SVG so that when you click the rectangle for a program, you get taken to the home page of the series.

4. Some of the titles of the programs are not displayed very well because the program only lasts for a short amount of time and SVG doesn't do any word wrapping. Assuming that each character takes up 11 user units, use either a recursive template or `<xsl:analyze-string>` to split up the text at word breaks so that it can flow over several lines. You may need to adjust the font size or the height of the rows so that several lines of text can fit in the rectangle for a program. If the text can't be split up (because the words are too long), then rotate the text so that it fits in sideways.

5. Currently, if a program starts before 19:00 but ends after 19:00, it isn't shown, and if it lasts past 22:00, then its rectangle goes over the end of the graphic. Amend the template for `<Program>` elements so that programs that start before 19:00 are included in the graphic and so that the rectangles for programs that finish later are foreshortened.

6. Assuming that the `<Program>` elements held in `TVGuide.xml` do *not* share the same date, alter the stylesheet so that it displays the programs shown on a particular evening by storing the date in a `$date` stylesheet parameter.

7. Change the `$startTime` and `$endTime` global variables into stylesheet parameters and serve `TVGuide.xml` using `TVGuide.svg.xsl` from Cocoon 2, allowing the `$date`, `$startTime`, and `$endTime` parameters to be set through request parameters or parts of the URL.

8. Add a `$series` parameter to the stylesheet so that it highlights programs in a particular series within the SVG graphic.

9. Create a user preferences file to hold information about the fonts and colors that the user wants to be used in the graphic. Use the information from this file when creating the presentational attributes that are used in the SVG document.

CHAPTER 17

Interpreting RSS with XSLT

The TV guide that we've been looking at throughout this book is a very useful resource; it not only lists all those programs, but also includes ratings on each of them to help you choose what to watch. Throughout, the origin of this information has remained hidden; in this chapter, we'll look at how the information might be collected from other sites using the syndication format RDF Site Summary (RSS).

RSS is an XML-based markup language that holds metadata about a web site, and in particular it is used to notify sites of time-sensitive information such as site changes, news headlines, mails on discussion forums, and notifications and announcements of various kinds. RSS has its roots in the channels used in the My Netscape Network (MNN) portal site, which allowed content providers to provide summaries of their web sites that users could follow if they chose.

RSS 1.0, the version of RSS that we will be looking at in this chapter, is based on the Resource Description Framework (RDF). RDF is a standard from the W3C that provides a framework for expressing metadata—information about information. RSS 1.0 is highly modularized—providers can put together their site information with the components that they need—and uses standards such as Dublin Core to provide **meta-information** about the content of the site.

In this chapter, you'll learn

- The basics of RDF and RSS 1.0
- How to transform RSS descriptions into other XML
- How to combine information from two different RSS feeds

RDF Basics

Before we launch into RSS, we'll take a quick look at the basics of RDF, the Resource Description Framework. RDF is an XML-based markup language that was initially developed by the W3C as a means of expressing meta-information about documents (for example, who wrote a particular document or when it was last modified).

RDF actually addresses a more general problem than how to express meta-information. RDF defines how to assert facts using XML. Some of these facts might concern documents (and therefore be meta-information for those documents). But other facts might be more general, such as "The capital of England is London" or "The Universe contains 1,000,000,000,000,000,000,000 stars."

RDF processors are able to make use of these facts to draw conclusions—to infer other facts. An RDF processor might take the fact "Amazon.com sells books published by Apress" and the fact "*Beginning XSLT 2.0* is a book published by Apress" and draw the conclusion that "Amazon.com sells *Beginning XSLT 2.0*." A search engine that understood RDF could search the metadata of a number of documents to create a list of the documents authored by a particular person or on a particular day.

Note The ability to express facts makes RDF one of the possible technologies at the heart of the Semantic Web. For more details, see the RDF home page at `http://www.w3.org/RDF/`.

RDF has been in development since 1997, before XML was even finalized. The first specification that reached Recommendation was the RDF Model and Syntax Recommendation (`http://www.w3.org/TR/REC-rdf-syntax/`), which became a Recommendation in 1999. This was replaced by a suite of related specifications that reached Recommendation status in February 2004:

- RDF Primer (`http://www.w3.org/TR/rdf-primer/`)
- RDF Concepts and Abstract Syntax (`http://www.w3.org/TR/rdf-concepts/`)
- RDF/XML Syntax Specification (`http://www.w3.org/TR/rdf-syntax-grammar/`)
- RDF Semantics (`http://www.w3.org/TR/rdf-mt/`)
- RDF Vocabulary Description Language 1.0: RDF Schema (`http://www.w3.org/TR/rdf-schema/`)
- RDF Test Cases (`http://www.w3.org/TR/rdf-testcases/`)

The Primer gives a good overview of RDF. The RDF Concepts and Abstract Syntax Recommendation describes how RDF is used to make statements; the RDF/XML Syntax Specification defines how those statements are expressed in an XML document. We won't go into the rest of RDF here.

In this section, we'll look first at the model that underlies RDF and then go on to look at how that model is expressed in XML.

Statements, Resources, and Properties

The heart of RDF is the ability to assert facts, which are known as **statements** in RDF. For example, RDF allows you to say, "The page at `http://www.jenitennison.com/` is written by Jeni Tennison" and "Jeni Tennison's e-mail address is `jeni@jenitennison.com`." An RDF document is essentially a collection of statements like these.

Statements are made about things, which in RDF terms are known as **nodes** or **resources**. There are two kinds of resources: ones that can be naturally identified using a URI (usually because they're web pages) and **blank nodes**, which can't. In the preceding examples, the resources involved are the web page `http://www.jenitennison.com/` and the person "Jeni Tennison". Of course, I am not a web-based resource, so I would be represented by a blank node in RDF.

Each resource has a number of **properties** with values; a statement states that a resource has a particular value for a property. The values of properties can be literals (like strings or numbers) or other resources (again, identified by their own URI). For example, in the statement "The page at `http://www.jenitennison.com/` is written by Jeni Tennison," the resource `http://www.jenitennison.com/` has the property "is written by" whose value is "Jeni Tennison". Properties can sometimes have multiple values; for example, a document could have multiple authors.

Different RDF applications are interested in different kinds of resources and properties. If you use RDF for metadata about pages on a web site, the resources will mostly be web pages, and the properties will be document metadata such as the author, date of last modification, keywords, and so on. If you use RDF to represent virtual business cards, then the resources will be people and the properties will be things like name, role, address, and telephone number. Each RDF application thus has its own **vocabulary**.

Representing Statements in XML

Statements in RDF can be represented using XML elements and attributes. RDF provides XML elements and attributes that allow you to point to resources in order to make statements about them. A particular RDF vocabulary will also define the elements or attributes that specify the properties about those resources, but RDF itself does not provide any domain-specific information, which means that it doesn't say anything about what properties can apply to a particular resource.

The elements and attributes that are part of RDF are all members of the following namespace:

```
http://www.w3.org/1999/02/22-rdf-syntax-ns#
```

In this chapter, we'll use the prefix `rdf` to indicate this namespace.

Describing Resources

The document element of an RDF document is the `<rdf:RDF>` element. Within the `<rdf:RDF>` element are a number of descriptions, each of which represent one or more statements about a resource.

The descriptions can be represented by either `<rdf:Description>` elements (for generic statements) or elements from another namespace, which allows you to give more information about the type of resource that the statement is about. In general terms, these are called **node elements**, because they represent a node in an RDF graph.

When a node element represents a resource that can be represented by a URI, it has an `rdf:about` attribute that indicates the resource that the statement is talking about. The `rdf:about` attribute holds the URI that identifies the resource. If the node element represents a blank node, it can have an `rdf:nodeID` attribute that provides an ID to enable that node to be referenced within the XML document.

For example, to make statements about the web page `http://www.jenitennison.com/` and about the person Jeni Tennison, you could use the following RDF:

```
<rdf:RDF xmlns:rdf="http://www.w3.org/1999/02/22-rdf-syntax-ns#">
<rdf:Description rdf:about="http://www.jenitennison.com/">
  ...
</rdf:Description>
<rdf:Description rdf:nodeID="JeniTennison">
  ...
</rdf:Description>
</rdf:RDF>
```

Alternatively, you could use elements in a different namespace as node elements, as follows:

```
<rdf:RDF xmlns:rdf="http://www.w3.org/1999/02/22-rdf-syntax-ns#"
        xmlns="http://www.example.com/websites">
<website rdf:about="http://www.jenitennison.com/">
  ...
</website>
<person rdf:nodeID="JeniTennison">
  ...
</person>
</rdf:RDF>
```

Note This second form gives additional information about the resource `http://www.jenitennison.com/`, namely that it's a web site, and states that the blank node with the identifier `JeniTennison` is a person. You can do the same with `<rdf:Description>` elements if you include an `<rdf:type>` element with an `rdf:resource` attribute whose value is a URI constructed by concatenating the namespace and local name of the node element.

Making Statements

The node elements contain a number of other elements that define the values of properties. These **property elements** usually come from another namespace because the properties that are relevant to a particular resource depend on the RDF application that you're using.

For literal values, the value of the property is given as the content of the property element. For example, to state that my name is Jeni Tennison and my e-mail address is `jeni@jenitennison.com`, you could use

```
<rdf:Description rdf:nodeID="JeniTennison">
  <name>Jeni Tennison</name>
  <emailAddress>jeni@jenitennison.com</emailAddress>
</rdf:Description>
```

or

```
<person rdf:nodeID="JeniTennison">
  <name>Jeni Tennison</name>
  <emailAddress>jeni@jenitennison.com</emailAddress>
</person>
```

Note Properties can be given structured literal values by nesting XML inside them. However, if you do this, you should add an attribute `rdf:parseType` with a value of `Literal` to the property element to indicate that the XML represents a literal value, not more RDF.

When a property's value is another resource, there are two options. The first option is to use the `rdf:resource` attribute to give the URI for this other resource, or the `rdf:nodeID` attribute if the other resource is a blank node. For example, to say that the web page `http://www.jenitennison.com/` is written by Jeni Tennison (a blank node with the identifier `JeniTennison`), you could use

```
<rdf:Description about="http://www.jenitennison.com/">
  <author rdf:nodeID="JeniTennison" />
</rdf:Description>
```

or

```
<website rdf:about="http://www.jenitennison.com/">
  <author rdf:nodeID="JeniTennison" />
</website>
```

Alternatively, you can nest the description of the resource within the property element, at the same time adding an `rdf:parseType` attribute with a value of `Resource` to the property element. This is particularly useful when there is additional information about the referenced resource because the more nested the structure is, the easier it is to read and navigate than the flatter structure. It's also handy when you have blank nodes, because it means you don't have to make up identifiers for them. For example, you could use

```
<rdf:Description about="http://www.jenitennison.com/">
  <author rdf:parseType="Resource">
    <rdf:Description>
      <name>Jeni Tennison</name>
      <emailAddress>jeni@jenitennison.com</emailAddress>
    </rdf:Description>
  </author>
</rdf:Description>
```

or

```
<website rdf:about="http://www.jenitennison.com/">
  <author rdf:parseType="Resource">
    <person>
      <name>Jeni Tennison</name>
      <emailAddress>jeni@jenitennison.com</emailAddress>
    </person>
  </author>
</website>
```

Note This latter example looks just like a normal XML document, but the RDF attributes allow any RDF processor to pull out useful information from it.

Bags, Sequences, and Alternatives

Sometimes properties have multiple values. For example, a web page may have many authors, have gone through multiple changes, or be available in several different formats. These situations are supported by the RDF elements `<rdf:Bag>`, `<rdf:Seq>`, and `<rdf:Alt>`, which are collectively known as **container elements**:

- `<rdf:Bag>` is used when properties have several values in no particular order, such as the authors of a web page.
- `<rdf:Seq>` is used when properties have several values and their order is important, such as a list of changes to the page.
- `<rdf:Alt>` is used when there are multiple alternative values for the property, such as several formats for the same web page.

Each of these container elements holds `<rdf:li>` elements, which behave just like property elements—they can hold a literal value, point to a resource, or even contain another resource. For example, I have an alternative e-mail address of `mail@jenitennison.com`. To represent this, you could use

```
<person rdf:nodeID="JeniTennison">
  <emailAddress>
    <rdf:Alt>
      <rdf:li>jeni@jenitennison.com</rdf:li>
      <rdf:li>mail@jenitennison.com</rdf:li>
    </rdf:Alt>
  </emailAddress>
</person>
```

Introducing RSS

RDF Site Summary (RSS) documents provide summaries of (some of) the information available on a web site. Each web site could provide several RSS documents to describe different aspects of the web site—news about changes to the web site, announcements on particular product lines, or information provided as a service to all. RSS documents can be retrieved by other applications, either behind the scenes (which is particularly useful for portal sites) or directly to the user via headline readers.

Note For a list of readers for RSS documents, see `http://blogspace.com/rss/readers`.

Each RSS document describes a particular **channel** available from a web site. The body of the RSS document contains summaries of one or more **items** that are available on that web site or elsewhere. For example, if you're using RSS on a site that serves news stories, the channel would be the news service, and the items would be news headlines, with links to the full story on your site. For our TV guide, we can imagine RSS documents from the site for each TV channel, with the items providing links to details of the programs that are showing on that channel. Another RSS source might provide reviews of the programs. The TV guide site itself might operate a channel for each subscriber, notifying them through a standard RSS reader when one of their favorite shows is about to start.

As with any standard that has been around for a while, there are several versions of RSS:

- RSS 0.9—The original format developed by Netscape for My Netscape Network (http://my.netscape.com/)
- RSS 0.91—A format that dropped RDF and incorporated elements from scriptingNews, a format from Userland (http://www.userland.com/)
- RSS 0.92—Further development on top of RSS 0.91, developed by Userland
- RSS 0.93—Again developed by Userland based on RSS 0.92
- RSS 1.0—Separate development on top of RSS 0.91, which reintroduces RDF, developed by members of the RSS-DEV mailing list
- RSS 2.0—Development based on RSS 0.93 by Userland and the Berkman Center for Internet & Society at Harvard Law School (http://cyber.law.harvard.edu/home/)

As you can see, the development of RSS forked after version 0.91, with Userland developing versions 0.92, 0.93, and 2.0, while members of RSS-DEV developed RSS 1.0. We're going to look at version 1.0 in this chapter because it uses RDF and Dublin Core, two standards that are useful in other areas aside from syndicated content, and because it provides a more interesting transformation due to its use of namespaces.

ATOM

In 2003, work began on yet another syndication format, called Atom. Atom does much the same thing as RSS, but aims to be simpler and to rationalize some of the more peculiar parts of RSS, with a particular emphasis on supporting blogging. You can find out more at the http://www.atomenabled.org/ web site; the latest specification at time of writing is an Internet Draft at http://www.ietf.org/internet-drafts/draft-ietf-atompub-format-08.txt.

Each Atom document describes a particular **feed** and contains a number of **entries**. To give you an idea, the Atom equivalent of listing.rss follows:

```
<feed xmlns="http://purl.org/atom/ns#draft-ietf-atompub-format-08"
      xmlns:dc="http://purl.org/dc/elements/1.1/">
  <title>BBC1</title>
  <link href="http://www.example.com/bbc1/" />
  <updated>2001-07-05T19:00:00Z</updated>
  <entry>
    <title>Panorama</title>
    <link href="http://www.example.com/bbc1#2001-07-05T21:30:00" />
    <link rel="related" href="http://www.bbc.co.uk/panorama" />
    <id>http://www.example.com/bbc1#2001-07-05T21:30:00</id>
    <updated>2001-07-05T19:00:00Z</updated>
    <content>
      Today discusses whether cloning pets is morally wrong.
    </content>
    <dc:identifier>85674</dc:identifier>
  </entry>
```

```
  <entry>
    <title>The National Lottery</title>
    <link href="http://www.example.com/bbc1#2001-07-05T20:45:00" />
    <link rel="related" href="http://www.bbc.co.uk/lottery/" />
    <id>http://www.example.com/bbc1#2001-07-05T20:45:00</id>
    <updated>2001-07-05T19:00:00Z</updated>
    <content>
      Stunning celebrity guests and a grand giveaway.
    </content>
    <dc:identifier>7129</dc:identifier>
  </entry>
  ...
</feed>
```

In this section, we'll have a look at the RSS format. We've already met RDF, on which RSS is based, so we'll look first at how the RSS markup language incorporates RDF, and then look at the Dublin Core and Syndication modules that plug into RSS.

RSS Markup Language

As you've seen, any RDF document has to be supplemented with elements from other namespaces in order to create a specialized vocabulary that can be understood by a particular RDF application. These namespaces need to define property elements and can also define node elements to take the place of `<rdf:Description>`.

RSS is one such markup language. RSS documents are RDF documents that use elements from the RSS namespace as description and property elements. The RSS namespace is

```
http://purl.org/rss/1.0/
```

We'll use the prefix `rss` for this namespace throughout the rest of this chapter.

In this section, we'll have a look at the node and property elements that RSS uses to describe channels and items.

Describing Channels

The first type of description element that RSS defines is the `<rss:channel>` element. The `<rss:channel>` element describes the web site whose content is being summarized by the RSS page.

Being an RDF node element, the `<rss:channel>` element has an `rdf:about` attribute that contains a URI that identifies the web site. Usually the URI is either the URL for the home page of the web site or the URL of the RSS document itself.

The `<rss:channel>` element contains a number of property elements, the most important of which are

- `<rss:title>`—A literal property giving the name of the web site.
- `<rss:link>`—A literal property giving the URL for the web site.

- `<rss:description>`—A literal property that gives a brief description of the web site (in plain text).
- `<rss:items>`—A sequence property that points to the items listed for the channel. The `<rss:items>` element contains an `<rdf:Seq>` element whose `<rdf:li>` elements each have an `rdf:resource` attribute; this attribute gives an identifier for each item described by the RSS page, which is usually the URL of the "full story" back on the web site.

Describing Items

The second type of node element that we'll look at is the `<rss:item>` element. Each RSS page should contain one or more such `<rss:item>` elements, each of which describes one of the items that are being summarized within the RSS page.

The `<rss:item>` element has an `rdf:about` attribute that references the URL summarized by the item. This URL is the same as the URL used in the `rdf:resource` attribute of one of the `<rdf:li>` elements within the `<rss:items>` element in the channel description outlined previously. The `<rss:item>` element contains three property elements:

- `<rss:title>`—A literal property giving a title for the item
- `<rss:link>`—A literal property giving the URL for the item (this will usually be the same as the URL in the `<rss:item>` element's `rdf:about` attribute)
- `<rss:description>`—An optional literal property giving a more detailed description of the item (as opposed to the `<rss:title>`, which gives only the "headline")

Example RSS Page

As examples of RSS, we'll look at two RSS documents that could provide useful material for our TV guide.

The first is a site that provides reviews of the TV programs showing over the next 24 hours. The RSS page `reviews.rss`, shown in Listing 17-1, gives a summary of each review, with URLs referencing back to the main site so that you can get more details. One thing to note here is that the URLs provided by the site use the VIDEO Plus+ code for each program to identify them uniquely.

Listing 17-1. `reviews.rss`

```
<rdf:RDF xmlns:rdf="http://www.w3.org/1999/02/22-rdf-syntax-ns#"
         xmlns:rss="http://purl.org/rss/1.0/">
<rss:channel rdf:about="http://www.example.com/reviews/reviews.rss">
  <rss:title>TV Reviews</rss:title>
  <rss:link>http://www.example.com/reviews/</rss:link>
  <rss:description>
    Reviews of TV programs showing in the next 24 hours.
  </rss:description>
  ...
  <rss:items>
    <rdf:Seq>
      <rdf:li rdf:resource="http://www.example.com/reviews/2571.html" />
```

```
      <rdf:li rdf:resource="http://www.example.com/reviews/85674.html" />
      ...
    </rdf:Seq>
  </rss:items>
</rss:channel>
<rss:item rdf:about="http://www.example.com/reviews/2571.html">
  <rss:title>EastEnders: They're Mad About the Boy</rss:title>
  <rss:link>http://www.example.com/reviews/2571.html</rss:link>
  <rss:description>
    Jamie Mitchell has never been so popular.
  </rss:description>
  ...
</rss:item>
<rss:item rdf:about="http://www.example.com/reviews/85674.html">
  <rss:title>Panorama: Current Issues</rss:title>
  <rss:link>http://www.example.com/reviews/85674.html</rss:link>
  <rss:description>
    Today's Panorama tackles the issue of pet cloning.
  </rss:description>
  ...
</rss:item>
...
</rdf:RDF>
```

Note VIDEO Plus+ numbers are the UK equivalent of VCR Plus+ numbers in the US.

The second example page is `listing.rss`, given in Listing 17-2, which provides a program listing. Note that new programs are added at the top of the list, so that the most recent item is a program that's just been added to the listing. Also note that the program identifiers use the timing of the program, while the links from the `<rss:item>` elements point to pages that may contain details about lots of programs.

Listing 17-2. `listing.rss`

```
<rdf:RDF xmlns:rdf="http://www.w3.org/1999/02/22-rdf-syntax-ns#"
         xmlns:rss="http://purl.org/rss/1.0/">
<rss:channel rdf:about="http://www.example.com/bbc1/listing.rss">
  <rss:title>BBC1</rss:title>
  <rss:link>http://www.example.com/bbc1/</rss:link>
  <rss:description>
    Listings of BBC 1 programs over the next 24 hours
  </rss:description>
  ...
  <rss:items>
    <rdf:Seq>
```

```
      <rdf:li rdf:resource="http://www.example.com/bbc1#2001-07-05T21:30:00" />
      <rdf:li rdf:resource="http://www.example.com/bbc1#2001-07-05T20:45:00" />
      ...
    </rdf:Seq>
  </rss:items>
</rss:channel>
<rss:item rdf:about="http://www.example.com/bbc1#2001-07-05T21:30:00">
  <rss:title>Panorama</rss:title>
  <rss:link>http://www.bbc.co.uk/panorama</rss:link>
  <rss:description>
    Today discusses whether cloning pets is morally wrong.
  </rss:description>
  ...
</rss:item>
<rss:item rdf:about="http://www.example.com/bbc1#2001-07-05T20:45:00">
  <rss:title>The National Lottery</rss:title>
  <rss:link>http://www.bbc.co.uk/lottery/</rss:link>
  <rss:description>
    Stunning celebrity guests and a grand giveaway.
  </rss:description>
  ...
</rss:item>
...
</rdf:RDF>
```

RSS Modules

As we saw in the previous section, the required content in an RSS page is rather brief and doesn't give a lot of detail about either the channel or the items that it describes. However, this is part of the design of RSS—different types of channels require different kinds of supplementary information for their items, so RSS defines a number of modules that can be used to add extra information to the basic RSS pages. These extra modules define additional property elements that can be used within `<rss:channel>` or `<rss:item>` elements.

The two modules that we'll look at briefly here are the Dublin Core module, which provides standard metadata properties (particularly relevant for web documents), and the Syndication module, which provides properties to do with how often an RSS feed is updated. We'll also see how it's possible for RSS applications to use their own properties if they wish.

Dublin Core Module

Dublin Core is a standard set of metadata that is commonly associated with documents. Dublin Core metadata isn't limited to XML representations, but Dublin Core elements and attributes are often used in XML-based markup languages to represent metadata. These elements and attributes are specified by the Dublin Core Metadata Initiative (`http://dublincore.org/`). The Dublin Core elements are all in the following namespace:

```
http://purl.org/dc/elements/1.1/
```

We'll use the prefix dc for this namespace throughout the rest of this chapter.

The following elements can provide common metadata about a document:

- <dc:title>—The title of the document
- <dc:creator>—The creator of the document
- <dc:subject>—A code or set of keywords that indicates the subject of the document
- <dc:description>—A description of the document
- <dc:publisher>—The entity responsible for making the document available
- <dc:contributor>—A contributor to the document
- <dc:date>—A date associated with the document (such as the date the document was issued)
- <dc:type>—The type of the document, for example Dataset, Image, or Text (see http://dublincore.org/documents/dcmi-type-vocabulary/ for a list)
- <dc:format>—The media type of the document
- <dc:identifier>—An identifier for the document
- <dc:source>—A URL specifying the resource from which the document is derived
- <dc:language>—A language identifier specifying the language in which the document is written
- <dc:relation>—A URI of a resource related to the document in some way
- <dc:coverage>—The scope of the document, in terms of physical location, time period, or organizational entity
- <dc:rights>—A copyright statement about the document

When RDF is used to represent metadata about documents, it generally uses these Dublin Core elements to hold that metadata. Similarly, RSS uses these same elements within <rss:channel> and <rss:item> to provide metadata about the channel or items.

These elements are particularly useful in the RSS document that contains reviews of TV programs (reviews.rss)—you can use it to add information about the author of the review, the date it was published, and any copyright issues governing the review. For example:

```
<rss:item rdf:about="http://www.example.com/reviews/2571.html">
  <rss:title>EastEnders: They're Mad About the Boy</rss:title>
  <rss:link>http://www.example.com/reviews/2571.html</rss:link>
  <rss:description>
    Jamie Mitchell has never been so popular.
  </rss:description>
  <dc:creator>Georgina Holland (george@reviews.example.com)</dc:creator>
  <dc:date>2001-07-05</dc:date>
  <dc:rights>Copyright &#169; 2001 Example Reviews Plc.</dc:rights>
</rss:item>
```

The TV listing RSS feed (listing.rss) could also use Dublin Core elements to add information about the item (for example, supplementing the item with a unique identifier for the program); here we'll use the VIDEO Plus+ code for the program again:

```
<rss:item rdf:about="http://www.example.com/bbc1#2001-07-05T19:30:00">
  <rss:title>EastEnders</rss:title>
  <rss:link>http://www.bbc.co.uk/eastenders/</rss:link>
  <rss:description>
    Mark's health scare forces him to reconsider his future with Lisa, while
    Jamie is torn between Sonia and Zoe.
  </rss:description>
  <dc:identifier>2571</dc:identifier>
</rss:item>
```

Syndication Module

The Syndication module for RSS defines a set of properties that can be specified for channels to describe how frequently they are updated. This is particularly useful for RSS documents that act as news feeds and are regularly updated—an application receiving the RSS document can work out when it next needs to check that more information has been made available. The namespace for the elements in the Syndication module is

```
http://purl.org/rss/modules/syndication/
```

We'll use the prefix sy to indicate elements in this module in the rest of this chapter.

The Syndication module defines three elements:

- <sy:updatePeriod>—Describes the period over which the channel is updated (hourly, daily, weekly, monthly, or yearly)
- <sy:updateFrequency>—States how many times the channel is updated during the update period (if missing, a value of 1 is assumed)
- <sy:updateBase>—Specifies the date and time at which the channel started, from which the date and time of updates can be calculated

---

Note The <sy:updateBase> element contains dates and times without seconds, slightly different from the more standard ISO 8601 date format.

The Syndication module elements are important in both the channels that we're using as examples. The TV review channel (reviews.rss) is updated once a day, so simply needs an <sy:updatePeriod> element to be added:

```
<rss:channel rdf:about="http://www.example.com/reviews/reviews.rss">
  <rss:title>TV Reviews</rss:title>
  <rss:link>http://www.example.com/reviews/</rss:link>
  <rss:description>
    Reviews of TV programs showing in the next 24 hours.
```

```
  </rss:description>
  <sy:updatePeriod>daily</sy:updatePeriod>
  <rss:items>
    <rdf:Seq>
      <rdf:li resource="http://www.example.com/reviews/2571.html" />
      <rdf:li resource="http://www.example.com/reviews/85674.html" />
      ...
    </rdf:Seq>
  </rss:items>
</rss:channel>
```

The TV listing channel (listing.rss) is updated more frequently, with more programs being added to the listing every half hour (48 times per day). It therefore needs both an <sy:updatePeriod> element and an <sy:updateFrequency> element, as follows:

```
<rss:channel rdf:about="http://www.example.com/bbc1/listing.rss">
  <rss:title>BBC1</rss:title>
  <rss:link>http://www.example.com/bbc1/</rss:link>
  <rss:description>
    Listings of BBC 1 programs over the next 24 hours
  </rss:description>
  <sy:updatePeriod>daily</sy:updatePeriod>
  <sy:updateFrequency>48</sy:updateFrequency>
  <rss:items>
    <rdf:Seq>
      <rdf:li resource="http://www.example.com/bbc1#2001-07-05T21:30:00" />
      <rdf:li resource="http://www.example.com/bbc1#2001-07-05T20:45:00" />
      ...
    </rdf:Seq>
  </rss:items>
</rss:channel>
```

Other Modules

The Dublin Core and Syndication modules are just examples of the modules that you can plug into RSS. The provider of an RSS document is able to add their own properties, in their own namespace, to the channel of items to provide appropriate supplementary information.

For example, as well as using the Dublin Core and Syndication module, the TV review channel in reviews.rss could define its own properties in the following namespace:

```
http://www.example.com/reviews
```

It could use a <rev:rating> element in this namespace to summarize the overall rating of the program, providing this information within the RSS feed:

```
<rss:item rdf:about="http://www.example.com/reviews/2571.html">
  <rss:title>EastEnders: They're Mad About the Boy</rss:title>
  <rss:link>http://www.example.com/reviews/2571.html</rss:link>
```

```
  <rss:description>
    Jamie Mitchell has never been so popular.
  </rss:description>
  <dc:creator>Georgina Holland (george@reviews.example.com)</dc:creator>
  <dc:date>2001-07-05</dc:date>
  <dc:rights>Copyright &#169; 2001 Example Reviews Plc.</dc:rights>
  <rev:rating>5</rev:rating>
</rss:item>
```

Naturally, the more people use and understand elements from these other modules, the more useful the information is. If an application didn't know that the <rev:rating> element held a rating, then it wouldn't be able to use that information.

Transforming RSS

The two types of RSS document that we've looked at provide us with a lot of useful information for our TV guide. The more important of the two types of document is the one giving the program listing, because we can use that to generate the XML that we've been using as the source of our TV guide. The review document is interesting too, because we can use that to provide the rating for each program. Rather than creating the TV guide document by hand, we can create it automatically by collecting the feeds together. The overall process might look as shown in Figure 17-1.

In the remaining part of this chapter, we'll look at how to generate the TV guide XML that we've been using throughout this book from a collection of RSS documents.

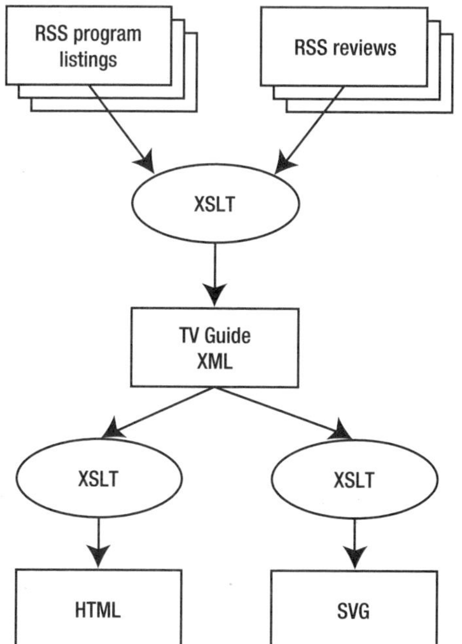

Figure 17-1. *Process of creating HTML and SVG TV guides from RSS feeds*

Sample Documents

We need to design a stylesheet that combines the two RSS files, `listing.rss` and `reviews.rss`, into a single XML document, `TVGuide.xml`. It's a good idea to look at the documents that we have and what we aim to get from them before we start. `listing.rss` is given in Listing 17-3.

Listing 17-3. `listing.rss`

```
<rdf:RDF xmlns:rdf="http://www.w3.org/1999/02/22-rdf-syntax-ns#"
         xmlns:rss="http://purl.org/rss/1.0/"
         xmlns:dc="http://purl.org/dc/elements/1.1/"
         xmlns:sy="http://purl.org/rss/modules/syndication/">
<rss:channel rdf:about="http://www.example.com/bbc1/listing.rss">
  <rss:title>BBC1</rss:title>
  <rss:link>http://www.example.com/bbc1/</rss:link>
  <rss:description>
    Listings of BBC 1 programs over the next 24 hours
  </rss:description>
  <sy:updatePeriod>daily</sy:updatePeriod>
  <sy:updateFrequency>48</sy:updateFrequency>
  <rss:items>
    <rdf:Seq>
      <rdf:li rdf:resource="http://www.example.com/bbc1#2001-07-05T21:30:00" />
      <rdf:li rdf:resource="http://www.example.com/bbc1#2001-07-05T20:45:00" />
      ...
    </rdf:Seq>
  </rss:items>
</rss:channel>
<rss:item rdf:about="http://www.example.com/bbc1#2001-07-05T21:30:00">
  <rss:title>Panorama</rss:title>
  <rss:link>http://www.bbc.co.uk/panorama</rss:link>
  <rss:description>
    Today discusses whether cloning pets is morally wrong.
  </rss:description>
  <dc:identifier>85674</dc:identifier>
</rss:item>
<rss:item rdf:about="http://www.example.com/bbc1#2001-07-05T20:45:00">
  <rss:title>The National Lottery</rss:title>
  <rss:link>http://www.bbc.co.uk/lottery/</rss:link>
  <rss:description>
    Stunning celebrity guests and a grand giveaway.
  </rss:description>
  <dc:identifier>7129</dc:identifier>
</rss:item>
...
</rdf:RDF>
```

The reviews.rss document looks like that shown in Listing 17-4.

Listing 17-4. reviews.rss

```
<rdf:RDF xmlns:rdf="http://www.w3.org/1999/02/22-rdf-syntax-ns#"
         xmlns:rss="http://purl.org/rss/1.0/"
         xmlns:dc="http://purl.org/dc/elements/1.1/"
         xmlns:sy="http://purl.org/rss/modules/syndication/"
         xmlns:rev="http://www.example.com/reviews">
<rss:channel rdf:about="http://www.example.com/reviews/reviews.rss">
  <rss:title>TV Reviews</rss:title>
  <rss:link>http://www.example.com/reviews/</rss:link>
  <rss:description>
    Reviews of TV programs showing in the next 24 hours.
  </rss:description>
  <sy:updatePeriod>daily</sy:updatePeriod>
  <rss:items>
    <rdf:Seq>
      <rdf:li rdf:resource="http://www.example.com/reviews/2571.html" />
      <rdf:li rdf:resource="http://www.example.com/reviews/85674.html" />
      ...
    </rdf:Seq>
  </rss:items>
</rss:channel>
<rss:item rdf:about="http://www.example.com/reviews/2571.html">
  <rss:title>EastEnders: They're Mad About the Boy</rss:title>
  <rss:link>http://www.example.com/reviews/2571.html</rss:link>
  <rss:description>
    Jamie Mitchell has never been so popular.
  </rss:description>
  <dc:creator>Georgina Holland (george@reviews.example.com)</dc:creator>
  <dc:date>2001-07-05</dc:date>
  <dc:rights>Copyright &#169; 2001 Example Reviews Plc.</dc:rights>
  <rev:rating>5</rev:rating>
</rss:item>
<rss:item rdf:about="http://www.example.com/reviews/85674.html">
  <rss:title>Panorama: Current Issues</rss:title>
  <rss:link>http://www.example.com/reviews/85674.html</rss:link>
  <rss:description>
    Today's Panorama tackles the issue of pet cloning.
  </rss:description>
  <dc:creator>Christian Taylor (chris@reviews.example.com)</dc:creator>
  <dc:date>2001-07-05</dc:date>
  <dc:rights>Copyright &#169; 2001 Example Reviews Plc.</dc:rights>
  <rev:rating>6</rev:rating>
</rss:item>
...
</rdf:RDF>
```

And the BBC1.xml document that we'll be generating from this is shown in Listing 17-5.

Listing 17-5. BBC1.xml

```
<Channel>
<Name>BBC1</Name>
<Program videoPlus="620">
  <Start>2001-07-05T19:00:00</Start>
  <Duration>PT30M</Duration>
  <Series>A Question of Sport</Series>
  <Title/>
  <Description>
    Sports quiz hosted by Sue Barker.
  </Description>
</Program>
<Program videoPlus="2571" rating="5">
  <Start>2001-07-05T19:30:00</Start>
  <Duration>PT30M</Duration>
  <Series>EastEnders</Series>
  <Title/>
  <Description>
    Mark's health scare forces him to reconsider his future with Lisa,
    while Jamie is torn between Sonia and Zoe.
  </Description>
</Program>
...
</Channel>
```

The stylesheet that we'll construct for this task is RSS2Channel.xsl. This stylesheet will exercise a lot of the XSLT and XPath that you've learned over the course of this book, so hold tight!

Basic Stylesheet

Before we launch into the body of the stylesheet, we need to set up the basics—look at the namespaces that we need to be able to handle, consider what whitespace management we want to use, and decide what control we want over the output.

Managing Namespaces

RSS documents use a lot of namespaces, especially if the extra modules are used as well. The namespaces that are used in the source documents are

- The RDF namespace—http://www.w3.org/1999/02/22-rdf-syntax-ns#
- The RSS namespace—http://purl.org/rss/1.0/
- The Dublin Core namespace—http://purl.org/dc/elements/1.1/
- The Syndication namespace—http://purl.org/rss/modules/syndication/
- The TV Review namespace—http://www.example.com/reviews

All except the Syndication namespace are used for elements or attributes that we're interested in, so our stylesheet needs to declare these namespaces, as well as the XSLT namespace, within the `<xsl:stylesheet>` element as follows:

```
<xsl:stylesheet version="2.0"
                xmlns:xsl="http://www.w3.org/1999/XSL/Transform"
                xmlns:rdf="http://www.w3.org/1999/02/22-rdf-syntax-ns#"
                xmlns:rss="http://purl.org/rss/1.0/"
                xmlns:dc="http://purl.org/dc/elements/1.1/"
                xmlns:rev="http://www.example.com/reviews">
...
</xsl:stylesheet>
```

In addition, we're going to need the namespaces for the XML Schema datatypes and the XPath datatypes, so we need to include their namespaces as well:

```
<xsl:stylesheet version="2.0"
                xmlns:xsl="http://www.w3.org/1999/XSL/Transform"
                xmlns:rdf="http://www.w3.org/1999/02/22-rdf-syntax-ns#"
                xmlns:rss="http://purl.org/rss/1.0/"
                xmlns:dc="http://purl.org/dc/elements/1.1/"
                xmlns:rev="http://www.example.com/reviews"
                xmlns:xs="http://www.w3.org/2001/XMLSchema"
                xmlns:xdt="http://www.w3.org/2003/05/xpath-datatypes">
...
</xsl:stylesheet>
```

On the other hand, the result of the transformation doesn't involve any namespaces. If we leave the `<xsl:stylesheet>` element as shown, then any elements that we construct within the stylesheet will be given namespace nodes for each of these namespaces, with the end result that the output of the transformation will include namespace declarations for the RDF, RSS, Dublin Core, TV Review, XML Schema, and XPath datatypes namespaces, despite the fact that they are never used within the document itself.

To prevent this from happening, we can use the `exclude-result-prefixes` attribute on `<xsl:stylesheet>`, listing the prefixes of the namespaces that we don't want to be included in the result. The `<xsl:stylesheet>` element therefore looks like the following:

```
<xsl:stylesheet version="2.0"
                xmlns:xsl="http://www.w3.org/1999/XSL/Transform"
                xmlns:rdf="http://www.w3.org/1999/02/22-rdf-syntax-ns#"
                xmlns:rss="http://purl.org/rss/1.0/"
                xmlns:dc="http://purl.org/dc/elements/1.1/"
                xmlns:rev="http://www.example.com/reviews"
                xmlns:xs="http://www.w3.org/2001/XMLSchema"
                xmlns:xdt="http://www.w3.org/2003/05/xpath-datatypes"
                exclude-result-prefixes="rdf rss dc rev xs xdt">
...
</xsl:stylesheet>
```

Managing Whitespace

Our next preparatory task is to decide what to do about whitespace-only text nodes in the source RSS documents. If we can strip out the whitespace-only text nodes that we're not interested in, we'll end up with a much smaller tree and run less risk of numbering going awry (if we ever add it) because we have whitespace that we don't want in the result document.

Fortunately, in general RDF documents tend to avoid mixed content, so you can usually strip whitespace-only text nodes throughout the document. This is true in the case of the RSS documents that we're dealing with, so we can use `<xsl:strip-space>` to strip all whitespace-only text nodes from the two source documents, as follows:

```
<xsl:strip-space elements="*" />
```

Managing Output

The final setup task for the stylesheet is to construct an `<xsl:output>` element that describes the format that we want to generate. In this case, we're generating a basic XML format, with no special media type, no DTD, and no elements that should contain CDATA sections. Therefore the `<xsl:output>` element is pretty simple—the only things that I think we should include are instructions to the processor to indent the output and to use the ISO-8859-1 encoding, as that will make it easier for us to read and debug in standard text editors:

```
<xsl:output indent="yes" encoding="ISO-8859-1" />
```

Creating the Program Listing

The first task that we'll attempt with our stylesheet is to generate the `<Channel>` and `<Program>` elements from `listing.rss`. To help us do this, let's look at the mappings between the information available within the RSS document and the format in `TVGuide.xml`:

- The document element `<rdf:RDF>` maps to the document element `<Channel>`.
- The content of the `<rss:channel>` element's child `<rss:title>` element maps to the `<Name>` child of the `<Channel>` element.
- Each `<rss:item>` maps to an equivalent `<Program>` element.
- The `<dc:identifier>` element maps to the `videoPlus` attribute on the `<Program>` element.
- The end of the `rdf:about` attribute provides the value for the `<Start>` element.
- The `<rss:title>` element within the `<rss:item>` element maps to the `<Series>` element in the `<Program>` element.
- The `<rss:description>` element maps to the `<Description>` element.

We can construct a template for each of these mappings, matching the relevant element or attribute in the source RSS document and using it to generate the required element or attribute in the result.

First the document element: the `<rdf:RDF>` element maps to the `<Channel>` element. Inside the `<Channel>` element comes the result of applying templates to the `<rdf:RDF>` elements' children, first the `<rss:channel>` element, and then the `<rss:item>` elements, in reverse order. We can make sure that the <rss:item> elements are processed in reverse order using the reverse() function. Sorting in reverse order is simpler than trying to work out the time of each program and using that. The resulting template is

```
<xsl:template match="rdf:RDF">
  <Channel>
    <xsl:apply-templates select="rss:channel" />
    <xsl:apply-templates select="reverse(rss:item)" />
  </Channel>
</xsl:template>
```

The <rss:channel> element doesn't have an equivalent as such—the only relevant thing about the <rss:channel>, for this transformation, is its title. We can therefore use a template that matches the <rss:channel> element to focus the processing on its <rss:title> element child, nothing more:

```
<xsl:template match="rss:channel">
  <xsl:apply-templates select="rss:title" />
</xsl:template>
```

The template for the <rss:title> element needs to map this element to a <Name> element with the same value. The mapping itself is straightforward, but we have to watch out here—<rss:title> elements occur in two places in the source RSS document (the <rss:channel> element and the <rss:item> elements). We're going to need to process the <rss:title> elements within the <rss:item> elements in a different way (to produce a <Series> element), so we'll make sure that this template only matches those <rss:title> elements that appear within <rss:channel> elements, as follows:

```
<xsl:template match="rss:channel/rss:title">
  <Name><xsl:value-of select="." /></Name>
</xsl:template>
```

That's all we have to worry about for the channel information, so we'll now move on to the <rss:item> elements, each of which maps to a <Program> element:

```
<xsl:template match="rss:item">
  <Program>
    ...
  </Program>
</xsl:template>
```

The first interesting property of this <Program> element is that it has a videoPlus attribute whose value comes from the <dc:identifier> child element of the <rss:item>. We could generate this attribute by applying templates to the <dc:identifier> element, but it's simpler in this case to just use an attribute value template, as follows:

```
<xsl:template match="rss:item">
  <Program videoPlus="{dc:identifier}">
    ...
  </Program>
</xsl:template>
```

To create the element content of the <Program> element, we need to make sure that the relevant attribute and child elements of the <rss:item> element are processed in the correct order—first the rdf:about attribute to generate the <Duration> element, then the <rss:title> element, and then the <rss:description> element:

```
<xsl:template match="rss:item">
  <Program videoPlus="{dc:identifier}">
    <xsl:apply-templates select="@rdf:about" />
    <xsl:apply-templates select="rss:title" />
    <xsl:apply-templates select="rss:description" />
  </Program>
</xsl:template>
```

The other thing we need to do in this template is to add the empty <Title> element (here I'm assuming that the RSS feed gives series names rather than program titles):

```
<xsl:template match="rss:item">
  <Program videoPlus="{dc:identifier}">
    <xsl:apply-templates select="@rdf:about" />
    <xsl:apply-templates select="rss:title" />
    <Title />
    <xsl:apply-templates select="rss:description" />
  </Program>
</xsl:template>
```

The templates for the <rss:title> and <rss:description> elements are straightforward, although again we need to take a little bit of care over the match pattern for the <rss:title> element because there are <rss:title> elements in other contexts that need to be treated in a different way. The two templates are

```
<xsl:template match="rss:item/rss:title">
  <Series><xsl:value-of select="." /></Series>
</xsl:template>

<xsl:template match="rss:description">
  <Description><xsl:value-of select="." /></Description>
</xsl:template>
```

The final template is the template for the rdf:about attribute. We're using this attribute as the source of the start time of the program, since the start time is used in the fragment identifier. For example, the rdf:about attribute for the <rss:item> representing the *EastEnders* program has the following value:

```
http://www.example.com/bbc1#2002-01-07T20:00:00
```

The start time of the program is given after the # in this URI. Since the URI can only contain a single #, we can simply use the substring-after() function to retrieve the value. The template for the rdf:about attribute is therefore

```
<xsl:template match="@rdf:about">
  <Start><xsl:value-of select="substring-after(., '#')" /></Start>
</xsl:template>
```

Adding Duration Information

The one bit of information available in the TV listing RSS document that we've missed out so far is the <Duration> element. In this section, we'll look at how to create this element.

The RSS TV listing doesn't explicitly provide us with a duration for each program. However, if we know when a program starts and know when it ends, then we can work out the duration of the program, and we can work out when the program ends by looking at when the next program begins. Calculating the duration is going to take a bit of work, so we'll create a separate template, matching the <rss:item> element in duration mode, to do it, just to make the stylesheet more modular:

```
<xsl:template match="rss:item" mode="duration">
  ...
</xsl:template>
```

We can "call" this template from the main template for the <rss:item> elements by applying templates to the <rss:item> element we're on, but in duration mode, as follows:

```
<xsl:template match="rss:item">
  <Program videoPlus="{dc:identifier}">
    <xsl:apply-templates select="@rdf:about" />
    <xsl:apply-templates select="." mode="duration" />
    <xsl:apply-templates select="rss:title" />
    <Title />
    <xsl:apply-templates select="rss:description" />
  </Program>
</xsl:template>
```

We've seen how to get the start time for the current program using the substring-after() function on the rdf:about attribute. To get the start time for the next program, we need to look at the rdf:about attribute of the immediately preceding <rss:item> element (remember that the RSS listing gives the programs in reverse order). We can get this <rss:item> using the preceding-sibling:: axis, as follows:

```
preceding-sibling::rss:item[1]
```

Of course, we might not be able to find an item at all—the latest program in the listing (which is the first <rss:item> in the RSS document) doesn't have a preceding sibling. In these cases, we won't generate a <Duration> element, so the first job in the duration-mode template is to test whether the <rss:item> actually has a preceding sibling at all. Since we'll be using the preceding sibling if it exists, we may as well hold it in a variable:

```
<xsl:template match="rss:item" mode="duration">
  <xsl:variable name="nextProgram" as="element(rss:item)?"
                select="preceding-sibling::rss:item[1]" />
  <xsl:if test="$nextProgram">
    <Duration>
      ...
    </Duration>
  </xsl:if>
</xsl:template>
```

The start of the program is the xs:dateTime given after the "#" in the rdf:about attribute. We can create variables to hold the start and end time of the program by looking at the rdf:about attribute of the current <rss:item> element and the one that's held in the $nextProgram variable:

```
<xsl:variable name="start" as="xs:dateTime"
  select="xs:dateTime(substring-after(@rdf:about, '#'))" />
<xsl:variable name="end" as="xs:dateTime"
  select="xs:dateTime(substring-after($nextProgram/@rdf:about, '#'))" />
```

The duration is then the start time subtracted from the end time. The completed template is as follows:

```
<xsl:template match="rss:item" mode="duration">
  <xsl:variable name="nextProgram" as="element()?"
                select="preceding-sibling::rss:item[1]" />
  <xsl:if test="$nextProgram">
    <Duration>
      <xsl:variable name="start" as="xs:dateTime"
        select="xs:dateTime(substring-after(@rdf:about, '#'))" />
      <xsl:variable name="end" as="xs:dateTime"
        select="xs:dateTime(substring-after($nextProgram/@rdf:about, '#'))" />
      <xsl:value-of select="$end - $start" />
    </Duration>
  </xsl:if>
</xsl:template>
```

Adding Rating Information

The remaining piece of information that we need to insert in the TVGuide.xml document is from the TV review feed—the rating of those programs that have been reviewed. This information is stored in the <rev:rating> child element of the <rss:item> representing a particular program review within the review RSS document.

The TV review RSS document, reviews.rss, is a separate document, which doesn't act as the main source for the transformation. Therefore it has to be accessed from the stylesheet using the document() function. Because we'll be referring to it multiple times during the course of the transformation, we'll create a global variable to hold the root node of the review document, as follows:

```
<xsl:variable name="reviews" as="document-node()"
              select="document('reviews.rss')" />
```

■ **Note** In real life, this reviews.rss document might come from a completely different web site. You could use document('http://www.example.com/reviews/reviews.rss') to retrieve it from http://www.example.com/reviews/reviews.rss, for example.

Within the review RSS document, each program review is represented by an <rss:item> element. The <rss:item> indicates what program it's talking about via the name of the file referenced by the <rss:link> element (and the rdf:about attribute). The HTML file containing the review of a program is named via the VIDEO Plus+ number for the program.

Luckily, we know the VIDEO Plus+ code for the program, because it's held in the <dc:identifier> child element of the <rss:item> representing the program in the listing document. We can therefore use the code as a link between the two sources of information—retrieve the VIDEO Plus+ number from the TV listing, and use that to identify the relevant review in the review RSS document.

As you saw in Chapter 10, the most efficient way to retrieve the element with a particular value for an attribute or child element is via a key. You can use <xsl:key> to set up a key to index an element on practically anything, and then use the key() function to retrieve the element based on its key value.

In this case, we need to index <rss:item> elements from the review RSS document by the VIDEO Plus+ number. The VIDEO Plus+ number can be retrieved from the <rss:link> child element of the <rss:item> element by taking the substring after the directory name 'http://www.example.com/reviews/' and before the file extension '.html', as follows:

```
substring-before(substring-after(rss:link, 'http://www.example.com/reviews/'),
                 '.html')
```

We'll call this key reviews. The <xsl:key> element needs to match <rss:item> elements and use the preceding path to calculate a key value (the VIDEO Plus+ code) for each item:

```
<xsl:key name="reviews" match="rss:item"
   use="substring-before(
          substring-after(rss:link, 'http://www.example.com/reviews/'),
          '.html')" />
```

Now, given a VIDEO Plus+ code in the $videoPlus variable, we can retrieve the <rss:item> that reviews that program in the reviews.rss document, and from there, its child <rev:rating> element to get the rating of the program, as follows:

```
key('reviews', $videoPlus, $reviews)/rev:rating
```

This code appears in the template for the <rss:item> elements (which are matched in the TV listing document), while creating <Program> elements, as follows:

```
<xsl:template match="rss:item">
  <xsl:variable name="videoPlus" select="dc:identifier" />
  <Program videoPlus="{$videoPlus}">
    <xsl:apply-templates
      select="key('reviews', $videoPlus, $reviews)/rev:rating" />
    <xsl:apply-templates select="@rdf:about" />
    <xsl:apply-templates select="." mode="duration" />
    <xsl:apply-templates select="rss:title" />
    <Title />
    <xsl:apply-templates select="rss:description" />
  </Program>
</xsl:template>
```

The template matching the <rev:rating> elements needs to generate a rating attribute for the <Program> element, using <xsl:attribute>, as follows:

```
<xsl:template match="rev:rating">
  <xsl:attribute name="rating" select="." />
</xsl:template>
```

Final Result

The RSS2Channel.xsl stylesheet can now be used to take the listing.rss and reviews.rss documents and generate BBC1.xml. The listing.rss document needs to be the main source document for the transformation; reviews.rss gets pulled into the transformation using the document() function from within the stylesheet.

The command line for running the transformation, with Saxon, for example, is

```
java net.sf.saxon.Transform -o BBC1.xml listing.rss RSS2Channel.xsl
```

If you run this transformation, you should generate BBC1.xml, which looks as shown in Figure 17-2 when you view it in Internet Explorer.

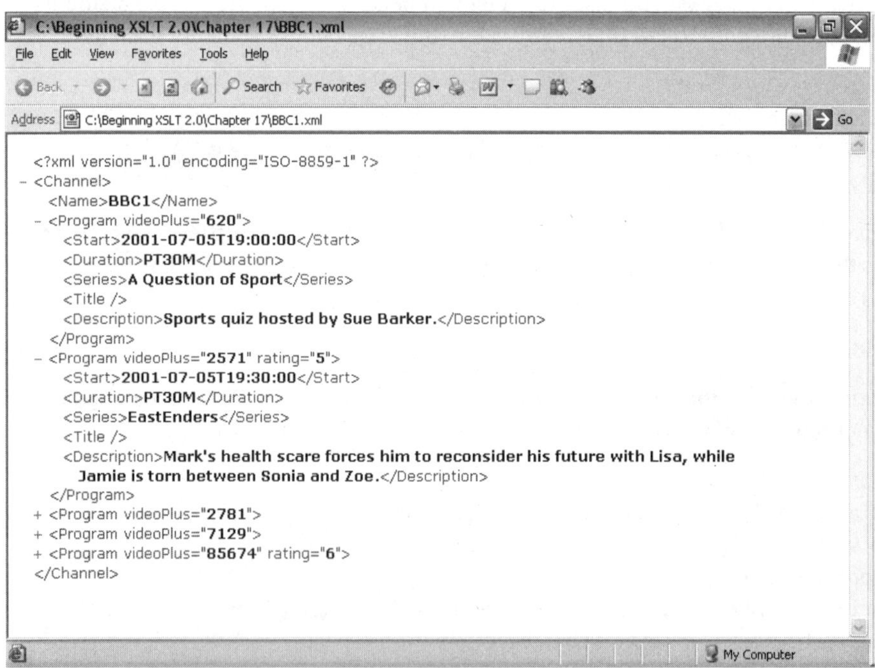

Figure 17-2. *Viewing* BBC1.xml *in Internet Explorer*

The information from listing.rss has been translated to the markup language that we've been using to represent channels throughout this book. Ratings have been added to those programs that have been reviewed from reviews.rss. Thus RSS documents, made available on channel and reviewers' web sites, can be combined to create the TV guide XML document that we can use on our online TV guide site to create HTML pages, SVG, and other formats.

Summary

This chapter has introduced you to the basics of RDF, for representing information about resources; Dublin Core, for representing metadata about documents; and RSS, for representing syndicated information or general site summaries. We've concentrated on transforming *from* RSS to another format, but hopefully this chapter has also given you an idea about how XSLT applications can use RSS as both the source and result of transformations.

In the process of generating a stylesheet to use information from RSS documents, we've looked at the following techniques, which you learned in the first part of this book:

- Using namespaces in XML documents to distinguish between elements and attributes from different markup languages
- Declaring namespaces for use in XSLT stylesheets, and preventing them from appearing in the result
- Stripping whitespace-only text nodes from data-oriented XML structures
- Controlling the indentation of output using `<xsl:output>`
- Identifying mappings between source information and result information, to use as the basis of templates
- Changing the order in which items appear in the result, both using `<xsl:apply-templates>` to select the appropriate information and by reversing items using `reverse()`
- Using attribute value templates to insert information into generated attributes
- Extracting information from strings using `substring-before()` and `substring-after()`
- Using modes to break up your stylesheet into more manageable components
- Identifying preceding siblings using the `preceding-sibling::` axis
- Conditionally adding elements and attributes using explicit flow control instructions (such as `<xsl:if>`) or by applying templates, which can only be used on nodes that exist
- Performing calculations on dates and times using arithmetic operators
- Working with multiple source documents, including using keys across multiple documents

Review Questions

1. Construct an XML document that points to a list of RSS documents containing TV listings.
2. Amend the stylesheet developed during this chapter so that it creates multiple `<Channel>` elements wrapped within a `<TVGuide>` element, based on the XML document from the first review question. The stylesheet should retrieve the RSS documents using the `document()` function.
3. Construct a separate XML document that lists RSS documents supplying TV program ratings.

4. Amend the stylesheet developed in Review Question 2 so that it accesses the TV rating RSS documents from Review Question 3 and calculates average ratings to include in the `rating` attribute of the `<Program>` element.

5. Construct, by hand, an RSS document containing reminders when someone's favorite programs are showing.

6. Create a stylesheet that generates the reminders RSS document from `TVGuide.xml`, assuming the `<Program>` elements in `TVGuide.xml` have `flag` attributes with a value of `favorite` for the user's favorite programs.

APPENDIX A

XPath Quick Reference

This appendix gives you a quick guide to XPath, including its syntax and a guide to all the functions that are available to you.

Sequences

Every XPath expression returns a sequence, which can be empty or hold any number of items. Items can be nodes or atomic values.

Nodes

Nodes can be of the kinds shown in Table A-1.

Table A-1. *Node Kinds*

Node Kind	Name	String Value
Document	-	Concatenation of all text nodes in the document
Element	Element name	Depends on element type
Attribute	Attribute name	Depends on attribute type
Text	-	Text
Comment	-	Text held within the comment
Processing instruction	Processing instruction target	Text in the processing instruction after the space after the target name
Namespace	Namespace prefix	Namespace URI

Node Types

Element and attribute nodes can be annotated with a type based on validation against a schema. The types, string values, and typed values of element and attribute nodes are summarized in Table A-2.

Table A-2. *Node Types*

Node Kind	Validity	Type	String Value	Typed Value
Element	Unvalidated	`xdt:untyped`	Concatenation of all text node descendants	String value as `xdt:untypedAtomic` value
Element	Invalid or partially validated	`xdt:anyType`	Concatenation of all text node descendants	String value as `xdt:untypedAtomic` value
Element	Valid	Simple	Text with whitespace normalized based on type	Sequence of items of appropriate type
Element	Valid	Mixed	Concatenation of all text node descendants	String value as `xdt:untypedAtomic` value
Element	Valid	Element-only	Concatenation of all text node descendants	Undefined
Attribute	Unvalidated	`xdt:untypedAtomic`	Value with whitespace replaced	String value as `xdt:untypedAtomic` value
Attribute	Invalid or partially validated	`xdt:untypedAtomic`	Value with whitespace replaced	String value as `xdt:untypedAtomic` value
Attribute	Valid	Simple	Value with whitespace normalized based on type	Sequence of items of appropriate type

Atomic Values

Atomic values in Basic XSLT can be of any of the atomic types shown in Table A-3. The relevant namespace URIs are

- `http://www.w3.org/2001/XMLSchema` (`xs` prefix by convention)
- `http://www.w3.org/2005/04/xpath-datatypes` (`xdt` prefix by convention)

Caution The namespace for XPath datatypes changes with each version of the spec.

Basic XSLT processors may support other, implementation-defined types as well as those given in Table A-3.

Table A-3. *Atomic Types in Basic XSLT*

Atomic Type	Representation	Description
`xs:string`	The string itself	A sequence of XML characters
`xs:boolean`	`'true'`, `'false'`, `'1'`, or `'0'`	`true` or `false`
`xs:decimal`	Any number of digits, with optional fractional part	A decimal number, with size limits being implementation-defined
`xs:integer`	Any number of digits	An integer, with size limits being implementation-defined
`xs:double`	As `xs:decimal`, but with optional exponent, `'NaN'`, `'INF'`, or `'-INF'`	A floating-point number: a double-precision 64-bit format IEEE 754 value
`xs:float`	As `xs:double`	A floating-point number: a single-precision 32-bit format IEEE 754 value
`xs:date`	`YYYY-MM-DD`	A date: year, month, day, and optional timezone
`xs:time`	`hh:mm:ss`	A time: hours, minutes, seconds, and optional timezone
`xs:dateTime`	`YYYY-MM-DDThh:mm:ss`	A date and time: year, month, day, hours, minutes, seconds, and optional timezone
`xs:gYear`	`YYYY`	A year with optional timezone
`xs:gYearMonth`	`YYYY-MM`	A year and month with optional timezone
`xs:gMonth`	`--MM`	A month with optional timezone
`xs:gMonthDay`	`--MM-DD`	A month and day with optional timezone
`xs:gDay`	`---DD`	A day with optional timezone
`xs:duration`	`PyYmMdDThHmMsS`	A duration of years, months, days, hours, minutes, and seconds
`xdt:dayTimeDuration`	`PdDThHmMsS`	A duration of days, hours, minutes, and seconds
`xdt:yearMonthDuration`	`PyYmM`	A duration of years and months
`xs:QName`	`prefix:local-name` or just `local-name`; namespace must be declared	A qualified name: a namespace URI and a local name
`xs:anyURI`	URI syntax	A URI
`xs:hexBinary`	Hex-encoded octets	Binary data
`xs:base64Binary`	Base64-encoded octets	Binary data
`xdt:untypedAtomic`	Any string	An atomic value whose type is not known, and can be cast implicitly to another type

In Schema-Aware XSLT processors, all the atomic types from XML Schema and XPath are built in. These are shown in Figure A-1. You may also import types from a schema using `<xsl:import-schema>`.

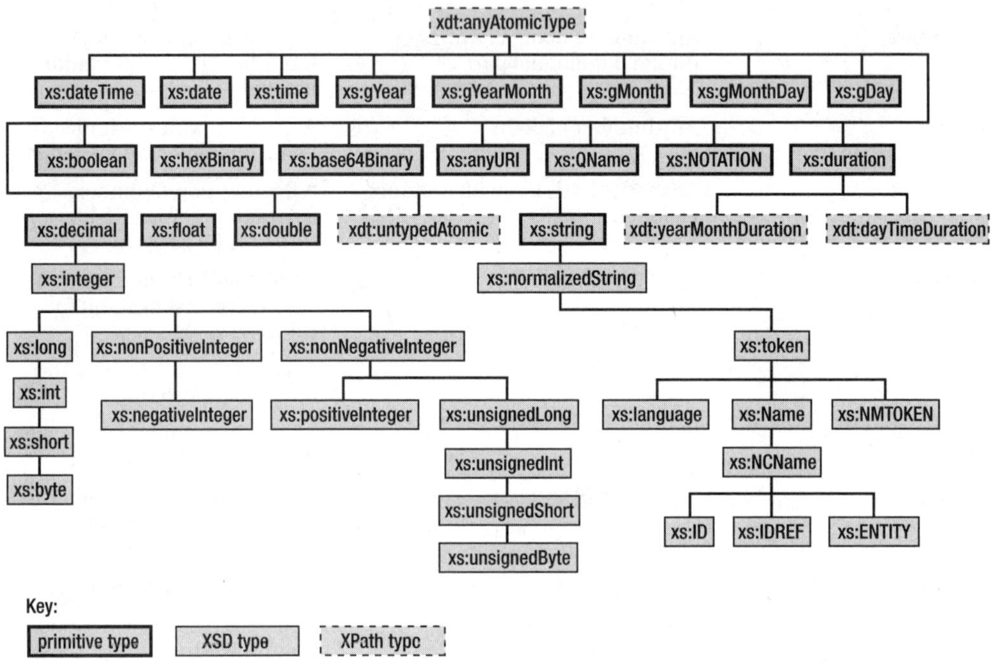

Figure A-1. *The hierarchy of built-in types*

Atomic values can be cast to other types using constructor functions—the name of the constructor function is the same as the name of the type—or the `cast` expression. Casting is allowed between the following primitive types:

- `xs:string` and `xdt:untypedAtomic` values can be cast to any other type (though the cast won't always succeed), with the exceptions of `xs:QName` and `xs:NOTATION`.
- Values of numeric types (`xs:decimal`, `xs:float`, and `xs:double`) can be cast to other numeric types, though casts from `xs:double` and `xs:float` to `xs:decimal` won't always succeed.
- Values of numeric types can be cast to `xs:boolean` and vice versa.
- `xs:dateTime` values can be cast to any of the date/time types.
- `xs:date` values can be cast to `xs:dateTime`, `xs:gYear`, `xs:gYearMonth`, `xs:gMonth`, `xs:gMonthDay`, and `xs:gDay` types.
- Values of the binary types (`xs:hexBinary` and `xs:base64Binary`) can be cast to each other.

Whether a cast will succeed or not can be tested using the `castable` expression.

Note Literal strings *can* be cast to `xs:QName` and to subtypes of `xs:NOTATION`.

Effective Boolean Value

Within tests, a value (equivalent to a single-item sequence) will be converted to its effective Boolean value, as shown in Table A-4.

Table A-4. *Effective Boolean Values*

Value	Effective Boolean Value
Node	`true`
String	`true` if the string contains any characters, `false` otherwise
Number	`false` if number is `0` or `NaN`, `true` otherwise
Boolean	`true` if `true`, `false` if `false`
Other atomic value	Raises an error

The effective Boolean value of a sequence is `false` if it is empty and `true` if the first item in the sequence is a node. Otherwise, if the sequence contains more than one item, you get an error.

Sequence Types

Sequence types are patterns that match sequences. Sequence types are summarized in Table A-5.

Table A-5. *Sequence Types*

Sequence Type	Description
`void()`	Matches the empty sequence
`itemType`	Matches a sequence containing a single item
`itemType?`	Matches a sequence that contains 0 or 1 items
`itemType+`	Matches a sequence that contains 1 or more items
`itemType*`	Matches a sequence that contains any number of items

Sequence types may use an item type to specify the type of the items in the sequence. Item types are summarized in Table A-6.

Table A-6. *Item Types*

Item Type	Description
`item()`	Matches any item
`atomicType`	Matches items of the named atomic type (see Table A-3)
`nodeKindTest`	Matches items that are nodes that match the node kind test (see Table A-7)

Node kind tests are used to test nodes. Node kind tests are summarized in Table A-7.

Table A-7. *Node Kind Tests*

Node Kind	Node Test	Description
Nodes	`node()`	Matches or selects all kinds of nodes
Document nodes	`document-node()`	Matches or selects all document nodes
	`document-node(element(`*name*`))`	Matches or selects document nodes with a single document element with a particular name
	`document-node(element(*, `*type*`))`	Matches or selects document nodes with a single document element with a particular type
	`document-node(element(`*name*`, `*type*`))`	Matches or selects document nodes with a single document element with a particular name and type
	`document-node(schema-element(`*name*`))`	Matches or selects document nodes with a single document element that matches a global element declaration within a schema
Text	`text()`	
Elements	`element()`	Matches or selects all elements
	`element(`*name*`)`	Matches or selects elements with a particular name
	`element(*, `*type*`)`	Matches or selects elements with a particular type
	`element(`*name*`, `*type*`)`	Matches or selects elements with a particular name and type
	`schema-element(`*name*`)`	Matches or selects elements based on a global element declaration within a schema
Attributes	`attribute()`	Matches or selects all attributes
	`attribute(`*name*`)`	Matches or selects attributes with a particular name
	`attribute(*, `*type*`)`	Matches or selects attributes with a particular type
	`attribute(`*name*`, `*type*`)`	Matches or selects attributes with a particular name and type
	`schema-attribute(`*name*`)`	Matches or selects attributes based on a global attribute declaration within a schema
Comments	`comment()`	
Processing Instructions	`processing-instruction()`	Matches or selects all processing instructions
	`processing-instruction(`*target*`)`	Matches or selects processing instructions with a particular target

Paths

Paths are made up of a number of steps, separated by /s. Each step can be a general step or an axis step. A general step is any expression; the expression must result in a sequence of nodes for all steps except the last in a path. Each axis step is made up of an optional axis (defaults to `child`), a node test, and any number of predicates (held in square brackets).

Axes

Axes dictate the relationship between the context node and the selected nodes. The direction of an axis determines how the `position()` of a node is calculated within a predicate—forward axes look at document order, reverse axes look at reverse document order. The axes are listed in Table A-8.

Table A-8. *XPath Axes*

Axis	Direction	Description
`self`	Forward	Selects the context node itself
`child`	Forward	Selects the children of the context node
`parent`	Reverse	Selects the parent of the context node
`attribute`	Forward	Selects the attributes of the context node
`descendant`	Forward	Selects the descendants of the context node at any level
`descendant-or-self`	Forward	Selects the descendants of the context node, and the context node itself
`ancestor`	Reverse	Selects the ancestors of the context node
`ancestor-or-self`	Reverse	Selects the ancestors of the context node, and the context node itself
`following-sibling`	Forward	Selects the siblings of the context node that follow the context node in document order
`preceding-sibling`	Reverse	Selects the siblings of the context node that precede the context node in document order
`following`	Forward	Selects the nodes (aside from attribute and namespace nodes) that follow the context node in document order and that are not descendants of the context node
`preceding`	Reverse	Selects the nodes (aside from attribute and namespace nodes) that precede the context node in document order and that are not ancestors of the context node
`namespace`	Forward	Selects the namespace nodes on the context node

---

Note The `namespace` axis is deprecated; not all XSLT processors will support it.

Node Tests

Node tests match different kinds of nodes as shown in Table A-9.

Table A-9. *Node Tests*

Node Test	Description
*	Matches all attributes when used with the `attribute` axis, all namespace nodes when used with the `namespace` axis, and all elements when used with other axes
name	Matches attributes with the specified name when used with the `attribute` axis, namespaces with the specified name when used with the `namespace` axis, and elements with the specified name when used with other axes
nodeKindTest	Matches nodes that match the node kind test (see Table A-7)

Abbreviated Syntax

You can use several abbreviations in XPath expressions, as described in Table A-10.

Table A-10. *XPath Abbreviations*

Abbreviation	Full Equivalent	Description
`..`	`parent::node()`	Indicates the parent of the context node
`//`	`/descendant-or-self::node()/`	Supplies quick access to descendants of the context node
`/`	(at the beginning of a path)	`(root() cast as document-node())/` Goes up to the root of the node tree, and gives an error if it is not a document node
`@`	`attribute::`	Shortens expressions that access attributes

Expressions and Operators

The expressions in XPath can be split into eight groups:

- Sequence operators (see Table A-11)
- Arithmetic operators (see Table A-12)
- Comparisons (see Tables A-13 and A-14)
- Logical operators (see Table A-15)
- `for` expression
- Conditional expression
- Quantified expressions
- Expressions on `SequenceTypes` (see Table A-16)

The precedence of the operators (from lowest to highest) is as follows:

1. , (sequence concatenation)
2. for, some, every, if
3. or
4. and
5. eq, ne, lt, le, gt, ge, =, !=, <,
6. to
7. +, -
8. *, div, idiv, mod
9. union, |
10. intersect, except
11. instance of
12. treat
13. castable
14. cast
15. unary -, unary +-, unary +

Sequence Operators

The operators shown in Table A-11 can be used to create sequences.

Table A-11. *Sequence Operators*

Operator	Description
,	Concatenates two sequences together
to	Creates a sequence containing all the integers from the left operand to the right operand
|	Creates a node sequence containing all the nodes that are in either operand, in document order
union	Creates a node sequence containing all the nodes that are in either operand, in document order
intersect	Creates a node sequence containing all the nodes that are in both operands, in document order
except	Creates a node sequence containing all the nodes that are in the left operand but not in the right operand, in document order

Note The operands for to must be integers. The operands for |, union, intersect, and except must be sequences of nodes.

Arithmetic Operators

The operators shown in Table A-12 can be used to perform arithmetic either on numbers or on date/times and durations.

Table A-12. *Arithmetic Operators*

Operator	Description
+	Addition
-	Subtraction
*	Multiplication
`div`	Division
`idiv`	Integer division
`mod`	Remainder from integer division
unary -	Negation
unary +	No-op

Comparisons

Table A-13 shows the comparisons you can perform between sequences and between values. General comparisons between sequences and values are true if the comparison is true for any item in the sequence. Value comparisons can only be used to compare single items.

Table A-13. *Value and General Comparisons*

Value Comparison	General Comparison	Description
`eq`	=	Equal to
`ne`	!=	Not equal to
`lt`	<	Less than
`le`	<=	Less than or equal to
`gt`	>	Greater than
`ge`	>=	Greater than or equal to

The comparisons shown in Table A-14 are used to compare two nodes.

Table A-14. *Node Comparisons*

Operator	Description
`is`	`true` if the two operands are identical
<<	`true` if the left operand appears before the right operand in document order
>>	`true` if the right operand appears before the left operand in document order

Logical Operators

The logical operators, shown in Table A-15, compare two Boolean values.

Table A-15. *Logical Operators*

Operator	Description
or	true if either operand is true when converted to Booleans
and	true if both operands are true when converted to Booleans

for Expression

Syntax:

```
for $var1 in sequence1,
    $var2 in sequence2,
    ...
return expression
```

Returns a sequence containing the results of evaluating expression for every combination of items in sequence1, sequence2, and so on. The variables $var1, $var2, and so on can be used within the expression to refer to the relevant item in each sequence.

Conditional Expression

Syntax:

```
if (test) then true-expression else false-expression
```

Returns the result of evaluating true-expression if the effective Boolean value of the result of evaluating test is true, and the result of evaluating false-expression otherwise.

Quantified Expressions

The following quantified expressions test the items in a sequence to see whether they meet a particular condition.

some Expression

Syntax:

```
some $var1 in sequence1,
     $var2 in sequence2,
     ...
satisfies test
```

Returns true if the effective Boolean value of the result of evaluating test for some combination of items in sequence1, sequence2, and so on is true. The variables $var1, $var2, and so on can be used within the test to refer to the relevant item in each sequence.

every Expression

Syntax:

```
every $var1 in sequence1,
      $var2 in sequence2,
      ...
satisfies test
```

Returns `true` if the effective Boolean value of the result of evaluating `test` for every combination of items in `sequence1`, `sequence2`, and so on is `true`. The variables `$var1`, `$var2`, and so on can be used within the test to refer to the relevant item in each sequence.

Expressions on Sequence Types

The expressions shown in Table A-16 deal with testing and casting values so that they meet a particular sequence type.

Table A-16. *Expressions on Sequence Types*

Expression	Description
expression instance of *SequenceType*	Returns `true` if the result of evaluating *expression* matches *SequenceType*
expression cast as *atomicType*	Returns the result of casting the result of evaluating *expression* to a single item of the named atomic type, or an error if it cannot be cast
expression cast as *atomicType*?	Returns the result of casting the result of evaluating *expression* to an optional item of the named atomic type, or an error if it cannot be cast
expression castable as *atomicType*	Returns `true` if the result of *expression* cast as *atomicType* is not an error
expression castable as *atomicType*?	Returns `true` if the result of *expression* cast as *atomicType*? is not an error
expression treat as *SequenceType*	Returns the result of evaluating *expression* if it matches *SequenceType*, or an error if it does not match *SequenceType*

Functions

This section describes the functions defined in XPath and XSLT 2.0. As well as these functions, there are built-in constructor functions for every atomic type known to the XSLT processor. Individual XSLT processors may also support extension functions. Individual stylesheets may define their own stylesheet functions.

The signatures of the functions in this section use the sequence-type syntax to describe the return type and the argument types. The term `numeric` is used when the argument or return type can be any of the numeric types `xs:integer`, `xs:decimal`, `xs:float`, or `xs:double`; in these cases, untyped arguments are usually cast to `xs:double`.

abs()

Returns the absolute value of the argument: the value itself if it's positive, and the value multiplied by –1 if it's negative. If the argument is an empty sequence, returns an empty sequence.

```
numeric? abs(numeric?)
```

See also `round()`, `floor()`, `ceiling()`.
From XPath 2.0.

adjust-date-to-timezone()

Returns the `xs:date` passed as the first argument adjusted to the timezone specified by the second argument. If the second argument is missing, it defaults to the implicit timezone. If the second argument is an empty sequence, the timezone of the `xs:date` is removed. If the first argument is an empty sequence, returns an empty sequence.

```
xs:date? adjust-date-to-timezone(xs:date?)
xs:date? adjust-date-to-timezone(xs:date?, xdt:dayTimeDuration?)
```

See also `adjust-dateTime-to-timezone()`, `adjust-time-to-timezone()`, `timezone-from-date()`.
From XPath 2.0.

adjust-dateTime-to-timezone()

Returns the `xs:dateTime` passed as the first argument adjusted to the timezone specified by the second argument. If the second argument is missing, it defaults to the implicit timezone. If the second argument is an empty sequence, the timezone of the `xs:dateTime` is removed. If the first argument is an empty sequence, returns an empty sequence.

```
xs:dateTime? adjust-dateTime-to-timezone(xs:dateTime?)
xs:dateTime? adjust-dateTime-to-timezone(xs:dateTime?, xdt:dayTimeDuration?)
```

See also `adjust-date-to-timezone()`, `adjust-time-to-timezone()`, `timezone-from-dateTime()`.
From XPath 2.0.

adjust-time-to-timezone()

Returns the `xs:time` passed as the first argument adjusted to the timezone specified by the second argument. If the second argument is missing, it defaults to the implicit timezone. If the second argument is an empty sequence, the timezone of the `xs:time` is removed. If the first argument is an empty sequence, returns an empty sequence.

```
xs:time? adjust-time-to-timezone(xs:time?)
xs:time? adjust-time-to-timezone(xs:time?, xdt:dayTimeDuration?)
```

See also `adjust-dateTime-to-timezone()`, `adjust-date-to-timezone()`, `timezone-from-time()`.
From XPath 2.0.

avg()

Returns the average value of the items in the argument sequence, which must all be numeric, all be xdt:dayTimeDurations, or all be xdt:yearMonthDurations. Returns the empty sequence if the argument is an empty sequence.

```
xdt:anyAtomicType? avg(xdt:anyAtomicType*)
```

See also sum(), count(), min(), max().
From XPath 2.0.

base-uri()

Returns the base URI of the node passed as the argument. If there's no argument, returns the base URI of the stylesheet in which it's used. If the argument is an empty sequence, returns an empty sequence.

```
xs:anyURI? base-uri()
xs:anyURI? base-uri(node()?)
```

See also resolve-uri(), document().
From XPath 2.0.

boolean()

Returns the effective Boolean value of the argument. Usually this is done automatically, for example, in test attributes.

```
xs:boolean boolean(item()*)
```

See also string(), number(), not(), xs:boolean() constructor function.
From XPath 1.0.

ceiling()

Rounds the argument up to the nearest integer (though this isn't returned as an xs:integer unless the argument is an xs:integer). For negative numbers, this means rounding nearer to 0, so ceiling(-1.5) is -1. If the argument is an empty sequence, returns an empty sequence.

```
numeric? ceiling(numeric?)
```

See also floor(), round().
From XPath 1.0.

codepoint-equal()

Returns true if the first string is equal to the second string according to the Unicode codepoint collation. Returns an empty sequence if either argument is an empty sequence.

```
xs:boolean? codepoint-equal(xs:string?, xs:string?)
```

See also compare(), eq operator.
From XPath 2.0.

codepoints-to-string()

Returns the result of converting each integer in the argument sequence to the appropriate Unicode character and concatenating the results into a string. Raises an error if any of the integers is the codepoint of a character that's not legal in XML, and returns an empty string if the argument sequence is empty.

```
xs:string codepoints-to-string(xs:integer*)
```

See also `string-to-codepoints()`.
From XPath 2.0.

collection()

Returns a sequence of nodes based on the argument URI or the default collection if no argument is specified. How a particular sequence of nodes is associated with a particular URI is implementation-defined. Returns an empty sequence if the argument is an empty sequence.

```
node()* collection()
node()* collection(xs:string?)
```

See also `doc()`, `document()`.
From XPath 2.0.

compare()

Compares the first and second arguments using the collation specified as the third argument. Returns `0` if they're the same, `-1` if the first argument is less than the second argument, and `1` if the first argument is greater than the second argument. If no third argument is specified, uses the default collation. If either of the first or second arguments is an empty sequence, returns an empty sequence.

```
xs:integer? compare(xs:string?, xs:string?)
xs:integer? compare(xs:string?, xs:string?, xs:string)
```

See also `codepoint-equal()`, comparison operators (`eq`, `ne`, `lt`, `le`, `gt`, `ge`).
From XPath 2.0.

concat()

Concatenates the strings passed as arguments into a single string.

```
xs:string concat(xs:string?, xs:string?, ...)
```

See also `string-join()`.
From XPath 1.0.

contains()

Returns `true` if the string passed as the first argument contains the string passed as the second argument, as determined by the collation specified by the third argument, or if the second argument is an empty string or empty sequence, and `false` otherwise. If the third argument isn't specified, uses the Unicode codepoint collation.

```
xs:boolean contains(xs:string?, xs:string?)
xs:boolean contains(xs:string?, xs:string?, xs:string)
```

See also `matches()`, `starts-with()`, `ends-with()`.
From XPath 1.0.

count()

Returns the number of items in the sequence passed as the argument.

```
xs:integer count(item()*)
```

See also `last()`, `position()`, `<xsl:number>`.
From: XPath 1.0.

current()

Returns the current item—the item that's currently being processed within the `<xsl:for-each>` or `<xsl:template>`, or matched by a pattern, as opposed to the *context item*, which is the item currently being looked at within an XPath.

```
item() current()
```

See also the `.` expression.
From XSLT 1.0.

current-date()

Returns the `xs:date` for the transformation. This doesn't change during the transformation.

```
xs:date current-date()
```

See also `current-dateTime()`, `current-time()`.
From XPath 2.0.

current-dateTime()

Returns the `xs:dateTime` for the transformation. This doesn't change during the transformation.

```
xs:dateTime current-dateTime()
```

See also `current-date()`, `current-time()`.
From XPath 2.0.

current-group()

Returns the items in the current group when grouping within `<xsl:for-each-group>`. When used outside `<xsl:for-each-group>`, returns an empty sequence.

```
item()* current-group()
```

See also `current-grouping-key()`, `<xsl:for-each-group>` instruction.
From XSLT 2.0.

current-grouping-key()

Returns the value that's being used to group items within `<xsl:for-each-group>` using `group-by` or `group-adjacent` attributes. Returns an empty sequence if used outside `<xsl:for-each-group>` or if the grouping is being done with `group-starting-with` or `group-ending-with` attributes.

```
xdt:anyAtomicType? current-grouping-key()
```

See also `current-group()`, `<xsl:for-each-group>` instruction.
From XSLT 2.0.

current-time()

Returns the `xs:time` for the transformation. This doesn't change during the transformation.

```
xs:time current-time()
```

See also `current-dateTime()`, `current-date()`.
From XPath 2.0.

data()

Returns a sequence of atomic values from a sequence of items. Each node in the argument sequence is replaced by its typed value; each atomic value in the argument sequence remains as it is.

```
xdt:anyAtomicType* data(item()*)
```

See also `string()`.
From XPath 2.0.

dateTime()

Returns an `xs:dateTime` value constructed by the date given as the first argument and the time given as the second argument. Raises an error if the date and time have different timezones; otherwise adopts the timezone of the arguments (no timezone if neither have timezones, the timezone of the argument with the timezone if only one has a timezone).

```
xs:dateTime dateTime(xs:date, xs:time)
```

See also `xs:dateTime()` constructor function.
From XPath 2.0.

day-from-date()

Returns the day component from an `xs:date`. If the argument is an empty sequence, returns an empty sequence.

```
xs:integer? day-from-date(xs:date?)
```

See also `year-from-date()`, `month-from-date()`, `timezone-from-date()`.
From XPath 2.0.

day-from-dateTime()

Returns the day component from an xs:dateTime. If the argument is an empty sequence, returns an empty sequence.

```
xs:integer? day-from-dateTime(xs:dateTime?)
```

See also year-from-dateTime(), month-from-dateTime(), hours-from-dateTime(), minutes-from-dateTime(), seconds-from-dateTime(), timezone-from-dateTime().

From XPath 2.0.

days-from-duration()

Returns the days component from an xdt:dayTimeDuration. If the argument is an empty sequence, returns an empty sequence.

```
xs:integer? days-from-duration(xdt:dayTimeDuration?)
```

See also hours-from-duration(), minutes-from-duration(), seconds-from-duration().

From XPath 2.0.

deep-equal()

Returns true if the two argument sequences are equal. Each of the items in each sequence is compared, and if any of the items are nodes, then they are compared based on their name and content (typed value for attributes and text-only elements). The optional third argument specifies a collation that's used to compare strings; the default collation is used if the third argument is missing.

```
xs:boolean deep-equal(item()*, item()*)
xs:boolean deep-equal(item()*, item()*, xs:string)
```

From XPath 2.0.

default-collation()

Returns the URI for the default collation currently being used to compare strings.

```
xs:string default-collation()
```

See also compare().

From XPath 2.0.

distinct-values()

Removes duplicates from the argument sequence. The optional second argument specifies a collation to be used when comparing strings to work out if they're duplicates; if it's missing, the default collation is used.

```
xdt:anyAtomicType* distinct-values(xdt:anyAtomicType*)
xdt:anyAtomicType* distinct-values(xdt:anyAtomicType*, xs:string)
```

See also <xsl:for-each-group>.

From XPath 2.0.

doc()

Returns a document node for the resource specified by the argument URI. If the argument is an empty sequence, returns an empty sequence.

```
document-node()? doc(xs:string?)
```

See also doc-available(), document(), unparsed-text(), collection().
From XPath 2.0.

doc-available()

Returns true if a call to doc() with the same URI argument will result in a document node; otherwise returns false.

```
xs:boolean doc-available(xs:string?)
```

See also doc(), document().
From XPath 2.0.

document()

Returns the nodes identified by the URIs specified via the first argument, resolved using the base URI of the node specified as the second argument. If the second argument is missing, URIs that are specified as atomic values are resolved relative to the base URI for the stylesheet, while URIs that are specified in nodes are resolved relative to the node in which they're specified.

```
node()* document(item()*)
node()* document(item()*, node())
```

See also doc(), doc-available(), unparsed-text(), collection().
From XSLT 1.0.

document-uri()

Returns the URI for the resource used to create a document node. Usually, this will be the same as the base URI for the document node, but it might be different if the document node was returned as part of a collection. For all other node kinds, or if the document doesn't have a document URI, returns an empty sequence.

```
xs:string? document-uri(node()?)
```

See also base-uri(), collection(), doc(), document().
From XPath 2.0.

element-available()

Returns true if the processor supports the extension element or new XSLT instruction named by the string passed as the argument. The string should be a qualified name, with a prefix.

```
xs:boolean element-available(xs:string)
```

See also function-available(), <xsl:fallback> element.
From XSLT 1.0.

empty()

Returns `true` if the argument is an empty sequence, and `false` otherwise.

```
xs:boolean empty(item()*)
```

See also `not()`, `exists()`.
From XPath 2.0.

ends-with()

Returns `true` if the first argument string ends with the second argument string, according to the collation specified in the third argument string, or if the second argument string is an empty string or empty sequence, and returns `false` otherwise. If the third argument isn't specified, it defaults to the Unicode codepoint collation.

```
xs:boolean ends-with(xs:string?, xs:string?)
xs:boolean ends-with(xs:string?, xs:string?, xs:string)
```

See also `starts-with()`, `contains()`, `matches()`.
From XPath 2.0.

error()

Raises an error that halts the transformation. The first argument, if supplied, identifies the error; if it's not supplied (there's no argument or the first argument is an empty sequence), it defaults to the qualified name `{http://www.w3.org/2004/07/xqt-errors}FOER0000`. The first argument may be mapped to a URL in the form *namespaceURI#localName* by a processor. The second argument is a description of the error, and the third argument supplies additional items that provide information about the error.

Caution The URI `http://www.w3.org/2004/07/xqt-errors` will change in future versions of the spec.

```
error()
error(xs:QName)
error(xs:QName?, xs:string)
error(xs:QName?, xs:string, item()*)
```

Note This function doesn't return anything: calling it halts the transformation.

See also `trace()`, `<xsl:message>`.
From XPath 2.0.

escape-uri()

Returns the string specified by the first argument with those characters that are significant in URIs escaped. The second argument should be true if the string will be used to form only part of a URI (such as a search parameter), and false if the string is a whole URI. If the first argument is an empty sequence, returns an empty string.

```
xs:string escape-uri(xs:string?, xs:boolean)
```

> See also resolve-uri().
> From XPath 2.0.

exactly-one()

Returns the argument if and only if it contains exactly one item; otherwise raises an error.

```
item() exactly-one(item()*)
```

> See also exists(), zero-or-one(), one-or-more().
> From XPath 2.0.

exists()

Returns true if the argument is not an empty sequence; otherwise returns false.

```
xs:boolean exists(item()*)
```

> See also empty(), boolean(), exactly-one(), one-or-more().
> From XPath 2.0.

false()

Returns false.

```
xs:boolean false()
```

> See also true(), boolean(), xs:boolean() constructor function.
> From XPath 1.0.

floor()

Rounds the number down to the nearest integer value (though this isn't returned as an xs:integer unless the argument is an xs:integer). If the number is negative, then it gets rounded away from zero, so floor(-1.5) returns -2. If the argument is an empty sequence, returns an empty sequence.

```
numeric? floor(numeric?)
```

> See also ceiling(), round().
> From XPath 1.0.

format-date()

Returns the xs:date passed as the first argument formatted according to the format pattern passed as the second argument. If the first argument is an empty sequence, returns an empty sequence. See format-dateTime() for a description of the format pattern.

If more than two arguments are specified, the third argument is a language, the fourth a calendar, and the fifth a country; these are used to determine the details of the formatting used, in particular which language is used for the names of months and days. If one of these arguments is an empty sequence, then an implementation-defined default value is used instead.

```
xs:string? format-date(xs:date?, xs:string)
xs:string? format-date(xs:date?, xs:string,
                       xs:string?, xs:string?, xs:string?)
```

See also format-dateTime(), format-time().
From XSLT 2.0.

format-dateTime()

Returns the xs:dateTime passed as the first argument formatted according to the format pattern passed as the second argument. If the first argument is an empty sequence, returns an empty sequence. The format pattern contains variable markers in square brackets to indicate where particular components should go in the formatted string and their format. Variable markers are of the form

component[*presentation1*[*presentation2*]][,[*minWidth*[-*maxWidth*]]]

where *component* is a component specifier shown in Table A-17, *presentation1* and *presentation2* are presentation modifiers, and *minWidth* and *maxWidth* indicate the minimum and maximum widths for the components.

Table A-17. *Component Specifiers in* format-dateTime(), format-date(), *and* format-time()

Component	Meaning	Default Presentation
Y	Year	1
M	Month in year	1
D	Day in month	1
d	Day in year	1
F	Day of week	n
W	Week in year	1
w	Week in month	1
H	Hour in day (24 hours)	1
h	Hour in half-day (12 hours)	1
P	a.m./p.m. marker	n
m	Minute in hour	01
s	Whole seconds in minute	01
f	Fractional seconds in minute	1

Component	Meaning	Default Presentation
`Z`	Timezone as a time offset from UTC, or if an alphabetic modifier is present the conventional name of a timezone (such as PST)	`1`
`z`	Timezone as a time offset using GMT, for example GMT+1	`1`
`C`	Calendar: the name or abbreviation of a calendar name	`n`
`E`	Era: the name of a baseline for the numbering of years, for example, the reign of a monarch	`n`

The first presentation modifier indicates the style in which the component is presented; possible values are shown in Table A-18.

Table A-18. *First Presentation Modifier in* `format-dateTime()`, `format-date()`, *and* `format-time()`

Modifier	Meaning	Example
`1`	Decimal numbering	1, 2, 3, ...
`01`	Decimal numbering with leading zeros	01, 02, 03, ...
`i`	Lowercase roman numbering	i, ii, iii, ...
`I`	Uppercase roman numbering	I, II, III, ...
`a`	Lowercase alphabetical numbering	a, b, c, ...
`A`	Uppercase alphabetical numbering	A, B, C, ...
`w`	Lowercase words	one, two, three, ...
`W`	Uppercase words	ONE, TWO, THREE, ...
`Ww`	Titlecase words	One, Two, Three, ...
`n`	Lowercase names	january, february, march, ...
`N`	Uppercase names	JANUARY, FEBRUARY, MARCH, ...
`Nn`	Titlecase names	January, February, March, ...

The second presentation modifier is either `t` for traditional numbering or `o` for ordinal numbering.

If more than two arguments are specified, the third argument is a language, the fourth a calendar, and the fifth a country; these are used to determine the details of the formatting used, in particular which language is used for the names of months and days. If one of these arguments is an empty sequence, then an implementation-defined default value is used instead.

```
xs:string? format-dateTime(xs:dateTime?, xs:string)
xs:string? format-dateTime(xs:dateTime?, xs:string,
                           xs:string?, xs:string?, xs:string?)
```

See also `format-date()`, `format-time()`.

From XSLT 2.0.

format-number()

Returns the number passed as the first argument formatted according to the format pattern passed as the second argument. The format pattern usually contains # to mean an optional digit, 0 to indicate a required digit, . to indicate the decimal point, and , to indicate a grouping separator. For example, format-number(1234.5, '#,##0.00') returns 1,234.50. If the third argument is specified, it gives the name of a decimal format, declared with the <xsl:decimal-format> element, which can define other characters to be used instead of #, 0, ,, and ..

```
xs:string format-number(xs:double, xs:string)
xs:string format-number(xs:double, xs:string, xs:string)
```

See also number(), <xsl:decimal-format> element, <xsl:number> instruction.
From XSLT 1.0.

format-time()

Returns the xs:time passed as the first argument formatted according to the format pattern passed as the second argument. If the first argument is an empty sequence, returns an empty sequence. See format-dateTime() for a description of the format pattern.

If more than two arguments are specified, the third argument is a language, the fourth a calendar, and the fifth a country; these are used to determine the details of the formatting used, in particular which language is used for the names of months and days. If one of these arguments is an empty sequence, then an implementation-defined default value is used instead.

```
xs:string? format-time(xs:time?, xs:string)
xs:string? format-time(xs:time?, xs:string,
                       xs:string?, xs:string?, xs:string?)
```

See also format-dateTime(), format-date().
From XSLT 2.0.

function-available()

Returns true if the processor supports the function named by the argument string. The string usually includes a prefix to test for the availability of extension functions. If there is a second argument, returns true if the processor supports the named function with the number of arguments specified by the second argument.

```
xs:boolean function-available(xs:string)
xs:boolean function-available(xs:string, xs:integer)
```

See also element-available().
From XSLT 1.0.

generate-id()

Returns an ID for the argument node that is both unique and a valid XML ID. If no argument is given, it returns a unique ID for the context node. The unique IDs are not stable—they are different from processor to processor, and even for the same processor operating over the same stylesheet with the same source XML document. If the argument is an empty sequence, returns an empty string.

```
xs:string generate-id()
xs:string generate-id(node()?)
```

From XSLT 1.0.

hours-from-dateTime()

Returns the hours component from an `xs:dateTime`. If the argument is an empty sequence, returns an empty sequence.

```
xs:integer? hours-from-dateTime(xs:dateTime?)
```

See also `year-from-dateTime()`, `month-from-dateTime()`, `day-from-dateTime()`, `minutes-from-dateTime()`, `seconds-from-dateTime()`, `timezone-from-dateTime()`.

From XPath 2.0.

hours-from-duration()

Returns the hours component from an `xdt:dayTimeDuration`. If the argument is an empty sequence, returns an empty sequence.

```
xs:integer? hours-from-duration(xdt:dayTimeDuration?)
```

See also `days-from-duration()`, `minutes-from-duration()`, `seconds-from-duration()`.

From XPath 2.0.

hours-from-time()

Returns the hours component from an `xs:time`. If the argument is an empty sequence, returns an empty sequence.

```
xs:integer? hours-from-time(xs:time?)
```

See also `minutes-from-time()`, `seconds-from-time()`, `timezone-from-time()`.

From XPath 2.0.

id()

Returns the elements with the XML IDs specified by the first argument in the document containing the node given in the second argument or containing the context node if no second argument is supplied. Any strings in the argument sequence are split up at the whitespace, and the function returns all the elements in the current document that have any of the IDs. You have to have declared an attribute or an element as having the type `xs:ID` within a DTD or schema, or use the attribute `xml:id` to hold the ID, for the `id()` attribute to work.

```
element()* id(xs:string*)
element()* id(xs:string*, node())
```

See also `idref()`, `key()`.

From XPath 1.0.

idref()

Returns the nodes that contain XML IDREFs that reference the XML IDs specified by the first argument in the document containing the node given in the second argument, or containing the context node if no second argument is supplied. Any strings in the argument sequence are split up at the whitespace, and the function returns all the elements and attributes in the current document that reference any of the IDs. You have to have declared an attribute or an element as having the type `xs:IDREF` or `xs:IDREFS` within a DTD or schema for the `idref()` attribute to work, and the context item must be a node in the same document as the nodes that you want to retrieve.

```
node()* idref(xs:string*)
node()* idref(xs:string*, node())
```

See also `id()`, `key()`.
From XPath 2.0.

implicit-timezone()

Returns the timezone currently being used when interpreting date/time values that don't have a timezone.

```
xdt:dayTimeDuration implicit-timezone()
```

From XPath 2.0.

in-scope-prefixes()

Returns the prefixes of the namespace nodes on the argument element as a sequence of strings. If a default namespace is in-scope, the sequence will include an empty string.

```
xs:string* in-scope-prefixes(element())
```

See also `namespace-uri-for-prefix()`.
From XPath 2.0.

index-of()

Returns a sequence of integers giving the positions (starting from 1) of the atomic value specified as the second argument within the sequence given as the first argument. The optional third argument specifies a collation to use when comparing strings; if it's missing, the default collation is used.

```
xs:integer* index-of(xdt:anyAtomicType*, xdt:anyAtomicType)
xs:integer* index-of(xdt:anyAtomicType*, xdt:anyAtomicType, xs:string)
```

From XPath 2.0.

insert-before()

Inserts the sequence specified in the third argument into the sequence specified in the first argument before the item at the position specified by the second argument, or at the end of the sequence if the second argument specifies a position greater than the length of the first argument sequence.

```
item()* insert-before(item()*, xs:integer, item()*)
```

See also the , operator.
From XPath 2.0.

key()

Returns the nodes that are indexed by the value specified by the second argument in the key named by the first argument and that are descendants of the node specified in the third argument (or that node itself). If the second argument is a sequence, then all the nodes with any of the values are returned. You have to have declared the key with an `<xsl:key>` declaration.

```
node()* key(xs:string, xdt:anyAtomicType*)
node()* key(xs:string, xdt:anyAtomicType*, node())
```

See also `id()`, `idref()`, `<xsl:key>` element.
From XSLT 1.0.

lang()

Returns `true` if the language (as specified with the `xml:lang` attribute) of the node specified by the second argument, or the context node if there's no second argument, matches the language specified by the argument. This test is aware of sublanguages and is case-insensitive, so, for example, `lang('en')` would return `true` even if the context node's language was specified as `EN-US`. If the argument is the empty sequence, returns `false`.

```
xs:boolean lang(xs:string?)
xs:boolean lang(xs:string?, node())
```

From XPath 1.0.

last()

Returns the index of the last item in the sequence that's currently being looked at (or the number of items in the sequence that's currently being looked at, depending on how you like to view it).

```
xs:integer last()
```

See also `position()`, `count()`.
From XPath 1.0.

local-name()

Returns the local name of the argument node—the part of the name after any prefix that there might be. If no argument is passed, then returns the local name of the context node.

```
xs:string local-name()
xs:string local-name(node()?)
```

See also `name()`, `namespace-uri()`, `node-name()`.
From XPath 1.0.

local-name-from-QName()

Returns the local name from an `xs:QName`. If the argument is an empty sequence, returns an empty sequence.

```
xs:NCName? local-name-from-QName(xs:QName?)
```

See also `namespace-uri-from-QName()`, `local-name()`.
From XPath 2.0.

lower-case()

Returns the argument string with each character converted to lowercase. If the argument is the empty sequence, returns an empty string.

```
xs:string lower-case(xs:string?)
```

See also `upper-case()`, `translate()`.
From XPath 2.0.

matches()

Returns `true` if the first argument string matches the second argument regular expression, based on the flags specified in the third argument, and `false` otherwise. If the third argument isn't specified, the result is the same as if the third argument were an empty string. If the first argument is an empty sequence, the result is the same as if the first argument were an empty string.

Legal flags are

- `s`—The meta-character `.` matches all characters, including newline (`#xA`) characters (by default, newline characters aren't matched by `.`).
- `m`—The meta-character `^` matches the start of a line and `$` matches the end of a line (by default, `^` and `$` match the start and end of the string as a whole).
- `i`—The match is case-insensitive (by default it's case-sensitive).
- `x`—Whitespace characters within the regular expression are ignored (by default they are treated as literal characters, which must be matched).

```
xs:boolean matches(xs:string?, xs:string)
xs:boolean matches(xs:string?, xs:string, xs:string)
```

See also `contains()`, `starts-with()`, `ends-with()`, `replace()`, `<xsl:analyze-string>` instruction.
From XPath 2.0.

max()

Returns the value from the argument sequence with the greatest value. The optional second argument is a collation to use when comparing strings; if it's not specified, then the default collation is used. If the argument sequence is empty, returns an empty sequence.

```
xdt:anyAtomicType? max(xdt:anyAtomicType*)
xdt:anyAtomicType? max(xdt:anyAtomicType*, xs:string)
```

See also `min()`, `sum()`, `avg()`.
From XPath 2.0.

min()

Returns the value from the argument sequence with the least value. The optional second argument is a collation to use when comparing strings; if it's not specified, then the default collation is used. If the argument sequence is empty, returns an empty sequence.

```
xdt:anyAtomicType? min(xdt:anyAtomicType*)
xdt:anyAtomicType? min(xdt:anyAtomicType*, xs:string)
```

See also `max()`, `sum()`, `avg()`.
From XPath 2.0.

minutes-from-dateTime()

Returns the minutes component from an `xs:dateTime`. If the argument is an empty sequence, returns an empty sequence.

```
xs:integer? minutes-from-dateTime(xs:dateTime?)
```

See also `year-from-dateTime()`, `month-from-dateTime()`, `day-from-dateTime()`, `hours-from-dateTime()`, `seconds-from-dateTime()`, `timezone-from-dateTime()`.
From XPath 2.0.

minutes-from-duration()

Returns the minutes component from an `xdt:dayTimeDuration`. If the argument is an empty sequence, returns an empty sequence.

```
xs:integer? minutes-from-duration(xdt:dayTimeDuration?)
```

See also `days-from-duration()`, `hours-from-duration()`, `seconds-from-duration()`.
From XPath 2.0.

minutes-from-time()

Returns the minutes component from an `xs:time`. If the argument is an empty sequence, returns an empty sequence.

```
xs:integer? minutes-from-time(xs:time?)
```

See also `hours-from-time()`, `seconds-from-time()`, `timezone-from-time()`.
From XPath 2.0.

month-from-date()

Returns the month component from an `xs:date`. If the argument is an empty sequence, returns an empty sequence.

```
xs:integer? month-from-date(xs:date?)
```

See also year-from-date(), day-from-date(), timezone-from-date().
From XPath 2.0.

month-from-dateTime()

Returns the month component from an xs:dateTime. If the argument is an empty sequence, returns an empty sequence.

```
xs:integer? month-from-dateTime(xs:dateTime?)
```

See also year-from-dateTime(), day-from-dateTime(), hours-from-dateTime(), minutes-from-dateTime(), seconds-from-dateTime(), timezone-from-dateTime().
From XPath 2.0.

months-from-duration()

Returns the months component from an xdt:yearMonthDuration. If the argument is an empty sequence, returns an empty sequence.

```
xs:integer? months-from-duration(xdt:yearMonthDuration?)
```

See also years-from-duration().
From XPath 2.0.

name()

Returns the full name of the argument node, including the prefix for its namespace as declared in the source document. If no argument is given, then returns the full name of the context node.

```
xs:string name()
xs:string name(node()?)
```

See also local-name(), namespace-uri(), node-name().
From XPath 1.0.

namespace-uri()

Returns the namespace URI for the argument node, or an empty string if the node is in no namespace. If no argument is passed, then returns the namespace URI of the context node.

```
xs:anyURI namespace-uri()
xs:anyURI namespace-uri(node()?)
```

See also name(), local-name(), node-name().

namespace-uri-for-prefix()

Returns the namespace URI associated with the prefix specified as the first argument in-scope on the element specified as the second argument, or an empty sequence if there is no namespace associated with that prefix on the element.

```
xs:anyURI? namespace-uri-for-prefix(xs:string, element())
```

See also `resolve-QName()`, `in-scope-prefixes()`.
From XPath 2.0.

namespace-uri-from-QName()

Returns the namespace URI from an `xs:QName`, or an empty string if the `xs:QName` has no namespace URI. If the argument is an empty sequence, returns an empty sequence.

```
xs:anyURI? namespace-uri-from-QName(xs:QName?)
```

See also `local-name-from-QName()`, `namespace-uri()`.
From XPath 2.0.

nilled()

Returns `true` if the argument node is an element node that is nilled (has `xsi:nil="true"` specified on it), `false` if the argument node is an element node that isn't nilled, and an empty sequence if the argument is an empty sequence or another kind of node.

```
xs:boolean? nilled(node()?)
```

From XPath 2.0.

node-name()

Returns the name of the node as an `xs:QName`, or an empty sequence if the argument is an empty sequence.

```
xs:QName? node-name(node()?)
```

See also `name()`, `local-name()`, `namespace-uri()`.
From XPath 2.0.

normalize-space()

Returns the argument string with leading and trailing whitespace stripped, and any sequences of whitespace converted to single spaces. If no argument string is specified, then it returns the normalized string value of the context item. If the argument is an empty sequence, returns an empty string.

```
xs:string normalize-space()
xs:string normalize-space(xs:string?)
```

See also `string()`, `<xsl:strip-space>` element, `normalize-unicode()`.
From XPath 1.0.

normalize-unicode()

Returns the first argument string after Unicode normalization using the normalization form specified by the second argument. If the second argument is missing, uses NFC normalization.

If the first argument is an empty sequence, returns an empty string. The legal normalization forms are (in any case combination)

- "NFC"
- "NFD"
- "NFKC"
- "NFKD"
- "FULLY-NORMALIZED"
- "" (an empty string—no normalization takes place)

```
xs:string normalize-unicode(xs:string?)
xs:string normalize-unicode(xs:string?, xs:string)
```

From XPath 2.0.

not()

Returns false if the effective Boolean value of the argument is true, and true if the effective Boolean value of the argument is false.

```
xs:boolean not(item()*)
```

See also true(), false(), boolean().

number()

Converts the argument to an xs:double. If no argument is given, returns the numerical value of the context item, or NaN if there is no context item. If the argument is the empty sequence, returns NaN.

```
xs:double number()
xs:double number(item()?)
```

See also string(), boolean(), xs:double()constructor function, format-number(), <xsl:number>.
From XPath 1.0.

one-or-more()

Returns the argument if and only if it is not an empty sequence.

```
item()+ one-or-more(item()*)
```

See also exists(), zero-or-one(), exactly-one().
From XPath 2.0.

position()

Returns the position of the context item amongst the sequence of items that are currently being looked at. Unlike the numbers generated through <xsl:number>, the position()

function depends on the order in which items are processed regardless of their original order in a sequence.

```
xs:integer position()
```

See also `last()`, `count()`, `<xsl:number>`.
From XPath 1.0.

prefix-from-QName()

Returns the prefix given in the `xs:QName` specified as the argument, or an empty sequence if there is no prefix or the argument is an empty sequence.

```
xs:NCName prefix-from-QName(xs:QName?)
```

See also `local-name-from-QName()`, `namespace-uri-from-QName()`.
From XPath 2.0.

QName()

Creates an `xs:QName` with the first argument as the namespace URI and the second argument as the local name. If the first argument is an empty string or an empty sequence, the `xs:QName` has no namespace URI.

```
xs:QName QName(xs:string?, xs:string)
```

See also `resolve-QName()`, `xs:QName()` constructor function.
From XPath 2.0.

regex-group()

Used within `<xsl:analyze-string>`, returns the substring that matches the subexpression whose index is specified by the argument. If the argument is `0`, returns the entire matching string. Returns an empty string if there is no substring matching the numbered subexpression.

```
xs:string regex-group(xs:integer)
```

See also `<xsl:analyze-string>` instruction, `replace()`.
From XSLT 2.0.

remove()

Returns the sequence that's left when you remove the item at the position specified by the second argument from the sequence given as the first argument.

```
item()* remove(item()*, xs:integer)
```

See also `subsequence()`.
From XPath 2.0.

replace()

Replaces each substring within the first argument string that matches the second argument regular expression with the replacement string given as the third argument. The optional fourth argument specifies any flags that should be used when matching the regular expression (see the `matches()` function for a description of the flags). The replacement string can contain references to up to nine subexpressions within the regular expression using `$1` to `$9` ($ characters themselves must be escaped as \$ and \ as \\) or the entire matched string using `$0`. Returns an empty string if the first argument is an empty sequence.

```
xs:string replace(xs:string?, xs:string, xs:string)
xs:string replace(xs:string?, xs:string, xs:string, xs:string)
```

See also `matches()`, `translate()`, `<xsl:analyze-string>` instruction.
From XPath 2.0.

resolve-QName()

Resolves the first argument string to a qualified name based on the namespace declarations in-scope on the second argument element. If the first argument is an empty sequence, returns an empty sequence.

```
xs:QName? resolve-QName(xs:string?, element())
```

See also `QName()`, `namespace-uri-for-prefix()`, `xs:QName()` constructor function.
From XPath 2.0.

resolve-uri()

Resolves the first argument URI based on the base URI specified as the second argument. If the second argument is missing, uses the base URI of the stylesheet to resolve the first argument. If the first argument is an empty sequence, returns an empty sequence.

```
xs:string? resolve-uri(xs:string?)
xs:string? resolve-uri(xs:string?, xs:string)
```

See also `base-uri()`.
From XPath 2.0.

reverse()

Reverses the sequence passed as the argument.

```
item()* reverse(item()*)
```

From XPath 2.0.

root()

Returns the root node of the tree containing the argument node, or the context node if no argument is given. This will usually be a document node. If the argument is the empty sequence, returns an empty sequence.

```
node() root()
node()? root(node()?)
```

See also / at the beginning of a path.
From XPath 2.0.

round()

Rounds the argument number to the nearest integer (though this isn't returned as an `xs:integer` unless the argument is an `xs:integer`). If the number is exactly between two integers, then it rounds up (the same as `ceiling()`). If the argument is an empty sequence, returns an empty sequence.

```
numeric? round(numeric?)
```

See also `floor()`, `ceiling()`, `round-half-to-even()`.
From XPath 1.0.

round-half-to-even()

Rounds the first argument to the number of decimal places indicated by the second argument. If there's no second argument, rounds to the nearest integer (though this isn't returned as an `xs:integer` unless the argument is an `xs:integer`). If the second argument is `-1`, rounds to the nearest multiple of ten; if `-2`, to the nearest hundred; if `-3`, to the nearest thousand, and so on. Rounds to a number whose last nonzero digit is even if the number is exactly between two possible rounded values; for example, `round-half-to-even(12.345, 2)` returns `12.34`, whereas `round-half-to-even(12.355, 2)` returns `12.36`. If the first argument is an empty sequence, returns an empty sequence.

```
numeric? round-half-to-even(numeric?)
numeric? round-half-to-even(numeric?, xs:integer)
```

See also `round()`, `format-number()`.
From XPath 2.0.

seconds-from-dateTime()

Returns the seconds component from an `xs:dateTime`. If the argument is an empty sequence, returns an empty sequence.

```
xs:decimal? seconds-from-dateTime(xs:dateTime?)
```

See also `year-from-dateTime()`, `month-from-dateTime()`, `day-from-dateTime()`, `hours-from-dateTime()`, `minutes-from-dateTime()`, `timezone-from-dateTime()`.
From XPath 2.0.

seconds-from-duration()

Returns the seconds component from an `xdt:dayTimeDuration`. If the argument is an empty sequence, returns an empty sequence.

```
xs:decimal? seconds-from-duration(xdt:dayTimeDuration?)
```

See also `days-from-duration()`, `hours-from-duration()`, `minutes-from-duration()`.
From XPath 2.0.

seconds-from-time()

Returns the seconds component from an `xs:time`. If the argument is an empty sequence, returns an empty sequence.

```
xs:decimal? seconds-from-time(xs:time?)
```

See also `hours-from-time()`, `minutes-from-time()`, `timezone-from-time()`.
From XPath 2.0.

starts-with()

Returns `true` if the first argument string starts with the second argument string, according to the collation specified in the third argument string, or if the second argument string is an empty string or empty sequence, and returns `false` otherwise. If the third argument isn't specified, it defaults to the Unicode codepoint collation.

```
xs:boolean starts-with(xs:string?, xs:string?)
xs:boolean starts-with(xs:string?, xs:string?, xs:string)
```

See also `ends-with()`, `contains()`, `matches()`.
From XPath 1.0.

static-base-uri()

Returns the base URI of the instruction element that contains the XPath in which the function is called (usually the URI of the stylesheet itself).

```
xs:anyURI? static-base-uri()
```

See also `base-uri()`.
From XPath 2.0.

string()

Returns the string value of the argument item. If no argument is given, returns the string value of the context item. If the argument is an empty sequence, returns the empty sequence.

```
xs:string string()
xs:string string(item()?)
```

See also `boolean()`, `number()`, `data()`, `xs:string()` constructor function.
From XPath 1.0.

string-join()

Concatenates the strings in the first argument sequence into a string, using the string provided as the second argument as a separator.

```
xs:string string-join(xs:string*, xs:string)
```

See also `concat()`, `tokenize()`.
From XPath 2.0.

string-length()

Returns the length of the string passed as the argument. If no argument is passed, then returns the length of the string value of the context item. If the argument is an empty sequence, returns `0`.

```
xs:integer string-length()
xs:integer string-length(xs:string?)
```

See also `substring()`.
From XPath 1.0.

string-to-codepoints()

Returns a sequence of integers giving the Unicode codepoints for each of the characters in the argument string. Returns an empty sequence if the argument is an empty string or an empty sequence.

```
xs:integer* string-to-codepoints(xs:string?)
```

See also `codepoints-to-string()`.
From XPath 2.0.

subsequence()

Return a subsequence of the first argument sequence starting from the number passed as the second argument and a number of items long equal to the third argument number. If the third argument isn't specified, then it returns the rest of the sequence, to the last item. The first item in the sequence is numbered `1`.

```
item()* subsequence(item()*, xs:double)
item()* subsequence(item()*, xs:double, xs:double)
```

See also `position()`, predicates.
From XPath 2.0.

substring()

Returns a substring of the first argument string starting from the number passed as the second argument and a number of characters long equal to the third argument number. If the third argument isn't specified, then it returns the rest of the string, to the last character. The first character in the string is numbered `1`. If the first argument is an empty sequence, returns an empty string.

```
xs:string? substring(xs:string?, xs:double)
xs:string? substring(xs:string?, xs:double, xs:double)
```

See also `substring-before()`, `substring-after()`.
From XPath 1.0.

substring-after()

Returns the substring of the first argument string that occurs after the second argument string, based on the collation specified by the third argument. If the second string is not contained in the first string, or if either of the first two arguments is an empty string or empty sequence, then it returns an empty string. If the third argument is not specified, then the Unicode codepoint collation is used.

```
xs:string substring-after(xs:string?, xs:string?)
xs:string substring-after(xs:string?, xs:string?, xs:string)
```

See also `substring-before()`, `substring()`.
From XPath 1.0.

substring-before()

Returns the substring of the first argument string that occurs before the second argument string, based on the collation specified by the third argument. If the second string is not contained in the first string, or if either of the first two arguments is an empty string or empty sequence, then it returns an empty string. If the third argument is not specified, then the Unicode codepoint collation is used.

```
xs:string substring-before(xs:string?, xs:string?)
xs:string substring-before(xs:string?, xs:string?, xs:string)
```

See also `substring-after()`, `substring()`.
From XPath 1.0.

sum()

Returns the sum of the values in the first argument sequence. If the sequence is empty, returns the value specified as the second argument, or the `xs:double` `0.0E0` if there isn't a second argument.

```
xdt:anyAtomicType sum(xdt:anyAtomicType*)
xdt:anyAtomicType? sum(xdt:anyAtomicType*, xdt:anyAtomicType?)
```

See also `count()`, `avg()`, `min()`, `max()`.
From XPath 1.0.

system-property()

Supplies information about the processor that's being used to run the stylesheet. The argument string specifies the kind of information that's returned. There are eight standard properties, but processors can support their own system properties. The standard properties are

- `xsl:version`—The version of XSLT supported by the processor (usually `1.0` in current XSLT processors)
- `xsl:vendor`—The name of the vendor of the XSLT processor
- `xsl:vendor-url`—A URL for the vendor of the XSLT processor
- `xsl:product-name`—The name of the XSLT processor

- `xsl:product-version`—The version of the XSLT processor
- `xsl:is-schema-aware`—`'yes'` if the XSLT processor is schema-aware, `'no'` otherwise
- `xsl:supports-serialization`—`'yes'` if the XSLT processor supports serialization, `'no'` otherwise
- `xsl:supports-backwards-compatibility`—`'yes'` if the XSLT processor supports backwards compatibility with XSLT 1.0, `'no'` otherwise

```
xs:string system-property(xs:string)
```

See also `element-available()`, `function-available()`.
From XSLT 1.0.

timezone-from-date()

Returns the timezone component from an `xs:date`. If the argument is an empty sequence or doesn't have a timezone, returns an empty sequence.

```
xdt:dayTimeDuration? timezone-from-date(xs:date?)
```

See also `year-from-date()`, `month-from-date()`, `day-from-date()`.
From XPath 2.0.

timezone-from-dateTime()

Returns the timezone component from an `xs:dateTime`. If the argument is an empty sequence or doesn't have a timezone, returns an empty sequence.

```
xdt:dayTimeDuration? timezone-from-dateTime(xs:dateTime?)
```

See also `year-from-dateTime()`, `month-from-dateTime()`, `day-from-dateTime()`, `hours-from-dateTime()`, `minutes-from-dateTime()`, `seconds-from-dateTime()`.
From XPath 2.0.

timezone-from-time()

Returns the timezone component from an `xs:time`. If the argument is an empty sequence or doesn't have a timezone, returns an empty sequence.

```
xdt:dayTimeDuration? timezone-from-time(xs:time?)
```

See also `hours-from-time()`, `minutes-from-time()`, `seconds-from-time()`.
From XPath 2.0.

tokenize()

Splits the first argument string into a sequence of strings at each substring that matches the regular expression given as the second argument. The optional third argument contains flags that govern the regular-expression matching (see `matches()` for a description). If the first argument is an empty sequence, returns an empty string.

```
xs:string+ tokenize(xs:string?, xs:string)
xs:string+ tokenize(xs:string, xs:string, xs:string)
```

See also `matches()`, `replace()`, `substring-before()`, `substring-after()`.
From XPath 2.0.

trace()

Outputs a message to the user. The first argument is a sequence whose value you want to report and the second a string message that will usually describe the sequence. The function returns the first argument.

```
item()* trace(item()*, xs:string)
```

See also `error()`, `<xsl:message>` instruction.
From XPath 2.0.

translate()

Returns the first argument string with all occurrences of the characters in the second argument string replaced by their corresponding characters in the third string. If a character in the second string doesn't have a corresponding character in the third string, then the character is deleted from the first string. If the first argument string is an empty sequence, returns an empty string.

```
xs:string translate(xs:string?, xs:string, xs:string)
```

See also `upper-case()`, `lower-case()`, `replace()`.
From XPath 1.0.

true()

Returns `true`.

```
xs:boolean true()
```

See also `false()`, `boolean()`, `xs:boolean()` constructor function.
From XPath 1.0.

unordered()

Returns the argument sequence in an implementation-dependent order; this function is really used as an optimization hint, for when you don't care about the order of the items in a sequence.

```
item()* unordered(item()*)
```

From XPath 2.0.

unparsed-entity-public-id()

Returns the public ID of the unparsed entity whose name is passed as the argument. Unparsed entities are declared within DTDs as a way of pointing to non-XML files, but they aren't very common nowadays.

```
xs:string unparsed-entity-public-id(xs:string)
```

See also `unparsed-entity-uri()`.
From XSLT 2.0.

unparsed-entity-uri()

Returns the URI of the unparsed entity whose name is passed as the argument. Unparsed entities are declared within DTDs as a way of pointing to non-XML files, but they aren't very common nowadays.

```
xs:anyURI unparsed-entity-uri(xs:string)
```

See also `unparsed-entity-public-id()`.
From XSLT 1.0.

unparsed-text()

Returns the content of the text file held at the URI specified by the first argument. The second argument specifies an encoding to use when reading the text file if no better information is available; if this is missing, it's assumed the text file is held in UTF-8 encoding. Returns an empty sequence if the first argument is an empty sequence.

```
xs:string unparsed-text(xs:string?)
xs:string unparsed-text(xs:string?, xs:string)
```

See also `doc()`, `document()`, `collection()`.
From XSLT 2.0.

unparsed-text-available()

Returns true if there is a readable text file held at the URI specified by the first argument in the encoding specified by the second argument (in other words, if a call to the `unparsed-text()` function with the same arguments would succeed without an error).

```
xs:boolean unparsed-text-available(xs:string?)
xs:boolean unparsed-text-available(xs:string?, xs:string)
```

See also `unparsed-text()`, `doc-available()`.
From XSLT 2.0.

upper-case()

Returns the argument string with each character converted to uppercase. If the argument is an empty sequence, returns an empty string.

```
xs:string upper-case(xs:string?)
```

See also `lower-case()`, `translate()`.
From XPath 2.0.

year-from-date()

Returns the year component from an xs:date. If the argument is an empty sequence, returns an empty sequence.

```
xs:integer? year-from-date(xs:date?)
```

See also month-from-date(), day-from-date(), timezone-from-date().
From XPath 2.0.

year-from-dateTime()

Returns the year component from an xs:dateTime. If the argument is an empty sequence, returns an empty sequence.

```
xs:integer? year-from-dateTime(xs:dateTime?)
```

See also month-from-dateTime(), day-from-dateTime(), hours-from-dateTime(), minutes-from-dateTime(), seconds-from-dateTime(), timezone-from-dateTime().
From XPath 2.0.

years-from-duration()

Returns the years component from an xdt:yearMonthDuration. If the argument is an empty sequence, returns an empty sequence.

```
xs:integer? years-from-duration(xdt:yearMonthDuration?)
```

See also months-from-duration().
From XPath 2.0.

zero-or-one()

Returns the argument if and only if it is either an empty sequence or a sequence containing only one item.

```
item()? zero-or-one(item()*)
```

See also one-or-more(), exactly-one().
From XPath 2.0.

Regular Expression Syntax

Regular expressions are used by the matches(), replace(), and tokenize() functions as well as the <xsl:analyze-string> instruction. This section summarizes the syntax that's used for regular expressions, beginning with basic syntax in Table A-19.

Table A-19. *Basic Regular Expression Syntax*

Expression	Matches
S	The string *S*
(*S*)	The string *S*, and creates a numbered subexpression
N	The same string as that matched by the subexpression numbered *N*
S|*T*	The string *S* or the string *T*
S?	The string *S* or an empty string, preferring the string *S*
S??	The string *S* or an empty string, preferring an empty string
S+	The string *S* appearing once or more, as many times as possible
S+?	The string *S* appearing once or more, as few times as possible
*S**	The string *S* appearing zero or more times, as many times as possible
*S**?	The string *S* appearing zero or more times, as few times as possible
S{*n*}	The string *S* appearing exactly *n* times
S{*n*,}	The string *S* appearing at least *n* times, as many times as possible
S{*n*,}?	The string *S* appearing exactly *n* times, as few times as possible
S{*n*,*m*}	The string *S* appearing between *n* and *m* times, as many times as possible
S{*n*,*m*}?	The string *S* appearing between *n* and *m* times, as few times as possible
[*chars*]	Any of the characters given between the square brackets
[*c*-*d*]	The character *c*, the character *d*, or any character in between
[^*chars*]	Any character except those given after the ^
[*chars*-[*exceptions*]]	Any character in *chars* except those in *exceptions*

Table A-20 lists characters and character escapes that are significant within a regular expression.

Table A-20. *Significant Characters and Character Escapes*

Expression	Matches
.	Any character (including newlines in dot-all mode, otherwise not including newlines)
^	The beginning of the string (or beginning of a line in multiline mode)
$	The end of the string (or end of a line in multiline mode)
\n	The newline character (#xA)
\t	The tab character (#x9)
\r	The carriage return character (#xD)
\s	Any whitespace character
\S	Any nonwhitespace character
\d	Any digit
\D	Any character that isn't a digit
\w	Any word character
\W	Any nonword character

(Continued)

Table A-20. *(Continued)*

Expression	Matches
`\i`	Any character that can be the first letter of an XML name
`\I`	Any character that can't be the first letter of an XML name
`\c`	Any character that can be used in an XML name
`\C`	Any character that can't be used in an XML name
`\\`	The character \
`|`	The character |
`\.`	The character .
`\-`	The character -
`\^`	The character ^
`\$`	The character $
`\?`	The character ?
`\*`	The character *
`\+`	The character +
`\(`	The character (
`\)`	The character)
`\[`	The character [
`\]`	The character]
`\{`	The character {
`\}`	The character }

Category escapes allow you to match a character based on the Unicode category to which it belongs. The general syntax is

`\p{`*`category`*`}`

to match characters in that category and

`\P{`*`category`*`}`

to match characters not in that category. The character categories are listed in Table A-21.

Table A-21. *Character Categories*

Category	Meaning	Category	Meaning
`L`	Letter	`Pi`	Initial quotes
`Lu`	Uppercase letter	`Pf`	Final quotes
`Ll`	Lowercase letter	`Po`	Other punctuation
`Lt`	Titlecase letter	`Z`	Separators
`Lm`	Modifier letter	`Zs`	Spaces
`Lo`	Other letter	`Zl`	Line separators
`M`	Mark	`Zp`	Paragraph separators
`Mn`	Nonspacing mark	`S`	Symbols
`Mc`	Spacing combined mark	`Sm`	Math symbols
`Mo`	Other mark	`Sc`	Currency symbols
`N`	Number	`Sk`	Modifier symbols
`Nd`	Decimal digit	`So`	Other symbols
`Nl`	Numeric letter	`C`	All other characters
`No`	Other number	`Cc`	Control characters
`P`	Punctuation	`Cf`	Formatting characters
`Pc`	Connectors	`Co`	Private-use characters
`Pd`	Dashes	`Cn`	Characters that are not assigned to a category
`Ps`	Opening punctuation		
`Pe`	Closing punctuation		

Block escapes allow you to match a character based on the Unicode block in which it's defined. The general syntax is

`\p{Is`*`block`*`}`

to match characters in that block and

`\P{Is`*`block`*`}`

to match characters not in that block. The current blocks are listed in Table A-22, though these might change as Unicode expands in the future.

Table A-22. *Unicode Blocks*

Block	First Character	Last Character
BasicLatin	#x0000	#x007F
Latin-1Supplement	#x0080	#x00FF
LatinExtended-A	#x0100	#x017F
LatinExtended-B	#x0180	#x024F
IPAExtensions	#x0250	#x02AF
SpacingModifierLetters	#x02B0	#x02FF
CombiningDiacriticalMarks	#x0300	#x036F
GreekandCoptic	#x0370	#x03FF
Cyrillic	#x0400	#x04FF
CyrillicSupplement	#x0500	#x052F
Armenian	#x0530	#x058F
Hebrew	#x0590	#x05FF
Arabic	#x0600	#x06FF
Syriac	#x0700	#x074F
ArabicSupplement	#x0750	#x077F
Thaana	#x0780	#x07BF
Devanagari	#x0900	#x097F
Bengali	#x0980	#x09FF
Gurmukhi	#x0A00	#x0A7F
Gujarati	#x0A80	#x0AFF
Oriya	#x0B00	#x0B7F
Tamil	#x0B80	#x0BFF
Telugu	#x0C00	#x0C7F
Kannada	#x0C80	#x0CFF
Malayalam	#x0D00	#x0D7F
Sinhala	#x0D80	#x0DFF
Thai	#x0E00	#x0E7F
Lao	#x0E80	#x0EFF
Tibetan	#x0F00	#x0FFF
Myanmar	#x1000	#x109F
Georgian	#x10A0	#x10FF
HangulJamo	#x1100	#x11FF
Ethiopic	#x1200	#x137F
EthiopicSupplement	#x1380	#x139F
Cherokee	#x13A0	#x13FF
UnifiedCanadianAboriginalSyllabics	#x1400	#x167F
Ogham	#x1680	#x169F
Runic	#x16A0	#x16FF

Block	First Character	Last Character
Tagalog	#x1700	#x171F
Hanunoo	#x1720	#x173F
Buhid	#x1740	#x175F
Tagbanwa	#x1760	#x177F
Khmer	#x1780	#x17FF
Mongolian	#x1800	#x18AF
Limbu	#x1900	#x194F
TaiLe	#x1950	#x197F
NewTaiLue	#x1980	#x19DF
KhmerSymbols	#x19E0	#x19FF
Buginese	#x1A00	#x1A1F
PhoneticExtensions	#x1D00	#x1D7F
PhoneticExtensionsSupplement	#x1D80	#x1DBF
CombiningDiacriticalMarksSupplement	#x1DC0	#x1DFF
LatinExtendedAdditional	#x1E00	#x1EFF
GreekExtended	#x1F00	#x1FFF
GeneralPunctuation	#x2000	#x206F
SuperscriptsandSubscripts	#x2070	#x209F
CurrencySymbols	#x20A0	#x20CF
CombiningDiacriticalMarksforSymbols	#x20D0	#x20FF
LetterlikeSymbols	#x2100	#x214F
NumberForms	#x2150	#x218F
Arrows	#x2190	#x21FF
MathematicalOperators	#x2200	#x22FF
MiscellaneousTechnical	#x2300	#x23FF
ControlPictures	#x2400	#x243F
OpticalCharacterRecognition	#x2440	#x245F
EnclosedAlphanumerics	#x2460	#x24FF
BoxDrawing	#x2500	#x257F
BlockElements	#x2580	#x259F
GeometricShapes	#x25A0	#x25FF
MiscellaneousSymbols	#x2600	#x26FF
Dingbats	#x2700	#x27BF
MiscellaneousMathematicalSymbols-A	#x27C0	#x27EF
SupplementalArrows-A	#x27F0	#x27FF
BraillePatterns	#x2800	#x28FF
SupplementalArrows-B	#x2900	#x297F
MiscellaneousMathematicalSymbols-B	#x2980	#x29FF

(Continued)

Table A-22. *(Continued)*

Block	First Character	Last Character
SupplementalMathematicalOperators	#x2A00	#x2AFF
MiscellaneousSymbolsandArrows	#x2B00	#x2BFF
Glagolitic	#x2C00	#x2C5F
Coptic	#x2C80	#x2CFF
GeorgianSupplement	#x2D00	#x2D2F
Tifinagh	#x2D30	#x2D7F
EthiopicExtended	#x2D80	#x2DDF
SupplementalPunctuation	#x2E00	#x2E7F
CJKRadicalsSupplement	#x2E80	#x2EFF
KangxiRadicals	#x2F00	#x2FDF
IdeographicDescriptionCharacters	#x2FF0	#x2FFF
CJKSymbolsandPunctuation	#x3000	#x303F
Hiragana	#x3040	#x309F
Katakana	#x30A0	#x30FF
Bopomofo	#x3100	#x312F
HangulCompatibilityJamo	#x3130	#x318F
Kanbun	#x3190	#x319F
BopomofoExtended	#x31A0	#x31BF
CJKStrokes	#x31C0	#x31EF
KatakanaPhoneticExtensions	#x31F0	#x31FF
EnclosedCJKLettersandMonths	#x3200	#x32FF
CJKCompatibility	#x3300	#x33FF
CJKUnifiedIdeographsExtensionA	#x3400	#x4DBF
YijingHexagramSymbols	#x4DC0	#x4DFF
CJKUnifiedIdeographs	#x4E00	#x9FFF
YiSyllables	#xA000	#xA48F
YiRadicals	#xA490	#xA4CF
ModifierToneLetters	#xA700	#xA71F
SylotiNagri	#xA800	#xA82F
HangulSyllables	#xAC00	#xD7AF
PrivateUse	#xE000	#xF8FF
CJKCompatibilityIdeographs	#xF900	#xFAFF
AlphabeticPresentationForms	#xFB00	#xFB4F
ArabicPresentationForms-A	#xFB50	#xFDFF
VariationSelectors	#xFE00	#xFE0F
VerticalForms	#xFE10	#xFE1F
CombiningHalfMarks	#xFE20	#xFE2F

Block	First Character	Last Character
CJKCompatibilityForms	#xFE30	#xFE4F
SmallFormVariants	#xFE50	#xFE6F
ArabicPresentationForms-B	#xFE70	#xFEFF
HalfwidthandFullwidthForms	#xFF00	#xFFEF
Specials	#xFFF0	#xFFFF
LinearBSyllabary	#x10000	#x1007F
LinearBIdeograms	#x10080	#x100FF
AegeanNumbers	#x10100	#x1013F
AncientGreekNumbers	#x10140	#x1018F
OldItalic	#x10300	#x1032F
Gothic	#x10330	#x1034F
Ugaritic	#x10380	#x1039F
OldPersian	#x103A0	#x103DF
Deseret	#x10400	#x1044F
Shavian	#x10450	#x1047F
Osmanya	#x10480	#x104AF
CypriotSyllabary	#x10800	#x1083F
Kharoshthi	#x10A00	#x10A5F
ByzantineMusicalSymbols	#x1D000	#x1D0FF
MusicalSymbols	#x1D100	#x1D1FF
AncientGreekMusicalNotation	#x1D200	#x1D24F
TaiXuanJingSymbols	#x1D300	#x1D35F
MathematicalAlphanumericSymbols	#x1D400	#x1D7FF
CJKUnifiedIdeographsExtensionB	#x20000	#x2A6DF
CJKCompatibilityIdeographsSupplement	#x2F800	#x2FA1F
Tags	#xE0000	#xE007F
VariationSelectorsSupplement	#xE0100	#xE01EF
SupplementaryPrivateUseArea-A	#xF0000	#xFFFFF
SupplementaryPrivateUseArea-B	#x100000	#x10FFFF

APPENDIX B

XSLT Quick Reference

This appendix summarizes the XSLT elements and attributes that you can use.

XSLT Elements

This section describes each of the XSLT 2.0 elements in alphabetical order. The syntax for each element is shown, followed by a description. Within the syntax descriptions, attributes that are attribute value templates are indicated by curly braces ({}) within the attribute value. Optional attributes are followed by a question mark.

<xsl:analyze-string>

The `<xsl:analyze-string>` instruction tells the XSLT processor to split the string selected by the expression held in the `select` attribute into substrings that either match or don't match the regular expression held in the `regex` attribute. These substrings are processed in order, with those that match the regular expression being processed by the `<xsl:matching-substring>` child element and those that don't match the regular expression being processed by the `<xsl:non-matching-substring>` child element. The `flags` attribute controls details about the matching of the regular expression. Its value is the same as that for the third argument in the `matches()` function.

```
<xsl:analyze-string select="string-expression"
                    regex="{regular-expression}"
                    flags="{regular-expression-flags}"?>
  (xsl:matching-substring?, xsl:non-matching-substring?, xsl:fallback*)
</xsl:analyze-string>
```

See also `<xsl:matching-substring>`, `<xsl:non-matching-substring>`, `matches()`, `replace()`.

From XSLT 2.0.

<xsl:apply-imports>

The `<xsl:apply-imports>` instruction tells the XSLT processor to take the current node and try to find a template in an imported stylesheet that (a) is in the same mode as the current template and (b) matches the current node. If the processor locates a template, it uses that template to process the current node; otherwise it uses the default templates.

The <xsl:apply-imports> instruction must be within an <xsl:template> element, and is not allowed as a descendant of an <xsl:for-each>—the current node at the point at which the <xsl:apply-imports> instruction is used must be the same as the current node of the template it's in.

The templates that are used are passed the parameters specified by the <xsl:with-param> elements within the <xsl:apply-imports> instruction. See the description of <xsl:with-param> for details.

```
<xsl:apply-imports>
  (xsl:with-param*)
</xsl:apply-imports>
```

See also <xsl:import>, <xsl:next-match>, <xsl:apply-templates>.

From XSLT 1.0.

<xsl:apply-templates>

The <xsl:apply-templates> instruction tells the processor to gather together a sequence of nodes and to process each of the nodes by finding a template that matches it and using that template. The nodes that the processor applies templates to are selected by the expression held in the select attribute. If the select attribute is missing, then the processor applies templates to the child nodes of the current node.

The nodes are processed in the order determined by the <xsl:sort> elements that are contained by the <xsl:apply-templates> instruction. See the description of <xsl:sort> for details. If there are no <xsl:sort> elements within the <xsl:apply-templates> instruction, the processor goes through the nodes in the order they appear in the sequence (which is usually document order).

The only templates that can match the nodes to which the processor applies templates are those whose mode attribute matches the mode specified via the mode attribute on the <xsl:apply-templates>. The keyword #current applies templates in the same mode as the current template was invoked in. The keyword #default applies templates in the default mode. If the <xsl:apply-templates> instruction doesn't have a mode attribute, then the default value is #default.

The templates that are used are passed the parameters specified by the <xsl:with-param> elements within the <xsl:apply-templates> instruction. See the description of <xsl:with-param> for details.

```
<xsl:apply-templates select="node-sequence-expression"?
                     mode="qualified-name | #current | #default"?>
  (xsl:sort | xsl:with-param)*
</xsl:apply-templates>
```

See also <xsl:sort>, <xsl:with-param>, <xsl:template>, <xsl:call-template>, <xsl:for-each>, <xsl:apply-imports>, <xsl:next-match>.

From XSLT 1.0.

<xsl:attribute>

The `<xsl:attribute>` instruction creates an attribute. When adding attributes to an element, any `<xsl:attribute>` instructions must come before any instructions that add content to the element. The `<xsl:attribute>` instruction can also be included within an `<xsl:attribute-set>` element; see the description of `<xsl:attribute-set>` for details.

The name of the attribute that's created is determined by its `name` and `namespace` attributes. The `name` attribute gives the qualified name for the attribute and the `namespace` attribute gives the namespace for the attribute. If the name held in the `name` attribute doesn't include a prefix and the `namespace` attribute has a value, then the generated attribute will be given a prefix generated by the XSLT processor.

If the `namespace` attribute is missing, then the qualified name specified by the `name` attribute is used to identify the namespace for the attribute—the namespace associated with the qualified name's prefix. If the qualified name doesn't have a prefix, then the attribute is in no namespace.

Both the `name` and `namespace` attributes are attribute value templates, so their values can be calculated on the fly.

The value of the created attribute is the result of processing the content of the `<xsl:attribute>` instruction or evaluating its `select` attribute (`<xsl:attribute>` may have a `select` attribute or content, but not both). The resulting sequence is atomized, each item cast to a string, and those strings concatenated with the value of the `separator` attribute used as a separator between each item. If the `separator` attribute isn't present, it defaults to a single space if the `select` attribute is used, and to an empty string if the content of the `<xsl:attribute>` element is used.

After the value has been constructed, the attribute may be validated and assigned a type annotation based on the `type` or `validation` attributes, only one of which may be present. If the `type` attribute is present, the attribute is validated against the named type. If the `validation` attribute is present, the attribute is validated accordingly: `preserve` and `strip` both result in a type annotation of `xdt:untypedAtomic`, while `strict` and `lax` result in a type annotation based on any top-level attribute declarations that have been imported into the stylesheet. If neither the `type` nor `validation` attribute is present, validation proceeds based on the `default-validation` attribute on the `<xsl:stylesheet>` element.

```
<xsl:attribute name="{qualified-name}"
               namespace="{namespace-URI}"?
               type="qualified-name"?
               validation="strict | lax | preserve | strip"?
               select="expression"?
               separator="{string}"?>
  sequence-constructor
</xsl:attribute>
```

See also `<xsl:attribute-set>`, `<xsl:element>`.
From XSLT 1.0.

<xsl:attribute-set>

The `<xsl:attribute-set>` declaration defines a set of attributes that can then all be added to an element at once through the `use-attribute-sets` attribute on `<xsl:element>` or `<xsl:copy>`, or the `xsl:use-attribute-sets` attribute on literal result elements. It is located at the top level of the stylesheet, as a child of `<xsl:stylesheet>`.

The name attribute holds the qualified name of the attribute set, by which it can be referred to later on. The <xsl:attribute-set> element contains a number of <xsl:attribute> elements. The use-attribute-sets attribute contains a space-delimited list of the qualified names of other attribute sets. The attributes from the used attribute sets are added to this one.

```
<xsl:attribute-set name="qualified-name"
                   use-attribute-sets="list-of-qualified-names"?>
  (xsl:attribute*)
</xsl:attribute-set>
```

See also <xsl:attribute>, <xsl:element>, <xsl:copy>, xsl:use-attribute-sets.
From XSLT 1.0.

<xsl:call-template>

The <xsl:call-template> instruction calls a template by name. The name of the called template is held in the name attribute. The <xsl:with-param> elements held within the <xsl:call-template> are used to define parameters that are passed to the template. See the description of <xsl:with-param> for more details.

```
<xsl:call-template name="qualified-name">
  (xsl:with-param*)
</xsl:call-template>
```

See also <xsl:template>, <xsl:apply-templates>, <xsl:function>.
From XSLT 1.0.

<xsl:character-map>

The <xsl:character-map> declaration defines a set of characters that should be mapped to other strings when a result tree is serialized. It is located at the top level of the stylesheet, as a child of <xsl:character-map>.

The name attribute holds the qualified name of the character map, by which it can be referred to by use-character-maps attributes on other <xsl:character-map> elements or <xsl:output> elements. The <xsl:character-map> element contains a number of <xsl:output-character> elements, each mapping a character to a string. The use-character-maps attribute contains a space-delimited list of the qualified names of other character maps. The mappings from the used character maps are added to this one.

```
<xsl:character-map name="qualified-name"
                   use-character-maps="list-of-qualified-names"?>
  (xsl:output-character*)
</xsl:character-map>
```

See also <xsl:output-character>, <xsl:output>.
From XSLT 2.0.

<xsl:choose>

The `<xsl:choose>` instruction is a conditional construct that causes different instructions to be processed in different circumstances. The XSLT processor processes the instructions held in the first `<xsl:when>` element whose `test` attribute evaluates as `true`. If none of the `<xsl:when>` elements' `test` attributes evaluate as `true`, the content of the `<xsl:otherwise>` element, if there is one, is processed.

```
<xsl:choose>
  (xsl:when+, xsl:otherwise?)
</xsl:choose>
```

See also `<xsl:when>`, `<xsl:otherwise>`, `<xsl:if>`, `if` expressions.
From XSLT 1.0.

<xsl:comment>

The `<xsl:comment>` instruction generates a comment node. The value of the created comment is the result of processing the content of the `<xsl:comment>` instruction or evaluating its `select` attribute (`<xsl:comment>` may have a `select` attribute or content, but not both). The resulting sequence is atomized, each item cast to a string, and those strings concatenated, with a single space separator between each item if the `select` attribute is used and no separator if the content of the `<xsl:comment>` instruction is used. The resulting value must not contain two hyphens next to each other (`--`), as this sequence isn't allowed in comments.

```
<xsl:comment select="expression"?>
  sequence-constructor
</xsl:comment>
```

See also `<xsl:processing-instruction>`.
From XSLT 1.0.

<xsl:copy>

The `<xsl:copy>` instruction creates a shallow copy of the current node. For most nodes, this is equivalent to a deep copy, but for element and document nodes it's slightly different.

If the current node is an element or document node, the children of the copy are the results of processing the contents of the `<xsl:copy>` instruction. If the current node is an element, then any namespace nodes from the original element are copied over, unless the `copy-namespaces` attribute is present with the value `no`. If `inherit-namespaces` is present with the value `no`, the children of the new element will not have copies of the namespace nodes of the copied element. The attributes from the attribute sets named in `use-attribute-sets` are added to the copied element (along with any attributes that might be added through `<xsl:attribute>` instructions within the `<xsl:copy>`).

If the current node is an element, attribute, or document node, the `type` and `validation` attributes control the validation of the element, attribute, or document. See the descriptions in `<xsl:element>`, `<xsl:attribute>`, and `<xsl:document>` for details.

```
<xsl:copy use-attribute-sets="list-of-qualified-names"?
          copy-namespaces="yes | no"?
          inherit-namespaces="yes | no"?
          type="qualified-name"?
          validation="strict | lax | preserve | strip">
  sequence-constructor
</xsl:copy>
```

See also <xsl:copy-of>, <xsl:attribute-set>.
From XSLT 1.0.

<xsl:copy-of>

The <xsl:copy-of> instruction creates a deep copy of whatever is selected by the expression held in its select attribute. A deep copy of a node includes child nodes, attributes, and namespace nodes (unless the copy-namespaces attribute is present with the value no).

If the node to be copied is an element, attribute, or document node, the type and validation attributes control the validation of the copy. See the descriptions in <xsl:element>, <xsl:attribute>, and <xsl:document> for details.

```
<xsl:copy-of select="expression"
             copy-namespaces="yes | no"?
             type="qualified-name"?
             validation="strict | lax | preserve | strip" />
```

See also <xsl:copy>, <xsl:value-of>, <xsl:sequence>.
From XSL 1.0.

<xsl:decimal-format>

The <xsl:decimal-format> declaration defines a method of interpreting the format pattern strings that are used as the second argument of the format-number() function. It lives at the top level of the stylesheet, as a child of <xsl:stylesheet>. There can be many decimal formats, but they must all have different names, specified by the name attribute. If the name attribute is missing, the decimal format is used as the default decimal format.

When you use the format-number() function, the XSLT processor identifies a decimal format to use to interpret the pattern that you specify as the second argument. If the format-number() function is passed three arguments, the third argument is taken as the name of a decimal format, and that decimal format is used. If the format-number() function is passed two arguments, then the default decimal format is used; if you haven't specified a default decimal format, then the XSLT processor uses one with all attributes set to their default values.

When the XSLT processor formats the number, it looks first to see if it is infinity or not a number. If it is infinity, then the XSLT processor returns the string held in the infinity attribute (default Infinity). If it is not a number, then the XSLT processor returns the string held in the NaN attribute (default NaN).

If the number is a number, and not infinity, the XSLT processor has to format it according to the pattern string passed as the second argument of format-number() and the decimal format that is identified. The processor splits the pattern into a positive pattern and a negative pattern at the character held by the pattern-separator attribute, which defaults to the semicolon character (;). The minus sign is indicated by the character held by the minus-sign attribute, which defaults to the hyphen character (-), within the negative pattern. If there's no negative pattern, then it defaults to the same as the positive pattern, prefixed by the character held in the minus-sign attribute of the decimal format.

If the pattern contains the character held by the percent attribute (which defaults to the percent character, %), then the number being formatted is multiplied by 100 prior to formatting, and that character is included as specified by the pattern. If the pattern contains the character held by the per-mille attribute (which defaults to the per-mille character, ‰ or ‰), then the number being formatted is multiplied by1000 prior to formatting, and that character is included as specified by the pattern.

The remaining pattern string is interpreted to indicate how many digits should occur before and after the decimal point and whether the digits should be grouped, and if so what by. Within the pattern, essential digits are indicated by the character held in the zero-digit attribute (which defaults to the zero character, 0), and optional digits are indicated by the character held in the digit attribute (which defaults to the hash character, #). The decimal point is the character held in the decimal-point attribute of the decimal format (which defaults to the period character, .). Groups of digits are separated by the character held in the grouping-separator attribute (which defaults to the comma character, ,).

```
<xsl:decimal-format name="qualified-name"?
                    digit="character"?
                    zero-digit="character"?
                    decimal-separator="character"?
                    grouping-separator="character"?
                    minus-sign="character"?
                    pattern-separator="character"?
                    percent="character"?
                    per-mille="character"?
                    infinity="string"?
                    NaN="string"? />
```

See also format-number().

From XSLT 1.0.

<xsl:document>

The <xsl:document> instruction creates a document node. The content of the document node is the result of processing the sequence constructor that the <xsl:document> instruction contains.

After the document node has been constructed, its document element may be validated and assigned a type annotation based on the type or validation attributes, only one of which may be present. If the type attribute is present or if validation is strict or lax, the document must be well-formed (have only one element as a child and no text-node children). If the type attribute is present, the document element is validated against the named type. If the validation attribute is present, strip results in a type annotation of xdt:untyped for the element and all its element descendants, with its attributes and all the attributes of its descendants being assigned a type of xdt:untypedAtomic, while preserve preserves whatever type annotations are on the document element, its attributes and descendants. strict and lax result in a type annotation based on any top-level element declarations that have been imported into the stylesheet. If neither the type nor validation attribute is present, validation proceeds based on the default-validation attribute on the <xsl:stylesheet> element.

```
<xsl:document validation="strict | lax | preserve | strip"?
              type="qualified-name"?>
  sequence-constructor
</xsl:document>
```

See also <xsl:result-document>.
From XSLT 2.0.

<xsl:element>

The <xsl:element> instruction creates an element. The name of the element that's created is determined by its name and namespace attributes. The name attribute gives the qualified name for the element, and the namespace attribute gives the namespace for the element. If the namespace attribute is missing, then the qualified name specified by the name attribute is used to identify the namespace for the element—the namespace associated with the qualified name's prefix, or the default namespace if it doesn't have a prefix. Both the name and namespace attributes are attribute value templates, so their values can be calculated on the fly—in fact, this is the only reason you should use <xsl:element> rather than a literal result element.

If inherit-namespaces is present with the value no, the children of the new element will not have copies of any namespace nodes of the new element. If the use-attribute-sets attribute is present, then the attributes held in the attribute sets named within this attribute are added to the created element. Other attributes and the content of the element are generated as the result of processing the content of the <xsl:element> instruction.

After the element has been constructed, it may be validated and assigned a type annotation based on the type or validation attributes, only one of which may be present. If the type attribute is present, the element is validated against the named type. If the validation attribute is present, the element is validated accordingly. strip results in a type annotation of xdt:untyped for the element and all its element descendants, with its attributes and all the attributes of its descendants being assigned a type of xdt:untypedAtomic. preserve assigns the element itself the type xdt:untyped but preserves whatever type annotations are on its attributes and descendants. strict and lax result in a type annotation based on any top-level element declarations that have been imported into the stylesheet. If neither the type nor validation attribute is present, validation proceeds based on the default-validation attribute on the <xsl:stylesheet> element.

```
<xsl:element name="{qualified-name}"
             namespace="{namespace-uri}"?
             inherit-namespaces="yes | no"?
             use-attribute-sets="list-of-qualified-names"?
             type="qualified-name"?
             validation="strict | lax | preserve | strip">
  sequence-constructor
</xsl:element>
```

See also <xsl:attribute-set>.
From XSLT 1.0.

<xsl:fallback>

The `<xsl:fallback>` element provides alternative processing in the event that an implementation does not support a particular element. When an XSLT processor comes across an instruction that it doesn't understand (such as an XSLT 2.0 instruction or an extension element), it looks for an `<xsl:fallback>` element amongst its children. If it finds one, it processes the content of that `<xsl:fallback>` element; if it doesn't, it stops processing and the transformation fails.

```
<xsl:fallback>
  sequence-constructor
</xsl:fallback>
```

See also `element-available()`.
From XSLT 1.0.

<xsl:for-each>

The `<xsl:for-each>` instruction tells the XSLT processor to process the items in a sequence one by one. The items are selected by the expression held in the `select` attribute. If there are any `<xsl:sort>` elements, these change the order in which the items are processed; if there aren't any, then they are processed in document order. Each of the nodes is then processed according to the instructions held in the `<xsl:for-each>` after any `<xsl:sort>` elements.

```
<xsl:for-each select="expression">
  (xsl:sort*, sequence-constructor)
</xsl:for-each>
```

See also `<xsl:sort>`, `<xsl:apply-templates>`, `<xsl:for-each-group>`, `for` expression.
From XSLT 1.0.

<xsl:for-each-group>

The `<xsl:for-each-group>` instruction groups the items in the sequence selected by its `select` attribute. The grouping depends on which of the other attributes is present. `group-by` groups the items based on a value calculated using the expression in the `group-by` attribute. `group-adjacent` groups adjacent items based on a value calculated using the expression in the `group-adjacent` attribute. `group-starting-with` and `group-ending-with` constructs groups that start or end with nodes that match the patterns in the `group-starting-with` and `group-ending-with` attributes. One of these attributes must be present.

When grouping by a string value using `group-by` or `group-adjacent`, the `collation` attribute specifies the collation to use for comparing the values.

The groups are sorted using the `<xsl:sort>` elements within the `<xsl:for-each-group>` instruction, and then processed using the sequence constructor that follows the `<xsl:sort>` elements. Within the `<xsl:for-each-group>` element, the `current-group()` function returns the items in the current group, while the `current-grouping-key()` function returns the value that's common to those items.

```
<xsl:for-each-group select="expression"
                    group-by="expression"?
                    group-adjacent="expression"?
```

```
                    group-starting-with="pattern"?
                    group-ending-with="pattern"?
                    collation="{collation-uri}"?>
  (xsl:sort*, sequence-constructor)
</xsl:for-each-group>
```

See also <xsl:sort>, <xsl:for-each>, distinct-values().
From XSLT 2.0.

<xsl:function>

The <xsl:function> declaration defines a stylesheet function. It lives at the top level of the stylesheet, as a child of <xsl:stylesheet>. The name of the stylesheet function is specified via the name attribute, which must be a qualified name with a prefix. The parameters for the function are specified through <xsl:param> elements; it's an error to have more than one function definition for a function with the same name and the same number of parameters. If the processor already has a built-in implementation of a function with that name, the stylesheet function will be used instead unless the override attribute is present with a value of no.

The result of calling the function is specified through the content of the <xsl:function> element, after the <xsl:param> elements. The type of this result can be specified through the as attribute.

```
<xsl:function name="qualified-name"
              as="sequence-type"?
              override="yes | no"?>
  (xsl:param*, sequence-constructor)
</xsl:function>
```

See also <xsl:template>, <xsl:param>, function-available().
From XSLT 2.0.

<xsl:if>

The <xsl:if> instruction performs some conditional processing. The content of the <xsl:if> is only processed if the expression held in its test attribute evaluates to a value with an effective Boolean value of true.

```
<xsl:if test="boolean-expression">
  sequence-constructor
</xsl:if>
```

See also <xsl:choose>, <xsl:when>, if expression.
From XSLT 1.0.

<xsl:import>

The <xsl:import> element imports a stylesheet into this one. This gives you access to all the declarations and templates within that stylesheet, and allows you to override them with your own if you need to. The href attribute gives the location of the imported stylesheet. Any <xsl:import> elements must be the very first elements within the stylesheet, the first children of the <xsl:stylesheet> document element.

```
<xsl:import href="URI" />
```

See also <xsl:include>, <xsl:apply-imports>.
From XSLT 1.0.

<xsl:import-schema>

The <xsl:import-schema> element makes type definitions and element and attribute declarations available for use within the stylesheet. It lives at the top level of the stylesheet, as a child of the <xsl:stylesheet> document element.

A W3C XML Schema schema can be embedded within the <xsl:import-schema> element, in which case the namespace attribute, if present, must have the same value as the target namespace of that schema. Alternatively, the XSLT processor may try to locate a schema using the namespace attribute alone (a missing namespace attribute indicates a schema with no target namespace) or in conjunction with the schema-location attribute.

```
<xsl:import-schema namespace="namespace-uri"?
                   schema-location="URI"?>
  (xs:schema?)
</xsl:import-schema>
```

From XSLT 2.0.

<xsl:include>

The <xsl:include> element includes a stylesheet in this one. This gives you access to all the declarations within that stylesheet, exactly as if they had been specified in your stylesheet. The href attribute gives the location of the included stylesheet. The <xsl:include> element is a top-level element, and must appear as a direct child of the <xsl:stylesheet> document element.

```
<xsl:include href="URI" />
```

See also <xsl:import>.
From XSLT 1.0.

<xsl:key>

The <xsl:key> element declares a key that indexes all the nodes in a document by a particular value. Each key is identified by its name attribute. The nodes that are indexed by a key are those that match the pattern held in its match attribute.

The value by which each node is indexed is specified through the use attribute or the content of the <xsl:key> element (you can't have both), which is evaluated for each matched node. If it results in a single value, then that value is used to index the node. If the expression evaluates as a sequence, then there are multiple entries for the matched node, one for each of the values. This enables you to access a node through multiple values using the key() function. When a node is retrieved using a string value, via the key() function, the collation specified by the collation attribute is used to compare that value with the value used to index the node.

The <xsl:key> elements are top-level elements, direct children of the <xsl:stylesheet> document element. There can be multiple keys with the same name within a stylesheet; they are combined for the purpose of retrieving nodes using the key() function.

```
<xsl:key name="qualified-name"
         match="pattern"
         use="expression"?
         collation="collation-uri"?>
  sequence-constructor
</xsl:key>
```

See also key().
From XSLT 1.0.

<xsl:matching-substring>

The <xsl:matching-substring> element appears within the <xsl:analyze-string> element. Its content is used to process substrings that match the regular expression specified by the regex attribute of the <xsl:analyze-string> element. Within the <xsl:matching-substring> element, you can use the regex-group() function to access the substrings that match the subexpressions within the regular expression.

```
<xsl:matching-substring>
  sequence-constructor
</xsl:matching-substring>
```

See also <xsl:analyze-string>, <xsl:non-matching-substring>.
From XSLT 2.0.

<xsl:message>

The <xsl:message> instruction sends a message to the XSLT processor, which will usually forward the message on to the person running the transformation. If the terminate attribute is present with the value yes, then the transformation ends with the error message; otherwise it continues. Either the content of the <xsl:message> instruction or the result of evaluating the select attribute (you can't have both) provides the message itself.

```
<xsl:message select="expression"?
             terminate="{yes | no}"?>
  sequence-constructor
</xsl:message>
```

See also trace(), error().
From XSLT 1.0.

<xsl:namespace>

The <xsl:namespace> instruction creates a namespace node for an element. When adding namespace nodes to an element, any <xsl:namespace> instructions must come before any instructions that add content to the element. The name attribute provides the prefix for the namespace, while the select attribute or content of the <xsl:namespace> instruction (you can't have both) provides the namespace URI. The name attribute is an attribute value template, which means that the namespace prefix can be determined dynamically.

```
<xsl:namespace name="{namespace-prefix}"
               select="expression"?>
  sequence-constructor
</xsl:namespace>
```

See also <xsl:element>.
From XSLT 2.0.

<xsl:namespace-alias>

The <xsl:namespace-alias> element tells the XSLT processor that a namespace as used in the stylesheet should be substituted by another namespace in the result tree. This is usually used when creating stylesheets that create stylesheets: a namespace alias enables you to create the XSLT elements for the result as literal result elements, without the XSLT processor confusing them with instructions that it should follow.

The stylesheet-prefix attribute holds the prefix associated with the alias namespace within the stylesheet. The result-prefix attribute holds the prefix associated with the namespace that should be used instead, in the result (which is usually xsl when generating XSLT). The keyword #default can be used to indicate the default (unprefixed) namespace in either attribute.

```
<xsl:namespace-alias stylesheet-prefix="namespace-prefix | #default"
                     result-prefix="namespace-prefix | #default" />
```

From XSLT 1.0.

<xsl:next-match>

The <xsl:next-match> instruction tells the XSLT processor to process the current node using the next-best matching template, which may come from the same stylesheet (but have lower priority) or from an imported stylesheet.

The <xsl:next-match> instruction must be within an <xsl:template> element, and is not allowed as a descendant of an <xsl:next-match>—the current node at the point at which the <xsl:next-match> instruction is used must be the same as the current node of the template it's in.

The templates that are used are passed the parameters specified by the <xsl:with-param> elements within the <xsl:next-match> instruction. See the description of <xsl:with-param> for details.

```
<xsl:next-match>
  (xsl:with-param | xsl:fallback)*
</xsl:next-match>
```

See also <xsl:apply-imports>, <xsl:apply-templates>, <xsl:template>, <xsl:with-param>.
From XSLT 2.0.

<xsl:non-matching-substring>

The `<xsl:matching-substring>` element appears within the `<xsl:analyze-string>` element. Its content is used to process substrings that do not match the regular expression specified by the `regex` attribute of the `<xsl:analyze-string>` element.

```
<xsl:non-matching-substring>
  sequence-constructor
</xsl:non-matching-substring>
```

See also `<xsl:analyze-string>`, `<xsl:matching-substring>`.
From XSLT 2.0.

<xsl:number>

The `<xsl:number>` instruction inserts a number into the result tree. The `<xsl:number>` instruction actually has two roles: generating a number and formatting that number.

By default, `<xsl:number>` generates a number based on the position of the node selected by the `select` attribute among its similarly named siblings within the source XML document; if there's no `select` attribute, the current node gets numbered. You can control what number is generated more precisely using the `level`, `count`, and `from` attributes. The `level` attribute determines what kinds of numbers are generated. The default value, `single`, numbers nodes amongst their siblings. The value `any` numbers nodes throughout the source tree. The value `multiple` creates multilevel numbering based on the hierarchical structure of the source tree. Only nodes that match the pattern held in the `count` attribute will be counted when creating a number. The `from` attribute holds a pattern matching the node from which numbering should start afresh.

If you already know the number that you want, you can use the `value` attribute to specify the number directly, rather than using the number-generating aspect of `<xsl:number>`.

The number is formatted according to the format pattern held in the `format` attribute. This works in a different way from the format pattern used by the `format-number()` function, because it's used to number integers rather than decimal numbers.

The format pattern can hold any punctuation characters and placeholders that indicate where the number should be included and in what format. There are eight standard placeholders: `1` for decimal numbers, `a` for lowercase alphabetical numbers, `A` for uppercase alphabetical numbers, `i` for lowercase Roman numbers, `I` for uppercase Roman numbers, `w` for lowercase words, `W` for uppercase words, and `Ww` for titlecase words. Processors can support other numbering schemas as well. The `ordinal` attribute indicates whether and how ordinal numbers should be used. The `lang` and `letter-value` attributes help the processor decide which alphabet and numbering scheme to use.

If the number is large, then the digits may be grouped into groups of the size specified by the `grouping-size` attribute and separated by the character specified by the `grouping-separator` attribute.

```
<xsl:number select="expression"?
            level="single | multiple | any"?
            count="pattern"?
            from="pattern"?
            value="numeric-expression"?
```

```
        format="{format-pattern}"?
        ordinal="{string}"?
        lang="{language-code}"?
        letter-value="{alphabetic | traditional}"?
        grouping-separator="{character}"?
        grouping-size="{integer}"? />
```

See also format-number(), position().
From XSLT 1.0.

<xsl:otherwise>

The <xsl:otherwise> element appears only within an <xsl:choose> element, containing the instructions that are processed if none of the expressions held in the test attributes of the <xsl:when> elements evaluate as true.

```
<xsl:otherwise>
  sequence-constructor
</xsl:otherwise>
```

See also <xsl:choose>, <xsl:when>.
From XSLT 1.0.

<xsl:output>

The <xsl:output> element describes how a result tree should be serialized into a file. The name attribute gives the name of the output definition, which can be used to refer to it via the format attribute on <xsl:result-document>. If the <xsl:output> element does not have a name, it's the default output definition.

The method attribute has the most effect on the serialization, determining whether the stylesheet creates XML, text, HTML, XHTML, or some other format defined by a processor implementer. The media-type and version attributes give tighter definition about the format being generated.

The encoding attribute determines the character encoding used during serialization, and defaults to UTF-8 or UTF-16. The byte-order-mark attribute determines whether a Byte Order Mark is written at the start of the file; it defaults to yes for UTF-16, is implementation-defined for UTF-8, and defaults to no for other encodings. Characters that are held in character maps named by the use-character-maps attribute are replaced by the associated strings. The indent attribute determines whether whitespace-only text nodes are added to the result tree in order to make it easier to read; this is yes by default for HTML and XHTML, and no by default for XML. The normalization-form attribute determines how the result is Unicode normalized and defaults to none.

The doctype-public and doctype-system attributes hold the public and system identifiers for the result, which are included in a DOCTYPE declaration at the top of the generated file.

When generating XML or XHTML, a processor will add an XML declaration at the start of the output, unless the omit-xml-declaration attribute is present with the value yes. Even if this attribute is present, the XML declaration will still be added if the encoding is something other than UTF-8 or UTF-16, or if the standalone attribute is present (in which case the XML declaration contains a standalone pseudo-attribute with the specified value). To cater for

XML 1.1, you can permit a processor to include namespace undeclarations using the undeclare-prefixes attribute with the value yes.

When generating HTML or XHTML, a processor will add a <meta> element in the <head> element of the document unless the include-content-type attribute has the value no. It will also escape attributes that hold URIs, such as the href attribute on the <a> element, unless the escape-uri-attributes attribute has the value no.

The cdata-section-elements attribute lists the names of elements in the result whose text content should be wrapped within CDATA sections.

The <xsl:output> element should appear at the top level of the stylesheet, as a child of the <xsl:stylesheet> document element. There can be multiple <xsl:output> elements in a stylesheet, in which case they are combined on an attribute-by-attribute basis; it is an error for more than one <xsl:output> element to specify the same attribute with different values.

```
<xsl:output name="qualified-name"?
            method="xml | text | html | xhtml | qualified-name"?
            media-type="content-type"?
            version="version-number"?
            encoding="encoding"?
            byte-order-mark="yes | no"?
            normalization-form="NFC | NFD | NKFC | NKFD | fully-normalized |
                                none | name-token"?
            use-character-maps="list-of-qualified-names"?
            indent="yes | no"?
            doctype-public="string"?
            doctype-system="URI"?
            omit-xml-declaration="yes | no"?
            standalone="yes | no"?
            undeclare-prefixes="yes | no"?
            escape-uri-attributes="yes | no"?
            include-content-type="yes | no"?
            cdata-section-elements="list-of-qualified-names"? />
```

See also <xsl:character-map>, <xsl:result-document>.

From XSLT 1.0.

<xsl:output-character>

The <xsl:output-character> element is used within an <xsl:character-map> element to define a mapping between a character and a string. When a character map is used during serialization, the character held in the character attribute is replaced with the string held in the string attribute.

```
<xsl:output-character character="character"
                      string="string" />
```

See also <xsl:character-map>.

From XSLT 2.0.

<xsl:param>

The `<xsl:param>` element declares a parameter for a template (if it's within `<xsl:template>`), a stylesheet function (if it's within `<xsl:function>`), or for the stylesheet as a whole (if it's at the top level of the stylesheet). The `name` attribute holds the name of the parameter. The `as` attribute specifies the type of the value expected for the parameter.

For template and stylesheet parameters, the `required` attribute indicates whether a value must be supplied for the parameter (the default is `no`, that it isn't required). The `select` attribute or the content of the `<xsl:param>` element (you can't have both) holds the default value for the parameter, which will be used if no value is explicitly passed in to the stylesheet or template for that parameter.

For template parameters, the `tunnel` attribute indicates whether the parameter is a tunneling parameter. If it has the value `yes`, the parameter can be set from an `<xsl:with-param>` whose own `tunnel` attribute is `yes`, even if there are intervening templates that don't declare or explicitly pass on the parameter.

```
<xsl:param name="qualified-name"
           select="expression"?
           as="sequence-type"?
           required="yes | no"?
           tunnel="yes | no"?>
  sequence-constructor
</xsl:param>
```

See also `<xsl:with-param>`, `<xsl:variable>`, `<xsl:template>`, `<xsl:function>`.
From XSLT 1.0.

<xsl:perform-sort>

The `<xsl:perform-sort>` instruction sorts a sequence. The sequence to be sorted can be selected using the `select` attribute or generated using the nested sequence constructor (you can't have both). The sort itself is defined using the `<xsl:sort>` elements within the `<xsl:perform-sort>` element. If you want to do only one thing with the sorted sequence (as opposed to storing it in a variable in order to reuse it), then you should combine the sort with processing using `<xsl:for-each>` or `<xsl:apply-templates>` instead.

```
<xsl:perform-sort select="expression"?>
  (xsl:sort+, sequence-constructor)
</xsl:perform-sort>
```

See also `<xsl:sort>`, `<xsl:for-each>`, `<xsl:apply-templates>`.
From XSLT 2.0.

<xsl:preserve-space>

The `<xsl:preserve-space>` element specifies the elements whose child whitespace-only text nodes should be preserved within the source node tree. The `elements` attribute holds a whitespace-separated list of name tests (which can include specific names, or * to mean any element, for example). Whitespace-only text nodes are preserved by default, so this element is only required if `<xsl:strip-space>` has been used to strip whitespace-only text nodes from the node tree.

```
<xsl:preserve-space elements="list-of-name-tests" />
```

See also <xsl:strip-space>.
From XSLT 1.0.

<xsl:processing-instruction>

The <xsl:processing-instruction> instruction creates a processing instruction whose target is the name held in the name attribute. The value of the created processing instruction is the result of processing the content of the <xsl:processing-instruction> instruction or evaluating its select attribute (it cannot have both). The resulting sequence is atomized, each item cast to a string, and those strings concatenated, with a single space separator between each item if the select attribute is used and no separator if the content of the <xsl:comment> instruction is used. The resulting value must not contain the string '?>'.

```
<xsl:processing-instruction name="unqualified-name"
                            select="expression"?>
  sequence-constructor
</xsl:processing-instruction>
```

See also <xsl:comment>.
From XSLT 1.0.

<xsl:result-document>

The <xsl:result-document> instruction creates a result document node. The result document node is associated with the URI specified in the href attribute, if there is one. The content of the resulting document node is determined by evaluating the content of the <xsl:result-document> instruction.

After it's constructed, the result document may be validated, depending on the values of the type or validation attributes, only one of which may be present. See <xsl:document> for details.

If the result tree is serialized, the output definition that's used is the one named by the format attribute, or the default output definition if there's no format attribute. The remaining attributes on <xsl:result-document> override the equivalent attributes on that output definition.

```
<xsl:result-document href="{URI}"?
                     format="qualified-name"?
                     type="qualified-name"?
                     validation="strict | lax | preserve | strip"?
                     method="{xml | text | html | xhtml | qualified-name}"?
                     media-type="{content-type}"?
                     output-version="{version-number}"?
                     encoding="{encoding}"?
                     byte-order-mark="{yes | no}"?
                     normalization-form="{NFC | NFD | NKFC | NKFD |
                                          fully-normalized | none | name-token}"?
                     use-character-maps="{list-of-qualified-names}"?
                     indent="{yes | no}"?
```

```
                     doctype-public="{string}"?
                     doctype-system="{URI}"?
                     omit-xml-declaration="{yes | no}"?
                     standalone="{yes | no}"?
                     undeclare-prefixes="{yes | no}"?
                     escape-uri-attributes="{yes | no}"?
                     include-content-type="{yes | no}"?
                     cdata-section-elements="{list-of-qualified-names}"?>
  sequence-constructor
</xsl:result-document>
```

See also `<xsl:document>`, `<xsl:output>`.
From XSLT 2.0.

<xsl:sequence>

The `<xsl:sequence>` instruction adds the sequence selected by its `select` attribute to the sequence being constructed using the sequence constructor to which it belongs. It's primarily used to add existing nodes to such a sequence, since other values can be added using the `<xsl:copy-of>` instruction.

```
<xsl:sequence select="expression">
  (xsl:fallback*)
</xsl:sequence>
```

See also `<xsl:copy-of>`.
From XSLT 2.0.

<xsl:sort>

The `<xsl:sort>` element specifies a method of sorting a sequence. For each of the items being sorted, the `<xsl:sort>` element creates a sort key by evaluating the expression held in the `select` attribute or the sequence constructor in the content of the `<xsl:sort>` (you can't have both) with the item as the current item. The items are then sorted according to this sort key and the other attributes on the `<xsl:sort>` element.

The items are usually sorted based on the type of the sort key. For backwards-compatibility, the `data-type` attribute can indicate that these sort keys are strings (`text`, the default) or numbers (`number`), or in some other order supported by the implementation. The `order` attribute determines whether the nodes are sorted in ascending order (the default) or descending order.

When comparing strings, the `collation` attribute specifies the collation to use. If it's not present, the `lang` and `case-order` attributes can be used to identify an appropriate collation; the default language is determined from the system environment, while the case ordering (whether uppercase letters are sorted before lowercase letters or vice versa) is based on the language being used.

If there are multiple `<xsl:sort>` elements, then they define subsort keys on which items are sorted only if they have the same value for their sort key according to the previous sort. If two items have the same values for all the `<xsl:sort>` elements, then they will appear in the same order as they were originally, unless the first `<xsl:sort>` element has a `stable` attribute with the value `no`, in which case the order in which they appear is implementation-defined.

```
<xsl:sort select="expression"?
          data-type="{text | number | qualified-name}"?
          order="{ascending | descending}"?
          stable="{yes | no}"?
          collation="{collation-uri}"?
          lang="{language-code}"?
          case-order="{upper-first | lower-first}"?>
  sequence-constructor
</xsl:sort>
```

See also `<xsl:apply-templates>`, `<xsl:for-each>`, `<xsl:for-each-group>`, `<xsl:perform-sort>`.
From XSLT 1.0.

<xsl:strip-space>

The `<xsl:strip-space>` element specifies the elements whose child whitespace-only text nodes are removed from the node tree when it is created. The `elements` attribute holds a whitespace-separated list of name tests (which can include specific names, or * to mean any element, for example). The `<xsl:preserve-space>` element can override this specification.

```
<xsl:strip-space elements="list-of-name-tests" />
```

See also `<xsl:preserve-space>`, `normalize-space()`.
From XSLT 1.0.

<xsl:stylesheet>

The `<xsl:stylesheet>` element is the document element for a stylesheet, and holds all the top-level elements such as global variable and parameter declarations, templates and stylesheet functions, decimal format and attribute set definitions, key declarations, output declarations, and so on. Any `<xsl:import>` elements that the stylesheet contains must come before anything else within the `<xsl:stylesheet>` element.

The `<xsl:stylesheet>` element must have a `version` attribute indicating the version of XSLT being used (usually `2.0`). If you're embedding a stylesheet within an XML document, the `id` attribute can be used as an identifier so that you can point to the stylesheet.

The `xpath-default-namespace` holds the namespace that should be used when interpreting unprefixed element and type names within XPath expressions. The `default-collation` attribute determines the collation that's used by default when comparing strings (except when sorting them with `<xsl:sort>`); the processor uses the first collation URI that it recognizes within the list, which defaults to holding only the Unicode codepoint collation URI.

The `input-type-annotations` attribute determines whether type annotations in the source document are preserved or stripped; if any module specifies `strip`, then they are stripped, unless another module specifies `preserve`, which results in an error; the default is `unspecified`. The `default-validation` attribute specifies the validation that's applied, by default, to newly constructed document, element, and attribute nodes; if it's missing, the default value is `strip`.

The `extension-element-prefixes` attribute lists the prefixes of namespaces that are used for extension elements. The `exclude-result-prefixes` attribute lists the prefixes of namespaces that shouldn't be included in the result document, which are usually those namespaces that are used in the source XML document.

```
<xsl:stylesheet version="2.0"
                id="identifier"?
                xpath-default-namespace="namespace-uri"?
                default-collation="list-of-collation-uris"?
                input-type-annotations="preserve | strip | unspecified"?
                default-validation="preserve | strip"?
                extension-element-prefixes="list-of-namespace-prefixes"?
                exclude-result-prefixes="list-of-namespace-prefixes"?>
  (xsl:import*, top-level-elements)
</xsl:stylesheet>
```

See also `<xsl:transform>`.
From XSLT 1.0.

<xsl:template>

The `<xsl:template>` element declares a template. Templates can be used in two ways within a stylesheet—they can be applied to nodes or they can be called by name. Each template must specify either a `match` attribute, so that it can be applied to nodes, or a `name` attribute, so that it can be called by name with `<xsl:call-template>`. Both a name and a match pattern can be specified.

When templates are applied to a sequence of nodes using `<xsl:apply-templates>`, they might be applied in a particular mode; the `mode` attribute on `<xsl:template>` indicates the mode in which templates need to be applied for this template to be used. If the value is `#all`, then the template will be used whatever the mode.

If templates are applied in a matching mode, then the `match` attribute is used to determine whether the template can be used with the particular node. The `match` attribute holds a pattern against which nodes are matched. If a node matches the pattern, then the template can be used to process that node. If there's more than one template that matches a node in the specified mode, then the `priority` attribute is used to determine which one should be used—the highest priority wins. If no priority is specified explicitly, the priority of a template is determined from its `match` pattern.

Whether templates are applied or called, they can be passed parameters through the `<xsl:with-param>` element. To use a parameter, however, the template must contain an `<xsl:param>` element that declares a parameter of that name. These parameters are given before the body of the template, which is used to process the node and create a result. You can declare the type of the result of the template using the `as` attribute.

```
<xsl:template match="pattern"?
              mode="qualified-name | #default | #all"?
              priority="number"?
              name="qualified-name"?
              as="sequence-type"?>
  (xsl:param*, sequence-constructor)
</xsl:template>
```

See also `<xsl:apply-templates>`, `<xsl:apply-imports>`, `<xsl:next-match>`, `<xsl:call-template>`, `<xsl:param>`.
From XSLT 1.0.

<xsl:text>

The <xsl:text> element creates a text node. Unlike elsewhere within an XSLT stylesheet, whitespace-only text nodes within <xsl:text> elements are included, so <xsl:text> is the only way to add whitespace-only text nodes to the result tree (aside from those automatically added if you tell the processor to indent the output using the indent attribute on <xsl:output>). The <xsl:text> element is also useful for limiting the amount of space that's included around text when it's added to the result.

If the disable-output-escaping attribute is specified with the value yes, then the content of the <xsl:text> element is output without special characters such as < and & being escaped with < or &.

```
<xsl:text disable-output-escaping="yes | no">
  text
</xsl:text>
```

See also <xsl:value-of>.
From XSLT 1.0.

<xsl:transform>

The <xsl:transform> element is an alias for <xsl:stylesheet>; see the definition of <xsl:stylesheet> for details.

```
<xsl:transform version="2.0"
               id="identifier"?
               xpath-default-namespace="namespace-uri"?
               default-collation="list-of-collation-uris"?
               input-type-annotations="preserve | strip | unspecified"?
               default-validation="preserve | strip"?
               extension-element-prefixes="list-of-namespace-prefixes"?
               exclude-result-prefixes="list-of-namespace-prefixes"?>
  (xsl:import*, top-level-elements)
</xsl:transform>
```

See also <xsl:stylesheet>.
From XSLT 1.0.

<xsl:value-of>

The <xsl:value-of> instruction creates a text node. The value of the created text node is the result of processing the content of the <xsl:value-of> instruction or evaluating its select attribute (you can't have both). The resulting sequence is atomized, each item cast to a string, and those strings concatenated with the value of the separator attribute used as a separator between each item. If the separator attribute isn't present, it defaults to a single space if the select attribute is used, and to an empty string if the content of the <xsl:value-of> element is used.

If the disable-output-escaping attribute is specified with the value yes, then the value is output without special characters such as < and & being escaped with < or &.

```
<xsl:value-of select="expression"?
              separator="{string}"?
              disable-output-escaping="yes | no">
  sequence-constructor
</xsl:value-of>
```

See also <xsl:copy-of>, <xsl:text>.
From XSLT 1.0.

<xsl:variable>

The <xsl:variable> element declares a variable. If the <xsl:variable> element appears at the top level of the stylesheet, as a child of the <xsl:stylesheet> document element, then it is a global variable with a scope covering the entire stylesheet. Otherwise, it is a local variable with a scope of its following siblings and their descendants.

The `name` attribute specifies the name of the variable. After declaration, the variable can be referred to within XPath expressions using this name, prefixed with the $ character.

The value of the variable is determined either by the `select` attribute or by the contents of the <xsl:variable> element (you can't have both). The `as` attribute indicates the expected type of the variable. If the `as` attribute is missing, and you set the variable using its content, the variable holds the document node of a temporary tree. Otherwise, the variable holds the selected or constructed sequence.

```
<xsl:variable name="qualified-name"
              select="expression"?
              as="sequence-type"?>
  sequence-constructor
</xsl:variable>
```

See also <xsl:param>.
From XSLT 1.0.

<xsl:when>

The <xsl:when> element appears within an <xsl:choose> instruction and specifies a set of processing that could occur and the condition when it occurs. The XSLT processor processes the content of the first <xsl:when> within the <xsl:choose> whose `test` attribute contains an expression that evaluates to a value whose effective Boolean value is `true`.

```
<xsl:when test="boolean-expression">
  sequence-constructor
</xsl:when>
```

See also <xsl:choose>, <xsl:otherwise>, <xsl:if>, `if` expression.
From XSLT 1.0.

<xsl:with-param>

The <xsl:with-param> element specifies the value that should be passed to a template parameter. It can be used when applying templates with <xsl:apply-templates> or calling templates with <xsl:call-template>. The name attribute holds the name of the parameter for which the value is being passed.

The value of the parameter is determined either by the select attribute or by the contents of the <xsl:param> element (you can't have both). The as attribute indicates the expected type of the parameter. If the as attribute is missing, and you set the parameter using its content, the parameter holds the document node of a temporary tree. Otherwise, the parameter holds the selected or constructed sequence.

The tunnel attribute determines whether the parameter is a tunneling parameter or not. If it is, then even if a template doesn't declare or explicitly pass on the parameter, it will be passed through that template in any case. Tunneling parameters can only be used in templates that declare parameters using an <xsl:param> element with a tunnel attribute equal to yes.

```
<xsl:with-param name="qualified-name"
                select="expression"?
                as="sequence-type"?
                tunnel="yes | no"?>
  sequence-constructor
</xsl:with-param>
```

See also <xsl:param>, <xsl:apply-templates>, <xsl:call-template>, <xsl:apply-imports>, <xsl:next-match>.

From XSLT 1.0.

XSLT Attributes

There are five attributes from the XSLT namespace that can be added to any literal result element. Aside from xsl:use-attribute-sets, these attributes can also be used on any XSLT element, in which case they appear without a prefix.

xsl:default-collation

The xsl:default-collation attribute determines the collation that's used by default when comparing strings (except when sorting them with <xsl:sort>); the processor uses the first collation URI that it recognizes within the list, which defaults to holding only the Unicode codepoint collation URI. This works exactly like the default-collation attribute on <xsl:stylesheet>.

```
<element xsl:default-collation="list-of-collation-uris">
  sequence-constructor
</element>
```

From XSLT 2.0.

xsl:extension-element-prefixes

The xsl:extension-element-prefixes attribute lists the prefixes of namespaces that are being used for extension elements. This works exactly like the extension-element-prefixes attribute on <xsl:stylesheet>.

```
<element xsl:extension-element-prefixes="list-of-namespace-prefixes">
  sequence-constructor
</element>
```

From XSLT 1.0.

xsl:exclude-result-prefixes

The xsl:exclude-result-prefixes attribute lists the prefixes of namespaces that should not be included within the result tree. This works exactly like the exclude-result-prefixes attribute on <xsl:stylesheet>.

```
<element xsl:exclude-result-prefixes="list-of-namespace-prefixes">
  sequence-constructor
</element>
```

From XSLT 1.0.

xsl:use-attribute-sets

The xsl:use-attribute-sets attribute lists the names of attribute sets that contain attributes that should be added to the literal result element, in exactly the same way as the use-attribute-sets attribute works with <xsl:element> and <xsl:copy>.

```
<element xsl:use-attribute-sets="list-of-qualified-names">
  sequence-constructor
</element>
```

See also <xsl:attribute-set>, <xsl:element>, <xsl:copy>.
From XSLT 1.0.

xsl:use-when

The xsl:use-when attribute determines whether a literal result element (or XSLT element) is included in the stylesheet. If the expression it holds evaluates to a value with an effective Boolean value of false, the element isn't included in the stylesheet. The expression is evaluated when the stylesheet is first constructed by an XSLT processor, so is mainly restricted to accessing information about the processor itself.

```
<element xsl:use-when="test">
  sequence-constructor
</element>
```

From XSLT 2.0.

xsl:version

The xsl:version attribute specifies the version of XSLT that is being used within the element on which the attribute is placed. This attribute is required on the document element of simplified stylesheets, which have a literal result element as their document element.

```
<element xsl:version="2.0">
  sequence-constructor
</element>
```

From XSLT 1.0.

xsl:xpath-default-namespace

The `xsl:xpath-default-namespace` holds the namespace that should be used when interpreting unprefixed element and type names within XPath expressions.

```
<element xsl:xpath-default-namespace="namespace-uri">
  sequence-constructor
</element>
```

From XSLT 2.0.

Index

Characters

Numbers

A

B

D

N

Q

R

S

T

Y

Z